CAMERON AT 10

Britain under Thatcher (with Daniel Collings)
The Foreign Office: An Illustrated History
The Blair Effect 1997–2001 (ed.)
Public and Private Education: The Divide Must End
Partnership not Paternalism
Brave New City: Brighton & Hove, Past, Present, Future
New Labour: Old Labour: The Blair, Wilson and Callaghan Governments (ed. with Kevin Hickson)
Blair: The Biography, Vol. I
The Blair Effect 2001–2005 (ed. with Dennis Kavanagh)
Recovering Power: The Conservatives in Opposition Since 1867 (ed. with Stuart Ball)
Blair's Britain 1997–2007 (ed.)
Trust: How We Lost it and How to Get it Back
An End to Factory Schools
Why Schools, Why Universities?
Brown at 10 (with Guy Lodge)
Public Schools and the Great War (with David Walsh)
Schools United
The Architecture of Diplomacy: The British Ambassador's Residence in Washington (with Daniel Collings)
Beyond Happiness: The Trap of Happiness and How to Find Deeper Meaning and Joy
The Coalition Effect, 2010–2015 (ed. with Mike Finn)

ANTHONY SELDON
& PETER SNOWDON

Cameron at 10

The Inside Story
2010–2015

**WILLIAM
COLLINS**

William Collins
An imprint of HarperCollins*Publishers*
1 London Bridge Street
London SE1 9GF
WilliamCollinsBooks.com

First published in Great Britain by William Collins in 2015

1

Anthony Seldon and Peter Snowdon assert the moral
right to be identified as the authors of this work

Principal researchers: Jonathan Meakin and Illias Thoms

All profits from Anthony Seldon's writing are given to charity

A catalogue record for this book
is available from the British Library

ISBN 978-0-00-757551-0

Printed and bound in Great Britain
by Clays Ltd, St Ives plc

MIX
Paper from
responsible sources
FSC C007454

FSC™ is a non-profit international organisation established to promote
the responsible management of the world's forests. Products carrying the
FSC label are independently certified to assure consumers that they come
from forests that are managed to meet the social, economic and
ecological needs of present and future generations,
and other controlled sources.

Find out more about HarperCollins and the environment at
www.harpercollins.co.uk/green

To Julia Snowdon and Joanna Seldon

Contents

List of Illustrations

P. 492: Oliver Letwin and Danny Alexander, 26 February 2013
(© REX Shutterstock)

P. 504: David Cameron campaigns in Carlisle, 6 May 2015 (© Chip
Somodevilla/Getty Images)

P. 526: David and Samantha Cameron celebrate the general election
results, 8 May 2015 (© Andrew Parsons/i-Images)

Dramatis Personae

The lists below are not exhaustive, and only contain names that appear in the book.

'LD' = Liberal Democrat
'2015' = Still in position at the time of the 2015 general election

The Quad

CAMERON, DAVID – Prime Minister of the United Kingdom of Great Britain and Northern Ireland, 2010–15. Leader of the Conservative Party, 2005–15.

CLEGG, NICK – Deputy Prime Minister, 2010–15. Leader of the Liberal Democrats, 2007–15.

OSBORNE, GEORGE – Chancellor of the Exchequer, 2010–15. Shadow Chancellor, 2005–10.

ALEXANDER, DANNY – Secretary of State for Scotland, 12–29 May 2010. Chief Secretary to the Treasury, 2010–15. LD.

No 10 (Officials and Political Staff)

BERTIN, GABBY – Press Secretary, 2005–12. Director of External Relations, 2013–15.

BOWLER, JAMES – Principal Private Secretary, 2010–12.

CASE, SIMON – Private Secretary to the Prime Minister, 2012–13. Deputy Principal Private Secretary, 2013–14. Executive Director, Implementation Group at the Cabinet Office, 2014–15.

CASEY, NIGEL – Foreign Affairs Private Secretary, 2014–15.

CASSON, JOHN – Foreign Affairs Private Secretary, 2011–14.

CHAMBERS, MAX – Policy Unit, 2014–15.

CHATWIN, TIM – Head of Strategic Communications, 2010–11.

COOPER, ANDREW – Director of Strategy, 2011–13.

COULSON, ANDY – Director of Communications, 2010–11.

DOWDEN, OLIVER – Political Adviser, 2010–13. Deputy Chief of Staff to the Prime Minister, 2013–14.

DUNLOP, ANDREW – Special Adviser to the Prime Minister on Scotland, 2011–15.

FALL, KATE – Deputy Chief of Staff to the Prime Minister, 2010–15

FELDMAN, ANDREW – Chairman of the Conservative Party, 2010–15.

FIELD, STEVE – Prime Minister's Official Spokesman, 2010–12.

FLETCHER, TOM – Foreign Affairs Private Secretary, 2010–11.

FOGES, CLARE – Speechwriter, 2009–15.

GILBERT, STEPHEN – Political Secretary, 2010–15.

GILL, AMEET – Special Adviser, Head of 'Grid' Planning, 2010–15.

GLOVER, JULIAN – Speechwriter, 2011–12. Special Adviser, Department of Transport, 2012–15.

HEYWOOD, JEREMY – Downing Street Permanent Secretary, 2010–11. Cabinet Secretary, 2012–15.

HILTON, STEVE – Director of Strategy, 2010–12.

JOHNSON, JO – Head of the Policy Unit, 2013–15. Cabinet Office Minister, 2013–15.

KIDDELL, TIM – Private Secretary to the Prime Minister and Speechwriter, 2010–15.

KIRBY, PAUL – Head of Policy Unit, 2011–13.

KORSKI, DAN – Special Adviser, 2013–15.

LLEWELLYN, ED – Downing Street Chief of Staff, 2010–15.

LOCKWOOD, CHRIS – Deputy Head, Policy Unit, 2013–15.

MANN, LAURENCE – Political Private Secretary, 2010–15.

MARTIN, CHRIS – Principal Private Secretary to the Prime Minister, 2012–15.

McDONALD, SIMON – Foreign Policy Adviser, 2010–11. Ambassador to Germany, 2011–15.

O'DONNELL, GUS – Cabinet Secretary, 2005–11.

O'SHAUGHNESSY, JAMES – Director of Policy, 2007–11.

OLIVER, CRAIG – Director of Communications, 2011–15.

SALTER, MICHAEL – Political Head of Broadcasting, 2010–15.

SCHOLAR, TOM – Second Permanent Secretary at the Treasury, 2009–13. Adviser, European and Global Issues, 2013–15.

SEDDON, NICK – Policy Unit, 2013–15.

SILVA, ROHAN – Senior Policy Adviser, 2010–13.

SUGG, LIZ – Head of Operations, 2010–15.

WILLIAMSON, GAVIN – Parliamentary Private Secretary to the Prime Minister, 2013–15.

WORTH, SEAN – Special Adviser, 2010–12. LD.

Cabinet

CABLE, VINCE – Secretary of State for Business, Innovation and Skills, 2010–15. LD.

CARMICHAEL, ALISTAIR – Secretary of State for Scotland, 2013–15. LD.

CLARKE, KENNETH – Lord Chancellor, Secretary of State for Justice, 2010–12. Minister without Portfolio, 2012–14. Chancellor, 1993–7.

DUNCAN SMITH, IAIN – Secretary of State for Work and Pensions, 2010–15. Leader of the Conservative Party, 2001–3.

FALLON, MICHAEL – Secretary of State for Defence, 2014–15.

FOX, LIAM – Secretary of State for Defence, 2010–11.

GOVE, MICHAEL – Secretary of State for Education, 2010–14. Chief Whip, 2014–15. Lord Chancellor, Secretary of State for Justice, 2015.

GRAYLING, CHRIS – Minister for Employment, 2010–12. Lord Chancellor, Secretary of State for Justice, 2012–15.

GREENING, JUSTINE – Secretary of State for Transport, 2011–12. Secretary of State for International Development, 2012–15.

HAGUE, WILLIAM – Foreign Secretary, 2010–14. First Secretary of State, 2010–15. Leader of the House of Commons, 2014–15. Leader of the Conservative Party, 1997–2001.

HAMMOND, PHILIP – Secretary of State for Transport, 2010–11. Secretary of State for Defence, 2011–14. Foreign Secretary, 2014–15.

HILL, JONATHAN – Leader of the House of Lords, 2013–14. European Commissioner for Financial Stability, Financial Services and Capital Markets Union, 2014–15.

HUHNE, CHRIS – Secretary of State for Energy and Climate Change, 2010–12. LD.

HUNT, JEREMY – Secretary of State for Culture, Olympics, Media and Sport, 2010–12. Secretary of State for Health, 2012–15.

JAVID, SAJID – Secretary to the Treasury, 2012–14. Secretary of State for Culture Media and Sport, 2014–15.

LANSLEY, ANDREW – Secretary of State for Health, 2010–12. Leader of the House of Commons, 2012–14.

MAY, THERESA – Home Secretary, 2010–15.

McLOUGHLIN, PATRICK – Chief Whip, 2010–12. Secretary of State for Transport, 2012–15.

MILLER, MARIA – Secretary of State for Culture, Media and Sport, 2012–14.

MITCHELL, ANDREW – Secretary of State for International Development, 2010–12. Chief Whip, 2012.

MOORE, MICHAEL – Secretary of State for Scotland, 2010–13. LD.

MORGAN, NICKY – Secretary of State for Education, 2014–15.

PATERSON, OWEN – Secretary of State for Northern Ireland, 2010–12. Secretary of State for Environment, Food and Rural Affairs, 2012–14.

PICKLES, ERIC – Secretary of State for Communities and Local Government, 2010–15.

SPELMAN, CAROLINE – Secretary of State for Environment, Food and Rural Affairs, 2010–12.

STRATHCLYDE, TOM – Leader of the House of Lords, 2010–13.

TRUSS, LIZ – Secretary of State for Environment, Food and Rural Affairs, 2014–15.

VILLIERS, THERESA – Secretary of State for Northern Ireland, 2012–15.

WARSI, SAYEEDA – Chairman of the Conservative Party, 2010–12. Minister without Portfolio, 2010–12. Minister for Faith and Communities, 2012–14.

Also attending Cabinet:

GRIEVE, DOMINIC – Attorney General, 2010–14.

HANCOCK, MATTHEW – Minister for Business and Enterprise, Minister for Energy, and Minister for Portsmouth, 2014–15.

LAWS, DAVID – Chief Secretary to the Treasury, 12 May–29 May 2010. Minister for Schools, 2012–15. Minister for the Cabinet Officer, 2012–15. LD.

LETWIN, OLIVER – Minister for Government Policy, 2010–15.

MAUDE, FRANCIS – Minister for the Cabinet Office, 2010–15.

McVEY, ESTHER – Minister for Employment, 2013–15.

SHAPPS, GRANT – Chairman of the Conservative Party, 2012–15. Minister without Portfolio, 2012–15.

STOWELL, TINA – Leader of the House of Lords, 2014–15.

WILLETTS, DAVID – Minister for Universities and Science, 2010–14.

WRIGHT, JEREMY – Attorney General, 2014–15.

YOUNG, GEORGE – Leader of the House of Commons, 2010–12. Chief Whip, 2012–14.

Other Ministers

BOLES, NICK – Minister for Planning, Department for Communities and Local Government, 2012–14. Minister for Skills and Equalities, 2014–15.

DUNCAN, ALAN – Minister for International Development, 2010–14.

FEATHERSTONE, LYNNE – Minister for the Home Office, 2014–15. Parliamentary Under-Secretary for International Development, 2012–14. Parliamentary Under-Secretary for Equalities, 2010–12. LD.

HERBERT, NICK – Minister for Policing and Criminal Justice, 2010–12.

WEBB, STEVE – Minister for Pensions, 2010–15. LD.

Office of Deputy Prime Minister (All Liberal Democrats)

ASTLE, JULIAN – Special Adviser, 2010–15.

COLBOURNE, TIM – Special Adviser, 2010–13. Deputy Chief of Staff, 2014–15.

MACKENZIE, POLLY – Senior Adviser to the Deputy Prime Minister, 2010–15.

OATES, JONNY – Deputy Communications Adviser, 2010. Chief of Staff, 2010–15.

PIETSCH, LENA – Press Secretary, 2010–15.

REEVES, RICHARD – Director of Strategy, 2010–12.

Whitehall (Treasury, Special Advisers, Civil Servants, Military and Security)

CAINE, JONATHAN – Special Adviser to Owen Paterson, 2010–12. Special Adviser to Theresa Villiers, 2012–15.

CARNEY, MARK – Governor of the Bank of England, 2013–15.

CASEY, LOUISE – Director General, Troubled Families, 2011–15.

CHOTE, ROBERT – Chairman of the Office for Budget Responsibility, 2010–15.

COWPER-COLES, SHERARD – UK Special Representative to Afghanistan and Pakistan, 2009–10.

CUMMINGS, DOMINIC – Special Adviser to Michael Gove, 2011–13.

CUNLIFFE, JON – British Permanent Representative to the EU, 2012–13. Deputy Governor of the Bank of England for Financial Stability, 2013–15.

CUNNINGHAM, FIONA – Special Adviser to Theresa May, 2010–14.

DARROCH, KIM – British Permanent Representative to the EU, 2007–12. National Security Adviser, 2012–15.

DEIGHTON, PAUL – Commercial Secretary to the Treasury, 2013–15.

DEVEREUX, ROBERT – Permanent Secretary, Department of Work and Pensions, 2011–15.

EVANS, JONATHAN – Director General of MI5, 2007–13.

FRASER, SIMON – Permanent Under-Secretary of the Foreign Office, 2010–15.

GEIDT, CHRISTOPHER – Private Secretary to the Sovereign, 2007–15.

HANDS, GREG – Deputy Chief Whip, 2013–15.

HANCOCK, MATT – Minister for Skills and Enterprise, 2013–14. Minister for Energy, 2014–15. Minister for Business and Enterprise, 2014–15.

HARRISON, RUPERT – Chief of Staff to George Osborne, 2010–15.

HOUGHTON, NICK – Chief of the Defence Staff, 2013–15.

KERSLAKE, BOB – Head of the Home Civil Service, 2012–14.

KING, JULIAN – Ambassador to Ireland, 2009–11. Director General of the Northern Ireland Office, 2011–14.

KING, MERVYN – Governor of the Bank of England, 2003–13.

LAMB, GRAEME – Commander Field Army, 2007–09.

LEWIS, LEIGH – Permanent Secretary at the Department for Work and Pensions, 2006–11.

LYALL GRANT, MARK – British Ambassador to the United Nations, 2009–15.

MACPHERSON, NICHOLAS – Permanent Secretary at the Treasury, 2005–15.

PARKER, ANDREW – Director General of MI5, 2013–15.

PARKER, NICK – Deputy Commander, International Security Assistance Force, 2009–10. Commander-in-Chief, Land Forces, 2010–11. Commander Land Forces, 2011–12.

PATEY, WILLIAM – British Ambassador to Afghanistan, 2010–12.

POWELL, HUGH – Deputy National Security Adviser, 2013–14.

RICHARDS, DAVID – Chief of the General Staff, 2009–10. Chief of the Defence Staff, 2010–13.

RICKETTS, PETER – National Security Adviser, 2010–12. British Ambassador to France, 2012–15.

ROGERS, IVAN – British Permanent Representative to the European Union, 2013–15.

ROGERS, THEA – Special Adviser to the Chancellor, 2013–15.

RUSSELL, BETH – Principal Private Secretary to the Chancellor, 2011–13. Director, Personal Tax, Welfare and Pensions, 2013–15.

SANTS, HECTOR – Chief Executive of the Financial Services Authority, 2007–12.

SAWERS, JOHN – Chief of the Secret Intelligence Service (MI6), 2009–14.

SHEINWALD, NIGEL – British Ambassador to the United States, 2007–12.

SHIPLEE, HOWARD – Director General of the Universal Credit Programme, 2013–14.

STANHOPE, MARK – First Sea Lord, 2009–13.

STIRRUP, JOCK – Chief of the Defence Staff, 2006–10.

STROUD, PHILIPPA – Special Adviser to Iain Duncan Smith, 2010–15.

TIMOTHY, NICK – Special Adviser to Theresa May, 2010–15.

TUCKER, PAUL – Deputy Governor of the Bank of England, 2009–13.

VICKERS, JOHN – Chair of the Independent Commission on Banking, 2010–11.

WALL, PETER – Chief of the General Staff, 2010–14.

WESTMACOTT, PETER – British Ambassador to the United States, 2012–15.

WILSHAW, MICHAEL – Chief Inspector of Education, Children's Services and Skills, 2012–15.

WOLFSON (NÉE SHAWCROSS), ELEANOR – Special Adviser to the Chancellor, 2010–15.

YOUNGER, ALEX – Chief of the Secret Intelligence Service (MI6), 2014–15.

Conservative Party (All members of, or closely aligned with, the Conservative Party)

BRADY, GRAHAM – MP for Altrincham and Sale West. Chairman of the 1922 Committee, 2010–15.

CROSBY, LYNTON – Australian political strategist. Director of 2015 campaign, 2012–15.

CRUDDAS, PETER – Conservative Party Co-treasurer, 2011–12.

DAVIDSON, RUTH – Leader of the Scottish Conservatives, 2011–15.

JOHNSON, BORIS – Mayor of London, 2008–15.

MAJOR, JOHN – Prime Minister, 1990–1997.

NORMAN, JESSE – MP for Hereford and South Herefordshire.

SOAMES, NICHOLAS – MP for Mid Sussex.

SPICER, MICHAEL – MP for West Worcestershire. Chairman of 1922 Committee, 2001–10.

STEWART, RORY – MP for Penrith and The Border. Chair of the Defence Select Committee, 2014–15.

Other UK

ALEXANDER, DOUGLAS – Shadow Foreign Secretary, 2011–15.

BALLS, ED – Shadow Chancellor, 2011–15.

BERCOW, JOHN – Speaker of the House of Commons, 2009–15.

BROWN, GORDON – Prime Minister, 2007–10.

DARLING, ALISTAIR – Chair of the Better Together Campaign, 2012–14.

FARAGE, NIGEL – Leader of the UK Independence Party (UKIP), 2010–15.

HARMAN, HARRIET – Acting Leader of the Labour Party, May–September 2010. Deputy Leader of the Labour Party, 2007–15.

LEVESON, BRIAN – Judge. Chairman of the Leveson Inquiry, 2011–12.

LUCAS, CAROLINE – Leader of the Green Party, 2008–12.

MILIBAND, ED – Leader of the Labour Party, 2010–15.

ROBINSON, PETER – First Minister of Northern Ireland, 2008–15. Leader of the Democratic Unionist Party, 2008–15.

SALMOND, ALEX – First Minister of Scotland, 2007–14. Leader of the Scottish National Party, 2004–14.

STEVENS, SIMON – CEO of NHS England, 2014–15.

STURGEON, NICOLA – First Minister of Scotland, 2014–15. Leader of the Scottish National Party, 2014–15.

WEI, NAT – Social entrepreneur. Government adviser, 2010–11.

USA

BIDEN, JOE – Vice President, 2009–15.

BLOOMBERG, MICHAEL – Mayor of New York City, 2002–13.

CLINTON, HILLARY – Secretary of State, 2009–13

DONILON, THOMAS – National Security Advisor, 2010–13.

EMANUEL, RAHM – White House Chief of Staff, 2009–10.

GATES, ROBERT – Secretary of Defense, 2006–11.

GIBBS, ROBERT – White House Press Secretary, 2009–11.

KERRY, JOHN – Secretary of State, 2013–15.

KNAPP, BILL – Media strategist and consultant.

OBAMA, BARACK – President of the United States, 2009–15.

RICE, SUSAN – National Security Advisor, 2013–15.

YELLEN, JANET – Chair of the United States Federal Reserve, 2014–15.

Europe

ASHTON, CATHERINE – High Representative of the European Union for Foreign Affairs and Security Policy, 2009–14. Vice President of the European Commission, 2010–14.

BARNIER, MICHEL – European Commissioner for Internal Market and Services, 2010–14.

BERLUSCONI, SILVIO – Prime Minister of Italy, 1994–1995, 2001–06, 2008–11.

DRAGHI, MARIO – President of the European Central Bank, 2011–15.

HOLLANDE, FRANÇOIS – President of France, 2012–15.

JUNCKER, JEAN-CLAUDE – Prime Minister of Luxembourg, 1995–13. President of the European Commission, 2014–15.

KATAINEN, JYRKI – Prime Minister of Finland, 2011–14.

KENNY, ENDA – Taoiseach, 2011–15.

LAGARDE, CHRISTINE – Managing Director of the International Monetary Fund, 2011–15.

MERKEL, ANGELA – Chancellor of Germany, 2005–15.

MEYER-LANDRUT, NIKOLAUS – Adviser to Angela Merkel on European Affairs, 2011–15.

MONTI, MARIO – Prime Minister of Italy, 2011–13.

ORBÁN, VIKTOR – Prime Minister of Hungary, 2010–15.

RAJOY, MARIANO – Prime Minister of Spain, 2011–15.

REINFELDT, FREDERIK – Prime Minister of Sweden, 2006–14.

RENZI, MATTEO – Prime Minister of Italy, 2014–15.

RUTTE, MARK – Prime Minister of the Netherlands, 2010–15.

SARKOZY, NICOLAS – President of France, 2007–12.

SCHULZ, MARTIN – Leader of the Progressive Alliance of Socialists and Democrats, 2004–12, 2014. President of the European Parliament, 2014–15.

THORNING-SCHMIDT, HELLE – Prime Minister of Denmark, 2011–15.

TUSK, DONALD – Prime Minister of Poland, 2007–14. President of the European Council, 2014–15.

VAN ROMPUY, HERMAN – President of the European Council, 2009–14.

WESTERWELLE, GUIDO – German Foreign Minister, 2009–13.

International (UN, other foreign PMs, etc.)

AL-ABADI, HAIDER – Prime Minister of Iraq, 2014–15.

AL-ASSAD, BASHAR – President of Syria, 2000–15.

AL-MALIKI, NOURI – Prime Minister of Iraq, 2006–14.

AL-THANI, HAMAD BIN JASSIM BIN JABER ('HBJ') – Prime Minister of Qatar, 2007–13.

BAN KI-MOON – Secretary General of the United Nations, 2007–15.

DALAI LAMA – Tibetan spiritual leader, 1950–2015.

ERDOGAN, RECEP TAYYIP – Prime Minister of Turkey, 2003–14. President of Turkey, 2014–15.

GADDAFI, MUAMMAR – De facto ruler of Libya, 1969–2011.

HARPER, STEPHEN – Prime Minister of Canada, 2006–15.

JIABAO, WEN – Premier of China, 2003–13.

JINTAO, HU – President of China, 2002–12.

KARZAI, HAMID – President of Afghanistan, 2004–14.

KEQIANG, LI – Premier of China, 2013–15.

LAVROV, SERGEI – Russian Minister of Foreign Affairs, 2004–15.

MEDVEDEV, DMITRI – President of Russia, 2008–12. Prime Minister of Russia, 2012–15.

NETANYAHU, BENJAMIN – Prime Minister of Israel, 2009–15.

POROSHENKO, PETRO – President of Ukraine, 2014–15.

PUTIN, VLADIMIR – President of Russia, 1999–2008, 2012–15. Prime Minister of Russia, 2008–12.

SINGH, MANMOHAN – Prime Minister of India, 2004–14.

USHAKOV, YURI – Adviser to President Putin, 2008–15.

XIAOMING, LIU – Chinese Ambassador to the United Kingdom, 2010–15.

YANUKOVYCH, VIKTOR – President of Ukraine, 2010–14.

YI, WANG – Chinese Foreign Minister, 2013–15.

The Twenty-First-Century Baldwin?

David Cameron did not expect to win the general election on 7 May 2015. Alongside many commentators, pollsters and most of the country, he felt outright victory, however narrow, was out of reach. The result gave him an authority he had never before possessed, not least within the Conservative Party, and ensures that his premiership will be seen as one of significant historical importance. Even before the election he was the sixth longest-serving Conservative prime minister since 1900, after Margaret Thatcher (eleven years), Winston Churchill (nine), Stanley Baldwin (eight), John Major (seven), and Harold Macmillan (six). His announcement in March 2015 that he will not fight another election means that if he serves most of a second term, he will become the second longest-serving Conservative prime minister since 1902. By the time of the 2015 general election, he had served nine and a half years as leader of the Conservative Party, making him one of the longest-serving leaders in the party's history.

There are other reasons why Cameron is a figure worthy of our attention. When he assumed office in May 2010, he was the youngest prime minister of any party since Lord Liverpool in June 1812. The chancellor, George Osborne, the youngest holder of that office for over 120 years, became quite exceptionally powerful during Cameron's premiership. Was this effectively a joint leadership? Did their youth and inexperience – neither had any ministerial track record – have downsides? Cameron was the first prime minister since the 1930s to head a peacetime coalition government. How did he approach leading a joint administration with the Lib Dems? What role did official deputy prime minister Nick Clegg play, and what did the Liberal

Democrats get out of the deal? They came to power during the worst economic crisis for eighty years. Did they over-dramatise the problems, and how well did they tackle them? This book looks in depth at these questions.

Cameron at 10 is divided into forty chapters, each discussing an event, decision or episode in the life of the prime minister and Number 10.[1] It would be impossible to relay all that happened in these five crowded years; hence the focus on those forty stories we deem the most telling. To help capture the unrelenting pace of events, we have written most of the account in the present tense, bringing life to the medium of contemporary history. The book is based on extensive inside interviews – over 300 – and a variety of documents. When the government archives are opened, further details will naturally come to light, but we believe that the principal facts and indeed judgements on these five years will not change substantially.

What kind of prime minister was David Cameron? What were his personal strengths and weaknesses? Harold Macmillan, a fellow Etonian, is the prime minister to whom Cameron has most usually been compared, not least by himself.[2] Similarities exist, certainly, above all in their pragmatic and measured approach to statecraft. But Macmillan was to the left of Cameron and was the more cautious figure. Stanley Baldwin provides the more revealing comparison, above all during his leadership of the 1931–5 National Government. Although Labour's Ramsay MacDonald was nominally prime minister during those four years, the Conservatives were the largest party, and Baldwin practically led the government as Lord President of the Council. Baldwin's keen sense of public opinion provides a strong similarity with Cameron, as does being neither doctrinaire nor ideologically driven.[3] Each man possessed a very English, patrician vision of the nation and a strong commitment to social justice and service. Both exuded a natural sense of confidence and did not have to exert themselves over others. When the occasion demanded, and it often did, they were cutters and trimmers, in an effort to hold their parties and coalitions together. Both were criticised for this; but they would respond that national priorities, party management and coalition cohesion necessitated their ducking and weaving. They brushed aside setbacks and doubts about them. Cameron, despite being twenty years Baldwin's junior when in office, was the more comfortable and self-confident figure, coming across as unruffled because he *was* unruffled.[4]

The coalitions of 1931–5 and 2010–15 had striking similarities too. The prime objective of each was economic recovery after the two worst economic crises of the last hundred years, caused by international instability and mismanagement by predecessor governments. Baldwin and Cameron were criticised for their economic judgements and for the uneven and slow pace of recovery. Both men were ideally suited to manage the dynamics of coalition government and working out what was possible, although Cameron was the less sensitive to disquiet within the party. The primary achievement too of both administrations was similar: overseeing recovery in difficult economic times, while providing stability at home at a time of considerable international unrest and uncertainty.

Both Baldwin and Cameron relished their roles as 'head of the nation'. It appealed to their shire Tory sense of duty that coursed through their veins. Both men, if pushed, would probably see themselves as much national as sectional leaders. Cameron was not at his strongest uplifting the nation with his oratory, in contrast to Baldwin, notably in the India debates in 1931 and during the abdication crisis in 1936. He lacked Baldwin's gifts as 'teacher' to the nation, inspiring the country with new understandings. If democracy is in part government by explanation, Baldwin understood this intuitively. Could Cameron have done more and earlier to persuade the Scottish people of the merits of the union in the 2014 referendum? Cameron was uncomfortable with anything that smacked of rabble-rousing or courting an emotional response, and this restraint often came at the expense of taking the public with him. He found it notably difficult to sound passionate during the 2010 general election, or until late in the day in the 2015 election.

Successful prime ministers need outstanding qualities of character combined with high-order skills of leadership. How did Cameron fare? He proved one of the most psychologically balanced prime ministers since 1900, *too* balanced in the eyes of some, who craved more passion and flair. From his first days in Number 10, officials noted his equilibrium in contrast to the volcanic Gordon Brown.

Cameron indeed exhibited many of the qualities that officials most admire. Impressive intellectually (Vernon Bogdanor, his tutor, said he was 'one of the ablest – and nicest – students I taught at Oxford. He achieved an outstanding first-class degree'[5]), he disposed of the torrent of paperwork that fills prime ministerial boxes and mastered his briefs with alacrity. Like Baldwin and Macmillan, he was interested in what the press had to say, but not obsessively so. Unlike Brown, Blair and Major, he did not work himself up into a lather if he or his government was being criticised. Like Baldwin and Churchill, he understood the importance of relaxation, and was unashamed to take evenings and holidays off in an effort to escape the constant intrusions into a prime minister's life. He possessed a strong constitution and could refresh himself with half an hour's sleep when necessary. His appetite for hard work was under-recognised by many contemporaries, who preferred to categorise him as a 'chillaxed' or even as an indolent prime minister, a charge also levelled at Baldwin, in his case with justice, not least by Neville Chamberlain.

Whereas Number 10 damages many PM's marriages, his relationship with Samantha became stronger. He leant on her throughout for emotional and practical support. The job of prime minister's consort is little understood: they rank amongst the most influential and least studied of any in the PM's inner court. Samantha was no exception. Although a strong personality, she could be overwhelmed by the grandeur of the role, especially in the early years. She kept her husband grounded, although he too recognised the importance of spending time with family and with old friends unrelated to politics. As a couple, they remained pleasantly unimpressed by the impressive people who constantly seek to flatter a prime minister and consort.

Cameron is a proficient public speaker, mastering information quickly and able to speak off the cuff. His most accomplished performances came when responding to the report on Bloody Sunday in June 2010 and at the party conferences in 2012 and 2014. Prime ministers need to remain focused and decisive during crises. Even when under intense and multiple pressures, he was the calmest in the room. He dominated Cabinet and its committees, including the National Security Council which he set up, conducted tight meetings and summed up succinctly. He was too decisive for some, who felt meetings were superfluous because he had already decided his own mind beforehand, if not always with a full assimilation of the issues, especially on foreign affairs. Over the five years, no one in Cabinet emerged as a serious threat to him, or made him look as if he was not in command. Though weakened by a parliamentary party intent on rebelling over Europe and other issues at critical points, he managed to survive, thanks in large part to the cushion of a coalition majority of over seventy in the House of Commons. In the chamber itself, he was effective at the despatch box and could rise to the occasion, if rarely to the same degree as Baldwin.

What of Cameron's team, and how did he manage them? His Cabinet was not full of big beasts, as had been Clement Attlee's (1945–51), Harold Wilson's (1964–70), or even Margaret Thatcher's after 1979. His only real stars in these five years were George Osborne and Michael Gove, with steely Theresa May not far behind. Cameron had no mentor figure in Cabinet, as Thatcher had with Willie Whitelaw from 1979–87 and Blair had, less successfully, with Derry Irvine from 1997–2003, and he hung on to Kenneth Clarke until 2014 partly because he offered some of their wisdom and experience. William Hague and Oliver Letwin provided some of the ballast a PM needs behind the scenes. Equally, and indicatively, he had no intellectual gurus to guide him, as Thatcher had in Milton Friedman and F. A. Hayek, though he liked to see himself in Disraeli's 'One Nation' tradition. Blair was almost as big an influence on him as Thatcher; but laying too much stress on either influence misses the point about Cameron. As prime minister, he travelled lightly, guided by his own convictions, largely unaffected by voices from history or academe.

Cameron's reading of political history taught him the pointlessness of frequent Cabinet reshuffles. He oversaw only two, in September 2012 and July 2014, with a minor one in October 2013, mainly for the Lib Dems. He strove to keep key ministers in place throughout, notably Osborne and May at the Treasury and Home Office, and William Hague remained at the Foreign Office until the July 2014 reshuffle when he was replaced by Defence Secretary Philip Hammond. Cameron's most controversial move of the five years by far was demoting Gove from Education Secretary to chief whip, which brought enduring ire from the right and bafflement from many commentators.

His final coalition Cabinet in April 2015 contained all except a handful of the ministers present at the first Cabinet meeting in May 2010; many of the changes that had occurred had been forced upon him. He stuck by ministers even when under fire, such as Eric Pickles and Iain Duncan Smith. Prime ministers need to be effective at both appointments and dismissals. Better at the former than the latter, Cameron nevertheless should not have appointed the tarnished Andy Coulson to Number 10 as communications director, and then hung on to him for too long when the phone-hacking saga exploded in 2010–11, nor retained some ministers when it could have been politic to have dismissed them earlier, such as Andrew Lansley at Health. Cameron's skill at making appointments has been unfairly overshadowed by Osborne's undoubted ability in this regard: the latter's recruitments included Mark Carney to the Bank of England and, in part, Lynton Crosby as campaign manager in 2013.

Cameron's preference for continuity and the familiar extended to staff at Number 10. He is extraordinarily loyal to those he knows well. When he became PM in May 2010, in came his close advisers from Opposition: Osborne, Ed Llewellyn (chief of staff), Kate Fall ('gatekeeper'), Steve Hilton (free-ranging policy strategist), Coulson and Rupert Harrison (Osborne's chief of staff). Essentially the same team was in place at the end, albeit with Craig Oliver replacing Coulson, and Crosby, the Australian campaign guru, taking over some of the strategic role of Hilton, who departed midway through the government. The Number 10 staff came under extensive fire from commentators, often as lightning conductors for criticism of the PM personally, as happens in all premierships. Some criticised his court for being high-handed, reactive or incompetent, or full of yes men. Are these criticisms fair? Readers must judge, and decide whether they adopted the bunker mentality of the inner courts of Wilson, Thatcher and Blair. Cameron's core team certainly worked with a ferocious degree of unity, had to devise how to run a coalition government for which there was no rulebook, and felt they inherited an anarchic Number 10 on which they imposed order by holding daily meetings at 8.30 a.m. and 4 p.m. in his office, which continued religiously throughout the five years. They rarely leaked information to the press and were unfailingly loyal to their boss. The attacks subsided though never disappeared. Had there not been a victory in 2015, the knives would have very swiftly come out for them, as for Cameron.

How did Cameron command ministers and the senior Civil Service, a core requirement for the PM? His style was, in the main, to let ministers get on with their jobs where they had his trust. Cameron was a laissez-faire captain of the team, not an autocratic one. He deliberately wanted his ministers to make the running in their own departments, and was equally happy for them to take the credit. The style worked most successfully when his ministers were proficient, a status not all ministers justified. He appointed Francis Maude to shake up the Civil Service, but rarely engaged with officials directly himself outside Downing Street and the Cabinet Office. Cameron as PM was unusually self-contained, knowing his own mind. 'The real business of this government was done between 6 and 8 a.m. up in his flat, when he went meticulously through his papers in his boxes,' said an official. By the time he came to meetings, he often knew what he wanted.

His decision to opt for a small-scale Number 10 operation militated against oversight from the centre, a deficiency he subsequently corrected. The drawback was particularly evident in 2010–12, when some avoidable oversights and policy reversals occurred. Learning from the mistakes of Blair's oddly unambitious first administration of 1997–2001, his team planned meticulously for a burst of activity in the first eighteen months. The belief that they would probably have one term to accomplish everything was at the forefront of their minds. His team was singularly fortunate to have the services of the experienced and formidable Jeremy Heywood, initially as permanent secretary at Number 10, and from January 2012 as Cabinet Secretary. The other two officials upon whom Cameron leant most heavily were Heywood's successor, Chris Martin, who became the senior official at Number 10, and Nicholas Macpherson, permanent secretary at the Treasury, and Whitehall's longest-serving head of department.

Prior to 2010, Cameron lacked experience of foreign and defence policy. How did he fare in office? He established a positive and effective, if not always easy, relationship with President Obama. He maintained good relations with Vladimir Putin from 2011–13, and with the leaderships in China and several in the EU and the Gulf. Angela Merkel was his bedrock relationship of these five years. As with

Obama, it took him time to gain her full trust. Did he rush the country into precipitous military involvement in Libya in 2011, and how did he manage to lose a parliamentary vote on military action in Syria in 2013, which brought his entire foreign policy strategy into question? How serious a threat did militant Islamism pose on British streets, and how well did he manage it? The book examines these questions in full. At home, his relationship with military chiefs blew hot and cold. He showed courage in confronting them over withdrawal from Afghanistan and excessive spending demands from a defence department that he and Osborne believed to be riddled with inefficiency and tired thinking. He worked conspicuously hard to maintain good relations with the Queen and the royal family, which coincided with a resurgence of enthusiasm for the royals, notably for its younger members. A traditionalist at heart, like Baldwin, he revered the royal family.

Cameron's poll rating was regularly ahead of his party's. So why did he not become a loved figure, as Thatcher (and to a lesser extent Major) had been, and why did so many in his parliamentary party dislike him? Like Baldwin he was no darling of the press. It is significant that Cameron did not have the support of a single broadsheet paper when he stood for the leadership in 2005, and it wasn't until 2013–14 that the Tory press threw their weight behind him. Disappointment that he was not a visionary explains part of the *froideur*. Many Conservatives and commentators yearned for him to come up with a grand narrative in the sweep of history, which he felt wasn't true to himself. He had big thoughts, certainly, and major ambitions for his country as a civilised place where all could aspire to further themselves economically. But he was always happier as a tactician than a strategist. He believed in a Conservative attachment to family, personal responsibility and patriotism. But it did not translate into an all-encompassing vision in a Thatcherite sense. The closest he came to a strapline in these five years was Hilton's 'Big Society', much of which resonated with him, notably community action, entrepreneurship and volunteering. Churchill would have dismissed it all as a 'pudding without a theme'. Is it fair, though, to dismiss Cameron for failing to articulate an all-embracing narrative and overly harsh on the man, and a misreading of the nature of Conservative history, to argue thus? Thatcher was the exception amongst Conservative leaders in being strongly ideological, and she was responding to a particular need for action after years of government failure. Cameron did not think like that. Did his preference for incremental reform, rather than national panaceas, sell the country short?

A more serious criticism, and one frequently voiced during the five years, was that he was an 'essay crisis' prime minister, reluctant to engage with issues until the last minute, and then overreacting when he found himself boxed into a corner. At worst, was he just a rather lazy, arrogant figure, who made it up as he went along? As we will see, tactical considerations could indeed often trump a more strategic approach to decision-making. On Europe, he pledged to pull out of the EPP group in the European Parliament to help win the leadership election in 2005, but then in office, was he bounced into calling for a referendum on Britain's future in the EU in January 2013? He was accused of preferring short-term stances on Europe over long-term strategy, as in his exercise of the veto at the EU Council in December 2011, or his attempt to stop Jean-Claude Juncker becoming Commission president in 2014. On his response to Islamist terror abroad, is there justice in the parallel accusation of lack of long-term thought?

On the domestic front, he had enthusiastically backed the 'detoxification' of the Tory brand from 2005, and then abandoned it in 2008 with the economic crash. How far did his succession of approaches once in office succeed in defining a modern conservatism? In a similar vein, he is blamed for calling a referendum on Scottish independence, albeit one almost inevitable given the SNP's success in the May 2011 Holyrood election, then for failing to negotiate the right question and being overconfident of a successful outcome until the last minute, when he panicked into making giveaway promises. Did he fatally undermine the union? All these charges are examined in the book.

Cameron sometimes betrayed his relative youth and could be chippy, as when he called UKIP supporters 'fruitcakes, loonies and closet racists' before he became prime minister, telling Labour frontbencher Angela Eagle to 'calm down dear' in April 2011 at PMQs, or too unguarded, as when he let slip in 2014 that the Queen had 'purred' when she heard the result of the Scottish referendum. None were capital errors.

How much did he learn as prime minister on the job over the five years? Might a steadier and maturer hand early on have helped him to deal more successfully with his backbenchers, some fifteen or twenty diehards of whom despised him and would have happily seen him toppled, and a further thirty or so of whom were regularly and openly rebellious? Rather than drawing such figures in, he could be high-handed and dismissive. Some harboured implacable resentment over his unforgiving stance on the parliamentary expenses scandal in 2009, and his failure to win a majority in 2010. He received little credit for the Conservatives gaining ninety-seven seats in 2010, the biggest increase for the party in any general election since 1931. But there were many others who felt bruised over government appointments, with fewer Conservative berths to fill as a result of the coalition, or who had legitimate objections to the coalition as well as some of its policies. Did party management in both the Commons and the Lords, especially early in his leadership, cause enduring resentment? From 2011–12, he embarked on a series of overtures to woo disaffected backbenchers and peers, culminating in the successful appointment of Gavin Williamson as his parliamentary private secretary in October 2013. Yet even the victory in May 2015 still far from convinced all of his party, some of whom argued he had only won due to fears of the SNP partnering Labour in government. But does that factor explain the result?

Anger from inside the party also stemmed from Cameron's preference for those whom he had known for many years, some since Eton and Oxford, which gave rise to the accusations of cliquey-ness and running a 'chumocracy'.[6] His apparently charmed circle of friends in the so-called 'Chipping Norton Set', containing many Old Etonians, were viewed for a time with deep suspicion, especially at the height of the phone-hacking saga, which implicated Rebekah Brooks and her husband Charlie, an old school friend of Cameron (though both were subsequently cleared). The lowest point of the premiership for Cameron personally was when details of his text messages to Brooks were revealed to the Leveson Inquiry. The charge of cronyism, frequently made against the PM, would carry force if he was giving preference to individuals purely for being friends, or if friends in his team were not proficient in their job. Was he guilty?

Failing to promote women was a linked charge, as was having a patronising attitude to them in general. Some like May were in Cabinet from the start, and he brought in three women in July 2014, Nicky Morgan, Liz Truss and Baroness Stowell, but failed to achieve his promise of April 2009 that a third of his government would be female. By the time of the general election in 2015, however, almost one-third of Conservative ministers who attended Cabinet were women. His inner team contained Kate Fall, at his right hand throughout, Liz Sugg (chief of operations), Gabby Bertin (press adviser) and Clare Foges (principal speechwriter); but does their presence counter the criticism that Cameron was sexist?

These are some of the questions the book will examine. Some of our thoughts are already evident on these pages, but for the most part, we leave it to readers to make up their own minds over the forty chapters before offering our judgement in the Conclusion.

Anthony Seldon and Peter Snowdon
August 2015

ONE

First Night in Downing Street

11 May 2010

'Snap out of it: we have a job to do,' barks Jeremy Heywood, Number 10's permanent secretary, the senior official, the top dog. It is 7.55 p.m. on Tuesday 11 May. Outside, dusk is descending. Staff are still dazed from Gordon and Sarah Brown's deeply emotional departure moments before.[1] They stand around the departed PM's open-plan office torpid, drained. Many have tears in their eyes. 'The prime minister will be here in half an hour.' Heywood's piercing voice urges them back into action.[2] Tom Fletcher, Brown's (and now about to be David Cameron's) foreign policy adviser, changes his red and yellow striped tie to one with blue and yellow stripes. Ever the diplomat, he wants to shift emotional and political gear before his new boss arrives in the building.[3] Dirty mugs and plates are spirited away, out-of-date papers removed, computer screens cleared. Here is the British Civil Service at action stations. The king is dead. Long live the king.

Just after 8 p.m., Brown delivers his farewell statement to the media circus outside Number 10. His former staff are too busy inside to notice. Three hundred yards down Whitehall, a similar riot of activity is taking place in the Leader of the Opposition's office in Parliament in the Norman Shaw building. Ed Llewellyn, Cameron's chief of staff, receives a call from the American ambassador: 'It looks like you guys are going across the road. The president wants to be the first to talk to your man when he gets there.'[4] Coalition conversations with Liberal Democrat leader Nick Clegg are still ongoing, though they are close to reaching an agreement. Cameron's wife, Samantha, is caught off guard by the fast-flowing action. She is called in the early evening by Kate Fall, Cameron's gatekeeper and senior female aide, at the family's

London home in Notting Hill: 'You're going to have to come down soon. David is about to form a government.' 'I don't have to get dressed up, do I? I'm at home with the kids.' 'Er, not yet,' Fall replies. Minutes later, Fall calls her back. 'Get ready. You'll need to put your dress on quickly.' With moments to spare, Samantha arrives at Cameron's office.

David and Samantha are bundled into a car to Buckingham Palace for the Queen to invite him to become prime minister, Britain's youngest for nearly 200 years. Their hands touch in the back of the car. Their lives are about to change forever, but the short journey gives them final moments of peace. The car sweeps through the open gates. Cameron, still calm, ascends the wide stairs to where Her Majesty awaits him. He listens with barely concealed pride as she invites him to form a government. Audience over, and now in the official prime minister's car under police escort, they are driven the half-mile to Downing Street.

His team have been advised by Heywood to enter Number 10 by the Cabinet Office entrance on Whitehall. Most of them have never been inside Downing Street. They walk down its long central corridor from the Cabinet Room to the front lobby in awe, before heading outside. Standing in front of the door to Number 11, they observe the lectern that Brown has just spoken from still standing on solitary duty outside the black front door of Number 10. Liz Sugg, who organises Cameron's trips, wants to tell him not to use the lectern and where to stand for his first speech as prime minister. She knows he is on his way back from the Palace, but is unable to get through. 'So this is what it's going to be like now he is prime minister,' she thinks to herself, 'he won't be able to take my calls.' Then her mobile rings. It is Cameron. 'Sorry, I was ringing my mum,' he tells her as if they are old friends sharing a latte at Starbucks. She tells him – she is nothing if not emphatic – exactly where his car is to stop, and where he is to speak.[5]

At 8.42 p.m., the prime minister's small convoy drives into Downing Street. He steps out beside a visibly pregnant Samantha, and delivers the statement he has put the finishing touches to just moments before:

Her Majesty the Queen has asked me to form a new government and I have accepted … our country has a hung Parliament where no party has an overall majority and we have some deep and pressing problems – a huge deficit, deep social problems, and a political system in need of reform. For those reasons I aim to form a proper and full coalition between the Conservatives and the Liberal Democrats … I believe that is the best way to get the strong government that we need … This is going to be hard and difficult work.

Huddled on the pavement in front of Number 11, his aides watch anxiously. 'I'll never forget that evening. The sun was setting. It was twilight, adding to the magic. While he was speaking, crowds in Whitehall were shouting. Helicopters were hovering overhead. It all seemed surreal,' recalls Cameron's political private secretary, Laurence Mann.[6] The new prime minister and Samantha walk to the front door. An official removes the microphone. Cameron poses with Samantha on the front steps, hugging her awkwardly. As the door is opened, he gives a final wave. A few chants float in from the streets: 'Gordon out!' vies with 'Tories out!' before the sounds of the outside world fall away with the closing of the door. He has arrived.

Staff line up along the long corridor from front door to Cabinet Room, clapping him and Samantha. His small team follow on behind. One looks down at his shoes in embarrassment, overcome by the occasion. Another notices the smell of newly cleaned carpet. Cameron turns round at the end of the line and says a few words to his new staff who less than forty-five minutes before had been tearfully clapping out Gordon and Sarah. Samantha is peeled away. Kate Fall goes with her, dividing her time that first evening between looking after both of the principals.

Inside the Cabinet Room, Cameron greets Cabinet Secretary Gus O'Donnell and Heywood. Britain's two top officials brief him about his most pressing tasks – some, such as procedures in the event of nuclear threats, are held over to the following morning.[7] His staff are shown to their offices. They are amazed to be presented with appointment cards showing the PM's diary neatly typed up. 'I realised then that this is the Rolls-Royce state in action,' recalls one.[8] Cameron is escorted through the double doors at the end of the Cabinet Room into his office, which

Blair used and called his 'den', at almost the furthest possible point in the Downing Street warren from Brown's office in Number 12. He looks around, disconcerted to see doors on each side, the other leading on to the long room where his aides and officials will work. He wonders about having people constantly entering his office from both sides.[9] Number 10 has no ideal room for a prime minister; nothing like the Oval Office. Unlike the White House, it was not purpose-built, but evolved from history. Discussions have taken place in the preceding weeks whether, should Cameron win, he would occupy the space Brown had chosen in Number 12, move upstairs in Number 10 to the office Thatcher had worked from, or use the den.[10] Cameron briefly flirts with the idea of using the White Room, one of the state rooms on the first floor, with views across to St James's Park and Horse Guards Parade. Heywood, Fall and Llewellyn later persuade him to use the den, for practical and security reasons.

Discussions had taken place also about Heywood in the preceding weeks. Should he stay? He had been very close – perhaps too close – to Labour's operation under both Blair and Brown. Was he a Labour man? He had been intimately involved in all Labour's decisions for the previous few years, bar a period (2004–7) when he left the Civil Service for the private sector. Some of these decisions under Labour Cameron and George Osborne thought were disastrous. They knew Heywood believed passionately in capitalism, but was he enough of a free marketeer, enough of an enthusiast for competition and the small-enterprise initiatives they wanted to see? But it was decided before the election that Heywood, one of the most omni-competent officials since 1945, was too important to lose.

Present in the den at nine o'clock that first evening are Llewellyn, Cameron's chief of staff since 2005; Osborne, his master strategist; Steve Hilton, his exuberant and intellectually brilliant thinker; and Andy Coulson, his worldly-wise head of communications. It had been felt by some observers that tension between them had seriously hampered Cameron's election campaign, but tonight their feelings are temporarily put aside.

The den clears suddenly at 9.10 p.m. when Fletcher enters to announce the Obama call is coming through. 'Here I am, just us in the room, less than half an hour after he's entered the building, with the

American president waiting to speak,' Fletcher thinks to himself.[11] The two national leaders barely know each other. The White House are aware they mucked up the relationship in the president's first year by being brusque to Brown, who they found needy. Obama thus wants to get off on the right foot with the new prime minister. 'Congratulations,' he booms down the secure line. Cameron has not used the apparatus before and has just been briefed that officials will be listening to his every word, taking careful notes. The prime minister is businesslike, savouring the moment when he says 'I'm speaking from Number 10' for the first time. When he does so, he winks to his aide. 'Come over and see me in the White House,' Obama says. This is a big deal, and very welcome news to the team. They are delighted to hear him utter the totemic words 'special relationship' between the US and Britain. The call is short and to the point. As the line goes dead, Coulson is agreeing the lines to brief about it with Robert Gibbs, White House press secretary. Coulson is anxious to get it right, and not hype it beyond what the White House wants. Cameron's team are now playing in an altogether new league.

Llewellyn and Fletcher decide which foreign leader talks to the PM and when. Next on his list is the German chancellor, Angela Merkel. 'Your job is to defend UK interests and my job is to defend German interests,' she tells a dazed Cameron, who has just been given a briefing on hedge funds, an issue between both nations at the time. Her tone is polite but formal. The chancellor is still cross that he withdrew the Conservative Party from the European People's Party (EPP) in May 2009. Their call gives no hint of the warmth that will develop after the first few months, though she invites him nevertheless to visit her in Germany. From France, President Sarkozy – always anxious for the limelight – is pressing to speak to Cameron. He will have to wait. The team debate whether Cameron should visit Germany or France first. Stephen Harper, Canadian prime minister, gets in with a quick call: 'Take it all in and pace yourself,' he tells the new prime minister.[12] This sounds better, Cameron thinks, sensing here is someone with whom he will be able to relate.

He is enjoying his new toy. He looks up from the telephone to see aides anxiously pointing to their watches. He is running late for his address to the Conservative Party. He is driven the short distance to

the House of Commons accompanied by the special protection officers who have been at his side in the weeks leading up to the election
and will now accompany him for the remainder of his premiership,
and indeed the rest of his life. His new escorts follow him up the stairs
to the Grand Committee Room where he is greeted with wild cheering from Conservative parliamentarians. The chief whip, Patrick
McLoughlin, calls for silence with the words 'Colleagues, the prime
minister.' 'I can honestly say that I was the first person to call him
prime minister in public,' McLoughlin recalls.[13]

It is 10.06 p.m. The atmosphere in the cramped room is near
hysterical with excitement. After the long election campaign, MPs
have endured a further five days of uncertainty until it becomes clear
only a couple of hours before that Cameron will be prime minister.
Aides recall 'a ferocious cheer, banging of desks and wild excitement'
after he makes a short speech about events during the historic day.[14]
It will not always be this cordial when Cameron meets his party's
MPs. Farewells over, the team repair to Cameron's former office in the
Norman Shaw building. Osborne's team join them and together they
tuck in to pizzas in celebration.[15]

Cameron relaxes in his old haunt among old friends, but becomes
aware that Llewellyn and Fall are telling him he needs to go back to
Downing Street. Once there, Cameron returns to the phone, absorbing the quickest of briefings between calls. Sarkozy will be his 'best
friend and biggest rival'. 'I need you to tell me when I get it wrong,'
Cameron says to his officials. A respectful conversation with
Manmohan Singh of India follows while calls stack up with the
Japanese and Chinese. Meanwhile, calls are still being put through
from Number 10 to Gordon Brown, who is being driven to the airport
to head north to Scotland. Obama and other leaders are keen to bid
farewell to the former prime minister. At one point, Brown rings
Number 10 to thank Fletcher for his assistance with the calls. It is a
surreal moment. Foreign leaders would have been surprised if they
knew that their words to Brown a few hours before – 'It's a pity you
are having to leave because you were so good' – were being noted
down by the same official who heard them say to Cameron, 'We
always wanted you to win. It'll be great and we can now reset this
relationship in a much better way.'

William Hague is present at Number 10 for much of the evening. Hillary Clinton, US Secretary of State, wants to congratulate him, but officials decide that the call should wait until the following morning as he is yet to be formally appointed Foreign Secretary. Hague, ever philosophical, accepts their advice with a smile, and walks through to Brown's old office in Number 12 where more pizza is being shared by Cameron's small team. With amazingly few exceptions, here are the team who will carry him through the entire five years. They are his four closest Cabinet colleagues: Osborne, Hague, fixer extraordinaire Oliver Letwin and close friend and colleague Michael Gove. His aides are Llewellyn, Hilton, Coulson, Fall, Oliver Dowden (a senior party aide), and Laurence Mann. Present too are the officials, Heywood, Fletcher, James Bowler, the PM's principal private secretary, and Rupert Harrison, Osborne's heavyweight economist and multi-talented chief of staff who is still only in his early thirties.

The new incumbents notice the pen marks on the table and ask officials, 'Is this where Gordon stubbed his pen? Is this where he threw his phone?' Their questions are not driven by point-scoring, but more by awed curiosity: 'There was no gloating,' notes one. Officials' first impressions of Cameron that night are that he is more level and composed than they had expected. Already they detect a calmer and more orderly tone to Downing Street. Cameron's team start drifting away from 1 a.m. The adventure for which they have worked tirelessly since Cameron became party leader four and a half years before is about to begin. Llewellyn leaves at 3 a.m. 'It was the most exciting night of my life,' he recalls.[16]

TWO

Origin of 'Plan A'

September 2008–February 2010

The most important decision to be taken by the Cameron government of 2010–15 was made before it even got into power. The decision had three distinct phases: the autumn of 2008, June 2009 and the autumn of 2009. Together they formed the building blocks of what became known as 'Plan A': placing deficit reduction at the very heart of their economic strategy. It provided the coalition government with its core narrative and principal claim to success, and it gave a coherent platform for the Lib Dems to sign up to and their rationale for remaining in the government. But these very decisions in 2008 and 2009 were also to cleave Cameron's team right down the middle, to contribute to him losing his stride in the 2010 general election, and almost certainly cost the Conservatives an overall majority. It is important thus to examine this history.

The first plank in the Plan A platform was put in place in the autumn of 2008. On 15 September, Lehman Brothers, the 158-year-old investment bank and the fourth largest in the United States, filed for bankruptcy. The shockwaves triggered the global financial crisis. Jon Cunliffe, a senior official in the Cabinet Office, sent an email around Whitehall: 'If we don't do something now the whole system is going to go down. We have to act.'[1] That week, the survival of British banks RBS and HBOS was at stake. As Prime Minister Gordon Brown and the Labour Party gathered in Manchester for their annual conference on 20 September, Brown was brought a note to say that Goldman Sachs, the bluest of blue-chip banks, might be on the verge of going under. The British economy was in dire danger. Cameron and Osborne regarded Brown as the principal architect of the economic position the country found itself in. But it was the PM who held the initiative, and was about to absolve himself of any blame.

Brown took the unusual step of addressing the Labour conference on the opening Saturday, speaking without notes and with gravitas about the profound problems in the global economy. It underpinned his own position in the party, as well as in the country, as the leader uniquely placed to handle the grave predicament. His main speech on Tuesday 23 September was preceded by a masterstroke. The conference expected him on the podium, but his wife Sarah walked on to the stage. 'Every day I see him motivated to work for the best interests of the people around the country,' she said, concluding her two minutes by introducing 'my husband, the leader of your party, your prime minister, Gordon Brown'. It was a coup.[2] He remained on a high throughout the speech. His most effective line was that it was 'no time for a novice', referring not only to Cameron, but also to Brown's would-be challenger, David Miliband. The most powerful of his three conference speeches as prime minister, it further underwrote his credentials as saviour of the nation. Brown left Britain on 24 September on a much-hyped trip to New York and Washington, leaving Cameron and Osborne behind at their conference desperately trying to find a way to make an impact. As PM, he had found a role.

Unlike Brown, whom they disliked, and the chancellor, Alistair Darling, whom they quite admired, the two leading Conservatives had neither the power of office, nor the boon of the advice and information from the Treasury, Cabinet Office and Bank of England. They were very young and inexperienced, as they were painfully aware. Cameron had more understanding of economics than Osborne. He had studied it as part of his politics, philosophy and economics (PPE) degree at Oxford, and had worked in the Treasury as a special adviser in the early 1990s.[3] Osborne, who studied modern history at Oxford, had been appointed shadow chancellor in May 2005 at the age of thirty-three. Though he served briefly as shadow chief secretary, Osborne had much to learn in his new brief. 'As shadow chancellor, my first and biggest political task was to establish economic credibility,' he later said. 'I did that by being a small "c" conservative and saying that I wouldn't promise unfunded tax cuts.'[4] Like Cameron, he looked to the example of Margaret Thatcher rather than her 1980s contemporary, President Ronald Reagan, 'who ran big deficits to pay for big tax cuts'.[5] The totemic event for Cameron, as for Osborne, was Geoffrey Howe's Budget of 1981, which raised taxes despite Britain being in a recession.[6]

After Cameron was elected party leader in December 2005, seven months after Osborne's promotion to shadow chancellor, they rapidly became the closest of allies: the closest indeed that British politics has seen at the top since the Second World War. They both yearned for credibility at a time when their youth and inexperience provoked so many questions. So in September 2007 they took a decision deliberately to imitate what New Labour had done before the 1997 general election, when Blair said he would match Tory spending plans, and promised to maintain Labour's spending plans if elected. Osborne's predecessor as shadow chancellor, Oliver Letwin, said Osborne 'took the decision early on deliberately to avoid an argument with Labour on public spending, in an attempt to neutralise the issue'.[7]

When the financial crisis hit, Osborne and Cameron were wrong-footed. They thought they were dealing with a failure of the banking system rather than a more general economic crisis. Osborne criticised Brown's government for creating 'an economy built on debt', saying of the public finances that 'the cupboard is bare', but he deliberately eschewed using the word 'austerity', because of the negative connotations of the term for the Conservatives.[8] He released a document called *Reconstruction: Plan for a Strong Economy*, which outlined his thinking, although it was soon to be overtaken by events.[9] The Conservatives held their annual 2008 conference in Birmingham. On 1 October, Cameron announced he would work with the Labour government 'in the short term to ensure financial stability'. During the conference, Osborne travelled to London with his aide Rupert Harrison to meet Alistair Darling and Financial Services Authority chief executive Hector Sants. He also spoke by phone to governor of the Bank of England Mervyn King and bank leaders in the City, realising he faced a fast-moving situation where only the authorities really knew what was happening.[10] Brown and the Labour government held the initiative and knew it. On 8 October, they announced a £500 billion bank bailout package to restore market confidence. Just days before, the Bush administration in the US had announced the

Troubled Asset Relief Programme (TARP), allowing for $400 billion to purchase troubled assets.[11]

Yet Cameron's and Osborne's relationship was cemented during these difficult weeks. A close team had begun coalescing around Osborne, consisting first and foremost of Rupert Harrison. Harrison began working for the shadow chancellor in 2006, recruited from the respected independent think-tank the Institute for Fiscal Studies. He is an intriguing character. Eight years younger than the chancellor, he is the possessor of a powerful and capacious mind. After having been head boy at Eton, at Oxford he switched from Physics to PPE, excelling at both. He went on to complete a PhD in economics at University College London. Harrison's influence on policy grew steadily in Opposition and his role would be pivotal when he became Osborne's chief of staff in 2010. He dislikes the comparison, but his relationship with Osborne is uncannily similar to Ed Balls's with Brown. Balls and Harrison have the much profounder technical understanding of economics and both are more intellectually assured than their masters. They are trained economists and highly effective operators in the Treasury and Whitehall at large. Both spend much time talking to Treasury officials before and after their chancellor has expressed his opinion, and both are skilled drafters of their speeches. They liberate and empower their bosses. There are differences. Harrison is a silky courtroom barrister where Balls is a backstreet fighter. Balls dominated the Treasury because of Brown's dysfunctionality; under Brown, it was a cliquey and conspiratorial place. The Treasury under Osborne is more open, collegiate and empirical. Osborne, unlike Brown, is happy to be challenged in front of officials, and Harrison for one does so regularly. Osborne, like Brown, is an historian, but unlike him, never claims to be an economist. Balls and Harrison are the principal *éminences grises* of the Labour and coalition governments respectively. Brown had tried hard to make Balls chancellor in June 2009, while Osborne would come to rely equally heavily on Harrison at the Treasury.[12]

Matthew Hancock was another key member of Osborne's team, serving as his chief of staff until 2010. A former Bank of England economist, he joined shortly after Osborne's appointment as shadow chancellor: 'I can do the politics, I want someone to do the economics,'

Osborne told the young aide.[13] They were joined in April 2006 by Rohan Silva, a Manchester and London School of Economics-educated former Treasury policy analyst, and in 2009 by Paul Kirby, a partner at KPMG. This high-powered team also included Eleanor Shawcross, another economist. Letwin remained a constant source of counsel to them all, self-effacing and intellectually brilliant. A group of former Conservative chancellors – Geoffrey Howe, Nigel Lawson, Norman Lamont and Kenneth Clarke – were only too happy to provide discreet ballast and experience to the young team. They were to prove notably important in the decision Cameron announced on 18 November 2008, to 'decouple' the Conservatives from their decision fourteen months earlier to match Labour's spending plans, which Brown was using, Keynesian-style, to drive the country out of recession. 'Matching Labour's plans seemed a very smart move at the time,' admitted an Osborne aide, 'but by late 2008 they were anything but sensible.' Letwin felt strongly: 'For Labour to be going on a spending spree in response to the downturn, deploying fiscal not monetary tools, was a basic strategic error. I felt deeply it was a terrible decision for Labour.'[14]

Six days later, on Monday 24 November, Labour delivered its Pre-Budget Report (PBR), as the Autumn Statement was then known. The top rate of income tax for those earning over £150,000 was raised from 40% to 45%, ditching Labour's manifesto pledge not to do so. A temporary cut in VAT from 17.5% to 15% was to come into effect on 1 December, in time for Christmas shopping, to stimulate the economy. This was to form the centrepiece of a £20 billion fiscal stimulus package to last for thirteen months. Bigger shocks followed. Darling announced that the £43 billion borrowing requirement forecast in his March 2008 Budget had been revised upwards, to £118 billion. He said the Budget would not be brought back into balance until 2015, that the economic situation was even worse than had been feared, and that public sector debt would rise from 41% to 57% of GDP by 2013/14. These figures did not even take into account the bank bail-outs. To Osborne, Darling's statement was the opportunity to regain the initiative. 'I knew we were right to focus on the rapidly rising deficit. He just read out these numbers and everyone was completely stunned. That's when we felt we were on the front foot and picked the right issue.'[15] He decided to oppose the stimulus and made a series of increasingly strong statements in late 2008 and early 2009 damning Labour for its response to the recession. By Christmas 2008, confidence in the Conservative camp was rising as it became clear that Labour's package was not giving the British economy the stimulus that it needed. Cameron and Osborne had now committed themselves against spending their way out of recession. They had yet to say that spending had to be cut. This was to come.

The second plank of Plan A was put in place in the spring and early summer of 2009. Cameron was planning to give a speech at the Conservative Spring Forum a few days after Darling's Budget on 22 April. The speech, on spending plans, had already been written. But he was so incensed by what Darling said, he came back up to his office 'extremely angry, thrashing around the place and kicking the buckets. He suddenly realised how everything was going to be fucked up because of the figures. I'd never seen him so angry at the way that Labour had mucked up the spending,' an aide recalls. He sat down to work almost immediately rewriting his forum speech. 'He's rarely happy talking about economics,' says the aide. But on this occasion he produced a draft which he regarded as really important. In his words can be traced key parts of what was becoming Plan A.

Osborne and Cameron had yet to announce if they were prepared to make cuts if they won the general election, because they were fully aware of the damage it could do to the Tories if they became known as the party of cuts. But for much of the first half of 2009, they goaded and taunted Brown and Darling into saying whether Labour would introduce cuts (known as the 'c' word). In his April Budget, Darling announced that income tax for top earners would rise again to 50%, and that borrowing would rise to £175 billion in the next two years.[16] But on cuts, not a word.

On 10 June, shadow Health Secretary Andrew Lansley went on Radio 4's *Today* programme and admitted that, if the Conservatives were elected, 10% cuts might be necessary to *all* departments except Health, International Development, and Education. Fatally, he omitted to mention that the Conservatives would just be matching what a leak suggested Labour would itself be doing.

'That's it! We can beat them on this,' a jubilant Brown yelled out to his team in Downing Street when he heard what Lansley had uttered.

At last he thought he'd found a clear Labour agenda for the future, a 'eureka' moment. Brown thundered across the despatch box at PMQs later that day: 'This is the day when [the Conservatives] showed that the choice is between investment under Labour and massive cuts under the Conservative Party.' Brown claimed that 'wide, deep and immediate' Tory cuts of 10% would be introduced 'in order to fund a £200,000 tax cut for the 3,000 richest families', a reference to the inheritance-tax reform Osborne had unveiled to wide acclaim at the Conservative annual conference in 2007.[17] Brown's team were deeply torn about the honesty of this claim, as well as the gulf opening up with his increasingly disillusioned chancellor, whom the Conservatives thought Brown had appointed as a mouthpiece, only to discover he had appointed a heavyweight with a mind of his own.[18] His discovery further fuelled Brown's desire to replace the independent-thinking Darling with his right-hand man and protégé, Ed Balls.

Cameron and Osborne went into a tight enclave to debate how to respond to Brown's latest attack. The outlet they selected was an article in *The Times* under Osborne's name, to appear on 15 June. In the first draft, Harrison had avoided using the word 'cuts', but Osborne insisted the dreaded 'c' word must be mentioned, rewriting the piece himself.[19] Rather than avoiding the language of 'austerity', as Tories had in the past, Osborne wanted to come out into the open and say the plan really was for 'cuts'. 'We have fought shy of using the "c" word – cuts,' he wrote. 'We've all been tip-toeing around one of those discredited Gordon Brown dividing lines for too long. The real dividing line is not "cuts vs investment", but "honesty vs dishonesty".' The reference to honesty was a calculated tactic to undermine Brown, whose integrity was being called into question, and by implication Labour's.[20] 'We should have the confidence to tell the public the truth that Britain faces a debt crisis; that existing plans show that real spending will have to be cut, whoever is elected,' wrote Osborne in *The Times*.[21] In September, a leak from the Treasury suggested that a future Labour government would itself make spending cuts of 10%.

Plan A's third and final plank was put into place in the autumn of 2009 with the announcement where the cuts might actually fall. For several weeks, working in the shadow chancellor's Parliament offices, Harrison, Hancock, Kirby and Philip Hammond (the shadow chief secretary) had been reviewing the spending options for a future Conservative government and where any cuts could take place. Their thinking was fed through to Osborne and Letwin, and then up to Cameron himself. The media, sensing they had both main parties on the run, brought immense pressure to bear on them during the summer and early autumn to be specific about cuts. Brown admitted at the TUC annual conference on 15 September that there might have to be some cuts, but failed to mention them in his party conference speech two weeks later, with the gulf between the realism of his chancellor and the obduracy of the prime minister becoming more and more apparent. Darling had become very much in tune with his officials at the Treasury. For the ten years 1997–2007, Brown had ruled the roost with these same officials, and he was furious.

Osborne was determined to craft an economic message to the 2009 party conference in the autumn that would stand up to any challenges, and show that he was serious about taking the necessary risks. The public, as well as the media, had to be shown that he meant business. The Conservatives enjoyed a strong poll lead in the summer of 2009, and he believed that lead would be challenged all the way through to the general election in 2010 unless he set out his stall very firmly. Nick Robinson, the BBC's wily political editor, got under his skin more than anyone, needling him to be precise about the Conservative plans.

Final decisions on the conference speech were taken only in September, and Osborne's voice proved decisive. His team came up with a package of cuts aimed to save £23 billion over the life of the next parliament. The key elements were public sector pay to be frozen, the state pension age to rise, and the cost of Whitehall to be cut by a third over the life of the parliament.[22] To ensure the proposals were seen to be fair, Osborne memorably later said 'we could not even think of abolishing the 50p rate on the rich while at the same time we are asking many of our public sector workers to accept a pay freeze to protect their jobs'.[23] Cameron and Osborne had adopted a high-risk strategy. 'We threw away the rulebook and came up with all sorts of measures that you'd never normally advertise in advance of a general election,' recalls Osborne.[24]

In the speech in Manchester, Osborne announced that the Conservatives would deal with the bulk of the deficit over the life of the parliament. Mervyn King had already suggested this timeframe: Osborne deliberately used it, without King's knowledge, as it seemed sensible to align the Conservatives with the Bank's thinking. He committed the Conservatives to 'in year' cuts in 2010, and laid out structural reforms that autumn to abolish the Financial Services Authority, to have more supervision of banks, which led to the setting up of the Prudential Regulation Authority in the Bank of England, the establishment of the Financial Policy Committee (also in the Bank of England), and to take all regulation into a new body, which was to be the Financial Conduct Authority. As he walked off the stage at the end of the speech, Osborne was reported as telling aides, 'Now let's see if I've cost us the election.'[25] Ever the risk-taker, he relished the daring he had shown and the headlines which spoke of his decisiveness. Martin Kettle writing in the *Guardian* called the speech 'smart, well delivered and in some respects really quite brave'.[26] The *Telegraph* leader writers praised his 'hard-headed realism'.[27]

Plan A was thus virtually all in place by Christmas 2009, five months before the general election, crafted in these three separate stages. The high command appeared united on the economic message, the party seemed content, large parts of the commentariat were won over. But at this point, the status quo became unbalanced. Hilton, who had come back from a sojourn in California, was not pleased. 'What the fuck is all this focus just on cuts and negativity? It'll cost us the election,' he said. He eyeballed Cameron and told him that the narrative around the 'Big Society' and modernisation that the party had built up over the previous four years would be jeopardised unless the message of the long election campaign beginning in January 2010 wasn't more positive. He argued forcefully to shift the focus from spending, which he thought a media-imposed narrative, and he was dyspeptic about the influence of communications director Andy Coulson. Coulson in return had no time for Hilton's *luftmensch* theorising about localism and social action, which he thought lacked popular resonance with the core voters whose support the Conservatives would need if they were to win the election.

Worryingly for Cameron's team, the Tories' poll ratings had started to dip by Christmas, despite Osborne's economic strategy receiving continuing support in large parts of the press. Cameron's camp was divided. On one side stood Osborne and Coulson, and on the other, Hilton. Letwin, along with Llewellyn and Fall, was trying desperately to bridge both camps. It was a hopeless position.

January 2010 started badly. Cameron wanted to set the tone for the New Year with his appearance on BBC's *The Andrew Marr Show* on Sunday 10 January. Hilton wanted Cameron to apologise for the uninspiring start to the campaign made by all the parties, with poster launches, attack dossiers and an obsessive focus on the cuts and say, 'This is the electorate's campaign. Tell us what you want to talk about and we will do so.' Coulson exploded when he heard, and heated discussions followed. A torn Cameron did not follow Hilton's advice. Embarrassingly, Cameron then became embroiled in a media furore over whether photographs of him on billboards, put up across the country, had been digitally enhanced.[28] At the end of the month, at the World Economic Forum at Davos, he tried pulling back from an overly harsh economic message by saying that any first-year cuts in spending would not be particularly 'extensive'. A few days later, on the BBC *Politics Show*, he said that cuts would definitely not be 'swingeing'; rather, the government would simply want to take a nibble out of the deficit to make 'a start'.[29] Private polling had been showing the Conservatives that their advocacy of deep cuts early on was politically highly risky.[30] The impression of dissonance appeared all the greater when a defiant Osborne said on *The Andrew Marr Show* that 'early action' was required to avoid a 'Greek-style budget crisis'.[31] Cameron was uncomfortable and worried. Osborne punched back strongly in February in the annual Mais lecture, an important fixture among economic policymakers. Entitled 'A New Economic Framework', drafted by Harrison, it laid out more clearly than ever the entire Conservative vision of a tight fiscal policy on tax and spending, an active monetary policy to assist borrowing and investment, supply-side reform to bolster economic activity, and a rebalancing of the economy from consumption towards exports. Osborne argued 'we have to deal with our debts to get our economy back on its feet'.[32]

Dissonance in Cameron's camp continued all the way up to the general election. The Conservative manifesto title, *Invitation to Join the Government of Britain*, echoed Hilton's mass participation idealism, and contained many 'Big Society' modernising ideas. But it equally spoke of the need to 'deal with Labour's debt crisis' and said that savings of £12 billion could be made without impacting front-line services. The dual message was confusing, epitomised by an election poster that said they would 'cut the deficit but not the NHS'.[33]

Cameron wasn't sure which way to turn. The campaign was a mess, with Osborne's and Coulson's voices being heard on some days, and Hilton's on others. Cameron's heart inclined him towards Hilton, whose passion and message chimed deeply with his own, but his head drew him towards Coulson and Osborne, because he knew instinctively that the public finances required stern measures. The memory of Margaret Thatcher's fiscal rectitude weighed heavily with Cameron and Osborne, as it did with the right-of-centre press whose support they wanted to maintain. Cameron couldn't find his mojo or any passion during the election campaign, epitomised by his lacklustre performance in the TV debates against Brown and Clegg. He knew he had squandered the first debate, the only one he felt that really mattered. He felt terrible, that he'd let everybody down. He only found his stride again when he woke up on 7 May, the day after the general election, with one idea in his mind: a 'big, open and comprehensive offer' to the Lib Dems.

THREE

'If we win'

6–12 May 2010

Cameron has not won on election day, Thursday 6 May. But he has not lost either. Yet. A 'big, open and comprehensive offer' to the Lib Dems is the thought in his mind when he awakes on the Friday morning, in his suite at the Park Plaza Westminster Bridge Hotel, where he has been camping out through some of the campaign. The words are Steve Hilton's but the seminal decision to deploy them is Cameron's. He may have had only two or three hours' sleep after going to bed at 6.30 a.m., but he awakes refreshed with the clear determination that he will make the Liberal Democrats an irresistible offer to form a coalition. His team arrive at 10 a.m. When he tells them, they are not surprised: 'I'd have been flabbergasted if he'd come up with any other way forward,' says a close aide. 'My definite instinct was that it was the right thing to do given the circumstances,' says Cameron.[1] When Liz Sugg expresses surprise at why he intends to embrace a party they have been fighting so hard for weeks, he replies, 'It is the right thing for the country.'[2] Nick Clegg himself offers a less rose-tinted interpretation: 'I don't want to sound ungenerous, but it was the only way they were going to get into power.'[3]

Cameron's team meet on election day at Hilton's country house in Oxfordshire. They finalise details for the 'If we win' file, running over ministerial appointments one last time and reconfirming the grid of action for the vital first few weeks. They hold a sweepstake on how many seats they will take. 'We're going to win,' Andrew Feldman, one of Cameron's closest friends from Oxford and, in early 2010, chief executive of Conservative campaign headquarters, says emphatically. 'We're not going to win,' Osborne replies curtly. Two weeks before,

Osborne had reached the conclusion that the party was unlikely to win outright and the only way to power would be via a coalition government which it would dominate. Without it, any hopes of seeing Plan A and their domestic agenda enacted will be dead in the water. Too risky to be seen to have his own fingerprints anywhere near 'defeatist' talk of coalitions, Cameron continues to rail against the iniquities of any form of coalition after the election. It is Osborne therefore who asks Oliver Letwin, the supreme fixer, to analyse exactly what a deal with the Liberal Democrats might look like. The brain of the team locks himself away for a week at Conservative Campaign Headquarters (CCHQ) exploring which policies the Conservatives might jettison, and what they might demand from the Lib Dems. 'For weeks before I had been analysing every single statement that the Lib Dems had been putting out, so I was up to speed when I began this exercise. I knew their weaknesses and our strengths intimately.'[4] The weekend before the general election, 1 and 2 May, Letwin meets William Hague, Llewellyn and Osborne at the latter's London house to brief them on his conclusions.[5] 'We then secreted away the fruits of his detailed analysis, while we went flat out in the final last few days to do everything humanly possible to get us over the line.'

Osborne leaves Hilton's home in the afternoon of polling day to travel up to his Tatton constituency in Cheshire. Cameron, Andy Coulson and Llewellyn, joined by Kate Fall and Gabby Bertin, who had been a press aide since the leadership campaign, go for dinner at Cameron's home in Dean, several miles away.[6] They are under no illusions. As they gather around the television screen, the results are greeted with a deadpan silence. The exit poll at 10 p.m. confirms what was expected: a hung parliament with the Conservatives as the largest party. There will be no election miracle. The Conservatives emerge after the final count with 307 to Labour's 258 and fifty-seven for the Lib Dems out of 650 parliamentary seats. The Conservatives may be the largest party, and gain the largest number of seats (net ninety-seven) in a general election since 1931, but it is little consolation. They are left nineteen seats short of an overall majority. Pressure mounts suddenly on Cameron. Critics in the party and the right-wing press, suppressed during the campaign, are now on the airwaves blaming him for a lacklustre campaign and for failing to engage core Tory voters. At 3.30 a.m. on Friday, a newly-energised Brown flies south from his Scottish constituency, believing he can cling to power. Cameron says Brown has lost the right to govern, but does not publicly call for his resignation. The prime minister, for whom Cameron's aides have such strong reservations, is far from finished yet.[7]

Before he went to bed, Cameron had told his team to reconvene in the morning so they can explore options. They all know, none more than Cameron, that a minority government in hock to the Conservative right wing will be their idea of a total nightmare. Cameron has no love for them, nor they for him. 'Let's face it, coalition really suits him,' says one close aide. 'Is he really going to be happy with a minority government, with Eurosceptics like Mark Reckless and Bill Cash knocking on his door every ten minutes?'

At 2.34 p.m. on Friday, Cameron speaks at a press conference at St Stephen's Club, Westminster, saying that the Conservatives will approach the days ahead with the 'national interest' in mind, and he will be making the 'big, open and comprehensive offer' to the Lib Dems to work with him in forming a government. 'Cameron's decision to call for a genuine coalition partnership is very significant,' says master of ceremonies, O'Donnell. 'This wasn't going to be a short-term deal: there was going to be a real commitment that it would last for the life of the parliament. That's what he wanted.'[8] Cameron's words are deliberately chosen, falling short of mentioning a coalition by name, leaving some room for manoeuvre, and offering some reassurance to the large numbers of Conservative MPs for whom the Lib Dems are anathema. Cameron's team knows that he must carry the party, including his leadership rival in 2005, David Davis, the Eurosceptics, and others on the right of the party who dislike his politics.

Five days of intense negotiation with the Lib Dems follow in the secrecy of the historic Cabinet Office at 70 Whitehall.[9] Cameron delegates the details of negotiations to a four-man team: Osborne, Letwin, Llewellyn and Hague, who acts as their head.[10] The Lib Dems include David Laws, Danny Alexander, Chris Huhne and Andrew Stunell. As they meet, television screens in the background show riots in Greece. The eurozone crisis, brewing since mid-2009, broke out into the open in February 2010. It focuses their minds on the importance of achieving a stable government to take Britain forward.

Hague and Alexander banish O'Donnell's posse of civil servants from minuting their discussions. Left alone, both sides find an affinity: 'Talks with the Conservatives go far better than we imagined. There were no rows or unpleasantness. They are polite and civilised. It started the relationship below the Clegg–Cameron level,' says Laws.[11] Hague emerges from the talks pleased not to have conceded more to the Lib Dems: there is an agreement to introduce a fixed-term parliament (later enacted in 2011), reform constituency boundaries, hold a referendum on the Alternative Vote (AV), reform the House of Lords, introduce a 'pupil premium' in schools, and raise the income tax threshold. These are not considered big deals: the Conservative team believe they will easily win the AV referendum, and neither the pupil premium nor the rise in tax thresholds are out of tune with party thinking.[12] The Lib Dems insist they would only agree to support the package if they can secure a fixed-term parliament, thus binding the Conservatives into a coalition for a full five years. Tory negotiators agree, believing it will contribute to stability. To O'Donnell, the deliberations 'provided a chance for both parties to drop their rubbish policies. It was all pretty much as expected. Obviously they agreed to go further than Labour on the extent and speed of the deficit reduction.' The pace of the negotiations would have consequences. Some policies, such as NHS reform, get through, which 'none of them understood – frankly no one examined them carefully.'[13] Ken Clarke, who encouraged Cameron to form a 'proper coalition' after the election, is surprised at how soon an agreement is reached. 'It was precisely because no one had any experience of forming a coalition that they drew up an extremely good agreement in three days flat – no one on the Continent would have done that so quickly.'[14]

Letwin estimates that 80% of the policies hammered out in the 'Coalition Agreement' are straightforward because both parties have relatively similar proposals. The hardest concessions for the Lib Dems to swallow are retaining nuclear power stations and renewing the Trident missile system, which the Conservatives make clear are essential, but which the Lib Dems opposed in their manifesto. Both parties lose only some 10% of their favoured policies. The Conservatives lose out on inheritance tax, the West Lothian Question (namely the issue that since devolution in 1999, Scottish MPs could vote on English domestic matters) and the replacement of the Human Rights Act.[15] Osborne is sanguine about losing inheritance tax. He knows it would be portrayed by Labour as a bung to the rich and has doubts about his ability to have got it through in his planned Emergency Budget.

Osborne thinks the discussions are not difficult because the areas of overlap are considerable. On the matter of Plan A however, the Conservatives are resolute: 'The big judgement the Lib Dems had to make in policy terms was to back our fiscal judgement, which they had attacked during the election campaign,' he says. 'They consented because we insisted that it was non-negotiable.'[16] Osborne believes that discussions the Lib Dem leadership held in private with O'Donnell, Nicholas Macpherson (the permanent secretary to the Treasury) and Mervyn King acted as a reality check, educating them in the need for urgent and tough action. He credits Vince Cable as a highly significant player recognising that Plan A was the right thing to do.[17]

Hague is struck by the naivety of the Lib Dem negotiating team, as by their lack of knowledge of nineteenth- and early twentieth-century coalitions. 'Liberals always come out badly.' Hague realises this, his Conservative colleagues know it, but the Lib Dem leadership he thinks does not. He is surprised too by their lack of familiarity with European coalitions, where the junior partner, whether in Ireland, Germany or elsewhere, is frequently annihilated at the next election. After the final meeting of the five days, Hague staggers home at 1 a.m. and tells his wife, Ffion, with prescience: 'Well, we have formed a government ... but we might well have destroyed the Liberal Party.'[18]

Without Clegg, the coalition would not have been formed. None of his predecessors as leader – Menzies Campbell, Charles Kennedy nor even Paddy Ashdown – would have countenanced a coalition with the Conservatives. Clegg insists too it will be a *full* coalition, not a 'supply and confidence' deal to enable a minority government to get through its Budgets and survive confidence votes, which would have been far more fragile. Clegg believes that the Lib Dems have the Conservatives on the run, and that unlike Labour's team of Peter Mandelson, Ed Balls and Ed Miliband, the Tories are biddable: 'Frankly, for Cameron and Osborne, the alternative to joining us was not pretty. They would have been out on their ears within two seconds at the hands of their own party.'[19] So given this realisation, why does he not push harder?

The dominance the Conservatives achieve in the Coalition Agreement which emerges from the talks is much down to Letwin's planning for such an eventuality.[20] 'In contrast, I was not aware of any detailed planning on the Labour side,' recalls Gus O'Donnell.[21] Clegg always deemed coalition a possibility, but put in less serious work during the campaign because the Lib Dems lacked the resources to do it. The Conservative Party is thus best prepared for coalition talks in May 2010 by a considerable margin.[22] The Coalition Agreement is drawn up by centre-leaning, pragmatic Conservatives, and by right-leaning Lib Dems. Many MPs, still more members in both parties, do not share their outlook. Here at the very genesis of the coalition, the seeds of future strife and discord are sown.

On Monday evening, 10 May, with the coalition talks at a delicate point, Cameron meets his Conservative MPs in Committee Room 14 in the House of Commons. It is the most important meeting of that body in the entire 2010–15 parliament. His MPs have the power to strangle the discussions with the Lib Dems before they reach a conclusion. Cameron tells them that Brown is offering the Lib Dems the AV system, for which Liberals have fought for years, without a referendum. He tells them that unless he can offer the Lib Dems an AV referendum, the talks might break down.

Critics later accuse Cameron of bouncing the party into a coalition in this meeting. During the discussions with the Lib Dems, only a handful of phone calls take place between the Conservative negotiators and the rest of their party, and senior figures in the 1922 Committee are disappointed to see only 'some negotiators running by and asking for our views on what should and should not be considered'. Many feel the process is neither 'systematic' nor 'comprehensive'. They also say the PM exploited the fact that 147, almost half of the 307 Conservative MPs elected, are new, overawed and highly biddable. Another ninety-plus had served on the back benches in Opposition and are eager for ministerial jobs. The scenario Cameron offered 'made most colleagues think there was no choice', says Graham Brady, chairman of the 1922 Committee. 'A lot of people were unhappy with what was being done, but felt they couldn't say so.'[23] For the time being, discontented MPs are quiet. But they come to bitterly resent being told they effectively have no choice other than a coalition with the Lib Dems. It confirms their impression that Cameron and his allies would sooner deal with Clegg and the Lib Dems than with them. How right they are.

The Conservative shadow Cabinet discuss and approve the Coalition Agreement on Tuesday afternoon, with the world's media speculating what is going on. Brown is pacing around Number 10 but knows the game is up. He is told by officials that he cannot go to the Palace to resign until details of the new government are locked into place. Cameron is given the green light. Suddenly, everything happens very quickly. Llewellyn needs the 'If we win' file. At 5.40 p.m., he calls senior party aide Laurence Mann to retrieve it from CCHQ. Behind Mann's desk in his office in Downing Street throughout Cameron's premiership is pinned a fading receipt for a short taxi journey that starts at 5.41 p.m. and finishes at 5.59 p.m. that Tuesday. Mann jumps into a cab in the street outside Norman Shaw building and asks to be taken to CCHQ. He runs in and lifts the file out of the party's safe, trying to look as unobtrusive as possible. A group of aides crowd around him. 'He is smiling,' shouts out one. Mann is silent, jumps back in the cab and just before Big Ben chimes six o'clock, runs back up to Cameron's office.[24]

Llewellyn joins him. Moments before, Cameron has called him back to the office from the marathon in the Cabinet Office. Llewellyn worries his departure might lead to media speculation that Cameron is about to form a government. So officials take him from the Cabinet Office through a tunnel that comes out in Horse Guards Parade. He then walks round the back of the Foreign Office and enters the Norman Shaw building, thankful for the detailed preparation work over the last few months which Mann carries in his hands. Cameron's first hours in Number 10, which follow, have been described in Chapter 1.

Fast-forward to the next day. It is 2.20 p.m. on Wednesday 12 May. Cameron and Clegg are waiting inside the Cabinet Room for a press conference which they have decided will work better outside under a mid-May sun. Aides notice how well and naturally they relate to each other. Warmth, generosity and good humour are palpable.[25] Clegg's aides are watching Cameron closely. They do not know him well yet and do not know what to expect.[26] Both leaders hear the journalists assembling for the press conference in the Rose Garden below. Neither have any illusions. They have both said and thought terrible things about each other. Moments before, Cameron has received a brief listing the criticisms he has voiced of Clegg, so he can be prepared for questions.[27] 'What we need is a show of unity and a light touch,' Coulson tells them both shortly before they walk down the steps into the garden. They hardly needed the advice. The obvious rapport between both men grates with Cameron's malcontented backbenchers. 'They saw Cameron and Clegg looking rather smug about being freed from having to deal with their own barking wings,' says a friend of Cameron's.[28] The word the backbenchers most detest is when Cameron says a minority government would have been 'unappealing'. Not to them it wouldn't. Payback will be just a matter of time.

The coalition angers many Conservative MPs further because it means fewer jobs to go around for them. The Coalition Agreement doesn't say anything about ministerial posts, only policy. Cameron and Clegg agree that positions should be allocated in proportion to the number of MPs, i.e. roughly three to one. But for Cabinet, the Lib Dems do even better with five full members. They say that in addition to Clegg and David Laws, the Chief Secretary to the Treasury, they want Energy, Business and they also claim Scotland, because the Conservatives have only one MP north of the border. Lib Dems debate amongst themselves whether Clegg should have his own Whitehall department; Cameron is very happy to place him in the Home Office. Conversations with allied parties in coalition in Europe hurriedly take place: they conclude that the deputy prime minister (DPM), as he will be called, should mirror the prime minister himself and not run his own government department, allowing him to range across all departments. They later wonder whether they have made the right call: the Civil Service fails to provide matching resourcing for the DPM's office to allow it to compete with the considerable resources at the disposal of the prime minister. The ratio of eighteen Conservatives to five Lib Dems in full-time positions in the Cabinet rubs salt in the coalition wound for many in Cameron's party, especially when it is announced that these five posts will be retained for the Lib Dems all the way through the life of the parliament. But at the top, all is harmony. 'What struck me was how relatively easy the appointments for the coalition government were to make,' says O'Donnell. 'Much of it was attributable to the closeness of Cameron's relationship with Clegg. I was really amazed by how mature both sides were, even down to agreeing who should chair the various Cabinet committees.'[29]

Cameron works closely with Osborne and Hague in making the final switches required for coalition. Hague himself becomes First Secretary of State. The Conservative Cabinet appointments see very few surprises; one is Theresa May to Home Secretary, an appointment that brings tears of joy to her eyes. The appointment of Iain Duncan Smith to Work and Pensions Secretary is another surprise as he hadn't held a portfolio in Opposition, though he had made it clear it was the post he wanted. Finally, it is a surprise that Chris Grayling is not offered a Cabinet position (though he later joins in September 2012 as Justice Secretary).

The decision to have a small-scale Number 10, attributable to Letwin, causes some consternation. Letwin looks back fondly to his time in the Policy Unit in the 1980s when Downing Street was regarded (not always correctly) as operating very effectively under Thatcher. Two factors were in their minds. 'Because tensions between the prime minister and Chancellor had gone on for decades and were endemic, we wanted the whole of Number 10, Number 11, the Treasury and Cabinet Office facing in one direction. We knew the money would never be controlled properly if we were not absolutely sharing the same overall strategic direction,' recalls Letwin.[30] Avoiding Number 10 breaking up into a series of sub-units, all pulling in different directions, was another concern. A small PM's office was thus considered by some to be much more biddable. Others understand that a strong Number 10 is necessary for the delivery of policy. In the months leading up to the election, Hilton and Rohan Silva spoke to some of the key New Labour figures, including Blair (twice), his chief of staff Jonathan Powell, head of policy Matthew Taylor, and speechwriter Phil Collins. They all said that Number 10 should remain big, advice that was ignored. Various Labour-devised units to enhance policy implementation, like the Delivery Unit, are promptly closed down in Number 10. Cameron will be a trusting, 'hands off' PM: why does he require a large office at the centre? But he soon realises he has been hasty to throw the baby out with the bathwater. He is critically short of capacity at the centre. The Policy Unit is thus expanded again from 2011, partly as a result of the patient chivvying of Jeremy Heywood, who repeatedly points out that Number 10 is not fit-for-purpose. But the inner circle around Cameron does not scale up: it remains small and tight. There are real gains from this, not least cohesion. But its social exclusivity is a source of irritation and anger which is to rebound on Cameron all the way down to the general election in 2015. Do they have the experience, the breadth and the stomach to master the maelstrom of political, social, military, security, economic and diplomatic challenges that are about to be hurled at them?

FOUR

Delivering Plan A

May–October 2010

Cameron's first twelve weeks in power are dominated by economic concerns. He and George Osborne had carved out Plan A over the preceding year and a half. They now have to enact it.

Since being appointed shadow chancellor in May 2005, Osborne had observed the operation of the Treasury carefully, looking with alarm at how he believed Gordon Brown had denuded it of some of its best people. In the long run-up to the general election, Osborne and his then chief of staff Matthew Hancock held conversations with Nicholas Macpherson and other senior Treasury officials. They regarded Macpherson as 'Gordon's man', and their initial impressions were not positive. They wanted a more buccaneering permanent secretary heading the Treasury. Macpherson's departure was one of three intentions that Osborne's tight group shared amongst themselves; an Emergency Budget and a probable VAT increase are the others. Osborne wanted his top official to be Jeremy Heywood, who had served as principal private secretary to Conservative chancellor Norman Lamont from 1990–3. When Osborne invited him to dinner before the election, they chimed immediately. The doyen of the Civil Service, Heywood had served both Blair and Brown as the senior official at Downing Street. He knew the territory inside out.

Yet the more the Conservatives saw of Macpherson in their pre-election talks, the more they rated him. They were impressed by his grip and understanding. 'Getting this transition right is the most important job I have to do in the rest of my career,' Macpherson told them. He had been principal private secretary to the chancellor at the time of the 1997 general election and oversaw the difficult transition from Ken Clarke to Gordon Brown. No other figure serving in Whitehall had his direct understanding of Treasury transitions.

Soon after he becomes chancellor, Osborne begins to see Macpherson as an asset and an ally. Moreover, Cameron grows too dependent on Heywood's advice at Number 10: he doesn't want to lose him. Osborne is also disconcerted by some Treasury voices who counsel him against Heywood: they criticise him for effectively running a shadow Treasury operation in Number 10 under Brown. Alistair Darling's strong advice to Osborne – the two men like each other – is to keep Macpherson.

Not since they prepared for power under Thatcher in 1979 has an incoming Conservative government had so much trepidation of the Civil Service. Osborne and Michael Gove, a close ally of Cameron's and recently appointed Education Secretary, are the most wary: the former thaws, but very significantly, not the latter. Macpherson and Treasury officials throw themselves into the process of identifying spending cuts, and Osborne realises that Brown and Ed Balls were the authors of Treasury profligacy over the previous few years. Osborne's team soon dub Macpherson 'Mr Fiscal Conservative'. They retain doubts about Gus O'Donnell, Macpherson's predecessor at the Treasury, who they know does not sympathise with their core economic judgement. Indeed, O'Donnell worries that Macpherson and the Treasury are so keen to show the new kids on the block their readiness to make cuts that they risk going much too far.

Osborne's planning takes a further dent. He has anticipated Philip Hammond, the shadow Chief Secretary, becoming a kind of 'super Chief Secretary' after the election, taking over much of the work on spending and efficiency, and even day-to-day running, leaving him free to work with Cameron from Number 10 and to range widely across government policy.[1] The team had been struck by how under New Labour, the post of Chief Secretary had become effectively Number 10's spy in the Treasury, so great was the mistrust between Downing Street and the Treasury. The fact of coalition, and the need to find posts for senior Lib Dems, rules Hammond out, to his deep chagrin (he is given Transport instead). In his place, David Laws, hitherto Lib Dem education spokesman, is appointed. Laws is philosophically in tune with Osborne's agenda, but he will not be freeing up Osborne to rove as Hammond would have done.

Laws is immediately struck by the closeness of the relationship between chancellor and prime minister, with constant messages to and fro about the cuts: 'We kept getting detailed and clearly quite personal feedback on some parts of work. The PM stress-tested the whole thing in quite a lot of detail. I had imagined he would have outsourced it completely to George,' he says.[2] The political impact of changing the reimbursement rate of mortgage subsidies is typical of the issues that Cameron raises. 'I'd been used to the Blair/Brown era, where Brown would say to Number 10, "I'm in charge, here's a copy of what I'm going to say. Don't give me any feedback." Here was a relationship where David clearly had a lot of trust in George, but expected to be involved and where we had to demonstrate that the judgements that we were making were sensible.'[3] Treasury officials are equally amazed at the intimacy and trust, as is Heywood himself, who has never seen a PM/chancellor relationship so close. From the very first days in power, it is apparent to all that this is going to be a very different era from the acrid relationships between Blair and Brown, and then Brown and Darling. Different too from the Conservative experience before 1997: witness Thatcher's fraught relationship with Nigel Lawson, and John Major's with Norman Lamont, both ending in departures of the chancellors.

The success of the government over the next five years will depend utterly on the two principals' closeness. Cameron is akin to the older brother and Osborne the younger. Osborne is the metropolitan liberal thinker, a product of the edgy hothouse St Paul's School; Cameron is more laid-back, more upper middle class and more cautious, a pragmatic Tory squarely in the tradition of Macmillan and Baldwin. Both are skilful tacticians, but Osborne is more attuned to presentational nuance, immediately sensing the advantages to the Conservatives of being in coalition with the Lib Dems and ensuring the economic strategy is the government's leitmotif. 'We're not going to waste time having divisions between chancellor and prime minister,' Hilton says on the eve of the general election. 'George will be embedded at the heart of Number 10. They will be inseparable.'[4] And so it proves. Both Cameron and Osborne know that where PMs and chancellors have got it wrong in the past, two factors have been responsible: disagreement over policy, as between Thatcher and Lawson, and rivalry for the top job, as with Blair and Brown. Both are utterly committed to avoiding the same mistakes. Both know who is the senior.

Osborne had spoken to Treasury officials before the election about a proposal to launch the Office of Budget Responsibility (OBR), an independent body to oversee the public finances. The idea was influenced by advice from economists Sir Alan Budd and Professor Kenneth Rogoff, which Hancock worked up in an announcement at the 2008 party conference – when it was drowned out by noise from the financial crisis.[5] At the press conference on 17 May 2010 launching the OBR, Laws happens to mention that outgoing Chief Secretary Liam Byrne has left him a cavalier note, with a stark message: 'I'm afraid there is no money.' Byrne's throwaway line immediately becomes a national story. Andy Coulson sends an urgent request for a copy of the original being demanded by the national newspapers. Laws confesses to Osborne that he had only mentioned it for light relief and what should he do? 'If you don't want to give the letter to Downing Street, don't give it to them,' Osborne tells him, so he doesn't. Byrne's message duly appears in the press, but not the letter itself, though it would eventually see the light of day, principally as an effective prop for Cameron during the 2015 general election campaign. In a similar spirit of collegiality to his new partners, Osborne offers Nick Clegg to put a stay on cutting an £80 million loan for Sheffield Forgemasters in his constituency, promised by Labour in March, to enable the company to continue manufacturing. Determined to show that he is sharing the pain, Clegg waives his offer. Clegg's decision causes considerable upheaval in his constituency.

On 24 May, Osborne and Laws announce Plan A's *hors d'oeuvre*, the initial £6.2 billion of immediate, in-year cuts.[6] These had been foreshadowed in the Conservative manifesto, and the Treasury has been working on them during the campaign, so they are processed smoothly through the machine. The precise figure emerged after Darling's last Budget in March 2010: it was needed to pay for reversing the jobs tax and to be seen to be 'robust but not reckless'. One of the officials working on the cuts is Chris Martin, who later succeeds Heywood at Number 10, his deft work having impressed Osborne.

Peter Mandelson, *éminence grise* to both Brown and Blair, cautioned against the risky strategy of announcing immediate cuts: but Cameron and Osborne are very sure they want to be upfront and explicit about precise figures in the general election.

Cameron and Osborne approve of the input of Laws over their first taster of cuts. Osborne misses Hammond, though finds Laws as 'dry as a bone' and 'more fiscally conservative' than any of them. Laws deals firmly with the unprotected departments including the Department for Communities and Local Government (DCLG), Culture, Media and Sport (DCMS), Work and Pensions (DWP), and above all with the Home Office. After long torrid discussions, Home Secretary Theresa May settles in the nick of time – at 11 p.m. on Friday 21 May.[7] Laws dispels altogether any apprehensions that the Lib Dems cannot take the heat of delivering Plan A on the ground. 'Lib Dem support for fiscal consolidation was important, because it broadened the legitimacy for the strong action that was taken and it underpinned the whole government,' says a senior Treasury official.

Things are going well for Osborne. Treasury officials are seriously warming to their new chancellor. After thirteen years of being dictated to, some say bullied, by Brown and Balls, they now have a chancellor who is powerful, but also an agreeable colleague: 'We were very excited by the new atmosphere. Osborne wanted to know what we thought and was genuinely interested. He was comfortable with us disagreeing with his arguments and being challenged on his thinking. It was pretty refreshing after what had come before,' says one senior mandarin.

On 29 May, with discussions in full swing, David Laws resigns following revelations in the *Daily Telegraph* that he claimed £40,000 of parliamentary expenses to pay rent to his partner.[8] This is a major blow to Osborne: he has lost Hammond and now Laws within the space of a month. Laws is promptly replaced as Chief Secretary by Danny Alexander, chief of staff to Clegg in the run-up to the general election. He had been appointed Secretary of State for Scotland after the election but serves for just seventeen days. Rather than a fatal blow to the coalition's economic policy and to the cohesion of the two parties, it proves heaven-sent serendipity. Alexander soon proves as dry as Laws, some think even drier, and combines toughness with humanity. He rapidly forms a close relationship with Osborne and Oliver Letwin; a relationship which proves of enduring value – existential value, perhaps – to the coalition over the years.

Within hours of his joining, the Treasury inform Alexander that there is more scope for cuts, so eager are they to show the financial markets that the government is prudent and serious, while Alexander initially argues for fewer. They settle closer to the Treasury end of the argument. O'Donnell is rare amongst officials in cautioning against too big cuts because of his scepticism about government's capability to deliver them. A series of meetings of the big four – Cameron, Clegg, Osborne and Alexander, later to be institutionalised in an arrangement unforeseen by the Coalition Agreement as 'the Quad' – finalises the decisions in the run-up to the Budget.

Osborne and his team are eager to get on with reforming the banking system. In their pre-election discussions with Macpherson, however, they decide to hold back from immediate implementation, and to produce a White Paper on financial reforms that leaves the door open. After discussion with Mervyn King and others, Osborne convinces Lib Dem Business Secretary Vince Cable that the Bank of England must have oversight of the banking system and that there is increasing recognition across the world that banks of last resort have to be in the same body as central banks. 'The return of all those powers to the Bank was quite striking,' says the former deputy governor Paul Tucker. 'It was to become more powerful than it had been for eighty years. Constraints and good design were therefore imperative.'[9] On 16 June, Osborne announces that he will set up the Independent Commission on Banking under the chairmanship of Sir John Vickers. The Treasury, nervous that the new government might be overly quick to regulate the City, thereby damaging its competitiveness, are happy with the delay.

The Conservatives had promised the Emergency Budget within fifty days. It comes on 22 June, after just forty-one days. The key announcement is the commitment to a clear deficit reduction plan over the life of the parliament, and the confirmation of what the figure will be. Officials in the Treasury and Cabinet Office continue to be struck by the readiness of the prime minister to be so supportive of the chancellor and Treasury. Back in mid-May, the Treasury had presented their proposals for the pace at which the deficit should be reduced, offering Osborne a set menu of cuts. The Budget presented on 22 June is almost identical to recommendations laid out in the Treasury's initial papers.

The Quad proves its worth in the run-up to the Budget. Under normal conditions, the chancellor and the Chief Secretary, with the PM, are the figures who sign off on the details of the Budget: not even the Cabinet are told until the day the speech is delivered. But Britain now has a coalition, and the Chief Secretary is from another party, as is the deputy prime minister. The Quad therefore remains after the Budget, and reaches maturity during the Autumn Statement. It does indeed become the key buckle binding the coalition together.

Clegg worries that the cuts might compromise the delivery of public services: Alexander reassures him that quality will not be compromised.[10] Osborne takes his Treasury team away to Dorneywood, the eighteenth-century Georgian house used by the chancellor, to analyse the proposals. They realise that they are about to be the authors of the toughest deficit-reduction plan ever enacted in peacetime Britain. It is unknowable how it will work out in practice, whether the country will accept it, and whether they are cutting too quickly or whether they should be going even further.

Savings are to be found mainly through cuts, but the Emergency Budget also brings in tax increases (80% of the deficit reduction is to come from cuts, 20% from tax increases). Prime amongst them is the plan to raise VAT from 17.5% to 20%. This is potentially very difficult. The Lib Dems are worried, as the change is regressive. 'It's difficult and damaging,' Clegg tells Osborne, 'but I can see that it has to be done.'[11] Further debates take place on whether the VAT increase should come into force immediately: the decision is taken to delay it to January 2011, principally for administrative reasons. The Treasury is surprised by how political Osborne is. 'It is clear that they don't have much time for tax credits,' says an official. Osborne and his team indeed regard Gordon Brown's innovation as overly complex and riddled with perverse incentives. They decree that they will be much less generous. Housing benefit equally will be hit, the Treasury believes for political reasons again. The Conservatives are clear, however, that they will not touch pensioners.

Osborne wants to insert the controversial line into his speech, 'when we say we are all in this together, we mean it', a phrase he had used in October 2009. The Treasury accept that Osborne is serious about not hurting the poor more than the rich. Teams are tasked to model the impact of the policy changes, though they must rely heavily on guesswork. The day before the Budget, Osborne, Hancock, Harrison and Treasury civil servants work late into the night. Officials have a palpable sense that history is being made, and that they are now in a completely different era from New Labour.

That morning, 22 June, the newspapers make their predictions about the Budget. 'The most draconian in thirty years' is the view of the *Daily Telegraph*. 'The most brutal Budget in a generation' predicts the *Financial Times*. Osborne, normally the epitome of confidence, is apprehensive as he rises to give his speech. But public opinion has been moving his way. Polls by both Ipsos MORI and ICM in the forty-eight hours leading up to it show that the coalition has succeeded in shifting the public mood from opposition to spending cuts to a cautious acceptance.[12] Osborne and his team are relieved too at the Budget's reception, both amongst the commentariat and in the country. The 'c' word proves after all not to be toxic.

Long before Osborne delivers the Emergency Budget, officials deep inside the Treasury had been working away on the Spending Review, to be announced in the Autumn Statement. While the Budget outlines the overall figure for the reduction, the final detail about departmental cuts will appear in this Spending Review. As one senior Treasury official put it, these 'spending decisions reframed the question of what the UK could afford'. It is a tightly controlled operation: besides Treasury officials, and the voices of Osborne and his aides, the other heavyweight input comes from Danny Alexander, who oversees much of the detail. Cameron and his team at Number 10 follow discussions closely, but with the exception of defence, they leave the work very much to Osborne and the Treasury team. Although the Budget cuts are agreed relatively smoothly, the Spending Review negotiations sees the first skirmishes in a five-year battle between Work and Pensions Secretary Iain Duncan Smith (IDS) and Osborne. IDS will not agree to any cuts unless £2.5 billion is ploughed back in to fund Universal Credit, the centrepiece of his reform agenda.[13] It is a sticking point for much of the negotiations and Osborne only reluctantly agrees in September at the eleventh hour.

Welfare is highlighted in the Budget as it will be cut particularly heavily, by £11 billion – largely through changing the measure of inflation used for welfare payments from the retail price index (RPI) to the consumer price index (CPI) – a hugely significant change. The NHS, unlike welfare, is a protected area. In Opposition, the Conservatives had been unequivocal in maintaining that the country could trust them with the NHS, and that they would protect real-term increases in NHS spending. Cameron and Osborne knew the general election could not be won on the NHS, but it could be lost on it, and they had been adamant that the area was sacrosanct. Protecting the schools budget is more contentious; Clegg and Alexander argue strongly for it, as does Education Secretary Michael Gove. Osborne assents, even though there is not the same political need to favour schools as the NHS. International development is the final protected area, primarily at the instigation of Cameron himself. When challenged over the years about the commitment to spend 0.7% of national income on aid, Cameron is apt to get testy: 'It is one of the few issues on which he will lose his temper. It is a mixture for him of genuine compassion with political positioning of his party.' A debate takes place whether the 0.7% should apply immediately or be delayed to 2015: they compromise on 2013.

Tuition fees for university students are to rise, despite a clear Lib Dem pledge to oppose any such increase. Osborne recognises that it will be a significant hit for Clegg (he tells his Tory staff, 'They are mad to let us do this'), and offers to pass on the proposal telling him the change is not imperative. Clegg rejects the offer, a momentous decision for the future of the Liberal Democrats, believing again that the change is part of the necessary punishment. Clegg, Alexander, Cable and Laws had all tried and failed to change Liberal Democrat policy on tuition fees. None of them realise fully what turbulence the judgement will cause their party across the country. Debate also takes place over defence cuts. Defence is an article of faith to the right of the Conservative Party. But Cameron and Osborne are determined to plug the black hole in the defence budget. Clegg and Alexander agree the MoD is overprotective of its spending, and inefficient.

August is normally a quiet month in the Treasury, but this August the teams working on spending cuts are buzzing with activity. They are spurred on by radical thinking from some of the department's young Turks as well as a crowd-sourcing exercise, pioneered by Steve Hilton, which solicits thousands of responses from the public on where savings can be made. By early September, it is clear where the main cuts will fall. Officials remain pleased to be working for a chancellor who knows what he wants to do. Osborne may not have developed any overriding philosophy for his cuts programme, yet he is certainly steely in his judgements. He and Alexander have been struck by Macpherson's commanding advice: 'You set the tight overall budgets, and the departments will find the savings. You can rely on the departments to ensure that they will get the money to the front line.' It emboldens them to cut more deeply. They are impressed by the Treasury's determination to enforce its will across Whitehall.

Cameron and Osborne had decided in Opposition that they wanted to have a major review of Britain's foreign and defence commitments. Defence spending, they thought, was excessive, capricious and unrelated sufficiently to Britain's strategic requirements and economic capability, all of which was exacerbated by a very badly run department. After the general election they move swiftly to set up the Strategic Defence and Security Review (SDSR), to run alongside the Spending Review, announced on 12 May in the Coalition Agreement. They know they will have a fight on their hands and that the defence and diplomatic communities will resist cuts fiercely, but they refuse to accept that defence cuts would lead to a diminution of Britain's role in the world.

Cameron becomes closely involved in the SDSR personally because, as PM, he takes his responsibility for defending the nation extremely seriously: he knows it is a very sensitive area politically for his party, and he has to handle Liam Fox, a senior figure and former leadership rival, with care; but not so gently that he doesn't insist that the SDSR is managed not by the MoD but by the National Security Council (NSC), a new body set up after the election to co-ordinate defence and security policy, operating out of the Cabinet Office. Once the SDSR begins, Osborne grows still more impatient with the military, whom he regards as guilty of special pleading: without Cameron's restraining influence, the cuts would have been even deeper.[14] Nothing prepares either man fully for the can of worms that they are about to open. The three services fight and fight each other over men and equipment, with long battles over aircraft carriers, jets, tanks and other hardware. Cameron and Osborne use the SDSR process to centralise power and decision-making in the NSC structure, utilising the full force of their election mandate to drive change through. The MoD fights hard, with Fox regularly articulating the anger of the defence community at having to take so much of the pain. He is angry that the protected areas – Health, schools, and International Development – escape free.

The SDSR is announced alongside the Spending Review. The MoD will face cuts of some 8% in real terms: Cameron announces the department is too big, too inefficient and is spending too much money.[15] The strategy must shift, he says, away from military intervention towards conflict prevention, with a new focus on unconventional threats. The army will be reduced by 7,000 to a front-line strength of c.95,000, the Royal Navy by 5,000, to 30,000, and the Royal Air Force by 5,000 to 33,000 by 2015.[16] The SDSR generates enduring bad blood, less from the Foreign Office and intelligence communities than from the MoD, especially from Fox and chief of the general staff, David Richards. Number 10 is furious at the briefing from the MoD to sympathetic journalists and to backbench Tories with service backgrounds. The SDSR does, however, achieve its desired end of savings, even if it creates bitterness that spills over in years to come, and is widely criticised for being rushed and insufficiently strategic.

Reorganisations have been a traditional way that governments have found money at times of need. Cameron is insistent, however, that there are to be no changes to the machinery of government. He has an instinctive dislike of organisational change in Whitehall, believing that it will not achieve efficiencies. The decision is equally taken not to embark on a series of privatisations, as Margaret Thatcher had done so successfully during the 1980s.

On the domestic front, some ministers argue hard against the Treasury, notably IDS at DWP, and Theresa May at the Home Office. None come close to resignation because they all understand the need for cuts; but equally none think that their own department should be the one to be cut heavily. Caroline Spelman claims she has done well for DEFRA by settling earlier, while others, like IDS, claim their department has benefited from his fighting (his relationship with Osborne reaches a new low just prior to the Autumn Statement). Local government, overseen by Eric Pickles, takes a heavy burden of cuts – 'too severe', Danny Alexander later thinks. The Foreign Office has its budget cut by 24% and Whitehall diplomats are reduced, but it is less severe than it might have been. Senior officials say that 'Cameron fell over himself' to ensure William Hague, his de facto deputy, is well done by. When the process is eventually complete, Alexander is able to demonstrate that each department's final settlement is no more than plus or minus 1% from the figures that had been written down in July.

At 12.30 p.m. on Wednesday 20 October, Osborne rises for the Spending Review, billed as 'the biggest UK spending cuts for decades'.[17] 'Today is the day when Britain steps back from the brink, when we confront the bills from a decade of debt … it is a hard road, but it leads to a better future,' says Osborne in his opening remarks.[18] The key elements are the likely 490,000 public sector job cuts, the average cuts of 19% in departmental budgets over four years, and the intention to eliminate the structural deficit by 2015. A further £7 billion of savings are to come from the welfare budget in addition to £11 billion announced at the Budget, the retirement age is to rise from sixty-five to sixty-six by 2020, police funding is to be cut by 4% a year and council spending by 7.1% every year for four years.[19] Osborne's hand is seen in most of these decisions, including details such as his determination that the science budget is spared and the Francis Crick Institute, a research centre planned to be opened in 2015, should not be axed. Equally, he gives his assent for the Crossrail project in London, which was nearly cancelled.

Alan Johnson, Labour's shadow chancellor, describes the Tories as 'deficit deceivers' and defends Labour's record of bequeathing a debt interest level 15% lower than that inherited in 1997 despite a world recession.[20] But while Osborne and his team are confident that the cuts are deep enough to reassure the bond markets, they are less certain about the social impact of their measures. To Lena Pietsch, Clegg's press secretary, the Spending Review is the moment when the five-month honeymoon for the coalition government comes to an end: 'To begin with, there was huge excitement and relief that the long election campaign was over. All of a sudden, the narrative became about cuts, anger, demonstrations. The atmosphere became very different by the autumn.'[21] She is thinking in particular of the large and angry student demonstrations against the rise in university tuition fees on 10, 24 and 30 November. These are followed by a further protest when the reform passes through the House of Lords on 9 December.[22] Although the Lib Dems feel the full brunt of the ire over tuition fees, the coalition's long honeymoon is not yet at an end. Were the cuts too great? Will the apprehensions of Treasury officials come true? Or did Osborne miss the opportunity to cut still more deeply when he had the political capital and support to do so? The new government has passed its initial tests; the heat will come later.

LIVE
SAVILLE INQUIRY STATEMENT
"Many of the soldiers knowing
forward false
accou
– David Camero
aville Report

FIVE

Bloody Sunday Statement

15 June 2010

Tuesday 15 June, just five weeks into the premiership, sees Cameron's first major test of his statesmanship, and of his oratory. It comes on unfamiliar territory. The premierships of his three predecessors, John Major, Tony Blair and Gordon Brown, had been deeply embroiled in the affairs of Northern Ireland. While welcoming the progress that had been made, and taking a great interest in Northern Irish affairs, Cameron is keen to avoid the Province dominating his premiership, preferring to let his Secretary of State take the lead. He is anxious to see politics in Northern Ireland move on, beyond the Blair/Brown era when prime ministers had 'to spend hours in crisis talks with Northern Ireland politicians, making endless visits, or staying up all night' in country house retreats hammering out the latest deals'.[1] Besides, relations with Northern Ireland had been changing. From 1972 to 2007, the Northern Ireland Secretary effectively acted as the prime minister of Northern Ireland. But in 2007, thanks to the work principally of Blair, devolution to Stormont was restored. The Northern Ireland Office (NIO) retained oversight of national security, policing and justice. The latter two areas were ceded in April 2010, in the dying days of Brown's premiership. A devolved assembly in Belfast, with local ministers running affairs, meant Cameron's wish was likely to come true – assuming the Stormont institutions remained stable and there were no further terrorist outrages. He had mentioned Northern Ireland in just one of his five annual party conference speeches as Opposition leader, in 2008, and then only in passing.

'When it comes to the union with Northern Ireland, I am very much a traditional Conservative,' he remarked during those years. He has little interest, still less patience, in the antics of those who emphasise sectarian divisions. What he wants ideally is for Northern Ireland politics to be reintegrated into mainland Britain, believing that a continuation of their own party system in Northern Ireland has disenfranchised voters in the province from full participation in British political life. In an effort to normalise politics in the province, Cameron agreed an electoral pact between the Conservatives and the Ulster Unionist Party (UUP) ahead of the 2010 general election. The pact failed to deliver any seats, not least because of the Democratic Unionist Party's (DUP) success in replacing the UUP as the major unionist force in Northern Ireland.

One major piece of unfinished business remains in Northern Ireland. In 1998, Tony Blair had announced an inquiry into the still controversial events of Bloody Sunday which had occurred on 30 January 1972, when twenty-six protestors and bystanders were shot by British Army soldiers, half of them fatally. The inquiry was under the chairmanship of Lord Saville: a tribunal at the time of the shooting had been discredited as a whitewash. Publication was delayed until after the 2010 general election. Officials in the NIO are now concerned that the new government will bin the report because Labour set up Saville, and Conservatives have been critical of its length and cost. 'What are you going to do with Saville?' officials ask nervously of Owen Paterson on his first day as Secretary of State. 'We will publish it in good order, as rapidly as we possibly can,' Paterson replies.[2] Cameron had been impressed with how Paterson, who was on the right of the party, forged good relationships on all sides in the Province as shadow Secretary. Nevertheless, the republican community in Northern Ireland have a wealth of negative impressions about the Conservatives, and dread their return to power. They believe it will be hard for a Conservative government to admit that the republican community had been wronged.

Cameron knows how much hangs on his response. He discusses Saville's inquiry with his foreign affairs private secretary Tom Fletcher on 20 May on his first trip to Northern Ireland to see the party leaders. The visit is uncontroversial. 'Belfast pretty solid,' records Fletcher in his diary.[3] A week later, Cameron hosts a garden party in Downing Street to thank CCHQ staff who had helped on the general election.

The imminent Saville Report is much in the air. Cameron walks over to Jonathan Caine, a trusted special adviser whom he and Llewellyn had embedded in the NIO. 'I think I'll have to make an apology, don't you?' Cameron confides to Caine. 'I think you will. What is important is how you frame that apology,' the adviser replies.[4] There is another potential problem. The Ministry of Defence (MoD) are wary that the Defence Secretary, Liam Fox, no friend or ally of Cameron's, might seek to appease the right wing of the party. Fletcher requests guidance from the MoD on their likely response to Saville. They indicate that they will not brook anything that sounds like an apology. Fox is emphatic on this point at a meeting with officials two weeks before publication. Number 10 signals back to the MoD that the prime minister will be standing his ground.

Three weeks pass, during much of which Cameron is busy on the economy and domestic policy. At 3.30 p.m. on 14 June, ten copies of the Saville Report arrive at the NIO, then housed at Millbank on the north bank of the Thames. The summary alone is crystal clear: every single person shot had been unarmed, and the killings were unjustified.[5] It is a lot to take in: it is the first time that anyone outside Saville's own team have seen the report, with the exception of the lawyers who have been through each page with a fine-toothed comb looking for national security concerns. NIO officials divide it up into sections to read it over and prepare the government's response, working out the possible questions that will demand precise answers. At 4.30 p.m., the full report and summary arrive at Downing Street. Cameron is just off a plane from his first visit as PM to Afghanistan. He already has one fight on his hands with the MoD over bringing British troops home. He picks up the summary.

Cameron reads it sitting on his chair next to the fireplace in his still new office. He is very quiet and seems lost in thought. 'This is the most shocking report I have ever seen,' he tells aides. He wants to give nothing less than a full apology.[6] At 6 p.m., he convenes a meeting for those most directly concerned. Present are Paterson accompanied by Caine, Nick Clegg, Ed Llewellyn, Fox, Attorney General Dominic Grieve, and the chief of the general staff, David Richards. Cameron picks up the summary off the table and throws it dramatically back down again: 'I've just read this twice. It's the worst thing I've ever read and I'm going to tell you exactly what I'm going to do about it.' He proceeds to tell his hushed audience the gist of what he wants to say in his parliamentary statement the following afternoon, the tenor of which remains unchanged. Those present murmur agreement, even Richards, a surprise to Cameron's aides. As Britain's army chief, they had anticipated more resistance, though even Richards is comfortable with the apology being unequivocal. Cameron reassures Richards that he is aware of the nuances of this, and how the apology must avoid denigrating the record of service by British forces in Northern Ireland throughout the decades of the Troubles – a point that Paterson also makes. 'We can't let Bloody Sunday be the defining point of the entire Operation Banner,' says Caine, referring to the code name given to the British military operation in Northern Ireland between 1969 and 2007.[7] 'Hear, hear,' responds Richards, very audibly. The MoD's preference for a more nuanced response is, Cameron makes clear, not an option. Fox sees the way the wind is blowing, and decides against opposing the prime minister's settled will.

Cameron's speechwriters, Ameet Gill and Tim Kiddell, are frantically taking notes while Cameron has been speaking. The meeting breaks up and Gill and Kiddell work to turn Cameron's off-the-cuff words into a formal speech, complemented by drafts from the NIO and Cabinet Office. They sit around Kiddell's screen, joined by Caine and Simon Case, another official, working until midnight producing a draft speech for Cameron to deliver the following day which they put in the PM's overnight box.

Cameron rises as usual soon after 5 a.m., finds their draft but makes relatively few comments on it. At 7.30, Paterson and Caine come into Downing Street to discuss final tuning of the speech. They have little to contribute because Cameron is so clear on what he wants to say. At 9.00, Tom Strathclyde, Leader of the House of Lords, comes in for a briefing as he will be speaking on the government's response in the Upper House. At noon, Cameron leaves for the Commons. He reads through the speech once more before asking for his Commons office to be cleared: 'I want to go through it on my own to give it one final polish.' He strikes observers as more than usually calm, confident and focused.[8] In Londonderry (or Derry as it is known by nationalists and republicans), where Bloody Sunday occurred, many expect the worst, believing Cameron will seek to make excuses. Crowds gather outside the Guildhall in the city, where relatives of those who died have been invited to read the report. A giant TV screen outside will broadcast live Cameron's statement in the House of Commons. The long wait is over. At 3.30 p.m., on the dot, the prime minister rises in the chamber:

> Mr Speaker, I am deeply patriotic. I never want to believe anything bad about our country. I never want to call into question the behaviour of our soldiers and our army, who I believe to be the finest in the world ... But the conclusions of this report are absolutely clear. There is no doubt, there is nothing equivocal, there are no ambiguities. What happened on Bloody Sunday was both unjustified and unjustifiable. It was wrong ... In the words of Lord Saville, what happened on Bloody Sunday strengthened the Provisional IRA, increased nationalist resentment and hostility towards the army and exacerbated the violent conflict of the years that followed. Bloody Sunday was a tragedy for the bereaved and the wounded and a catastrophe for the people of Northern Ireland.[9]

Cameron will not make a better-received speech over the next five years in the House. In Derry, the crowds applaud and there is cheering. 'Last Tuesday was an unforgettable day,' writes Edward Daly, the priest who attended to the dying on Bloody Sunday. 'The great dignity of the families, the immense power and magnanimity of the prime minister's speech, the international media presence, the brilliantly sunlit afternoon, the ringing declaration of innocence of each and every victim and the minute of silence for all the victims of the past thirty years all added to the wonderful emergence of the truth after such a long time.'[10] Even that morning it seemed inconceivable that a Derry crowd could respond positively to a Tory PM. In fact, security arrangements are made to ensure that officials could escape from the Guildhall should the atmosphere turn ugly. Julian King, British ambassador in Dublin, is profoundly struck and moved by the reception on both sides of the border in Ireland. The statement from Cameron so early in the life of the government sets the context for the British government's relations with Dublin and Belfast for the years that follow.[11] It paves the way for the Queen's historic visit to Dublin in May 2011, the first by a British monarch since Ireland broke away from Britain in 1921, and for the Irish president's return visit in April 2014.

It is not all plain sailing. On 1 October 2011, Cameron experiences an unpleasant personal encounter in Downing Street. The controversy surrounding the death of Pat Finucane, a Belfast solicitor murdered in 1989 by loyalist paramilitaries who had been colluding with British security forces, was left for Cameron to deal with following the previous Labour government's unfulfilled commitment to hold a public inquiry. Finucane's widow, Geraldine, and her family are demanding a fully independent inquiry into the whole episode, something which has the support of the republicans and all parties in the Republic, but is opposed by unionists. The government thinks a review by a senior QC will establish the truth of what happened more effectively and speedily than a statutory inquiry. The review itself would be entirely independent. The family are not convinced by this: so Cameron takes a personal decision to invite Mrs Finucane into Downing Street. He knows the meeting will not be easy. He sees her, one of her sons, a lawyer, and Pat Finucane's two brothers in the white drawing room on the first floor. Paterson, Caine and two other officials are also present. From the very beginning, it is clear she is in no mood to be mollified; Cameron tells her 'I know you have no reason to trust or believe me, but I think that a statutory inquiry is neither right nor necessary. It will take years and be bitterly fought over. But there is someone I know who can get to the truth for you far more quickly.' While Mrs Finucane is extremely disappointed, she remains dignified throughout. At one point the officials believe that one of Finucane's brothers is about to thump Cameron. Sensing the tension in the room, Cameron draws the meeting to a swift close. Mrs Finucane then storms out of Downing Street to the waiting press outside, telling them that she is so angry she can hardly speak. 'All of us are very upset and disappointed,' she exclaims.[12]

Northern Ireland continues to simmer throughout the next five years, with violence never far away, and political difficulties after the failed talks in 2013 led by the American diplomat Richard Haass, which tries to resolve disputes over the use of flags, parades and other 'legacy' issues associated with the Troubles. Many both north and south of the border, as well as in London, are disappointed that the government didn't build more on the momentum and goodwill of the Bloody Sunday statement to settle outstanding issues. Progress is made with the Stormont House Agreement in December 2014, following cross-party talks initiated by Theresa Villiers, Paterson's successor as Secretary of State. A crisis is averted over Stormont's budget and some consensus emerges on dealing with the sensitive legacy issues.

Cameron's Bloody Sunday response remains his defining moment concerning Northern Ireland. It sees him at his best, instinctive, courageous, fired with moral zeal. Here, his pugnacity does not land him in trouble, as it would later do periodically. The tone of the speech and the words, unusually for a prime minister, are almost entirely his own. 'It wasn't my first opportunity to speak on Northern Ireland. It was my first opportunity to be prime minister,' he said shortly afterwards. He might have favoured similar openness on Iraq, but he deemed it inappropriate to intervene while the long-awaited Chilcot Inquiry was still deliberating. But he could press ahead on Britain's other twenty-first-century war: Afghanistan.

SIX

Chequers Summit on Afghanistan

June 2010

Tuesday 15 May, one week in, sees Cameron's first visit to Chequers as prime minister. His convoy slows down as it approaches the house so he can savour the full impact of the sixteenth-century mansion in Buckinghamshire, given to the prime minister in 1921 as the official country residence. Staff and the trustees present themselves formally to their new master. He is typically at ease with them. He had visited once when much younger; it is bigger than he remembered. Hamid Karzai, Afghan president since 2004, is his guest. Cameron wants to show him that he means business in Afghanistan, and is focusing his attention on it. Hence the honour, not missed on Karzai, of being his first overseas visitor to Chequers. Invited too that day are Britain's most senior military figures, including Chief of the Defence Staff (CDS) Jock Stirrup, Vice Chief of the Defence Staff Nicholas Houghton, Chief of the General Staff (CGS) David Richards, Commander-in-Chief of Land Forces Peter Wall and First Sea Lord Mark Stanhope. Here is the cream of the British armed forces. Differences though there are between them, they are united today wanting to make a positive impression on the new prime minister, not least with the Spending Review in the offing. On the horizon too is the imminent appointment of Stirrup's successor as CDS, with Houghton and Richards the frontrunners.

Cameron has no illusions about his own lack of experience in military and defence matters. In Opposition, he announced at the 2009 party conference that he would be taking advice from Richard Dannatt, Richards' forceful predecessor as CGS, who had spoken out strongly in favour of more support for the British war mission in

Afghanistan. The idea proved unpopular, and Cameron tried to drop it quietly. Similarly he brought into his circle Pauline Neville-Jones, a retired diplomat and past chairman of the Joint Intelligence Committee (JIC), whom he appointed shadow Security Minister in July 2007. She was important in giving him gravitas in this area until the authority of the PM's office obviated the need. Cameron is now bolstered by the constant presence of Ed Llewellyn, who has worked closely with Paddy Ashdown in Bosnia and with Chris Patten when governor of Hong Kong. Cameron does not take decisions in this realm without aligning first with Llewellyn.

Cameron has never served in the armed forces, nor spent any time shadowing foreign or defence departments. The responsibility on his shoulders as prime minister to protect British lives, servicemen and women in the field and civilians on the streets of Britain weighs heavily. He is an avid imbiber of military and diplomatic history, and a serious patriot. He would have loved to have been Foreign Secretary, and he revels in broad strategic discussions about Britain's place in the world. He enjoys talking to soldiers in the field and to his Foreign Office staff, chatting to them late into the evening after his domestic officials have gone home.

But Cameron is no romantic. Friends from Eton, Oxford and elsewhere are now in middle-ranking positions in the services. He listens carefully to what they have to tell him about the top brass. He watched with growing alarm as he saw army chiefs run circles around Brown at Number 10, colluding, as some saw it, with the *Sun* to whip up support for the boys at the front to gain financial leverage for more equipment and more men. His most pressing concern is the scale of the black hole in the MoD's budget, which runs to tens of billions. Cameron is clear that civilians are going to regain control of British defence policy and its finances and that he, not the army chiefs, will decide what will happen over the biggest military decision he is likely to take as prime minister, the future of the British commitment to Afghanistan. So he is on his guard as the top brass arrive kitted out in their pristine uniforms at Chequers. They chance their luck with a couple of requests which he firmly declines with a respectful smile. An aide records that Cameron is 'charmingly steely and quite effectively sees them off'. He knows that Afghanistan has the potential to tear his premiership apart, as it almost did Brown's. He is painfully aware of a complete lack of consensus in Britain, and abroad, on the best way forward. Britain's allies in Afghanistan are going in different directions. While the US commits to a surge in troops from 30,000 in mid-2009 to 90,000 in 2011, France announces in January 2010 it will send no more forces to Afghanistan, and the following month the government in the Netherlands collapses after trying to extend the mission of the Dutch forces. Simon McDonald, the senior foreign policy adviser in the Cabinet Office under Gordon Brown, writes a minute soon after the election to say that the war in Afghanistan is not being won and will never be won. Britain needs to get out.

Cameron suspects that the service chiefs are trapped into conventional ways of thinking on Afghanistan, so he decides to return to Chequers for a 'summit' on Tuesday 1 June where he will deliberately confront his senior military figures with some left-field thinkers to shake up their thinking. The seminar will be in two halves. The 'wild men', as he dubs them, will be present at the first session in the library upstairs from 9 a.m. in the morning to act as the grit in the oyster. A lunchtime session will then be held in the dining room after the outsiders have left.

Few areas have exercised his mind when Opposition leader more than Afghanistan, and he has spent many hours pondering the problem and talking to those with unorthodox outlooks. Prime among them is Sherard Cowper-Coles, the Foreign Secretary's special representative to Afghanistan and Pakistan who had become highly sceptical of the prospects of success of continued military engagement. Cameron talks to him on his visits to Afghanistan, where the seasoned diplomat is brutally clear that the war cannot be won.[1] Rory Stewart, the intellectually brilliant former diplomat, author and now Tory MP, who had walked across Afghanistan and served as a senior official in Iraq, is another invited, as is James Fergusson, an Old Etonian and Oxford friend of Cameron's and author of three books on Afghanistan, the third of which advocated talking to the Taliban.

The meeting begins. 'It is pointless to put in more troops,' Fergusson says, feeling self-conscious at finding himself placed between the head of MI6 and the chair of the JIC. 'We have to speak to the Taliban,' he says. 'Oh it's very difficult to talk to the Taliban,' interjects Foreign Secretary William Hague. Fergusson believes that Mullah Zaeef will be an excellent intermediary: he has spent five years as a prisoner in Guantanamo, but is not bitter. Fergusson describes him as a 'nice man'. 'This is a unique opportunity,' he says, 'as the Taliban respect the British and really quite like us, as opposed to the Americans, who they regard, above all due to Guantanamo, as beyond the pale.'[2] Fergusson is listened to by the great and good in respectful silence. 'You're not exactly on the same page as most of us,' confides Pauline Neville-Jones to him at the coffee break.[3]

Graeme Lamb, who has been commander of British Special Forces and has aggressively pursued al-Qaeda operatives in Iraq, presents a sharply different view. Lamb is a no-nonsense kind of soldier who talks and looks like a battle-hardened warrior. He exudes charisma and authority. 'Prime Minister, you have nothing to worry about with the Taliban in Kunar Province because we've killed them all,' he starts. Fergusson, at the other end of the table, disagrees because he's recently been talking to Taliban who are still ubiquitous in Kunar Province. Cameron and Clegg, in the middle of the table, turn their heads from side to side as Lamb and Fergusson testily dispute the facts, as if watching a tennis match.[4] Lamb's formula is: 'Either we're going to beat these guys, or we're going to have to do a deal with them. So let's start thinking about what that deal should be.'

Cameron asks Cowper-Coles to speak about political strategy for Afghanistan. 'The military campaign is important, but not enough,' he asserts; and the political strategy has to be given top priority. 'We also need to talk to our regional partners, India, Pakistan, Russia and Iran. We'll never solve Afghanistan unless we work with the regional powers.' At a break, Cowper-Coles confronts Cameron: 'We are part of an American war, this isn't our war. You need to talk to Obama.' Cowper-Coles knows that Obama is sympathetic to a political strategy, and had been disappointed not to have received more support for it from Brown, who had gone public about never talking to the Taliban. Cowper-Coles believes that Britain is making a mistake, as it had in Iraq, in letting the US administration think that its support was unconditional, meaning that it was taken for granted. Rory Stewart also strongly denounces Britain's existing policy.

The 'wild men' depart after the morning session, leaving behind just the cool-headed men and women. They are a diverse crew – too many for Cameron's liking, as he had wanted more of a free-thinking and less official seminar. Present are senior Cabinet ministers, service chiefs, assorted diplomats, including William Patey, the new ambassador to Afghanistan, and the 'spooks' (the heads of MI5, MI6 and GCHQ). At the forefront of their minds is how quickly the Afghan army can be trained to take over the security of the country. There are secondary concerns about what kind of a signal setting a date for a British departure might give to NATO allies, particularly the United States. If too early, it could damage relations with allies, undermine the progress already made, and open Britain up to the charge of cutting and running. If the departure is too late, even more lives and money will be lost.

Cameron chairs the meeting with a hint of irritation in his voice. He is being kept awake at night by the fans in Number 10. The upstairs flat is being renovated and he is not sleeping well. He is particularly testy with the service chiefs. He is very wary about the numbers of troops on the ground and of any talk of 'mission creep'. He, Osborne and Hague will decide what is to happen with Afghanistan. Osborne recoiled in shock when he was told that the cost of the war in Afghanistan might approach £26 billion over the life of the parliament. To the chancellor, Britain can't get out quickly enough. Even before they come to power, he and Cameron have reached a secret understanding that Britain will get out of Afghanistan; they have only to decide how and when to do it.

British ambassador to the US Nigel Sheinwald is asked to speak about the thinking of the Obama administration. 'The president is very, very cautious about Afghanistan and far more reserved than his generals,' he tells the meeting. 'Obama isn't going to dig deeper in Afghanistan beyond the additional 30,000 troops. There will not be a further surge: the direction of travel is they want to get out, without rush, and in an orderly way.'[5] Liam Fox says, 'It is clear that Obama wants to take the US out of two wars, Iraq and Afghanistan, and if that is what they're going to do, Britain can hardly remain there on its own.'[6]

The seminar is not intended as a decision-making forum. But it becomes painfully clear to all present the limits of what Britain could still achieve in Afghanistan, and that already some 250 British servicemen have lost their lives since 2001, compared with 179 dead in Iraq. The meeting recognises that there is no ultimate prospect of a Jeffersonian democracy in Afghanistan, as the senior diplomat Simon McDonald puts it.[7] Rather, the most that can be hoped for is building up Afghanistan's military and civil capacity, and avoiding the return of al-Qaeda and the threat that would pose to Britain's national security. Cameron probes intensely the military's 'status quo' argument, that staying on in Afghanistan will produce solutions where doing so had failed to work in the past. He is at his strongest at this kind of forensic questioning of received wisdom. He winds up the seminar, more convinced than ever in his mind that Britain must leave. He is even clearer than ever of the date: before the next general election.

David Richards is the most vocal of the service chiefs. Setting any kind of time limit will be a big mistake, he says. The politicians must give the military more time and more money. Cameron notes what he says but will not be swayed by him. Richards is in his mind also as he decides who should succeed Stirrup as CDS. He ignores advice from Whitehall in favouring Richards over Houghton, whom he passes over (Houghton succeeds Richards in July 2014). Cameron has just finished reading Andrew Roberts' *Masters and Commanders* about Churchill and Roosevelt and their relations with their military chiefs. It affects him; he wants to take on a big figure like Alan Brooke, Chief of the Imperial General Staff during the Second World War. Richards is known to be outspoken and with a media profile, very conscious of his image on the stage. He is exactly the big personality Cameron wants as CDS, rather than a more conventional and retiring officer type, because Cameron's reassertion of civilian control over defence policy will be much more effective if he can show he doesn't have a cipher in the CDS slot. In another innovation, Cameron again draws inspiration from Churchill, who was the last prime minister to have by his side in Number 10 an officer in uniform. It is indeed odd that no prime minister since has seen the need for having a serving officer on their personal staff who understands military operations and the thinking of servicemen in the field. Colonel Jim Morris is selected as the military assistant against the favoured MoD candidate because he is independent-minded, and totally trustworthy.

Cameron surprises himself with his confidence taking decisions on defence and foreign policy. His clarity of mind and personal assured-ness quickly command the respect of army chiefs, top officials and spooks. On 12 May, a few weeks before the Chequers summit in June, Cameron holds his first Cabinet, and Afghanistan is high on the agenda. Discussions had already begun earlier in the day among the new body, the National Security Council (NSC), a rare Cameron organisational innovation foreshadowed in the manifesto. Andy Coulson briefs that this is the prime minister's first 'War Cabinet'. This new structure, including a National Security Adviser (NSA) and secretariat, emerged from Ed Llewellyn's and Oliver Letwin's discussions with Pauline Neville-Jones.[8] On the advice of William Hague, Cameron chooses the permanent secretary at the Foreign Office, Peter Ricketts, as his first NSA. 'Come over the road and work with me on setting up the NSC,' he says to Ricketts on his first day in power.[9] It is an inspired choice. Cameron thinks Ricketts a 'consummate professional'. The brand-new piece of Whitehall apparatus needs a figure of Ricketts' authority and skill to embed it quickly, a process aided by the political capital of the incoming government. Not the least of Ricketts' skills is to reassure Whitehall that the new PM is not setting up a PM's office running foreign and defence policy from Downing Street. He also resists the notion that the NSC should have responsibility – as does its US counterpart – for broader economic issues.

As Ricketts addresses the first meeting of the NSC, he gazes around the Cabinet table at the exhausted faces of newly appointed ministers, weary after weeks of an election campaign and coalition talks. 'They were both excited and a bit disoriented to sit down as the War Cabinet within hours of walking into their ministerial offices,' Ricketts recalls.[10] Cameron, by contrast, is alert and in command of the meeting from the start. Ricketts opens his remarks with a sobering fact: 'This is the first time a British government has come into office with the armed forces engaged in major combat operations since the Korean War in 1951.'[11]

The NSC meets almost daily in the first weeks deliberating Afghanistan. The most powerful voices are Cameron's – the body is much more successful when he is in the chair – as well as those of Osborne, Hague, Theresa May, Richards, and head of MI6 John Sawers, a voice of caution. More often than not an expert would be invited to brief the meeting before being quizzed by ministers. Indeed, Cameron encourages open debate before reaching a decision. The NSC structure achieves many of Cameron's hopes of centralising decision-making over foreign, defence and security policy in one locus, with a fixed membership which is properly constituted and completely under his control. It addresses many of the anomalies of the Blair and Brown years, and works well because the PM chairs it, and it meets on the same morning as Cabinet so all the key people are present. It brings together homeland security and overseas intelligence. The intelligence chiefs like it because it brings them into weekly contact with the PM and senior ministers. Cameron likes it because overseas development is part of the structure, enabling him to keep an eye on the Development Secretary with his large and controversial budget. But for all its strengths, he becomes at times disappointed that it doesn't operate like the White House Situation Room, and he finds it can be dominated by officials and chiefs not willing to engage in open-sided debate.

Within these first few weeks, Cameron emerges as the dominant figure on foreign policy, eclipsing Foreign Secretary Hague, and even on defence, eclipsing Fox. He cannily utilises to the full the opportunities a prime minister possesses – trips, speeches, visits and PMQs – to achieve limelight to advance his agenda. He makes it clear he is not interested in maintaining relationships for the sake of relationships – a blasphemous concept to the Foreign Office – nor is he interested in strategy for the sake of having a strategy, blasphemous to the MoD. He establishes himself rapidly as *sans pareil* at establishing one-to-one relationships with overseas leaders. He respects Hague, and gives him wide measures of freedom on defined areas, including the Middle East Peace Process and Russia. Relations between Number 10 and the Foreign Office settle into a more harmonious rhythm than for several years, since indeed Major was PM.

Cameron soon shows himself to be more interested in the details of foreign than domestic policy. Like many PMs, he finds it easier dealing with people on his level in other countries than with subordinates in his own. Like many PMs too, he finds himself having to spend much more time than he expects or wants talking to leaders from countries not in the front rank, and considerably more time than he wishes or expects on Europe and on national security. But much of his overseas work fascinates him: it is like being head boy of Britain, protecting its interests and citizens at home and abroad. Hence his obsession in getting Afghanistan right.

Cameron knows he must make two particular visits before going public with his decision. First up is Afghanistan. He flies there on 10 June via Oman, where he boards a military transport aircraft. He had visited Camp Bastion several times as Leader of the Opposition, but this is his first trip to the battle zones of Helmand Province and to Lashkar Gah. It brings home to him that 'these guys are now here because of me, because of my policies'. On a hospital visit, he talks to British soldiers, and local civilians, as well as nurses and doctors. He addresses 400 British soldiers, some on armoured vehicles, and reads out a special message from the England football manager, Fabio Capello. When flying around Helmand, his helicopter is diverted because of an intelligence intercept that the Taliban are about to fire a surface-to-air missile at a VIP flight. When Tom Fletcher tells him of the danger, 'He didn't blink, didn't miss a beat. He enjoyed a certain amount of black humour!'[12]

Nick Parker is the senior British officer on the ground in his capacity as the deputy commander of International Security Assistance Force (ISAF), NATO's forces in Afghanistan. He and the PM speak face-to-face for the first time on 11 June in Camp Bastion: 'We touch on casualties and I am deliberately hard,' Parker writes in his diary. 'Casualties will get worse. You have to live with it. Our job is to keep going and retain the initiative.' Cameron doesn't flinch. He is frank about the political pressures he is under at home, the difficulty of finding more money for resources, and his scepticism of success in Sangin. Parker concludes, 'Very impressive … he's quickly brought a far greater sense of purpose. First impression, a good leader and quick to understand.'[13] Cameron presses Parker and fellow officers on the ground hard about the need for an end date. He is told that if the British forces are able to concentrate their efforts on a small part of

Helmand, where they can show clear progress, then it is entirely sensible to give a date for withdrawal. Cameron has heard what he needs to hear. On the return flight, Liz Sugg notes that he's much more silent and thoughtful than usual. 'The visit has made a big impression on him,' she says.[14]

The second journey Cameron has to make is across the Atlantic to see Obama, his first meeting with him as prime minister. He wants to make a good impression, and is fully aware that he had failed to strike up the right note with the president on their meeting in London when Leader of the Opposition. Reports that Obama thought Cameron a 'lightweight' at their encounter in July 2008, which Obama's team denied, had caused embarrassment.[15] In early June 2010, Obama had sacked Stanley McChrystal, commander of ISAF forces, following an article in *Rolling Stone* magazine quoting McChrystal criticising Obama.[16] David Petraeus, who'd overseen the 'surge' strategy in Iraq in 2007, is the new man.

Obama had spoken by phone to Cameron about the transition: but the PM doesn't give any hint that he thinks the president has made the wrong call. It is suspected Obama is being weak in standing up to his military. It is thought that because he is battling to get his health-care reforms through Congress, he doesn't wish to be accused of being anti-military or unpatriotic by the Republicans at the very moment when his domestic flagship is on the line. Number 10 suspect that deep down Obama knows that the surge will not work in the long term but he's not prepared to say so for political reasons. Another complicating factor is BP. In April, the BP-operated Deepwater Horizon drilling rig had an oil spill in the Gulf of Mexico, causing the biggest accidental oil leak in the history of the petroleum industry. The White House made their fury well known. Cameron is on the back foot over this, conscious of how American hostility could impact on the share price of BP, damaging the British economy at a vulnerable time. It is a delicate situation.

Cameron boards the plane for the G8 at Muskoka in Ontario on Friday 25 June. He is clear in his own mind that British forces will be out of Afghanistan by December 2014. He has rejected utterly the argument from the military to 'just give us a few more years and we'll sort it out'. In the weeks following the Chequers summit, Richards has continued to argue success is the only option: 'Whatever it takes, whatever it costs. We're the professionals. Leave it to us in the military; you can't set timelines on something like this.' Some in the military are anxious to prove to their American counterparts that the British can succeed in Afghanistan where they had failed, so the US military believed, in Iraq.

Cameron is clear he will be the prime minister who will bring the UK troops home. A further four years seems to him a sensible timeframe. Part of him would like to leave earlier, but he needs to keep in step with the US administration, who are insistent that the drawdown be managed and orderly. He is determined that Afghan security forces be sufficiently well trained to continue after NATO has left, to maximise the chances of being able to say that the war has been worthwhile, and that it allowed the country to manage its own security. But he is aware that some are saying this is a pipe dream, and that the Afghan army, without an air force, without the logistics, without the expertise or willpower, will never succeed where the British and NATO have failed. He would ideally like to persuade Obama to engage in political negotiations with the Taliban or their associates, but he knows this is a bridge too far in Washington.

Cameron is unusually quiet on the flight to Canada. His team have chartered an entire plane for the journey. 'This is serious. In Opposition, it was just four or five of us on trips bundled aboard a BA flight,' one of his staff observes. Cameron has already established a rhythm. He usually sits in seat 1B, with space for boxes by the window, and 1C free for him to call up whoever he wants to talk to. He clears the domestic papers in his box, and then at last his brief for the visit, highlighting particular sections. He wants to command the detail. He has been PM for less than seven weeks: Afghanistan is his biggest personal decision to date. He is 95% clear what to do when the plane takes off and his team have squared with the White House that Britain will be bringing its troops home by the end of 2014: he has merely to decide in his mind when to tell the world and how to present it. He takes these decisions alone, relying on his instincts. The plane touches down at Ottawa's Macdonald–Cartier Airport and he immediately calls Llewellyn, who is for once absent because he is getting married. 'I will talk it over with the president and then I will announce our plan,' he tells him. Cameron announces later that day that British forces will be out of Afghanistan by 2015.

He has thought hard about establishing his presence as the new boy with his fellow G8 and G20 leaders. He has formative relationships to build on, but his team are full of trepidation. Typically, he himself is confident. On the morning of 26 June, he goes for a pre-breakfast swim in the lake. Word is put out to G8 delegations that the youthful new British leader has been swimming. His dip becomes the talk of the morning session. The Italian prime minister and doyen of alpha males, Silvio Berlusconi, is palpably disconcerted by the attention given to another leader. The Italian delegation hastily circulate photographs of Berlusconi in Speedos as a weightlifter. Cameron begins to relax, sensing he can hold his own with these leaders. His natural confidence and height give him an easy authority. Fellow leaders express interest in the novelty of coalition in British politics. 'I'm entirely up to it, I know that I can do this,' he later tells a close aide. The Afghanistan announcement out of the way, there are no pressing or concerning items on the G8 agenda. There's downtime and joking with fellow leaders. In the evening, he feels very tired. One of his aides borrows some of Obama's Pro-Plus to perk him up.

The next day, the G8 leaders travel south to Toronto for the larger meeting of the G20. Marine One, the president's helicopter, is preparing to take off. When the weather closes in, the helicopter Cameron intends to use is grounded, and only Marine One has clearance to fly the short journey. There is a brief moment of panic – Cameron is stuck. Sugg asks, 'Why can't the PM fly with Obama?' Fletcher goes over to talk to Obama's chief of staff, Rahm Emanuel, and asks if their bosses can travel together on the helicopter. The Americans are happy to help, still influenced, the British suspect, by continuing guilt over their treatment of Brown on his visits to the US as prime minister. They have two spaces spare. Fletcher and Coulson toss a coin to see who will accompany Cameron. Coulson wins. (At Fletcher's leaving party in 2011, he is presented with a model of Marine One.) Once ensconced on the chopper, the PM and president talk about their young families, their jobs and US politics. It is one of the most personal conversations they are to have. Cameron tries to buckle himself into his seat: 'We don't need seat belts here: this is Marine

One,' the president tells him. Cameron is boyishly excited. Driving to the conference hotel afterwards, he calls up Samantha to tell her all about it. 'We didn't wear seat belts!'

The World Cup is being played in South Africa, and Cameron has a bet with Obama over the match between England and the United States: a case of Chicago beer versus a crate of Hobgoblin beer from his Witney constituency. The match is a draw. A photograph is released to the press of both leaders in front of their flags toasting each other, beer bottles in hand. England play Germany in the first of the knockout rounds – England go two goals down after thirty minutes, but pull one back in the thirty-seventh minute. Moments later, England player Frank Lampard hits the ball over the German line, but the referee misses it and the goal doesn't stand. The eventual score is 4–1 to Germany. A photo of Merkel and Cameron perched on armchairs in the conference centre at the G20, avidly watching a screen in front of them, flashes around the world.

Cameron picks up on Afghanistan when he flies over to the US for an important visit from 19–21 July. Llewellyn and National Security Adviser Peter Ricketts visited Washington a month after the general election, saw leading figures in the administration and paved the way. Afghanistan is the biggest topic on the Washington trip. Detailed discussions take place on the pace of the British drawdown, and the political strategy. The British insist on talking to the Taliban and their associates and are sceptical about any further military upgrade by NATO forces. It is Cameron's first visit to the Oval Office. He glances around in fascination, but his mind is calm and focused. Obama and he are more similar in personality than Obama and Brown, with his brooding passions. It is clear to their respective staffs that the president and PM are on the same wavelength. The White House are impressed by the way Cameron handles himself. They tell Sheinwald after the visit that they like him, and feel that he will be 'someone they can do business with'.

This is the fourth time both leaders have met: but their personal relationship doesn't recapture the spontaneity of their helicopter ride in Canada the month before. Cameron is naturally gregarious, but takes his cue from Obama, who settles into a businesslike, emotion-free zone, where he feels most secure. His staff too are very different from their predecessors in the days of Bill Clinton and George W. Bush. Indeed, Cameron's team find the White House 'surprisingly transactional'. They are very aware of what they can get from Cameron, and set out to get it. But the impression of the trip is encouraging, which is why Cameron's team is so keen that it took place early into his premiership. Back home, the PM is portrayed in the British media as a heavyweight figure, parlaying and at ease with the world's most powerful man. They have a longer than planned walk around the White House lawn, jackets on shoulders, and a surprisingly warm press conference.

The BP oil spill which threatened at one point to stain the discussions is barely mentioned. Differences emerge instead over the conduct of the economy. The Obama administration is not fond of austerity, and think Plan A is going too far too fast, and will not work. Their economic guru (and close friend of Brown's), director of the National Economic Council, Larry Summers, is a core figure to them. On the economy, if nowhere else, the Obama White House felt happier with Brown.

Abdelbaset al-Megrahi, the terminally ill Lockerbie bomber, had been the cause of considerable friction between both countries when the Scottish government released him from jail to Libya in 2009. The US administration suspects that pressure from oil companies was responsible for the release and are angry with Brown. Cameron himself can show a clean sheet. He is on record as resisting the transfer of al-Megrahi to Libya. On his first evening in Washington, he sees four senators to placate them. He impresses figures on Capitol Hill and in the White House, and helps lance the boil. Doing so clears the way for Cameron's party offering Obama a state visit to the UK, which follows in May 2011.

Cameron is pleased to have resolved the issue of troop withdrawal from Afghanistan before the summer recess. Difficult discussions will need to take place in the autumn with NATO allies. But the British intent has been made public, and he believes that he has achieved the right balance, of a dignified rather than over-hasty exit. He has already started the sad task of writing handwritten letters, as did Blair and Brown, to the next of kin of British soldiers who have lost their lives. He shuts himself away and never wants to be hurried when he writes them. His staff always give him time, recognising that these are sensitive moments for him. The month before the Washington trip, the 300th British soldier had died in Afghanistan. A further 153 soldiers will be killed before the troops leave, and many billions of pounds will be spent. Did he struggle because in his heart he found it difficult to write that the deaths had not been in vain?

SEVEN

Life and Death in the Cameron Family

February 2009–September 2010

Wednesday 8 September 2010. Cameron is up at 5 a.m. in the Downing Street flat, and is soon working through his prime ministerial boxes. Four months into the premiership, he has an early-morning routine of working for two hours on the sixty or so items placed in them by his private office the night before, added to by the overnight duty team. Officials are pleased to go back to the convention of prime ministerial boxes: Gordon Brown did not use them, preferring email or summoning or phoning the person he wanted. But Cameron willingly delves into his red boxes, dealing with all the notes meticulously, writing detailed comments in the margins. Unlike Brown, he is happy to be challenged on paper as in person. Brown would regard questioning of his thinking as a challenge to his authority. 'Gordon knew he should be in charge but thought everyone else was out to get him. Cameron equally knows he should be in charge, and thinks everyone should know that too,' says an official who served them both.[1]

At 6 a.m., his mother Mary disturbs his reading when she calls his mobile with worrying news about the health of his father, Ian, aged seventy-seven.[2] They are on holiday in the south of France. Ian and Mary have four children: sons Alex and David, and two daughters, Tania and Clare. Cameron is immensely proud in his first months as prime minister to show his father his study and the adjacent Cabinet Room in Downing Street, culminating in drinks outside on the terrace. Shortly before the Cameron seniors left for France, he invites him to Chequers. Ian had been born with no heels and is confined to a wheelchair so David pushes him around the mansion. 'I was determined to get him up the stairs, too. There's a beautiful room where there's Cromwell's sword,' Cameron says. 'He wanted to as well. There's a rope that goes up the stairs; it was a bit like going up the north face of the Eiger. He pulled as we pushed and finally we got there.'[3]

Cameron pauses after his mother's phone call. His father is far from young, and had suffered health complications all his life, but the family has not expected any sudden deterioration. He picks up his mobile and calls Liz Sugg, the indomitable aide who organises his trips. 'My father is in hospital and I may need to fly to see him.' She logs the information calmly. At this stage, the family are still far from certain how serious the illness is and he debates whether he should go. He is anxiously preparing for the first PMQs since the summer recess. He expects to be up against Labour's Harriet Harman – it is still a month before Ed Miliband will be elected party leader – and the likely questions are the highly charged topics of phone hacking, as well as public spending and electoral reform. Cameron phones Tom Fletcher, his foreign affairs private secretary, to talk over the dilemma. Fletcher, although inherited from Brown's Number 10, is already much trusted and respected. While Cameron shuffles his papers and contemplates the health of his father, Fletcher calls Peter Westmacott, the British ambassador in Paris, and the Elysée, the French president's official residence. Sugg researches flights to the south of France.

Nicolas Sarkozy's and Cameron's relationship goes back a few years. In his first foreign visit as Conservative leader in January 2006, Cameron deliberately chose to meet the French interior minister and presidential hopeful. They subsequently met in June 2008 and March 2010, establishing an easy rapport, upon which Cameron built when he made his first visit abroad as prime minister, on 20 May, to Paris. A working dinner at the Elysée sees them united on bolstering defence and security co-operation, key for Cameron with the impending budget cuts in the SDSR. Their discussion later bears fruit in two treaties signed in Downing Street following talks at Lancaster House on 2 November. Deepening nuclear co-operation is all part of the new *entente cordiale*, from which emerges an agreement over joint nuclear research in Burgundy and Berkshire.

Sarkozy is keen to ingratiate himself with Cameron during the May 2010 visit. The Elysée has heard that Cameron is a keen tennis player, and the president presents him with two racquets made by French company Babolat. After dinner, Cameron ruffles French security by insisting on walking the 250 metres from the ambassador's residence, the Hôtel de Charost, down the Rue du Faubourg Saint-Honoré to the elegant *hôtel particulier*, purchased by the Duke of Wellington in 1814, that houses the British Embassy. Cameron is in high spirits and, despite the late hour and the fact that it has just rained, wants to play tennis at once on the embassy's timeworn and rather slippery grass court. Kicking his shoes off, he plays barefoot against Fletcher under the moonlight, staff egging them on. 'I don't think we kept a score, but if we had, he would have won,' recalls Fletcher diplomatically. Cameron sits up late into the night with his staff reflecting on the dinner. Sarkozy had been on expansive form, regaling Cameron with indiscreet stories about fellow leaders, and revelling in his trick of making his guest feel they are the most important figure in the world. 'You and me will do this together ... We are the only two people who really understand,' the president repeatedly says.

Forward to 8 September. Time is rushing on. Cameron is still split between duty to his father and to his still new job, anxious to provide a strong lead at PMQs. News about his father's health is uncertain and confusing, but he decides on balance to go. His convoy sets out from Downing Street to London City Airport where Sugg is holding reservations on the 9.45 a.m. flight to Nice. A short time into the journey, fresh calls suggest his father's condition may not be too serious. Cameron instructs the convoy to turn around. Then his mobile phone rings. He is told that Jean-David Levitte, Sarkozy's trusted diplomatic adviser, has some worrying news. Sarkozy has dispatched one of his private doctors in haste to the hospital in Toulon, and he is concerned. 'Go, go, go,' says the caller from Number 10. 'Get on the bloody plane.' At the same time, Sarkozy is speaking to Fletcher: 'Do your job and send him, just send him.'

Fletcher calls the PM again and reasons with him: 'Why take the risk? Sarko is telling you to come.'[4] Cameron calls Clegg and talks it through with him. The deputy prime minister readily agrees to stand in for him at PMQs. The two party leaders have become quite close. The prime minister's convoy turns around again and heads back towards City Airport. They are now running very late. It is touch and go if they will make the British Airways flight in time. The convoy speeds through the security gates and goes straight up to the aircraft. Cameron runs up the boarding stairs with his security team and staff and settles at the front of the plane. It takes off just after 10 a.m. They touch down in Nice shortly before 1 p.m. French time. The party are escorted to a French army helicopter laid on by Sarkozy to fly them to Toulon, where waiting French police drive them to the Font-Pré hospital. There he meets his mother and rushes to the bed to see his father, who dies shortly afterwards.

Cameron has taken the right decision. In the hospital ward in the south of France, the world of Westminster politics seems a million miles away. He is able to say goodbye properly to his father. He adored him. Much of Cameron's philosophy of life can be traced to the head of this very close, old-fashioned, very English, upper-middle-class family. They grew up in Peasemore in Berkshire, a small country village with a parish church opposite the house. The upbringing gave Cameron his sense of community, which was later to blossom in the Big Society's advocacy of localism. During the election campaign on Sunday 18 April, Samantha's birthday, he had spoken in his parents' presence of their influence, at the Sun Inn, near Swindon. 'The Big Society … is thanks to my mum and dad. It's down to them,' he boasted proudly, before going over and kissing them.[5]

His father taught him the value of pragmatism. A Conservative, though not an ideologue, and a stockbroker, he imparted to his son the merits of fiscal conservatism and prudence with the importance of balancing the books. Earlier in his son's career, he advised him on investments; when Cameron became prime minister, it was deemed wise to sell them and it horrified Ian that it was done at such an inopportune point financially. Despite his disability, Ian remained a formidable figure, never letting his difficulties act as an excuse, and exuding throughout his life a calm authority and decisiveness, inherited by his younger son. 'My father is a huge hero figure for me,' Cameron says in an interview during the 2010 election campaign. 'He's an amazingly brave man because [of] his disability. But the glass with him was half full … I think I got my sense of optimism from him.'[6] Ian was a huge bon viveur, a lover of a punt on the horses and the good things in life. He was completely single-minded about whatever he turned his attention to. Cameron would often talk about him, and how his confidence, grit and zest shaped him.[7]

Sarkozy's timely intervention cements their relationship, which bears fruit in the months to come, notably over Libya. That early September night, Sarkozy offers the Cameron family use of the president's official residence on the Mediterranean coast, the Fort de Brégançon. The world's media has descended on the hospital so they welcome the seclusion. Cameron and his brother Alex stay up late drinking the fine wine that Sarkozy has instructed they are given. The loss brings the brothers even closer together.

Ian's funeral is held on 16 September at Peasemore. The ceremony coincides with Pope Benedict XVI's speech to Parliament. Cameron has to miss the papal address but meets the Pontiff subsequently at a private audience. Cameron is institutionally, but not spiritually, religious. He enjoys the ceremony and rhythm of church services but does not derive profound solace from them.

His staff worry how the seismic blow of the loss of his father might affect him in the busy autumn political season now upon them. 'I am the sort of Englishman who cries at weddings, not funerals,' he says to reassure them. There is barely any time for grieving: He fits in a European Council between the death and funeral, and makes it clear it is business as usual. But there are to be many moments in the coming years, notably during the Jubilee and Olympics summer of 2012, when he becomes sad and nostalgic that his father cannot see him leading the country. He is distressed too that Ian never had the chance to see his grandchild, Florence Rose Endellion, born in Cornwall on 24 August, just two weeks before he dies.

These weeks have been a roller coaster for the Cameron family. His own feet indeed had hardly touched the ground since the New Year, and the intense start to his premiership means that he had been looking forward more than usual to a proper summer holiday. He and Samantha left for Cornwall in mid-August in high spirits. Some turbulence had followed some over-hasty comments in late July, that Gaza was a 'prison camp', spoken when he was in Turkey, and that Pakistan was 'looking both ways' on terrorism, uttered the next day when he was in India.[8] Andy Coulson and the team had tried to make a virtue of him being a 'shoot from the hip' kind of leader.[9] But he is happy overall with how he has begun as PM, with his response to Bloody Sunday, his Obama meetings and stance on the economy. Samantha is feeling much happier in Number 10 than she had expected, though she is still painfully shy. She has redesigned the flat (largely at their own expense) to look elegant but homely, like all the places they had lived in: 'She had properly nested in it,' says an aide. 'She was feeling much more settled and her state of mind soothes him. They have a home upstairs in Downing Street to escape to, which she likes, and that helps him too.' When Samantha is happy, so is he.

Once in north Cornwall, they plan to get the mandatory press photographs over with at the beginning. Samantha does not enjoy the ritual, especially as she is clearly so pregnant, putting on a brave face in a bright yellow dress. The idea is to have a few days resting on holiday before coming back to London for the birth. But events move quickly and Florence is born at the Royal Cornwall Hospital in Truro on Tuesday 24 August. It is 'a bit of a shock', Cameron says, but not entirely unexpected because 'Samantha's babies have tended to come a bit early'.[10]

The birth is another big adjustment for both of them, bringing home once and for all that they are no longer private citizens but surrounded, even on these most intimate occasions, by staff and security, with the media and its invasiveness never more than a door or a window away. He realises that he cannot even go to the shop for nappies or the small things that Samantha needs. Some in the media are caught trying to talk to the nurses looking after them. Samantha's anaesthetist is a refugee from Gaza: even at the moment of delivery, Cameron is asked, half-jokingly, about lifting the blockade on Gaza. As with all their previous children, the baby is delivered by caesarean section. Florence is their fourth child, a sister to Nancy and Arthur, aged six and four.[11] 'She is an unbelievably beautiful girl and I'm a very proud dad,' he says.[12] 'Florence is a great source of happiness for him,' says a friend.

Number 10 announces he is taking paternity leave. He throws himself into looking after Nancy and Arthur, and visiting Samantha and Florence in hospital. He is due to address the UN General Assembly on 24 September so asks Clegg to go in his place, the first Liberal Democrat leader from the UK ever to address the body. On 3

September he and Samantha pose for an official photograph outside Downing Street on a brief return to London. A member of the public called Mary has knitted a shawl which she has sent to Samantha. She is contacted by Number 10 to say Florence will be wearing her creation. The photo of David and Samantha showing off Florence becomes the image on their first Christmas card from Number 10 in December.

The Cameron family depart for Chequers for a few days of rest and seclusion behind its high walls, protected by police. Domestic joys vie in his mind with work anxieties. As we will see in the next chapter, storm clouds are gathering over a scandal enveloping Andy Coulson. It gnaws away at him. 'We had bleak and grim moments among the team,' recalls one. Adrenaline is further pumped into the system with the publication of Tony Blair's memoirs *A Journey*. Everyone at Number 10 seems to be reading it or listening to it on tape. Blair is referred to in hushed tones by some as 'the master'; he is seen as the supreme political operator taking on his party, dominating the media with his command of communications, and providing strong leadership from Downing Street. Blair's reflections about his premiership lend weight to Hilton's thesis that Cameron must move at pace. The master squandered his first term, as Blair himself admits in his book. Cameron's team are even more determined not to make the same mistake. The youthful Blair will not remain a model for long.

The joy of Florence's birth turns his mind back to his grief at the loss of his six-year-old son Ivan, in February 2009. Ivan was born in April 2002 with the very rare Ohtahara syndrome which left him with both epilepsy and cerebral palsy. Ivan had a number of seizures over the years but his death came as a surprise and terrible shock to his parents. Gordon Brown cancelled PMQs that day out of respect. Cameron does not have the regard for Brown personally that he has for other PMs. But he did that day. Brown himself had lost a daughter, Jennifer, aged just ten days, in 2002: 'The death of a child is an unbearable sorrow that no parent should ever have to endure,' Brown said to a hushed chamber in the House of Commons.[13] Nothing in Cameron's life has affected him as deeply as the birth, life and death of his son Ivan. Birthdays and anniversaries are particularly painful. He and Samantha attend the church in Oxfordshire where Ivan is buried. He will never be the same man again. 'David was just another talented

Etonian until Ivan,' says long-standing friend Andrew Feldman. 'What Ivan gave him was compassion and humanity.'[14] Those closest to him agree that Ivan has softened him and given him a humility he might not otherwise have developed. Cameron's fondness and respect for the NHS is another impact: 'I am someone who has relied on the NHS ... who knows what it's like to go to hospital night after night with a child in your arms ... knowing that when you get there, you have people who will care for that child, and love that child like their own,' he says in his party conference speech four years later, visibly and unusually allowing emotion to break through in public. Few have so shaped his premiership as much as Ivan.

If Ivan and Ian were the greatest influences on him, Samantha is the sheet anchor of his life and premiership. She brings him down to earth. 'She is so creative and supportive. The key thing for me is sanity at home. Samantha is absolutely amazing at it,' he says. 'Take our first summer in 2010. We'd been living in the flat above Downing Street and then we went off to Cornwall, and she had our baby and somehow or other she manages to completely redesign our flat and make it a home for us all.'[15] He cannot fathom how she manages to bring up the family, maintain her own work as a creative consultant at the luxury leather goods firm Smythson, and be extensively involved in charity without courting personal publicity.

Her head is not turned by the glamour of her role; indeed, a criticism is that she is too retiring in her role as 'First Lady' and does not attend as many official events as might a more ambitious consort. Equally, no PM's wife in the modern era, with the exception of Cherie Blair, has simultaneously managed to cope with having a child while bringing up a family in Number 10. Samantha takes care not to express her views in public, and only rarely to her husband in private. Although from a privileged background herself, her down-to-earth approach to life has helped smooth away some of his more privileged attitudes and opinions, epitomised by his membership of the much-ridiculed upper-class Bullingdon Club when at Oxford from 1985–8. She has become content enough at Downing Street, but she looks forward to the day when the commotion of their lives there is over.

Besides the impact of Samantha, he attributes his almost uncanny calm in the face of constant pressures and adversities to 'getting the diary right', by which he means help to ensure he feels in control of his life, allowing him time to exercise and to rest.[16] Routine is very important. He becomes impatient when he feels time running away, with his good humour giving way to bad temper. Weekends are sacrosanct. Early on in the premiership, the family regularly go to Chequers. They value the help that the Chequers staff give with baby Florence and the other children. But the seclusion of their home in Dean, near Chipping Norton in the Cotswolds, proves increasingly alluring and homely. They are happiest when having friends to dinner on Saturday evening or to lunch on Sunday, after a long walk in the morning. On Sunday evening, they arrive back at Downing Street by 7.00 or 7.30 in time to put the children to bed. He will always talk to George Osborne and often to Nick Clegg on Sunday evenings, either in person, or by phone from the car.

To have lost a much-loved son and a powerful and adored father in little more than a year, and entering Downing Street at such a young age, would have been a daunting prospect for any prime minister. Cameron is the linchpin, the steadying presence, who holds his whole family together. These formative experiences draw him even closer to Samantha, to his brother Alex, to his mother Mary, and to his three surviving children, as well as to his close circle, above all Llewellyn, Fall, Hilton, Osborne and Coulson. Within the next few months, at a time of great vulnerability, two of these close aides will fall.

EIGHT

Coulson Departure

May 2010–February 2011

'Yes, yes, yes!' It is Saturday 25 September 2010 and George Osborne is on his knees. He is fixated on the television screen, in the company of Cameron and Andy Coulson. It isn't positive news of the latest quarterly figures that has brought him to this position. It is something that he knows will have a much greater bearing on the outcome of the 2015 election. Ed Miliband is announced leader of the Labour Party, beating brother David by only just over 1% of the vote (50.65% to 49.35%), and Cameron's team are fizzing with excitement. For the first three rounds of counting, David was ahead of his brother, but in the fourth and final ballot Ed edged over the 50% mark required for overall victory. While David is supported by most Labour MPs and constituency parties, Ed has secured the backing of the trade unions, sufficient to tip the balance in his favour. Cameron and Osborne fear David. They don't fear Ed. Cameron agrees with his ultra-political strategist-in-chief. 'Ed will be a thousand times better for the Conservatives,' he says. Ed Miliband will take Labour more in the direction of Gordon Brown's failed policies and he is 'much less confident' than his brother, he thinks – not that he knows either brother well.

The news plays into their hands at the party conference in Birmingham the following week, the first for fourteen years in which they have been in power. Cameron's team had sought to undermine Labour's conference by arguing that when the party was in power, it had brought the country to its knees with its spending and borrowing. Now that Ed, a principal architect of that strategy, is the leader, it is a much more telling line of attack.

The Tories start arriving in Birmingham in high spirits. They cheer to the rafters when Osborne announces a benefit cap of £500 per week per household.[1] Boris Johnson, always a conference favourite, further whips up the delegates when he announces he will run for re-election as London mayor in 2012. David Cameron delivers a feel-good speech, light on policy commitments. It is not the product of intensive preparation as his conference speeches are to be later. Cameron and Osborne have piloted the party into government, are sorting out the national finances, and are overseeing a frantic pace of domestic reform. For all the early criticism of Plan A and the pain likely to be endured, the novelty of coalition government has not yet worn off in the public's mind. But the storm clouds are gathering. Cameron and Osborne are about to reveal how naive and inexperienced they both still can be.

In late 2006, one year into Cameron's leadership of the party, they were not getting their message across and concluded they needed a dynamic head of press. Rupert Murdoch was far from impressed with Cameron at the time, considering him little more than 'a PR guy'. Conscious of their upper-middle-class backgrounds, Cameron and Osborne searched for a ballsy figure with the common touch to project their modernising message more effectively to the country at large. They were not inundated with contenders. Enter Andy Coulson. On 26 January 2007, he had resigned as editor of the *News of the World*, denying all personal knowledge of phone hacking but taking responsibility for it having occurred under his watch as editor.[2] Osborne had got to know Coulson, while Cameron had met him a few times when Coulson was still editor. It was Osborne who first identified Coulson as a candidate for the new role of director of communications. When Osborne met him to float the idea, he was quickly convinced that the former tabloid editor could give them the populist edge they needed to take the fight to Labour.

Coulson met Cameron in his Norman Shaw South office in the spring of 2007. Cameron talked about the job and liked what Coulson had to say: he asked about the hacking concern, and Coulson re-assured him about his own role in the affair. Cameron did not probe him deeply, anxious perhaps not to frighten him off, and avoided asking the most searching questions. Coulson subsequently saw Steve Hilton and then Francis Maude and Ed Llewellyn together. Later that spring, Cameron phoned Coulson while on holiday in Cornwall. Coulson again reassured him he knew nothing of the antics of Clive Goodman, the *News of the World*'s royal reporter who had been convicted of phone hacking.[3] That was the green light Cameron needed. At the end of May, Coulson's appointment was announced.

The first two years went smoothly. Coulson was rigorously professional, and his skill at bringing discipline to the relationship between the Conservative leadership and the media was prized highly by Cameron's team. 'What was there not to like,' one insider said, 'his understanding of the media was brilliant. He proved much stronger at broadcasting than people thought. He was from Essex. He had edited a red top and had a sophisticated political brain.' Coulson began rapidly to secure much better headlines for the Conservatives, and for a time all was relatively calm. He achieved the ultimate accolade of admission to the inner circle of Osborne, Llewellyn, Hilton and Kate Fall.

The *Guardian* had been engaged in a long investigation into phone hacking, and refused to let the matter rest. Hot in pursuit also were two Labour MPs, Tom Watson and Chris Bryant. In July 2009, the Culture, Media and Sport Select Committee summoned Coulson to appear before it to investigate phone hacking. Again Coulson denied any knowledge. The committee concluded, however, that it was 'inconceivable' that *News of the World* executives had not known about phone hacking, accusing them of suffering from 'collective amnesia'.[4]

Cameron felt that Coulson was being unfairly victimised, and on 9 July said: 'I believe in giving people a second chance.'[5] He considered that Coulson had already paid for any errors or oversights when he lost the editorship of a high-profile paper, and said he believed that the attacks were politically motivated. Murdoch had slowly begun to approve of the direction Cameron was leading the Conservative Party in, and during the Labour Party conference in late September 2009, with Labour probably at its lowest point since the night of the 1992 election, the *Sun* announced that it would be supporting the Conservatives at the upcoming general election, having supported Labour for the previous twelve years and three general elections.

However, concerns about Coulson refused to go away. In early 2010, the *Guardian* reported that Coulson had employed a private detective who had been jailed for conspiracy.[6] The paper then followed up with calls to Steve Hilton, but it is unclear whether Hilton informed Cameron himself.[7] Representations came into Number 10, reportedly from Buckingham Palace and the upper echelons of Whitehall, questioning the suitability of Coulson moving into Number 10 as director of communications, if the general election was won. Clegg was another who counselled restraint in appointing him, while Paddy Ashdown, Clegg's mentor, went further, later saying, 'I warned Number 10 within days of the election that they would suffer terrible damage if they did not get rid of Coulson, when these things came out, as it was inevitable they would.'[8]

Even Coulson himself told Cameron that he would be happy to call it a day and not join the premiership team. His suggestion was ignored. Cameron and Osborne were contemplating taking on the biggest challenge of their lives, running the country, and they were in no mood to jettison their worldly press adviser on the threshold of power. Coulson duly moved across into Number 10, to the surprise of some inside and outside the Conservative Party.

His first few months at Number 10 belie the concerns and appear only to confirm Cameron's and Osborne's judgement in sticking by their man. Coulson sets up camp in Number 12, in the same space where Brown had based himself alongside his media outfit and other chief aides. Coulson establishes strong and good relations with all media outlets, and imposes a calm and reassured regime within Downing Street. He pivots the day around two meetings: at 8 a.m., half an hour before the PM's morning meeting with the core members of the Number 10 team, including Jeremy Heywood and George Osborne; and at 5 p.m., after the even more important 4 p.m. meeting, when further key decisions are taken. He swiftly builds a strong relationship with Jonny Oates from the Lib Dems, whom he appoints as his deputy, and Lena Pietsch who subsequently replaces Oates when Oates becomes Clegg's chief of staff. Remaining sceptics are won over by Coulson's professionalism and personal consideration: 'He was very well liked, doing things people don't normally do in that world like buying people presents,' says an aide. Relations remain fiery with Hilton, a hangover from their long and bitter disputes in Opposition. But this relationship is an exception to the rule. Civil servants remaining in Downing Street through the transition come to see his considerable strengths. It is Coulson's recommendation that the savvy Treasury official Steve Field becomes the PM's official spokesman – a successful appointment.

But rumblings about him refuse to go away. On 1 September, the *New York Times* publishes on its website a lengthy account of phone hacking at News International claiming that Coulson himself had known about it.[9] This is dynamite. His appointment to Number 10 is beginning to fail the 'smell test'. Cameron and Osborne dig in further, compounding their earlier lack of rigour in probing Coulson's knowledge of the affair by refusing to reconsider the wisdom of confirming his appointment. Indeed they feel it would appear weak to cut him loose in the absence of direct evidence linking him to the scandal. They hope that the noise will simply go away. It doesn't.

The weeks following the party conference in Birmingham see Coulson's reputation go into free fall. Cabinet Secretary Gus O'Donnell worries that Cameron is not wanting to face up to the issue, nor to probe further into the truth of the allegations. Nor is he happy with Coulson saying that he will quit if it becomes too big a distraction: this is an admission of guilt, he believes, and tells Cameron so. Cameron still holds his ground: he appointed Coulson on the basis of what he knew at the time, and he will not now abandon him to satisfy those trying to prise him out. To do so, he says, would be to show weakness to his many enemies. He hasn't even been charged with any crime, Cameron maintains, let alone been convicted. Internally, though, the unity of Cameron's court is beginning to fracture. Hilton has begun to think he should go: Osborne, Fall and aide Gabby Bertin think he should stay. 'Our whole stance was not to question what Andy said, but to accept his validation and to defend it,' says one of them. 'We believed it, because we made ourselves believe it.' Coulson is willing to stand down. Again Cameron persuades him to stay. Fatally, Coulson accepts.

By December, the pressure becomes almost unsustainable. On the 21st, the *Daily Telegraph* publishes a transcript of Business Secretary

Vince Cable stating that he has 'declared war' on Murdoch and will block the proposed takeover of BSkyB by News International's parent company, News Corp.[10] Following the advice of the Treasury solicitor, which stresses the need for impartiality, Cameron strips the Business Secretary of his quasi-legal responsibility for competition and media policy, giving it to Culture Secretary Jeremy Hunt. Suspicion is fuelled that he is protecting the Murdoch group. Ian Edmondson, news editor at the *News of the World*, is suspended early in the New Year over allegations of phone hacking at the paper in 2005–6.[11]

By the third week of January 2011, Coulson's position is untenable. He quits on the 21st, saying, 'When the spokesman needs a spokesman, it's time to move on.'[12] Cameron is mortified. 'I'm very sorry that Andy Coulson has decided to resign,' he announces. 'Andy has told me that the focus on him was impeding his ability to do his job and was starting to prove a distraction for the government ... he can be extremely proud of the role he has played, including for the last eight months in government.'[13] Andrew Feldman says, 'David depended on Andy for so many things. He respected him, and valued his advice deeply.'[14] Cameron knows instinctively that his communications director's departure will give licence to all who resent his leadership to come out into the open, not least the Tory MPs still simmering after the expenses scandal.

Many in Number 10 are devastated to see Coulson go. There are plenty of tears. Not from Hilton, though, who views it as the opportunity for a major push on the Big Society. But he is at one with the rest of Cameron's team hoping that the boil has finally been lanced, and that they can look forward to a busy spring without further distractions. Yet the press reaction worries them. It is overwhelmingly negative, typified by the *Independent*, which says: 'This affair casts serious doubt on the prime minister's judgement. He saw fit to appoint Mr Coulson as the Conservative Party's director of communications when the former editor was tarred by association with the phone-hacking scandal. Why would he want such a compromised spokesman? Was he naive enough to believe Mr Coulson's assurances? Or did he not care about what had taken place? Neither scenario is very comforting.'[15] While naivety is certainly the more plausible explanation, there can be no doubt that there was an abject lack of judgement.

Cameron and Osborne move quickly to cover the gap. The search is on for a successor to Coulson. Because of their reluctance until the last minute to see him go, planning for this eventuality has not taken place. Although not his first choice, Coulson suggests Craig Oliver who had run World News at the BBC, as well as editing the *Six O'Clock News* and *News at Ten*. Oliver is summoned to Chequers where he talks to Cameron. They get on well. Llewellyn and Osborne approach the BBC's political editor, Nick Robinson, for his professional views of Oliver: his reference is positive. As the job is partly an official role, Heywood is brought in: he is impressed by Oliver's experience at running media programmes.

Number 10 communications directors (earlier called 'press secretaries') had traditionally come from newspapers – for example, Joe Haines under Wilson, Bernard Ingham under Thatcher, and Alastair Campbell under Blair. Cameron's team are excited about Oliver's experience of broadcasting. He arrives with a bang, making it clear that much of Coulson's operation was out of date. 'It's all very old school, very slow and reactive: 1980s mentality,' he is heard to say. He wants the whole operation shifted towards digital and social media. Regular Thursday slots are arranged for Cameron to talk to regional radio stations from Number 10. He continues with the 'PM Direct' meetings, which give Cameron the opportunity to meet and talk to people across the country. Cameron even starts 'tweeting'.[16] There is, however, a downside: handling the media in the wake of the hacking scandal would inevitably create friction. Fiercely loyal to his boss, Oliver takes on the press lobby, making enemies in the process. Not all in Number 10 adapt easily to the new style. They dislike the criticisms of Coulson's style, and hanker for the man with whom they had worked so closely through good times and bad for four years. It is all new territory for Cameron's close-knit inner circle. They are initially wary of the new broom, and it takes a full two years to embrace Oliver fully. But by mid-2013, he has earned his spurs, and he achieves a unique feat for a post-2010 addition to Number 10 by being accepted as a respected insider of the Cameron court. He travels regularly on tours with the PM abroad and in the UK, they talk or text several times daily, and he is a regular and influential member of the PM's 8.30 a.m. and 4 p.m. meetings.

However, partly as a result of the departure of Coulson, morale in Number 10 slumps badly in early 2011. It is the first sustained period of reversal the team has experienced in government, and they are yet to develop resilience. Cameron is under fire from all sides: the economy is not improving, a series of U-turns in January and February, on the sale of forests and cuts in housing benefit, damage confidence in him.[17] Suddenly Cameron, and Osborne too, appear at sea and struggling.

Cameron now compounds any errors over Coulson by not distancing himself from Murdoch and the tentacles of the News International empire. He continues to see Rebekah Brooks and her husband Charlie, an old school friend. In May, the *Sun* asks for his support to reopen the search for lost child Madeleine McCann, which he readily agrees to out of sympathy. But it prompts questions about whether he was 'pressured' into giving favours to News International.[18] Was it demanding payback for its support at the 2010 general election? Cameron keeps trying to turn the spotlight onto the government's domestic achievements, but the probing doesn't go away. A fresh inquiry into the hacking scandal set up in January keeps the issue in the public eye, and Labour MPs Chris Bryant and Tom Watson are gaining traction with their questioning about whether Murdoch's support was being traded for commercial advantage. In the summer, always a highly charged time at Westminster, Culture Secretary Hunt announces in the House of Commons on 30 June that the government is ready to give the green light to Murdoch's bid for BSkyB, giving him enormous power over broadcasting.[19]

However, on 5 July, Murdoch's hopes of extending his empire are shattered. The *Guardian* reports that the *News of the World* had hacked the phone of murdered teenager Milly Dowler, while she was still officially missing. Ed Miliband seizes the moment, ushering in his most vibrant and effective period as leader. He tackles Brooks head on, suggesting she consider her position in the company, and takes aim at News International. Dominoes start falling. On 7 July 2011, News International chairman James Murdoch announces the closure of the *News of the World*. On 8 July, Coulson is taken into custody on suspicion of conspiring to hack phones and corruption. On 13 July, News Corp withdraws its bid for BSkyB.[20] On the same day, Cameron announces that Lord Leveson will head an inquiry into the media. On

15 July, Rebekah Brooks resigns as CEO of News International. Two days later, she too is taken into police custody before being bailed. On 19 July, Rupert and James Murdoch, father and son, as well as Rebekah Brooks, are humbled before the Commons Culture, Media and Sport Select Committee. The nation revels in a rare moment of *Schadenfreude* at the expense of the Murdoch family.

Following a week of fast-moving developments, Cameron cuts short a visit to South Africa to make an emergency statement on the crisis in the House of Commons on 20 July. He comes the closest yet to making an apology. 'Of course I regret, and I am extremely sorry about, the furore it has caused,' he tells MPs. 'If it turns out that Andy Coulson knew about hacking at the *News of the World*, he will not only have lied to me, but he will have lied to the police, a select committee and the Press Complaints Commission, and of course perjured himself in a court of law … if it turns out that I have been lied to, that would be the moment for a profound apology.'[21] In a test of stamina, he answers 138 questions from MPs after the statement. It is a bruising experience, but he survives.[22]

When announcing the inquiry a week earlier, Cameron says that the aim is 'to bring this ugly chapter to a close and ensure that nothing like it can ever happen again'.[23] It is a naive hope. The Lib Dems and the Conservatives are not in agreement. Cameron's team want to stop the inquiry investigating the role of politicians; the Lib Dems do not, and win. Cameron initially resisted setting up any inquiry at all. He had visibly reeled when Craig Oliver told him on 7 July that the *News of the World* was closing. He goes up to the flat and talks about how to respond with Osborne, Llewellyn, senior aide Oliver Dowden and with Craig Oliver. Heywood has been arguing forcefully that an independent inquiry establishing the facts would be in the prime minister's own interests. Cameron's political staff agree, believing it is the only way to draw the sting from Ed Miliband's ferocious attack. Gove vehemently disagrees. He subsequently briefs the press against Heywood for advocating the inquiry, which to Gove, as a former journalist, is anathema. Cameron knows that an inquiry will be a minefield, but he heeds Heywood's advice: he has to do something to stop the firestorm gathering around him. 'Camp Cameron was hanging by a thread,' recalls a senior figure in Number 10. 'He had to find a way of getting through this and calming everything down.' He is under the greatest pressure in his premiership to date by a distance.

Discussions follow over who should chair the inquiry. O'Donnell is one of many to advise against appointing a judge, on the grounds that their investigations go on forever (Saville's twelve years on Bloody Sunday are still fresh in everyone's mind). Nevertheless, they land on Lord Justice Leveson because he has gravitas, and is known to be seeking one of the top positions in the judiciary, and is thus unlikely to want to spread out the inquiry too long. The Lib Dems are strongly supportive of the inquiry, and want it conducted in as public a manner as possible. The decision is taken that the inquiry will be televised, adding extra layers of strain on Cameron and Number 10.

Problem over? Those who hoped Coulson's departure, and announcing the inquiry, would calm the storm are in for a rude shock. Cameron's woes are only just beginning. Miliband's tail is up – he knows he has Cameron on the run. Any honeymoon Cameron may have enjoyed with the media is over, as they probe consistently and relentlessly. One of his team offers this interpretation of what is happening: the '*Telegraph* and *Mail* think Cameron got into bed with News International before the general election, that he fell in love with Rebekah Brooks who persuaded him to appoint Coulson, an act of naivety and folly that led to the setting up of Leveson, which is going to stuff the British press. For that reason, they are giving us hell.' Their questions rain down on Number 10. Did Hunt break the ministerial code in dealing directly with News Corp over the BSkyB bid? Was Cameron foolish bringing Coulson into Downing Street? What due diligence did he undertake? Had he allowed the Murdoch empire undue influence over him? When his judgement and integrity are called into question, it galls him, and makes him miserable. He has only himself to blame. It is his worst episode in Downing Street.

Cameron projects his anger onto Miliband who he thinks is posturing cynically. His distress reaches new levels when, on 30 April 2012, the Labour leader forces him to the House to answer 'an urgent question' about whether Hunt breached the ministerial code in his handling of News Corp's bid for BSkyB. Speaker John Bercow's support of Miliband's action infuriates Cameron: he regards Bercow as biased and currying favour with Labour. Nerves are very frayed.

Llewellyn insists the close team avoid any hostile briefing of the press. Heywood's critics believe he pushed Cameron towards an inquiry, not because it is in the PM's interests, but because it suits the Civil Service to rein in News International. In truth, Heywood advocated an inquiry because he judged it to be the best way for Cameron to respond to allegations of impropriety.

Cameron's personal discomfort grows the next month. He endures acute personal humiliation when personal texts he sent Brooks are released, which he sometimes signed off 'LOL', mistakenly believing it stood for 'lots of love' (rather than 'laugh out loud'). They are universally and rightly condemned as embarrassing and inappropriate, above all because they are between a prime minister and a senior figure in a highly partisan media outlet. Some of Cameron's aides became frustrated earlier by his unwillingness to criticise Brooks personally and say publicly that she should stand down. They wonder whether he has learnt the lesson from his misplaced loyalty to Coulson. Cameron is in a terrible place, skewered in a complex web of loyalties and sense of duty. Charlie Brooks is close not only to Cameron but also to Cameron's brother Alex. 'Charlie is one of my oldest friends. I'm not going to dump him,' he tells his team. He has yet to learn it is his duty as prime minister to stand back from any friendships that might compromise him or cloud his judgement.

The most hazardous moment for Cameron is when he is called to give evidence on 14 June 2012 in front of the Leveson Inquiry. He is questioned for nearly six hours. Number 10 had begun to prepare for the appearance in March and much of his time and energy is devoted to it. Tristan Pedelty, an official in the Private Office and a former barrister, pilots him through the evidence. Cameron worries about his memory and whether he overplayed his hand in his written statement to the inquiry: was his memory at fault? He is often prone to fret about the reliability of his memory when unsupported by written documents. He worries about his ability to master so much detail: he describes it as like a marathon PMQs session. He remains acutely embarrassed about the texts to Brooks. But he is sure of his ground with Murdoch, and tells the inquiry he doesn't believe he overstepped any mark, or has gone any further in his relations with News Corp than Blair and Brown had done. Officials have never seen him so anxious or exercised, before or since. Equally, they have no sense of a 'guilty secret' that might be rooted out in the inquiry. Some pressure on him eases after Hunt, who has himself been brought under intense scrutiny, provides what are generally considered reasonable explanations for his decisions on BSkyB. Cameron's appearance in front of the inquiry adds to the febrile atmosphere inside Number 10 during the summer of 2012. The unravelling of the Budget, unpopularity of the NHS reforms and threat of a fuel strike all contribute – as we see in subsequent chapters – to falling poll ratings for Cameron personally and the Conservatives. Aside from the respite of the Olympics, this is a bleak time. Discussion inside Number 10 is about a general feeling of drift and loss of grip as much as it is about Leveson.

The 2,000-page Leveson Report arrives in Downing Street on 28 November 2012. Leveson had indeed moved, as expected, with commendable speed. As with the Saville Report, Number 10 is given twenty-four hours to prepare its response before publication. Llewellyn, Oliver, Dowden and Heywood pore over the principal findings. There is huge relief that the inquiry found no evidence of wrongdoing or impropriety by either Cameron or Hunt. It also finds there was no breach of the ministerial code. Had Hunt not been exonerated, his inevitable resignation would have been very damaging indeed to Cameron. There is, however, a serious sting in the tail. Cameron always recognised that the inquiry could be a minefield, and his apprehensions are justified in the recommendation that a new body to regulate the press be set up. Even though this body would be non-statutory, its existence would be 'underpinned' in legislation. The *Guardian* is positive, News International, understandably, are not overtly hostile. The *Telegraph* group is against, but the main opposition comes from the *Mail* group. The report divides the coalition. Clegg approves of proposals to protect the public from unjustified media intrusion. Cameron's view on regulation is more nuanced. He doesn't want to impose anything that smacks of political interference with a free press, fearing that any party that introduces mandatory regulation will be 'done over' all the way up to the next general election. The notion also grates with his instinct on the sanctity of press freedom.

With Labour and Lib Dems in favour of regulation, and the press overwhelmingly against, Cameron's response is to hand the problem over to his 'arch-fixer', Oliver Letwin. Following negotiations with James Harding, outgoing editor of *The Times*, Letwin proposes on 14 March 2013 that press regulation be overseen by a Royal Charter, similar to the one that brought the Bank of England and the BBC into being. But the Royal Charter is not a compromise that the press will accept because it still maintains the spectre of press regulation, anathema to most of the profession. The *Spectator* leads the way in declaring it will not sign up to any Royal Charter. In April, the press produces its own proposals.[24] Any collective will to act is being lost. The whole fandango to make the press more responsible and accountable fizzles out. Inevitably, many think.

There is a final twist in the tale. In October, a romantic affair between Rebekah Brooks and Coulson is revealed at the phone-hacking trial. It makes Cameron's judgement in befriending both appear even more tawdry. On 24 June 2014, the verdict of the court is announced: Brooks and other defendants are cleared, Coulson is found guilty and jailed for eighteen months. 'I think, once again, it throws up very serious questions about David Cameron's judgement in bringing a criminal into the heart of Downing Street despite repeated warnings,' is Miliband's fiery response.[25] To add further embarrassment, Cameron decides to go on television to make a 'full and frank apology' for hiring Coulson.[26] His comments are immediately criticised by the judge presiding over the phone-hacking trial for launching 'open season' on Coulson while the jury is considering other charges against him. The jury is later discharged and a retrial is announced. 'It was unwise. He should have taken some legal advice first, but I doubt whether it crossed David's mind,' Ken Clarke, a former QC, tells the media.[27] On 21 November, Coulson is released from prison with a tag under curfew, after serving five months.[28]

Cameron was greatly unsettled and traumatised by the whole episode. Exceptional though Coulson was as his communications director before and after Cameron became PM, his appointment was a very major error of judgement given the toxicity of the phone-hacking scandal. It revealed how naive Cameron was in dealing with figures far more worldly-wise than him, above all the Murdoch family and Rebekah Brooks, and how flawed his openly trusting approach could be, as indeed could be that of his inner circle. They were a world apart from the harder-nosed courts of Blair, with figures like Campbell and Mandelson, and of Brown, schooled in Labour's tribal politics.

By initially backing Leveson but then turning away from its recommendation for statutory regulation, Cameron further managed to earn contempt from all sides. The cynical Whitehall view is that 'governments in the end always give way to the press, every single time'. The fact that Cameron's worst episode as PM came in one of the areas where he had personal expertise, public relations – he had been director of corporate affairs at ITV company Carlton in the 1990s – makes it all the more perplexing. He displayed insufficient maturity in understanding the dignity of the office of prime minister and the need to be above suspicion, which includes ensuring that one's close friends are also above suspicion. Most prime ministers have tumbles and lapses in Downing Street – the pressure is so intense, it's not surprising. The question remained: had Cameron learnt sufficiently from his errors of judgement?

Benghazi بنغازي
Jeudi 15 septembre 2011

NINE

Taking on Gaddafi

February–September 2011

Monday 21 February 2011. Cameron goes for a walk through the highly charged streets of Cairo. North Africa is in turmoil. Five weeks before, President Zine El Abidine Ben Ali of Tunisia had resigned after violent protests. Events there sparked a wave of unrest across the Arab world. On 25 January, thousands of protestors gathered in Cairo's Tahrir Square demanding the resignation of Hosni Mubarak, autocrat leader of Egypt since the assassination of Anwar Sadat in 1981. On 11 February, the protestors in Egypt achieved their goal: Mubarak was gone. As Cameron walks the streets and inhales the febrile air, he feels vindicated in his first decision taken in the 'Arab Spring' – not to come out in support of the existing regimes and urge them to take back control of their countries.

Back at home, however, his Cabinet is divided on the subject. Defence Secretary Liam Fox urges caution, arguing 'it is unclear what our long-term strategy is'.[1] So too does MI6 head John Sawers, who warns of the danger of mistaking the middle classes protesting as demonstrative of a genuine revolution in the country more generally. At the other pole stands Michael Gove, ranging far from his education brief, who argues that failure to support the protestors could alienate Britain from the Egyptian population. Cameron wants to be the first world leader to go out to see the Arab Spring for himself. On the flight on the way out, he tells his team, 'This is a great opportunity to talk to those running Egypt to help ensure this really is a genuine transition from military to civilian rule.'[2] At the time, it is felt that it would be possible to deal with the Freedom and Justice Party (FJP) who had been formed after the toppling of President Mubarak, despite their links to the Muslim Brotherhood. 'They really didn't understand properly what they were up against,' says one senior figure in the intelligence community. As Cameron talks to passers-by in Cairo, his strong instinct is to support these 'brave people' with their aspirations to replace corrupt and authoritarian regimes. On the streets, he is relaxed, though his security detail are far from happy. Later he meets interim Egyptian prime minister, Ahmed Shafik. Many in Britain at the time share Cameron's optimism that the fall of Mubarak might open the door for civil society to reaffirm itself, and for Egypt to have a modern constitution and democracy. He reckons that if the protests fail to produce a stable alternative government, the Egyptian army would always step in again, and little would have been lost.

The following day, 22 February, Cameron is in his hotel room in Doha, Qatar, watching the television screen. He is captivated and excited by the images of the protestors in Libya, who had taken to the streets of Benghazi within days of the fall of Mubarak. Gaddafi has ordered the Libyan army to crack down hard, and already a hundred protestors have been killed.[3] Cameron feels a deep sense of *Schadenfreude* at the plight of Gaddafi. By his side stands John Casson, Tom Fletcher's successor. Cameron is fortunate in his foreign affairs private secretaries. Fletcher had given him insight into the issues and personalities gleaned from two years serving Brown. As focus switches to the Arab world, enter Casson, an Arabist who has recently been overseeing North Africa and the Middle East in the Foreign Office. Since taking over in November 2010, he has been coaxing Cameron towards a vision for the whole African continent, and for reform and democratisation in the Arab world.

That evening, Cameron has a long dinner with Hamad bin Jassim bin Jaber al-Thani, prime minister of Qatar. For the next two years, 'HBJ', as he is known, will be the foreign leader Cameron speaks to most in the region. They sit down at a small round table, an army of attendants anxiously watching on. He launches into a tirade, telling Cameron that Gaddafi is mad and finished and that other Arab leaders needed to say so. What's more, the Russians have to realise this fact, he tells the PM. The Qatari prime minister touches a raw nerve in Cameron, who has a visceral dislike of the Libyan leader. The murder of the young policewoman Yvonne Fletcher by a Libyan outside their embassy in St James's Square, London, in April 1984 happened when he was still at Eton – a formative time for him. Four years later came the bombing of Pan Am Flight 103 over Lockerbie in Scotland, killing 270 people, mostly British and American citizens. When the bomb was proven to have been planted by a Libyan, Cameron became still more angry. He was repulsed by Tony Blair's decision in his final term to rehabilitate Gaddafi, which is why he argued strongly in 2009 against the Scottish government's return of the bomber al-Megrahi on grounds of illness to Libya. Gordon Brown claimed that it was the Scottish government who had taken the decision. Cameron did not believe him, and once inside Number 10, asked Gus O'Donnell to conduct a review into the episode. It concluded that the previous government 'did all it could to facilitate' the release of al-Megrahi, and that lobbying by BP over its commercial interests in Libya 'played a part' in its decision to release Libyan prisoners.[4] In the autumn of 2010, Cameron came under diplomatic pressure to attend a summit that Gaddafi was hosting. He declined forthrightly. Gaddafi felt slighted. Cameron said he would go nowhere near him. It is a very personal animosity. A timely release of the report into the al-Megrahi affair took place in early February 2011.[5] 'Let's make a joint public statement saying that war crimes have been committed,' Cameron now says to HBJ over the table. The Qatari prime minister agrees, expressing his exasperation at Gaddafi's corrupt behaviour and betrayal. 'Well, I have no love for Gaddafi!' Cameron replies. He tells HBJ about his revulsion over Yvonne Fletcher and Lockerbie.

The next day, 23 February, Cameron and his party fly on to see the sultan of Oman. The day before, Gaddafi makes a televised speech vowing to catch the demonstrators like 'rats'. If the protestors do not surrender, he will 'slaughter' them.[6] He will never give up power, he says, and would rather die a martyr. Cameron is tired. It is half-term week, and the trip has been emotionally and physically exhausting. He would like to be back home relaxing with his children. But the sultan has been anticipating his visit eagerly and has laid on a very long and very splendid meal. A note is brought in which is intercepted by Casson: 'Call London', it says. Casson asks the sultan's permission to leave the table and goes outside. 'British expats are in danger in Libya,' he is told down the line. The day before, Cameron had spoken out strongly in support of the protestors in Libya. As war breaks out, British civilians are in imminent danger. The Foreign Office is not having its most glorious hour. It has chartered a plane to evacuate some of the 500 British citizens estimated still to be in Libya, but it has broken down at Gatwick and ten hours are lost while it is repaired. The media goes to town on the government's prevarication, contrasting it to the French, German and Brazilian governments who have chartered planes and ships immediately to bring out their own nationals. Cameron rarely loses his temper, but he does so now. He is furious that the wheels of government have ground to a halt.

The Coulson and phone-hacking sagas have changed the entire mood music in the UK. Cameron is under fire from the press for being on a trip when he should be dealing with the crisis at home. Hypocrisy is another charge: why is he accepting hospitality from undemocratic sheikhs when he is encouraging democracy elsewhere in the Arab world? As soon as he can politely extract himself from the sultan's sumptuous table, he makes a conference call to William Hague and Liam Fox. They debate the pros and cons of sending in military aircraft to Libya. Cameron hears too much equivocation. 'Just send the RAF in and do it now,' he instructs them. A C130 transport plane is promptly dispatched from the south of England to collect the oil workers from the desert. It comes under small-arms fire from a Gaddafi loyalist on the ground. Had the plane come down, it would have been one of the biggest crises of the premiership. The incident is hushed up, but the Foreign Office blames Number 10 for briefing against it over the handling of the evacuation. An ugly moment is exacerbated a week later on 4 March when six SAS soldiers dropped into Libya are arrested and sent home.[7] Cameron has already apologised for the bungle over the evacuation, and on 7 March, Hague takes responsibility for the failed military operation. Not a good start.

The SAS adventure is a harbinger of a new and far more serious turn of events in Libya. So far, Cameron has not crossed the Rubicon. Anti-Gaddafi rebels in Libya come under intense pressure over the next few days and on 26 February, a UN Security Council Resolution (UNSCR) freezes Gaddafi's assets and imposes an arms embargo on the country. Two days later, Cameron proposes to fellow leaders a 'no-fly zone' over Libya to deter Gaddafi's use of jet fighters against the rebels. 'Go now,' Cameron urges Gaddafi. On 2 March, he tells the House of Commons that the international community are considering his suggestion of a no-fly zone. He is becoming increasingly convinced that a military response may be needed, and instructs the MoD to draw up plans. Gaddafi's reply is to intensify his assault against rebels in Misrata to the east of Tripoli. Cameron is speaking regularly to Nicolas Sarkozy in France: they want to act militarily, but do not want to do so without US support. Obama is sitting on the fence and does not want to play ball.[8] Cameron's support for a no-fly zone is melting away.

Cameron is working particularly closely with Llewellyn, who draws on his experience as an adviser to Paddy Ashdown, when he was high representative to Bosnia and Herzegovina in the early 2000s. David Richards, newly promoted to chief of the defence staff, believes that Llewellyn is egging on Cameron. They have a model of the Balkans in their heads, Richards surmises, notably the massacre at Srebrenica in July 1995.[9] By acting now, they think they can prevent another Srebrenica unfolding in Benghazi. Cameron knows of Richards' scepticism, and he discusses the difference between them with his team. He's all too aware of the long shadow cast by Iraq, which suggests that military intervention by the West in a Muslim country is well nigh impossible to countenance. But he is determined not to abandon those fighting Gaddafi. He has been much influenced by a book, *Last Chance: The Middle East in the Balance* by David Gardner of the *Financial Times*. 'Unless the Arab countries can find a way out of this pit of autocracy, their people will be condemned to bleak lives of despair', Gardner writes.[10] Cameron is full of zeal: his instincts are with the people on the streets. Weighing heavily in his mind is the human cost of inaction. His moral purpose is fully shared by Llewellyn.

A divide is opening up on the NSC with Richards, and less strongly John Sawers, warning about the risks of a 'half-baked' military intervention. They believe that the 'idea of a simple no-fly zone' will make no difference to the situation on the ground. Hague is in favour, cautiously, of military intervention. In Cabinet, George Osborne and Michael Gove are most supportive of action, as is – to Number 10's surprise – Ken Clarke, who nine years before defied the Tory whip and voted against the Iraq War. Fox argues that Britain cannot possibly engage in an open-ended commitment at the very time, following the SDSR review, when it is regrouping its defence forces. The deteriorating position in Yemen and Bahrain concerns him, and he thinks it will be a mistake to put all the British military assets into Libya.[11] A generational split is opening up in the daily meetings of the NSC. Younger members, dubbed the 'forty-something generation' – including Cameron, Clegg, Llewellyn and others – for whom Bosnia was a formative experience, are in favour of action; older voices, and almost all officials, are advising, 'We will have to strike a deal with Gaddafi.' Some military and intelligence officials believe Cameron's team are 'twenty years out of date when it comes to dealing with conflict', having not been immersed in the Iraq and Afghan campaigns.

On 6 March, Gaddafi's army launches a tank and artillery counter-offensive against the rebels, smashing their disorganised forces, and advances swiftly along the Libyan coast towards Benghazi where he plans to put down the uprising. On Monday 7 March, the differences between Cabinet members come out into the open at a special Cabinet meeting held in Derby. Cameron startles ministers by saying he does not regard UN support as a prerequisite for military intervention in Libya, desirable though it may be. He is becoming steelier by the day. He convenes a private meeting in Downing Street for Libyan exiles and specialists: their overwhelming message is that the uprising is genuinely nationalist and democratic, and Libya will not descend into a tribal war if the West intervenes.[12]

The NSC start meeting at least once a day: there are sixty-nine meetings of the full NSC or its Libya subcommittee over the entire episode. Cameron is becoming increasingly impatient with the Whitehall machine. He forces the pace and demands papers from the NSC secretariat. It produces a menu of options including air strikes and mentoring teams to guide the rebel forces. One option alone is off the table, 'boots on the ground', as in Iraq and Afghanistan. No one is advocating this. Cameron understands the risks of doing so. Rather he wants to strengthen the opposition to Gaddafi and he believes that support from the international community is necessary if they are to achieve that. Cameron says that he's willing to risk failure; officials, however, are reluctant to consider failure as an option. An NSC meeting later in that month tellingly reveals the widening split between

Cameron and his officials over Libya as well as illustrating the PM's own motivations on the matter. Upon declaring to those assembled that 'intervention in Libya is in the British national interest, speak now or hold your peace', the prime minister is confronted by John Sawers, who disputes this is a matter of national interest. He wants to do it for humanitarian reasons, Sawers tells him. Cameron is surprised by the challenge, but quickly answers somewhat unsatisfactorily, 'Yes, yes, but it is important that we do these things.' It is answers like this that lead many in the intelligence and defence community to worry that the whole situation is 'not clearly thought through'.

On 11 March, EU leaders meet at an emergency summit in Brussels to discuss the deteriorating situation. Cameron arrives wanting a very tough communiqué in support of decisive action. He has been talking daily to an increasingly emotional Sarkozy, who is saying that Libya is the great humanitarian issue of the day. On the other hand, some argue he has not been talking or working closely enough with Obama. At dinner with fellow leaders, Sarkozy becomes so angry with the failure of other leaders to support the emerging Anglo-French initiative that he storms out dramatically. Cameron follows him out of the room to placate him. 'Forget it,' the French president snaps at him, 'I've had enough of these people.' 'Well Nicolas,' Cameron replies, 'I still think we should have a go and get some language that could be useful for us.' 'I disagree. It's better to tell the media they are complete weaklings who are happy to see Gaddafi massacre innocent people.' 'No, no,' replies Cameron, 'it's important to try and get at least some support as long as we have a chance.' He soothes Sarkozy enough to bring him back to the table, but their fellow EU leaders are still far from convinced of the need for a strong EU response. Conspicuous in its opposition is Germany. Angela Merkel feels let down and out of the loop. Obama has had an eleventh-hour change of heart, and is now in favour of supporting a no-fly zone, although it is still unclear whether the US would take part. But his switch wasn't communicated to Merkel earlier. The Americans feel that they are being bounced into action, due to a lack of communication, and this explains their later desire to 'supersede what the Europeans had been doing'. Ever since 1945, a core tenet of German foreign policy has been to support the US and French line. Where they diverge, as over Iraq in 2003, the decision is always to go with one or the other. On Libya, Germany finds herself at odds with both of her traditional allies.[13] Merkel later tells Cameron that one of her biggest regrets of her time as chancellor was for Germany to end up outside the coalition over Libya. But within her own closed circle, she is unapologetic about Libya, and feels vindicated by the subsequent course of events.

Cameron and Sarkozy have more success with the Arab League, who they have been intensively lobbying. Hague's lobbying of the Egyptian Secretary General of the Arab League, Amr Moussa, is crucial. On 12 March, the Arab League calls for the UN Security Council to impose a no-fly zone over Libya, saying that the Gaddafi government has 'lost its sovereignty'. On 14 March, however, embarrassment is caused in London and Paris when Saudi and Emirati troops help crush protests in Bahrain, shattering any illusion that the Gulf States are being supportive in Libya because of a newfound affection for democracy and human rights. Their concerns remain stability, not democracy.

Arab support, regardless of the niceties, is crucial in gaining UN Security Council support for Resolution 1973, advocating 'all necessary measures' to be taken to protect Libyan civilians. Cameron and Sarkozy concentrate their lobbying on the White House. Peter Ricketts' contacts in the Obama administration help, as does lobbying by long-serving British ambassador, Nigel Sheinwald. Their task is not helped by the administration being split down the middle, which explains Obama's wobbling. In favour of UNSCR 1973 are Secretary of State Hillary Clinton, Vice President Joe Biden, and UN ambassador Susan Rice. In opposition are most of the State Department, Secretary of Defense Robert Gates, and National Security Advisor Thomas Donilon. The Pentagon and State Department talk to their opposite numbers in London, smelling their scepticism, which does nothing to increase their own enthusiasm for action.

It is St Patrick's Day weekend, the big annual Irish celebration in the US calendar. Sheinwald talks to Obama in the margins of the celebrations. It's clear there will be military action from the British and French, he says, with or without the Americans. Obama's unclear position has been causing concern and anxiety in Downing Street. 'He won't take our calls because he doesn't know where he stands. It's not very impressive,' spits out one aide.

On 12 March, with the UN Security Council debate imminent, Cameron phones Merkel. 'I know you are very sceptical on this, but can you at least abstain? It will be a very close vote,' he pleads. 'I don't want to vote against my comrades. I think I will abstain. But I will not participate militarily,' she says. As an aside, she says to Cameron, to whom she's becoming increasingly close: 'One day, I really want you to tell me what it is with Libya: why are you so obsessed with it?' She speaks in English. Cameron likes her directness. 'He's killing large numbers of people. It's not like Darfur or Cote d'Ivoire,' two places where recent massacres had occurred, he responds. She pauses. 'I think I see why you see it differently.' She likes Cameron and seeks to understand why they are at loggerheads.

On 17 March, to the surprise of many who thought that the Russians would block it, UNSCR 1973 is passed by ten votes to zero, with five abstentions (Russia, Germany, Brazil, China and India). Cameron now has legal cover from the UN. In his mind and that of his aides, he must avoid anything akin to the anarchic decision-making process of Blair in the run-up to the Iraq War. He knows that the first fresh British military intervention since Iraq will be much the stronger for explicit UN authorisation. All involved weigh the possibility that they will face the prospect of Iraq-style inquiries hanging over them in the future. No one wants to be involved in any decision which is not completely defensible, not least with the Chilcot Inquiry, the last of several into the Iraq War, still in full swing. Support of the Gulf Co-operation Council (GCC) and Arab League has fortified the cause immeasurably: there is genuine regional support from other Arab and Muslim states. This is to be no Holy War against Islam.

On Friday 18 March, Cameron holds an emergency Cabinet meeting. It is briefed out to the media that no ministers are considering resigning in disagreement, as Robin Cook and Clare Short did from Blair's Cabinet over Iraq in 2003.[14] Fox, despite earlier qualms, is now totally behind the action proposed. As ministers arrive at the meeting, the written legal advice from the Attorney General, Dominic Grieve, giving his opinion on the legitimacy of any actions is placed in front of each seat around the Cabinet table.[15] Later that day, Cameron makes a statement in the House of Commons, flanked by the Attorney

General, emphasising again that there are no difficulties on the legality of any action that might take place. The PM commits British forces to enforcing a no-fly zone in Libya. As Matthew d'Ancona, the journalist closest to the Cameron team, writes in his column for the *Sunday Telegraph* two days later, 'whatever now happens in the skies of Benghazi and the streets of Tripoli, there will be no allegations in the months and years to come that the PM misled the Commons, or that the conflict was conducted by a "sofa government"'.[16] Cameron's team remain acutely aware of the lessons of the build-up to the invasion of Iraq in 2003. They knew they could not proceed without full legal cover and proper consultation of the Cabinet.

An important message is received at Number 10. Now that the UN Resolution has passed, Obama at last wants to speak to him. He is blunt, telling him that America will help for the first week of action. 'After that, it's going to be a British and French operation,' Obama tells him. Cameron and the team sit down after the call to puzzle out exactly what the president means. 'What do you think we should now do?' Cameron asks each in turn. 'Accept the offer but try and tease more out of him' is the consensus. They are massively bolstered by having Obama's support, difficult though it has been to secure. They know that without it, they would be very exposed.

By 18 March, the Libyan army is at the outskirts of Benghazi. The atmosphere in London and Paris is very tense, the expectation being that Benghazi might fall at any moment. Had Gaddafi pulled his forces back from threatening the city, indeed the UN Resolution might not have passed. On Saturday 19 March, Sarkozy convenes a summit in Paris to affirm the coalition's commitments in the wake of UNSCR 1973 passing. While Clegg chairs the NSC in Whitehall, Cameron boards a Eurostar train to Paris. Every half an hour, he receives updates from the NSC on latest developments. As the train slows down into Gare du Nord, he gives his authorisation for British military action. Later he describes this as the moment he 'took the decision to go to war on a mobile phone in France'. On an open line he instructs the NSC: 'We've got to do this.'

Moments later, they pull into the station, and are whisked through the streets at seventy miles an hour to the Elysée Palace. The PM's party are pointed to a room, followed shortly after by Hillary Clinton, who has just flown in. Sarkozy is also present, accompanied by a French general who briefs the small group about French attacks that day. 'What about air defences?' Cameron asks the French president. Sarkozy hasn't a clue. He wheels around to his general and asks, 'What about air defences?' Satisfied with the general's response, they go through to lunch where they meet fellow leaders conjoined in military action, including representatives from Arab states. As they begin their meeting that afternoon, French fighter planes are going into action. To Ricketts, it is nothing if not a 'dramatic meeting'.[17] The British ambassador to France, Peter Westmacott, comments how Cameron is happy letting Sarkozy chair the meeting and take the credit for launching the Franco-British operation.[18] Some of the leaders are not happy, and murmur that Sarkozy is taking too much of the limelight: they think he is trying to glorify 'La France'. When they are told about French aircraft going into action in Libya, without their being warned, discontent rises. The participants nevertheless conclude the summit, signing a joint declaration to enforce UNSCR 1973 with all necessary actions, including military force.

On the train back to London, Cameron is thoughtful. He realises that for his first time as prime minister, he has agreed to a plan of action himself in which people will die. Libya, for better or worse, will be his war. There can be no disguising this. Part of him always felt that Afghanistan belonged to someone else. This war will have his name on it. Once back in Downing Street, he goes quietly to his office and closes the door. He reads his brief for what he will shortly say to the camera. Once he has the text clear in his mind, he walks back down the corridor and out into Downing Street to announce that British planes that evening will be in action with the United States Air Force in the skies above Libya.

Intense fighting is taking place around Benghazi. On the evening of Saturday 19 March, British war ships and submarines in the Mediterranean launch Tomahawk cruise missiles against air defence system targets, and in the early hours of 20 March, RAF fighter jets strike against Gaddafi's forces along the coastal highway south of Benghazi. Most of his air defences are knocked out, and Gaddafi's forces are in retreat.[19] On Monday 21 March, Cameron opens the Commons debate on military action in Libya. MPs vote 557 to thirteen in support of military operations, with only one Conservative MP, John Baron, voting against the measure. On 24 March, NATO takes over command of the no-fly zone from the United States. As Obama indicated before the operation began, the US participates for a short while, then steps back. There is a debate over whether Britain and France should jointly lead the operation from headquarters in Northwood, Hertfordshire, instead of using NATO command structures, given the reticence of members such as Germany and Turkey. The White House insists, however, that their 'air support' functions (required for target mapping, analysis and refuelling) – set to continue after their military operations have ceased – only be available to the allies through NATO HQ. This helps to pressurise sceptics, above all Germany, to agree to a NATO-led operation. There is still no consensus amongst the allies on whether to target the air campaign against Gaddafi's ground forces.

On 26 March, rebel Libyan forces begin a major offensive against the Gaddafi regime, which demands a response from London, Paris and their allies. What now? On Tuesday 29 March, Cameron opens a conference in London attended by UN Secretary General Ban Ki-moon and leaders across the coalition, to remind them of their core mission, to assess the mission to date, and to begin planning for a post-Gaddafi Libya. Cameron reminds the conference poignantly that many would have died in Benghazi had Gaddafi's forces been allowed to take the city, before handing the chair to Hague. However, no clear sense of purpose emerges from the conference, particularly over a post-war strategy.[20]

Despite the reservations in Whitehall, Cabinet and the military, Cameron has achieved virtual unanimity behind British action. But in the following weeks and months, as progress against Gaddafi becomes bogged down, it all becomes very messy. Ken Clarke breaks cover, to the irritation of Number 10, saying that he was 'still not totally convinced anyone knows where we are going now'.[21] There are several tense moments during meetings of the NSC. 'There were some very real difficulties that Number 10 didn't really want to hear,' recalls one official. With Benghazi now secure, Richards says hostilities should cease, and talks be opened with Gaddafi. Cameron rules out the suggestion. Richards continues to press for a realpolitik approach and is suspicious of the French for being driven by '*la gloire*', and wants to work with the Libyan tribes who he thinks will be pivotal.[22] He complains that he is not being listened to. Number 10 suspect he is talking to the press.

Cameron's frustration is rising by the week. With the economy showing no sign of recovery, continuing fallout from the Coulson affair, and no progress in Libya, he comes under mounting pressure. He wants action, and believes the MoD and the Whitehall machine are too sluggish. Without his personal drive, constant probing, and regular chairing of NSC meetings, he thinks there will be no co-ordinated effort from London. Large chunks of each day are spent on the telephone as he tries to fire up partners in the international coalition. Cabinet colleagues start to complain he is too preoccupied on what looks increasingly like a personal obsession.

The long shadow of Iraq becomes ever darker. Failure to prepare after the original combat operation had been one of the principal failings of the entire unhappy saga. Cameron asks International Development Secretary Andrew Mitchell to identify the 'lessons learnt' from Iraq. He puts together a team from the MoD, Foreign and Cabinet Offices to work on post-fighting stabilisation.[23] And yet, there are frustrations that there is no similar process to the one led by Nigel Sheinwald after the Iraq invasion looking into a post-war solution. 'The prime minister simply didn't have faith in the system and bypassed it,' says one senior figure.

Ricketts places Whitehall on a war footing, and what Hague dubs the 'anaconda strategy', squeezing Gaddafi to the death, is launched. Officials joke that Whitehall is coming to resemble *The West Wing*, the US television series.[24] Libya is the fist big war test for the NSC apparatus, and for Ricketts personally. Cameron comes to admire him for his understanding of NATO, the MoD and the Foreign Office, and for his command of the complex detail. Ricketts is part of the close Number 10 team till his departure in January 2012 to become ambassador in Paris. Now Hugh Powell – son of Thatcher's foreign policy adviser Charles Powell, and nephew of Blair's right-hand man Jonathan – comes to the fore. One of Ricketts' two deputies, and a hawk, he has wide-ranging responsibility for gripping Libya. Powell argues that they should be denying oil to forces loyal to Gaddafi, taking out fuel lines, depots and oil facilities, and thus stopping them in their tracks. Cameron agrees. The military reply is that this is a NATO-led campaign, and NATO lawyers argue that these actions are inconsistent with the UNSCR. Cameron is all in favour of cutting loose from NATO and taking action unilaterally, so frustrated is he. Some argue that Powell's influence at this time 'positively set back the effort'. French special forces working with Libyan rebels sever the pipeline to the main Libyan refinery at Zawiya,[25] and the British broker a secret deal to keep the rebels supplied with oil: without it, Benghazi may well have fallen.

Blair telephones Number 10 to say he's been contacted by a key individual close to Gaddafi, and that the Libyan leader wants to cut a deal with the British. Blair is a respected voice in the building and his suggestion is examined seriously. Number 10 decide, though, not to follow it up: they want to avoid doing anything which might be seen to be giving Gaddafi succour. But in parallel, and with Cameron's knowledge, Powell is secretly exploring backchannel deals to see if Gaddafi can leave Libya with a degree of honour. Nothing comes of this either, nor indeed of Gaddafi's own proposal that he should become a 'monarch figure without real power'.

The capture of Misrata by the rebels on 15 May, after a long battle, brings temporary relief, but stalemate soon returns. Summer arrives, and there is still no resolution. Gaddafi is very much alive, and rebel forces are failing to make headway against the Libyan forces. Cameron maintains relentless pressure on Whitehall to produce imaginative solutions: sanctions are one possibility, as are finding fresh ways of helping the rebel forces to become more effective. Some feel the opportunity for an international presence on the ground working with the militias while a political settlement is pushed through has long since passed. And in any case, the idea was never seriously advocated. 'There was no security presence on the ground. That was a huge failure. That was a failing of the system. No one was thinking that through clearly,' says one who was part of the discussions. Richards' complaints do not let up: he feels Cameron and the NSC are interfering with the military operation and being involved even down to the most tactical level. 'We had really frequent meetings where the prime minister felt that the system wasn't really committed, or trying its hardest to make this work,' recalls one official. 'He wanted to keep checking up on all the details.' The army chiefs say that if there's still stalemate after six months, which means by August, Britain's capacity to continue operations will be exhausted. Number 10 feels the military are reserving their position, gearing themselves up to say 'we told you so'.

Cameron's frustration results in occasional outbursts. 'This is ridiculous,' he explodes, when Dominic Grieve counters his suggestion to airlift 200 million Libyan banknotes printed in Britain from a Kent airfield to the rebels. 'Why cannot I just order they are going to go, and I'll provide a waiver and indemnity on the legalities?' Grieve points out that the UN freeze covers all Libyan assets, including money that could be used to help the rebels.[26]

There is little sign of a breakthrough in June, despite the rebels concentrating their fire on the West around Tripoli. These are some dark days in Number 10. Gove acts as principal cheerleader in Cabinet, buoying up any ministers who are beginning to have doubts. Cameron is aware that they are making it up as they are going along – one senior aide describes policy as 'a halfway house between Bosnia, where we did nothing, and Iraq, where we sent troops in on the ground. At no point did we ever consider that. We were always clear it was up to the Libyans to sort it out.'

July is yet another worrying month in Number 10. Qatari weapons and trainers appear to be making some impact, the fruit of Cameron's productive relationship with HBJ. But everyone in Number 10 is planning to leave for holidays at the end of July with no obvious conclusion in sight. One option being mooted is to host a big international conference in the style of the US Dayton Accords over Bosnia and Herzegovina in 1995. Another is for Number 10 to accept that it may have to talk to Gaddafi, for all Cameron's revulsion at the very prospect.

Sarkozy has become equally frustrated, though has a more amenable military chief than Richards, and is able thus to drive forward harder. The president sets up a secret operational headquarters outside Paris, separate to NATO, to inject energy into the campaign. This is referred to for security reasons by the nickname 'the four amigos' (beside France are Britain, Qatar and the UAE). 'David, we are not schoolboys in short trousers. We are men,' Sarkozy utters to Cameron to contrast their resolve with that of the fickle Americans. He is constantly egging Cameron on to take bolder positions – on this occasion it is his desire to outflank the Obama administration on the entire Middle East Peace Process. The four powers agree on a new strategy to help tip the balance against Gaddafi's forces. It includes switching support away from the formal opposition, which is bogged down in the east of the country, to new rebel groups in the west. Military assistance will be provided, and this new strategy will take place outside the straightjacket of NATO.

On 20 July, members of the rebels' forces based in Misrata in the west of Libya fly on a secret mission to see Sarkozy in Paris. They are planning a bold attack on Tripoli. The following weeks see French, British and Qatari assistance in Libya providing the rebels with weapons, fuel and food, as well as giving them access to satellite imagery of enemy positions. Fighter planes step up their aerial bombing campaign to facilitate the rebels' advance towards Tripoli.[27] On 20 August, the rebels enter Tripoli, reaching Green Square in the centre of the city. On 23 August, they capture Gaddafi's compound, and three days later, the final areas of the city collapse. Fighting continues for several more weeks, as Gaddafi's strongholds elsewhere in the country continue to hold out. On 20 October, a NATO air strike outside of Sirte halts a military convoy. Rebel forces engage the vehicles, one of which contains Gaddafi, who then hides in a drainage pipe. He is taken prisoner, wounded but alive. By the time he reaches Misrata he is dead. On 21 October, NATO announces that operations in Libya will cease ten days later.[28]

Sarkozy and Cameron have a private understanding that neither will visit Libya without the other. Even though the fighting is not yet over, a date for their joint expedition is fixed for 15 September. In Number 10, the visit is a closely guarded secret. The evening before, Cameron is driven from his constituency to RAF Brize Norton in Oxfordshire. After dinner and a short sleep in military accommodation, the two leaders fly in the early hours in an RAF C-17 Globemaster aircraft. Gabby Bertin carries a Union Jack in her handbag, given to her the day before by the Foreign Office to fly at the British Embassy in Tripoli, which had been looted and burnt earlier in the year.[29] The military are worried about ground-to-air missiles, with a secure military presence on the ground yet to be established. The French military protection ring around them is exceptionally heavy.

After months of strain, Cameron is boyishly excited: 'He really, really, really thinks he has done the right thing,' says an aide on the flight. He and Sarkozy are all but mobbed by the hysterical crowds. They all want to see and touch them. In Benghazi, they speak to a crowd of several thousands. Cameron is alert to the dangers of hubris: he is anxious to avoid Bush's mistake when he announced in May 2003, aboard the USS *Abraham Lincoln*, an end of major combat operations in Iraq (the infamous 'Mission accomplished' speech). It is nevertheless Cameron's most exciting day so far as prime minister. That evening, back in London, he speaks at a political dinner at the Carlton Club. His message is that the Conservative Party must be unambiguously on the side of the most vulnerable.[30] There is to be no Thatcherite triumphalism, as when she told the press outside Downing Street on 25 April 1982 to 'Rejoice!' after British troops landed on South Georgia at the outset of the Falklands War.

Libya is the formative experience for Cameron in his premiership to date. He feels vindicated, and his self-confidence is initially boosted. Rose-tinted spectacles have been removed from his eyes about fellow world leaders. He cannot rely fully on Obama, nor Merkel, and Sarkozy's ego knows no bounds. But equally, he learns how to build a coalition of foreign leaders, and sustain it, even in adverse circumstances. The future of the Libya story will, he recognises, be down to the Libyans themselves, and to their ability to form a stable government. He is cautiously optimistic – too optimistic, it turns out. Libya is not to be the success that the Falklands War was for Thatcher. He invested much personal capital in Libya. But from 2013 the situation in the country deteriorates gradually before 'falling apart' from the autumn of 2014. Cameron has learnt how difficult it is to unseat even the most capricious overseas leaders, and how hard it is to change the status quo: to do so requires him to drive the change himself, because the military and diplomatic establishment is inherently conservative; he is more sceptical of the MoD and the service chiefs than he was before the Libya episode. At the conclusion of hostilities, in an attempt to show that there are no hard feelings, he presents Richards with a signed photograph, and a first edition of T. E. Lawrence's book, *Seven Pillars of Wisdom*. It is not the last of their battles. Syria is to come.

TEN

AV Referendum: Coalition Buckles

January–May 2011

'If you wanted a formula to maximise the prospects of the coalition falling apart, decide at the outset to select an issue of existential importance, ensuring that it will be seen as vital to both parties, then say you will conduct a debate in public on its implementation with both parties being on different sides: you will then have your formula for disaster.'[1] This is the prediction of Cabinet Secretary Gus O'Donnell, whose job it is to oversee the smooth conduct of the virgin coalition government. The dynamite charge he envisages is a vote on introducing electoral reform in the form of the Alternative Vote (AV), which is duly enshrined in the Coalition Agreement.

Electoral reform is of fundamental importance to the Lib Dems. Since their replacement by Labour in the 1920s as one of the two main parties in Britain's two-party system, they have believed that only proportionality would address their historic problem as the third party: the proportion of votes they receive at elections translates into only a pitifully small percentage of seats in Parliament. While a form of proportional representation has long been their preferred system, they agree to AV, which asks voters to rank candidates in order of preference to ensure that the winner receives over 50% of the vote. Although Lib Dems believe AV to be an improvement on first-past-the-post, which has long been Britain's method of choosing MPs, it is not the proportional system they crave. To the Cameron team in the first few weeks of coalition, the implications of any successful AV referendum seem a long, long way away. The immediate concern in those warm May days is binding the Lib Dems into a government to ensure that their own favoured policies, including Plan A, would thus be enacted.

When Cameron sees Conservative MPs on 10 May 2010 in House of Commons Committee Room 14, he tells them that electoral reform is the minimum price that the Lib Dems are demanding for agreeing to come into a coalition government. The chief whip, Patrick McLoughlin, acknowledges that there was 'very little dissent' about it at that meeting.[2] That evening, William Hague, who is leading negotiations, offers Lib Dems a national referendum on AV, which will form a cornerstone of the Coalition Agreement. He knows that AV is the biggest single gamble in the Coalition Agreement. If the country votes in favour of it, it will change politics forever.[3] Like all in Cameron's team, insofar as he thinks through the implications at all, he assumes that AV will be rejected in a referendum and that it will be a necessary inconvenience.

The clear understanding of the coalition negotiators is that the Conservatives and the Lib Dems will campaign on opposite sides of the argument, but that they will do so in a dignified way, as becoming of 'Rose Garden' partners. That at least is what the Tory negotiators think is agreed. The Lib Dems have gleaned a different understanding: that Cameron will not himself lead from the front, and that as PM, he will maintain an Olympian distance above the troops slugging it out on the ground. The following weeks give no cause for concern. Nick Clegg is reassured by Michael Gove's hands-off, even indifferent, attitude to the result of the referendum. Julian Astle, Clegg's special adviser, is working on the understanding that the Tory leadership will let AV 'go' to focus on other matters.[4] One of Clegg's senior policy aides agrees: 'Cameron's personal view was that he didn't really give a damn. AV is not a massive change to the first-past-the-post system. His view was, "Nick, you and I, we'll just stay out of the fray on this one."' Indeed some leading Conservatives, like Gove, are actively considering coming out and supporting AV.[5] In the second half of 2010 every poll indicates that the 'No' side will win. Cameron has reason to be laid-back. In January 2011, a high point in Conservative/ Lib Dem harmony, the Fixed-Term Parliaments Act is passed by 320 votes to 234, which means that unless there are exceptional circumstances, general elections will be held every five years in Britain and no longer at the whim of the prime minister. At the first Conservative conference at Birmingham, AV is barely mentioned.[6] George Osborne is in unashamedly pugilistic form, picking up a 'No to AV' sticker from a conference stall, albeit placing it on the inside of his lapel.[7]

December sees the first harbingers of problems. A *Guardian*/ICM poll at the beginning of the month puts 'Yes' on 44% but 'No' on only 38%.[8] The New Year in 2011 brings a chill wind to Number 10. The Coulson affair is rocking the confidence of the party in Cameron and heralds open season for critics to come out into the open. In the second week of January, rumours fly around Westminster that Cameron and the high Tory command are not putting their weight behind the referendum just four months away.

Graham Brady and the executive of the 1922 Committee come on a visitation to Downing Street. They are not happy. 'You do realise that there is now a serious prospect that you could have the distinction of being the last ever Conservative prime minister,' they tell him.[9] Cameron listens stony-faced. After the grilling, Osborne warns Cameron that a challenge by angry backbenchers might follow a lost referendum. This is not remotely what Cameron wants to hear in the present climate. At the end of February, with just ten weeks to polling day on 5 May, polls are even more in favour of the 'Yes' campaign: one by Ipsos MORI puts 'Yes' on 49% with 'No' on 37%.[10]

Matthew Elliott – co-founder of the TaxPayers' Alliance (a think-tank dedicated to low taxation) and a vigorous campaigner – is brought in to spearhead the all-party 'No' campaign, to run alongside the Conservatives' own campaign. He gives a bleak presentation to Cameron's team on the outlook. Unless robust financial effort is put into the cause, the referendum will be lost.[11] Panic is mounting in growing sections of the party: more start saying the Conservatives will never achieve an overall majority again if AV is brought in. Among Cameron's circle, Osborne is the most agitated; strategist and pollster Andrew Cooper is the most sanguine, believing that the tide will turn and the 'No' campaign will triumph.

Osborne convinces them more impetus is needed. Stephen Gilbert, Conservative director of campaigning, is brought in to transform the campaign. An experienced organiser, he has known from the outset that the key to defeating AV is to get out the Labour vote against it: Labour too will lose out if AV is introduced. Gilbert works with Andrew Feldman to ensure that the campaign is properly funded and energised. Cameron's team are particularly irked by the 'Yes' campaign being awarded a huge grant from the Joseph Rowntree Foundation. Cameron knows raising more money is key, but he is becoming uneasy with the aggressive turn campaigning is taking. He knows it will damage his relationship with Clegg and his Lib Dem partners if he himself accepts the upfront role Osborne is urging him to take. The vitriol against the Lib Dems is about to become personal.

Writing on the influential website ConservativeHome, former MP and journalist Paul Goodman anticipates the angst of Conservative MPs should the referendum be lost: 'First he [Cameron] messes up the election. Now he's messed up the referendum. We'll never govern again on our own – and I'm going to lose my seat.'[12] Right-wing websites and commentators are saying Cameron has been weak in his running of the coalition and should be giving the Lib Dems a much harder time; indeed, that he should never have conceded the referendum in the first place. Cameron is caught between a rock and a hard place. Attack Clegg and he strains the coalition: hold back, and his party attack him. To the Lib Dems, Cameron's predicament is a symptom of his weakness in his party. Libya is taking up much of his attention in these months. He is at a loss to know what to do. Osborne has heard enough: he can take no more fence-sitting. 'Look,' he says, 'we have to win this fucking thing; who cares what Clegg thinks?' There are no ifs and buts. Cameron listens in silence. So do other members of the team in his study, watching how he will respond. Later that day, Cameron calls Feldman: 'I absolutely agree with George,' he says. 'We cannot lose this.'[13]

Everything now changes from February. Cameron puts Number 10 on a war footing, telling his staff to get right behind the 'No' campaign, and instructs CCHQ to organise at least one major activity for him on AV each week.[14] There is no love between Labour and Conservative in the marriage of convenience that is the 'No' campaign. Labour's team are pleased by the new Tory activism. But on funding, they take the view that 'you fucking Tories can raise the money we need'. Self-made millionaire Peter Cruddas is duly brought in by Feldman to help them do so, recognising that the 'Yes' campaign is still better organised and funded. Money soon starts to flow and confidence rises. Clegg's team are incandescent about Cameron's new tack. They suspect the PM at best of turning a blind eye, at worst of ordering the 'No' campaign to personalise their attacks on Clegg. The Lib Dem leader's poll ratings are on floor level: Clegg's aides surmise the Conservatives are capitalising on his weakness by turning the leader of the 'Yes' campaign into an object of public ridicule, in effect making the referendum not about AV but Clegg himself. To the Lib Dems, Cameron's action is in direct contravention of earlier (if disputed) understandings. It is 'the great betrayal'.

The energy that Osborne and Stephen Gilbert bring to the campaign from Downing Street, and the funds that Feldman and Cruddas acquire from CCHQ, combine with the newfound bellicosity of the prime minister. The voices of Conservative criticism are placated. On 18 February, Cameron gives his principal speech in the referendum campaign at the Royal United Services Institute. He tells his audience outright that AV will be 'bad for democracy'.[15] The all-party 'No' campaign, which becomes primarily the vehicle to mobilise the Labour vote for polling day, is increasingly bypassed by Number 10. Cameron and Osborne divide up phone calls to newspaper editors and commentators, urging them to fight AV. Eventually the *Daily Telegraph*, *Daily Mail*, *Daily Express*, *Sun* and *The Times* all come out against. The Lib Dems are furious when they hear about the calls.

The 'No' campaign, reflecting strenuous market research, focuses their campaign on the 'three Cs': cost, complexity and Clegg. Television adverts feature a horse race in which the third-placed rider goes on to win, and another has Alan B'Stard – the louche star of the 1980s and 1990s television comedy show *The New Statesman*, played by Rik Mayall – winning an AV election. Labour's team on the 'No' campaign are delighted to see Clegg, a figure they despise, besmirched: 'They are only too happy to tear strips off Nick Clegg. Labour loved this stuff,' says Elliott.[16] The 'Yes' campaign try to respond in kind. One of their posters features a photograph of the British National Party leader, Nick Griffin, with the strapline 'He's voting "NO". How about you?' But their campaign is lacklustre by comparison. So successful has the 'No' campaign become that Labour are alarmed that it is becoming a 'Tory front' with Cameron using it to gain profile for himself and his party. On 18 April Labour Party heavyweight John Reid appears on a platform beside Cameron, to the delight of the 'No' campaign. The morning after, the *Guardian* publish a poll showing that support for AV is collapsing.[17] Osborne asks CCHQ what more he could do by way of a 'big intervention' to help the 'No' cause. 'Lend your authority as chancellor to our claims about the cost to taxpayers of AV', he is told. To Lib Dem fury, the No to AV campaign says the change will cost the country £250 million, leading Chris Huhne to write an angry letter on 24 April asking Osborne to deny this claim.[18] For Clegg, 'the spring of 2011 was the lowest of the low'.[19]

Number 10 is finding it hard to maintain the story that Cameron is not responsible himself for the personal attacks and that they are instead down to Labour: 'Basically we convinced ourselves that it was Labour who forced us to play tough. But this was a fairly thin fig leaf', admits one of Cameron's inner circle. They know the attacks will anger Clegg: it is a calculated risk, but one they feel they have to take. They draw the line merely at personal or nasty stories about Clegg or the Lib Dems.

Not that Clegg sees it that way. At the height of the campaign he visits his parents near Oxford with his wife and children. 'Look, we've just got this leaflet through the door', his father tells him, 'it's outrageous.' Clegg junior is handed the leaflet depicting what he describes as 'incredibly personalised stuff about me'.[20] He believes the personal attacks are wholly gratuitous and can under no circumstances be justified. He is sickened by the Tory mantra: 'It's Labour's fault, not ours', or 'We have to work with Labour on the campaign and they felt it was the only way to make their voters vote against AV: we are terribly sorry'. Not that it totally shatters his view of Cameron: he continues to believe in his partner's integrity and discomfort at what is happening.

On Tuesday 3 May, two days before the referendum, matters come to a head in Cabinet. Lib Dem Energy Secretary Chris Huhne is observed to be in a highly charged state as he waits outside the Cabinet Room for the meeting to begin. He then bursts in with a stack of leaflets from the 'No' campaign attacking Clegg for going back on the Lib Dem pledge on tuition fees, and says he is appalled by the actions of those at the very top of the Conservative Party.[21] The meeting begins. He turns on Cameron: 'I want to know if you disassociate yourself from these leaflets smearing Nick.' He challenges the PM to sack Stephen Gilbert, demanding to know whether he had been responsible for producing them. Cameron is taken aback by the onslaught. 'I am not responsible for the all party literature produced by the "No" campaign,' he says. Huhne thinks he is dodging the question and shoves the leaflets across the Cabinet table towards Osborne. 'This was always going to be a difficult period for the coalition,' Osborne responds, seeking to pacify him. Huhne comes back at him, even more forcibly, demanding if he had known in advance about these leaflets. 'I am not going to be challenged by a Cabinet colleague acting like he is Jeremy Paxman on *Newsnight*,' responds the chancellor.

Round the Cabinet table there is a collective dropping of ministerial jaws. Huhne turns on Sayeeda Warsi, and says she must resign as party co-chairman. Several ministers with longer memories, like David Willetts, wonder whether they are about to witness a 'Heseltine moment', a reference to the highly charged occasion when the blond-haired firebrand stormed out of Thatcher's Cabinet in 1986 over the Westland helicopter affair. 'You could hear a pin drop,' Willetts recalls.[22] It is the trickiest moment in Cabinet for Cameron by a distance: yet Huhne is not finished. He reverts to Cameron and demands that he condemns posters that have suggested that babies' and soldiers' lives are at risk if AV is introduced. Cameron and Osborne argue that they are only responsible for the 'No' campaign being run by the Conservative Party.[23] When asked again on Radio 4's *Today* programme to condemn the posters featuring ill babies, Cameron replies, 'The fact is that if you move to a new voting system it will cost money.'[24] After the Huhne inquisition is over, ministers return to Cabinet business.

Cameron's team reflect on the outburst at their 4 p.m. meeting. They have different views. Some see Huhne's outburst as anti-Clegg positioning: Clegg is at a very low ebb, the tuition-fees row has damaged his confidence, with over 30,000 protestors marching on the streets, some carrying effigies of Clegg. He has been suffering both personally and professionally for a number of months: he was ill in the early part of 2011 as well as being 'crucified in the right- and the left-wing press in a way that I don't think we've seen in British politics since the days of Neil Kinnock'.[25] He is further damaged by the poor showing of the party at the Oldham East and Saddleworth by-election on 13 January, the first of the parliament, where the Lib Dems were heavily defeated. Most think Huhne is up to something. But Oliver Letwin thinks Huhne is motivated by genuine panic at the prospect of not achieving electoral reform: 'In Eastleigh, I'll be in terrible difficulties if we join a coalition with you: we must get AV,' Huhne had told Letwin, referring to his vulnerable position in his own constituency.[26] The truth is that Clegg is desperately weak and has become depressed about his party's fortunes, and Huhne, for all his indignation, is parading his own leadership credentials.

Thursday 5 May is referendum day. The AV system is resoundingly rejected by 67.9% to 32.1% on a turnout of 42.2%. Victory strengthens Cameron's position in the Conservative Party. For a time. And at a cost. As O'Donnell predicted, the episode has inflicted significant and enduring damage to the coalition. To Clegg, 'a certain kind of hardness entered into the transactions' thereafter, while to Vince Cable 'it was perfectly clear that we were dealing with people who have no sentiment'.[27] To Danny Alexander, 'it is the moment the scales fall away from our eyes about the Tories. The personal attacks on Nick were personal and brutal.'[28] It ends any notion that the relationship between the two parties will realign British politics. 'We are one team. We are one government' had been the mantra of Cameron, Llewellyn and Coulson when they first went into Downing Street. There were joint meetings, shared offices, joint political Cabinets at Chequers, joint press operations and joint policy units. The AV debacle sweeps all this away. There are to be no more joint meetings. 'Nothing again will rest on goodwill, everything has become a transactional relationship,' says Astle. 'It became: "I'll concede this in return for that." It was all negotiation and bargaining.'[29]

But survive the coalition does. Clegg picks himself up and the Lib Dems put their show back on the road. They've lost their primary *raison d'être* for entering the coalition: electoral reform, and with its defeat, much of the support in the country for their party leadership becomes more flaky. And yet there is now a new purpose for the Lib Dems in the coalition, informed by the sober recognition that pulling out would result in a general election, which would be disastrous for them electorally. The new mission is to continue to show that they can be credible members of government, bring economic stability back to the country, and achieve as many of their own policies as they can. For a while after the defeat, Clegg's leadership position looks to be in serious danger: but when Huhne resigns in February 2012 to face prosecution for perverting the course of justice over a speeding offence, the pressure recedes, and Clegg's buoyancy slowly returns. To coalition architect Letwin, the AV episode provides the moment of greatest tension within the coalition to date: 'If we could get through AV in one piece together, we could get through anything. The coalition would indeed endure until 2015.'[30] It is for this reason that for some, the AV referendum proves 'the key turning point' that ensures the coalition lasts for the 'full five years'.

5 May 2011 also sees the local elections. The Conservatives gain eighty-six councillors while the Lib Dems lose a 'catastrophic' 748, compounding their misery.[31] For a party in power to have done so well, and from a strong base in the previous local elections, augurs well and strengthens Cameron. The most dramatic result of election day, however, is not the AV referendum. Nor is it the local elections. It is the result north of the border. In Scotland, Alex Salmond's Scottish National Party gain twenty-three seats, allowing it to form a majority government in the Scottish Parliament for the first time. It will precipitate one of the most historic and perilous episodes of Cameron's increasingly dramatic premiership.

ELEVEN

Scottish Referendum Call

May 2011–February 2012

'This party, the Scottish party, the national party, carries your hope ... I'll govern for all the ambitions of Scotland and for all the people who can imagine that we can live in a better land.' These heady words from Alex Salmond, the leader of the Scottish National Party (SNP), are uttered in the early hours of Friday 6 May 2011. Scotland had been voting for its own Parliament at Holyrood since 1999. The system had been carefully devised using proportional representation precisely to prevent any one party gaining an overall majority and thus too much power. But achieving an overall majority is exactly what the SNP have now achieved. They are as shocked as anyone: 'Not in their wildest dreams did they imagine they would get a majority,' says a senior Lib Dem. Of 129 seats contested, the SNP win sixty-nine, allowing them to form a majority government for the first time. Labour wins thirty-seven seats (losing seven), the Conservatives fifteen (losing five), and the Lib Dems five seats (losing twelve).

Salmond is determined that Scotland will be independent, and that he will become Scotland's first ever prime minister. He wants to reclaim the independence lost 304 years before with the Acts of Union in 1707, when the Scottish Parliament voted itself out of existence, accepting political union with England and parliamentary representation in London.[1] He is demanding a referendum to settle the question. Scotland will, he believes, be the first part of the United Kingdom to break away and become independent since the Irish Free State in 1922, which later became a republic in 1937. Cameron has not been anticipating this result, though the last phase of the election suggested that it was a possibility. Victory for the SNP sets in motion a train of events that leads Cameron to take what Llewellyn, as ever at the very heart of the Cameron operation, describes as 'the historic decision of the entire premiership'.[2]

The outcome that day in Scotland may have been unexpected, but the prospect of a referendum to deal with the 'Scottish Question' had been considered before by Cameron and Osborne. They had often pondered the problematic Conservative representation in Northern Ireland and Scotland. In Scotland there had been a steady Conservative decline since the Second World War: MPs have dwindled from thirty-six in 1955, to twenty-two in 1979, to zero in 1997, and they have picked up just one seat since, in 2005. However, Cameron and Osborne were very confident that Scotland would vote to remain in the UK, and became attracted to the idea of initiating a referendum on Scotland's continuation in the United Kingdom. To Osborne, the key was the middle class in the central Edinburgh–Glasgow belt of Scotland supporting the Union.[3] Holding and winning a referendum would seize the initiative north of the border, and put a lid on the nationalist clamour. The proposal foundered because of the implacable opposition to the plan by Brown. To have promoted the idea in the teeth of opposition by the Labour prime minister would have alienated supporters north of the border. So they dropped the plan, but their cogitations gave them an appetite for radical thinking.

On 14 May 2010, a week after the general election and on only his third full day in office, Cameron visits Scotland for the first time as prime minister to address the Scottish Parliament and to meet Salmond. The new PM is no stranger to Scotland: he is the possessor of a Scottish name with roots in the Western Highlands and has family links through Samantha's stepfather to the Isle of Jura.[4] He is fired by Big Society zeal for localism and spreading power away from London, a zeal that is only enhanced by the coalition with the Liberal Democrats. Cameron tells the Holyrood Parliament that day he wants an 'agenda of respect' between both Parliaments.[5] Accompanied by his initial Scotland Secretary, Danny Alexander, they give Salmond the distinct impression they want to go further than the existing Scotland Act and are supportive of moves towards further devolution. Salmond is pleased. He says that the meeting is 'more substantive' than he had expected.[6]

Scottish devolution disappears from the limelight over the following six months. Other priorities preoccupy both leaders. Osborne remains in the vanguard of those who believe a referendum may be necessary. He sees the issue in strongly *political* terms, whereas Cameron sees it much more in national terms. Alexander, who has become a close colleague of Osborne's since his promotion to Chief Secretary to the Treasury at the end of May, thinks similarly.[7] Both are ahead of their party leaders. Cameron is sincere about the 'respect agenda' and wants to take the Scottish concerns seriously. The question he keeps asking is 'what is the right thing to do for democracy?' Then the surprise SNP victory in May 2011, which provides a mandate for the party's commitment to hold a referendum, changes everything. At a meeting of the Quad in June, Osborne, who wants a quick referendum to kill off independence, says it must be dominated from London, and imposed on Edinburgh. 'Why don't we just do what the Spanish do and say (to their own separatists) we hold the power!' The Lib Dems respond that they cannot impose a referendum settlement unilaterally on Salmond.

In Edinburgh, Salmond has begun poring over the options for greater devolution and full independence. At a meeting at his official residence, Bute House on Charlotte Square, he decides to run with 'Devo Max', which would greatly enhance the powers of the Scottish Parliament, but stops short of severing the link to Westminster and the Crown. It may not be the holy grail of full independence but Salmond and his advisers recognise that a vote for Devo Max will be more likely to achieve a majority in a referendum than one for the full monty, which will scare off some voters with vestigial attachment for remaining in the UK. But the idea runs into trouble, in part because the Lib Dems, who are the most enthusiastic of the three main parties in Westminster for devolution, are not supportive.

The Christmas holiday in 2011 sees the pace quicken dramatically. In the run-up to it, Cameron receives a visit at Number 10 from the Conservative Party's Scottish grandees – Lord Strathclyde, Leader of the Lords, and two former Scotland Secretaries, Lord Lang and Lord Forsyth. The last advises: 'Hold a referendum within the next three months, and don't yield on the question, the timing or franchise.' 'Once we concede a referendum,' Cameron replies, 'how do we stop conceding it again and again?' Cameron realises that being seen to block such a referendum will be counterproductive. The SNP will hold it on their own, and the knowledge that the Conservatives were trying to prevent it will bring resentment, making a vote for independence in some form more likely. Alexander believes that the argument that 'Salmond would call a consultative referendum even if we didn't' is key to convincing Cameron.[8] Now he has begun focusing on the issue again, the PM sees that if he gets out ahead of the SNP, and is seen to be supportive of a referendum, he can ensure that it will be properly organised, that the results will be binding and lawful, and he will have more say and influence.

Cameron's team believe that Salmond is posturing and isn't ready to hold a referendum yet: 'So we thought, let's seize the initiative and hold it when he is wrong-footed,' says one. The argument is moving Osborne's way. 'If we don't lance the boil now it's going to become a *cause célèbre* and support for the SNP will magnify. Doing nothing is not an option,' says another.[9] They are convinced that the SNP did so well in the Holyrood elections *despite* their commitment to independence, not because of it: indeed, they believe Salmond fought shy of making it a major part of his platform because he knows that many Scottish voters do not want to go that far. Cameron's team remain privately sure they will win any referendum.

Cameron spends a lot of time thinking and talking to Osborne over Christmas. Before the New Year, they decide they will take the plunge and instigate a referendum. The Quad holds a core meeting on 3 January 2012. All four principals finally sign up to the referendum: following the wrangling over AV the year before, they are relieved to alight on an electoral issue on which they can agree. Michael Moore, Alexander's successor as Scotland Secretary, has been summoned to attend: 'The Tories were totally gung-ho. It was all about "seizing control" of the initiative. It was all pretty macho, testosterone-fuelled stuff and "only by showing them who's the leader will we get things done"; he says.[10] Clegg and Alexander have repeatedly stressed it cannot be a referendum seen to be controlled from London, still less by the Conservative Party. Osborne and Cameron agree: the SNP must not be given any pretext for arguing that this is anything other than a totally fair contest. The Quad is clear that there must be a single 'either/or' question on the referendum ballot paper.

On Sunday 8 January, Cameron goes to the BBC for his start-the-year television interview with Andrew Marr. To the surprise of viewers, he announces that the government is to offer Salmond a legally constituted referendum. 'We owe the Scottish people something that is fair, legal and decisive. And so in the coming days we'll be setting out clearly what the legal situation is.' To increase pressure on Salmond, who they are convinced is running scared, he says that it must be held within eighteen months and must only pose one question – ruling out the option of voters being offered the choice of either full independence, Devo Max or the status quo. The *coup de théâtre* does indeed wrong-foot Salmond. The rest of the Sunday is taken up by briefing and counter-briefing, with the SNP alleging that Westminster is trying to dominate the referendum from London, and are bullying the SNP. The Lib Dems on the Quad are furious at the way Number 10 spin Cameron's television statement in a much more belligerent way.

On 9 January, Cabinet convenes to achieve agreement over the government's strategy on the referendum. They meet, unusually, in the Olympic Park in East London's Stratford, in the middle of a large sports hall. The PM opens by urging all ministers to exploit the opportunities to showcase the British summer of 2012, with the Queen's Diamond Jubilee and the Olympic Games. After the meeting he announces they will be joined by London mayor Boris Johnson and chairman of the Olympic organising committee, Sebastian Coe, on a tour of the facilities and organisations associated with the games. Jeremy Heywood is now Cabinet Secretary, having succeeded Gus O'Donnell at the end of December. Scotland is the main item on the agenda. Ministers agree with proposals to give Holyrood legal and constitutional authority to stage the referendum. Not all are convinced. Iain Duncan Smith and Gove doubt whether any interference from London will be acceptable to the SNP. 'It will just be seen as meddling,' Gove argues. But they endorse the argument that a fair and legal vote will lead to a decisive result, hopefully ending the call for a referendum for a generation or more.

On 10 January the focus shifts to the Commons, and Moore lays out the details of the government's proposal. The Scottish Parliament is not empowered to hold a referendum, he states, but the UK government will change the law to allow it to hold 'a legal, fair and decisive referendum' on Scottish independence.[11] He announces that there will only be one question, and suggests that the referendum should be staged before the end of 2013, a good year earlier than Salmond wants, in the hope of catching him off guard. He also states his hope that the referendum will be overseen by the Electoral Commission, and the next phase will be a consultation with the people of Scotland on the best way to facilitate such a referendum. 'Salmond was furious,' recalls one involved in the negotiations, 'he hated the fact that we had put ourselves so firmly in the game.'

The starting gun has been fired. Cameron has indeed taken potentially the most fateful decision of his premiership. Now for the detail, including finalising the question, the timing and the franchise – should the voting age be reduced to include sixteen- and seventeen-year-olds? What exactly will the question be and when will polling day be? Will the campaign be conducted under Westminster or Holyrood's authority? Number 10 realises it needs to increase its firepower. In February 2012, the Glasgow-born Scot, Andrew Dunlop, who worked in Thatcher's Number 10 and has since worked in political consultancy, joins the Policy Unit. He rapidly gains the trust of the Lib Dems and becomes a major figure in negotiations. Cabinet itself delegates responsibility for the issue to a Scotland committee, chaired by Osborne and subsequently by the Scotland Secretary. Danny Alexander and Oliver Letwin are the two dominant members.

Cameron's thinking is developing rapidly. On 15 February, he is in Scotland to deliver what will be his defining speech of the long referendum campaign. He hosts a dinner at the Peat Inn near St Andrews and discusses progress with his team, including Heywood's successor at Number 10, now called director general of the prime minister's office Chris Martin, Craig Oliver and Dunlop. They are joined by Alan Cochrane, editor of the Scottish edition of the *Daily Telegraph* and an influential figure in Scottish circles. Cameron has been encouraged for some months by journalist and friend Bruce Anderson to listen to Cochrane's views. Cameron reveals he is prepared to make significant concessions to Salmond in the interests of showing how amenable the British government is being, as long as Salmond accepts his 'red line' of a single 'yes/no' question.[12] He will even concede the referendum date to Salmond, which private polling has suggested will not significantly affect the outcome, and that the SNP can have their way on including sixteen- and seventeen-year-olds, which again Conservative polling suggests will make little to no difference to the outcome. But Cameron insists that the referendum should be overseen by the Electoral Commission, another red line for him, which means that they will be the arbiters, not London or Edinburgh, on the precise question to be put to voters. 'Let Salmond boycott it,' Cameron tells his team over dinner.[13] 'Cameron had come to a very nuanced understanding,' says one of his team. 'He realised it would be self-defeating to impose the question and timetable from Westminster. If the vote was lost by the nationalists, as we expected it would be, they could always come back and say it was unfair. Thus the timing and precise question should be decided by Scotland itself to place the outcome beyond any future dispute.'[14] The Liberal Democrats, in the form of Alexander and Moore, are delighted that Cameron has come to this conclusion.

On the morning of 16 February, Cameron drives south to give his speech at the Apex Hotel in Edinburgh, a dramatic view of the castle behind him.[15] The text has been long debated in Number 10. Julian Glover had been brought in as chief speechwriter the previous October from the *Guardian*: it is he who holds the pen, describing it 'as one of the most romantic of the speeches that Cameron gave as prime minister'.[16] Gove is responsible for much of the content including that Scotland and the rest of the UK are 'better together', and that Scotland is a great success story, shares much in common throughout history with the rest of the UK, and that both countries should thus remain together. Scare tactics are totally off the page. Gove's input can be detected in the reference to Aberdeen, his home town, early in the speech: 'In Aberdeen, King's and Marischal Colleges remind us of a time when the Granite City had as many universities for its citizens as England had for all of hers.'[17] The message of Cameron's speech is summed up neatly by one of the team: 'You Scots are my mates, we love you, you are brilliant.' Cameron knows how much is at stake, and has spent much time on the drafts:

I am convinced that both for Scotland and for the United Kingdom, our best days lie ahead of us ... I know that the Conservative Party is not currently – how can I put this – Scotland's most influential political movement. I am often reminded that I have been more successful in helping to get pandas into the zoo than Conservative MPs elected in Scotland ... I am here to stand up and speak out for what I believe in. I believe in the United Kingdom. I am a unionist head, heart and soul. I believe that England, Scotland, Wales, Northern Ireland, we are stronger together than we ever would be apart. When you set aside difference, when you roll up your sleeves in a common endeavour, you achieve things that are truly worthwhile – even noble – which you could never accomplish on your own.[18]

The speech's tone surprises many: they had expected a more abrasive tone. 'It played well,' thinks one Cabinet member, 'it was a useful intervention.'

On 25 May, 'Yes Scotland', the pro-independence campaign, is launched with a media razzmatazz at a multiplex cinema in central Edinburgh. A month later, on 25 June, 'Better Together' launches, at the Craiglockhart campus of Edinburgh Napier University, with Alistair Darling, the leader of the campaign, centre stage. The leadership was debated at length by the Quad. Clegg's two predecessors as leader of the Lib Dems, Charles Kennedy and Menzies Campbell, are considered, but judged insufficiently to mobilise Labour. John Reid in contrast is looked at very keenly, but rules himself out. It is abundantly clear that Better Together must be led by a Scot, and that it had to be someone from Labour: a Tory, especially if posh, would have been fatal. Gordon Brown is judged to be too egotistical and unreliable to head it up. Darling, in contrast, with the gravitas of a former chancellor, is liked and respected by Osborne and Cameron as well as by the Lib Dems. That same month, at a reception at Dover House in London, Cameron surprises some of his side when he openly appears to concede the timing to the SNP. 'Frankly the timing matters but I'm pretty relaxed about it,' he tells the assembled Scotland Office officials and press. 'I think I exceeded my brief a bit there,' he confesses to Moore on the way out. 'But it does us no harm to give this a bit more momentum.' The Scotland Secretary is nonplussed. As one Lib Dem later said, 'Maybe he felt he had to give something to the press. He is immensely tactical.' Concern spreads about strategic drift.

Number 10's Andrew Cooper, co-founder of polling organisation Populus, is brought in by Osborne to provide advice on election strategy. His research suggests the electorate in Scotland can be divided into three camps: nearly 40% are convinced unionists and are safely in the bank as No voters. Just under 30% are firm nationalists, while the remaining third are undecided. The effort must be directed to this third who will decide the outcome. Cooper's advice is that love-bombing Scotland and talk of common bonds will not in fact do the business: the effort must be placed instead on independence being irreversible and the economic interests of Scotland demanding a No vote. His hard-nosed advice is not universally popular in Number 10, but leads to a change of tack. Ed Miliband is invited for a meeting with Cameron and Clegg to discuss Labour support for securing agreement on the referendum's terms, which are still up in the air.

As the talks grind on over the summer of 2012, Cameron becomes frustrated: 'I don't see why we can't tie all this up by the end of September,' he says. He knows that Salmond is trying to string it out for his own advantage, so he insists on agreement being reached by the end of the month. His impetus irritates Salmond, but it speeds the process, and in September a consensus is reached on the negotiating text. Moore leads the charge, negotiating directly with Nicola Sturgeon, Salmond's astute and well-briefed deputy. 'Salmond wanted to dip her blood into the process in case it all went wrong and then wanted Cameron to come to Edinburgh to hammer out the final details with him. We weren't having any of that,' says an official involved with the negotiations. The way is cleared for the final agreement. The day before it is signed, Michael Forsyth, who had been so emphatic with Cameron in late 2011, is one of the senior Tory figures to spread alarm when he now compares Cameron to 'Pontius Pilate' who has washed his hands of Scotland. He tells the *Sunday Times* that 'Salmond has been able to get what he wants … it sounds like a walk-over to me.'[19] His words foreshadow those of many Tory critics over the following two years, climaxing before referendum day. Scotland is becoming another stick with which to beat Cameron.

On 15 October, the Edinburgh Agreement is signed at St Andrews House, home of the old Scottish Office. Cameron and Salmond agree that sixteen- and seventeen-year-olds will be allowed the vote, there will be a single 'yes/no' question, and the vote will take place in the autumn of 2014. The hopes of Osborne et al who wanted a quick referendum have been thwarted. The Scottish Parliament are given the legal authority to hold the referendum. The campaign has begun. As the PM's pen hovers over the paper, Llewellyn later says that 'I felt the weight of history bearing down on us. If one thing kept me awake at night, it was this.'[20] The next day, Tuesday 16 October, Cameron says to Cabinet ministers, 'The Scottish negotiations are a model for the rest of you.' His pleasure at being spared murky, smoke-filled rooms negotiating is apparent to all. 'I turned up. I signed. I left.' All know the words *Veni, vidi, vici*, attributed to Julius Caesar a few years after his failed attempt to invade Britain. Has Cameron, with insufficient thought, signed away its dismemberment?

TWELVE

London Riots

August 2011

Friday 5 August. Craig Oliver is strolling around the corridors in a near empty Number 10. Cameron's team have taken a hard pounding since the New Year on many fronts and have been desperate for a holiday. The usual form is that the team go away at the same time as Cameron himself, leaving just one of them manning the fort. Oliver, the communications director, was the last to join the team, in February. By the time he has his feet under the table, all the other team have booked their holidays. He has drawn the short straw.

The day before, eight miles to the north in Tottenham, Mark Duggan, a twenty-nine-year-old man of mixed race who worked at Stansted Airport, was shot dead by police at 6.15 p.m. The news barely registered with Oliver, but on the Saturday morning crowds gather outside Tottenham police station, protesting against the police. The demonstration begins peacefully but erupts into violence. That evening, arson and looting break out across Tottenham. Twenty-six police officers are injured.

The Camerons are blissfully unaware. They are relaxing in a villa in the Tuscan province of Arezzo. Ed Llewellyn is in Paris where his wife is shortly to give birth. Kate Fall is deep in the country, while press secretary Gabby Bertin is in New York. Cameron picks up the news but is not remotely eager to break away from Samantha and the children to return to London. It is the right judgement. 'You can't bring the prime minister back from his holiday every time something goes wrong, because you might be seen to be panicking,' said a Number 10 aide. Oliver decides to sound out Cabinet Secretary Gus O'Donnell and the Number 10 permanent secretary, Jeremy Heywood. 'I think this is becoming very serious,' he tells them down the phone. Their response is to go easy on bringing the PM back. 'What will he do?' is Heywood's response. Officials believe that it is dangerous to be seen to be panicking, which might escalate the violence. Besides, prime ministers need holidays like anybody else.

Sunday 7 August sees violence spread from Tottenham across London. Photographs appear in the papers of a relaxed Cameron in casual clothes, tanned and smiling, in a café in Montevarchi, 'with his arm round a waitress he had forgotten to tip on a previous visit'. Placed side by side with images of wrecked buildings in Tottenham, it makes uncomfortable viewing for the prime minister's team.[1] He speaks to the Home Secretary, Theresa May: her opinion is that he need not return.

Events take an uglier turn still on Monday night. The capital descends into chaos. Oliver has been watching the scenes of vandalism and looting from shops on the television screens in his office in Number 12. He is mesmerised and shocked by the shots from helicopters of areas of London ablaze. Some of the images are akin to the horror of the Blitz. Oliver might be the new kid on the block, but he is convinced that the prime minister needs to come back. He phones Heywood and tells him the political requirement is now for the prime minister to come back. In Paris, Llewellyn too is watching the unfolding picture on Sky television with mounting dismay. In the early evening he calls Cameron, imploring him to return that night. 'I'm coming to that conclusion myself,' Cameron tells his chief of staff. The fear is the police may not be able to control the rioters in London, and, galvanised by social media, 'spontaneous' riots are spreading across several cities. A conference call at 7.30 p.m. with his team confirms his intentions. 'I want to go to every area affected, meet the people affected, and understand for myself exactly what is happening and why,' he tells them.[2] An RAF plane is mobilised to fly to Italy to bring him back. He leaves the villa at midnight, boards the plane at Pisa at 3 a.m. and walks through the door of Downing Street just before 6 a.m. 'It was the right call,' he tells a relieved Oliver. Llewellyn has calculated he can hop back to London on the Eurostar before his first child is born. 'If the PM had delayed his return another twelve or twenty-four hours, it would have been a disaster,' he is later heard to say. From nine o'clock that evening, several fires are burning across the capital. It proves the busiest night for the London fire brigade since the Second World War. Is this conflagration the first event in a complete breakdown of civil society unleashed by Cameron's austerity programme, which, one year in, is showing no signs of working?

Not for the first time, Cameron understands the near impossible demands on a prime minister. Back too early and he would have been slated for grandstanding. Too late, and he would have ceded control of the agenda to Ed Miliband, who is back from a family holiday in Devon on Monday night and saying he is 'shocked by the scenes we are seeing in parts of London and Birmingham', or to Clegg, who is preparing to return from holiday in the West Country. Boris Johnson, himself heavily criticised for his absence, decides to fly back from his family holiday in the Rockies. National disasters raise the stakes for all. As Cameron wrestles with tiredness after his night flight, he hears Theresa May on Radio 4's *Today* programme saying that the disorder is on a scale 'not seen in this country for many years'.[3] Nothing, he realises, can prepare one for the loneliness of being PM.

On Tuesday 9 August Cameron has an update with Clegg and May at 8 a.m., and chairs the meeting in Cabinet Office Briefing Room A (COBRA) at 9 a.m. The room is crowded with ministers, officials and police. Standing space only is available for the less senior officials. Cameron is disconcerted by the police. Their reaction to the rioting the night before is to claim an operational success, despite the riots spreading to Birmingham with 400 arrests being made due to 'copycat criminal activity'.[4] 'No, no, no!' says Cameron furiously. 'Your job is to intervene and stop it.' The public mood is one of incomprehension and a feeling that the police are standing by and watching whilst the rioting is taking place and buildings are burning. Cameron says, 'Look, you have one more go to get this right, otherwise we'll do it my way.' In his mind, he is already envisaging curfews and allowing use of water cannons – an anti-riot device that had been used in Northern Ireland, but never on the British mainland. Police numbers in London need to be more than doubled, he says, and they should dramatically increase the number of arrests. (By early Tuesday evening, the total number of arrests would climb to 563, leaving no spare police cells in the capital.[5])

After the meeting is over at 11 a.m., Cameron comes outside Number 10 to make a statement:

> These are sickening scenes – scenes of people looting, vandalising, thieving, robbing, scenes of people attacking police officers and even attacking fire crews as they're trying to put out fires. This is criminality, pure and simple, and it has to be confronted and defeated ... I have this very clear message to those people who are responsible for this wrongdoing and criminality: you will feel the full force of the law and if you are old enough to commit these crimes you are old enough to face the punishments. And to these people I would say this: you are not only wrecking the lives of others, you're not only wrecking your own communities – you are potentially wrecking your own life too.[6]

The words are substantially Cameron's own, coming from deep inside him. He knows that the nation looks to him for a grip that had been lacking over the previous few days and he is determined to provide it. So serious does Cameron judge the crisis that he announces that Parliament will be recalled that Thursday.

Craig Oliver and Liz Sugg have been planning which of the affected areas in London he should visit. Sugg is described as Cameron's 'secret weapon', ever resourceful and *sans pareil* at masterminding his travel. She dispatches him to Croydon in South London, where he visits members of the Reeves family whose 144-year-old furniture store had been burnt down the previous day. He views a corner shop which is still burning. He talks to Kit Malthouse, chair of the Metropolitan Police Authority. Relations with the police are still uneasy after the previous two days: politicians have been blaming the police for handling the riots ineptly, while the police response has been that the politicians are in no position to criticise when they have been on holiday. Cameron and Malthouse agree to work together and that the police will have the political backing to get tough. Having insisted on visiting Tottenham to survey the damage on Monday, despite some resistance in Number 10 that it might be seen as an over-reaction, Clegg then travels to Birmingham the following day.[7] The visit does not go well. He is booed by crowds on a walkabout in the city centre.

'Go home,' young people in the crowd shout at him. 'Go on – run, run, run', they shout at his car as it departs.[8]

Boris Johnson encounters similar heckling when on Tuesday he visits Clapham Junction, scene of some of the worst rioting. 'I came as fast as I could,' he says, when angry residents ask why he hadn't come home earlier. 'Where were the police?' they shout at him. 'Tonight, we're going to have huge numbers of police on the streets,' he replies.[9] 'People felt angry because they'd seen their shops, their property attacked and, sod it, the sodding mayor has been somewhere else,' he says later.[10] As the heckling grows louder, he appears disoriented and his usual loquacious charm eludes him. But when someone hands Johnson a green broom, he marches defiantly towards the crowds in the street, saying that he is on the side of innocent Londoners. The mood suddenly turns and the heckling subsides. Cameron's aides urge him to do the same. 'No,' he tells them. 'It's not prime ministerial.'[11] That evening, violence spreads to Merseyside and Manchester.

A second Cabinet meeting is convened on Wednesday 10 August, following a meeting of COBRA. News is received that three young men have been killed in Birmingham when a speeding car hit them in the early hours of the morning: witnesses say they were only trying to protect local property from being attacked.[12] COBRA debates the impact of the greatly enhanced police presence on the streets of London the night before, with officer numbers rising from 6,000 to 16,000. Cameron asks for an early assessment of the increase. The meeting is more measured than the day before, and relations with the police more harmonious. Afterwards, Cameron gives a second statement on the street outside Number 10, promising that the police would have whatever resources are needed to bring the rioting under control, including water cannons. He is keen to point out that the 'more robust approach' is working.[13] However, water cannons are played down by the Home Secretary and the president of the Association of Chief Police Officers, Sir Hugh Orde, both speaking on Radio 4's *The World at One*. 'The police are very clear – they tell me, at the moment, they don't need water cannon,' May declares on the radio.[14] Later that day, Cameron goes to the West Midlands and meets residents, police and local officials in Birmingham and

Wolverhampton. Earlier in the day, Tariq Jahan, the father of one of the three men run over and killed in Birmingham, who just hours before had tried to save his son's life, made an emotional appeal for calm. 'Why, why? … It makes no sense why people are behaving in this way and taking the lives of three innocent people.'[15] The impact of his words, more than any other statement uttered by politicians, is immediate. That night the streets are silent.

By the morning of Thursday 11 August, order begins to return. No major incidents of violence are recorded. As Oliver emerges from Hammersmith Tube station, he notices a sense of calm, and sees police everywhere: 'The levers had been pulled. The response was very, very strong.'[16] The House of Commons convenes for its special recall. At 11.30 a.m., Cameron thanks the House for returning and proceeds to highlight a timeline of events and what is being done to restore order. Directly addressing the victims, he says:

> No one will forget the images of the woman jumping from a burning building, or of the furniture shop that had survived the Blitz but has now tragically been burnt to the ground; and everyone will have been impressed by the incredibly brave words of Tariq Jahan, a father in Birmingham whose son was so brutally and tragically run over and killed. Shops, businesses and homes – too many have been vandalised or destroyed and I give the people affected this promise: we will help you repair the damage, get your businesses back up and running and support your communities.[17]

Later that afternoon, Theresa May addresses the House claiming that 'the last five days have been a dark time for everybody who cares about their community and their country'. She argues that the violence seen throughout the country 'raises many searching questions, and the answers may be painful to hear and difficult to put right'.[18] She announces that courts are being opened up to process cases very quickly and that very tough sentences will be enforced. She announces all police leave will be cancelled. Miliband's tone changes from condemnation to showing more empathy for the plight of the protestors. 'We all have a duty to ask ourselves why there are people who feel they have nothing to lose and everything to gain from wanton vandalism and looting,' he tells the House, before calling on the government to reconsider spending cuts to the police.[19] Cameron's stark expression of outrage strikes more of a chord in the press than Miliband's overtly political response.

By Friday 12 August the riots have petered out completely. In total, over 3,000 people have been arrested and five killed. An exhausted Cameron meets Samantha and the children back from Italy at Gatwick airport before going on to Dean. On Sunday, the Cleggs come to lunch. Cameron now looks for an opportunity to set the riots in context. In Opposition, fired up by Steve Hilton, his argument had been that society overall had been broken. He thinks he must distance himself from this umbrella view: British society isn't broken, only *parts* of it are. Specifically, there are 125,000 problem families in the country – though many millions of families are not broken. These families have been the focus of one of Whitehall's most tenacious figures and a former appointee of Tony Blair's, Louise Casey. She is later to be appointed director general of the 'troubled families unit'.

Hilton had gone away before the summer feeling very downbeat and disillusioned: the government isn't radical enough, and is going nowhere; he thinks Cameron has allowed himself to become institutionalised by Osborne and the Civil Service. Hilton now sees the riots as a great opportunity, capitalising on the absence of Iain Duncan Smith, who is temporarily away, to lay out his thesis for a reinvigoration of the government's Big Society agenda.

In a speech he writes for Cameron on Monday 15 August, delivered in the prime minister's Witney constituency, criminals are blamed for much of the disturbance during the riots: Cameron has learnt that gangs are at the heart of the trouble, and that three quarters of those arrested have previous convictions. He believes that not enough is being done to help people recognise the boundaries between right and wrong. Out of the speech emerges the 'social policy review', a cross-departmental initiative galvanised by Hilton, who wants to give Whitehall a good kicking and bring it back to his radical, reforming agenda. Hilton acquires a new lease of life and pads around Downing Street with a spring in his bare feet. But he encounters forces of resistance, against which even he is unable to prevail. Richard Reeves, Clegg's director of strategy, fiercely challenges Number 10's attempts to blame the riots partly on family breakdown, and believes, along with Labour, that economic hardship is the key factor. 'The Lib Dems blocked it very, very aggressively,' says Hilton. 'I was really surprised.'[20] But it is not only the Lib Dems who are dismantling Hilton's big agenda.

THIRTEEN

The Big Society and Beyond

May 2010–April 2012

'Steve made the PM. He would never have become prime minister without him. Dave loved him,' says someone who knew them both. 'But the PM found it hard to live with him in Downing Street.'[1] These comments sum up the oddest story in Cameron's far from conventional premiership. The lead character, Steve Hilton, is one of the most creative and unusual figures ever to hold a senior role in Downing Street: he regularly padded around the corridors of Number 10 barefoot. On one particular morning, 17 June 2010, he arrived at Number 10 in his cycling shorts. He had a meeting scheduled with the prime minister and panicked until a member of the policy team took off his own trousers and handed them to him. He wore them all day, apparently unaware they were completely the wrong size. Hilton at 10 is a story of love, genius, inspiration, and if not ultimately betrayal then certainly rejection. He was the booster on Rocket Cameron. He gave his boss the self-belief, inspiration and the ideas to make it to Downing Street. But the core mission fulfilled, his role became gradually redundant, and he fell to earth, leaving Cameron and his team, who had also come of age with him, to find their own way onwards into an uncertain future without their pilot-in-chief.

Hilton is the son of Hungarian refugees. He attended Christ's Hospital, an independent school in West Sussex, read PPE at Oxford, and met Cameron at the Conservative Research Department in 1992. Opposites though they were in most ways, they were powerfully attracted to each other. 'At heart Hilton is a radical reformer, an angry young man breaking free from the shackles of Communism. He wants to change everything all at once and hates anything that is secret, not transparent, or that reeks of an impersonal officialdom.' Hilton's ability took him on a stellar rise through the advertising agency Saatchi & Saatchi. One of his assignments was selling the Conservative Party: he displayed a natural gift for 'political imagery, communications, and sloganeering', which caught the eye of those in power.[2] He joined Cameron's team in 2005 and made an immediate impression. 'He tells me stuff from the heart,' said Cameron, who was captivated by Hilton's mind and breadth of vision. He was everything Cameron was not. He made Cameron a more complete person and professional politician. His role resembled New Labour's Peter Mandelson, without his guile.

Cameron looks back with special fondness on Hilton's impact on his party conference speech in 2007, his best, he says, of the Opposition years, and delivered, on Hilton's prompting, without notes.[3] In this 2005–7 period, Hilton was at the forefront of the Conservatives' 'detoxification' drive, moving away from the traditional emphasis on immigration, law and order, and anti-Europeanism, towards a more metropolitan, compassionate and liberal vision of conservatism.[4] He gave Cameron a passion for enterprise, transparency, the environment, well-being and the digital agenda.

The crash of 2008 changed everything. Osborne moved up into the driving seat, and Coulson advanced up the pecking order within the inner court. The primary task now became winning the trust of the electorate for Cameron's and Osborne's leadership and economic agenda. Hilton departed for a time to California with his wife, Rachel Whetstone, former political secretary to Michael Howard. When he returned in the autumn of 2009, the landscape was very different. But his experience of Palo Alto and California had brought him into contact with a wealth of new ideas. He was a whirling dervish, firing off communications in all directions. He worried that the Tory pitch for the general election, as we have seen, lacked positive messages. His energy was boundless, as one of several thousand emails, this one sent to Tim Chatwin who ran the grid, shows: 'Tim, I love this on schools and urban regeneration – can we please put something in the grid on this in the New Year?'[5] He continually wanted activity, fresh thinking, and he wanted it now.

On 10 November 2009, Cameron gave the 'Hugo Young' lecture in London. Written by Hilton, it was the most persuasive case Cameron made for Hilton's 'Big Society' agenda. The state, he said, had become too big, taken too much responsibility from people, and caused economic and social problems. There was more than an echo here of the mantras of the Institute of Economic Affairs, founded by Whetstone's grandfather, Antony Fisher. To take the place of the state, Cameron said, you need to build up family, community, neighbour-hood and local government, creating a strong civil society. At the same time, Hilton began drawing on his California experience and was pushing his notion of the 'post-bureaucratic age' with its concomitant ideas of decentralisation, technology, transparency and freedom of information. The ideas coalesced in Cameron's 'TED' (Technology, Entertainment, Design) talk on 16 February 2010, called 'The Next Age of Government', and in the launch the same month of the 'Network for a Post-Bureaucratic Age'. The Big Society was taking shape in Hilton's mind in those months under three broad headings, in order of priority: decentralisation, public sector reform, and social action.

But by early 2010, as we saw in Chapter 2, Hilton ran into prob-lems, with Cameron finding it difficult to juggle the two very different agendas. Osborne and Coulson were arguing that 'Plan A' was all that mattered and should be the main narrative. 'What people wanted was competence and effective leadership,' says one person at the heart of the 2010 election campaign. 'They didn't want grand schemes or the Obama vision of hope and change.' Hilton responded that his Big Society agenda was the right way forward, and that it was nothing to do with the fiscal cuts. He wanted the Big Society as the only item in the shop display. Cameron hates conflict, and charged Letwin with weaving both agendas into a coherent narrative. Letwin was the ideal choice. His economic views chimed with Osborne's and he possessed the shadow chancellor's total trust. Equally he made Hilton believe he was on his side too. But Letwin is a clever man, and it soon became obvious to him that he was merely papering over a glaring crack, one which would emasculate Cameron and the clarity of the Conservative message at the 2010 general election. Indeed apart from when the party launched its manifesto, in which the Big Society took centre stage, the concept was hardly mentioned in the rest of the election campaign – a reflection of the doubts about its electoral appeal within the team.

Cameron's core philosophy and beliefs remained elusive to many. They were clear in his own mind. 'People say they don't know what I stand for,' he said in 2014: 'I would say that my own agenda is aspiration for all, Big Society and service, education and welfare reform.'[6] One person close to Cameron is sceptical about Hilton and regards his influence as overblown and damaging: 'The Big Society stuff came out of absolutely nowhere. Dave agreed with parts of it, on personal responsibility and taking control of your life. But most people had absolutely no idea what it was talking about.' Yet the Big Society agenda *did* come from somewhere. Much of the approach – including the sense of community, the importance of family and stability, and the value of charity and service – struck a chord deep within Cameron. Hilton was Cameron's muse. He knew Cameron better than almost anyone, and articulated Cameron's most profound instincts. 'He is a really modern, liberal, socially concerned person: not at all like George or Andy,' says Hilton. 'He really *believes* in decentralisation of power, family, entrepreneurs, transparency, communities and neighbourhoods, and gay marriage.'[7] By 2015, Hilton however had accepted that although Cameron still believed in the Big Society agenda, he had taken a conscious decision to prioritise stable government, holding the coalition together and leading Britain through the economic crisis.[8]

Hilton had an insatiable energy and in the weeks leading up to the 2010 general election demanded to be involved in everything. Together with Chatwin, he mapped out in great detail the first hundred days of a Cameron government. Rohan Silva became a major ally in his crusade.[9] With Letwin and Francis Maude, the shadow minister for the Cabinet Office, they worked through each department's Structural Reform Plan with each shadow Secretary of State, later to be renamed 'business plans' once in power. 'Steve's instinct was to go for it and get a lot done very quickly,' says Letwin. 'That impulse was shared by Osborne and Cameron. We took a clear decision that we should have the architecture very firmly in place if we became a government.'[10] Each plan had a timetable creating a powerful sense of impetus and incentive. Cameron told Hilton, 'I want you to get things done now so when we look back at the end of the five years, we can see how much we did.'

* * *

After the election, Hilton bursts onto an unsuspecting Number 10. Civil servants were warned about this odd creature, but nothing could prepare them fully for what hits them. None have ever known a figure like him at the heart of government. Hilton is as wary of Civil Service obstructionism as any in Cameron's team so moves quickly on the transparency agenda, to increase the openness of government through the publication of data and information, before official resistance can be organised. 'Steve, Rohan and I acted together on this very swiftly after the general election,' recalls Maude. They bring together a 'Transparency Board' containing high-octane figures such as Web-inventor Tim Berners-Lee, and artificial intelligence expert and later co-founder of Open Data Institute, Nigel Shadbolt.[11] Hilton wants every new policy proposal to be submitted to the 'family test', and is passionate to make it 'the most family friendly government ever'[12]: policies aimed specifically at helping families take up nearly half his time in Downing Street.

Hilton looks back nostalgically to the dynamic Number 10 operation of Thatcher's heyday in the 1980s. He disagrees with Letwin's determination to slim it down. Instead, he becomes frustrated that it lacks the right machinery to pursue his policy ideas. Cameron and Ed Llewellyn are anxious that Number 10 shuns the bloated Blair and Brown models, and do not want it to give the impression of throwing its weight around. The Policy Unit will have only a handful of staff, overseen by James O'Shaughnessy, manifesto writer and head of the research department when in Opposition. Hilton eschews the idea of any title for himself: he doesn't want his role to be defined or bureau-cratised. To Gus O'Donnell, the lack of capacity in Number 10 is bound to create problems. 'Steve was brilliant and bonkers, apt to lose his temper. But the PM knew he was like this. The problem lay more below the level of Steve and Rohan. They had pared too much back so lacked the capacity in Number 10 to drive change through.'[13] Fatally, Cameron's team do not heed his advice on Number 10, nor Heywood's.

On Thursday 1 July, Heywood convenes a meeting for Number 10 staff, introducing them one by one 'with customary professionalism'. Hilton gives a talk about his three cross-cutting ideas that bind the government together: Big Society, transparency and families. Letwin goes on to outline the philosophy of the government: 'Wherever possible, markets should be open to provide choice: if a market is not possible, there should be payment by results, as in welfare and prisons; if that is not possible, as in with the police, there should be direct elections; and if that is not possible, delivery should be scrutinised to be made as efficient as possible.' Officials swallow hard. Not since 1979 has there been such an ideological shift in the thinking behind government operations. Hilton knows at this early stage that Whitehall has not grasped the concept of the Big Society. 'In a well-intentioned but typically bureaucratic way, they heard the phrase and thought "there must be a Big Society programme or policy we can roll out and implement" rather than seeing it as the central argument for domestic reform,' Hilton recalls. 'That is the moment when it first started to go wrong.'[14]

The Treasury are expected to obstruct the enterprise agenda. Hilton wants to open up government contracts to small companies, introduce tax breaks for early-stage companies and have start-up loans. Treasury officials are indeed not enthusiastic about this agenda, though Osborne is personally. They both think the Treasury is never at its strongest generating fresh ideas.

Cameron's speech on 19 July in Liverpool officially launches the Big Society, and speaks of 'a new approach' to government and governing. He calls for an end to regulation and bureaucracy that hinders volunteering, and for people to act as volunteers.[15] Even in these early days, the Big Society has its critics, including Cameron's erstwhile rival for the leadership, David Davis, who is reported in the *Financial Times* as dismissing it as 'Blairite dressing' to compensate for the baleful agenda that has come from the 'Brokeback Coalition'.[16] Hilton soon starts running into problems. He deeply resents the Civil Service ring of officialdom that descends around Cameron and fills his day with meetings and state business, which Hilton thinks is largely a waste of Cameron's time. 'Why the fuck is he proposing to have four or five separate intelligence meetings each week?' he demands to know when discussing the PM's diary.

Hilton gets off to a good start with the Lib Dems. He shares a small office adjacent to the Cabinet Room with Lib Dem policy chief Polly Mackenzie. 'He generates fresh thinking, an antidote to the technocratic tendencies of the Civil Service,' says one Lib Dem.[17] His initial fights are not with civil servants, nor the Lib Dems, but friendly fire. Within days of taking power Hilton and Coulson are falling out badly: 'You can talk this crap if you like, but I'll just keep chucking meat out to the red tops' is how one aide sums up Coulson's approach. Hilton implores Cameron to reach out to a more liberally minded audience than the tabloids. Hilton's relations with Osborne are no better in power than in Opposition. Soon the chancellor is refusing to have Hilton at meetings of the Quad. Hilton's flair for ideas does not translate into know-how at getting things done in Whitehall. He is reluctant to compromise on his agenda or align it with anyone else's, insisting the Big Society is nothing to do with the programme of fiscal cuts. He does not build alliances and relationships to win people over: his irascibility irks and alienates those who might have been his allies.

His relationship with Heywood is intriguing. The biggest iconoclast in Downing Street for many years meets the most savvy and powerful official figure to bestride Downing Street since the 1980s. In these early months, Heywood is galvanised by working with Hilton and makes a big effort to support him. He asks Hilton to attend, at the outset, the weekly meeting of Whitehall's permanent secretaries: 'They need to understand what it [the Big Society agenda] means for them,' Heywood says. He arranges for Hilton to chair a series of weekly meetings in Number 10 to help him deliver the agenda on family policy and the Big Society. He even supports Hilton's thinking on open data and transparency in government. It is at Heywood's suggestion that Hilton later brings in Louise Casey to devise policies that help troubled families following the riots. In the first few months of the government, Hilton is instrumental in bringing in Labour figures, like Frank Field and Graham Allen, to conduct reviews into child poverty and early years intervention. He also draws heavily on the advice of two Tory grandees, Lord Heseltine and Lord Young, who become his mentors 'on how to get things done' in government as well as his friends and allies. Both undertake important reviews into urban regeneration and deregulation respectively. Heywood is intrigued by and admires Hilton's creativity and willingness to draw on thinking from across the political spectrum. Heywood is a subtle civil servant. His prime responsibility is to serve the prime minister. As long as Hilton has his master's favour, Heywood will facilitate his wishes.

Coulson's departure in January 2011 revitalises Hilton. Within days, he inaugurates a huge push on the Big Society with emails charging through the system again to widespread irritation, or admiration. Briefing of the press by Cameron's team, which Coulson had strongly discouraged, reaches new heights. Concerns begin to be voiced in Number 10 that Hilton is stirring up the large 2010 intake against the inertia, as he sees it. Hilton presses Cameron to deliver another speech. The left have consistently attacked the Big Society as a smokescreen for hiding the cuts. Polly Toynbee, writing in the *Guardian*, describes it as a 'national joke'. The attacks are striking home: two-thirds of voters believe that the Big Society agenda is merely the government's attempt to put a positive spin on the cuts.[18] The response comes in a speech delivered on 14 February at Somerset House in London. In it, Cameron launches a week-long drive of activities to persuade the public that the policy is not a 'sepia-tinted' wash. A torrent of initiatives is announced. £200 million is promised for a Big Society Bank. To fill shortfalls caused by local authority cuts, charities are to be offered 'lifeline' funding totalling £110 million. Cash machines are to have a facility to allow donations to good causes. A National Citizen Service (NCS) is to be established offering tens of thousands of teenagers the chance to gain skills and participate in social action projects, while 5,000 community organisers are to become the manifestation of the Big Society across England.[19]

This might have been the take-off moment for the Big Society. But instead, it begins to unravel. The relaunch fails to achieve the impact that Hilton hopes for. Aside from the NCS, many of the initiatives do not capture the public imagination. Personal relationships are seriously deteriorating. On top of excluding him from meetings of the Quad, Osborne now refuses to let Hilton attend his bilateral meetings with Cameron and deliberately cuts him out from key papers. Hilton is furious. Nat Wei, a peer, who was appointed as an unpaid adviser on the Big Society before the general election, and who continued in government, leaves the role in May 2011. It is a bad sign. Lib Dem enthusiasm for the agenda is replaced by cold hostility. Even before Polly Mackenzie departs on maternity leave in autumn 2011, her relationship with Hilton sours. 'The Lib Dems hate the Big Society,' Hilton is regularly heard to say. He is particularly angry that Clegg and

Communities Secretary Eric Pickles gang up to emasculate the proposal for elected mayors as they fear the animosity of their councillors and activists on the ground. 'Dave really believed in local mayors,' fumes Hilton. 'But he wasn't going to bust up the coalition over it.'[20] Heywood, who has worked as hard as anyone to facilitate what Hilton was trying to do, begins to show doubt. 'At some point, from early/mid-2011, Jeremy decided to dodge the bullet and move onto the next thing,' says one insider.

Hilton falls out badly with Paul Kirby, head of an expanded Policy Unit since February 2011. On 1 June, a private diary records that 'Hilton doesn't like Kirby' and feels he is being undermined by him; Kirby is openly contemptuous of Steve, and 'whereas Heywood always respects Steve and tempers him when necessary, Paul always seeks to undermine him'. Hilton complains that 'Paul Kirby is George's person. It's been like *Yes, Minister* with me being kept out of things. I'm told I've been copied in on key documents, but I only receive them at the last minute, when it's too late.' Hilton protests to Cameron about being marginalised from the work of the Policy Unit: 'Your job is to make it happen,' Cameron responds brusquely. Hilton now excludes himself from the twice-daily meetings in the PM's room, which he considers reactive and unstrategic. Distance is growing from Cameron's team, who were once so close to him. Hilton soon falls out with Andrew Cooper, who had arrived in Number 10 as director of strategy in March 2011. 'The prospect of polling and focus groups makes me physically ill,' Hilton tells him. Ed Llewellyn and Kate Fall have been his closest friends and allies for years, but he grows apart from even them too. He becomes scornful of Coulson's successor, Craig Oliver. He blames Rupert Harrison for leading Osborne astray.

Fatally, differences are beginning to appear between Hilton and Cameron himself: 'He is completely falling for the fucking establishment line, we are never going to get anywhere like this!' he says. He speculates that there are two sides to Cameron: the radical, who he loves, and the traditionalist, who he doesn't. He fears Cameron's liking for due process as prime minister is trumping the radical side. There is much unhappiness among Cameron's close team in the first half of 2011. They retain great affection for Hilton, and, following the departure of Coulson, are deeply anxious not to lose another member of their tight group, least of all when under so much attack from party and press. But Hilton's iconoclasm, his bombastic style, his lack of discipline and his anger are making enemies across the piece, and causing untold worries: 'We are always trying to find the right niche for him,' says one. 'It was so much easier in Opposition, but he remains the intellectual live wire among us. We need him,' says another.

Cameron is not giving up on Hilton just yet. He consents to a further Big Society relaunch, in Milton Keynes on 23 May. It includes the announcement that ministers will lead from the front, pledging themselves to undertake a day of voluntary service a year. 'The Big Society is not some fluffy add-on to more gritty and more important subjects,' Cameron insists.[21] But the reaction of the media remains as cynical as ever. Polls are published showing that the agenda will either be neutral or damaging to the Conservatives at the next general election.[22] This is toxic.

The policies Hilton is driving are running into new kinds of problems, cranking up tension still further. He wants the *Open Public Services* White Paper to be radical, but is thwarted by the Lib Dems, who keep pushing back publication. Officials say progress is difficult with both coalition partners in such different places. Hilton is insistent that contracts be subject to more competition, and public services be opened up more to private sector providers. A high point of tension comes in July 2011 with a Cameron article in the *Daily Telegraph* written by Hilton, which lays out the aims and principles of the White Paper.[23] The Lib Dems hate its advocacy of competition and profits and continue to push publication back to after the summer recess. Hilton wants the Office of Fair Trading to act against monopolies in the public sector, as they do against monopolies in the private sector. For a while, Richard Reeves, Clegg's director of strategy, is supportive, but Clegg's implacable opposition to personal budgets in health and social care and competition in public services proves decisive. Losing this battle is a major blow to Hilton.

Lib Dem opposition now thwarts another of his crusades. He wants to liberalise the labour market and asks Adrian Beecroft, a venture capitalist, to look at how this might be done. Beecroft's suggestions include making it far more difficult for employees who have been dismissed to appeal to employment tribunals. Cameron gives his backing to Hilton, but he runs headlong into the opposition of Business Secretary Vince Cable, who considers this his domain. Hilton cannot understand Cameron's reluctance simply to push it through against Cable's blocking. He does not have time for the nuances of holding the coalition together. Progress with the business community and entrepreneurs seems to be getting nowhere, while the TUC, which strongly opposes the plans, is having its way. The forces are stacked too heavily against him. He works tirelessly to build up support for the changes, but he has to admit defeat. Months later, Cameron tells him candidly, 'I couldn't tell Vince Cable what to do. I couldn't overrule him on this.'

On 1 June 2011, Hilton has a frank talk with Silva. They acknowledge they are trying to fight on too many fronts and together draw up a Venn diagram with the overlapping areas in the middle denoting what is really important to both of them. This brings forty areas down to just ten, which they decide to concentrate on. They draft a note, with initials in brackets showing which of them will be principally responsible for driving each agenda item forward in the coming year. They are: open public services White Paper (SH), mayors and decentralisation (SH), families (SH), Somerset House (SH), marketing Britain (SH), Tech City (RS), pharmaceutical industry (RS), sex trafficking (RS), planning (RS), well-being/social value (SH and RH). 'Somerset House' refers to Hilton's obsession that the entire British Empire had been run from buildings that size in the nineteenth century, and that the Civil Service should be shrunk down to the same size today, an idea which, unsurprisingly, provokes anger among senior mandarins. 'Pharmaceutical industry' speaks of the determination to make Britain world class in the life sciences. 'Sex trafficking' refers to curbing the sex-slave problem.

Hilton's rationalisation of priorities comes too late. 'He let himself become involved in minor issues and lost sight of the big picture,' is the verdict of one senior official. Perhaps the forces are now arrayed too strongly against him. On Monday 20 June, he has a frank conversation with his policy colleagues, having read rumours in the press again over the weekend that he is on the verge of resigning. 'As you can see, I am still here. We have known each other for years. We are friends in the Tory Party, not in some psychodrama. When we disagree it is a genuine policy disagreement. My role for the prime minister is to push the agenda forward. Others are here to push it back, and that is fine. We are grown-ups and disagreement is fine.'

Matters come to a head at Chequers, where senior ministers assemble for a political Cabinet on Sunday 24 July. Hilton has been uncharacteristically depressed in the early summer. Letwin and Danny Alexander have prepared a paper advocating a new coalition agreement for the second half of the government. Hilton believes their whole approach is fundamentally wrong, and argues they should be first trying to 'implement the radical things we said we'd do rather than water them down'. Hilton finds a quiet moment and confronts Cameron: 'We haven't done a thousandth of what we should have done. The government is far too timid. We are wasting our chance. You need to put me in charge rather than people like Ed [Llewellyn] and Craig [Oliver].' An acrimonious discussion follows. Cameron is losing patience. His team are feeling undermined. Reports leak that Hilton will shortly be leaving Number 10 – variants of that story have been in circulation in the building since New Year.

The riots in August, which he sees as a great opportunity to reassert the importance of the Big Society, came at the right time for him. The riots have happened, he says, because of insufficient regard for community, personal responsibility and family. The social policy review is set up. He returns to Number 10 in September in a much happier frame of mind. But the old problems soon emerge. Hilton is infringing a golden rule of Cameron's inner circle – you do not talk to the press. It alienates him badly from them. Deep down, the mood is changing. Trust has been lost and Hilton's old friends are afraid of what he might be telling the press about them. But they still do not want to lose a second member of the team. He must be taken off day-to-day policy work and immerse himself instead in long-term thinking, with a seat in the office outside the prime minister's study, alongside Llewellyn, Fall and Heywood. Cameron says he wants him at all his meetings, even those with Osborne. But he doesn't come. Neither does he take up his seat at his desk in his office.

The annual party conference in October 2011 is a crunch point. Hilton fights hard for his decentralisation agenda to be in the prime minister's speech. Cameron's team argue that it is jarring when the country's attention is so focused on austerity and terrorism. Prioritising decentralisation will seem irrelevant. A fight takes place over a line that Hilton has written for Cameron: 'The purpose of my leadership is to unleash your leadership.' Cooper is particularly unhappy and says the line should be cut. 'Most people do not want to run their library, they don't want to run their school, they want government to do these things, and to lead them, not to be leaders themselves,' he says. Cooper is attacking the very soul of the Big Society. After heated discussions, they compromise with Cameron delivering the line: 'That's why so much of my leadership is about unleashing your leadership.'

Christmas 2011 at Chequers. Hilton tells Cameron to get rid of Kirby as head of the Policy Unit. Cameron tells Hilton outright he will not do this, but repeats that he wants Hilton there at all his meetings. Hilton has begun listening to other voices. Nigel Lawson tells him that he can only remain as a backseat driver for so long. Blair regrets that his advisers were not more radical than he was as prime minister. Rachel is tired of her husband's unhappiness. She has had a second baby and remembers the happy time they spent in California after their first baby was born. She thinks this is where their future lies. At Chequers in early January 2012, Hilton tells Cameron he is contemplating resigning. The prime minister tells him to sort himself out.

Of all Hilton's defeats, he finds the lack of progress on Civil Service reform hardest to stomach, because Cameron cannot claim as usual that the Lib Dems are blocking it. Responding to Hilton's frustrations, Letwin had suggested that Hilton throw his passion into reforming the Civil Service, a campaign for which Letwin, as well as Maude, are keen enthusiasts. While Maude works with permanent secretaries across Whitehall to draw up a coherent reform plan, Hilton and Silva immediately start work on a number of separate proposals. The central idea is still to shrink the Civil Service radically 'so it is small enough to fit inside Somerset House', and make it more open and competitive, ending the public sector monopoly over the delivery of services. But in Hilton's final few months they run into problems with Heywood, now Cabinet Secretary, and Bob Kerslake, the newly appointed head of the Civil Service from January 2012. Both are open to reforming the Civil Service and increasing its efficiency, but the extreme changes Hilton envisages frightens them because they believe it will drastically reduce the Civil Service's capability and ability to support governments. While Heywood is still willing to seek an accommodation with Hilton, Kerslake finds his way of working too unfocused and disorganised. It does not augur well.

Had the Civil Service reformers themselves been unified, they might have prevailed even against the mighty Whitehall. But difficulties had started to appear in 2011 even before the promotions of Heywood and Kerslake. Differences with Maude and, unusually, with Hilton's principal lieutenant, Silva, blunted the focus. Hilton is categorical that the Civil Service has to be cut by 70% and wants that figure written into the policy proposal. Silva thinks it more sensible to begin small, with the Department for Education where Michael Gove is such an enthusiastic supporter, and prove that dramatic efficiency savings can be made, before scaling up across the entire Civil Service. For Hilton, the 70% figure is a red line. In 2012, when Kerslake and senior officials from the department propose a more modest downsizing at one meeting, conscious of the impact on morale, Hilton explodes. 'You haven't done what I wanted to do.' Turning his fire on Kerslake, he shouts, 'You're lying about what I want to achieve!' before storming out of the room. 'He just lost his bottle,' Kerslake recalls, 'he swore at me and slammed the door. In my view some of his work never really added up to a coherent body of argument.'[24] Meetings on Civil Service reform drag on and failure to achieve progress in this area, more than anything, destroy Hilton's morale.

The approaching death of the Big Society had been evident the previous autumn: 'more a fizzling out than one deliberate decision', says an insider. One by one, totemic Big Society policies fall. A Civil Exchange report later says the Big Society 'largely failed' to meet its goals.[25] The initial fervour around the post-riots social policy review dissipates into nothing. Elected mayors fail to capture the imagination and succeed only in Liverpool. Police and Crime Commissioners are elected on painfully low turnouts. On 8 February 2012, Hilton presents a set of slides on Civil Service reform to Cameron, hoping to win him over. 'They weren't very good,' recalls one senior official. 'He hadn't really thought it through very much.' Hilton is bitterly disappointed that Cameron fails to give him the backing he needs. 'If you wanted me to be radical you should have won me a general election victory,' Cameron tells Hilton.

In March, relations plummet to a new low. The prime minister is to give a speech to the Institute of Civil Engineering. Hilton has been working hard to introduce radical reforms into the road network, and to promote 'Boris Island' as London's new airport. He is in despair when he reads the text on 19 March. 'If this is where we are going, it is all useless. The government is useless. We've given up on everything. What the fuck is the point in carrying on?' This time, there is to be no going back. 'The Big Society might not have been a very good idea,' he says to anyone who will listen, 'but it was the only fucking idea we had.' Around Downing Street, he is regularly heard to make comments like 'Fucking hell, I don't know what they stand for anymore or what the fucking point is in being here.'

The end comes swiftly in the spring of 2012. He goes to Washington with Cameron in March but tells him before they travel that he is leaving. Hilton has run out of allies. Clegg objects strongly to his neo-Thatcherite policies in his final phase. Hilton's attempts to portray Cameron in the media as a free-market liberal prove too much. Osborne lost faith months ago and is not fighting to retain him. Craig Oliver is thoroughly alienated from him and finds him 'massively destabilising'. Llewellyn has become alienated by his briefing. A mawkish moment had occurred at Osborne's fortieth birthday party at Dorneywood in 2011 when Hilton had embraced Llewellyn and made out that they were great friends; but the gulf has now become unbridgeable. Kate Fall is the last of the inner court to hold faith, but even she feels that the team will be more cohesive without him. Andrew Feldman has repeatedly told Cameron, 'You've got to let him go.' The noise is building and building. Before Easter, Hilton finally leaves for California.

The arrangement is that he is to reappear for annual party conferences. But his reign is over. With him goes a creative genius and innovation that is never to be replaced. Indeed, arguably Number 10 has never seen such a creative, one-man Policy Unit. Whitehall breathes a collective sigh of relief when he leaves, though within three months, forward-thinking mandarins are mourning the loss of the impetus, urgency and fresh thinking he provided. His departure sounds the death knell for the Big Society, though some of it remains and Cameron regards aspects of it, like the National Citizen Service, as among his proudest achievements. Volunteering and charitable giving rates grow despite the economic gloom. But in his 2012 party conference speech, which places individual aspiration and Britain's role in the 'global race' at the heart of the Tory message, the Big Society is hardly mentioned.

Letting Hilton go is one of the hardest things Cameron has to do as prime minister. He never loses his love and admiration for him, and is profoundly pained that his philosopher has had such a difficult ride in government. Despite all that has happened, their strong friendship endures. Cameron's remaining team begin to think Hilton has become a security blanket, preventing his boss from realising he can flourish without him. Whether Cameron will be able to find his voice without his muse by his side remains to be seen. Osborne, Llewellyn, Fall and Oliver tell him, 'You can't talk about the Big Society.' Cameron tellingly responds: 'It's our idea for reforming the country. We can't just drop it. It's what we are all about!'

First Coulson, now Hilton: Cameron is losing key lieutenants. He is in trouble from all sides. Things are about to get worse still.

FOURTEEN

The EU: Back Burner to Veto

May 2010–December 2011

'I don't want Europe to define my premiership,' Cameron said shortly before the general election. In the months leading up to it, a series of Whitehall specialists on Europe had told him the next five years would not be difficult in the EU. With the 2009 Lisbon Treaty out of the way, they said, no more treaty changes are envisaged, and the EU will settle down to one of its quiet periods. 'We didn't expect Europe to form a big part of the agenda,' he says with confidence.[1] Cameron was just twelve years old when Thatcher came to power. He observed with dismay the fights over Europe during her premiership, and had a vantage point as a special adviser on the vicious infighting during John Major's premiership. If elected prime minister, he does not want his own leadership to be bogged down by Europe.

He implored the Conservative party conference in October 2006 to stop 'banging on about Europe', and to focus instead on the issues that mattered to people, like public services. His victory over David Davis and Liam Fox in the leadership contest was strengthened by his pledge to withdraw Conservative MEPs from the European People's Party (EPP) in the EU Parliament, one of the few specific policy pledges he made. His advisers told him that the EPP was a stitch-up between Paris and Berlin, and he would do well to be out of it. (The withdrawal from the EPP group came about later in 2009, and the Conservatives helped form the European Conservatives and Reformists (ECR) group. The move pleased Eurosceptics while causing dismay in European capitals, notably Berlin, and led to an angry Angela Merkel withdrawing the head of the Konrad-Adenauer-Stiftung political foundation in London, Thomas Bernd Stehling.)

Cameron's attempt to neuter the EU as a toxic issue continued in September 2007 with an article in the *Sun* offering a 'cast-iron guarantee' of a referendum over the Lisbon Treaty, should it be signed but not ratified.[2] This was rash. By the spring of 2009, it became clear that Lisbon would be ratified. That summer Cameron discussed how to respond with his team, George Osborne, William Hague, Ed Llewellyn, Oliver Letwin, and Steve Hilton. They were in a vice. Persisting with a referendum policy on Lisbon would damage the party's standing with key business and financial interests, and might impact negatively on the general election. But admitting that the 'cast-iron guarantee' was premature would only inflame Conservative backbenchers. A middle way had to be found.

As so often when in a tight spot, Cameron fell back on the expedient of a speech. Written by Llewellyn and Hilton, he delivered it at St Stephen's Club in London on 4 November 2009. Cameron announced that as Lisbon had been ratified, it could not now be undone: but he boldly promised he would 'make sure this never happens again' by offering a 'referendum lock', whereby a British government could only transfer powers to the EU in the future if the British electorate gives their consent in a referendum. He promised to work to make the EU more congenial to Britain, not least by the 'returning of powers' to London. But he argued that 'Britain's interests are best served by membership of a European Union' and said he would work for changes to make British membership more beneficial, including financial regulations to protect the City of London's competitiveness. Although offering the electorate an 'in/out referendum' on the EU in a second term did not make it into the speech, Cameron's team say they 'had this prospect clearly in all our minds'. The speech did not let him off the hook. To his right wing in Parliament and the country, and to Eurosceptic commentators in the media, his dodging of a referendum on Lisbon was a broken promise. Even a betrayal.

So confident nevertheless were Cameron and Osborne that the EU would not become a major issue during the premiership they did not convene any strategic meetings before the election to hammer out their thinking. The manifesto merely included the reforms promised by Cameron at his St Stephen's Club speech.

* * *

The election brings large swathes of independent-minded and Eurosceptic Conservative MPs into Parliament. The party watches warily as Cameron's team disappear with the Lib Dems into a huddle to plot the Coalition Agreement. Lib Dem negotiators make it clear they will not allow any mention of powers being returned from the EU: the most they will allow is a re-examination of the 'balance of competences'. Clegg is worried about the Conservative Party on Europe, and is adamant that there will be no renegotiation of the terms of accession.[3] The Lib Dems will, however, allow the 'referendum lock' envisaged by Cameron in the St Stephen's Club speech (which is enacted in 2011), confirming their own manifesto commitment to a referendum in the event of 'a fundamental change in the relationship' with the EU.[4] They agree importantly with the Tories that 'the EU is not going to be a big feature of the life of the coming parliament'.

Cameron is full of hopes for crafting a forward-thinking EU policy. He envisages as many free trade agreements as possible, rolling back unnecessary EU legislation, and building long-term alliances with northern states Sweden, Denmark and Finland, as a countervailing force to the central European states who are the big spenders and who tend to dominate EU policy. He envisages taking a very tough line on the seven-year EU budget from the beginning, as Thatcher had done, and will insist that it be reduced. With Osborne, he is emphatic that British money will not unnecessarily go to Europe. He knows that financial services regulation will be a big battleground, and he will fight to ensure that the City of London is protected. Officials in Whitehall think neither the Conservatives nor Lib Dems understand the EU or what is happening in the eurozone. 'I don't want Europe to be noisy,' Cameron tells one. Like Blair in 1997, he believes he can usher in a new era of Britain–EU relations.

These aspirations are called into question very early on. It is easy with hindsight to understand why. The eurozone crisis had not been foreseen. The first harbinger of trouble comes in Greece the month after the St Stephen's Club speech. It takes off from February 2010, and continues throughout 2011. The crisis heightens the need to protect financial services, which constitute some 4% of British jobs. Number 10 is exasperated with the previous government's handling of the EU commissioner negotiations, blaming Gordon Brown for botching them in late 2009 by accepting the High Representative portfolio for Baroness Ashton rather than holding out for an economic portfolio. The result has been that Ashton's foreign policy role takes her too often abroad and away from protecting British interests in Brussels. Their concerns are exacerbated by a lack of faith in other office holders, notably Michel Barnier, commissioner for Internal Market and Services, who they regard as neither pro-liberalisation nor pro-City of London. EU president Herman Van Rompuy they eye warily, believing his mission in life is to 'reconcile the differences between Paris and Berlin, leaving little room for us'. The net result is a diminution of British influence in Brussels.

The key reason why Cameron's premiership becomes so dominated by Europe is down to the Conservative Party itself and the rise of UKIP. Hague anticipates how difficult the party might be, but Cameron is caught off guard by the strength of feeling on the issue, with cheerleaders Norman Tebbit in the House of Lords, Daniel Hannan in the European Parliament, Douglas Carswell and Mark Reckless amongst newer MPs, and Bill Cash and Bernard Jenkin amongst the old guard. Cameron has Eurosceptic tendencies of his own, but he has only contempt for UKIP and its leader Nigel Farage. In 2006, Cameron had memorably described the party as full of 'fruit-cakes, loonies and closet racists'. The words refuse to go away because they seem to capture what, deep down, people suspect Cameron thought. But is the UKIP bubble bursting? While the party came second in the European election in 2009, winning nearly 2.5 million votes, it performs poorly at the 2010 general election. Cameron dearly hopes it is on the wane.

It isn't. The fervour surrounding UKIP and within his own party drives Cameron steadily rightwards on Europe, which only increases conflict with the Lib Dems. Clegg for a long time remains respectful and understanding of Cameron's difficulty in 'trying to manage the constant rage of the Tory Party'.[5] After the summer recess in 2011, the rage breaks out into the open. A public petition calling for a referendum on continued EU membership attracts 100,000 signatures.[6] On 24 October, the House of Commons votes on a motion calling for an in/out referendum. Feverish discussions take place amongst Cameron's team in Number 10. 'We cannot lie down on this.

We must have a three-line whip,' says Cameron. Osborne and Hague concur. 'Such a referendum is not in the manifesto and is not Conservative policy,' Cameron continues. If they don't get tough, they will send out a signal that it's fine to vote against it, and 'we will have had 150–200 MPs filing through the "no" lobby'. He worries that Labour might decide not to participate, resulting in the motion being carried.

Cameron is infuriated with his backbench Eurosceptics. They gave him no credit earlier in the year for negotiating Britain out of the European Financial Stability Mechanism (which Labour had entered). Cameron orders an 'industrial-scale operation' to organise resistance to the referendum motion.[7] The chief whip Patrick McLoughlin is confronted by a spectrum of opponents, from ultras like Cash to those who have said in their election literature they favoured a referendum. Others are venting their anger, he believes, at not receiving a minister-ial job after the general election, with the Lib Dems scooping up many plum posts. Things turn nasty: one parliamentary private secretary, Stewart Jackson, is sacked after voting against the government; another, Adam Holloway, stands down. The motion is nonetheless heavily defeated by 483 votes to 111. However, no fewer than eighty-one Tory MPs defy the three-line whip and their prime minister. Many openly say they do not know where the PM's instincts lie on Europe. It is not a good omen. He is becoming bogged down in Europe.

At some point during 2011, Cameron takes a critical decision: despite his strong, if volatile, relationship with Nicolas Sarkozy, he decides Merkel will be the key to advancing British interests in the EU. The European Council, which had twenty-seven nationalities when he became prime minister (increasing to twenty-eight with the accession of Croatia in July 2013), arouses strong feelings in him. 'Nothing I did beforehand gave me any preparation for them,' he says.[8] While he quite enjoys his work on EU business, which takes some 10% of his time as PM, and likes negotiating optimum outcomes and building alliances, he finds the organisation and very frequency of the European Councils – where the leaders meet on their own without officials or ministers – very wearisome. He frequently returns to London drained and cross. He wants to talk about deregulation, productivity and job creation, but is steamrollered by fellow leaders who do not share his economic ideals. He has few soulmates: he enjoys his regular meetings with Sarkozy and the grandiose ideas that emerge from the mouth of this Gallic version of Steve Hilton. But much of the conversation with Sarkozy is just flannel; besides, he is replaced by the left-wing François Hollande in May 2012. Cameron chimes with Jyrki Katainen (Finland), Mark Rutte (Netherlands), Frederik Reinfeldt (Sweden) and Helle Thorning-Schmidt (Denmark), but his lack of strong philosophical allies in the EU leads him to become still more dependent on the lone figure of Merkel.

Cameron first meets her on 21 May 2010, within days of becoming PM. She has been chancellor already for nearly five years, and has approval ratings of which Cameron can only dream. Cameron flies with his party of Ed Llewellyn, Europe adviser Jon Cunliffe, national security adviser Peter Ricketts, foreign affairs adviser Tom Fletcher and future ambassador to Germany, Simon McDonald, meeting Merkel in her rooms on the eighth floor of the Chancellery in Berlin. The two leaders talk on her terrace that overlooks the city before the wider team join for lunch. Merkel is perplexed to see some of Gordon Brown's team there. The neutrality of the British Civil Service is foreign to her and she asks Cameron, 'Explain to me again how these people are still with you?' After the lunch, in a lift, she says to one, 'How does this work? I thought you worked for Gordon.'

She is intrigued by this new 'upper class' prime minister, admiring his confidence and manners. But there is a tension in the air: even though she is no longer furious, she is still disconcerted by his withdrawal from the EPP. She is not a vindictive person and her anger has mellowed. Cameron reads his briefing notes on the flight from seeing Sarkozy in Paris: they highlight her antipathy, and he is thus wary, remaining so for the early councils. On her side, she concludes that this charming new PM is apt to make up his mind a little too quickly. She admires his speed of decision-making, but thinks he should be more reflective and considered. She surmises, correctly, that he hasn't thought through fully Britain's position as a non-euro country, or come to terms with the reality that the financial crisis means that the euro countries will have to integrate more – or risk breaking up. But they strike a chord: the encounter suggests they will share an affinity, and there is even a suggestion of personal chemistry.

Relations deepen over the summer, and on 30 October, Merkel arrives on an overnight visit to Chequers. She brings her husband, Professor Joachim Sauer, a professor of physical and theoretical chemistry at the Humboldt University of Berlin. It is a mark of the regard that Merkel has for Cameron, as well as of Chequers' mystique, that her husband joins her on this trip. They converse in English: Cameron has a little French, but no German, whereas her English is excellent. The next day, they walk across muddy fields, which she enjoys. Her party stay in a local hotel and join for discussions, mostly on the eurozone crisis, the following morning.

The eurozone dominates their discussions in 2011, with the debt-heavy euro countries – Portugal, Greece, Spain and Ireland – threatening to drag the entire economy of Europe into disaster. Harsh austerity measures adopted by most have varied impacts, but in Greece the scale of the problem proves insurmountable. Merkel plays a lead role in agreeing a series of packages to prevent Greek debt from wrecking the entire euro project. Talks between her and Sarkozy are described as 'the last chance' to prevent collapse of the euro.[9] In late 2010, Cameron had assented to a small treaty change Germany said it needed to stabilise the euro. But he is uneasy about it. She is perturbed by Cameron's scepticism about the eurozone's prospects, and lack of sympathy for its plight. She is particularly upset when he later describes himself as a 'Eurosceptic'. He comes on the phone to explain to her that the word 'sceptical' in Britain doesn't mean the same as in Europe. 'It doesn't mean I am against the European project. What I want is a reformed Europe.' He says he has to be pragmatic and practical. 'I think I get it,' she responds. She quotes a saying of one of her predecessors as chancellor, Helmut Schmidt: 'He who has visions should go to a doctor.'

On 18 November 2011, Cameron travels to Berlin to meet her for a long lunch. Officials have already warned him that further treaty change is being considered by Germany to deal with the eurozone crisis. To prevent countries from accumulating the huge debts that had triggered the crisis, a Fiscal Compact Treaty is being proposed to reform the euro and fine countries failing to meet certain regulations. Even though it wouldn't have directly affected the UK, as it is outside the eurozone, the treaty could be seen as damaging to the UK. The

British oppose it because they think it will be a threat to the British financial sector. Cameron wants to convince Merkel to agree to safeguards that Britain needs, and then to impose the treaty on the other twenty-five leaders. Also in his mind is the fact that pushing a new treaty through Parliament without safeguards for Britain's financial services would be indefensible in the eyes of many in his party, especially after the October rebellion. Merkel has her own problems: she needs a new treaty to assuage public opinion in Germany, which is anxious about bailing out irresponsible eurozone members, but is isolated among other European leaders. Fond though she is growing of her British counterpart, she resents the way she feels boxed into a corner by him, compounded by what she feels is a lack of British empathy or appreciation for her role in saving the eurozone (although some argue German actions contributed to its difficulties).

Over lunch, Cameron and Merkel have a philosophical discussion about markets, and why they have lost confidence in the eurozone. 'You can't complain about them, they reflect reality, they don't have a political agenda,' Cameron says. Merkel probes him, wanting to understand the Anglo-Saxon capitalist mindset. He says he will ask British official Jon Cunliffe to send her an analysis on why the eurozone is experiencing its deep structural problems.

The lunch breaks up mid-afternoon. Cameron believes that he has got her in the right place. 'Okay, let's be practical,' she says. 'You send me a text of things that are possible that you want, and I'll send you the things that are impossible, and I'm sure there will be an overlap.' 'What about Sarkozy?' Cameron asks. 'Nicolas will agree,' she replies. 'He has changed his philosophy and is closer to the UK and Germany compared to a year ago.'

Back in London, discussions take place between Cameron, Hague and Osborne. Cameron also talks separately with Clegg, who he needs on board. 'I remember people being very paranoid about our negotiating position being leaked, and not discussing the content of it on the phone,' recalls one. The British strategy remains investing all effort in Merkel's ability to leverage a deal beneficial to them between national leaders. British ambassadors across the EU are frustrated that they are not being asked to lobby their national leaders on the issue: 'The Rolls-Royces were never taken out of the garage,' says one.

The text is sent, as promised, from Whitehall to the German chancellor's office. It says the British government would support treaty change in return for changes that would satisfy Parliament. These include protection for financial services, and changes to health and safety and the working time directive. 'It contained six paragraphs,' says an official involved with its creation. 'These were the areas Britain needed and we wanted to know from them which were feasible.' Days pass and Berlin refuses to give a clear response. Cameron decides to send Cunliffe into action with Nikolaus Meyer-Landrut, Merkel's EU adviser, to unblock the logjam and broker an agreement. The team in London ponder whether the six paragraphs of tough and detailed Treasury language proved indigestible to German stomachs: some wonder whether a couple of sentences might not have been much better. But it becomes clear that Merkel is simultaneously negotiating with other leaders, principally Sarkozy. 'The Germans were keeping us in play all the time while they looked for other options,' surmised one British official. Number 10 is becoming very apprehensive.

When Cameron and Clegg decide to push the protection of financial services as the important safeguard, the signals back from Berlin are not promising. By Friday 2 December, it is clear British demands will not be met. The team meeting in Whitehall to discuss the response decide not to compromise in their demands. Some on the British side believe an opportunity to cut a deal is lost at that point. Merkel has concluded that it would be more trouble than it is worth to take up British concerns. So she switches her primary allegiance to Sarkozy. The EU Council opens in six days, and she must get the treaty through: she will press ahead without the British.

On Monday 5 December, Merkel and Sarkozy meet in Paris and finalise details of the treaty. Sarkozy may have been Cameron's best friend recently over Libya, but he is indignant at what the British are asking and at their refusal to ameliorate the eurozone crisis: he will not allow Britain its concessions on financial services. He and Merkel agree that Britain is asking for too much in wanting special privileges for the City of London. Together, they finalise the terms on what becomes known as the 'Merkozy' Treaty.[10] Britain's ambassador to the EU, Kim Darroch, picks up a whiff from French counterparts of what is being planned. He dispatches an immediate email to Llewellyn: 'An ambush is being prepared here in Brussels. Merkel and Sarko will not give in to us. They will go down the separate treaty route.' Darroch suggests Cameron goes ahead and demands that the remaining EU powers sign a separate treaty outside the formal membership of the twenty-seven national leaders, as unanimity is required for all treaty changes. Whitehall dismisses the idea of a separate treaty as unlikely. Llewellyn nevertheless shows the email to Cameron.

The mood in Cameron's team that Monday is bleak. The separate-treaty route would give away leverage. The Foreign Office remain cautiously optimistic: it reckons there is a 60% chance of the PM coming back from the meeting with a deal, although Hague's closest aides are more doubtful. Most optimistic of all is Clegg. 'The DPM never thought we would be isolated, and so didn't properly weigh up how it would play and what he'd do about it.' 'The possibility that we'd be alone was never envisaged or talked about. That had to be a mistake,' said an official. 'We frankly underestimated the emotional commitment that the European countries have to the EU and each other,' admitted another.

On Tuesday, Cameron phones Merkel: 'I'll have to block. I'll have to veto,' he tells her in a state of some agitation. 'In that case, I'll have to do it without you,' she tells him emphatically. He takes a breath. 'You'll have to use the European Union institutions and they belong to all of us and we won't let you,' he says. 'Well, we'll go to the European Court of Justice,' she replies. Everywhere she turns, she tells him, he is standing in her way. Her tone at this point is more jovial than threatening. But underneath, her exasperation at the British is palpable.

On Wednesday and Thursday, the EPP group, from which Cameron has resigned, meet in Marseilles. The German chancellor and the French president attend: the latter pleads on Thursday morning for members to support the Franco-German proposals that will be discussed in just a few hours in Brussels. EPP members are support-ive. The British believe that Sarkozy and Merkel have got to Van Rompuy, in the chair for Thursday evening's Council, so as to deny Cameron a fair hearing for his financial services request.

Before Cameron leaves London on Thursday afternoon, he speaks to Clegg. The DPM believes that Cameron will push for the best deal possible, recognising there will be huge downsides if Britain is seen as the only member state preventing the treaty within the formal EU process. Cameron is in a sombre mood when he arrives in a grey, wintry Brussels. He and Hague have a private meeting at 4 p.m. with Merkel and Sarkozy in the French delegation office. 'You've got your politics,' Cameron tells them, 'well, I've got my politics too!' He pleads for them to agree to the British concessions. 'No, we can't, it won't work,' they reply. 'Everyone will end up asking for something.' There is going to be no compromise, and the British text on safeguards for financial services is dead. It comes as a real blow to them. They return to the British delegation. 'They say their answer is no,' Cameron tells them, looking 'pale and concerned'. 'We'll have to make a pitch to the northern states,' he tells them, before going off to speak to the Dutch. He also sees Van Rompuy, who to his frustration says he will deal with the treaty change first before moving on to British concerns. The British recognise their text will be considered only after the main business, when leaders will be tired and ready to go home.

Dinner begins at 8.30 p.m. on the Thursday. It drags on past 10 p.m., 11 p.m., midnight, 1 a.m. … The British text is not discussed until 3 a.m. As part of the Franco-German stitch-up with Van Rompuy, the Italian prime minister Mario Monti is called to speak on it first. 'I'd hoped, knowing the British, that they would want to strengthen the single market. But their plan will weaken it,' he says. 'If you won't give me the text we need, I will have to say "no" to the treaty,' Cameron responds emphatically. The British veto is duly exercised. On a pre-programmed pattern, Merkel, then Sarkozy, then a succession of other leaders, line up saying, 'In that case, we will go for a separate treaty.' Debate ensues on the legality of bypassing the treaty outside the formal process. Hague tells the PM emphatically: 'David, if you concede on this issue, it will split the Conservative Party.'

The meeting breaks up amidst general exhaustion at 4 a.m. on the Friday. Cameron returns to the British delegation looking 'very green about the gills and physically shattered'. 'I don't want to do that too often,' he tells them. He has found the confrontation with his fellow leaders very draining. 'We had been all waiting anxiously. He knew it had been a disaster,' said an official. Two immediate concerns in his mind are the press conference and handling the coalition. The journalists are all still up and baying for the story. The team spend an hour debating what to tell them. They decide his strongest line is to say, 'I did what I promised I would do – what it said on the tin.' They agree that he must be very careful with his language and categorically avoid saying whether it was a victory or not. At 5 a.m., a sprightly-looking Cameron goes before the British press corps.

Llewellyn had spoken to Jonny Oates, Clegg's chief of staff, at 8 p.m. the previous day, just after the Sarkozy/Merkel meeting, to say it was very unlikely that Cameron could now pull off a deal. Cameron had spoken that evening to Clegg, who was in Sheffield, and again just after 4 a.m., waking him up. Clegg's reaction on both calls, Cameron reports to his team, is fairly measured. At the time, he appears not unduly concerned, beyond being in a minority of two (the Czechs are the only other country not to sign).

At 6 a.m., Cameron's party return to Kim Darroch's official Brussels residence for a rest, before heading back to London. Cameron is a strikingly resilient man and does not get down easily; but he is quiet and reflective on the way to the airport, with 'absolutely no sense that his stance had been a triumph', as one of his team recalls.

Shortly after his plane touches down in London, Cameron's party become aware of very strong concerns among Lib Dems at the way the media is portraying the events. 'What he did forced the rest of the EU to go it alone for the purpose of renewing the treaty, which sets an incredibly bad precedent', is the view of Clegg's senior adviser Tim Colbourne. 'We understood that the PM felt he had to come back with his "pound of flesh", but we didn't expect to him to demand the whole pound of flesh in exchange for his agreement. We expected him to reach some sort of deal.'[11]

Former Liberal Democrat leader Paddy Ashdown is furious: Cameron's team suspect that he has fired up Clegg. It explains to them why Clegg is so dismissive on Marr's BBC show that Sunday: 'I am bitterly disappointed by the outcome of last week's summit … there's nothing bulldog about Britain hovering somewhere in the mid-Atlantic and not standing tall on Europe and not being taken seriously in Washington.'[12] A silver lining for the Lib Dems is that, from now on, they can portray the Conservatives, as well as UKIP, in the same rejectionist political corner, while they are the one unequivocal pro-EU party.[13]

Cameron gives his statement on the summit the next day, Monday 12 December. He acknowledges that the eurozone crisis is having a chilling effect, not only in Europe but spilling over to the British economy too. Yet he says the safeguards he sought for Britain were 'modest, reasonable and relevant' to protect British interests, given London's position as the world's leading centre for financial services. He maintains adamantly that he is right to have stood aside from a treaty which 'would have changed the nature of the EU – strengthening the eurozone without balancing measures to strengthen the single market'.[14] Memories of his bruising climbdown over a referendum on Lisbon are still in his mind.

And yet, overnight, Cameron becomes a hero to the Conservative Party. His personal ratings and those of the party soar in opinion polls: 'The more the BBC stress how isolated Britain was and how it was 25 in the EU against Britain, the better it played for us. Our focus groups liked Cameron standing up for his country and saying "no" to the EU', recalls Andrew Cooper.[15] On Wednesday 14 December, Cameron addresses the 1922 Committee, and is greeted with a full-on orgy of 'desk-banging and hysteria'.[16] Bernard Jenkin says, 'It is a watershed. The beginning of a long process.' Bill Cash declares, 'The fact that we're now vetoing this treaty means that we are set on a path which involves fundamental renegotiation. Make no mistake about it.'[17]

Cameron's status as darling of the Conservative right is never going to last for long. It whets their appetite for their leader to be this pugilistic all the time. They refuse to understand why he cannot be. Turmoil in the party returns in 2012, more rabid than ever. Internationally, however, the pyrotechnics soon die down. 'Both parties got what they wanted. Merkel got her Fiscal Compact Treaty, and Cameron got a good press,' says one jaded EU official. Merkel is determined not to let this issue become a major problem between them. Steve Field, the PM's official spokesman, is soon out telling reporters that the government is looking to 'engage constructively' with other EU nations to help them progress without the UK.[18] Guido Westerwelle, the German foreign minister, comes to London on a peace mission that Monday, and 'very soon again it was all sweetness and light'. Sarkozy had been fiery at the Council: he'd brushed past Cameron without acknowledging him, leading to photographs and headline stories across the world.[19] But he and Cameron reach a private understanding that they will not make a big deal of it. The president accepts the British will spin it as a veto of treaty change, while the EU will spin it as saying 'no' to Britain and a refusal to allow an à la carte Europe. Sarkozy is wily enough to see it will be easier to ratify with just twenty-five signatories, so he is far from unhappy with the outcome of his very late night in Brussels.

The damage from the veto, such as it is, is felt in two quarters. The Lib Dems remain angry that they were given very little warning that a deal would not be forthcoming. 'I had to be in the negotiating room. I couldn't simply slip out and make a phone call. I had to make my views clear there and then. There was no opportunity to tell you. Sorry Nick,' is how Cameron later explains it to Clegg.[20] Lib Dems are perturbed that the 4 a.m. call had been taken as tacit support for the line that there was no alternative. In any future coalition, the Lib Dems say they will insist on an operating manual where their leader will not be excluded from key decisions and then presented with a fait accompli. Even some Conservatives agree it would have been prudent to have taken a senior Lib Dem with them. But no enduring damage is done to the relationship with the Lib Dems.

Harm is done, however, to Cameron's vision of a consistent policy towards Europe. As his team take stock in the months following the veto, they realise that they had boxed themselves into a corner with their 'Berlin or bust' strategy. If he is to use it again, he will have to ensure that he has a far stronger relationship with Merkel: he has yet to learn fully how to play her. The episode throws into sharp relief his lack of a coherent strategy towards the EU. He had not wanted Europe to dominate his premiership. This experience shows him that it will, and that the sooner he defines what he wants to achieve in Europe, the better.

FIFTEEN

The NHS Debacle

November 2009–September 2012

If a prize were to be awarded for the biggest cock-up of Cameron's premiership, there would be only one contender: Andrew Lansley's NHS reforms. But is the condemnation totally fair? In no single area had the Conservatives been so emphatic about their commitments: 'I make this commitment to the NHS ... no more pointless reorganisations,' said Cameron in October 2006 in his first party conference speech as leader.[1] 'The NHS needs no more pointless organisational upheaval,' echoed shadow Health Secretary Andrew Lansley in July 2007.[2] 'There'll be no more of those pointless reorganisations that aim for change but instead bring chaos,' Cameron told the Royal College of Nursing in May 2009.[3] If that wasn't all sufficiently clear, he told the Royal College of Pathologists that November, 'There will be no more of the tiresome, meddlesome, top-down restructures that have dominated the last decade of the NHS.'[4] The key word here, often overlooked, is 'pointless'. This operative word was omitted, crucially, in one seminal document, however: the Coalition Agreement: 'We will stop the top-down reorganisations of the NHS that have got in the way of patient care.'[5] If Cameron and George Osborne had learnt only one thing in Opposition, it is that not being trusted with the NHS will lose them the general election. 'We love the NHS,' Osborne repeatedly said in meetings to anybody who would listen: 'We *love* the NHS!'

Yet a reorganisation 'so big you could see it from outer space', as one insider describes it, is exactly what the government tries to introduce the moment it comes to power.[6] Lansley's appointment as Health Secretary goes through on the nod: he'd done the job in Opposition, both Cameron and Osborne had worked for him in the Conservative

Research Department, and they both consider him a reassuring figure on the NHS who knows the subject backwards. Once in office, he starts saying, 'I am the Secretary of State for Health. I've decided what I want to do. I've thought about it. My ideas have all been written down. I know what I am doing.' Cameron's and Osborne's teams say they are shocked when they hear exactly what Lansley has in mind, which they think has come out of the blue. 'Andrew Lansley may think we talked about these reforms in the manifesto, but not in any way that we recognised,' says one.

But Lansley is right and they are wrong. He has been very clear and open about his plans. In the build-up to the election, health plans were not highlighted in the overall message that the leadership gave, and collective amnesia seems to have come over them. Among other documents, Lansley had written a paper in 2007, later rewritten by Oliver Letwin for the Conservative's Spring Forum in 2008. In the foreword, Cameron wrote: 'we will free our NHS professionals and allow them to fulfil the vocation they were trained to do. We will give GPs real control over their budgets so they can reinvest savings and negotiate contracts with service providers to get the best deal for their patients'.[7] In place of 'top-down' reform, which the Conservatives associated with Labour's muddled reforms of years gone by, they propose a 'bottom-up reform model, allowing those closest to the patients themselves, not bureaucrats, to run the system'.

Lansley's reform package has two key elements: to allow GPs at a local level, through Care Commissioning Groups (CCGs), to make decisions that had hitherto been taken at a top level by strategic health authorities; second, within Whitehall, day-to-day management of the NHS is to be taken away from the Secretary of State and placed in the hands of a new post – the 'chief executive of the NHS Commissioning Board' (which becomes known as 'NHS England'). Once a year, government is to set the mandate for what the NHS will deliver and the new body will be responsible for commissioning services. The aim is to depoliticise the NHS. What is envisaged is for government no longer to be directly responsible for the most highly sensitive of public services and the one most visible to the media. Not until as late as the autumn of 2013, when he becomes concerned about a crisis in accident and emergency departments, does the PM fully realise that he no longer has the levers of power to control the NHS. Only then does he admit that he fully 'got' the reforms. He may have understood them in his head on one level, but doesn't understand the full significance until then.

The critical question is how on earth do two figures as savvy as Cameron and Osborne miss this laser-illuminated spaceship landing before their eyes outside the front doors of Number 10 and Number 11? Andy Coulson puts it down to a collective failure to be candid about the considerable difficulties the NHS is facing – an ageing population, the rising cost of treatment, and a struggling economy – to meet the electorate's ever-increasing expectations. They simply don't want to engage with reform of the NHS when they have so much else to think about, so they put it out of their mind. 'We're reforming welfare, education and the public sector. Do we really need to do health now too?' Cameron asks forlornly early on.

Two vital moments are lost when the plans could have been side-lined: the first is at a rare meeting of the coalition committee. Some Lib Dems are disturbed by Lansley's intentions. When the programme for government is being negotiated, the former Lib Dem spokesman for health, Norman Lamb, learns the full extent of Lansley's plan. He texts Polly Mackenzie: 'Holy Crap, Andrew Lansley is announcing that we are going to go ahead with this NHS quango thing.' Lansley is concerned he is excluded from the crucial coalition discussions, when the lead is taken by Letwin and Danny Alexander, neither of whom have a background in health. His objections are 'studiously ignored' by Number 10.[8]

Letwin, a key figure in this story, picks up the phone to Lansley: 'Stop announcing stuff. We haven't finalised with the Lib Dems yet what we are doing with the NHS.' Lansley replies, 'I am Secretary of State, I am going ahead.' He brushes aside the objections from Lamb. Lansley believes he is being misunderstood; others think that he is being inflexible. By the time the coalition committee meets in July to discuss his White Paper, *Equity and Excellence: Liberating the NHS*, alarm bells are ringing in some quarters. The document is well written by Lansley's civil servants, who had been enthusiasts for Labour Health Secretary Alan Milburn's earlier reforms, which bear similarities. When it comes to Number 10, Cameron's team conclude that

Lansley's officials have done a good job and see no problems with it being published, even if 'people didn't totally understand what Lansley is talking about'. The Lib Dems are too preoccupied to give the proposals the detailed attention they merit. But Jeremy Heywood and Gus O'Donnell become increasingly alarmed: they are seriously concerned that the plans are unworkable. Lansley himself is partly responsible for the speed: he had formed the view in Opposition that the Department of Health was going to be full of socialists, so said the White Paper should be published at once, with no preparatory Green Paper or lobbying to bring the medical professions onside. 'He had a clear view that he was going to be up against the health establishment or "blob" and we would have to tough it out.' Like Gove with his own educational 'blob', he decides to take it on directly, though later admitting that aspects of his communication strategy were not ideal.

Letwin, who is sympathetic to Lansley's aims, wants a meeting to discuss the White Paper before publication and to bring the Lib Dems onside. William Hague and Osborne raise objections: 'I've read the papers for this meeting and we are doing *what* to the NHS? What the hell are we doing here? This is completely insane.' 'No, no, no. We're just agreeing the details,' Letwin responds, trying to reassure them. 'This is totally stupid. Surely we'll have to go back to first principles,' Hague and Osborne respond. The Lib Dems add their own protests. 'Lansley's plans are totally stupid. We could have made 90% of the changes without any legislation, as Blair did – genius!' says one Lib Dem. 'Andrew's fantasy was that we all knew what he was planning, and that it was a done deal. Bollocks!' says another. 'Cameron could have killed it off there and then'. The debate is getting nasty: Lansley hotly denies there was any secrecy about his proposals, and insists they need legislation. Cameron and Clegg critically are again reassured, and decide to let it pass. 'We know what we are doing, this is going to go through,' Cameron insists. The White Paper is duly published on 12 July. But do they really understand what they have endorsed?

Concerns mount over the summer. After the party conferences, Letwin and Danny Alexander conduct a review into the plans and give their approval. This does not stop Lansley and officials being asked to come to Number 10 to further explain their plans. Cameron and Osborne listen, but later claim that they are still in the dark over what the Secretary of State is telling them. When Lansley is questioned, he goes off into a long spiel, speaking in specialist jargon. 'They felt that they couldn't challenge or contradict him,' says one observer. His defence of his policy is described as 'impenetrable': Osborne says, 'I didn't understand a word that he said.' The chancellor is furious at the problems that the NHS reform proposals are causing the government: 'Nobody told me this was coming,' he says. 'Nobody.' Matthew d'Ancona, who first chronicled the history of the coalition, says it is the first time Osborne has truly lost his temper since becoming chancellor.[9] Osborne is worried about the political effect of creating NHS England: 'the Health Secretary will always be seen to be running Health because that's what the public expects, even if it is hived off to a quango, and the Treasury will always have to bail it out.' Ultimately, Osborne's primary concern is not just financial, but also political: that waiting times do not increase, and he tells Lansley he does not really care what is in the bill. The meeting polarises opinion: those who are in favour of the reforms become more passionate; those who are scared become more scared. Letwin is tasked by Cameron and Osborne with going away and looking at it in more detail. His recommendation is they should hold tight and back Lansley. Osborne later regarded his failure to stop it dead in the tracks at that moment as a major mistake.

The chancellor senses that this is an approaching car crash. How then was it allowed to happen? Deference to Lansley, odd though that might sound, explains in part why Cameron and Osborne have not challenged him earlier. Lansley is older than them, his command of the NHS, and the psychological effect of his being their former boss, all play their part. Cameron and Osborne ascribe difficuties to his being a poor communicator, but assume he knows what he is talking about and decide to give him the benefit of the doubt. Both men also have an instinctive trust of Letwin's judgement on this sort of issue.

Letwin is not Lansley's only supporter in the inner circle. Aspects of the reforms strongly chime with Steve Hilton's advocacy of opening up the NHS and devolving responsibility, for all Osborne's suspicions of localism. Hilton too is primarily responsible for the feeling that 'we will only have one chance in government', and the belief in those heady first months that 'everything is possible and we must forge ahead doing the big things now'. 'There was a premium for every Cabinet minister to have a major reformist agenda,' says an insider. 'For some time, Lansley was promoted by Number 10 with the same aura as Gove at Education.' The fervour and radicalism of the early months powerfully explain why more detailed examination is not given.

Lansley's almost superhuman self-belief in the face of the mounting criticism powers the policy forward. 'I know what I'm doing. You can trust me. This is my baby. By the time of the next election, people will feel the benefits. It will be worth it,' he tells them. His strapline is, 'You don't need to sell these reforms: the reforms will sell themselves.' He has imbibed the lessons of Thatcher's favourite Secretary of State, Norman Tebbit, who told him to 'steamroll change through the civil servants and press them very hard. They'll block you, but some will be on your side. Don't waste time having lengthy consultations. Get all the change through quickly and before long, you will win advocates over to your side.'

Secretaries of State have been told by Number 10 to find creative solutions to address the financial realities the coalition government face. The NHS is in dire financial need. The Gordon Brown solution, initially as chancellor and then PM, had been to throw more money at the problem. The Conservatives have promised to increase levels of spending, but the Treasury tells Osborne that economies still have to be found. Lansley says his reforms will help by delivering £20 billion of savings. This is another reason why his proposals get through. Cameron could have made a speech explaining the financial pressures the NHS is under. But the opportunity is not taken. Had he more regularly explained that the Lansley proposals are designed in part to ensure better value for money, the reforms might have carried the professions with them. Ultimately he made only one such speech, in January 2011, which, indicatively, is soon forgotten.

The proposals are not as foolish as the sceptics allege: indeed, they have much to recommend them. By giving budgets to GP-led groups, more procedures can take place at primary-care level, which saves money, increases the choice of NHS providers, and creates competitive pressure on cost increases. Number 10 deliberately decide not to present Lansley's reforms as a continuation of Blair's health innovations: 'The Number 10 psyche is that we have to up the rhetoric, talk about paradigm shifts,' says one insider. This strategy is in stark contrast to education policy, where Michael Gove says he is deliberately building on the work of Blair and Andrew Adonis, which helps him gain support from the Lib Dems and makes the reforms appear more organic. The reality, as Simon Stevens (the future CEO of NHS England) writes in the *Financial Times*, is that 'what makes the proposals so radical is not that they tear up [Blair's plan]. It is that they move decisively towards fulfilling it.'[10] NHS patients would choose when and where they are treated. Foundation hospitals would be rapidly expanded, accountable to an independent regulator. Properly handled, Lansley's proposals could transform the face of the NHS for a generation.

But they have not been properly handled. Whitehall is worried, especially the Treasury. Neither O'Donnell nor Heywood is convinced the government fully knows what it is taking on. They ask Letwin and Alexander to hold discussions with Treasury officials to ensure that they have thought through all dimensions. They regularly ask Cameron: 'Are you really sure that you know what it is about?' They continue to worry that the Treasury is ceding financial control to GPs in the front line. Officials point out, 'We can't yield control to GPs who have never managed budgets.' Within the Department of Health, apart from a few enthusiasts, officials are beginning to block the reforms, much as Tebbit had predicted. 'They didn't like it because the White Paper envisaged a reduced role for them, and thus their mates would lose their jobs,' is the view of a special adviser.

The professional medical bodies, widely respected by the country and the media, are equally becoming agitated, with the Royal College of General Practitioners and the British Medical Association (BMA) the most vociferous. Lansley and his team are cynical about them, believing they are trying to protect their vested interests. He appeals to the prime minister to lead the crusade from the front. The message comes back from Number 10 that the PM wants front-line ministers – Lansley, Gove, Iain Duncan Smith and Francis Maude – to front up their own reforms. The trade unions Unite and Unison are having increasing success in mobilising their members against the reforms. As Lansley feared, the medical 'blob' is uniting and will fight hard. He believes his reforms are being deliberately misrepresented by them to whip up opposition.

By January 2011, the reforms are running into serious problems. Coulson becomes increasingly agitated. 'Nobody can give me a chunky paragraph, let alone two or three sentences, explaining the policy,' he says. He shares his concerns with Letwin, but days later Coulson leaves Number 10 for good. Lansley tells Number 10 to stop obsessing about opinion polls. Governments always see their position on the NHS erode over time, he says.

On 19 January, his Health and Social Care Bill has its first reading in the House of Commons, its second reading on 31 January, and on 8 February its first sitting in committee. Opposition is mounting all the time. On 7 March, Andrew Cooper arrives in Number 10 as director of strategy. He joins forces with the newly appointed Craig Oliver and with Stephen Gilbert, another figure who is alarmed by the damage in the polls, which had been so positive in the months after the general election. Opinion in Number 10 is strongly divided. Hilton is circulating a poll which shows that 80% of people are in favour of more choice and competition in the NHS: opposition from professional bodies and trade unions, he says, will pass. He is tasked to spend time helping Lansley communicate his case better. The sense around the prime minister is to persevere. The U-turn over the sale of Forestry Commission land in February, following a concerted campaign of opposition, has wounded the government. As one aide puts it, 'the great fear is that the PM will be portrayed as somebody who goes in for U-turns'. Stopping the reform process now will also risk losing Lansley, which would entail a reshuffle that no one wants. The working assumption remains: they must 'tough it out'.

Oliver and Cooper disagree, and decide that they must write a memo to the PM. It doesn't mince its words; both later regret their tone. They argue that the NHS reforms are a train crash waiting to happen, and that no one understands what the hell the reforms are all about, and that the entire medical profession are against them. Following the bust-up over AV, they can no longer rely on the support of the Lib Dems. The party will suffer badly in the May elections without a change. Finally, they ask the question increasingly being asked: why is a major bill, a focal point for resistance, necessary? They say that they could have introduced the reforms by stealth, as Blair had done. Cameron's immediate response to the memo is to continue to support Lansley.[11] 'This is Andrew's project,' he tells them.

On 11–13 March 2011, the Lib Dems meet in Sheffield for their spring conference. The hot topic is the NHS reforms. Members vote almost unanimously to give local councillors a central role in GP commissioning and in scrutinising foundation trusts, and call for a ban on private companies offering treatment services. Clegg tells Cameron, 'I don't understand this reform fully but my MPs are very cross.' Another Cabinet is held to look at the issue. Lansley says that 'By the end of this parliament, the country will see so much improvement that the doctors who are now so angry will be on our side.' Clegg says that communication needs to be much better, and Lansley is instructed to present a much stronger case. Cameron and Osborne concur that Lansley's performance delivering the bill is not reflecting well on the government: he is not putting the case across with the clarity and force it needs.

By late March, Cameron and Osborne decide that they cannot carry on as they are. The logic of the Cooper/Oliver memo is inescapable. Heywood too is a strong advocate of a 'pause'. Criticism in the country is rising to a cacophony, suggesting that the NHS is not safe in Tory hands and that the leadership have lied in promising there will be no reorganisation. Conservative backbenchers have hardened in their opposition to the bill, which leads to worries that it might not pass through the House of Commons. They worry too that if they do not give the Lib Dems some of what they demanded at their spring conference, then Lib Dem support for the bill will come into jeopardy. They speak to Clegg, who is at the UN seeing Joe Biden, and collectively decide that Lansley must be told that there has to be a pause for reflection.

Thursday 31 March is the day chosen, coinciding with Clegg's overnight flight back from the US. So important is the meeting that he is given his first ever 'blue light' police escort from the airport to Number 10.[12] Cameron summons Clegg into his room along with Lansley, telling officials and advisers outside that they will be only ten minutes. They take almost an hour. What happens behind the closed doors is hotly disputed. One account has Cameron and Clegg raising their concerns, and Lansley himself proposing a pause to reforms, and time for the NHS Future Forum to deliberate. Another account has it that Lansley is told that they are taking control from now on, with him arguing that a pause will lead to a delay in the benefits which wouldn't be felt until after the general election, and he believes that they should bash their way through all the opponents. He is visibly upset. When the officials are called in, Cameron reads out some words about the pause. Lansley starts arguing again with him: 'You can't just stop everything.' The PM slaps him down and Clegg explains what will happen. 'Andrew, the reason why we are here is because you have put the ideological cart before the political horse,' Clegg forcibly tells him.[13]

The pause is announced on Wednesday 6 April, following robust briefing to the Sunday papers, for which Cameron and Clegg apologise to Lansley. Cameron says that the government will be holding a 'listening exercise' on the NHS to 'pause, listen, reflect, and improve' the proposals.[14] A month earlier, Paul Bate, a civil servant who had worked with Michael Barber in the Delivery Unit under Blair, had been brought into Number 10 by Cameron and Clegg to offer a fresh perspective on health policy. Using his considerable experience of health care at the national level, Bate quickly grips the process, his task being to come up with the minimum concessions to get the bill through. 'I want you to sort this out so the bill goes through Parliament, and if you see a need for major changes, you must tell us,' he is told.

The pause lasts for May and June. Bate, who knows many of the key players in the health world, talks to concerned parties, while Clegg and Cameron, working closely together, target leading sceptics to bring them onside. The priority is to make the medical establishment feel it is being listened to, and gain support for agreed changes.

Cameron and Clegg ask for regular reports from Bate, and they see him at least weekly during the process. Rarely again will Cameron be so intimately involved in an aspect of domestic policy. Three Quads take place during these weeks focusing on choice, on competition, and on GP commissioning. All four members know what is at stake, and they are joined by Letwin, Llewellyn, Hilton, Heywood, Bate, and Lansley and his advisers. Osborne's principal focus is the politics, though he retains profound reservations about the substance and its financial implications. Heywood works hard to ensure that the reforms will be workable and fully consistent with government aims: he regularly suggests changes to Bate's weekly notes. Hilton intervenes strongly: 'I don't really care about any of the commissioning stuff,' he says, 'but I want to drive a massive wedge through the profession and dramatically enhance patient power and competition.' The Quad cannot assent to anything so controversial, much to Hilton's chagrin. Clegg and Alexander argue tenaciously for changes to reflect the views of their spring conference, which made thirteen recommendations for change.[15] It is important, after all the reversals of the previous months, for Clegg to show his party that he is listening to them and that they can influence policy, and indeed agreement is reached that the requirement for all trusts to take on foundation status by 2014 is removed and a commitment is made to keep waiting time targets. The date of implementation is also pushed back a year to April 2013.

The pause succeeds in reaching consensus. Despite the changes, the bill remains substantially intact. Cameron delivers a speech on 7 June in which he promises to safeguard the integrated and universal nature of the NHS. Clegg is kept onside so the Lib Dems will support the bill through the House of Commons, and he is able to show his party that they have made a difference. The bill duly sails through the Commons receiving its third reading in the House on 7 September.

There, one might assume, the protracted saga ends. The House of Lords will be just a formality, as on so many bills. It is debated there in the autumn of 2011, but runs headlong into the concerns of Lib Dem peers. Party grandee Shirley Williams is one of the most forthright. Week after week it is fought through clause by clause. Earl Howe, health minister in the Lords, fights to steer the bill through. But SDP founder David Owen produces, in effect, a wrecking motion. As the months drag on, they tease out some concessions. Number 10 thinks their impact is reduced by failing to agree on concrete changes. By the end, there are more than a thousand amendments which Williams claims have changed the bill 'significantly'. From February, she becomes a supporter of the bill.[16] On 19 March, the bill receives its final reading in the House of Lords and, on 27 March, Royal Assent.

The most fraught domestic legislation of Cameron's premiership is concluded. Number 10 are very far from happy with the political capital expended and the hit on party popularity, and blame one person alone: Lansley. They feel he has made a 'dog's breakfast' of it. 'We had pulled it back to a place in the pause where the medics, if not enthusiastic, were broadly constructive. Now we've tipped them all back again. We'd repaired the relationships, then Andrew started lecturing them again,' said one insider. As early as February 2012, they are talking about a new Health Secretary being needed who is better at communications as soon as the bill is on the statute book. For the time being, Lansley stays on. The spring reshuffle is pushed back to the summer. Then to the early autumn. Cameron does not like reshuffles, nor does he relish the prospect of dismissing his former boss.

The primary concern in Number 10 is the polls. The Conservatives had been polling 38% to Labour's 29% since the EU veto in December until the beginning of March, but then they started dropping dramatically. By April, they had fallen to 32%. Polling begins to show a fall from the beginning of March 2012, three weeks before the Budget. As far as they can tell, it is because of the NHS bill: 'There are weeks when its fraught final passage dominates the news. Trusted medical professionals are put up one after the other saying we are destroying the NHS.'

Lansley is finally replaced by Jeremy Hunt in a reshuffle that comes in September. The new Health Secretary soon impresses Number 10 with his stewardship of the department. But they will have to be circumspect. The closest of watches is kept on him by Nick Seddon in the Policy Unit, Oliver Dowden, the deputy chief of staff, and Simon Case in the Private Office. The winter of 2012 passes fairly uneventfully for health. Nevertheless, from September to December 2013, Number 10 is on high alert. Cameron convenes monthly COBRA meetings in recognition that he needs Blairite-style 'command and control' capability to keep on top of the situation. This is the point when he says that he had never understood that in creating NHS England he would be devolving so many of the government's levers of control over the NHS. The PM maintains a close personal interest in the leadership of NHS England: earlier in 2013 he had met Simon Stevens, who had worked on health in the Policy Unit under Blair, and warms to this doyen of the field greatly. He decides at that point that he should succeed David Nicholson, whose departure is announced in October, and Stevens becomes chief executive of NHS England in April 2014.

'I was very concerned about the Lansley health reforms,' said Cameron's close friend Andrew Feldman. 'After campaigning for five years building trust on the NHS, such a radical overhaul threatened to put all that at risk.'[17] These concerns seem well placed. The whole episode has revealed Cameron at his most uncertain. He failed to stand back and see the political damage, given the mistrust of the Conservatives on the NHS, that would follow any attempt at major reform. 'With hindsight, I left some ministers too much on their own, for example Health. Thinking I was the chairman and letting ministers get on with their jobs may not have been the best strategy', admits Cameron.[18]

Lansley's bill was certainly the most acrimonious domestic legislation of the period. But was all the opprobrium heaped on him justified? Was Lansley made too much of a scapegoat? Many of his proposals were unaltered. Above all, NHS England, with its independence guaranteed by legislation, has steered the NHS through choppy waters with few of the dire consequences critics predicted. Its Five Year Forward View, published in October 2014, set out a vision for the future of the NHS which achieved widespread support.[19] Contrary to fears in CCHQ and Number 10, and despite Ed Miliband's determined campaign, neither the NHS nor the reforms became a major issue in the 2015 election.

SIXTEEN

Cameron and Obama

March 2012

'It's amazing to think they are doing this for us,' says George Osborne to Craig Oliver, as they stand on the South Lawn of the White House. In the marquee, Mumford & Sons are playing. Obama's team are bending over backwards to tell the world that David Cameron is their friend, and that they are giving him the biggest party for an overseas leader of Obama's first administration.

The White House indeed are falling over themselves to play up the importance of the prime minister. During Cameron's first five years as prime minister, a senior White House aide says, he and Obama 'have agreed on virtually every single issue of importance to the US'. 'David Cameron is the first person the president wants to talk to on any issue. Look at Afghanistan, Libya, Syria, Iran, Pakistan, Egypt or the euro-zone crisis, and there is no significant difference between them.' The White House is eager to provide visible evidence to show the close-ness of their man to Cameron. Between 2010 and April 2014, they meet twenty-two times, and have forty-seven phone calls or video teleconferences. 'The UK is our number one collaborator.'

Number 10 didn't always see the relationship in such roseate hues. Obama's businesslike tone can give the impression of a lack of warmth and collegiality. If Cameron comes up with a good idea, Obama might say 'We've already thought of that', or 'We will come back to you on it'. The White House, in contrast, makes much of the 'instinctive under-standing' between two senior leaders: 'No one who hasn't held that burden can possibly understand it: it's a complicity that exists between those who hold ultimate power in their countries.' They point out that both Obama and Cameron regard themselves as husbands and fathers first, and president and prime minister second, that they share a pragmatic rather than doctrinaire approach to politics, a sense of fun, high intelligence and rationality. But even Cameron can find Obama too rational and considered. Obama's love of the emotionless, logical *Star Trek* character Dr Spock is well known, and there is certainly more than a passing resemblance between the president and his childhood hero, so much so that his nickname at the Foreign Office had been Spock for many years.[1] Cameron may well be Obama's closest overseas ally amongst world leaders, but personal friendships are not Obama's forte. The president is not close personally to any of the Chinese or Indian leaders, he doesn't like Netanyahu of Israel, he fell out with Erdogan of Turkey, and he never developed a close relationship with Hollande in France. Merkel is important to him on certain issues, notably Ukraine and Russia. But again they are not close personally. There is not the warmth between Cameron and Obama that existed between Thatcher and Reagan, Major and George Bush, and Blair with both Clinton and George W. Bush.

When Obama comes to Britain on 23–25 May 2011 for his first state visit it is a major staging post in their relationship. White House expectations are not very high, but they agree to the visit as a legacy issue to redress the way the British media portrayed Obama's relationship with Gordon Brown, which gave the impression of the prime minister being snubbed. They are very anxious to avoid the relationship with Cameron going down the same route. They thus determine to give the Brits some serious time as a sign to show how much the relationship means to them. Obama's visit is part of a four-nation European tour, including Ireland, France and Poland. Michelle accompanies her husband throughout. As it is a state visit, they stay with his fellow head of state, the Queen, in Buckingham Palace.

Great thought has gone into the schedule. The Obamas meet the newly married Prince William and Kate, go to the Globe Academy school in London where they play table tennis with students, and attend the mandatory white tie banquet at Buckingham Palace, where guests include film stars Kevin Spacey and Helena Bonham Carter. On the final day, Obama attends a Cabinet meeting, followed by a barbeque for servicemen in the Number 10 garden where he and

Cameron dispense burgers while wearing white shirts and ties. Obama is intrigued by Number 10: he is eager to see the Camerons' flat.

The political centrepiece is the speech Obama gives in Westminster Hall to both Houses of Parliament, in which he lays stress on the United States and Britain relying on each other, and the world relying on both of them. He deftly touches on an issue which is widely thought to have been responsible for a certain coolness towards Britain when he first became president: 'it is possible for hearts to change and old hatreds to pass ... it is possible for the sons and daughters of former colonies to sit here as members of this great Parliament, and for the grandson of a Kenyan who served as a cook in the British army to stand before you as the president of the United States'.[2]

The White House team are pleasantly surprised by how well the visit goes. Michelle is especially taken with the Queen, and both Obamas delight in the pageantry and ceremonials. Like all US presidents, Obama realises that 'once you are in the UK, it is like being in a safe harbour, a feeling that you don't get in any other country: it is partly about the shared language, history and culture', a top White House aide says. 'The trip generated tremendous goodwill.' The Obama trip comes at a difficult period for Cameron, and its palpable success vindicates his strategy of not being seen to be overly reliant on transatlantic approbation. The idea crystallises that a return visit in the spring of 2012 would be ideal, with Obama facing re-election that year. Number 10 is absolutely delighted to accept.

After much diary juggling, 13–15 March 2012 is fixed as the date for Cameron's return trip. Obama has grown much more comfortable with Cameron, and the relationship with Britain generally. He is looking forward to Cameron's visit. A difference of opinion on tackling the economy is the only cloud on the horizon. Osborne's inclusion in the party is in part to reassure commentators that there are no fundamental differences over economic policy, though clearly there are. But he is also keen not to miss out on the fun.

Cameron flies out by British Airways with Samantha, landing at Andrews Field air force base on 13 March to a full military reception. The mood in the front of the plane is euphoric. 'We had got through Leveson and we were checking ourselves for contact wounds, realising that none of us were bleeding, and here we are, on this amazing visit,' says one person on the flight. But one member of the large PM party is far from happy: Samantha. 'It is unusual for her to go, she is very nervous because she is not a natural lover of the limelight, and particularly hates the moment when the plane door opens and all the cameras start clicking.' Various figures on the plane reassure her. On arrival, they are whisked to Blair House, the white-painted building built in 1824 just opposite the White House reserved for prestigious visitors. They are greeted by assistant chief of protocol, Randy Bumgardner (the *Guardian* reports that Cameron just manages to contain his mirth).[3] Generating good publicity and images is everything. Obama has a surprise in store. Later that day, Cameron flies on Marine One back to Andrews, and then by Air Force One to Dayton, Ohio for a basketball game. The White House say they want him to see the interior of the US rather than just the coastal cities overseas leaders normally visit.

During the flight, Cameron disappears up to the front of the plane into the president's private office where they talk alone. As the Americans hoped, he is excited and duly impressed by being on the famous plane. Of Cameron's first five years in office, 2012 is the quietest of them on the world stage, although the Middle East as ever is still a major source of concern. They discuss whether Netanyahu will launch an attack on Iran's nuclear facilities during the window between June and September, when the Israelis will calculate that Obama is least likely to stop them because of the US elections. Advice from British officials is that Netanyahu might not risk an attack, not least because of domestic pressures from within his country.

For Cameron, the basketball game is largely an irrelevance, but 'for Obama, bringing in the Conservative British prime minister to Ohio – a swing state – flaunts his foreign policy credentials and underlines how he's improved America's image abroad,' reports the press.[4] On the British side, Craig Oliver makes the most of Cameron being the first world leader to fly on board Air Force One: the BBC's Nick Robinson rates it even higher in PR terms than both leaders flipping burgers at the Downing Street barbeque the year before.[5] On the flight back to Washington, Obama even allows the jet-lagged Cameron to curl up in the hallowed presidential bed.[6]

Wednesday 14 March sees the principal events in Washington. Obama's team are relieved that the British will not be holding talks with any Republican challengers on the visit. The day opens with a nineteen-gun salute echoing around the south lawn with the British national anthem being played. Obama makes a play of it being almost exactly 200 years since the British had come to Washington and burnt down the White House in August 1814: 'The relationship between the United States and the United Kingdom is the strongest that it has ever been,' he says at the press conference.

'The Americans gave the PM the kind of reception normally reserved for a head of state,' said new British ambassador to the US Peter Westmacott. The atmospherics are helped by the good weather, the roses and magnolia being in bloom, and the Marine Band creating a sense of occasion.[7] The words spoken are all very warm. At the state dinner in a marquee on the White House garden, the theme is 'America's backyard': guests include Richard Branson, George Clooney and Damian Lewis, star of the hit television series, *Homeland*. 'I've learnt something about David Cameron,' Obama says in his after-dinner speech. 'He is just the kind of partner that you want on your side. I trust him. He says what he does, and he does what he says.' 'There are three things about Barack that really stand out for me,' replies Cameron. 'Strength, moral authority and wisdom.'[8]

It clearly means much to Cameron that he and Obama spend so much time together. Number 10 estimates they have an unprecedented nine hours together on the trip. In the private flat in the White House, they discuss their families, which is a genuine shared and real bond. In formal talks, they agree that they cannot do much more to intervene in the upheavals in the Middle East and North Africa, or in Syria, where President Assad has been killing large numbers of his people. The president praises Cameron for his work in bringing the international community and aid to supporting progress in Somalia, but they barely touch on the economy. Osborne attends a dinner at the British Embassy, at which he meets his opposite numbers, and where he plays down any differences in approach. Osborne flies home that night a very contented man.

The next day, Cameron flies to New York, where he meets Mayor Bloomberg and visits Ground Zero. Samantha had been visiting New York on 11 September 2001: Cameron had tried frantically to speak to her, but could not do so because the telephone networks were down. At Ground Zero, they pay tribute to those killed in the attacks. Oliver peels off from the prime minister's party to see a broadcasting friend at NBC. He has only eight dollars in his pocket, not enough for a cab, but a rickshaw driver says he will take him across town for that money. As he is pedalled through Times Square, he thinks 'what an extraordinary few days this has been, and we are even ahead of Labour'. The trip has indeed been a spectacular success. The PM's party are on the first high for many months.

Oliver's mobile rings. 'Are you going to cut the 50p rate in the Budget?' he is asked. He has to think very quickly. Unless he denies such a direct question, the media will know that it is true, yet he tries to brush the caller off. 'This was precisely the time when we needed to be hammering things through on the Budget, when important things come to your attention and the Treasury tries all kinds of things on. It was incredibly unwise for Osborne to go on the trip to America,' says Clegg's chief of staff, Jonny Oates.[9] Osborne had been in regular touch with the office from the US, but his disappearance at such a critical time did not look good. 'What the fuck is he doing in America? The Budget is days away,' one of the press team had said. 'Don't worry: it's all fine, it's all sorted,' Osborne's senior aide Rupert Harrison had replied, trying to reassure them.

Cameron flies back that night from New York's JFK airport. Oliver discusses the phone call with him on the plane while still on the ground. There appear to have been two separate briefings, one to the *Financial Times* that the top rate of income tax would be cut to 45p, another to the *Guardian* that it would go down to 40p. They suspect that the Lib Dems are responsible. Before the plane takes off, Cameron speaks to Osborne. 'Let's not add any energy to the story,' the chancellor says. But the matter is already out of their hands.

SEVENTEEN

Omnishambles Budget

March 2012

'George felt incredibly cross with himself over his 2012 Budget. He had let down people who trusted him to deliver. His reputation as the person who delivers the political goods for the government had, very rightly, taken a big knock,' reflects one insider who worked closely with Osborne. 'It was the moment that he felt under greatest political pressure over the five years in power.' What had gone wrong? Had the man who had steered the Conservative Party through Opposition and power so effectively over the previous seven years suddenly lost his grip? Why had the Osborne story suddenly become one of sizzling hubris?

Osborne revels in the sangfroid of breezing off to Washington on Tuesday 13 March, telling those left behind, 'Don't worry, Rupert is in charge.' A passionate devotee of American politics and history, he has been looking forward to the trip for weeks. He is too smart not to appreciate there is a risk, but he reckons 'the choice between going to America to hang out with Obama or lingering in London to monitor Twitter and the blogs in case of Budget leaks was no choice at all', as Matthew d'Ancona memorably put it.[1] He has even succeeded in showing worried US administration figures and congressmen that the American and British approaches to the financial crisis are not irreconcilable, missing the trip on Air Force One to do so: Cameron's team mollify him with packets of presidential M&Ms they had lifted from Obama's plane. Following the Budget a week later, his reputation is in tatters, and the government is facing the biggest crisis in confidence of its first two years in power. What has gone wrong? And why did things unravel so quickly?

From the moment that Alistair Darling raised the top rate of income tax from 40p to 50p in his March 2009 Budget (coming into effect in April 2010), Osborne was determined that, if elected, he would bring the rate down: 'I had put a lot of stock into cutting the 50p rate as early in the parliament as I could.' As he mulls over his options with Rupert Harrison after the Autumn Statement in late 2011 and early 2012, it is clear in his mind that he has only three more Budgets after March 2012, and this may well be the moment to do what they are sure is needed to help the economy grow. They agree 'we shouldn't worry about short-term unpopularity'. As Harrison recalls, 'George felt it was the time to be bold. We were only two years into a five-year parliament. We had no illusions that we were planning a popular Budget.'[2]

Osborne's first Budget in 2011 has failed to kick-start the economy, and by the end of the year the economic outlook remains bleak. On 25 January 2012, the GDP figures for the final quarter of 2011 are published, showing the economy had shrunk by 0.2%, the first fall in quarterly GDP since the last three months of 2010. Britain is thought to be slipping into a 'double-dip recession' and Osborne comes under huge pressure from the business community, and from his own party, to boost the economy. The figures have got to him. His confidence has dipped seriously, and he starts musing, as Janan Ganesh records, 'about his own political mortality'. 'I don't know how many more Budgets I will give,' he tells his team. He confides in friends that he doesn't know if he will 'still be doing this job next year'.[3]

The Times and the *Telegraph* newspapers, so friendly to his austerity programme back in 2010, begin to ask whether he should be doing more to stimulate the economy, while the banks, still smarting at moves to regulate them, are biting back – especially after the subsequent government decision to strip former RBS chief executive Fred Goodwin of his knighthood, which went down very badly. The Institute of Directors warns of the government creating 'anti-business hysteria'.[4] Chancellors bow to pressure, and Osborne is no exception. He had ducked the idea of reducing the 50p rate in his 2011 Budget, after objections from Cameron about how it would look. Osborne instead announces in this Budget that Her Majesty's Revenue and Customs will produce a report into how much the 50p rate is in fact raising. Osborne has long suspected that the extra revenue is insignificant compared to the disincentive caused by the high rate. As well as HMRC, the Institute for Fiscal Studies also produce a report which provides just the evidence that Osborne hopes for: 'the rise to 50p had raised a mere £1 billion, while reducing the rate to 45p might cost as little at £100 million'.[5] Even the Treasury favour change: 'We thought that sticking to Plan A was losing us money,' admits an official.

By January 2012, Osborne's mind is settled on reducing the top rate. But how far? He speaks to Cameron about reducing it to 40p. 'In favour of 40p was that we would take a big political hit if we did 45p, so we might as well go all the way to 40p, because we would be as well hung for a lamb as for a sheep,' as one senior aide puts it. Cameron thinks 40p is going too far, conscious as ever about the move being portrayed as favouring the wealthy. But he removes his objection to 45p, and the decision is confirmed by early February.

Intense meetings of the Quad take place during January and February. Altering the VAT rate has been discussed, but ultimately ruled out. Nick Clegg and Danny Alexander are publicly receptive to the cut in income tax, as long as there are compensating benefits for their own favoured causes, namely increases in the personal allowance. 'Our number one policy objective from our manifesto, on which we were keen to make progress, was to cut income tax,' says Julian Astle, a senior Clegg aide.[6] Osborne is more than usually nervous of leaks, and believes that the Lib Dems had leaked discussions before the Autumn Statement in November 2011. 'I want nobody in the room apart from principals,' he says. Special advisers are thrown out, more or less nicely, which the Lib Dems claim prevents them sniffing out the political folly of some of the proposals produced by Treasury officials. In the privacy of the Quad, Clegg is still worrying about reducing 50p: 'I've got no ideological objection to doing it, but doing so at a time of massive angst and social insecurity, and before our austerity plan is clearly working, is the wrong time.'[7]

Lib Dems are nevertheless open to the idea of a cut to 40p, on the key proviso that there is a mansion or property tax on the wealthy. The Treasury like the sound of this proposition, and have been pushing very hard for a property tax themselves. The Lib Dem proposal will mean a net tax rise on the rich, and Osborne is quite receptive to the idea: Tim Montgomerie is one of several commentators on the centre right who are arguing for the burden of tax to shift from earned income to property and assets.[8] Cameron's shire Tory sensibilities are offended. He doesn't like what he is hearing: this is rare territory where his Toryism and Osborne's are in utterly different places. Andrew Feldman doesn't like the sound of it either, and nor does Kate Fall. They put their foot down: a mansion or property tax is off the table.

The Liberals respond by going very cold on 40p. Osborne worries he is losing Lib Dem support even for a reduction to 45p, and thinks the coalition government may lose its chance to send out his 'big signal' that 'Britain is open for business'. Clegg and Alexander come under pressure and concede to 45p, but demand heavy compensation.[9] 'He got sucked into a deal with the Lib Dems. He had to offer something juicy enough for them to accept it as a trade-off,' says a figure close to Osborne. 'They were demanding a big increase in personal allowance of just under £800.' The Lib Dems say they have to 'fight tooth and bloody nail' for an increase in the amount individuals can earn before paying tax. Osborne maintains that he is very comfortable with the idea, and had spent much of his time as shadow chancellor saying 'we might well increase the personal allowance in government'. He is later heard to say, 'Frankly, it is much the easiest thing the Lib Dems ever demanded.'

All this had to be paid for, which, as one insider admits, is 'where the legs fell off the stool'. Osborne holds discussions with Treasury officials and with the Quad, thinking through how the extra money could be found. 'People say that we hadn't done the detailed work on these proposals. That's not true. We had spent hours and hours on it,' says a Treasury source. 'But George didn't see the wood for the trees. He didn't stand back and say, "Hold on, we are increasing taxes on working people, to reduce taxes on the well off."' A key Quad meeting takes place in the Cabinet Room on Monday 12 March. 'Suddenly, a load of discussions are concertinaed into one big Quad meeting because Osborne has to fly off to DC the following morning,' says one disconcerted colleague. Osborne thinks it is all sorted, but Number 10 are left frustrated: they are feeling frozen out of the final stages of the

Budget. It is the first Budget in several years where Number 10 officials have not been intimately involved.

The Treasury keep these final stages of the 2012 Budget unusually tight, in the words of one insider, 'partly, and ironically, because there was a concern about leaks and partly because George didn't want to engage with what he knew would be strong resistance to what he wanted'. As Number 10 don't know all the details of the Budget, it is ill-prepared to defend it. When the 50p cut is leaked by the Lib Dems on the Thursday before Budget day, they are stymied. As Oliver is trying to think through how to respond from his rickshaw weaving its way across Manhattan, he reasons that it's always worse to change a plan, even if he isn't totally sure what the plan is. 'This is a real problem,' he tells Number 10. 'I am 3,000 miles away. What is going on?' No one in Number 10 knows whether the leak is deliberate or not. They are in a terrible predicament.

One figure who had foreseen problems is Andrew Cooper, who had written a memo within Number 10 saying that to cut 50p at this time would be a 'political mistake', and that they are in danger of making a grave error by offering a 'tax cut for millionaires while taking away tax credits for working families'. He argues that their number one priority must be the cost of living: he wants to see a cut in fuel duty, but Osborne rules that out. Another concern in Number 10 is the Budget's 'granny tax' proposal, a tax increase on pensioners, which hadn't made it on the Number 10 list of top items in the Budget. The Treasury has sold it to Number 10 as a 'technical tidying up'. Osborne knows it is a risk, but he thinks that he can carry it because he will be announcing the increase in the personal allowance in his speech, which he has deliberately avoided briefing out to the media. But the night before the Budget, the Lib Dems leak it on top of the 50p leak the week before. Osborne is absolutely livid: as angry as he can be. Worse, he is now alarmed. 'The Lib Dems deliberately leaked the personal allowance the night before the Budget because they didn't want Osborne to have it as his big moment. They regarded it as their proposal and they wanted to own it.'

Hilton is disappointed because he argued for a cut in corporation tax to attract inward investment and to boost jobs. He tabled a proposal to cut it by 10% or 11% and came up with a list of welfare savings for Osborne, amounting to £25 billion, to pay for it: the cut to corporation tax was only going to cost the Exchequer, he estimated, £7 billion. Hilton is attracted to the argument that the government is cutting the taxes on jobs by cutting welfare. Like Cooper, he is worried about the timing of the cut on the top tax rate. But Hilton loses out to the Treasury, who argue that cutting corporation tax below a certain point would not be effective. He thinks Harrison has been responsible for warding Osborne off his idea. To Hilton, an advocate of behavioural economics, it is a classic example of the inadequacy of traditional economic thinking.

Hilton and Rohan Silva have been adopting the practice of composing a letter to the Treasury before major economic pronouncements, designed to show that Number 10 is speaking with one voice. They sent such a letter to Osborne before his first Budget in 2010, the two Autumn Statements and the 2012 Budget, outlining for the Treasury three to five Number 10 'hopes' reflecting what Cameron, Heywood, as well as obviously Hilton and Silva, wished. But the system doesn't work for the 2012 Budget. Hilton's frustration is that Cameron does not fight the Treasury hard enough. Osborne would say, 'We want your ideas for the Budget, because all I get is crap from the Treasury, and we need fresh thinking.' But the 2012 Budget reveals to Hilton that it is truly the Treasury that 'runs the show'. Cameron has allowed himself to become obsessed, traumatised even, by the acrid Number 10/Treasury relations of the previous thirty years. 'I don't want to fall out with the Treasury' is, Hilton believes, a Cameron tenet that is misplaced. Hilton thinks that Cameron has ceded too much power to Osborne and the Treasury in leaving it to officials and advisers to work on the detail. The 2012 Budget sees the biggest test yet for this 'Cameron doctrine'.

The 2012 Budget also sees Harrison's extraordinary power at its most raw. Harrison regards Heywood as a managerial economist, keen to increase government support for lending to small businesses. Although he respected O'Donnell as an economist, he believes Heywood is more fundamentally in tune with what he and Osborne want than O'Donnell, who Heywood has now succeeded as Cabinet Secretary. A low point with O'Donnell came when he produced a paper written by Jonathan Portes shortly before Portes departed in

February 2011 as the Cabinet Office's chief economist, suggesting that the government in effect move to 'Plan B', shifting away from austerity to Keynesian policies designed to stimulate the economy. 'Gus was … wobbly on it … though he was nothing like such a massive advocate of change as Jonathan,' says one senior Treasury official. 'It really wasn't a good thing for Gus to propose at the time. It implied that he was not wholly signed up to the government's strategy,' says another.

Harrison is as formidable an economist as he is confident of his right-of-centre convictions. He is also personable, tactful and tenacious. 'Rupert is very important to George because he provides the arguments that he needs to look impressive with Treasury officials,' says an insider. 'George isn't a trained economist. He needs Rupert constantly by his side.' Osborne himself is unsparing in his praise: 'Dr Rupert Harrison is a very able economist. The most able of his generation pretty much. He has delivered on the economics. I have delivered the politics for him,' he was heard to say. But not even the formidable Dr Harrison preempts what is about to happen.

The pieces are nearly all in place for the fiasco that the 2012 Budget becomes. The final two elements are, firstly, the series of proposals for funding, produced by the Treasury, which might have made sense financially, but not politically: the 'pasty tax' (imposing VAT on hot takeaway food like Cornish pasties) and the 'caravan tax' (increasing VAT on static caravans) came late in the day, without adequate scrutiny; out of the same filing cabinet came the idea of limiting tax relief on charitable donations – the 'charity tax' would inevitably provoke a strong reaction from charities and philanthropists. Knowing this will be sensitive, Osborne flags up to Cameron that 'there will be a row and people will say it is going to damage the Big Society'. Cameron assents to it – meekly, in the eyes of Hilton. Hilton knows that Osborne has little time for the Big Society, but had not expected him to come up with such an 'asinine' proposal.

The leaking is the second factor that turns a potentially hazardous Budget into a disaster. It means that the two key parts of the architecture – the cut in the top rate and the increase in personal allowances – have already been briefed, so the media go to town on the minor and ugly parts. The Lib Dems are brazen about the leaks. 'It was a very conscious decision on our part to put together a political strategy of briefing to stop the Tories claiming the credit alone,' says one. Clegg brings in political, economic and media consultants to advise on the Budget. A dozen meet regularly to ensure that the Lib Dems achieve a 'political dividend' from the Budget, as Astle put it.[10] They are angry with their Tory partners and want to show they are no pushovers. The result is 'the media has no good news to report on Budget day. They focus instead relentlessly on the bad news and chew over it excessively,' as Danny Alexander says.[11]

Osborne and Harrison are guilty, as they admit, of hubris and naivety. Number 10 do not have the time to prepare the ground: it insists it could have made a reasonable case on the new flat-rate pensions and other proposals given more notice. Budget day, 21 March, is a day that Osborne had been anticipating for months, if not years. It turns into one of the unhappiest days of his life. Miliband all too easily dismisses it as the 'millionaire's Budget' which destroys forever the government's claim that 'we're all in this together'. 'How can the priority for our country be an income tax cut for the richest 1% when the squeezed middle are facing rising petrol prices, higher energy bills and cuts in tax credits and child benefit?' Miliband continues.[12]

'The morning after the Budget, I could see we were going to be in for months of misery. I could see even then it starting to unravel. I could see how this was going to go, and it was going to go in only one direction,' Osborne reflects.[13] Cameron shares the same apprehension: as one insider says, 'It was instantly clear to him that we hadn't handled it properly. He felt it had become much too transactional, without any central vision about what the Budget was about.' Cameron's frustration mounts over the next few days; he is angry with Osborne, but he will not let himself be angry with his chancellor, so he is angry with the Treasury instead. He vows that in future, Number 10 'will have a much bigger footprint on the decisions in the run-up to the Budget'. He is cross with Clegg, but he doesn't let himself be cross with Clegg, so is angry with the Lib Dems instead, blaming their malice aforethought and their premeditated leaking.

Feldman is on the phone within hours of Osborne sitting down after the Budget speech. He tells Cameron he is being inundated with complaints from the business community and is worried about the impact on party donations: a duke has been complaining to him about the charity tax, and his own staff are up in arms about the price of pasties. 'George took his eye off the ball, and his officials took over,' recalls one. Cameron's and Osborne's relationship remains undamaged, even when Osborne's net approval rating falls to minus 37 in August, and half the voters in the *Guardian*/ICM poll think he should 'lose his job'.[14] Cameron does not blink: 'The prime minister never asked me to step down or even considered anything like that,' Osborne says.[15]

Just days after the Budget, a new horror emerges. The trade union Unite threatens a fuel-tanker strike by its drivers over health and safety. Francis Maude has spent several months in the Cabinet Office looking at the possibility of a fuel strike and producing contingency plans. He considers himself the specialist figure. Number 10 are far from pleased when he walks out of the black front door, passing Craig Oliver in the hall, and gives an interview to the waiting television cameras. He tells *Sky News* 'a bit of extra fuel in a jerry can in the garage is a sensible precaution to take'.[16] His words are designed to calm nerves but instead cause panic-buying. Number 10 is hypersensitive about fuel strikes. The ease with which the country was brought low by fuel strikes in 2000 led to one of the very rare times in Blair's period in power when Labour fell behind in the opinion polls. Cameron senses he must take control himself. He sets COBRA to work, and is frustrated to learn preparations for a strike are not more advanced. Yet again, he finds the machine only works flat out when he himself is driving it. He instructs ministers to talk to employers and then directly with the unions to help ward off the strike. The impetus is successful, but the damage has been done. The perception is given of a government not fully in control.

Osborne had been praying for good news when the GDP figures for the first quarter of 2012 are produced. But the data, published on 25 April, is bleak: the economy has shrunk again by 0.2%. He had feared the worst, and when it comes, it is a hard blow. Cameron and he instinctively feel that the data is not entirely accurate. Cameron spends time in the late spring and early summer touring the country: he regularly remarks how the economy always seems to be much better than the data suggests. Worries abound of a triple-dip recession. Osborne knows that he will never acquire the parliamentary votes for the Finance Bill, implementing measures from the Budget, in June and July unless he changes direction. On 19 July, the IMF produces a pessimistic assessment of the UK's economy and warns the government to slow the pace of its austerity programme. Osborne's image is under attack along with Cameron's. Nadine Dorries, the outspoken Tory backbencher, had said in March that 'The problem is that policy is being run by two public school boys who don't know what it is like to go to the supermarket.'[17] On 23 April she returned to her script, accusing Cameron and Osborne of being 'two arrogant posh boys' who show 'no passion to want to understand the lives of others'.[18] Having a Conservative MP attacking the party leaders further confirms an impression of a government seemingly out of touch and looking after the rich.

Osborne knows he must change tack. He sets about a programme which he calls 'defusing the bomb'.[19] On 28 May comes the first U-turn, on the pasty tax: only food cooling down rather than being kept hot is liable for VAT. He is not convinced of this U-turn but he thinks 'we might as well chuck in the pasties, because otherwise it makes Cornwall quite difficult for us'. Next, the proposed VAT rise on static caravans, again seen as targeting the less well-off, is cut from 20% to 5%. This helps win back the MPs with caravan makers in their constituencies, many of them in East Yorkshire.[20] Three days later, he announces the U-turn over the 'charity tax' proposals. 'I never thought of this as a charities tax: it was supposed to be a tycoon tax. You can see how that went wrong,' he tells colleagues. The Church of England too had to be bought off, because VAT had been put up on Church buildings. Osborne invites the Bishop of London to see him; together they find a compromise. In public, Osborne admits that he had 'got it wrong' on some Budget measures with political capital expended on 'battles that don't matter'.[21]

Number 10 has drifted into the heart of the 'omnishambles'. The term itself was first used in 2009 by the fictional character Malcolm Tucker, Labour director of communications in the BBC television comedy *The Thick of It*. Oliver Dowden remembers it from the programme and starts using the term around the building. It leaks through the walls to the world outside: Craig Oliver always accused him of popularising the term.

The Budget, the bad economic news and the U-turns are all damaging the party. The Tories had been on 38% or 39% in the polls since the EU veto in December 2011, well ahead of Labour. But three weeks before the Budget, Cooper believes because of the damage to the reputation of the government over the NHS bill, the polls start turning against them. Focus groups begin to say the Tories are incompetent, produce half-baked measures, and that Cameron is merely buffeted by events, lacking principles and staying power. Cameron's team feel they could live with unpopularity over the NHS bill because at least it was advancing Conservative policy; but they know in their hearts that unpopularity over the Budget is totally their own fault.

Each week brings new woes to Cameron and Osborne. They are sinking together. The mood in the parliamentary party is terrible. Many have lost their confidence in Osborne's judgement. A large number of Conservative MPs, perhaps most now, think Cameron is incompetent and lacks grip and clarity. At times, he seems overwhelmed. Even his closest team in Number 10 begin to worry about him. Pressure mounts in some corners for a more activist economic policy. Rumours are rife of leadership plots. 'I felt we were paddling furiously up a creek and couldn't make any headway,' says one insider. 'There are only so many times you can pick up a newspaper and read yourself being picked apart before it gets to you: even my friends, few of whom are Tories, would say how sorry they felt for me,' said another. In late April, Cooper sits down with Oliver. They agree, 'this is hopeless: we have to achieve greater clarity and agreement about what we are trying to do'. Cameron's party conference speech that autumn is one of the fruits of their deliberations.[22]

Number 10 is still adapting to the departure of Hilton. After the summer, Oliver Dowden is promoted to deputy chief of staff to help Llewellyn and Kate Fall. Together with head of strategic communications Ameet Gill and Craig Oliver, they work hard to bring more focus to their work, and more discipline to the message. Attempts are made to make the Policy Unit more political. Paul Kirby, the director, comes under pressure to help generate stories to show Number 10 has momentum. Cameron's court debate bringing in a political heavyweight to run it: the idea is shelved, for a time, with the argument that 'made-up policies on the fly smacks of the Brown regime'. Cameron's team accept the problem lies 'on the ground floor, not on the first floor', i.e. it is failure of direction from the PM rather than failure of policy, which is the heart of the problem. Party co-chairman Sayeeda Warsi comes under a critical spotlight from Number 10, reflecting the unease about relations with the wider party.

The 2012 Budget gave the coalition a hammering. For one senior Treasury official, it 'was a reminder that reforming taxes in the middle of the parliament is very difficult'. But the desperate position of both coalition partners in the polls, and the shared determination of Cameron and Clegg, keeps the coalition on the road. They will have to rethink the Quad, which had expanded to include other senior ministers and officials. It now consists of just the four principals and a private secretary taking notes, alongside Heywood and a senior Treasury official. It rarely leaks again. Twice a year the four principals have dinner together. Unencumbered by officials and formal agendas, the dinners become rare occasions when they can let off steam and talk about the world outside politics.[23]

Policy needs refreshing too. Osborne has been thinking deeply. Despite the ritual slagging match, whereby it suits Ed Balls to say that austerity is far too harsh, and for Osborne to reply that the pain is necessary, Osborne realises he is in fact only keeping to the plan laid out by Darling before the general election, with nothing radical or particularly Tory about his policy. He remains frustrated that the Treasury is not doing more to come up with fresh ideas. Though Plan A remains intact, 'there was a resistance to any kind of Keynesian panacea; but, within that, there was incredible flexibility on the fiscal pathway,' as one senior Treasury figure puts it. The Policy Unit therefore produces a slew of proposals for Osborne, including 'shovel-ready' infrastructure projects, radical ideas to increase house building, and to privatise road building which is at an historic low. The last proposal appeals to Cameron himself: 'in Europe people charge to use roads: why can't we do the same here and use the money to invest in new road building?' But idea after idea falls by the wayside as neither Cameron nor Osborne are prepared to expend the political capital or take the risk to drive the projects forward. Road pricing is thus deemed too risky and shelved for a future parliament. Home building, including entirely new towns, is considered likely to upset

Conservative voters in the shires. They are not yet prepared to find the money for big infrastructure projects. 'Funding for Lending' is the most important initiative that comes out of this work. Osborne is adamant: 'I will not tolerate a second quarter of negative growth.' Wanted or not, that is exactly what he is about to have to tolerate.

EIGHTEEN

Olympian Summer, Olympian Difficulties

May–September 2012

'The game was massively up if Boris didn't win London in May 2012,' recalls party chairman Andrew Feldman.[1] The Olympic Games are raising the stakes. To have Ken Livingstone, the Labour challenger to Boris Johnson in the mayoral election, parading endlessly before the cameras would be a considerable blow. With Conservative confidence in Cameron's leadership so fragile, defeat for Johnson might very well mark the beginning of the end for him. Number 10 know that they are in an existential fight, and they have to win.

Boris Johnson was first elected London mayor in 2008. At the time, he was far from certain whether it was the right platform for him. But Cameron wanted a big hitter as the Conservative challenger, and there weren't many alternatives. Sebastian Coe was a possibility, but he made it clear he wasn't interested. Steven Norris, former vice chairman of the party, was another option, but lacked widespread appeal. Cameron and George Osborne liked and trusted Nick Boles and regarded him as a serious candidate; but while Boles was making up his mind, he developed Hodgkin's lymphoma. So it was Boris Johnson, who had charisma and an ability to appeal to a cross-section of the electorate, essential if the Conservatives were going to win in London. Ultimately, Boris defeated Ken Livingstone by a margin of 53.2% to 46.8%. It is too close for comfort.

The job of mayor proves to be his *métier*, to the surprise of many, himself included. Relations with Number 10 are better than expected from 2008–12. 'Of course Boris, being Boris, couldn't but help criticising and jabbing periodically,' says one insider. 'Equally, he could claim he was standing up for London, which meant he would disagree periodically in public with what we were doing.' A new London airport on 'Boris Island', as the media dubbed it, in the Thames Estuary is a big point of difference. Cameron and Osborne have never regarded it as remotely feasible financially.

Johnson is rare as a person about whom Cameron and Osborne differ. To the latter, he is, according to one former Number 10 aide, just 'plain annoying'. 'There was a sense in this building that the PM and the chancellor were getting on taking the difficult decisions while Boris, with his crass bumbling, was lapping it all up and loving twisting the knife,' says another. Cameron, however, often finds Boris entertaining and funny. But when he gets under his skin, the gloves rapidly come off. After Johnson lists in print all the Old Etonians who have gone on to become prime minister, Cameron sends him a text: 'The next PM will be Miliband if you don't fucking shut up.' There are other tense moments with Boris in Cameron's first two years as PM. According to one former Number 10 aide, 'there is a big feeling that Boris is difficult, that we cannot depend on him, that he is a fair-weather friend who strikes poses and can't be trusted.'

Number 10, for all the ambivalence, know they have to 'hug Boris'. Party conferences require particular stage management. Before the 2010 and 2011 conferences, Number 10 hold discussions about what will satisfy him. He is allocated a big morning slot with his media circus, giving him a place in the sun, and his exposure is very carefully managed. In 2011, he receives much more applause than Cameron on his arrival at conference, and Number 10 are relieved that he only makes one jibe at the PM, on police numbers.[2] However much they resent him for being a 'box office matinée idol', they know spurning him would be churlish as well as dangerous.

So despite the ambivalence, backing him again for re-election in 2012 is almost inevitable. Osborne approaches the Australian political strategist Lynton Crosby to campaign again for Boris as he had in 2008. Throughout April and early May, the political side of Number 10 is reoriented to try to ensure Boris will win. The whole CCHQ machine too is thrown behind making sure he is re-elected, even at the expense of shifting resources away from supporting councillors across the country. It will be a tight election: London is not naturally a Conservative city, and with the economy still in trouble, and the polls nationally at such a low ebb, it will be an uphill struggle. The result on 3 May is very close – much closer than 2008. Johnson scrapes home with 51.5% of the vote to Livingstone's 48.5%.

Relations between Boris's camp and Number 10 plummet in the months following the election, with jealousy and resentment at Boris's high profile and his effortless playing to the gallery. Cameron and Osborne, in contrast, are under great pressure and their positions precarious. Johnson's re-election will at least bind him up in London for another four years, reducing the biggest leadership threat to Cameron. Predictably, the Conservatives do badly in the May local elections across the country, although they avoid the midterm collapses seen under both Thatcher and Major. Some 405 councillors lose their seats in May, and the Conservatives lose control of twelve councils, including their only two in Wales.

Johnson thinks seriously about taking on Cameron, but knows that his re-election in London makes it impossible. Boris aside, Cameron has no obvious challengers around the Cabinet table: Osborne, Hague and Gove will never stand against him. Liam Fox has resigned and is discredited, while no one serious is thinking that David Davis merits another stab at the leadership. Osborne remarks that it is 'not a bad position for a prime minister to be in, if the most credible challenger is an Old Etonian who isn't even in the House of Commons'. Number 10 nevertheless continue to watch Johnson carefully, and are never quite certain what he is up to. After the local elections, when Conservative losses are exacerbated by UKIP gains, Graham Brady, chairman of the 1922 Committee, makes threatening noises that MPs are willing to put their signatures to a challenge against Cameron. Tory grandee Michael Spicer, himself a former chairman of the 1922 Committee, is encouraged to see Brady: 'You should never look isolated – always flank yourself with named supporters. The first job of the chairman of the 1922 Committee is to represent the parliamentary party to the leadership as objectively as you can', Spicer tells him. It is debatable whether Brady has been put back in his box. Number 10 studies intently the names of all those voting against the government. 'We had weekly meetings convened in the utmost secrecy,' says one. 'We always thought he would get at least 50% in the event of a challenge, but the truth is that the party never liked him. They accepted him as long as he was a winner, but since the omnishambles he looked like a loser and that could have been fatal to him.' They do not take suggestions of a plot by Conservative MP Adam Afriyie seriously, regarding him as something of 'a fantasist'. The board at CCHQ, carefully watched over by Feldman, remain loyal to Cameron. Apart from the period leading up to the 2007 party conference, when Gordon Brown was on the brink of calling a snap election, his support in the parliamentary party has never been so precarious.

Relations between Number 10 and Johnson do however improve from 2013. Lynton Crosby's arrival from January is 'key in bringing Boris round', says one insider. He and Johnson have a very close bond, far closer than he enjoys with Cameron and Osborne. The Australian rapidly becomes the go-to person to smooth over any difficulties that arise between Downing Street and City Hall. Jo Johnson, Boris's brother, joins Number 10 that April as head of the Policy Unit. He is not seen to be as close to his brother as Crosby is, he hates any notion that he is an intermediary, and according to one Number 10 aide, describes his brother as a 'colourful, local government leader'. Kate Fall puts into Cameron's diary regular, if infrequent, dates for Cameron and Boris to have lunches at Chequers or drinks at Number 10. Cameron begins to relax more with him, seeing him ultimately not as his problem, but one for whoever wants to succeed him when he stands down, i.e. Osborne or May. When Johnson announces his intention in August 2014 to stand in the 2015 general election, Cameron tweets from holiday in Portugal: 'I've always said I want my star players on the pitch.'[3] He may not have totally believed his words at the time, but 'he has increasingly come to believe it', says one. Osborne cuts Treasury deals for Johnson – such as the extension of the Northern Line, announced in the Autumn Statement on 29 November – which keep him in his place.

Cameron has a private dinner with Boris in autumn 2013, which proves to be a turning point. Boris's name features much less afterwards at the 8.30 a.m. and 4 p.m. daily meetings in Cameron's room. Cameron's aides are relaxed about his appearance at the 2013 party conference, and still more so in 2014. In November 2014, Boris is pleased when Number 10 organises a dinner for him to meet Jeb Bush, and he is flattered by the notion that the putative future US president is meeting the potential future British prime minister. But despite all this, some tensions still remain: on 25 February 2015, the headline in *The Times* is 'Tories call for Boris to rescue their campaign'.[4]

A few days of light relief, if not sunshine, come on 2–5 June 2012 with the Queen's Diamond Jubilee. Cameron loves the monarchy. Whilst still at Eton, he stayed up all night on The Mall in 1981 for the wedding of Charles and Diana. He makes it clear there will be no repetition of the tensions with the Palace that occurred under Blair, notably after the death of Diana. He is assiduous in ensuring that Number 10 keep Buckingham Palace very closely informed about matters of state, so no possible misunderstandings can occur. He is thrilled that the Queen accepts his invitation to come to Chequers (her first visit since 1996): unlike some predecessors, he loves his annual visits to Balmoral in September. He treats the royal family with utmost respect in public and in private, looks forward to his weekly audiences with the Queen, and studies the racing results before going to see her.

Cameron is boyishly pleased that the Jubilee coincides with his premiership. He wants to hold a street party as part of the 'big Jubilee lunch', an initiative in which the whole nation is invited to share lunch with neighbours. Rain dictates that the event moves inside. To mark the conclusion of the Jubilee year, on 18 December 2012, the Queen will attend a Cabinet meeting at Downing Street.

Johnson only just squeezing home in the mayoral election, and the very wet Diamond Jubilee, take some shine off the summer. So too does the NHS bill, causing continuing difficulties, as is proposed House of Lords reform, and the Leveson Inquiry, still in full swing. In June, Osborne goes before the inquiry and more embarrassing text messages come out about Cameron. With all these challenges, if the Olympics now go wrong, it may well spell the end for Cameron, and he knows it. The games are New Labour's legacy to the Tories, achieved by Blair in July 2005, one day before the 7/7 terrorist attacks on London. Cameron's own efforts to secure a major sports tournament do not go so well. He returned home empty-handed from the English bid to host the FIFA World Cup in 2018. He was deeply upset and angry about losing, and Russia being victorious. He suspects foul play. 'We really felt we had a good shot. But we felt we had been completely misled,' says one of his team.

Not screwing up the Olympics is thus a major preoccupation for Cameron. 'If this goes wrong on our watch, it will be a disaster', he repeats regularly in the first half of the year. The consequences would be 'absolutely dire', confirms an official. 'The media was just waiting for some kind of disaster.' Cameron views the Olympics as 'a humungous opportunity to show off the UK in the best possible light, to tell the world "we were open for business"', as Ed Llewellyn puts it.[5] In the run-up to the Olympics, two weeks of global industry conferences are planned focusing on a different sector each day, to be kicked off by a major British business promotion event. The Battersea Power Station redevelopment, to cost £8 billion and expected to create 20,000 jobs, is launched as part of 'the biggest ever drive to attract investment into Britain'.[6] Cameron is so determined nothing is going to spoil the games that he invests intensive personal time to ensure that they are a huge success.

Terrorist attacks are a principal worry in his mind. He wants the SAS brought up from their base in Hereford to minimise any possible risk. Surface-to-air missiles are placed on tower blocks in East London to shoot down incoming rockets and hijacked airplanes. The police are given greater powers to search people and property. This is the largest police operation on British soil since the 1926 General Strike. 'Our view was that if terrorists know that we are there, and they won't get away with anything, that will minimise the risk,' says an official. Cyber terrorism, though, proves to be the greatest threat, with a plot to knock out the lighting for the opening ceremony.[7] A police raid on a bedroom in a private house clinically eliminates the risk.

Cameron has great self-belief that his personal attention alone will maximise the chances of the Olympics being the big success he so desperately craves. He had moved into full swing in January 2012, chairing monthly meetings of the Olympic committee of Cabinet, which is serviced by the Olympic secretariat, set up the previous month. This works alongside the National Security secretariat for the duration of the Olympics, and is overseen by an official, Simon Case. Cameron is a forceful chairman of the Olympic committee, on which sit senior Cabinet ministers, heads of the security services, Seb Coe and Boris Johnson. With the possibility that Johnson might lose the mayoral election to Livingstone, officials contemplate the historically unusual possibility of having Conservatives, Lib Dems and Labour all on the same Cabinet committee. Risks it considers include immigration queues at Heathrow, London transport grinding to a halt, and government visitors from abroad not receiving requisite respect. The experience of opening the Millennium Dome on 31 December 1999, when a fifth of the 10,500-strong audience did not receive their tickets in the post, is very much on their mind.[8] So too are the Beijing Olympics in 2008, with embarrassments including dubbed voices and false fireworks. Jealousy plays a part too: the team reckon more money had been spent on the opening ceremony in Beijing than they had to spend on the entire Olympics. By May, the secretariat has a hundred people, and they are operating 24/7 from their war room underneath COBRA.

Three weeks before the opening ceremony, panic sets in when G4S, the security firm brought in to staff the venues, reveals that it cannot fulfil its remit. Cameron steps in. He chairs two key meetings of the Olympic committee to arrange bringing in troops. The week before the opening ceremony, he chairs daily meetings. On the Monday, commander-in-chief of land forces General Nick Parker briefs David Richards that a further 1,200 troops are required. Richards and Jeremy Hunt persuade the PM of the case, against the advice of Theresa May. She is angry. She later comes to the operational command centre at High Wycombe and says to Parker, 'you are the general who deployed far too many troops'. The G4S furore adds to a perception in the country that preparations are not going well. The press are having a field day: everything from G4S to concerns over temporary 'Olympic lanes' to speed officials through the London traffic lead to a series of negative headlines. A worried Craig Oliver calls a number of newspaper editors. 'Look, you need to give this a fair wind. Obviously there will be teething problems, but don't write it off as a disaster before it's begun.' The coverage changes.

Danny Boyle, the film and theatre director responsible for the opening ceremony, comes to show Cameron what he has planned. The PM is disconcerted by his focus on the NHS, especially given contemporary sensitivities with the bill. He would have preferred something more 'Churchillian' but knows he has to be very careful what he says. He makes it clear to Boyle that he would have liked the opening ceremony to be a celebration of all the UK was most proud of, not just the NHS.

Number 10 puts great thought into the events Cameron is going to see, giving due weight to the Paralympics to avoid accusations he is not taking them as seriously. The London Organising Committee of the Olympic and Paralympic Games (LOCOG) advise Cameron's team which British athletes he should see at both the Olympics and Paralympics. He is very conscious of striking the right balance and not being seen to be 'sitting around watching sport all day' when he should be running the country. Liz Sugg, his events and travel co-ordinator, works with LOCOG to ensure he attends the right events at the right time, and that he is in place to meet key figures from the Olympic movement as well as foreign leaders. John Casson, the foreign affairs private secretary, has a big say. He wants to ensure opportunities for bilateral meetings with foreign leaders are maximised. A 'judo summit' takes place with Putin. The Whitehall saying 'don't waste a good funeral' morphs into 'don't waste a good Olympics'. Cameron has no history of interest in attending sporting events or following the Olympics. He enjoys tennis, and will keep up with news during Wimbledon fortnight: he is thrilled to be present when Andy Murray wins the Championships in 2013. He also follows Test matches, and will often have cricket on the screen when he is working in his study or listen to it on the radio when he is in the car. Nevertheless, Cameron finds himself thoroughly swept up in the Olympics, the pageant, excitement and sense of occasion.

After the euphoria of the opening ceremony, the games themselves start badly on 28 July, with criticisms of empty seats (exacerbated by officials from around the world booking mass seats but not bothering to use them in the early rounds). On the first day of competitions, Cameron goes to The Mall to see the cyclists. The expectation, on the back of Bradley Wiggins's success in winning the Tour de France a few weeks before, is for British cyclists to triumph. When they don't, the press write stories about the 'curse of Cameron'.[9] But then British success starts taking off. He is in the velodrome on 2 August, along with the Duke and Duchess of Cambridge and Prince Harry, to see Britain win gold in cycling. He rejoices in the success of Mo Farah, Jessica Ennis, and especially Nicola Adams, the world's first Olympic female boxing champion. The beach volleyball is taking place on Horse Guards Parade just beyond the garden of Downing Street, and he is frustrated it isn't visible from the upstairs rooms of Number 10 because the large stands obscure it, though he manages to attend a game with Samantha and the children.

An awkward moment comes when Cameron is booed, albeit drowned out by applause from the crowds, whilst presenting Ellie Simmonds with her second gold swimming medal of the Paralympic games;[10] 'the PM loved giving her the medal and the boos weren't noticeable in the room so he didn't hear them,' explains a close aide. It pales into insignificance beside the treatment of Osborne, who is roundly booed presenting medals to the winners of the men's 400 metres at the Paralympics.[11] When Seb Coe had phoned him to ask if he would be willing to present a medal at the Paralympics, he wondered about the wisdom of doing so. 'Are you sure?' he asked. Osborne has taken his children to several Olympic and Paralympic events, and has an intimation of impending disaster as the time for him to present the medals approaches: 'I thought I can't get out of this. I am slated to present a medal. But I knew it was going to be a disaster the moment I walked out.' He laughs it off at the time, saying it was 'not surprising' that the chancellor will be unpopular at a time of austerity, but afterwards describes it as 'a pretty unpleasant experience'.[12] His children are watching him, and for the first time perhaps, they realise the full enormity of the job their father does. For all his self-confidence and high intelligence, Osborne is a more sensitive and vulnerable figure than he appears. Andrew Feldman, watching the grizzly affair on television, thinks, 'We can't possibly win from here.' He comments, 'We had all hoped the Olympics, as well as the Jubilee, would give us the boost we needed. It wasn't happening.'[13]

Ultimately, however, the Olympics and Paralympics prove a great sporting success: Britain comes third in both the Olympics and Paralympic gold medal tables (with twenty-nine Olympic and thirty-four Paralympic gold medals). The Olympics are also organisational and cultural successes. Politicians, officials and military combine to do a very professional job. It is a financial success too, helped by the Treasury insisting on a large contingency back in 2005–6, much-needed in view of the recession, unforeseen back in those Elysian days. GDP figures show a minor Olympic dividend, though less than hoped. Cameron soon turns his attention to the legacy. School sport is a particular opportunity, an area he knows is not the natural habitat of Michael Gove. A school sport initiative is launched in January 2013, with Jessica Ennis playing a key part, though inevitably the government is criticised over the following years for not making more of the legacy.

After a torrid 2012 to date, Cameron's mood is lifted by the Olympics. He takes Samantha and the children to Majorca for a few days between both sets of games and is back in London on 29 August to attend the Paralympics. He then goes to Cornwall for a quick break, but is back on Monday 3 September for a government reshuffle. Planned initially for the spring, it was pushed back to July because of the fuel crisis. The stormy end of the session – ninety-one Tory MPs voted against the government on Lords Reform on 10 July – and with the Olympics imminent, Number 10 decided to push it back again until after the summer break. Neither Cameron nor Osborne are enthusiasts of reshuffles. Cameron came to power believing that they almost never resolve the problems they were designed to solve, and almost always produce fresh problems. Craig Oliver had been reading up about reshuffles under the Conservatives and Labour over the previous thirty years, which reinforces their belief that they should be minimised. A conversation with Godric Smith, one of Blair's media team, further fortifies their prejudices.

Besides Cameron and Osborne, Llewellyn and Fall are key figures in working out the details of the 4 September reshuffle. Conservative MPs have become deeply suspicious and resentful of Osborne's influence over appointments. Osborne prides himself on being very good at picking people. Mark Carney, appointed Bank of England governor in July 2013, and Paul Deighton, formerly chief executive of LOCOG and appointed a Treasury minister in January 2013, are two appointments with which he is especially pleased. Other figures owing their advancement to him include Matthew Hancock, Greg Hands, Sajid Javid and Paul Kirby, head of the Policy Unit.

Final touches are made over pizza in the chancellor's dining room in Number 11. Each fresh appointment will be announced on Twitter in real time, so all have the same story at the same time. The corner piece of the reshuffle is the decision to move Andrew Lansley. He has 'had his card marked since the spring' and only the delayed reshuffle allows him to continue in office so long. Cameron takes time to accept Lansley has to go; their interview is particularly painful. Lansley believes that he is being offered an EU commissioner job for the next round in 2014. In the interim, to the surprise of Cameron's team, he accepts the leadership of the House of Commons, which is widely considered a demotion.

Appointing Jeremy Hunt as his successor makes admirable sense. Cameron was first impressed by Hunt when he helped him prepare for the 2010 TV debates and liked the calm bedside manner and confidence he exuded. His opinion of Hunt rockets during the Olympics: Hunt's loyalty, mastery of detail and ability to foresee and overcome problems persuade many in Number 10 that he can handle a much bigger brief. Getting him out of the Department for Culture, Media and Sport following the Leveson Inquiry is another reason for the move. They worry that the Murdoch press might react against his appointment because of the furore over the BSkyB bid, but no such campaign materialises.

The reshuffle tries to address Number 10's fragile grip over the party. Sayeeda Warsi must go as party co-chairman. While many admire her resolve, she had a number of disagreements over campaign strategy in the run-up to the 2012 local elections with senior figures in CCHQ, including the director of campaigns Stephen Gilbert, a stalwart of the party machine. Cameron and Osborne want someone who will create a feeling of optimism and purpose with the party in the country. Feldman has sorted the organisational and financial side of CCHQ as co-chairman; it now needs a charismatic leader to galvanise the party. They alight on Grant Shapps as co-chairman, who has done a good job as Minister of Housing. Cameron never found it easy to find the right party chairman, but he believes Shapps, who is eager for the job, will be biddable as the election approaches.

Finding the right chief whip is another ongoing problem. Patrick McLoughlin has done the job since May 2005. He is widely liked and trusted, but with further fierce battles coming up, they need a more assertive figure. Enter Andrew Mitchell, Osborne's idea. He had been a strong and effective International Development Secretary, had been in the Whips' Office in the 1990s, and has a military bearing from his days in the Royal Tank Regiment. He is on the right of the party too, a benefit. Cameron's team are desperate to put the travails with the party over the last two years firmly behind them, and they believe Mitchell will 'sort out the party'. His assertiveness is evident from his very first minutes in his new post. Mitchell insists that Number 10 does not interfere with the running of the Whips' Office. 'Mitchell made clear that in recent years the Whips' Office had been too much of a "sergeants' mess" and it needed to revert to its previous [role] as an "officers' mess" composed of the young and talented passing through and older more reassuring senior types,' recalls one. Have they appointed the right man? 'Some of us were saying: "Look, it might not be too late to review this decision."' McLoughlin is happy enough to leave, and is flattered by Cameron's phone call to him the previous Friday to say, 'I would like you to head a major department.' He is invited to become Transport Secretary, with a clear instruction to press ahead with the high-speed rail project HS2.

Warsi's departure, on top of widespread critical comment that Cameron has insufficient women in his government, helps explain the promotions of Maria Miller to succeed Hunt at Culture, Theresa Villiers to succeed Owen Paterson at the Northern Ireland Office, and Justine Greening to succeed Mitchell at International Development. Chris Grayling is promoted to Justice Secretary. As one of only two figures to hold positions in the shadow Cabinet but not to receive Cabinet posts in 2010 because of the Lib Dems, he has much support. Nick Herbert, the other shadow Cabinet minister to miss out, is judged not to have handled his disappointment as well. Grayling, in contrast, quietly put his head down, and did well as Minister of State for Employment. It means shifting Ken Clarke sideways to Minister without Portfolio. He is lucky to survive. He had been squabbling with May at the Home Office which created tension, and had been winding up Cameron with talk of prisoner rights and prisoner voting. Yet senior aides in Number 10 felt his 'wise experience', shorn of departmental responsibility, would still be of value to them.

The Justice Secretary berth had originally been cleared to make way for Iain Duncan Smith. Cameron is much more instinctively loyal to Tory grandees than Osborne, who is an iconoclast by comparison.

But two years of listening to Osborne's belittling of IDS and his reforms at the Department of Work and Pensions (DWP) have left their mark. 'You've been there a couple of years, would you like to move on to Justice?' Cameron asks. 'I'll think about it,' he tells the PM.[14] IDS subsequently discussed the move with BBC political editor Nick Robinson, musing that he had been quite attracted to the idea because it would enable him to develop his thinking about the rehabilitation of offenders. That night, Danny Finkelstein, *The Times* journalist and close friend of Osborne's, goes on BBC2's *Newsnight* and speculates about the reasons for IDS moving from DWP. IDS firmly suspects Osborne's hand behind what he is saying, although Finkelstein insists he had been thinking through the logic of the move, rather than taking any cue from his friend. IDS tells Cameron the next day that he wants to remain at DWP. 'If he really wanted to move me, he could have done,' insists IDS. 'But I said that I wanted to see through the reforms.'[15] Forcing a former Conservative leader to move against his will is not something Cameron wants to countenance.

Reshuffle over, and a tougher team in place, Cameron believes he can place the problems of the spring and summer squarely behind him, and look forward to a much better autumn. Cameron has had a punishing eighteen months. Osborne has been on the run since his Budget. It is vital things pick up. Even with no obvious challenges in sight, Cameron's future is very much in the balance.

NINETEEN

Lords and Boundaries

January–December 2012

Nick Clegg has had a very poor 2011. His party are hammered in the polls, his popularity ratings are on the floor, and he fails to win the AV referendum. His own survival and his party's position require him to show he can achieve constitutional reform, which his party holds dear, as fruit from the coalition. Following Chris Huhne's dramatic resignation on 3 February 2012, when he admitted to perverting the course of justice over a speeding offence, the threat of a challenge to Clegg's leadership recedes for a while. But he remains adamant that he must see constitutional reform. 'I understand this and am happy to accommodate you,' Cameron tells him – until the heat is on and Cameron engages with exactly what this support will mean.

Polls regularly suggest there is widespread popular support for the replacement of the Lords with an elected chamber.[1] The political classes recognise that the reforms introduced by Blair in 1999, cutting the number of hereditary peers to just ninety-two, were only the first stage in a continuing reform process. The House of Lords is acknowledged to be too big: it is the largest second chamber in any democracy (and it is the only second chamber in the world larger than the first).[2] In 2003 and 2007, proposals for further reform were defeated. In 2009, the judicial function of the Lords passed to the Supreme Court. There is unfinished business here.

The Conservatives include a commitment to reform, albeit a tepid one, in their 2010 manifesto: 'we will work to build a consensus for a mainly elected second chamber to replace the current House of Lords'.[3] A similar pledge was in the previous two manifestos: it has been Conservative policy to have a mainly elected second chamber since 1999. The Lib Dems go much further in their own manifesto, stating they will 'replace the House of Lords with a fully elected second chamber with considerably fewer members than the current house.'[4] 'We've still got the temporary arrangement we had in 1911,' says Nick Clegg. 'It's an absolute absurdity that we have this Gilbert and Sullivan chamber.'[5] With such manifesto commitments, it is easy for those involved in the coalition negotiations to agree the basis for action to take place many months in the future. 'We will establish a committee to bring forward proposals for a wholly or mainly elected chamber on the basis of proportional representation', the Coalition Agreement says.[6] 'Ah,' says Oliver Letwin, 'the form of words we used was less than total commitment to House of Lords reform.'[7] Officials agree that, 'at the end of the day, the position in the Coalition Agreement on Lords reform is very far from clear'. The seeds of future strife are therefore sown at the very genesis.

Clegg is fixated on delivering Lords reform. He has lost the innocence and trust in the coalition that he had in its first year. The AV experience wiped it away. In January 2012, he tries to unilaterally pressure Cameron into action on Lords reform, without any warning, so frustrated and suspicious has he become, which creates friction between them and results in a rare and frank direct phone call on the matter. From the spring, Clegg begins to hold monthly cross-party meetings in his room in the Cabinet Office. Conservative members on it are far from happy. 'It was all very confusing; Nick Clegg was leading it, but he appeared not really interested. The meetings dragged on and on but he hadn't read the papers, or mastered the details or the implications,' says a senior Tory.

Wednesday 27 June sees the House of Lords Reform Bill introduced to the House of Commons. It proposes a 450-strong Upper House, 80% of whom will be elected, and the remaining members to be appointed on a non-party basis. Peers will be elected on the same day as major national polls: there will be eight voting regions, giving the electorate a choice between parties and individuals. Church of England bishops in the Lords will be cut from twenty-six to twelve, while members of the revised body will no longer have the title 'Lord'. The new name is yet to be decided upon by Parliament, though powers for both Houses will remain unchanged.[8] 'We have been discussing this issue for a hundred years and it really is time to make progress,' says Cameron on the day the bill is introduced. 'There is a majority in this House for a mainly elected House of Lords and I believe there's a majority for that in the country. But if those who support Lords reform don't get out there and back it, it won't happen.'[9]

Conservative backbenchers became worried long before the bill is introduced. Their concerns now crystallise in an article in the *Observer* the weekend after publication of the bill, written by Tory MP Jesse Norman, a loyalist with a record of supporting Cameron. Norman is a traditionalist who is writing a book on Edmund Burke, the eighteenth-century conservative philosopher who argued for preserving tradition. Norman describes the bill as a 'hopeless mess ... confused, inaccurate, self-contradictory and disingenuous ... it would be a catastrophe for our country'.[10] The expense is not the least of his concerns: he writes that the new senate would cost three to four times more than the current Lords. He further dislikes the ninety appointed senators who he says will be anomalous with the elected principle, and he does not favour the regional nature of the franchise. The bill, he concludes, 'will prevent real reform'.[11]

Recriminations soon begin over who was responsible for the problems the bill encounters. Clegg is the prime culprit, according to the Conservatives. If only he had been willing to listen to concerns from us, they allege, a set of proposals could have been produced that would have passed through the Commons; 'it was a failure to prepare the ground,' agrees one official. 'If you're serious about this,' Conservative Leader of the House of Lords Strathclyde had said to Clegg, 'you will get it through, but only if you build a rapport with Labour and do it on the second reading and in committee.' Strathclyde sees correctly that the divisions are not between the political parties but within them and therefore wide support will be necessary across all parties.[12] Despite Lib Dem feelings to the contrary, Cameron is still 'broadly in favour of the proposals'. As one senior official puts it, 'after all, the current conversation with the House of Lords could be quite hard to defend'. However, the Lib Dems fail to see this and believe that pressure is required. 'They were only going through the motions,' says Julian Astle, senior aide to Clegg. 'That was why we needed him to call it a "first term" priority and we thought he would only do that if we raised the stakes.'[13] Some truth lies on both sides: Clegg hadn't wanted to compromise on the purity of the Lib Dem 'full monty' proposals because it would have looked like weakness; and Cameron, ever wary of his own backbenchers, had indeed been trying to fudge it. Insiders say that 'it was a hell of a problem to get the PM and chancellor to focus on it – an absolute nightmare'. Both men had suspected that they would face a massive defeat on it and wanted to delay it until the party came back into line. But that was not happening. In February 2012, 101 Tory MPs had written to Cameron criticising the subsidies paid to the onshore wind turbine industry; in March, MEP Roger Helmer defected to UKIP; in April the Budget was being unpicked; while in May, 405 Tory councillors lost their seats.

When in trouble, Cameron's strategy is often to kick problems as far as he can into touch. By the time he can delay it no longer and the bill is published, he has become unclear what exactly he is trying to achieve. That lack of clarity transmits itself to the party. He sends out mixed messages on how important the bill is to him. Chief Whip McLoughlin is finding his job almost impossible and in Parliament 'People kept asking, "Prime Minister, do you care about the House of Lords reform?" and he kept changing his mind.'

Cameron has a torrid couple of weeks after the bill has its first reading in the Commons. Many Conservative MPs are impressed with Jesse Norman's argument that a finely tuned constitution would be unbalanced if an elected House of Lords challenged the Commons for authority. Obama's problems in Congress are fresh in everyone's minds, and a picture is painted of a US-style gridlock between both chambers, which would be resolved not by democratic representatives, but by lawyers and judges. Some civil servants have their own concerns about the bill too. 'We worried about the way that 800 years of House of Lords procedure was about to be trashed,' says one.

By 6 July, the Tory rebellion is spreading and is thought by the whips to be 'up to 100': only fifty will be needed to defeat the bill entirely, if Labour oppose it.[14] Mark Harper, Minister for Political and Constitutional Reform, is running the operation to pull support together. 'I would disagree with the contention that it is a Lib Dem bill,' he says, and he works hard to remind Conservative MPs that it has been party policy for the previous thirteen years.[15] Big beasts like

William Hague are brought in to win over the rebels. Lib Dems complain of reports they receive that 'Hague is approaching rebels with a twinkle in his eye and says he needs to speak to them about Lords reform. He pauses and then adds: "There we are. I've spoken to you about Lords reform."'[16] Even Cameron is reported to be nodding and winking to backbench opponents in private saying, 'I know none of us want this.'

On 7 July, nine former Cabinet ministers including Geoffrey Howe and Norman Lamont attack the proposal in a letter sent to MPs, urging them to defy Cameron and defeat the measure. The Lords, they argue, is 'a vast reservoir of talent and experience, which complements the more youthful and vigorous House of Commons, without ever being able to threaten it'.[17] On 9 July, Clegg argues passionately in the Commons in favour of his reforms. His reception is hostile, with Labour and Tory MPs trying to drown him out. The Lib Dems are furious that Cameron is not present (reports circulate that he is visiting the Farnborough Air Show).[18] 'We all knew it was important that the PM signalled his support for the bill,' says Jonny Oates. 'Mark Harper asked him to be on the front bench for the debate and we reinforced the request. When he failed to make himself available, that was the moment we knew that the PM did not intend to make any real effort to get the bill through.'[19] Tory rebels publish their own letter that day expressing 'serious concern' about the reforms.[20]

On 10 July, at 4.39 p.m., Leader of the Commons George Young announces the withdrawal of the timetable for the bill.[21] This notionally gives Cameron more time to bring recalcitrant Tory MPs onside. Lengthening the process also removes one of Ed Miliband's objections – too little time to debate such a substantial bill. That evening at 10 p.m., the vote on the second reading passes the Commons by 462 to 124. Ninety-one Conservatives vote against a three-line whip: it is the biggest rebellion of a second reading of a bill in the parliament (though 134 vote against Cameron's wishes on a free vote on gay marriage in February 2013, and 114 vote against the omission of a referendum bill from the 2013 Queen's Speech). But denying the bill a timetable effectively kills it off for good.

Cameron has been at his weakest in his handling of this bill, blowing one way, then the other. But the realisation that its effective defeat will bring him serious problems is beginning to sink in. Cameron is still reeling at what he believes was an attempt by Jesse Norman to deliberately misrepresent his position on the Lords. He confronts Norman in the Commons shortly after the vote, pointing at him in 'a very aggressive manner'. Norman is visibly 'taken aback' by the vehemence of Cameron's reaction to him.[22] Cameron and Number 10 know they are running into an unholy mess. They accept that many Tory MPs share Norman's concern, but think others are using it as a stick with which to hit Cameron, or the despised Lib Dems, or both.

It is more than humiliation and fatigue that is embittering Number 10. The Lib Dems have chosen to push the nuclear button. Clegg has met several times with his advisers. His line is, 'The only way we're going to get the Conservative Party to deliver on their commitment in the Coalition Agreement is to warn them about the consequences of not delivering.' He requests a meeting with Cameron. 'If you do not deliver on the Lords, we will not deliver on the boundary changes.' To underline the message, Astle searches out Llewellyn and says, 'Ed, does every Conservative backbencher understand that if you don't vote through the House of Lords reform, they'll lose boundaries, and may well lose the general election if it's that close?' 'Yeah, yeah, we've told them,' Llewellyn replies. 'Tell Jesse Norman and the 1922 Committee that you understand how deeply concerned they are,' Astle advises, 'but the fact is that the Conservative Party has promised to do it, and do it they will.' As the Lib Dems have warned Cameron of the consequences, they regard their reciprocal withdrawal of support on boundary reform not as vengeful, but as 'self-harm' the Conservatives inflict upon themselves.

Conservative MPs will not budge, and for good reason. The Coalition Agreement does not explicitly link the two issues. 'There was no sense that the boundary changes were a quid pro quo,' says one senior civil servant. In fact, the Agreement states that boundary reform is linked to the *AV referendum*. Cameron makes it clear to Clegg he cannot guarantee his party's support. Neither are Labour willing to support the bill, on what the Lib Dems think are spurious grounds. Clegg has had enough of the farce. On 6 August, he seizes the initiative. Those who have been opposing the bill, he says, wish to inflict a 'slow death' on it, which will take up 'unacceptable' amounts of parliamentary time. He cannot allow this to happen, so is withdrawing it. Cameron sees his statement before it is made, but Clegg is in no mood to modify it.[23] 'The Conservative Party is not honouring the commitment to Lords reform and, as a result, part of our contract has now been broken,' Clegg says. 'A coalition works on mutual respect; it is a reciprocal arrangement, a two-way street. So I have told the prime minister that when, in due course, Parliament votes on boundary changes for the 2015 election, I will be instructing my party to oppose them.'[24] On 3 September, Clegg announces to the House of Commons that the Lords bill is to be withdrawn altogether.

'Boundary reform was the most important single thing we needed to get from this parliament from a party political point of view,' says Liam Fox, 'and we failed to get it.' His views echo those of many fellow MPs.[25] To Cameron sceptics amongst MPs, boundary reform was one of the very few bits of the Coalition Agreement that they liked: 'We will bring forward a [bill] … for the creation of fewer and more equal-sized constituencies,' the Coalition Agreement had stated.[26] Few could dispute the democratic case for change. The proposals envisaged all constituencies being within 5% of the optimum number of 76,641, excepting the four island seats. Mainland constituencies currently vary in size from 41,000 to 91,000, approximately. Stephen Gilbert had been tasked to oversee the boundary changes and to work with every Tory MP. There would be only 600 MPs in the new House of Commons (as opposed to 650): he estimated that at the 2010 general election, had the proposed adjustments from the boundary commission been in place, the Conservatives would have won between 301 and 306 seats, a greater proportion than they actually achieved in 2010. Whatever the merits, Labour was never going to like the proposals on pragmatic grounds, because the status quo benefited them, with their votes much more efficiently spread across constituencies.

Conservative anger against Cameron and Clegg is real. Many believe that the Coalition Agreement had pledged the Lib Dems to supporting boundary changes in return for the AV referendum, regardless of House of Lords reform. 'Of course there was a bloody link!' says Clegg. 'You can't just say "we're not going to deliver House of Lords reform" and expect the Lib Dems to dutifully march through the lobbies for them on boundaries. It's absurd. A deal's a deal. It obviously upset David very much. He got very angry about it.'[27] The Lib Dems become deeply indignant with the Conservatives. 'The Coalition Agreement, much like a legally binding document, can't be overstated to us. We were in government to implement the whole thing. It's not an *à la carte* menu from which the Tories can pick and choose what they like.'[28] The Lib Dems think they have walked through fire for the sake of the coalition, supporting the Conservatives on the cuts and, most painfully, on tuition fees. Their support for the government on a whole range of policies has caused them grief from their members and supporters.

At the very heart of the coalition is a fundamental disequilibrium which neither party ever fully acknowledges. The Lib Dems hadn't seriously expected to be in power after the general election, and need to prove their ability to be responsible partners in government. Conservative MPs had been very much expecting to win, and many blame Cameron for their failure to do so. They never totally accept the Lib Dems and thus do not regard their demands as remotely legitimate. 'Some Conservative MPs think they can pick only what they like,' says Oates. 'We were never going to allow that: it isn't how a coalition operates.'[29] 'We're not supposed to cause trouble,' adds Lena Pietsch, Lib Dem deputy director of communications in Downing Street. 'We're not supposed to answer back. We had to constantly remind Conservatives they wouldn't be in power without us.'[30]

Throughout the autumn of 2012, Number 10 and many MPs continue to believe that the Lib Dems have 'pulled a fast one' on them and argue that boundary reform was linked to AV, never to the House of Lords. They come out in public and allege that the Lib Dems were never sincere about backing boundary reform, because it could damage them heavily at the 2015 election as some Lib Dem MPs would lose the benefit of incumbency. 'Failure to get House of Lords reform through was just the pretext for not supporting boundaries,' Feldman and many others believe.[31] Is there some truth in this claim? The answer is yes. After failing on AV and Lords reform, boundary changes are simply no longer possible for the Lib Dems, even though legislation has been passed to enact them. 'If we have the boundary changes, we will lose so many seats. If that happens, they'll get rid of me as leader of the party,' Clegg himself admits. 'They would then have to work with another leader, so the whole thing is impossible.' Clegg's aides confirm that he would not have survived if he had whipped his MPs into delivering harmful boundary changes, having failed to deliver both AV and House of Lords reform for the party. 'The idea that Nick could whip his party into voting for all the blue bits once the yellow bits had got nowhere was an impossibility,' says an aide. Some Conservatives, like Jesse Norman, believe the Lib Dems were never going to agree to boundary reform regardless of AV or Lords reform, while others, like Michael Gove, think that they might have supported it; either way, it is unknowable.

The parliamentary vote on boundary reform is held on 29 January 2013. The result is long expected: MPs vote by 334 to 292 to delay reform to 2018 at the earliest. Last-minute attempts are made by the Tories to persuade the Democratic Unionists, the SNP and Plaid Cymru to support them, but the will simply isn't there. The Conservatives are outvoted. The breakdown in coalition relations in the Lords, where Lib Dem peers amended the legislation, had precipitated Strathclyde's decision to resign on 7 January. The vote is the first time Lib Dem ministers vote against their Conservative colleagues in the Commons. Earlier that month, debate had taken place inside Number 10 about the Conservatives offering their own nuclear retaliation, withdrawing from the coalition unless Lib Dem MPs support the boundary changes. They know that the Lib Dems will be hammered if it precipitates a general election. Llewellyn, the 'ultimate protector of the coalition', as insiders describe him, will not hear of it, and neither will Cameron. But the fact that some in Cameron's court are considering ending the coalition early only shows how very jaundiced relations have become.

An angry exchange takes place between Cameron and Clegg in Number 10. Cameron makes it clear he feels very let down by Clegg. After the meeting, insiders say they have never heard him speak so critically of the DPM. Both men feel the other has gone against private understandings. Even though Cameron knew the defeat was coming, the result is still a rude shock. He is in a bad place. Conservative MPs begin saying: 'You told us it was essential to have boundary changes to win the general election. We don't have them. What now?' One insider believes that 'Many thought it was the last straw in the relationship with the Lib Dems'. To Hague it is the worst coalition crisis of the five years.[32] Officials think the same. It is the only time that Jeremy Heywood, in his capacity as Cabinet Secretary, takes out the official papers to examine how a minority government might operate, holding several meetings in his room in the Cabinet Office to explore the options. Some officials are very surprised that the Lib Dems have gone ahead with their threat on boundaries.

Ironically, experiencing the depths of the descent from the Rose Garden harmony helps make the principals come to their senses. Powerful forces may be pulling the coalition apart, principally Conservative MPs and Lib Dem purists, but at the centre, the forces are centripetal. For all their anger and critical words about each other in the privacy of their enclaves, Clegg and Cameron retain a respect for each other which goes far beyond mutual survival. They come from the same world, are both rational and logical, and don't let emotion overcome them. Civil servants watching them together are apt to think of the mafia expression: 'differences are strictly business, not personal'. Osborne can be the most impulsive of the four on the Quad, but even he retains throughout a close relationship with Danny Alexander, arguably the most pragmatic. These four alone hold everything together in these terrible months.

Clegg at heart also knows how much he needs the coalition. No sooner has Chris Huhne departed than another rival for the leadership strolls into the limelight: Vince Cable. Clegg's staff become obsessed during 2012 with the Business Secretary. 'Vince was on manoeuvres with Plan A not working,' says a Cameron aide. And yet, the common enemy of Cable helps reunite Clegg and Cameron.

Both leaderships need to discover a common narrative. The Conservatives worry that Clegg is being driven towards greater 'differentiation', while the Lib Dem leadership worry that Cameron is drifting to the right to buy off UKIP supporters. Within days of the Coalition Agreement being signed off in May 2010, Letwin had said to Clegg, 'The time will come when we will need to renew our programme for government.' Clegg is keen and agreed saying 'You have to refuel your tank at some point mid-flight.'[33] 'Our vows will need to be rededicated in the future,' Letwin had written to Cameron shortly afterwards.[34] Embryonic conversations took place in mid-2011 and the early summer of 2012. On 16 July, Cameron and Clegg appear together at a railway depot at Smethwick in the West Midlands. They announce a Midterm Review to be published in the autumn, alongside a £9 billion railway investment programme. In the September 2012 reshuffle, David Laws returns to government as Minister of State at the Department of Education and the Cabinet Office. Laws is a figure who is trusted by the Conservatives. Clegg appoints him leader of the Midterm Review on the Lib Dem side, working with Letwin and the Number 10 Policy Unit. Aside from discussions on Budgets and Autumn Statements, Laws and Letwin now often attend meetings of the Quad.

The work begins in earnest before the party conferences. The review will be both a celebration of what has already happened as well as a statement of collective intent for the remaining two and a half years. The coalition partners are delighted to discover that over 80% of what had been laid out in the Coalition Agreement has either been enacted or is in train. This is widely briefed out to show, not least to both parties in it, that the coalition government has had significant policy successes. Alighting on common policies for the future is more problematic. The Conservatives want further welfare reform. Clegg puts his foot down. He made a video in September 2012 apologising for student loans: if Cameron will make a similar apology for his broken promise to pensioners, Clegg says he will agree to include welfare. Now it is Cameron who refuses to budge. A way through the deadlock is found, and they agree on long-term care, a new single-tier pension regime, and more spending on roads. The review talks help heal divisions between both parties. The package is agreed finally at an away day at Chequers in December 2012. Cameron's team push the launch date back to January 2013 because they want to show they have impetus going into the New Year, and to finally draw a line under the *annus horribilis*, an overused phrase but one the leadership feels aptly describes 2012. The cap on the cost of social care is agreed in a conference call between Cameron, Clegg and their staff on New Year's Day.

Cameron and Clegg launch *The Coalition: Together in the National Interest* on 7 January. The fifty-page document contains a scorecard of what the coalition had pledged in the initial agreement, what it has achieved, and what it plans to do. 'We are dealing with the deficit, rebuilding the economy, reforming welfare and education, and supporting hard-working families through tough times,' the introduction says. 'On all of these key aims, our parties, after thirty-two months of coalition, remain steadfast and united.'[35]

Cameron feels a new confidence this January. It isn't only the unanimity around the Midterm Review: he also has a cunning plan to neutralise his European problem and with it, he hopes, to swat UKIP. But he is still very far from out of the woods. The final four months of 2012 have been especially testing on him politically and personally. Even those closest to him are struck by his inner reserves of optimism and strength, and how much he draws on Samantha as his rock.

TWENTY

Halfway Point: Autumn Blues

September–December 2012

It is the autumn of 2012, the midterm point in the parliament. Cameron is just weeks away from being challenged as party leader if he doesn't turn a corner. For six months or more he has faced problem after problem. The economy is showing no signs of improvement, nor are the opinion polls, and his flagship domestic policies in health, welfare and education are coming under intensive fire. He desperately needs a successful reshuffle to rejuvenate the government and to give the speech of his life at the party conference.

The reshuffle on 4 September goes down well. Optimism grows in Number 10. But just fifteen days later Andrew Mitchell, whose promotion to chief whip is one of the centrepieces, finds himself in the middle of an explosive and toxic fracas. On the evening of 19 September, he leaves his office in 9 Downing Street, jumps on his bicycle and rides up to the main gates leading onto Whitehall. In spite of usually cycling through the main gates, he is directed by the policeman to the pedestrian gate. As he does so, Mitchell utters some of the most contested words in the entire five years of the government. According to leaked police logs, later apparently backed up by an eyewitness account, he called the police 'plebs'. This was political dynamite. The next morning the *Sun* reported the exchange. What was so damaging was that the words fitted into the narrative of a patrician government treating working people in a patronising and offensive way. Mitchell later apologises, arguing that he said 'I thought you guys were supposed to fucking help us,' but adamantly denying that he used the emotive word 'plebs'.[1] However, in a libel trial in November 2014, Mr Justice Mitting ruled that he was satisfied that 'at least on the balance of probabilities ... Mr Mitchell did speak the words alleged, or at least something so close to them as to amount to the same, including the politically toxic word pleb'.[2]

Cameron is furious when he hears about the episode. Number 10 have already become frustrated with Mitchell. They are very happy with the job he did as International Development Secretary in championing the 0.7% of national income for aid, a cause close to the prime minister's heart. But now that they are working up close and personal with him as chief whip, they find him restive. He speedily brings greater operational and political clarity to the Whips' Office, and a regimental sense of order, but ruffles many feathers in doing so.

The episode has been filmed on security cameras. Ed Llewellyn, Chris Martin and Oliver Dowden go downstairs in Number 10 to view all the tapes, which unfortunately do not have recorded sound. But after many viewings they cannot tell what Mitchell said, let alone what actually happened. Mitchell is summoned to Downing Street. The prime minister decides he will have to adjudicate personally. He wants to believe Mitchell's account of what happened, but equally he wants to be seen to be supporting the police. For four and a half weeks, Cameron stands by his man, even while the pressure mounts. Cameron's team do not imagine for one moment that there could have been a police conspiracy, but they simply don't understand why the police's version of events does not reconcile with Mitchell's explanation. It is a puzzle. Cameron is later stunned when he watches a Channel 4 programme presented by the veteran political reporter Michael Crick which calls into serious doubt the evidence provided by the police. Over the next two years, at least four police officers are sacked for misconduct and one imprisoned.

From 25–28 September, Cameron is in New York addressing the UN General Assembly, before travelling to São Paolo, Brasilia and Rio de Janeiro. The noise from 'Plebgate', as it comes to be known, is growing. Cameron just wants to focus on his conference speech. On Sunday 30 September, he invites Boris Johnson, who has been separately ruffling feathers, to Chequers. Number 10 are irritated that Boris has weighed into Plebgate on the side of the police, saying it would have been 'wholly commonsensical' to arrest Mitchell for his behaviour.[3] Johnson has also accused Cameron of preparing the ground for a U-turn on a third runway at Heathrow, which would kill off 'Boris Island', and has claimed an 'in/out' referendum on EU membership is unnecessary.[4] Boris is slated to make two speeches at the conference in Birmingham. Number 10 believe he is 'on manoeuvres' against their man.[5] So they release a statement from Cameron to say that 'Boris has been a great friend of mine for a long time and a first-class mayor of London.' Johnson assures Cameron there is no cause for alarm. Whereas Cameron is apt to believe him, George Osborne is more sceptical.[6] This is not what either need.

While Miliband is rallying the troops at Labour's conference in Manchester, Cameron is working from Chequers. Over dinner, and several glasses of wine with three of his Number 10 aides – Andrew Cooper, Ameet Gill and speechwriter Clare Foges – Cameron asks 'Do you think that Mitchell uttered the word "pleb"?' Cooper doesn't think he did, though agrees that 'it smells a bit fishy: you get the sense it's not the first time that he's been cocky with them'. Cameron replies, 'I just don't believe he said it. He looked me in the eye, and I cannot believe he said those words. Something here is not adding up.'

Mitchell's position had come under greater threat when an email was sent to the Whips' Office on 20 September, allegedly from a bystander outside the gates of Downing Street. 'Imagine to [sic] our horror when we heard MR MITCHELL shout very loudly at the police officers guarding "YOU _____ PLEBES!!" [sic] and "YOU THINK YOU RUN THE _____ COUNTRY" and just continued to shout obscenities at the poor police officers. My nephew, as was I, totally taken aback by his, [sic] MR MITCHELLS' [sic] behaviour and the gutter language he used, especially it [sic] appeared directed at the police officers.'[7] Cameron had been resisting holding an inquiry, but the pressure has by now become too great, and he directs Jeremy Heywood to investigate the matter swiftly. The Cabinet Secretary concludes the evidence is not clear and certainly not compelling enough to justify forcing the chief whip's resignation. Osborne, who suggested Mitchell for the post, remains his supporter and tells him, 'We will stand behind you. But you have to understand that if you have lied, the world will come down on you.'[8]

Matthew Hancock offers a sober view of the government's plight. 'After the omnishambles Budget, we knew we had to have a plan to get back on track.' It consists of two parts: 'First, get things stabilised for the party conference and ensure no screw-ups there. Second, have a very good 2012 Autumn Statement.'⁹ Pulling off these aims is still very much in the balance. Pressure mounts on Cameron's speech. Clare Foges normally starts thinking in June/July about what he might say in his conference speech, has a session with the team in late July, mulls it over in August and goes flat out on it in September. This year it is different: Craig Oliver and Andrew Cooper have been cooking up themes since April. They recognise that Cameron's strategy post-Hilton is in a listless state and they need to help the PM find clarity. His party conference speech goes through twenty-eight drafts (although by draft four, in June, the main items had been established).

The question Cameron's team keep asking is 'What is our unifying idea?' Cameron is innately suspicious of talk of vision per se. More pressing is the need to find a recognisable argument, connecting the government's reforms despite the climate of austerity. At a political Cabinet before full Cabinet in June, Cameron invites every minister to elucidate an overarching argument. After a lengthy discussion, William Hague comes out with 'We are in a global race, and we will fail unless we become more competitive.' Ministers nod their heads wisely, a good sign because Cabinet buy-in during this volatile period is essential. 'We needed something that would lift our agenda beyond merely sorting out the mess Labour had left behind and that didn't just define everything through the lens of cuts. We needed something positive and forward-looking, and the idea of the global race was key to providing it,' says Cooper.¹⁰ 'Frankly, I should have started "global race" when we came into government: the importance of promoting British exports and British economic power abroad gave us a very simple and clear message for my speech in 2012,' admits Cameron.¹¹ 'Aspiration' becomes Cameron's other key message, via Cooper's polling. He and Oliver wanted to find a theme true to Cameron that had popular appeal. Research finds that even though most voters don't use the word 'aspiration', the great majority know what it means, and it resonates with them. The research also shows that the Conservatives need to articulate more forcefully that they are on the side of those 'who work hard and want to get on' and that they, not the bankers and benefit scroungers, are the real contributors to the economy and the country.

What links both themes is the idea that aspiration will unleash the potential of everyone in Britain, allowing the country to compete better in the global race. These two themes become the organising concept of the government, at least until Lynton Crosby further narrows them down for the 2013 conference. 'It is very noticeable that the Big Society is there no longer,' says one of Cameron's team. Cameron is one of a very small group to mourn the passing of Hilton and his agenda. Oliver and Dowden feel a hum of contentment that they have rationalised the Cameron project around an agenda over which they feel much more ownership. 'For the first time,' says one insider, 'we had a clear narrative about what we stand for. It makes our life much simpler.' The conference speech is to be the most important of the five Cameron delivers as prime minister, in part because, as Kate Fall says, '2012 was the first party conference speech where he said, "This is me, this is what I believe."'[12]

The speech has several writers. Steve Hilton makes a brief return from California to help. Padding around shoeless in the PM's suite on the twenty-second floor of the Hyatt Regency in Birmingham, he writes the slightly patronising section in the speech where Cameron lectures Miliband about taxes. 'Ed … let me explain to you how it works. When people earn money, it's their money. Not the government's: their money. Then, the government takes some of it away in tax. So, if we cut taxes, we're not giving them money – we are taking less of it away. OK?' Danny Finkelstein sees the speech very late in the day and says, 'We need a stark reminder about how bad it was.' The beginning of the speech runs: 'In May 2010 … We were entering into government at a grave moment in the modern history of Britain. At a time when people felt uncertainty, even fear. Here was the challenge. To make an insolvent nation solvent again. To set our country back on the path to prosperity that all can share in. To bring home our troops from danger while keeping our citizens safe from terror. To mend a broken society.' The section concludes: 'Two and a half years later of course I can't tell you that all is well, but I can say this: Britain is on the right track.'

When the draft is finished, it is seen again by a very narrow group of Cameron, Gove and Hilton. Hilton is 'wonderfully fussy' and looks at every single word. Gove is 'very good at the funny bits', and adds humorous flashes. It is the best-written of his conference speeches as PM, with solid meat, if not new policy, on welfare, education and security. He tackles head on the 'posh' criticism: 'I'm not here to defend privilege. I'm here to spread it.' He had been persuaded to be personal about himself, to combat the charge he has no hinterland, and had thought hard about this point over the summer. What he says comes from deep inside him. His father was born 'with no heels on his feet', but showed the resolve to succeed in life: 'the glass was always half full – usually with something alcoholic in it'. He wants to allude to the Olympics, and had a flash of inspiration in the summer, linking the Paralympics to his son Ivan, who died in 2009. So he talks about his hopes that the Paralympic Games will change society's attitude to disability. 'When I used to push my son Ivan around in his wheelchair, I always thought some people saw the wheelchair, not the boy. Today, more would see the boy – and that's because of what happened here this summer.' Andrew Feldman takes some credit for persuading him to open up. 'I'm always telling him to bring out his inner Semite,' he says, referring to Cameron's Jewish ancestry (Cameron's great-great-grandfather was the Jewish financier Emile Levita), which Feldman thinks explains Cameron's inner warmth.[13]

The speech comes together in the last few hours, the themes of global race and aspiration chime in the Birmingham Symphony Hall and outside. Cameron is far happier with the reception than he received the year before. As soon as he can get away, he goes up in the lift with Samantha and Liz Sugg to his room where drinks are laid out for his team. Cameron has succeeded in the first of Hancock's two prerequisites. 'Terrific performance. Bloody good speech' is the verdict of Quentin Letts in the *Daily Mail*.[14] After a difficult few months following the health bill, omnishambles Budget and Lords reform, there is relief among the party that a sense of direction has been restored at the top. Wounds are by no means healed, but the conference speech goes some way to restoring confidence in Cameron's leadership. He now needs to get the Autumn Statement right.

Before it, however, Plebgate returns for one final death throe. Mitchell was advised to keep away from the party conference, but he is not forgotten. Police federation members wearing t-shirts saying 'PC pleb and proud' outside the conference centre provide a stark reminder of the row. On Wednesday 17 October, at the first PMQs after the conference season, Miliband focuses on Mitchell. He cites Boris Johnson's comments at the 2011 party conference, when he demanded that those who swear at the police should be arrested. Mitchell, sitting next to Lansley on the government front bench, says, 'I didn't swear.' Miliband replies, 'He says he didn't. Maybe he'll tell us what he did say. Did the chief whip use those words?' Mitchell looks visibly uncomfortable, but Cameron intervenes, 'The chief whip apologised. That apology has been accepted. What he did and said was wrong.' Miliband senses he is on to a winner: 'Just because the officer had better manners than the chief whip doesn't mean he should keep his job. While it's a night in the cells for the yobs, it's a night in the Carlton Club for the chief whip.' But Miliband then squanders his initiative when he broadens out the attack to the economy, which is blunted by better employment figures released that day, opening the way for Cameron to respond with the jibe: 'He comes to this House. He's written out his clever questions, he doesn't really care what's happening in our economy.' Mitchell himself survives the session and that evening he meets the officers of the 1922 Committee.

After PMQs, Cameron asks to see John Randall, the deputy chief whip who has been threatening to resign if Mitchell does not go. Later, at the 1922 Committee, seven or eight speak in Mitchell's favour, but five MPs speak out decisively against him, including Sarah Wollaston, the GP elected as a candidate in the 2010 election via an open primary. The following morning, Mitchell realises he is losing the support of most of the party. The mood in Number 10 is also turning against him, following a number of phone calls from those eyeing up promotion. Mitchell's supporters feel that Number 10 is not standing behind the chief whip: 'spineless, cynical, serpentine' is how one described Downing Street's response. That evening, with pressure from Number 10 mounting on him to resign, he decides that he must go. On Thursday evening, Mitchell arranges with Cameron's office to meet the PM at Chequers at 4 p.m. on Friday 19 October as soon as Cameron returns from the EU Council, to hand in his resignation.[15] He spends two hours at Chequers and at 6 p.m. a statement announcing his resignation is released. The collapse of confidence in Mitchell by the parliamentary party proved fatal. Cameron had come under great pressure for him to go, not least from Iain Duncan Smith, who never forgave Mitchell for plotting against him as party leader in 2003. A ComRes poll published that weekend suggests that Labour's lead over the Tories has increased by four points since September, with Labour on 41% to the Conservatives 33%.[16] Cameron swiftly appoints the reliable Sir George Young as Mitchell's successor as chief whip. Cameron tells him that upcoming difficulties include gay marriage, renewable energy and Europe. With Osborne caught in a first-class train carriage with a standard-class ticket, prompting the allegation that he didn't want to sit with the hoi polloi, it has not been a good week.[17]

The Autumn Statement, to be delivered on 5 December, has become even more critical; Osborne is under tremendous pressure. Demands are rising that he stop being a strategist and regular attendee at Number 10 meetings, because it is distracting him from the job of being chancellor. In the months leading up to the Autumn Statement, pressure to abandon Plan A intensifies, the eurozone looks as if it may fall apart, while a recovery in the British economy remains elusive. Inflation peaks at 5.2%, and the continuing financial crisis, with its impact on credit, means there is insufficient growth to provide the expected tax yields. However, solid support from the IMF, as well as the OECD, offers Osborne some solace. José Ángel Gurría, Secretary General of the OECD, also provides encouragement at the Global Investment Conference in London on 26 July: 'You are now sowing the seeds for what will be the elements for recovery.' He urges Osborne to stick by his austerity programme.[18]

Intense conversations take place in the Treasury during the summer. It is becoming increasingly evident that the government is falling behind meeting its financial targets outlined in 2010. Some officials are keen to move on to Plan B, with a greater emphasis on policies to stimulate growth, echoing the debate among leading economists in the country. Debate intensifies over the following weeks. Some Lib Dems become very jumpy. Letwin believes it is 'the moment of greatest tension within the coalition over the whole five years'.[19] Osborne's team mobilise voices within the CBI and the Institute of Directors, who are staunchly supportive of his strategy, to speak up in public. The Quad remain solid behind Plan A, as do Nicholas

Macpherson and Jeremy Heywood. 'We were pretty sure even that September that we had got it right and would be vindicated,' says an Osborne aide. Rupert Harrison predicts that in six months the economy will be doing well. Many in Number 10 are reassured by his confidence.

But there is more bad news. On 16 October, a report from the Office of Budget Responsibility comes out which says that 'along with many other forecasters, we seem to have significantly overestimated economic growth over the past two years ... Fiscal consolidation may also have done more to slow growth than we assumed.'[20] The report cranks up pressure in the Treasury even further to ease austerity. 'We will have to chase the numbers if we are to retain credibility,' Treasury officials are telling Danny Alexander.[21] In the final few days before the statement, they decide that rather than cutting further, they will spread the cuts out over a longer period, making the critical calculation that doing so will retain credibility with the markets and keep interest rates low. Osborne duly announces on 5 December that the official target of having debt falling as a percentage of GDP by 2015–16 will be delayed by one year. Osborne additionally cancels a planned rise in fuel duty, increases personal allowances further to help those on low incomes, and again cuts corporation tax to spur job growth.

The 2012 Autumn Statement is a high-wire act. Using the windfall benefits from the 4G mobile auction, as well as £5 billion that he hopes to repatriate from Switzerland through an agreement on tax avoidance, he produces the money to finance a fuel duty freeze, the personal allowance change and the corporation tax cut. Osborne also cunningly manages to set some elephant traps for Labour. Somehow, with deft political skill and a dollop of luck, Osborne emerges stronger from the Autumn Statement than he had been the day before. 'In years to come politics professors might hold seminars on this resilient character ... who managed to persuade the public that he was doing a reasonably good job', says the *Guardian*.[22] Ed Balls too comes to his rescue. The shadow chancellor rises to his feet full of adrenaline to pummel Osborne. He will outline 'the true scale of this government's economic failure'. The beginning is promising: 'Our economy is contracting. The chancellor has confirmed that government borrowing has revised up this year, next year and every year.' But then he makes a terrible slip: 'The national deficit is not rising ...' before correcting himself '... err, is rising, not falling.' The correction comes too late and Balls fails to recover his momentum. He is drowned out by gleeful jeers from the Conservative side of the House. Osborne has a lucky escape – for time being. Missing the debt target is probably going to consign Britain's AAA rating to history within a few months. By softening the edges of Plan A, the chancellor has bought some respite, but both he and Cameron know they are still very far from in the clear.

TWENTY-ONE

Cameron Pledges
a Referendum

April 2012–February 2013

On 23 January 2013, David Cameron delivers a speech on the European Union at the Bloomberg offices in London. His Private Office reckon it is the most significant foreign policy speech of his five years in power. Janan Ganesh of the *Financial Times* later calls it 'the most important speech by a British prime minister since Tony Blair's case for war in Iraq'.[1]

It is not a speech Cameron had wanted to make. He had entered 2012 on the back of his EU veto, still hoping Europe would be no more than a marginal distraction in his premiership. But pressure has piled up on him from all sides to make some kind of defining statement of his thinking. Cabinet ministers have become impatient with the EU once they grapple with the reality of its impact on their departments, and the Conservative Party has become more Eurosceptic by the month. Even Cameron feels angry that the advice he received before the election – that there would be no major treaty change in the next five years – has turned out to be wrong. Spurred on by the eurozone crisis, the EU has an ever greater appetite for stronger powers at the centre. The Lisbon Treaty, over which Cameron declined to hold a 'promised' referendum, turns out to have been more federalist than he had feared. The result, as Matthew d'Ancona puts it, is that 'it has become increasingly clear to many ministers that if Britain is to remain a member of the EU, significant powers must be repatriated'.[2]

Within Number 10, Cameron's aides have been on a long journey since he came to power in May 2010. As Major's team found in the 1990s, the EU arouses deep feelings among Tory MPs that cannot be contained. Both Cameron and Osborne are profoundly irritated by their Eurosceptic MPs, but Osborne is even more pragmatic than Cameron. 'George worried whether it was sensible politics to talk about disengaging from major international institutions in the twenty-first century,' says one close to them. 'He was worried not only about the effect on the party but also the reaction of the business community leading up to any referendum.' Osborne's eye is on a further horizon than Cameron's: his own leadership succession. Business opinion weighs heavily on him, and he 'is loath to make the Conservative Party appear the riskier proposition to business than Labour'. Cameron, however, is more willing to engage with the Eurosceptics and see if he can accommodate them. He relies particularly on Ed Llewellyn over Europe. His chief of staff is at his most influential on this topic. Llewellyn has deep contacts in the Foreign Office, on the EU ambassador network, and with Foreign Secretary William Hague, who is himself at the pragmatic end of Eurosceptic opinion. Llewellyn is bringing Cameron round to realise that a reformed EU, with Britain playing its part within it, is a serious possibility. Cameron must always heed Nick Clegg, who is not keen on a referendum. The 'referendum lock' policy in the Coalition Agreement is crystal clear, as Clegg reminds Cameron regularly: a referendum would only be triggered if new powers are to be transferred to Brussels.[3] It would be strategically disastrous for Cameron to agree to a pre-emptive referendum, as it would force him into a position where he was either in the 'yes' or 'no' camp.

By spring 2012, the pressure for Cameron to commit to a referendum is becoming virtually unstoppable. Hague was the first to argue for it: even in Opposition he'd said that it was inevitable that one would have to be held before long. Initially reluctant, Osborne is coming round to see the case. The longer Cameron delays an announcement, the more it will appear that he is being bounced into one, and he will lose all advantage. There are particular fears about the 2014 European elections, with the likelihood growing that the party will poll less than UKIP (as indeed proves to be the case). The time has come for a decision. The improbable location of a pizza restaurant at Chicago's O'Hare airport is the location. It is 21 May and on their return from a NATO summit, Cameron sits down with Hague and Llewellyn to talk. Before going to the country Cameron and his senior ministers must first reform relations with EU partners. They agree to offer a referendum in the middle of the next parliament, i.e. before the end of 2017. They discuss a later date, but 2017 is already five years distant; any longer might not seem credible. Their deliberations remain top secret.

On 29 June at the EU Council, Cameron blocks moves to extend the eurozone banking union across the EU, successfully resisting plans to allow a single supervisor to oversee banks.[4] He secures a further agreement that the single market will not be undermined by any new governance arrangements for the eurozone. Number 10 brands the Council 'one of the PM's greatest negotiating triumphs'.[5] At the press conference, Cameron places himself on a collision course with his Eurosceptic MPs when he rejects out of hand an immediate in/out referendum and mounts a passionate defence of Britain's membership of the EU. The outcry is so great that he is bounced into writing an article in the *Sunday Telegraph* on 1 July, in which he drops a heavy hint that a referendum might be needed one day.[6] The article – headed 'We need to be clear about the best way for getting what is best for Britain' – is, in truth, anything but clear. Number 10 has an agonised weekend, besieged by messages from those on both sides of the debate.

A large section of the parliamentary party has lost whatever trust it might once have had in Cameron over Europe. Only their pressure, they believe, will push him into action. On 27 June, backbencher John Baron delivers a letter to Number 10 signed by a hundred MPs calling for legislation to ensure that a referendum on the future of Britain's membership of the EU will be held during the next parliament. It states brazenly that only 'a commitment on the statute book to hold such a referendum would address the very real lack of public trust when people hear politicians making promises'.[7] Cameron's team smart when they read it, knowing that the letter is attacking the PM for abandoning his 'cast-iron guarantee' on Lisbon. Cameron agrees to see Baron on 9 July. He listens to him as politely as he can, before concluding he wants to give himself time before making a response. On 18 September, he writes to Baron to say that 'the EU is currently undergoing radical and fundamental change', he wants 'less Europe not more Europe', but that it would be quite wrong to hold a referendum before exploring fully what concessions and reforms might be negotiated from the EU. Any question of gaining 'fresh consent of the British people' through a referendum should thus be delayed until clarity is reached on new arrangements between Britain and the EU.[8]

Just before the summer recess, a critical meeting had taken place with Cameron, Osborne, Hague and Llewellyn in the PM's office. Osborne still has reservations over holding a referendum. They are now joined in September by Letwin. He and Osborne are at opposite ends of the spectrum, but it is clear that a speech announcing a referendum will have to be made before the end of the year. Cameron's position is desperately weak. He cannot hold out much longer.

Meanwhile, backbenchers are not remotely reassured by Cameron's reply to Baron. Angered by the brush-off, they resolve to bide their time until they can make their feelings known and damage Cameron. They humiliate him in a parliamentary vote on the EU budget at the end of October. Fifty-three Conservative MPs, including the usual suspects – Douglas Carswell, Bill Cash, Bernard Jenkin, Mark Reckless and David Davis – join with Labour to pass an amendment calling for Cameron to impose a real-terms cut in the EU budget between 2014 and 2020.[9] The BBC reports that it is 'the most [significant] defeat since the coalition came to power', and a 'blow to David Cameron's authority'.[10] Number 10 had mounted a massive whipping operation to prevent MPs from voting against the government. Cameron spent an hour with Graham Brady, trying to persuade him to bring his troops into line. Brady himself abstained, but believes the fact that Cameron goes on to secure a budget reduction shows how influential the rebels and critics are. Number 10 is incandescent at the result, finding it 'staggering that the defeat becomes yet another story about the Conservative Party at war with itself'. The lesson they draw is to be very careful about ever bringing another European issue to a vote in Parliament. The seemingly unstoppable rise of UKIP also remains a major concern for Conservative MPs. By the autumn of 2012, UKIP is consistently polling around 10% in opinion polls.

Speechwriting begins in great secrecy in early November. The aim is for Cameron to deliver it at the end of the month, but it is postponed until 18 January the following year because of the EU Council. It is then changed again because of the fiftieth anniversary of the Elysée Treaty which will take place on 22 January, with major celebrations in Berlin and Paris; it is then postponed because of the hostage crisis in Algeria of 16–19 January. Cameron has to remain in London to oversee COBRA meetings and co-ordinate Britain's response. British nationals are among the forty civilians killed when the crisis reaches a bloody conclusion. The morning of 23 January is hurriedly chosen for the speech because it falls between the Elysée celebrations on the 22nd and the start of the four-day World Economic Forum in Davos which Cameron has to travel to later in the day on the 23rd.

Where should he deliver the speech? The location had been the subject of diplomatic angst for several weeks. Brief consideration is given to Berlin and Brussels. But then the team alighted on the Chamber of Commerce in Amsterdam: the Dutch have a similar outlook on the EU to the British, Mark Rutte is very open to reform, and the hall itself has long been associated with free commerce. All was set until the hostage crisis dictated a move to London, and then the Elysée Treaty celebrations which forced a change in the date. A scramble was on to find a venue: Bloomberg's modern office building in the heart of the City of London was available and happy to host.

No speech by Cameron has been more anticipated. Llewellyn, the chief speechwriter, is aware that it has to succeed with three different audiences. Firstly, Eurosceptics in the Tory Party, who need convincing that this will be the first serious attempt since the referendum on membership in 1975 to establish popular consent for the EU. Secondly, the business community: extensive conversations take place with the CBI and groups of business people (which result in a supportive letter to *The Times* on 24 January, the day after the speech). Getting business onside is crucial for the Conservatives politically. Finally, Cameron has to convince key EU leaders that the speech is not just a cynical ploy to help him out of personal difficulties with his party, but a sincere and credible contribution to the European debate. 'He had to develop a narrative on why Britain should stay in the EU,' says one senior official. 'He began thinking through the speech with one thing in mind: "If I am ever to persuade the public of remaining in, how do I convince them?"' Merkel is the key. Without her support, the announcement could be a fiasco.

Wooing Merkel is a major preoccupation on a flight back from the Gulf on 7 November. She is coming to a private dinner in Number 10 that evening. Cameron has an idea: 'Why don't we show her a PowerPoint and give some of it in German?' The team likes the idea: it is a way of engaging her and injecting humour and informality. Further conversations take place with the team back in Downing Street. Hurriedly a presentation is cobbled together, including pictures of Cameron and Merkel hugging. The two topics for their discussion are Cameron's impending speech, and the EU budget negotiations which are then in full swing. It is decided that the PowerPoint presentation should stick to the technicalities of the EU budget, before moving onto a more wide-ranging conversation. He greets her at the front door and shows her up to the Pillared Room where they have a drink, and then he shows her through the double doors into the Small Dining Room. They sit opposite each other at the table as she is taken through the presentation partly in German on the screen.

Cameron begins by describing his own Euroscepticism, and how he feels the British public don't give him the benefit of the doubt over Europe. She asks why frustration with the EU has got so high.

He provides two responses: 'First, the single currency was key because it changed everything, and this is exacerbated by the eurozone crisis that Britain is watching from the margins. You are in the midst of a huge existential crisis which we are not part of.' He tells her that the single currency has thrust itself forward as the most important European project to the detriment of the member states outside the eurozone. As a consequence, the single market has been neglected. He finishes by asking her: 'What is most important to you – the single market or the single currency?'[11] She looks at him and listens intently to every word, attempting to understand what he is saying. At European Councils, she has a habit of studying her fellow leaders very closely, trying to get inside their heads to decide whether or not they are serious. She is reserving judgement on Cameron. Secondly, he tells her, 'The British people never got a choice to vote on Lisbon. It spread much unhappiness towards the political establishment.'

Interrupting him, she asks whether he wants to stay in the EU.

'Like many in my party, I've supported our membership of the EU all my political life, but I am worried that if I don't get the reform objectives I'm setting out, I won't be able to keep Britain in. I am passionate about the single market, I am passionate about foreign policy co-operation, but if I don't listen to British public opinion, then Britain will depart from Europe. The European project was mis-sold here, so what I want are changes that will make it possible for Britain to stay in.' Aides listening to the conversation have never heard him give a clearer definition of his European politics.

The genie is out of the bottle, she replies, implying that antipathy has been allowed to grow in Britain in a way that she wouldn't have allowed in her own country. Cameron returns to the way the country felt betrayed by the political class over the Lisbon volte-face. She doesn't fully understand: why has the political class betrayed the people?

'I have a problem with my party,' he replies, 'even though elements in the Conservative Party are more pro-Europe than the country, which is even more sceptical.' He insists the problem is deeper than placating his Eurosceptic backbenchers. It goes to 'the very heart of the British understanding of democracy'.[12]

She probes him about sentiment in the business community. Surely some of them are pro-EU, she asks, insisting that both countries can rally round an agenda of greater competition. They clearly strike common ground here.

Cameron goes on: 'But the more I fight for competitiveness in the EU, the more I feel you are leaving me to do it on my own when it is exactly what you want. I find it very frustrating.'

She is staring very hard at him. If Britain leaves the EU, or if it leaves Britain behind, she tells him, Europe will be lost. 'Without you, I don't know what is going to happen.' They then turn to his veto in the EU the previous December. She knows why it made him a fleeting 'hero' in the eyes of the country.

'That was a side benefit, not a deliberate choice,' he responds. He wants her to realise that he had not set out with the veto in mind. 'I came to see you in Berlin to try to get a deal with you.' She tells him that he was too forceful, too certain – making the most of the dis-agreement. He says that is the British style. Other cultures in the EU do things differently, she says, but he replies that to be forceful is very British. Perplexed, she refuses to accept any pride in being controver-sial. She is genuinely fascinated by the way his mind works; but she still doesn't think he's right. Why can't he create more space to retreat and compromise, like her? She tells him about her own statecraft: by asking for less at the beginning, she gives herself more flexibility and keeps her options open. After discussing Israel, Libya, Iran and Greece, they return to the main point. She will try her utmost to keep him on board, she concludes, warning him not to rush into saying 'I'm leaving the ship.'

'No,' says Cameron, 'this is our EU as much as anyone's. Therefore I have to be pushy for our interests; but I don't want Britain to leave.'

It is the frankest conversation they have ever had about Europe. She offers him advice on talking to the northern states, to the Bulgarians and to Poland. They need to understand what he is doing, she insists. If he is seen as just a wrecker, it will be hopeless. He wants to find a way for Britain to stay in. If he goes into the Council and makes it 'Britain vs The Rest' it will become self-fulfilling, she warns starkly.

He becomes defensive at this point. 'I don't accept that we just turn up at the Council to be difficult; we put lots of initiatives on the table,' he replies, listing examples. He returns to his central theme, using his full emotional force with her: 'I need to make a pitch to the country. If there is no acceptable deal, it's not the end of the world; I'll walk away from the EU.'

Now the chancellor draws on her psychological arsenal: as an older woman, she tells him, it is difficult to know whether she regrets him being so decisive, or to admire it. It can be very helpful to have some friends in the room, she says.

He pauses and reminds her of his difficulties in Parliament: 'I lost a vote in Parliament and it was humiliating,' he says, referring to the vote over the EU budget two months earlier.

She is intrigued how the parliamentary system works. What happened to the Conservative MPs who voted against him, she asks.

A senior aide comes in at this point and talks about those Tory MPs who never accepted his leadership and want to destroy him, regardless of the consequences. But the great majority of Conservative MPs are not like that: 'It's just that they're terrified of their constituency associations.'

'I won't break promises that I made on development spending and universal benefits for pensioners, even when so many in my party want me to break them,' Cameron tells her. He wants to take the poison out of the EU issue.

She knows he wants a deal. 'I do get it.' If she can be certain of that, she will try to find a way through for him. She adds that although she will try and help, there are limits to what she can do, given Germany's multilateral relationships in Europe – a caveat remembered more in Berlin than in London.

The dinner is a turning point in Cameron's relationship with Merkel. She has some sympathy for his argument that the Common Market Britain joined in 1973, and voted to remain a part of in the 1975 referendum, was a very different entity from what it had now become. She leaves Number 10 with a much clearer understanding of how the British public might have felt cheated, especially when denied a referendum on Lisbon.

Llewellyn returns to writing the speech soon after the Merkel dinner, spending several weeks on it with John Casson, Cameron's foreign affairs private secretary. Cameron, in parallel, holds a series of talks with Cabinet ministers, including Theresa May, Philip Hammond, Iain Duncan Smith and Ken Clarke, taking them into his confidence to bring them onside. Clarke is the most tricky: 'I am totally against referendums,' he says. He is 'horrified' that Cameron was contemplating holding one. Although in 'resigning mood', he falls short of threatening to resign. Cameron tells him: 'We can't get away without having one. We can have the argument during the referendum itself, and it will allow us to get on with governing.'[13] Clarke is gratified to hear Cameron say the intention is to reform the EU, completing the single market in services, and having more deregulation. Cameron focuses intently on his own party. He knows that the threat of withdrawal is necessary not just to focus minds in Brussels, but to gain credibility with his backbenchers. He spends time talking to Graham Brady, who says he is pleased that his 'suggestions are taken on board', and that it is a speech with which most Conservative Eurosceptics could live.[14]

Cameron then turns his attention to winning over key EU leaders. He holds long conversations with Frederik Reinfeldt of Sweden, Mark Rutte of Holland, Mario Monti of Italy, and François Hollande of France, who is the most difficult. Merkel's advice is to 'make it a

European argument, and not just an argument about Britain'. The Private Office carefully notes their concerns, and Llewellyn rewrites the speech over Christmas, partly in London and partly in Paris. When he shows it to Cameron in the New Year, Cameron says, 'I want to give it now.' He doesn't want to see the speech again, and is quite detached from it, which is unusual, as he often tinkers with major speeches. But he thinks that Llewellyn has got the core argument right and is happy to trust his judgement. Security around the text is unusually tight because of the fear of leaks, not least by the Foreign Office. Simon Fraser, the acute permanent secretary, comes across the road into Number 10 a few days before delivery to look it over.

Finally, the text is ready. On the morning of 23 January, Cameron speeds across London to the modern Bloomberg building on Finsbury Square, and at 8.10 delivers the speech in front of a video wall. 'Seventy years ago, Europe was being torn apart by its second catastrophic conflict in a generation … And millions dead across the world in the battle for peace and liberty. For us, the European Union is a means to an end – prosperity, stability, the anchor of freedom and democracy both within Europe and beyond her shores – not an end in itself … I never want us to pull up the drawbridge and retreat from the world. I am not a British isolationist. I don't just want a better deal for Britain. I want a better deal for Europe too.' The speech is one of the most pro-EU speeches given by a British prime minister for some time. The next Conservative manifesto, he says, will ask for a mandate to negotiate a new settlement with the EU, and once it has been negotiated, he will give the British people an in/out referendum.

The team are more than usually anxious about how the speech will be received. Having delayed it for so long, the concern is there would be nothing fresh to say, given the extensive trailing of the referendum announcement. 'My worry was that it would be an anti-climax, but it wasn't,' says a senior aide, 'we were very pleased by the way it landed.'[15] Cameron too is delighted: 'It got us ahead of the debate in the country, and the debate in Europe,' he says.[16] Expectation management had been pitch perfect: 'Many of the key parties expected it to be worse than it was,' says one insider.

The speech is so early in the morning because later that day Cameron has PMQs in the Commons. As he enters the chamber, he is cheered to the rafters by his backbenchers. 'The reason that those on the Conservative back benches are cheering is not that they want to vote yes in an in/out referendum; it is because they want to vote no,' booms Ed Miliband. 'Can he name one thing – just one thing – which, if he does not get it, he will recommend leaving the European Union? … Why can he not say unequivocally that he will vote yes in a referendum? Because he is frightened, because of those on the Conservative back benches.'[17] Cameron gives Miliband as good as he gets. 'He needs to go away, get a policy, come back and tell us what it is. In the meantime, our approach is what the British people want. It is right for business, it is right for our economy, and we will fight for it in the years ahead.'[18]

Cameron then flies to Davos, which is useful because he can speak to his fellow EU leaders individually to explain what he is trying to say. The extensive prior lobbying has helped the speech's positive reception in Berlin and across the EU. There is widespread, if not universal, agreement amongst EU leaders that there needs to be a reform agenda, including competition and subsidiarity. To gain wider support, Cameron enlists the support of John Major. He knows that the last Conservative prime minister had been treated very badly by his predecessor, Margaret Thatcher, and that it stung.[19] Attacks from Thatcherites have not prevented Major becoming admired across the party. Cameron had consulted Major before the Bloomberg speech, and Major wants to know how he can help now that it has been delivered. It is arranged that Major should talk about it on 14 February at Chatham House, where he says: 'I don't like referenda in a parliamentary system, but this referendum could heal many old sores and have a cleansing effect on politics … We need a renegotiation, and a referendum endorsement of it. And if that is denied, the clamour for it will only grow.'[20]

After Bloomberg, the EU budget remains unfinished business. The EU had been volatile during 2012, with feelings towards Britain still raw after the December 2011 EU veto, and with uncertainty about what Hollande's succession of Sarkozy in May would mean for France's relationship with Germany, and its impact on the EU. As the focus of interest shifted to whether the Merkel/Hollande relationship would build on the Merkel/Sarkozy partnership, the heat was taken off

Britain. Below the radar, Britain put great focus on securing safe-guards for the City of London, and EU lead diplomat Ivan Rogers spent six months travelling around EU capitals doing his best to nego-tiate a deal by December.

The seven-year budget, known as the Multiannual Financial Framework, became a major focus towards the end of 2012. In November, EU member states are not ready to settle. The budget is a big topic for Merkel and Cameron at their Downing Street dinner on 7 November. Merkel and her European adviser, Nikolaus Meyer-Landrut, are irritated that the Treasury has spoken in public about the real-term freeze of €886 million over seven years which Cameron is hoping to secure. Cameron knows Merkel is cross about it but never-theless decides to present the figures to her.

'Why did you put this number out there?' she exclaims, adding that it left very little room for negotiation. Why does he always do this, she complains; there is no flexibility at all.

'Parliament has the ability to vote down parts of it,' he tells her.

Everyone will go to the barricades, if that is his position, she replies. She tries again to convince him to take a more flexible stance. She then suggests it would be easier for him to veto the whole deal.

Now it is his turn to be direct. 'I'll block it if I have to,' he says, 'but I am not afraid to negotiate, nor for coming back for annual budgets. But I am not blocking it for the sake of blocking it.'

There are twenty-five others in the European Union that she has to get on board, she replies, exasperated now.

He talks to her about Plan A and austerity in the UK, and how the electorate can't understand why the EU is increasing its budget at the very time that they have to face spending cuts in welfare, defence and health.

She is unmoved by his pleas. How can it be that you keep putting yourself up as our opponent and we all hate you and isolate you, she says. Why can't he make any tactical shifts, just as Germany has had to make? She tells him that they have to work together to find a coalition of support. 'There is a chance that we can do this. But it is not a given.' She tells him that if Germany is seen as too closely identified with Britain, then everything will be lost. She worries that Britain is the EU's 'problem child' and asks him to work with her to mitigate this perception. She asks him to talk to the likes of the Dutch and Swedes, and to make more effort with Donald Tusk, the prime minister of Poland. They discuss budget numbers that Cameron thinks he might be able to live with. 'Can you make an effort to reach out to your friends?' she asks.

Cameron decides to capitalise on Hollande's attempt to work with the Italians to block the deal, which is alienating Merkel. At the conclusion of the Council on 8 February, after twenty-six hours of negotiation, Cameron secures a cut of 3.3% (€32 billion) in the seven-year European budget. The pleas of Hollande to relax austerity and increase spending are swept aside. Cameron achieves some of the best headlines on Europe for a British prime minister for many years. The *Daily Telegraph* describes the result as a 'victory' for Cameron, while the *Guardian* calls the deal 'historic'.[21]

Alas, his early successes in 2013 do not herald a new era of harmony with the Conservative Party. Hardened Eurosceptics have little confidence in his Bloomberg pledge on the referendum and pressure him to bring forward legislation for an in/out referendum into the present parliament. They want legislation on a referendum included in the Queen's Speech. Knowing that Clegg will not countenance such a proposition and preferring to have the legislation in the next parliament, Cameron declines. The Conservative MPs nevertheless draft a bill for a referendum by the end of 2017. Number 10 is in a flat spin, uncertain how to react. They hoped Bloomberg would substantially close down Eurosceptic rumbling. Cabinet is divided, and nerves are further rattled when Michael Gove, never totally reliable in the eyes of Number 10, says in public that he might vote to leave the EU in the referendum, suggesting that Number 10 is losing control over Cabinet and that it is open season for Cabinet ministers to express their views on the EU freely.[22] For avowed Eurosceptics like Environment Secretary Owen Paterson, Bloomberg 'was an important step, because it delivered a chance to have a vote, but more importantly for me it provided an opportunity to discuss restoring our trading relationship with the rest of the world and our ability to make our own laws in Parliament'.[23] Here there is consensus with Europhiles like Ken Clarke, who welcomed what was a 'very pro-European speech'. 'From the moment he announced it, all the hard-line Eurosceptics have been putting pressure on him to bring forward subjects like the free movement of people which they know he can't negotiate. Unfortunately, he has made UKIP, though I know David thinks the reverse. Nigel Farage was a fringe player until David Cameron announced a referendum.'[24]

Things get worse when on 7 May 2013 former Chancellor Lord Lawson calls for an exit from the EU in an article in *The Times*. He dismisses any concessions that Cameron might be able to win from Brussels as 'inconsequential'.[25] Eight days later, 114 Conservative MPs vote for an amendment expressing 'regret' that the referendum bill was not in the Queen's Speech.[26] Cameron is on a trip to the US and so is not at the debate, which goes down badly with his party. A private member's bill is introduced by James Wharton, calling for a referendum by 2017. With begrudging senior Conservative support, it passes the Commons by 304 votes to zero after Labour and the Lib Dems abstain, but fails to pass through the Lords, and an attempt to revive it in 2014 is unsuccessful.[27] In November 2013, Conservative MP Adam Afriyie introduces an amendment calling for an EU referendum before the next election. A new poll suggests that around a third of Conservative Party members support an early referendum on the EU.[28] MPs vote against the amendment by 249 to fifteen.

Cameron is confident that he can charm his fellow EU leaders and secure a deal to put before the British electorate. But as 2013 moves into 2014, he becomes progressively more Eurosceptic. His three objectives – to pacify Eurosceptic critics, neutralise UKIP, and take the EU off the front pages – are all under heavy pressure. Whatever successes he may have in Europe, and however hard he tries to hold his party together, he never seems to satisfy his Eurosceptic MPs. His leadership remains under strain. And life is about to get much worse.

TWENTY-TWO

Gay Marriage Saga

October 2011–July 2013

Cameron's stock with Conservative backbenchers is low and falling. He needs to avoid anything that will further unsettle the party. Above all, he should avoid introducing something that was neither in the election manifesto, nor the Coalition Agreement, and that threatens to undermine support for what he is trying to achieve on the economy and core domestic policy areas. Yet introduce something utterly unexpected is exactly what he chooses to do. Out of a blue sky, or so it would seem, he announces in his 2011 party conference speech that he is consulting over the possibility of legalising gay marriage. A bomb detonates in the party. Few issues so divide opinion both in the party at large or even within Number 10. Many see the initiative as a self-inflicted wound. Others see it as authentic Cameron, pursuing a course of action courageously regardless of the hostility it arouses.

Cameron believes that gay and straight people should be treated the same. At Oxford and beyond, some of his closest friends are gay. Before he became party leader he voted to retain a version of the controversial 'Section 28', banning the teaching of homosexuality in schools, but the following year he voted in favour of the Civil Partnership Bill.

In his speech to the party conference in Blackpool in 2005, which propelled his leadership bid, he went out of his way to endorse marriage: 'We'll support marriage because it is a great institution. So we'll back it through the tax system.'[1] He and Steve Hilton shared very similar beliefs about the importance of family stability. 'Both of us felt very strongly about marriage and wanted to make it a central feature of his platform,' says Hilton. Not all in Cameron's court agreed: they saw marriage as old-fashioned, preachy and politically risky to talk about.[2] In his party conference speech the following year, Cameron returned to the theme of the sanctity of marriage, but with a twist. 'There is something special about marriage … what you are doing really means something,' he said; 'and by the way, it means something whether you are a man and a woman, a woman and a woman, or a man and another man.'[3] By placing gay marriage in the context of family and social stability, rather than gay rights, this line drew applause from the party faithful – something that would have been unthinkable just years before. Cameron was saying that 'we believe in marriage, we believe in it for everyone. At its heart, it's about commitment, whether it's straight or same sex, not about whether it's men or women.'

Although not a man of traditional faith himself, Cameron is close to the Reverend Mark Abrey, vicar of St Nicholas's Church in Chadlington near Dean, who helped clarify his thinking on marriage. At an Easter reception at Downing Street in 2014, Cameron says of him: 'I can't think of anyone who [is] more loving or thoughtful or kind than Mark.'[4] Cameron's non-doctrinal approach to religion helps to explain why he is comfortable with the concept of gay marriage. He was no exception: apart from evangelical Christians who vociferously opposed it, opinion polls suggested that a majority of Christians supported gay marriage.[5]

The crash in 2008 removed the whole issue of marriage and morality from the spotlight for a time, and only in the run-up to the 2010 election did it reappear. Hilton wanted Cameron to do something 'that will show that we are not just pro-vested interests and pro-frumpy people in the shires, but we can be liberal and compassionate'. He tasked policy adviser Sean Worth to go and look at the subject. Worth produced a paper called 'Gay Marriage', which argued that right-of-centre parties in the US and elsewhere were often supportive of gay marriage for conservative reasons. This was encouraging as it would provide ammunition against social conservatives. But Andy Coulson came out 'dead against it'. Putting it in the manifesto, he said, with the polls narrowing, would be a mistake. James O'Shaughnessy, who was writing the manifesto, thought similarly. 'We took soundings from a number of groups: there was ambivalence towards it even from the gay community. They hear views that it is a bourgeois aspiration, that it won't appeal to the gay community, and that for those who want it, there are already civil partnerships.' The team conclude, 'What's the point if it is going to piss off a lot of people and not win us any votes?' So it was quietly dropped from the manifesto, a decision that would return to haunt Cameron.

Fast forward to September 2011. Cameron is mulling over with his team about what he might say at the conference in Manchester the following month. He is being hammered over austerity, and there has been a spate of newspaper articles questioning what, if anything, he believes in. When prompted during an interview on the *Today* programme, he described himself as a 'common sense Conservative', eschewing the phrase 'modern compassionate Conservative' that had characterised his early period as party leader.[6] In September, Andrew Cooper writes a memo to Cameron. 'Abandoning modern, compassionate Conservatism would be a serious, potentially fatal, political error,' he warns. It means continuing with 'the modernising edge' that he displayed in Opposition and not 'subcontracting modern and progressive policies to the Lib Dems'. Cooper argues that Cameron should intervene to claim ownership of the issue of gay marriage. In doing so, he would have to overrule objections to a consultation from Iain Duncan Smith and Philip Hammond on the Cabinet Home Affairs Committee, and commit to legislation before the end of the parliament. It would also mean seeing off the Liberal Democrats.

Cameron and Osborne are told that Lynne Featherstone, the Lib Dem Minister for Equalities, will be announcing Lib Dem support for gay marriage at their conference. Cameron has a clear choice: agree to her announcing it at the Lib Dem conference, which will require some form of corresponding announcement at the Tory conference, or block her from doing so, and risk the Lib Dems announcing it anyway, and leaking that the Conservatives had tried to stop them doing so. Cooper insists Cameron has an opportunity to reaffirm his modernising credentials. 'There is no reason to allow this to be claimed as a Lib Dem internal victory. We should be doing it because we are a modern party opposed to discrimination against gay people, not because the Lib Dems compelled us to do it.' Cameron is persuaded.

Another influence is Michael Salter, head of broadcasting in Number 10, described as Cameron's 'go-to gay' on the issue. According to *Pink News*, Salter 'played a key role in assisting the PM and other members of the government on LGBT [lesbian, gay, bisexual and transgender] policies, most notably equal marriage'.[7] Cameron instructs a press briefing ahead of the Liberal Democrat conference stating that he will support gay marriage, scooping Featherstone's announcement. Despite disagreements within Cameron's camp – Coulson has gone but there are those who are still opposed – a section supporting gay marriage is drafted for Cameron's conference speech.

What he says is, 'I don't support gay marriage *despite* being a Conservative. I support gay marriage *because* I'm a Conservative.'[8] The phrase, Hilton recalls, comes from American politics. After Hilton's departure the following spring, it becomes convenient to scapegoat him for having inserted gay marriage into the speech; but the decision has Cameron's and Osborne's fingerprints all over it. After the announcement is made, a lull follows. The hornets' nest has been stirred. Cameron receives much praise for his stand and despite support from some religious people, religious bodies in general respond critically, believing that marriage is being redefined. Cameron and his team have very little idea quite how disconcerted and angry their party in the country is about to become.

On 15 March 2012, a twelve-week consultation on 'Equal Marriage' is announced. The public are invited to submit thoughts on changes to the law to allow same-sex couples to enter into civil marriage, and to allow those already in civil partnerships to convert it into marriage. At each fresh threshold, a heated debate takes place within Downing Street. Osborne and Cameron urge the policy forward. Oliver Dowden, who is close to MPs and to the party at large, is one of the more resistant. Ed Llewellyn, Kate Fall and Craig Oliver strongly agree with the policy, but are very worried about the timing. Messages from MPs are relayed in their meetings: 'Don't you imbeciles in Number 10 know anything?' 'Can't you see how foolish this is?' 'Why are you doing this when everything else is falling apart?' Cooper makes several presentations to backbench MPs citing private polling. 'Of all the things this government is doing right now, it's about the only one that is popular,' he tells them, adding that the British public will quickly become used to a new social norm, just as it had done over abortion and civil partnerships.[9] Some are convinced; many are not.

Opposition grows over the consultation period. The Church of England says the government 'misunderstand[s] the legal nature of marriage in this country. They mistake the form of the ceremony for the institution itself.'[10] A lobby group called Coalition for Marriage, in favour of traditional marriage and against any redefinition of it, claims it has collected 200,000 signatures: 'This consultation is a sham,' it says.[11] To release some of the pressure, Cameron announces on 24 May that there will be a 'free vote' on any future bill. The media portrays this as yet another Cameron U-turn, coming on the coat-tails of pasties and caravans, and in the wake of all the U-turns of 2011–12.[12] Clegg is not happy, and attacks the free-vote decision on *The Andrew Marr show*: 'I don't think this is something that should be the subject of a great free-for-all because we're not asking people to make a decision of conscience,' he says.[13] The departure of Hilton in spring 2012 is seen as an opportunity to drop the proposals as he has been so closely identified with them. Cameron decides to pause, to take stock of party feeling. To coincide with the party conference in October, the *Sunday Telegraph* publishes a survey of party constituency chairmen showing that 71% want the issue to be abandoned, believing that it is having a detrimental effect on local constituency membership.[14] Alan Duncan, a serving minister and the first openly gay Tory MP, is one of many critics: 'It is losing us 20% of our membership. It is just so badly explained. Why are we doing it? To purge accusations of Blimpism? It is poison to the party.'[15]

Cameron and Osborne nevertheless take the decision that autumn to introduce a bill on gay marriage into Parliament. 'Why are you doing this? Why are you doing this now?' they are repeatedly asked in their meetings with the sceptics, who say that many gay people are happy with civil partnerships. The word 'UKIP' is being heard increasingly in Cameron's ears: 'Gay marriage may well be a factor fuelling its rise,' says one, 'adding weight to those who want to pull the plug.' 'I never thought David understood how very unpopular the issue was. If you believe something very strongly, you can be blind to how others think,' says another. Cameron is aware that many elderly party members are deeply opposed, but still believes that he has the majority of public opinion behind him. 'Out of all the correspondence he received from party members in his ten years as leader, this was the number one issue raised by a country mile,' says Number 10 aide Laurence Mann.[16] Andrew Feldman commissions detailed analysis of the impact of the gay-marriage issue on party membership, which confounds what many internal critics have been saying: it shows that the party lost more members through death than through members resigning during the passage of the bill.

Osborne is unwavering. He tells the team: 'It will send out a message if we do this; and it will send out a message if we don't do it.' Cameron says, 'Unless you are making some Neanderthal judgement on gays, those who are gay should have the same rights as those who are not.' 'There is something very stubborn about David Cameron. He wants to do this and he really doesn't like the attitudes of those who are against,' says another in his team. The risk of not pushing ahead and being seen to be weak is a seminal consideration. Following the messy aftermath of the omnishambles Budget, he adamantly refuses to countenance anything that might be construed a 'U-turn'. Another reversal could, he believes, irrevocably define his administration as weak and indecisive. If they are going to do it, they daren't risk doing so any later, with the European elections in 2014 and the general election a year later. They must do it now. 'How can we speed this up?' soon becomes the mantra of Number 10. In a rare public intervention outside his Treasury brief, Osborne writes an article in *The Times* on 13 November 2012, arguing that 'Successful political parties reflect the modern societies they aspire to lead,' and that there is significant support in the country for gay marriage.[17] The consultation report is published on 11 December. It finds that gay marriage is supported by the majority of respondents. Critics are quick to point out that the majority is narrow, and that submissions had been accepted not just from the UK but from all over the world.[18]

Late in the day, Cameron decides he will try and win over Conservative grass-roots and religious opponents. 'If there is any church or any synagogue or any mosque that doesn't want to have a gay marriage it will not, absolutely must not, be forced to hold it,' he says.[19] In his New Year's interview with Andrew Marr in January 2013, he says that marriage needs to be reformed to allow all couples to benefit from tax breaks, incentives and benefit triggers.[20] Iain Duncan Smith had argued that tax breaks and gay marriage should have been linked from the outset, which would have strengthened the political argument in its favour. For the time being, Cameron can only announce this as an aspiration because of Liberal Democrat opposition.

The Marriage (Same Sex) Bill is introduced by Culture Secretary Maria Miller on 24 January 2013. She is selected to steer the bill through the Commons because she is seen to be a mainstream Conservative rather than a moderniser, who could present the measure as a 'sensible and modest change'.[21] Many backbenchers fail to see it as either sensible or modest. 'If I hear one more person call this a "free vote" I am going to hit them,' says one. 'People are being told that their careers are over if they go against the prime minister on this.'[22] Senior Conservatives, including Philip Hammond, Owen Paterson and Gerald Howarth, are saying publicly they disagree with the bill. Many opponents claim they had supported civil partnerships (although when Number 10 checks the record, it turns out that most had not). On the day of the first vote, 5 February, Osborne, Hague and May publish a letter in the *Telegraph* declaring their support and encouraging other MPs to vote for the bill.[23] No less than 136 Conservatives are unmoved by their plea and vote against, with 127 registering support and five abstaining, including Attorney General Dominic Grieve, who makes known his unhappiness with the law underpinning the bill, not voting. Paterson and Welsh Secretary David Jones are the only two members of the Cabinet to vote against the bill. It passes by 400 to 175 votes due to Lib Dem and Labour support. Having more than half his party voting against or abstaining, even on a free vote, is a bitter blow: 'Few prime ministers have faced such an extensive rebellion in their own ranks,' says the *New York Times*.[24]

When Cameron is under pressure, he has two responses: 'kick the issue into touch', as he would say, or 'get it over and done with as soon as possible'. His taking the second option on gay marriage doesn't seem to be helping. Opposition is intensifying as the bill goes through Parliament. The chief whip Patrick McLoughlin had not exaggerated when he told him that it was going to cause a lot of trouble in the party. Within the PM's circle, it remains a running sore. To Lynton Crosby, whose influence is increasing over 2013, it is a distraction (even though he personally supports the move). 'You're fucking off the party big time,' is his blunt assessment. Chairman of the 1922 Committee Graham Brady thinks gay marriage caused more difficulty between Cameron and the parliamentary party than any other single issue over the five years. The 1922 executive counselled very strongly not to push ahead at such a volatile point, though many have no objection to gay marriage in principle. They think the proposal has appeared from nowhere and, because it was not included in the manifesto, lacks any clear mandate. 'It showed a cavalier attitude and dismissiveness of the views of others. It felt again like the party was being bounced, without significant reassurance or preparation.'[25]

The conservative political philosopher Phillip Blond believes this issue, more than any other, split the Conservatives in these years. 'Cultural conservatives were deeply alienated by it because it broke with the conservative tradition as many understood it.'[26] Backbencher Edward Leigh is one such: 'We should be in the business of protecting cherished institutions and our cultural heritage. Otherwise what, I ask, is a Conservative Party for?'[27] Backbencher Roger Gale argues similarly: 'It is Alice in Wonderland territory, Orwellian almost, for any government of any political persuasion to seek to come along and try to rewrite the lexicon. It will not do.'[28] Liam Fox articulates the views of many Conservative ministers as well as backbenchers: 'The damage was caused because in the minds of many, it represented the victory of liberal-dinner-party, metropolitan thought over the wider party. For many others who didn't have strong views on the subject, they were asking "What on earth does it gain us?"'[29] But most Cameron loyalists believe he was right to push ahead despite internal opposition. 'It wasn't a matter of party management for him – he genuinely believes in it. I don't think somehow if he had held more tea parties for sceptical backbenchers at Number 10 or met church leaders more often it would have made a difference.'

The final debate on the bill takes place on 21 May. Various amendments are discussed, including proposals raised by David Burrowes (Conservative MP and Owen Paterson's parliamentary private secretary), who believes the bill undermines traditional marriage and wants changes to 'protect the liberty of conscience for people who believe marriage should stay as it is.'[30] The bill passes its third reading by 366 to 161. Only 40% of Conservative MPs support it. Despite intensive lobbying by Cameron and the Number 10 machine, Tory support has fallen away.

The focus now moves to the House of Lords. On 25 May, Conservative peers are said to be plotting a revolt against the passage of the bill.[31] Baroness Warsi is reported as being asked by Cameron to take the bill through the Lords but refuses to do so.[32] Opposition is led by a former chief constable and crossbencher, Lord Dear. By 'trying to defeat the bill on the second reading, rather than trying to ambush it with amendments at committee stage', the government is let off the hook. On 15 July, the Lords pass the bill after a short debate and without a formal vote. The chamber is packed with peers wearing pink carnations.[33] Two days later, the bill receives Royal Assent. Cameron's team experience momentary relief. A warning from the Coalition for Marriage, which claims nearly 700,000 supporters (about five times the number of members of the Conservative Party), is seen by some as a harbinger of what is to come. 'They are just ordinary men and women, not part of the ruling elite.' The repercussions, says its chairman Colin Hart, 'will be felt at the next general election'.[34]

Cameron has a new problem. Have they achieved a heroic victory to proclaim from the rooftops? His team debate whether they should reap the benefit from the passage of the bill, or say nothing about it and sweep it under the carpet. In September, the issue comes to the fore, when they discuss whether he should mention it in his party conference speech. He plays it safe, saying the government is 'backing marriage'.[35]

Six months later, on 29 March 2014, the first same-sex marriages take place. Cameron sends congratulations cards to the initial couples to marry. He hopes that the 'country ... is growing stronger socially because we value love and commitment equally. Let us raise a toast to that – and [to] all those getting married this weekend.'[36] 'I believe that our country should feel proud that almost uniquely in the world, leaders from across the political spectrum put aside their differences to unite in favour of equality for all, regardless of their sexuality,' he continues.[37] 'Only the right to marry ... is true equality,' Clegg had said in 2013. 'Let every member – young or old – of our LGBT community, know that they are recognised and valued, not excluded.'[38]

The gay-marriage saga has lasted three years. It has shown all sides of Cameron, and displayed him at both his best and his weakest. It is one of his principal achievements as prime minister. Yet why exactly did he take such an unnecessary risk? He himself offers an explanation: 'I am proud of what I did, and what is more, if we hadn't done it, we would have had endless pressure with Members of Parliament wanting to introduce legislation. People don't think of that when they criticise me for doing what I did. It got the decision done.'[39] A fair point, if something of a post hoc rationalisation. He drove it forward for a variety of reasons: because he believed it was the right thing to do, and was convinced by Cooper's strategic argument that it could bring a political dividend. He didn't then want to be seen to do a U-turn, which he felt could permanently undermine the government's reputation following months of bad headlines. He also had Osborne by his side all the way. A more experienced leader would have prepared the ground better and done more to win over allies once the initiative had been launched. It exposed both his naivety and deficiency as a strategic thinker. It had been removed from the 2010 manifesto because of the objections from one media counsellor, Coulson; and it may never have been allowed to make it to the statute book had another adviser been in play earlier: Lynton Crosby.

TWENTY-THREE

Lynton to the Rescue?

January 2013–October 2014

'You guys have political Attention Deficit Disorder,' Lynton Crosby tells Cameron's team in early 2013. 'Everything is all too fragmented, you have no plan.' Introducing gay marriage at such a dangerous time is, to Crosby, the very height of idiocy. But there are many other candidates for capital folly. Cameron's team are uncomfortable hearing the tirade. But they know that he is right. The outlook is bleak, and they lack any clear idea how to regain control and get back on top.

'It's two years away, but the 2015 election is already lost,' writes ConservativeHome executive editor Paul Goodman on 29 December 2012. He is hardly alone in his analysis. Reasons why Cameron will not win an outright victory include: lack of support amongst ethnic minority voters, with only 16% voting Conservative in 2010; the rise of UKIP, which Goodman is (presciently) tipping to win the Euro election in 2014; unity on the left, despite Miliband's uncertain leadership; and Britain's electoral geography, which, after the failure to achieve boundary reform, means the Conservatives will have to lead Labour by seven points to win a bare majority. 'Losing older voters on the one side, failing to win ethnic minority ones on the other, and all at sea in Scotland and in parts of the North' is a desperate scenario. 'Conservatism has been living through a crisis for the past twenty years – one which Opposition after 2015 may not relieve.'[1] Cameron's speech at the party conference in October 2012 had given the party a lift, but a ComRes poll published later that month had the Conservatives still stuck on 33% with Labour on 43%, while an Ipsos MORI poll published in November had the Conservatives on 32% and Labour on 46%, with a predictable impact on party morale.[2]

A critical spotlight focuses more than ever on the Number 10 team and especially Cameron himself. Tories 'increasingly fear that David Cameron is a loser', writes Martin Ivens in the *Sunday Times*.[3] Fraser Nelson, editor of the *Spectator*, is predicting that 'drift and disillusion will lose Cameron the next election'.[4] Academic John Curtice, whose election exit polling is unsurpassed, is even more cutting in the *Guardian*: 'People used to think Cameron was charismatic. But he is proving to be a kind of average prime minister. His ratings are not terrible, but he's not Thatcher, he's not Blair. He is not a dominant figure. Nobody loves him.'[5]

Cameron's deficiencies are more evident in late 2012 and early 2013 than at any previous point. It has become clear he is not an architect conceiving the agenda of government in the mould of Thatcher and Blair. He contracted out much of his strategic thinking to Osborne and Steve Hilton, and the latter's departure leaves him exposed in shaping the overall direction of policy. Not winning outright in 2010 deprived Cameron of personal kudos and authority. Partnership with the Lib Dems plays to his strength, but militates against him driving the government in a clear direction beyond Plan A, or confronting those who are in the way of achieving clarity and cohesion.

After the departure of his two biggest players, Hilton and Coulson, no comparable giant personalities have emerged to take their place. Heywood had proved an unexpected boon to the team in Number 10 when the coalition first came to power, but his successor, the gritty Chris Martin who had been press secretary at the Treasury to Brown and Darling, soon is up to speed. Ed Llewellyn and Craig Oliver continue to steady the ship, but they become targets: Llewellyn is criticised by Tory MPs for being a Europhile and defensive of the Liberal Democrats; Oliver is resented by several in the press lobby because he is 'not one of them'. The Policy Unit is under attack for not firing on all cylinders and the political side of Number 10, including the chief whip George Young, are said to lack grip. 'Nobody's really frightened of Number 10,' writes Tory blogger Iain Dale.[6] Cameron's team have allowed themselves to become overly defensive, too inward-looking and too tactical. They fret too much about what is written in the press: 'Did you read what Ben Brogan has written in his blog?' they ask one visitor, who is surprised that they are so worried about what journalists are saying, rather than seeing the bigger picture.

Number 10 badly needs a big hitter, a strategic thinker who understands the electorate, and someone with real force of character. Enter Lynton Crosby. Osborne and Andrew Feldman have been talking and decide that he could be the answer to their prayers. Campaign director to Liberal prime minister John Howard in Australia, Crosby was best known in Britain for masterminding four Australian general election victories in the 1990s and 2000s. He came to Britain in 2005 to work on Conservative Party leader Michael Howard's general election campaign in which Blair was victorious. He later claimed that he'd arrived too late to make a major impact: 'You can't fatten a pig on market day.'[7] He returned disappointed to Australia, but in December 2007 had a phone conversation with Osborne to ask if he would be willing to insert more strategy and structure into Boris Johnson's campaign to become mayor of London in 2008. Crosby duly became his campaign director in January 2008.

Osborne and Feldman were impressed that Crosby pulled off a second, and harder, victory in London in 2012. They agree that they must have Crosby at the heart of the Conservative campaign for the 2015 general election and approach him straight after Boris's victory. Feldman is delegated to start negotiations to bring Crosby in, initially part-time. Crosby then has a meeting with Osborne who alludes to his 'unfinished business' with the party at general elections. The Australian has a host of questions: 'Will I have control? Will Steve Hilton come back? What will Number 10's role be? Who will report to me? How much freedom will I have?' Negotiations go on throughout the latter half of 2012. Crosby had been very bruised by the 2005 general election campaign: he never felt that he had complete control and was forced into agreeing to an agenda that had been set before he was hired. Cameron is not involved in discussions at this stage. He is being kept informed, but does not conceal he is nervous about Crosby. A part of him remains happier with ambiguity. He worries about the prospect of 'having one clear figure in charge dictating one clear message'. Feldman implores Cameron to hire him: 'I cannot contemplate fighting another election unless we hire Lynton. He's the only person who can bring discipline and order to the campaign – I cannot go through 2010 all over again.'[8]

Crosby remains unsure he wants to do it and needs persuading. He only wants to run campaigns if he is in charge, and he looks with dismay at the bleak forecasts for the Conservatives. He looks back at the shambles of the 2010 election campaign with its 'multiple points of authority' which resulted in no overall strategy or clarity of message. He will only become involved, he says, if he reports solely to the prime minister and is answerable to no one else, though he is happy to work closely with Feldman and Osborne. Exclusive control is a red line for him. Osborne, the strategist in 2010, must take a back seat.

On 18 November 2012, it is announced that Crosby will begin working on a part-time basis from 1 January 2013.[9] He is determined not to be bogged down in detail and only comes into Number 10 for two or three political strategy meetings a month, basing himself instead at CCHQ.

The appointment receives a mixed reception. Former Tory funder Lord Ashcroft is no fan. Ashcroft did not blame Crosby for the failure of the 2005 campaign, but after Cameron became leader Ashcroft offered to fund a comprehensive research programme for the party and support candidates in marginal seats. Cameron decided it would be better to keep Ashcroft within the camp, and they worked reasonably well with him on campaigning until the general election. But they fell out over the planned TV debates in the 2010 election campaign, which Ashcroft strongly disapproved of, and over the criticism from Labour and some newspapers about his tax status. Ashcroft felt let down by the leadership for not coming to his defence. In 2006, Hilton had approached Crosby to run the 2010 general election campaign, and there followed several meetings including one between Crosby and Cameron in Dean. But Ashcroft threatened to walk away and pull his resources, and Crosby told Llewellyn he did not want the job.

Ashcroft is even angrier after the election, when Cameron does not offer him a ministerial post, which he considers a betrayal, and he becomes a regular and vocal critic of Cameron and his team. Crosby's appointment inflames Ashcroft still further, given what happened before the last election.

Crosby is a man of pronounced views: 'Don't let us down or we'll cut your fucking knees off,' he reportedly told Boris Johnson before taking on the 2008 mayoral campaign.[10] He makes his mind up quickly about people and rarely alters his view. When he was taken on, he rapidly formed a view of everyone in Cameron's team. He had been worried about Llewellyn and Oliver, but decides that they are both 'okay and essentially on the right track'. One figure who Crosby believes does not have the right strategic qualities, though, is Hilton. 'Steve is an engine room of ideas but that was not what was needed.'[11] Crosby doesn't believe his approach is correct for an election, and is adamant he will not have him anywhere near the 2015 campaign. Hilton lets Cameron know that he's unhappy about this, but Crosby repeats to the prime minister: 'I absolutely mean it.' Crosby will not budge. Hilton's modernisation, he believes, appealed to West London but not to the Conservative Party in the country. It is too socially liberal, while Crosby is more interested in social justice, and the issues of tax, crime, immigration and Europe, which he thinks matter to people at large.

Crosby casts his eye over policy, turning particular attention to Cameron's 2012 conference speech, of which Number 10 is still so proud. He views it as a big improvement on the modernising agenda that dominated 2010–12, but quarrels with the language. He likes the notions of 'aspiration' and 'global race', but they need to be made personally relevant to voters if they are to strike a chord with the values that they hold. 'Global race', he says, is inadequate shorthand for an interconnected world where people will fall behind if they don't make progress.[12] He embraces the speech's ideas, but wants to communicate them in a way that will be relevant and attractive to voters.

'Scraping the barnacles off the boat' is the widely reported expression Crosby uses when he arrives, by which he means that the team has to strip away policies which are dividing the Conservatives or damaging or irrelevant to voters and concentrate instead on clarifying the strategic message. He is blunt with Cameron, telling him he is concentrating too much on foreign policy, and that he has to drop issues he has become interested in, like combating modern slavery, which, although hugely important, are not priority issues for voters. 'I thought they were overindulgent, failing to distinguish between the issues that mattered to people, and second and third order issues.' The fundamental weakness is that there is no story about their purpose. 'My job is to be the navigator, give confidence in the route map and equip them with the diagnostic tools they need. The route map is the simple narrative about economic competence and security, rewarding hard work, reforming welfare, being firm on immigration, focusing on DC as an asset of his party and holding Labour to account more effectively.'[13] Bit by bit, he nudges Cameron and Osborne to what the research shows is relevant to voters in 2014/15. He has iron discipline and keeps tight control of the polling through his political strategy company, Crosby Textor. 'My job is to make sure we stay on the train tracks' is a frequent refrain. Matthew d'Ancona describes him as 'a bull of a man, bespectacled, mild on first encounter but evidently fizzing with barely suppressed energy. He [told] visitors only that the election was "winnable" … [He] did not make a habit of working for losers.'[14] By mid-2013, he has achieved traction in Number 10 and the party because of his aura as a campaign guru, but also because he is an 'alpha male Australian who shouts and swears at them, which they all know they need', as one insider puts it. Not all are such fans.

Crosby knows time is not on their side. In March 2013 he chairs his first meeting with what Cameron describes as the 'core election planning group' at an away day in Chequers. Crosby tells them that they are effectively already in the campaign and all policy announcements have to be agreed and strategically focused. Anything that creates further discontent within the party must be stopped. He is complimentary about the critique of Labour the Conservatives developed in 2012, but scornful about the failure to follow it in a disciplined way. On 12 June, Crosby addresses a meeting of the 1922 Committee, in the presence of Osborne and Cameron. The PM tells them that the campaign in 2010 suffered because there was no one figure in charge, and that Crosby will be the sole person running the 2015 campaign. Crosby tells MPs that Labour's lead in the opinion polls can be reversed, that Labour are vulnerable on welfare, the deficit, and Europe, and that both Miliband and Balls are seen to be weak by floating voters.[15] In September, he presents his research to the Downing Street team: 'Central concern of voters is economic security and international security. Security is core,' he tells his rapt audience in Mrs

Thatcher's first-floor study in Number 10. He talks about his in-depth research into the values expressed by the two rival candidates in the 1984 US presidential election, Ronald Reagan and Walter Mondale: while the left owned public services, the right owned economy and jobs. He has reached the conclusion that the Conservatives, like the victorious Reagan, have the right policy on the economy, but lack a deep emotional identity with voters. His work feeds through into the slogans of the 2013 party conference, 'A Land of Opportunity for All', and the 2014 party conference, 'Securing a Better Future'.

Crosby's unassailable rise is at the expense of Andrew Cooper, who leaves Number 10 in October 2013. When Cooper was appointed it was on the understanding that he would return to the polling company he founded, Populus, after one or two years in Number 10. Crosby may not have warmed to Cooper's modernising drive, but he is respectful of his work – at the March election meeting he goes out of his way to praise Cooper's contribution over the previous eighteen months. Soon after Crosby joined the team, Cooper tells him of the arrangement he has made with Cameron, and that he is willing to leave after the local elections in May. However, Crosby encourages Cooper to stay. Despite their best efforts, they frequently disagree, strongly over the NHS. While Cooper believes 'we have to sort it out', Crosby's line is 'the best thing we can do is simply to ignore it and keep talking about the economy'. Crosby's strident style too is more what many feel is needed in contrast to Cooper's more nuanced, inclusive approach. Cameron is initially reluctant to see Cooper go, but the rest of his team are crying out for the metallic certainty of Crosby.

Cooper had already warned Cameron of his misgivings about Crosby during a long conversation in the PM's car the previous year. Cameron told Cooper that he and Osborne were still haunted by the 2010 campaign. 'The endless meetings, the discordant voices, the endless indecision, the cancelling of posters a day before they are due to go out. It drove us all nuts!' he said. 'We have to have one person to be the sole director of the campaign.'

'You can't have Lynton without having "Lyntonism",' Cooper replied, referring to the core-vote agenda he pursued in 2005.

'We won't have Lyntonism because my judgement is better than Michael Howard's,' was Cameron's response.

But then Cooper says that he is being placed in an impossible position, given that Crosby's control of private polling is sending out the signal that Cameron no longer trusts Cooper's analysis. 'That's not what I think,' Cameron says. Cameron is uncomfortable, because of his affection and respect for Cooper, and unwilling to see him leave. When a story appears in the *Mail on Sunday* in April that Crosby and Cooper are embroiled in a power struggle, Cooper offers to leave immediately – but Craig Oliver implores him to stay until the autumn, not wanting to give any credence to the report.[16] While Cooper agrees to continue as a part-time adviser, paid by the party, it is clear power has already passed to Crosby, and there can be only one figure in charge.

In July 2013, Crosby comes under attack for his business connections, particularly after the government, on 12 July, announced that proposals to introduce plain packaging on cigarettes would be put on hold. That day, the media also reported that a plan to introduce minimum pricing for alcohol was to be abandoned.[17] Labour links the decisions with Crosby's work for tobacco giant Philip Morris. Shadow public health minister Diane Abbott says, 'We have to ask, what happened? We suspect Lynton Crosby happened.'[18] Sarah Wollaston tweets, 'What a tragic waste of an opportunity "barnacles scraped off the boat" aka more lives ruined for political expediency.'[19] Cameron tells Andrew Marr that Crosby played no part in the decision. But Cameron recognises that the problems are not going to go away, and Feldman holds conversations with Crosby over the summer, resulting in the decision, announced in November but decided long before, that he will now work full-time for the Conservatives. He will have no need to work for other organisations that might be portrayed as conflicts of interest.[20] As part of the deal, Crosby's business partner Mark Textor and his team come on board.

Crosby and Textor become convinced that the 'long-term economic plan' is the key organising idea for the Conservatives. 'We needed to show that David Cameron and the Conservative Party have an eye to the future, and are not just driven by opportunism, responding to the latest issue or the next controversy: it was all about consistency, continuity and purpose.'[21] For Boris Johnson's 2012 London campaign, Crosby had come up with a nine-point plan. With Cameron it is to be a five-point plan. The idea is foreshadowed in Cameron's 2013 party conference speech and then expanded in a speech to the CBI on 4 November.[22] It is subsequently refined as the 'Big Five' objectives: cutting the deficit, reducing income tax, creating more jobs, capping welfare and immigration, and delivering the best schools and skills for young people. The subliminal message is that 'we are working for something better in the long-term and the Conservatives are not just a bunch of opportunist politicians or short-term interventionists.'[23]

As the general election comes into view, Crosby becomes a powerful figure in Cameron's team, the equal in punch of Osborne, and the strongest since the departure of Coulson and Hilton. When he goes full-time from November 2013, his voice becomes even louder. Osborne remains the 'big-picture guy' adjudicating the broad outline of government policy, but it is Crosby who now helps them to 'sell' those policies. 'We don't do anything now without talking first to Lynton,' says one team member. He works hard in the first part of 2014 to win over MPs individually and in groups, becoming a 'human shield' for Cameron. Crosby's politics are much more in tune with many MPs than those of Cameron. They like his messages and his emphatic style. But as the year drags on, criticism of him mounts. As polls fail to improve, MPs blame him for placing too much emphasis on economic policy. They worry that that alone will be insufficient. 'He has completely misread the mood of the British electorate,' says 1922 chairman Graham Brady in November. In the same month, a ComRes poll places the Conservatives on 30%, exactly where they had been a year before, and by early December it puts the Conservatives on just 28%.[24] Crosby may have brought order to the Cameron premiership; he had yet to bring it success.

TWENTY-FOUR

Warfare Over Welfare

May 2010–December 2014

'We will all need to hold our nerve,' Welfare Secretary Iain Duncan Smith tells Cameron early in the New Year. 'Everything is happening in 2013. It's going to be the bumpiest year we face on welfare. I don't need anyone to blink.'[1] He was not being alarmist. In April 2013 alone, housing-benefit changes (including the controversial spare-room subsidy or 'bedroom tax') come into effect, the Personal Independence Payment scheme (PIP) replaces the Disability Living Allowance, the 'pathfinder' trial begins for IDS's flagship policy, Universal Credit (UC) – the merging of six means-tested benefits and tax credits into one monthly payment – and in July, the household benefit cap is introduced. The 2010–15 government sees a welter of activity on welfare. This chapter's focus is on UC. For IDS, working to fulfil a lifelong dream of welfare reform, this year is critical.

Public concerns have been building about UC, and continue to do so well into 2013. In December 2012, Philip Langsdale, who had been brilliantly project-managing it, died after only a few weeks in post. In February 2013, the Major Projects Authority (MPA) orders a 'reset' of UC, while in September the National Audit Office (NAO) heavily criticises the IT programme, claiming it has resulted in £40.1 million in wasted expenditure. In November, the Public Accounts Committee (PAC) chaired by Margaret Hodge, nicknamed 'the fishwife' at the Department for Work and Pensions (DWP) for her aggressive manner, turns on IDS. It all leads to a widespread belief that UC is a failed scheme that will never see the light of day.

DWP feel these critical reports are woefully out of date, providing analysis based on recommendations already initiated by IDS and the department in 2011. It is not surprising that given the huge changes in welfare reform over this parliament, there would be teething problems, they respond.

IDS, and his UC policy, have been a source of division between prime minister and chancellor. Both men think very differently. Cameron is fervently committed to welfare reform, but does not immerse himself in the detail. 'I remember a couple of meetings about a welfare programme in Number 10 in the first few months: there was very little interest there, and it was only with a lowly adviser,' recalls a DWP official. IDS himself makes it clear to Cameron on his appointment in 2010 that he only wants to be Welfare Secretary if he is allowed to introduce UC: Cameron readily agrees and says he will stand by him. Cameron might lack IDS's deep Christian faith, but is fired by a similar moral zeal for welfare reform, to ensure that benefits are targeted only on those who need or deserve them. His overtly moral approach is alien to Osborne's world view. 'The fundamental tension is that George and Iain are not natural bedfellows,' says a senior figure in the Treasury. Osborne forms the view, shared by some in Whitehall, that IDS is 'too stubborn to come up with the costs and consequences of what he is proposing'. He also worries whether IDS has the intellectual firepower to handle his brief. One supporter of IDS blasts Treasury civil servants for their lack of support: 'Officials stirred up Treasury ministers to be very, very concerned that it could all go terribly wrong and cost an arm and a leg and destroy all the welfare savings.' The Treasury's drive for savings across the entire DWP budget, irrespective of UC, and IDS's refusal to see any part of UC cut, creates much tension. 'The conflict was that Iain was only interested in reform and Universal Credit, but George desperately needed to save money,' recalls one Treasury aide. 'There was a mixture of personal and policy decisions causing tensions between IDS and Osborne,' says a senior Whitehall figure.

By 2011 IDS's proposals come under similar pressures to Lansley's at Health. But where Lansley falls, IDS survives the 2012 reshuffle, and the tribulations of 2013. What explains the difference in their fates? Welfare does not have the same emotional resonance with the public and media as health care. While people are ever alert to bad NHS news stories, many never fully grasp or experience first-hand the problems in implementing UC. Public opinion is largely behind the need for reform; in July 2013, a poll suggests 73% of the public support the household benefit cap.[2] IDS, unlike Lansley, has powerful friends on the right of the parliamentary party, and among the commentariat, notably ConservativeHome blogger and later comment editor of *The Times*, Tim Montgomerie.

Peel away the Whitehall lid too and we see the powerful hand of the Number 10 permanent secretary, Jeremy Heywood. While cautious about health reforms, which he believes are undoing progress made under Blair and Brown, he is supportive of welfare reform. From the very first meetings in the summer of 2010, he tells Cameron and IDS that 'Universal Credit is a right reform to do – worth the upheaval and the change.' Heywood knows that every Work and Pensions Secretary for a generation has wanted fundamental welfare reform. Following a critical meeting in Number 10, at IDS's request, and the assurance of the DWP's permanent secretary Leigh Lewis that the project is achievable from an IT perspective, Heywood agrees that the prime minister should accept the advice and move forward. Cabinet Secretary Gus O'Donnell pins the blame for the later problems of UC on the government trying to introduce too much radical reform so quickly, a fruit of the Steve Hilton philosophy that speed and steely purpose should go hand in hand in those first months. O'Donnell believes that Cameron's team, fresh to government, lack the resources in Number 10 to grip all the measures they are seeking to drive through simultaneously. But IDS has other powerful supporters, including Hilton, albeit an initial sceptic, and Oliver Letwin.

Furious rows with the Treasury emerge in no time. During the party conference of 2010, to IDS's anger, Osborne announces cuts in child benefit for higher-rate taxpayers without consulting him, and the warfare continues throughout 2011 and 2012. The Treasury insists on continued savings while giving IDS just enough leeway to prevent him from resigning. The DWP blames the Treasury for tightening the money so much that UC could not be rolled out properly, and believe they were not consulted fully over the replacement of the Disability Living Allowance by PIP. The latter, and the decision to link benefits to the Consumer Prices Index instead of the Retail Price Index, produce the biggest savings. The Treasury rub salt in the wound by claiming that many of the welfare successes in 2010–15 are down to their own innovations, rather than those of the DWP, and that IDS and the DWP are muddled and inefficient. IDS, despite his hard pounding at the DWP, remains throughout bloodied but unbowed. Few ministers suffer more from negative briefing, some from the Treasury, and, for a time during 2013, from his own department. His press is largely hostile, with Polly Toynbee in the *Guardian* a high priest. A withering attack by Philip Collins appears in *The Times*, mocking IDS for his 'evangelical fervour', describing UC as a 'gothic folly' and IDS as guilty of 'the sin of hubris' heading towards 'political disaster'.[3] He does have some cheerleaders, including the *Spectator's* Fraser Nelson and Peter Oborne in the *Telegraph*, who describes the UC story as 'one of the most dramatic in post-war political history', heaping praise on IDS for his tenacity in piloting it through.[4]

IDS's moral zeal for reform is a cause of mockery in some quarters. In 2004, the year after he stood down as party leader, he established the Centre for Social Justice (CSJ) as an independent think-tank. He had visited many of the UK's most disadvantaged communities, encountering 'levels of social breakdown which appalled me … [especially] in the fourth largest economy in the world'.[5] The CSJ identified five separate pathways to poverty: family breakdown, failed education, addiction, debt, and welfare dependency. 'We always knew that we could only tackle one of these in a five-year term,' said Philippa Stroud, his special adviser who followed him from the CSJ into government; 'we were given the opportunity to tackle welfare dependency'. The groundwork for UC was laid in the CSJ's publication *Dynamic Benefits* in 2009, the brainchild of academic turned management consultant Dr Stephen Brien.[6] IDS may have put in much of the preparatory work, but had not expected to be appointed in 2010: 'It was a total surprise. I wasn't expecting it.'[7] In fact Cameron admired IDS's dedication to social reform, thinking for some time that he would offer him the post. Now IDS had the chance to salvage pride after his lacklustre leadership of the party.

He gets straight down to work. The Welfare Reform Bill, which builds on the extensive agreement with the Lib Dems on welfare enshrined in the Coalition Agreement, is announced in the Queen's

Speech on 25 May. To IDS, it is 'absurd' that some of the poorest people faced 'huge penalties for moving from benefits to work'. Almost 5 million people, he says, are on unemployment benefits, 1.4 million of whom have been receiving support for nine of the last ten years. 'A system that was originally designed to support the poorest in society is now trapping them in the very condition it was supposed to alleviate,' he says.[8] These anomalies are what he wants to address with his legislation. The October 2010 Spending Review announces the government's intention to cap total household benefits at £500 per week for a family and £350 per week for a single person with no children, from April 2013.[9] The measures are popular with the public and in government; 'Everyone was agreed that it should happen,' says one official. The proposal even manages to gain eventual begrudging support from the Labour Party, with Ed Miliband later claiming in January 2015 that he would keep the welfare cap and even consider a reduction in the £26,000 a year limit on household benefit introduced in the Welfare Reform Bill.[10]

The bill has its first reading in the Commons in February 2011, and in the Lords on 16 June. In January 2012, the Lords defeat the bill on seven key items, including the capped out-of-work benefits. Cameron, sensing the public is on side, fights back. The day following the defeat, he writes in the *Sun*, 'I respect [the Lords'] concerns, but … I'm prepared to battle all the way … I've lost count of the number of people who've said "I go to work early in the morning and on the way I pass neighbours with their curtains closed, lying in because they've chosen to live on benefits" … The cap is going to help us crack welfare dependency.'[11] The measure eventually receives Royal Assent in March to become the Welfare Reform Act 2012.

As seen earlier, Osborne pushes for IDS to be moved in the reshuffle of September 2012.[12] Now the Act has passed through Parliament, the chancellor sees no need to keep the Work and Pensions Secretary in post a moment longer: implementation will be much better handled by another minister. IDS says he would rather stay at DWP and see through his reforms than move to Justice, the job Cameron offers him. Cameron knows the stink a forced departure would cause, not least with the right revved up over gay marriage, and does not want to move IDS against his will.

Osborne's low opinion of IDS appears to be justified in 2013, the most difficult year for welfare, when the huge number of changes are introduced and the damaging reports from the MPA and NAO are published. Negative reaction on the airwaves and in the press seeps into Number 10, despite DWP's insistence that they are on track and have identified potential problems several years before. Even Cameron's faith in the former Tory leader begins to waver. IDS irritates Number 10 by being so outspoken with his Eurosceptic views. Details of a dinner in Downing Street at which Cameron tried to win him and Owen Paterson over to his European policy find their way into the press.[13] The political side of Number 10 become increasingly exasperated with IDS, finding him difficult to manage.

Tribulations over welfare can be tolerated only as long as they are not creating poor headlines. But in August 2013, IDS is accused of being disingenuous by the Trussell Trust, which provides food banks in the UK, after he argues that the explosion in demand for their services comes not from benefit cuts but from an enhanced awareness of the service on offer (by advertising them in Job Centres, which Labour had never allowed). In October, the media is full of reports about the steep rise in numbers using food banks, with cases of food poverty reaching 'scandalous levels', and reports of mothers 'not eating for days'. Some of the reporting is exaggerated, but the chorus of charities is growing. Oxfam comment that 'these figures lay bare the shocking scale of destitution, hardship and hunger in the UK. It is completely unacceptable that in the seventh wealthiest nation on the planet, the number of people turning to food banks has tripled'. The British Red Cross announce it will be providing volunteers for the first time to support food banks as 'it is so concerned by levels of UK hunger'.[14] A letter signed by twenty-seven bishops in early 2014 blames 'cutbacks and failures' in the benefit system for driving people to food banks.[15] IDS believes that the Trussell Trust, whose chairman is a Labour Party member, and other charities are behaving in a highly political manner. It is telling that by 2015, much of the hostility has died away. Even the left-wing blog Left Foot Forward features a story in 2015, based on a report by the Trade Union Congress (TUC) and Child Poverty Action Group (CPAG), on how Universal Credit might be used to reduce child poverty.[16]

And yet in 2013, these reports are greeted in Number 10 with almost the same horror as reports of winter crises in the NHS. Relations between IDS and Osborne reach new lows. IDS resents Treasury intrusions into welfare and for continuing to regard UC as 'a waste of time and unmanageable'. IDS has his own views of the Treasury: he thinks officials have a young average age and lack 'collective memory', seeing their job merely as overseeing money in the short term without any long-term forethought – an essentially dysfunctional process. He thinks that from the 'top down', by which he means Nicholas Macpherson, one-time principal private secretary to Gordon Brown and now permanent secretary, the Treasury has had its fingers burnt by the 'shambles of tax credits'. It was a Brown policy which IDS regards as a disaster, and he thinks, rightly or wrongly, it has made the Treasury risk-averse against UC.

Introduced by the DWP to save roughly £500 million a year by lowering the amount of housing benefit received for a family living in a house deemed to have a spare room (the Spare Room Subsidy), the 'bedroom tax' comes under particular attack from the Labour Party and a number of charities. It continues to be a source of difficulty and internal tension for the government right up to the 2015 election. A study published in the *Journal of Public Health* in March 2015 finds that worries around debt, rent arrears and the prospect of being forced to move from their family home, caused by the removal of the Spare Room Subsidy, produced a sense of 'hopelessness verging on desperation'.[17] A National Housing Federation report in May 2014 finds that more than half of affected tenants have cut back on essentials and that more than a quarter have racked up debts.[18] The measure proves so divisive that it causes a Lib Dem U-turn in July 2014. IDS claims that the proposals have not come from him or his team, but were presented to him in his first few weeks at DWP by an official who 'raised an eyebrow and said, "We've done a little bit of work on this before,"' leading some in the department to question whether the policy was actually being developed by the outgoing Labour government. The DWP is also frustrated by what they see as 'appalling behaviour' by the BBC, claiming it consistently refers to the removal of the Spare Room Subsidy as the 'bedroom tax' – they feel this is a partisan approach that helps unite public opinion against the reforms.

The skates are under IDS, and amidst regular speculation during 2013 that he will fall, or UC will be abandoned, the negative coverage in the media cumulatively makes the department look weak and uncertain. IDS rues the death of Philip Langsdale, who had earlier project-managed the deployment of IT systems at London Heathrow's new Terminal 2, and was described by special adviser Philippa Stroud as the 'Stephen Hawking of the IT world'.[19] Langsdale was one DWP figure trusted by the Treasury and the Cabinet Office. Following a 'red team' investigation initiated by IDS in 2011, Langsdale identified problems with the roll-out of UC but crucially not the IT systems. As a result of his report in July 2012, UC is 'reset' and a more pragmatic approach to the roll-out is agreed. DWP are annoyed when the NAO and PAC reproduce the original warnings of the 'red team' investigation into their 2013 reports, which, in their eyes, stokes further unjustifiable criticism in the press.

With Langsdale's death in early 2013, the way forward temporarily looks unclear. IDS invites Francis Maude and the Cabinet Office to help get UC back on track. While Maude is personally supportive, IDS and his team think his staff approach UC in an overly 'conflict-orientated manner'. Over six months of intensive meetings between IDS, Maude, Oliver Letwin, DWP permanent secretary Robert Devereux and project manager David Pitchford, who is crucial, problems are analysed and solutions identified. The Cabinet Office insists that UC adopts newer digital technology, in line with all fresh government programmes. Indeed, it is only in 2013 that the new technology exists which can manage the changes. The Treasury equally are hammering DWP throughout 2013 for more financial control, which they achieve. With employment and support allowance and the removal of the Spare Room Subsidy causing difficulties, it often appears that UC will succumb. 'It was hanging in the balance and might have gone. Doubters might have taken the opportunity to stop it,' admits IDS. 'Without Philip Langsdale, the whole programme was leaderless. There was nobody in the department capable of running the programme.'[20] Cameron is deeply frustrated. 'The prime minister was really cross,' recalls Bob Kerslake, head of the Civil Service. 'The whole fraught project did influence Cameron's view about the capability of the Civil Service in this area.'[21]

One of the recommendations during the months of meetings between the Cabinet Office and DWP is the need for a top manager to take the place of Langsdale. DWP invites Howard Shiplee, who had project-managed the Olympic Park, and in May, he arrives at the department in the nick of time. He looks over the Langsdale plan and opines the department should in essence stick with it: 'You have to have a plan, you need to stick to the plan, and people need to deliver on their parts of the plan,' he would say, sounding like a welfare version of Lynton Crosby. Like Crosby too, he is forceful: 'This is your bloody job. You do it or you bugger off!' is his approach. Blunt emails fly around the system day and night. Shiplee is determined that there will be no more problems. But it takes some months before the impact of his leadership begins to be felt. Despite this, as the year progresses, the conventional wisdom in the media still remains that UC will not happen. IDS is told that 'there are no journalists in the country who think that it will survive'. In an effort to win over the press, Stroud takes Peter Oborne of the *Telegraph* to a Job Centre in Hammersmith on a cold December morning to see Universal Credit in action. It is a gamble. 'We hadn't taken any journalists down to see it,' she says.[22] The gamble pays off. Oborne becomes one of the first journalists to become a wholehearted supporter of UC, writing that 'With Universal Credit, work might finally pay.'[23]

Over the course of 2014, the welfare story begins to improve. Figures suggest that the amount of money being spent on welfare claimants is falling, and that the policies are helping the unemployed back into work, a change for which the Treasury tries to claim credit. Osborne makes a speech against a backdrop of a list of successful government programmes. Harrison emails Stroud, his opposite number, to say: 'Hope you saw we placed Universal Credit beside George's head,' a move regarded as totemic. IDS notes with wry satisfaction not only that Osborne is now happy to be identified with his flagship policy, but also that UC begins to become a more regular feature in the PM's speeches. Matthew d'Ancona, whose book *In It Together* published in 2013 catalogues the battles between Osborne and IDS, starts to write articles about Osborne's belated admiration for IDS's stoicism and work to bring about behavioural and cultural transformation in welfare.[24] Doubts remain whether Osborne has genuinely warmed to IDS, or has simply adopted the position that 'I've got to live with him and work with him'. But from 2013, they have fewer disagreements. 'They are not natural bedfellows, but the relationship has become perfectly functional,' says one of Osborne's team, 'It just needs looking after.'

Cogs at last are beginning to turn. Having weathered the Midterm Review and the hostile press in 2013, the revised roll-out plan, agreed by the DWP and the Quad, continues unabated. Cameron has to adjudicate in a minor spat between Osborne and IDS at the time of the March 2014 Budget over savings to pay for childcare for those receiving UC. He comes down on Osborne's side: IDS is not happy, but this setback is small beer compared with the epic battles of earlier years. In September, an accelerated programme for UC is announced, to go nationwide in February 2015, ahead of the election.[25] In October an NAO report, whilst still critical (like many of its reports), is not nearly as damaging as in previous years.[26]

Welfare, like health and education, is a battleground for the coalition government. Cameron and Osborne wholeheartedly supported Education Secretary Michael Gove, at least until early 2014, which explains the ready passage of his schools policies. They both gave up on Lansley's health reforms, hence the change of Secretary of State. But Cameron and Osborne are split on welfare: over personal judgement on IDS, philosophical priorities, and turf wars between the Treasury and the DWP. Osborne's unrelenting hostility to IDS and UC worked for the chancellor as long as the department and the flagship were mired; but from mid-2014 onwards, the overall welfare policy eventually starts to come right with numbers of people either earning more or moving back into work increasing, having been 'slowed down to a painfully slow snail's pace in order to allow it to be on track'. It gives Osborne a new set of problems. The impact on his popularity, and on his prospects of becoming the next leader of the Conservative Party, has to be reckoned with. Osborne's supporters claim much of the credit on welfare is due to him.

As for the impact of the reforms themselves, many in the government see them as one of their greatest achievements. Letwin claims that it will be 'transformational by 2020' and talks of the reforms 'utterly changing the face of the relationship between benefits and work'.[27] Time will tell whether they actually achieve this feat. What is without doubt is the scale and radicalism of the reforms. They amount to the biggest changes to the welfare state since its inception. The path has been rocky and uncertain, but IDS's survival against the odds may prove to be seen as the quiet revolution of Cameron's government in years to come.

TWENTY-FIVE

The Darkest Hour Before Dawn

January–June 2013

'The most difficult period, the darkest hour, was just before the dawn,' says George Osborne. 'I felt we'd done everything we could, we had made our economy more competitive, we'd taken very unpopular decisions, but according to the preliminary figures it still looked as if we were heading for a triple-dip recession which turned out to be completely wrong and the difficult decisions were in fact paying off.'[1] Osborne is in Davos for the World Economic Forum on 25 January 2013 when the preliminary GDP Q4 figures for 2012 come out, which show an estimated shrinkage of 0.3% compared with Q3. Worse, production industries are estimated to have decreased by 1.8% in Q4 compared to Q3 in 2012, reversing a 0.7% increase over the previous quarter due to a bounce from the Olympics. Osborne and Rupert Harrison reel at the news. They had hoped that the double dip at the end of the 2011 and beginning of 2012 had been reversed by the Olympics factor. 'It was a very significant blow. Definitely the low point,' recalls Harrison.[2] 'When we got the news he went blank, he was lost,' says one close to Osborne. 'It was immediately difficult as we knew we had to get through that day without him giving any indication on his face or voice that there was anything he was worried about.' The night the figures come out, *Channel 4 News* present a discussion about the likelihood of a triple dip.[3] Triple dip is suddenly the talk everywhere that January.

On 4 February, Osborne, Ed Llewellyn, Kate Fall and Harrison are talking to the PM in his room shortly after their return from Davos. The atmosphere is bleak. A triple dip may well spell the end for Plan A, the chancellorship of Osborne, and possibly even the premiership of Cameron. They contemplate this grim scenario, and debate stimulus possibilities for the 2013 Budget. Then, suddenly, Harrison pipes up: 'We don't need to change our strategy. The next few months will be difficult, but by July, we're going to be going gangbusters.' It takes some time for what he says to sink in, then they laugh. They want to believe him, but they are not certain he is being serious, or that they understand his grounds for optimism. Harrison is not normally brazen but today he is a man possessed. He thinks that Whitehall has allowed itself to become hexed by looking backwards, at the last set of historic figures, rather than forwards. He is struck by the important improvement in financial conditions in the second half of 2012, helped significantly by the Funding for Lending scheme, which Mervyn King announced at Mansion House in June 2012, and which was feeding through into some of the monetary numbers and consumer confidence. Smart hedge-fund managers too were buying and making money. So sure of his ground is Harrison that he gets Llewellyn to record the prediction in his notebook. He asks Llewellyn to sign a copy and puts it up in his office in the Treasury.

Osborne nevertheless remains under intense pressure. Too many of those who had backed him since 2010 are beginning to turn away. There are some in the Treasury who feel that the 'community of support we had built up from 2010, the OECD, the IMF, the governor of the Bank of England, most of the broadsheet press, it was all beginning to wither'. *The Economist* gives out noises that it is still supportive, whereas in reality, it is joining a long list of doubters. On 23 February 2013 it concludes 'the long road to a balanced budget is getting longer'.[4] A few remain loyal, including some in the business community, many Conservatives and Liberal Democrats. 'Above all, very crucially, George had the support of the PM,' says a figure close to Osborne. 'But George's worry was that even the remaining support would begin to fray if we registered a triple dip, and things could get really tough in the summer.' As the weeks pass, cracks begin to appear within Cabinet. Ken Clarke, with all the authority of a former chancellor, begins to say a triple dip is now likely, and that they should 'brace, brace'. Vince Cable is making his unhappiness increasingly evident. In early March, he writes an article in the *New Statesman* about Plan A entitled 'When the facts change, should I change my mind?'[5] Cameron's team worry that Cable might be about to abandon camp: for several weeks, he appears to teeter on the brink, before pulling back. 'He always does that. He looks strong but then ends up bottling it,' sighs one of Cameron's team.

Osborne has his most challenging Budget to prepare to date, which he is to deliver on 20 March. He is acutely aware he has to avoid anything that could be turned into a debacle as in 2012, or 'the game will be up'.[6] His take is that the Budget unravelled in 2012 because the well-off were perceived as being subsidised by everybody else, which seemed patently unjust. The 2013 Budget must thus above all be seen to be fair: if it can be, the continuing punishment may seem to be reasonable. He gives forensic attention to every twist and turn in the budgetary process. Cameron's team at Number 10 learn their mistake of 2012: they too are going to be intimately involved at every stage. 'The Treasury are constantly showing us stuff. Each option they present, we think through and assess the political consequences,' says one of them. This process weeds out some ideas, including for a penny to be cut off the top rate of income tax, about which Number 10 firmly puts its foot down, not least because it is unaffordable. 'We had to root out anything that would come back and hit us in the face,' says another of Cameron's team, revealing a degree of anxiety about what Osborne might spring on them. 'It's obviously George's Budget, and he's a natural showman: that's part of his appeal. He loves to have something in each Budget that he can pull out of the bag. What we have to do is to make the size of the rabbit smaller, and dampen it down.' Osborne feels his team is working in the dark, against the backdrop of not knowing what the GDP numbers will be for Q1 in 2013. 'We didn't know if it would be a triple dip. It was not easy,' says an aide. Osborne knows there is only one question that will be asked about the Budget: 'What has it done to get the economy moving?' What no one knows (but what Rupert Harrison has predicted) is that the economy is already beginning to motor.

Osborne's and Cameron's team are happy with the proposals, so they go to the Quad to run them past Nick Clegg and Danny Alexander. 'I'm very conscious I'm the first chancellor in modern history to have to negotiate my Budgets with another political party,' said Osborne. For all the closeness of Osborne's personal relationship with Alexander, his chief secretary remains a Lib Dem, and that is a constraint, and not always a welcome one.[7] For the third consecutive Budget the Lib Dems press particularly hard for the personal allowance to be increased (to £10,000 from 2014, brought forward from 2015). Coalition rivalry runs high over the ownership of this: it is a Lib Dem policy, though one that the Conservatives have become increasingly happy to champion.[8]

Osborne lacks scope for a big initiative in the Budget. So this most political of chancellors makes it one of his most political to date, aiming it at voters who 'do the right thing'.[9] To counter rising Labour attacks on the fall in living standards since 2010, Osborne freezes petrol duty (to be precise, he cancels an increase of fuel duty planned for September). To please his own backbenchers, he cuts beer duty. Mindful of protecting the government's credibility with financial markets following his decision the previous autumn to delay the fulfilment of his cuts programme, he announces a further 1% cut in many government departments, though not in Health or Education. Corporation tax is reduced in line with his long-term aim of cutting tax and increasing the attractiveness of the UK to inward investment. National Insurance is cut to boost employment: 450,000 small businesses will pay no employer National Insurance contributions. A consultation on the introduction of a new tax relief to encourage investment in social enterprises is announced. Tax incentives are announced for vehicles with ultra-low emissions, and for investment in shale gas. The centrepiece of the Budget is the 'Help to Buy' scheme, one of the more overtly political moves. The scheme offers equity loans and mortgage guarantees to borrowers purchasing new-build homes. Osborne sidesteps the charge that he is stoking a new housing bubble by resorting to the Thatcherite argument that he is helping spread ownership, particularly to first-time buyers. The economy will grow by 0.6% in 2013, he predicts, albeit half the rate he forecast three months earlier.

Ed Miliband senses that he has Osborne on the ropes. 'We have had the slowest recovery for a hundred years … It is a downgraded Budget from a downgraded chancellor.' He taunts Osborne's use of Twitter, saying he could have summarised his Budget in 140 characters: 'Growth down. Borrowing up. Families hit. And millionaires laughing all the way to the bank. #downgradedchancellor.'[10] Labour's punches leave their mark. Osborne is relieved that the Budget is nevertheless better received than he and Cameron had feared. 'The Laddie's Not For Turning!' is the headline in the *Daily Mail*, while *The Times* goes for 'Betting the house: Mortgage giveaway and tax cuts at heart of the Budget' and 'Osborne goes for growth', and the *Daily Telegraph* has 'Osborne pins hopes on housing boom'.[11] For a time, it seems that Osborne has got away with it. But fresh woes lie ahead.

On 16 April, IMF chief economist Olivier Blanchard says that Osborne is 'playing with fire' with his fiscal policy. He openly criticises the Budget for failing to change the austerity strategy. 'I think conditions have deteriorated. There is no question that the fiscal plan – which was designed a few years back – was assuming that private demand would be stronger than it is.'[12] Blanchard's words are bad enough, but worse follows just two days later when the respected and trusted Christine Lagarde, head of the IMF, says the poor performance of the British economy has left her with no alternative but to call on Osborne to rethink his austerity strategy.[13] A few very bleak days follow.

Osborne knows he is still in a fight for his political survival. Looking at a new monetary policy remit is one avenue he has been exploring for several months. In February 2013, he had sent Harrison with Treasury economist Andy King (later head of staff at the Office for Budget Responsibility) to the East Coast of the US to talk to economists and investors about a new framework for Britain. They met Janet Yellen, a member of the US Federal Reserve, and became increasingly attracted to the idea of 'forward guidance', which the US practised, whereby the central bank makes a long-term commitment on interest rates as long as certain criteria, such as the rate of unemployment, are fulfilled. On their return, they wrote a paper advocating the adoption of it in the UK.

Osborne's critical eye turns to the Treasury. He remains very happy with Nicholas Macpherson at its head, and thinks that the machine is doing an effective job at putting the Budgets together and controlling public expenditure. But he is less impressed by the private-sector-facing part of the Treasury, and with its record on innovation, specifically generating growth. (This long-standing frustration explains the appointment of Paul Kirby as head of the Number 10 Policy Unit back in spring 2011.) Osborne also worries about the Treasury's reliance on experienced hand Tom Scholar, who is *sans pareil* in his grasp of banks, regulators and financial services. In November 2013, Scholar is appointed head of the European and Global Issues Secretariat, which, Osborne believes, leaves a gaping hole. He worries that no existing Treasury officials have the skills needed, so he makes two external appointments. One is to bring back John Kingman, who had become the first CEO of UK Financial Investments in November 2008 before joining Rothschilds in 2010: he provides a strong lead on banks, the private sector and growth policy. Charles Roxburgh is the other hire in February 2013 as director general of financial services, who joins from McKinsey.

Osborne prides himself on his eye for a good appointment. Paul Deighton, who succeeds James Sassoon as Commercial Secretary at the Treasury in January 2013, is another example. Deighton had been an investment banker before coming to public prominence as a notably successful CEO of the London Organising Committee of the Olympic and Paralympic Games. These changes in personnel at the Treasury help inject new impetus.

But Osborne's most important hire of all sees him at his most persuasive. For Osborne there are three vital people he needs to consult and keep onside, and he invests great attention on all of them: the prime minister, the Treasury permanent secretary (Macpherson), and the governor of the Bank of England (Mervyn King). Osborne has had a good relationship overall with King, governor since 2003, whom he regards as a mentor, but during 2011 and 2012, he becomes frustrated with King's almost fatalistic approach to banks and credit. King tells Osborne he thinks the eurozone will almost inevitably break up, and the banks need to be strong enough to withstand the shock.

Osborne has attacked the Financial Services Authority, part of the Brown legacy, although he cannot attack the Bank itself as it is widely accepted that the monetary policy apparatus he inherited is working well. But for King's successor, he wants someone who will signal change and resolve. The search for a successor begins in early 2012. Paul Tucker is the leading candidate inside the Bank, though John Vickers and Howard Davies are higher up the list of potential candi-

dates. But Tucker was never seen as the candidate who would introduce the radical change they wanted. Osborne has encountered Mark
Carney, governor of the Bank of Canada since 2008, on many occasions at international monetary and financial forums, and likes him.
Carney's name is head of the list of possibles, but is he only a 'dream
candidate'? Much discussion takes place over whether it would be
acceptable to appoint a Canadian, who would be the first foreigner to
become governor in the Bank's 319-year history.

Osborne had been first introduced to Carney by James Sassoon,
and formed a high opinion of Carney's skill as a central banker. A
graduate of Harvard and Oxford, Carney had worked at Goldman
Sachs, and as governor of the Bank of Canada, the country had been
the only G8 nation not to bail out its banks. Unlike in other countries,
lending in Canada had not got out of hand and there had been no
artificial housing boom. Osborne says whereas King is instinctively
cautious, Carney is far more open to the idea of using 'unconventional
monetary instruments' in addition to quantitative easing to stimulate
the economy.[14] Osborne first raises the vacancy with Carney off-piste
from the G20 in Los Cabos in Mexico on 18–19 June 2012. Beth
Russell, Osborne's private secretary, is tasked with finding an obscure
location in the 'middle of nowhere', so he can lobby Carney without
arousing any suspicion, and comes up with a Japanese restaurant. The
media nevertheless get wind of it, and in August, Carney is asked if he
would take up the post. He says no.[15] The appointment continues to
be discussed among a very tight group, extending no further than
Osborne and Cameron, Llewellyn and Harrison, and Macpherson. In
September, Osborne calls Carney, ostensibly to hear his thoughts on
a list of candidates, though Osborne lobs in: 'You know, you're still my
guy. You're still top of my list. Will you think about it again and tell us
what you need?' Osborne always had an instinct Carney wanted to do
it, but personal factors are a block. Key to his eventual acceptance is
the agreement that he serve just five years rather than the customary
ten.

By the autumn of 2012, Carney's appointment is finalised, and it is
announced on 26 November 2012. Osborne had been consulting
Carney regularly about forward guidance, on which Carney is an
enthusiast. Osborne announces in the March 2013 Budget that the

Bank will set a new remit for the Monetary Policy Committee (MPC) in an effort to stimulate the economy. Then in August, the Bank formally announces forward guidance, saying the MPC will not raise the bank rate from its current level of 0.5%, and will be ready to undertake further asset purchases, as long as unemployment remains above 7%.[16] Osborne and Harrison had wanted the MPC to agree to a 6.5% unemployment figure, but the MPC were not unanimous. The publication of the new remit, alongside Carney's appointment, sends a powerful message to business and the markets that the government is deadly clear about getting the economy moving again.

On 25 April, the Office for National Statistics (ONS) publishes the Q1 figures for 2013. They show that GDP increased by 0.3% compared with Q4 in 2012, with the largest contribution coming from services.[17] Cameron happens to be with Osborne and Harrison when the figures come through. Harrison hands his Blackberry to the PM, who pumps his fist into the air. Two months later, the ONS also revises its figures for 2012, showing the UK had just managed to avert a double-dip recession.[18] Suddenly, the pressure is easing. It looks like Plan A may have paid off after all. In the Queen's Speech in May, Cameron calms nerves with an upbeat speech promising further measures to boost economic growth. On 19 June, Osborne delivers a positive Mansion House speech, one year on from the announcement of Funding for Lending. He tells the audience the economic news has been 'better in recent months', although 'while Britain has left intensive care, we still need to secure the recovery'. This is not the time for faint hearts, he says. There will be no change to the government's central strategy, and no wavering in its 'determination to put right what went so badly wrong'. But he is not opposed to all innovation. The government is to sell off the taxpayer's 39% stake in the Lloyds Banking Group, and he raises the possibility of the break-up of RBS. 'Nothing signals better Britain's move from rescue to recovery', he says, than planning to exit from government ownership of the biggest banks.[19]

Mario Draghi, European Central Bank president, who in July 2012 had arguably saved the euro when proclaiming he would do 'whatever it takes' to stand behind the currency, is meanwhile continuing to be optimistic about the future of the eurozone, further reducing anxiety in the financial markets. The Spending Round in June 2013 announces

£11.5 billion of cuts to come and freezes public sector pay rises to 1%, but passes through relatively smoothly. On 25 July, the ONS give their preliminary estimate of Q2, which shows that GDP has increased by 0.6% on Q1.[20] The figures are revised upwards in August, adding still further to confidence.[21] It is now official. Not only did the double dip in 2012 never happen, but the much feared triple dip has been avoided.

That summer, the sense of optimism in Number 10 is palpable. The bleakness of the economic data in the preceding months has been replaced by much more encouraging news. The economy may have been flat in 2012, and the original downturn after the crisis in 2008 is shown to have been deeper than feared at the time, but UK PLC is finally emerging from the gloom. Miliband is under pressure from senior figures in his party, including Alistair Darling.[22] Osborne goes off to the US on his summer holiday, with the weight lifting from his shoulders. The mood is bolstered further when, in October, the IMF officially drops its criticism of Osborne. In October 2013, Blanchard is reported in the *Financial Times* as saying he is 'pleasantly surprised' by the UK's economic growth.[23] In June 2014, after the ONS Q4 2013 second estimate shows GDP up 0.7% on Q3 and up 1.8% for the whole year, Lagarde says that 'At the IMF, we have learnt that there is no single best way to reduce the fiscal deficit,' and admits 'We clearly underestimated the growth of the UK economy in our forecast a year ago.'[24] After Osborne's long night, dawn lies ahead.

TWENTY-SIX

The Iron Lady's Long Shadow

April 2013

Monday 8 April 2013 is scheduled to be an unusually busy day for the PM. Cameron is in the Moncloa Palace in Madrid, settling down for lunch with Mariano Rajoy, Spain's conservative prime minister. 'The visit has been ring-fenced in the diary; a British premier has not been to Madrid for several years.' Later that day, he is due to fly to Paris to see French president François Hollande. Then he will be whisked back to the UK for a three-day tour of the Midlands, Cornwall and the North-West, to drum up support ahead of the local elections.[1] But the plans are about to be ripped up. At 11 a.m. London time, in a suite in the Ritz hotel, Margaret Thatcher dies at the age of eighty-seven.

From December 2012, information had begun to flow into Number 10 that Lady Thatcher was not well, and a telephone tree procedure had been put in place in preparation for her demise. At 11.45, Julian Seymour, the former director of Thatcher's Private Office, calls Chris Martin at Number 10 to tell him the news. Martin had been looking forward to Cameron's absence as a chance to catch up, but Number 10 immediately explodes into life. Craig Oliver calls Cameron's team in Madrid. 'Look, Baroness Thatcher has died. We need to get words out from the PM, very clearly. We need him back here very quickly.' Ed Llewellyn is at the lunch in the Moncloa Palace and receives a text with the news as they are sitting down. He decides that they should remain for the rest of the meal, but fly back to the UK immediately afterwards. A draft statement has already been prepared for the occasion. As they leave the palace, the statement from London is handed to Cameron: 'It was with great sadness that I learned of Lady Thatcher's death, he tells the assembled cameras. 'We've lost a great leader, a great prime minister and a great Briton.'[2]

Hollande must be stood up. Sensitive conversations are held with the Elysée Palace explaining why the PM must return immediately to London. While Cameron's plane hurries back from Madrid, Cameron and his team agree the text of the statement he will deliver. As Llewellyn finalises the text, Oliver talks to the BBC about filming Cameron's statement outside Number 10. Wearing a black tie, he delivers the agreed words: 'Margaret Thatcher didn't just lead our country; she saved our country ... She was the shopkeeper's daughter from Grantham who made it all the way to the highest office in the land ... If there is one thing that cuts through all of this, one thing that runs through everything that she did, it was her lionhearted love of this country. She was the patriot prime minister.'

Cameron's team are happy that the statement demonstrates to the nation that he understands the full significance of this moment in British history. They have to fight against an institutional inertia in Whitehall: 'The system wants you to slightly undercook things,' says one, 'but too much is at stake. It was a major moment and we needed to demonstrate that as a Conservative, the PM understood the scale of it,' says an aide. The three-day regional tour is promptly cancelled.

Handling the delicate question of Margaret Thatcher's legacy has never been far from the surface. She had a profound influence on Cameron: when he was at Oxford, he held a party in his room to celebrate her third election victory in June 1987.[3] Alongside Llewellyn, he had worked for her in the Conservative Research Department. They resolved that, should she die while he is in Downing Street, they would make it a major national moment. His relationship with her when he became party leader in 2005 began poorly: at a meeting shortly after his election, she was heard to remark that she could not believe anyone not wearing a tie could possibly be a Conservative leader.[4] To the bafflement and frustration of Cameron's team, she accepted Gordon Brown's invitation to visit Number 10 for tea on 13 September 2007.[5] The acceptance of the invitation would have been decided by Thatcher's praetorian guard, a source of concern in itself.

On 8 June 2010, very shortly after Cameron becomes prime minister, he invites her to tea. For Cameron and his close team, this is a moment to savour. They meet upstairs in the White Room. Respect for Lady Thatcher also means that in October that year she is invited to Downing Street for her eighty-fifth birthday. Along with former Cabinet colleagues, the staff who worked with her in Number 10 are also invited. But on the day, a message arrives that she is too unwell to attend. The party goes ahead without her at her office's wish.

Margaret Thatcher still casts a deep shadow over the Conservative Party. That shadow had significantly damaged the premiership of Major, whom she treated deplorably, deliberately undermining him.[6] In the eyes of many commentators on the right, like Simon Heffer and Charles Moore, Major had been part of the 'great betrayal' of Thatcherism.[7] Vernon Bogdanor, who taught Cameron at Oxford, reminded him that democracy is government by explanation, and wrote to him saying that it is not enough to have good policies – what is also vital is to communicate them to the country.[8] Cameron models some of his personal style on her, such as her insistence on punctuality, on injecting urgency into the system, and personally driving it forward. But in some ways, as William Hague notes, Cameron is more like Harold Macmillan, albeit more ambitious for change.[9] It was Macmillan's portrait that hung above Cameron's desk in the Commons when he was Leader of the Opposition. In his first speech as Tory leader on 6 December 2005, in the full flood of the modernisation phase, he very deliberately distanced himself from one of her best-known statements: 'There is such a thing as society, it's just not the same as the state.'[10] Cameron indeed felt that for all her achievements, she could be needlessly rebarbative and divisive.

After the crash and the adoption of austerity, Cameron moves closer to Thatcher ideologically. One of the key lessons that Cameron, Osborne and Hague take from the Thatcher years is the Budget of 1981, in which, despite widespread criticism from economists and commentators, the direction did not change and Thatcher and her chancellor Geoffrey Howe stuck tenaciously to their plan. 'We were all schooled in the Geoffrey Howe Budget of 1981,' says Rupert Harrison, 'we all knew it would be difficult and we'd have to stick to our strategy.' Cameron admired Thatcher for triumphing over her opposition and confounding her critics against the odds. There are lessons for his administration. 'People misremember the Thatcher syndrome and expect it to be easy today,' he says.[11]

Shortly after her death, he says on Radio 4 that 'we're all Thatcherites now'.[12] Does he believe it? Scratch below the surface, and he refuses to describe himself as a 'Thatcherite', but rather a 'Thatcher supporter'. He and Hilton admire aspects of her thinking, but a yawning gulf remains. When pushed to define the difference, he describes himself as a 'one-nation Conservative, wanting to take the whole nation with me' – a phrase that he later repeats on the morning after the 2015 general election. He is critical of her for being 'so focused on economics' and overlooking the fact that 'Conservatism is also about social renewal and communities'.[13] His brand of Toryism is far more pragmatic and traditionally set than the radicalism she represented and inspired.

Within twenty-four hours of his return to London, Cameron decides, after consultation with Ed Miliband, that Parliament must be recalled for a day of tributes. The arrangements for her commemoration are pored over in great detail. He works hard on his speech for the occasion to ensure it is full of praise, but also sincere: 'Margaret Thatcher … rescued our country from post-war decline. They say that cometh the hour, cometh the man. Well, in 1979 came the hour, and came the lady. She made the political weather. She made history. And let this be her epitaph: she made our country great again.'[14] Miliband gives one of his better speeches: 'Whatever one's view of her, Margaret Thatcher was a unique and towering figure. I disagree with much of what she did, but I respect what her death means to the many, many people who admired her, and I honour her personal achievements.'[15]

The parliamentary tributes over, the nation's attention turns to the funeral. Francis Maude oversees the arrangements at the Cabinet Office. The funeral is fixed for Wednesday 17 April. In a break with convention, Buckingham Palace gives an early indication that the Queen will be in attendance. There are daily meetings in the COBRA room. Intense liaison takes place with the Thatcher family and other parties over who is to be invited, and where they will sit in St Paul's Cathedral. Earlier planning in anticipation of her death had taken place when both Blair and Brown had been prime ministers. Different possibilities are discussed with the Palace, including the option of a state funeral. The Duke of Wellington, who died in 1852, had received one, but that was more by dint of his contribution as a military leader than as an undistinguished prime minister. Since 1945, only Churchill in 1965 has received a state funeral, which again was significantly because of his leadership of Britain during the Second World War. They soon agree on a 'ceremonial' funeral, which includes a military component as well as national representation. This accords with the wishes of the Thatcher family, who did not want it to have a status higher than the Queen Mother's funeral.

As the day approaches, meetings in the COBRA room become longer and the tension more apparent. Maude is pulling his hair out over the Cabinet Office's chaotic ticketing arrangements, which nearly derail the event. All living prime ministers and their wives are to attend, as are Lady Thatcher's former chancellors, Nigel Lawson and Geoffrey Howe. Foreign prime ministers include Italy's Mario Monti, Canada's Stephen Harper, and Donald Tusk of Poland. President Obama isn't there but James Baker, Ed Meese, George Schulz and Dick Cheney, senior figures from the Reagan and Bush presidencies, are all to be in attendance. Cameron will read a lesson, and the address will be given by Richard Chartres, the Bishop of London. The night before the funeral Cameron hosts a dinner in Number 10 for all those from the US and Canadian administrations she had worked with.

Massive police presence is required in the event of public disorder, a real fear discussed in COBRA. On Saturday 13 April, a largely peaceful crowd gathers in Trafalgar Square to protest against her policies.[16] 'Ding Dong! The Witch is Dead' from *The Wizard of Oz* rises to number two in the singles chart. On the day of the funeral, angry demonstrators stage their own mock funeral in the former mining town of Goldthorpe in South Yorkshire. Six police forces from outside London send officers, and 4,000 policemen and women are on duty. Terrorism is another concern, given her strong stance on Northern Ireland and support of the USA. The funeral takes place just two days after the Boston Marathon bombing and security is intense. In the event, the day passes relatively without incident. Thousands line the streets as her coffin, placed on a gun carriage and covered by the Union flag, is drawn through London to St Paul's. While some hold placards in protest, the mood is respectful, and as the cortege passes spontaneous applause ripples through the crowd. The service is emotionally charged, although Cameron is composed throughout. During Chartres' eloquent address, Osborne, sitting directly behind the Camerons, is moved to tears. He later tweets: 'A moving, almost overwhelming day.'[17] Although some ridicule Osborne, his display of emotion is genuine, and contributes to his rehabilitation – at least in the eyes of some in the press.

John Major is one of many in the congregation of St Paul's who feel a degree of ambivalence towards Thatcher. Since Cameron became leader, he went out of his way to build a close relationship with Major, and his advice is regularly called upon. He has known Major from the time he prepared his press briefings during the 1992 general election. Llewellyn equally knows Major well from that era. Llewellyn worked for Chris Patten and keeps in close touch with Major's long-standing chief of staff. They work together to co-ordinate several 'helpful' interventions by Major, such as after the Bloomberg speech, on Europe, Scotland and on immigration. A rare exception comes with Major's suggestion of a windfall tax on the profits of energy companies, following Ed Miliband's call for a price freeze in October 2013.

In St Paul's Cathedral, Cameron sits on the front row alongside Major, Blair and Brown. All three had governed the country that Thatcher had so decisively shaped. All three, in their own particular ways, had been shaped by her policies and her style. At the end of the ceremony, as music begins to play, the soldiers lift the coffin and begin a slow march down the great cathedral's nave. The mourners, some mighty and powerful, others from what seems to be a distant era, are left in sombre contemplation.

TWENTY-SEVEN

Maximum Danger: Syria Vote

August 2013

Cameron is relaxing with Samantha and the children on holiday near Polzeath in Cornwall. He is enjoying the August sunshine, feeling considerably more confident and happy than he was on holiday the year before. They are spending a few days at a house rented from Conservative MP George Hollingbery, reading and trying to avoid attention from the paparazzi on the beach and in Cornish villages. His ever-present staff are keeping a low profile, and have barely had to disturb him. But in the early hours of 21 August, reports come in to Number 10 of a chemical attack in the Ghouta region east of the Syrian capital of Damascus. Videos are soon being uploaded online, showing people suffering from the effects of poison gas. Médecins Sans Frontières quickly estimate that at least 3,600 patients are being treated for 'neurotoxic symptoms', and it is widely reported that as many as 1,300 have been killed.[1] The finger of blame points to the Assad regime, as the chemicals are delivered by rocket artillery of a type used by the Syrian government's armed forces. The UN later says that the gas is probably sarin, a nerve agent 'twenty times more deadly than cyanide'.[2] Syrian government forces have been under severe pressure in the region, and reports have filtered through that opposition forces are making significant gains against them.[3] Cameron decides to return to London at once, as Britain, the US and France announce that they hold the Syrian government responsible.

Cameron is deeply anguished about what is happening. He is ahead of any member of his team, any minister or official, in asserting that Bashar al-Assad, ruler of Syria who succeeded his father Hafez in 2000, is a ruthless, brutal dictator, and that the world would be a safer place if he is swept away. On the surface, Assad – who had two years of postgraduate medical training in London in the early 1990s – is mild-mannered and articulate. Once the Arab Spring begins in late December 2010, Assad is indubitably beyond the pale.

Protests erupt against Assad's regime in April 2011, and the bloody military crackdown by Assad's forces incenses Cameron. Unrest is kicking off at the same time in Libya. Many ask why he is prepared to take action in Libya but not Syria. The answer becomes obvious: Britain lacks the capacity to become involved in both countries at the same time, much though Cameron's instincts lead him to want to do so. The plight of Benghazi at the time seems more acute, Libya is closer and, while far from straightforward, it offers better chances of a successful outcome. Syria is also a diplomatic headache. Russia has been quick to provide weapons and ammunition for Assad's government forces, as have the Iranians, while Saudi Arabia and Turkey side with the rebels. Unpredictable forces are at play. Then there is the position on the ground, which is vastly more complex than in Libya. Syria's Alawite Muslim, Christian and Druze communities in general back Assad, while many Sunni Muslims, who make up the majority in Syria, support the opposition rebels. The opposition itself, which initially appeared to be pro-West and pro-democracy, is also splintering: by the end of the second year of unrest, there will be as many as a thousand different opposition groups, with Islamist penetration becoming ever deeper.[4] As the conflict continues, the jihadist groups grow stronger, with arms and resources sent from Saudi Arabia, and an influx of dedicated foreign fighters. Increasing numbers of Western policymakers express concern that any more help for the opposition will simply empower dangerous Islamic fundamentalists.[5]

So Syria must take a back seat while Cameron negotiates his way through the Libya morass. But, by the autumn of 2011, it appears that British intervention there is reaching a successful conclusion. His gaze starts to turn eastwards towards Syria. After the massacre of over a hundred civilians by Syrian soldiers or government-backed militia near Homs in May 2012, the British government expels the remaining senior Syrian diplomats from London. Three months later, Foreign Secretary William Hague says that Britain will supply aid to those fighting government forces in Syria in the form of 'non-lethal, practical assistance' including satellite phones, radios and equipment.[6] In October, Cameron asks Hugh Powell of the National Security Council to 'grip Syria'. The following month, Hague announces that the government recognises the 'National Council of Syrian Revolutionary and Opposition Forces' as 'the sole legitimate representative of the Syrian people'.[7]

Cameron holds back from doing more in Syria in the autumn of 2012 until after the result of the US presidential election, held on 6 November. Once Obama's victory is declared, Cameron and the president discuss Syria. Shortly afterwards, the British government announce they are opening talks with the armed opposition groups. Within days, Downing Street is indicating that the EU arms embargo against Syria should be lifted.[8] Cameron privately tells his officials that he has grown sick of the endless slaughter and the intransigence of the Assad regime.[9]

In November the National Security Council debate a set of papers advocating a large programme to train and equip Syrian rebels and air power options. The British military has also been reappraising options, now that the Libyan conflict is over, including using Western 'boots on the ground' and air power. Possibilities also include creating a large Syrian army in exile, which would be used decisively to reverse the military balance on the battlefield.[10] This would be combined with a robust diplomatic stance by Arab states and Syrian opposition groups in order to ensure their full co-operation. When Chief of the Defence Staff David Richards presents his plan to the NSC in the spring, a response comes back from Powell to say that it is 'more than the market could bear'. It would be unsellable to Washington as well as contrary to parliamentary and public opinion. The military's plan is also rejected on the basis that it will take a year for the benefits to be felt. Richards is angry: 'If they'd had the balls, they would have gone through with it ... if they'd done what I argued, they wouldn't be where they are with ISIS.'[11] He tries to make the point that if the government is not prepared to adopt a comprehensive strategy then 'the next best option was to let Assad win'.[12] He is critical of the government for not being willing to work with Assad, who has the support of a considerable part of the Syrian population, many of whom Richards thinks are more biddable than the opponents. 'They had this moral disgust of Assad. They didn't want to think through second- and third-order questions, to find out what was really happening on the ground, where our intelligence wasn't good.' Others say that as well as never having the support of Washington, Richards's plan is misdirected, and that more attention should have been given to options below the massive commitment of resources, time and effort that he favours.

Cameron nevertheless makes it clear to the NSC at a meeting on 14 November that he wants to see movement on Syria, and in a series of crunch meetings of the NSC later in November and into December, various options are debated. Cameron decides to move ahead on two multinational platforms, the US and the EU. He and Obama hold detailed discussions in December 2012 and January 2013 in which they consider the action they might be prepared to take. His aim is to get the re-elected president more 'muscularly active' in Syria, so Cameron is pleased to find Obama more willing than he had been in the preceding eighteen months. Reports are that some 60,000 people have already died in Syria.[13] Cameron takes the view that things are so bad that action will hardly make the position on the ground worse and offers a significant chance to make it better.

Cameron comes to the EU Council in December 2012 with a number of proposals. He talks about ending the arms embargo and allowing weapons to be supplied to moderate as opposed to Islamist opposition groups. He also floats the idea amongst his team of putting military trainers on the ground to assist the rebels. He pressures his fellow leaders to do far more than simply roll over the arms embargo. In the first few weeks of 2013, Britain succeeds in getting agreement for technical assistance to the rebels, which the NSC has identified as a major priority. Cameron is satisfied with the momentum that this provides, but at the EU Council in March, François Hollande wants to go much further, saying, 'we should lift the whole arms embargo on Syria'. He requests a bilateral with Cameron in his office before the Council begins. Coming off the back of the difficult budget negotiations the previous month, Cameron feels obliged to fall in with the French plan. In front of the cameras Hollande reiterates his desire to remove the embargo.[14] Having made his gesture, Hollande then withdraws, leaving much of the work to get it lifted to the Foreign Affairs

Council from March to May, where Hague takes up the slack. The Netherlands, Sweden and the Czech Republic are among the EU countries who are sceptical, worrying that the weapons could fall into the hands of Islamist terrorists with connections to groups fighting in Syria. Nevertheless, by 28 May agreement is reached when the EU announces that it will lift the arms embargo, though there are many details to be agreed before the Syrian rebels will be supplied with arms.

Back in the House of Commons, MPs of all parties are alarmed when they hear the news. An Early Day Motion on 5 June receives forty-nine signatures, stating that 'a full debate and vote should be held in Parliament' before any decision is taken to supply the Syrian opposition forces with British arms.[15] Little commented on at the time is a sentence saying that if Parliament is in recess it should be recalled 'to debate any further involvement'. As MPs become increasingly agitated, the topic becomes the latest test of the PM's relationship with the Conservative Party. The issue is about far more than the events in a country 2,000 miles away. Backbenchers are concerned by conversations that they have been having with the military, who are not reticent in sharing their dismay at the direction of British policy, and apprehensive that the sending of arms might not be sanctioned by international law. On 16 June, Nick Clegg tells *The Andrew Marr Show* that arming rebels is not 'the right thing to do now'. To the irritation of Number 10, Boris Johnson says 'this is not the moment to send more arms. This is the moment for a total ceasefire'.[16] The *Sunday Times* estimates that two-thirds of Tory MPs oppose arming Syrian rebels.[17]

International caution is also building. A key impediment to any imposed Western solution in Syria is Russian opposition. Cameron has worked hard to build a good bilateral relationship with Putin, with some success. But the Russian president is angry with Cameron over Libya, believing that he highlighted the protection of Libyan civilians to ensure Russian abstention in the Security Council, as a cover for his real objective: regime change. He is in no mood to be hoodwinked again. Moreover, Syria is an ally of Russia, a purchaser of its military merchandise and host to a Russian naval facility at Tartus. All of this could be jeopardised if Assad is toppled and a Western-backed regime comes to power in Damascus. Cameron must work on Putin. On 10 May, he travels to Sochi to see him with the proposal of a Dayton-style peace conference (which had ended the war in Bosnia in 1995 by dividing the country between combatants). Cameron has a long bilateral with Putin, accompanied by National Security Advisor Kim Darroch and his Russian counterpart Yuri Ushakov. Cameron tries hard and, he believes, with some success to persuade the Russian leader that they both want the same end, i.e. neither of them have any interest in Syria falling apart. Cameron reassures him that the British understand the Russians want continuity, and want Assad and his military to remain in power. The British want to bring the Syrian leaders round the table and changes made on the ground. Putin is surprised and, the British feel, open to the PM's argument that his aim is not regime change, but to deal with both sides in order to achieve a ceasefire and peace deal. Then the government and moderate opposition forces could combine to defeat the extremist Islamists. However, there is still a point of fundamental disagreement: Cameron insists that Assad must leave power once a deal is brokered; Putin is adamant that Assad must stay.

Talks between London and Washington have taken place to ensure the Obama administration is happy with what Cameron is proposing to Putin. Number 10 is disquieted to hear that US Secretary of State John Kerry had been in Moscow two days before his visit, which has the effect of diminishing Cameron's pitch. The irritation is magnified because the PM's party are not told exactly what the Russians and Americans have agreed. 'Kerry felt he'd secured a version of a deal over Syria, but we felt we hadn't been able to go into specifics to tie Putin to it,' says one of Cameron's team. It is a low point in the Number 10/White House relationship, especially coming just five months after the criticism by Philip Gordon, a senior State Department official, of Cameron's EU referendum announcement. It is a long way from the bonhomie of Cameron's visit to Washington in March 2012.

Syria becomes the hot topic at the G8 hosted by Britain at Lough Erne in Northern Ireland from 17–18 June 2013. Cameron has put great effort into the gathering, which has free trade, tax, and financial transparency as the main points on the agenda.[18] He fights hard to stop Syria from sucking all the energy out of the discussions, but has to bow to the inevitable. Dinner on Monday 17 June is tense. After deliberating with his team, Cameron decides to seat Obama and Putin opposite each other. They spar throughout the dinner. Merkel is unusually quiet. Putin is imperious, and out on a limb while Cameron and Obama try to secure an agreement that some form of action is required in Syria to stop the bloodshed. A statement is agreed that all parties support a Syrian peace conference, but this fools nobody; the differences between the G8 leaders are enormous. 'It is a papering over the cracks merely,' says one.

Progress on Syria remains deadlocked for the next two months until the news comes through of the 21 August chemical attack. The year before, Obama had said that Assad's use of chemical weapons would constitute a 'red line' that, if crossed, would demand a Western response.[19]

Cameron knows what it means the moment he hears. Interrupted summer holidays have become the norm and Samantha has learned to accept them. In 2011, they had to return from Italy to deal with the London riots, in 2012 the Olympics and Paralympics broke up any chance of a long rest together. Now it is Syria. Obama is on the secure line in Cornwall. They discuss what has happened. They agree they need to talk properly. Cameron returns swiftly to London, but for three days is unable to reach the president. The message comes back from the White House that Obama is unable to speak. 'We had had this before from the White House, constant excuses when he didn't want to talk,' says an aide.

On the evening of Saturday 24 August, Obama eventually comes through. Cameron takes the call at Chequers, while Ed Llewellyn, Darroch and others assemble in Number 10. 'It is typical uncompromising Obama style, not "What do you think?" as Bush might have said.' Obama has spent three days with his staff deliberating the American response and is now simply informing Cameron what the US is planning to do. They will be making a strike on Syria on Monday, with an unspecified number of cruise missiles. The British are told they can't tell anyone. Cameron says he supports the American action and welcomes 'decisive action' by the president. Cameron calls Clegg, who is staying with his parents-in-law in Spain. 'He asked if I thought there was a case to join in American action,' Clegg recalls. 'I didn't need long to think about it. If Obama thought it was right to remove chemical weapons from the battlefield, why would we not?'[20] On Sunday 25 August, Cameron convenes a meeting of senior advisers at Chequers, including Llewellyn, Richards and Darroch. They explore how British forces might be able to support American action, and what might be possible with submarines and missiles. Fear of possible Syrian counterattacks is a consideration. The Russians are thought likely to block any proposed action in the UN. 'It all looked pretty difficult for us in the time frame the Americans were giving to us,' says one insider. The Americans are planning a short, sharp 'command and control operation, targeting military installations' (rather than Assad himself). Cameron decides to write a personal note to Obama.

It takes the form of a typed letter which he signs and which is sent down the secure line. It confirms that he is supportive of the American action, but for it to work for him, he would like reassurance on three points: that there is indisputable evidence about what has happened, a clear legal basis for military action, and that the UN is behind it, with a proper role. Cameron's advisers are uncertain whether, after the letter is sent, the US will strike the next day. They agree that if their attack is delayed for a few days, given the Early Day Motion of the previous June, it will be necessary to recall Parliament, and that the NSC should be convened on the Wednesday, and Cabinet the following day. 'We all knew our marching orders. The meeting then breaks up.' Communications with Washington remain far from perfect. No one knows exactly what is happening in the White House. On Monday 26 August, reports are received that US Navy warships are positioned to strike Syria. But it becomes clear as the hours pass that they will not go into action that day. Over the weekend the Syrian government had announced that UN weapons inspectors, who had been despatched by the UN Security Council, would be allowed into the country to inspect the site of the Damascus attack. Obama tries unsuccessfully to persuade Secretary General Ban Ki-moon to pull the mission back. The president realises he cannot launch air strikes while UN inspectors are in the country. Crucially, the delay opens the way for a parliamentary debate.

Cameron comes back to Downing Street, and for two days is in back-to-back meetings. The legality of any action is a predominant concern. Cameron and his team are given legal advice by the Attorney General, Dominic Grieve, and by the Joint Intelligence Committee. By the time Cabinet meets, the legal position is thus clarified and each minister is given a carefully prepared portfolio reassuring them on the precise position, that military intervention could be justified on humanitarian grounds.[21] As with Libya, the long shadow of the Iraq War, when the legality of British action was in dispute, is present. Ken Clarke, who had been Justice Secretary till the year before, says: 'I was of the view that [Assad] was trying out the use of chemical weapons step by step, seeing if anybody responded [to] "punish" him in the international community. If we didn't, he would start using his chemical weapons to the full. We were thus going to attack targets specifically [related to the] use of chemical weapons.'[22] Clarke is so confident of parliamentary backing that he will return to his holiday in Portugal shortly afterwards, but 'by the time the Labour Party decided to play silly games and vote against us, it was too late for me to get back'.[23] Many assume that because parliamentary backing in Libya had not been difficult in 2011, support for limited action now in these extreme circumstances will be forthcoming.

Downing Street keep trying to understand when the Americans are planning to strike. Richards, who manages to talk to his US counterparts, is gung-ho at first, but becomes more cautious when the Americans begin to prevaricate. At first, a limited strike is the American plan, but everything hinges on its timing, and what they are expecting from the British. 'We were struggling to understand what it was the White House wanted from us,' says an official. It is clear, though, that it wants some sort of British military contribution in support of the American action.

The recall of Parliament is another key topic in Cameron's in-tray. Cameron and Osborne favour a recall – the Early Day Motion in June requires no less – on the Thursday. (They consider Saturday or Sunday, in order to give MPs more time to plan their return, but rule it out in the likely event of early American action on Friday.) Cameron's advisers meet and agree he should make the opening speech in the debate and Clegg wind it up. Osborne, the chief whip George Young, and Defence Secretary Philip Hammond are all broadly supportive. One dissenting voice is Hague's. The assumption amongst all present is that there will need to be a precise motion and then a vote on it. Hague is not against it, but he urges caution. 'Are you sure that we would win a *vote?*' he asks. Everyone goes quiet. The chief proponent on the other side is Craig Oliver. 'Look, you can't just recall Parliament about going to war and merely have a conversation. You have to vote,' he says. Hague reminds them that there are parliamentary devices to end the debate, which would avoid voting on the motion, though he advises against this.

On Monday evening, however, they are still debating whether Parliament needs to be recalled. There is no absolute need to do so, says Michael Gove. The final decision for recall is taken in a phone call between Cameron and Osborne. By that evening it becomes clear that the US timetable is slipping. But the likelihood of an early American strike remains. 'If a military strike took place and we'd had a week's notice and hadn't bothered to recall Parliament, it would have caused us a big political problem,' says one aide. On Tuesday morning, Cameron phones Commons speaker John Bercow about the crisis. At 12.36, on Oliver's suggestion, he tweets: 'Speaker agrees my request to recall Parliament on Thurs. There'll be a clear Govt motion & vote on UK response to chemical weapons attacks.'[24]

The focus now shifts to Labour. Their support is crucial for the vote. Cameron's team expect Ed Miliband to be wholly supportive. 'It is probably fair to say that we started with the expectation that chemical weapons used against innocent people by a murderous regime was a pretty clear red line, so we were not expecting it to be difficult with them.' It turns out to be far from easy.

Cameron's first call to Miliband is on Tuesday afternoon. The Labour leader falls short of full support. 'The evidence has to be clear,' he tells Cameron, who mulls over with his team exactly what Miliband means. 'He seemed to imply that he wanted to find a way to support military action,' they conclude. Later on Tuesday, Miliband comes into Downing Street with shadow Foreign Secretary Douglas Alexander to see Cameron, Clegg and Hague. Cameron briefs them on what they know about the chemical attack on Damascus. He says there is still no final decision from Obama, who is asking the British to be ready to take part, 'but we have yet to give our reply'. 'We want to have a multilateral approach with the UN to ensure that any action would be proportional, legal and focused on deterring chemical weapons use, rather than having a wider role in the conflict.' Cameron tells Miliband about the NSC meeting planned for the following day and Cabinet on Thursday. 'I hope we can act on an all-party basis to deplore chemical weapons use and put pressure on the regime,' Cameron says. Clegg backs him up: 'I am thoroughly convinced that chemical weapons have been used. They have been outlawed since the 1920s. It is abhorrent. It is not about changing the wider conflict dynamic, but standing up to chemical weapons.'

Miliband listens carefully before responding with four prepared questions: 'What about the UN inspectors and their efforts, and why not wait? What legal authority would we be acting on? What would be the military objectives? How would it be demonstrable that we'd be stopping something worse happening and avoiding escalation?' Cameron replies that he is happy to share information on a Privy Council basis, meaning that Miliband and Douglas Alexander would be bound to confidentiality. He says that the legal advice is clear, that he will be hoping for support at the UN, and that it is important at least to try to stop chemical weapons. Both Labour politicians ask why they cannot try for a UN Security Council Resolution, and probe more about the timescale for action. Cameron replies that they are unaware of precise US intentions but do not anticipate any strikes before Thursday. Miliband responds: 'I really don't want to oppose this, but we have to take the public with us.' Cameron promises to brief him on further evidence and on the precise military objectives. Miliband expresses concern that 'the parliamentary time plan is very tricky'. 'Yes, it's all a tricky balance,' agrees Cameron, adding 'To be fair, this is only about action that would be legal and aimed at chemical weapons.' 'What if they keep using them? What can we do to build wider legitimacy?' asks Alexander. The meeting serves only to confirm the sense among Cameron, Clegg and Hague that Labour want to find a way to support them.

Later that evening, Miliband phones the PM. Cameron's team believe that Miliband has been talking to shadow Cabinet colleagues and is getting cold feet. 'We can't do this without a UN Resolution, or if a UN Resolution is vetoed by Russia,' Miliband says. Further calls take place between their chiefs of staff that evening. Cameron decides that he must himself speak to Mark Lyall Grant, British Permanent Representative at the UN, to see what more can be done in New York. He realises that before any British decision is made, Labour will want to be reassured that every possible UN avenue has been fully explored. The White House is becoming worried about the situation in London, as they know there is little chance of agreement among the five permanent members on the UN Security Council. So further conversations take place late into the night between Llewellyn, Darroch and foreign policy private secretary John Casson in London with Lyall Grant and his team in New York, who agree to initiate informal consultations with the other members of the Security Council. Their joint endeavour to show that the British have been trying to establish the basis of a UNSCR is damaged when it becomes clear from these soundings that Russia is highly likely to exercise a veto. Clegg comes into the PM's study late that Tuesday evening. They recognise that they are in a very tight spot. 'We can still thread the eye of this needle with something dramatic to convince the public that we have tried and hit a brick wall with the Russians,' says Clegg.

Wednesday 28 August is a difficult day. 'The mood changed in those little gatherings in the prime minister's office on the Wednesday. It suddenly darkens because MPs are starting to flood back to their constituencies after the holidays and the Whips' Office were talking to them. Suddenly there is a list of Tory dissidents, and it is quite long,' recalls a senior official. Miliband is becoming more sceptical by the hour. Opinion divides in Cameron's team between those who think he is being influenced by pressure from sceptical Labour colleagues, and those who believe his whole stance is part of a cynical ploy. Cameron himself is starting to wonder whether Labour are serious about action. Miliband's team are adamant that at no point was he ever convinced about the need for action and neither did he ever convey that impression to Cameron. 'Both the Conservatives and Labour had reasons to think that Miliband was consistent: more consistently playing a game, say the Conservatives, or more consistently doubtful, say Labour,' as one observer puts it.

Tory backbencher Nick de Bois is one of many returning MPs who have asked their constituents for feedback and is besieged by emails 'overwhelmingly opposed' to intervention.[25] Few opinion polls are being published because of the speed of events. On 28 August, however, YouGov suggest that the British public oppose military action in the form of missile strikes by a ratio of two to one. The *Sun* carries the story on their front page.[26] Over the course of the Wednesday, it becomes clear that Labour support will be 'essential' if the vote is to be carried. Cameron meets Osborne and Hague for forty minutes at 8.30 a.m. before the NSC meeting, while Clegg joins the conversation at 9.10. They debate Labour's evolving thinking, but are as uncertain about what is going on in the mind of Miliband as in the mind of Obama. They agree that if Labour tables an amendment to say that there must be an attempt at a UNSCR, then the government will lose. Should they push the White House to gain extra leverage? Their discussion is inconclusive and the mood at the NSC is cautious. Foreign Office diplomats are concerned about how the international community will respond. No one openly opposes the plan; equally, it is obvious to many that, in the absence of Cameron, few would be pushing for military action.

Despite its reservations, the NSC agrees that the British should support any American action. It recommends that British military planes should be deployed in a bombing campaign, and that Cabinet should be asked to endorse that decision the following day. At 2.30 p.m. on Wednesday, Miliband and Douglas Alexander are invited back to Downing Street to meet Cameron, Clegg and Hague. Alexander maintains that 'we were open to support the government' still at that stage.[27] Cameron opens by saying: 'As you asked, we have taken action and we have written to Ban Ki-moon, we have had consultations with the P5 [the five permanent members of the Security Council] for a Chapter 7 Resolution,' authorising military action, as in Libya. Miliband and Alexander unleash another torrent of questions: 'How can the Security Council discuss this quickly enough for a vote tomorrow? Have the inspectors finished their work yet?' Two days earlier, Ban Ki-moon had said a further week's work was required before the inspectors completed their evidence-gathering. This timetable puts Cameron in a weaker position. 'You are talking about this UN Security Council meeting as a moment, as theatre, not substance,' Alexander says. 'How can the Commons vote before weapons inspections?' Miliband asks. Cameron replies: 'We're going to take a look at the motion because I think it answers everything. It puts down caveats and says the things you want.' 'I need some time to reflect,' Miliband replies. Cameron is visibly uncomfortable: 'Time is tight. I've tried to get your signature. I've tried to meet your need with lots of clauses and a long motion. If it's not likely to get your support, I need to know because then I'll go for a shorter approach.' Clegg is staunch in his support. 'Look, this is a moment in history and we all have to choose. Do events require a response? Is this response good enough? It's not about process, although process is very important.'

They are now arguing openly with each other. 'It's not about process, it's about legitimacy,' Alexander says, mindful again of Iraq. 'This is all unlikely to succeed because we know we won't get the UNSCR because of the Russians,' insists Cameron. Alexander says 'Legitimacy is about letting the inspectors work too. It's about letting the inspectors finish.' Miliband is defiant. 'Process matters, it's crucial for support and legitimacy. Our government got it wrong in 2003.' Clegg takes over the running: 'This couldn't be more different to Iraq. We have to make a judgement as leaders. We know a war crime was committed last week, on Wednesday. The French, the Arab League, everyone agrees it was Assad. Yes this process is important, but we have to make a judgement.' Clegg is furious. 'I could tell Ed Miliband was thinking this'll be a good way of absolving his party of Iraq and embarrassing the Liberal Democrats,' he recalls. 'He had a choice to do something big or score points, and he chose the latter.'[28] The meeting breaks up with Cameron telling his Labour interlocutors: 'Have a look at the motion – I've tried to capture your views in it.' He is exasperated.

At 4 p.m., Lyall Grant calls in from the UN with bad news. The Russians will indeed vote against any resolution authorising force against the Syrian regime. 'I'm not getting anywhere with the Russians,' he says. The Russian announcement has the effect of 'killing the idea and foreclosing any further discussion', in the words of the *Los Angeles Times*.[29] The news, Cameron realises at once, is a game-changer.

Clegg's position with his Liberal Democrat colleagues is now in jeopardy: 'If Labour played the UN card I will lose the whole of the Liberal Democrat Party.' At 5.25 p.m., Miliband phones Downing Street. 'I won't support the motion. I've talked to the shadow Cabinet.

I will not be supporting the motion. We would need another vote after the inspectors have reported.' While he is still on the line, Cameron confers quickly with Osborne, Hague and Young. 'Whatever we do tomorrow,' Miliband says, 'we need to go back to the Commons and have another vote before military action, after the inspections.' After the call, Cameron turns to his colleagues forlornly. A second vote doesn't look remotely possible with the timetable the White House is envisaging, with attacks still expected on Friday. It looks like 'amateur hour', Osborne says. 'This won't end well,' predicts Hague. 'Our options are narrowing.'

Number 10 now learn that Labour will be producing their own amendment. A furious government source tells the press that 'Number 10 and the Foreign Office think Miliband is a fucking cunt and a copper-bottomed shit. The French hate him now and he's got no chance of building an alliance with the US Democratic Party.'[30] In Cameron's office, they cannot allow their fury with Miliband to cloud their judgement. 'Why don't we incorporate Labour's amendment into our motion?' suggests a senior aide. They pause in silence. This would mark a big retreat, by giving Labour everything it is asking for. But their room for manoeuvre has shrunk to almost nil. Hague is supportive of the idea, realising that they are heading towards an ugly showdown in the Commons. Late that evening, given the flaky support from the Conservative MPs and the abandonment of Labour support, they bow to the inevitable. The motion on the following day will no longer be to endorse military action, but merely to condemn the chemical attack. It further agrees 'that a strong humanitarian response is required from the international community and that this may, if necessary, require military action that is legal, proportionate and focused on savings lives by preventing and deterring further use of Syria's chemical weapons.'[31] It is clear: a second vote would be needed before any British military action.

Cameron wakes up on Thursday 29 August to a front page in *The Times* featuring another YouGov poll suggesting that national support for missile strikes is as low as 22%.[32] The poll has a sobering effect on Conservative MPs, who have had little chance to hear the government's side. Nick Boles comments 'the national mood shifted in a significant way and those of us who wanted action were taken by surprise'.[33] Cameron's normal 8.30 a.m. meeting focuses on the consequences of a lost vote later that day. Osborne, as so often, provides steel. 'No,' he says, 'we won't dig in. We'll just move on.' He is emphatic: 'We can compartmentalise it. Put it down to Iraq angst, the House has spoken, move on. We couldn't carry the country.' Cabinet follows. In most meetings, few ministers speak. Today, almost everybody does. They all look to Cameron as their leader and are content to accept his judgement backed by the advice from the NSC. The two most sceptical about the proposed intervention are Owen Paterson – who asks a lot of questions, and who pointedly does not say 'I support this' – and Theresa Villiers: 'I feel very unhappy about this,' she says. The PM cannot claim unanimous support, but is able to say that there is overwhelming support for the more limited motion in Cabinet.

Shortly after its conclusion, Cameron travels to Parliament to rally his MPs. He sees a succession in his room at the House of Commons: 'I find it incredible that there were some backbenchers we wanted to see who could not be found,' says an irritated aide. Some are won over, many are not. 'It made a massive, massive difference that people were away during recess,' recalls Clegg. 'People weren't there, they couldn't talk to each other. We just didn't have the time, wherewithal and the venue to make the case.'[34] Cameron has to abandon any further lobbying to go to the chamber: Osborne, Young and Gove are in the lead continuing the persuasion effort in his absence. Gove, a hawk, regards it as 'deplorable' that the Opposition are withdrawing their support.[35] He is prominent as an enforcer, revealing qualities and an appetite that make Cameron believe he would make an ideal chief whip. At 2.38 p.m., Cameron stands up to speak in the chamber:

> The question before the House today is how to respond to one of the most abhorrent uses of chemical weapons in a century, which has slaughtered innocent men, women and children in Syria. It is not about taking sides in the Syrian conflict, it is not about invading, it is not about regime change, and it is not even about working more closely with the opposition; it is about the large-scale use of chemical weapons and our response to a war crime – nothing else.[36]

Mid-afternoon, a meeting is convened in the chancellor's room in the Commons. Much anger is directed towards the Conservative MPs opposing them, and towards Miliband personally: 'Each time we've tried to incorporate him, he's slipped through the noose and makes out he disapproves,' says one of the team. It's become clear that they will not have sufficient numbers for the second motion authorising action. But even securing the first motion is looking increasingly unlikely. The stakes are rising. They discuss again how to respond. Osborne's line is the one that carries the day: 'accept the verdict and move on'. After the meeting, Osborne bumps into the BBC's Nick Robinson. 'We're not going to be able to do this,' he tells him.

At 9 p.m., the team convenes in the PM's office in the House of Commons. 'Prime Minister, we are convinced you are going to lose,' says Casson. 'Quick and gracious,' Clegg says. 'Yes, we should immediately concede,' Osborne says, 'there will be no military action and the PM should concede to the will of the House.' Cameron believes their arguments in the debate have trounced Miliband and Labour, but he is philosophical. 'He was exhibiting a sense of occasion which is one of his hallmarks under pressure,' records one present. Cameron takes a piece of paper and writes out the words he will speak immediately after the tellers announce the vote: 'The House has spoken ...' Some hope remains until the very end. The whips report that Labour numbers have dwindled considerably in the House. But they return for the vote and the day is lost.

The debate lasts over seven hours. Clegg rounds up for the government at 9.59 p.m., and at 10.30 MPs gather to hear the whips announce the result. It is a defeat for the government motion by 285 to 272, and the Opposition amendment is defeated by 332 to 220. Miliband asks Cameron to assure the House that British forces wouldn't attack Syria regardless: 'I can give that assurance,' Cameron replies instantly. 'While the House has not passed a motion, it is clear to me that the British Parliament, reflecting the views of the British people, does not want to see British military action. I get that, and the government will act accordingly.'[37] Thirty Conservatives vote against the motion, including David Davis, Peter Tapsell and Sarah Wollaston.[38] Twenty-six Tories are absent, including Bill Cash and Nadine Dorries.[39] Jesse Norman is sacked as a government adviser for failing to support the government.[40]

In Cameron's camp there is dismay, yet also a sober realisation that if they had won the first vote and then lost the second authorising military action, it might have put the government in an even worse position, stringing out the sense of crisis for several more days. They are reeling. 'I'm depressed. This is a real turning of the page. It's a different world we are in now,' says Clegg. 'It's been the worst moment of being Foreign Secretary,' Hague reveals.[41] Indeed, officials at the Foreign Office note how much the whole experience takes out of him: 'He was a changed man when he returned to work in the autumn.' Hague had been right all along: the decision to go for a parliamentary vote had been a risk – hubristic even. 'This was meant to be a debate on Syria; it actually turned out to be more a debate on the legacy of Iraq,' says private secretary Laurence Mann.[42] Obama is another target for their ire: they blame him for his prevarication which put them in an almost impossible position. Before they have too much time to mull it over, a message is received that Obama wants to speak to Cameron: 'Hey brother, I know you had a tough few days. I totally get it.' This is the president at his most gracious. Deep down, he is conscious that the White House haven't made it easy for their friend across the Atlantic.

Anger in the US is widely predicted when, over the following days, the British media try to make sense of what happened. The last time a British government had been defeated on a matter of war in a parliamentary vote was in February 1782, following the British defeat by the US and France at Yorktown in October 1781. The widespread expectation is of a deterioration in Anglo-American relations.

Obama has been monitoring progress closely in the Oval Office when the news of the defeat comes through. His own anger and dismay are not so much directed at Cameron personally, though he immediately realises that the defeat will make American action much more difficult, perhaps impossible. Obama himself likes Cameron, and admires his fight to secure parliamentary backing. Deep down, Obama's inherent caution has been kicking in: 'Our failure made it a bit easier for him to put the brake on his own system,' reports one insider. Below president/PM level, there is intense frustration in the White House against the British. There is not much personal warmth at these echelons anyway, so when things go wrong, there is little fund of respect or understanding to draw on. Had the vote not been lost, US missiles could have been fired against chemical weapons targets in Syria the following day or early the next week. History would have been different. Assad might not have been emboldened. IS might not have been emboldened. Putin might not have been emboldened. Such things are unknowable. What is known is that on Saturday 31 August, Obama makes a statement announcing that he wants Congress to debate Syria action, a debate that never takes place. Cameron tweets 'I understand and support Barack Obama's position on Syria.'[43]

In Britain, as expected the headlines on Friday and Saturday are grim, many of them critical of Cameron personally for his bravado and lack of preparation or sense of tactical understanding. 'From a sleepy summer recess, Cameron has conjured up one of the most spectacular parliamentary defeats in modern political history,' says the *Spectator*.[44] 'Cameron humiliated as MPs veto missile strikes on Syria' is the headline across *The Times* on Friday.[45] 'There are no modern precedents for a British premier ceding control of foreign and military policy to the Opposition, and only one war in the lifetime of most MPs – Vietnam – saw the US acting without British support', says *Time* magazine.[46] 'Shocking and shaming' is the verdict of *The Economist*: 'Far from the first time, Mr Cameron complacently misread the mood of his rebellion-prone party.' The magazine is critical of many of Cameron's decisions, including his allowing the 'sodden cardboard' Clegg to make the wind-up speech rather than Hague, who is 'probably Westminster's best debater.'[47]

Hague comes under intense pressure to resign, as Cameron knew he would. There is a wide outcry from Conservative MPs and beyond that someone's head should roll for such a major debacle and national humiliation. Peter Oborne, the influential right-wing columnist, thinks it 'shocking' that neither Hague nor anybody else resigns following the comprehensive shattering of the government's policy. Just before the vote was declared on Thursday evening, Cameron whispered to Hague, 'I'm sorry William. I've got us into a real pickle this time.' Hague was looking very glum and physically distressed. 'I can tell that he is thinking he will have to resign,' Fall tells Osborne that evening. 'You will have to go and tell him not to do it.' Hague himself later says, 'I needed reassurance and persuasion that I should indeed carry on, despite the defeat. A key factor was that you generally resign when you are in disagreement with the government, but I was not.'[48] Fall is not alone in Cameron's circle in feeling that Parliament has become increasingly like the US Congress: with the leader unable to rely on his own supporters, he isn't accountable in the way he once used to be. As Fall walks home late that night, she thinks to herself 'This is very bad, but it's not a disaster. We will get through.'

Craig Oliver and his team in Number 12 immediately get to work on the press. The turn is noticeable by Sunday. The criticism becomes less harsh, and talk of a leadership challenge is nipped in the bud. Cabinet remains firmly around Cameron, the would-be challengers do not chance it, and the Lib Dems are solid. 'The way Miliband played it brought Clegg and Cameron closer together,' thinks senior Lib Dem policy aide Julian Astle. 'They both felt Miliband was playing short-term opportunistic games with a very serious issue.'[49] By Monday, the talk in Number 10 is that Cameron is through the worst.[50] At the political Cabinet on Tuesday, Cameron comes across as quite chipper. 'DC was not fazed by the defeat – he was neither chastened nor was he sanguine about it. He was somewhere in the middle,' notes one participant. To some, he is the 'teflon PM'.

One immediate impact is to remove Britain from the top table when dealing with Syria. John Kerry refers to France, which has jets only hours from launching air strikes, as the United States' 'oldest ally', widely interpreted as a deliberate snub to Britain.[51] But support for military action against Assad is evaporating. Merkel explicitly rules out any German participation in such a mission, saying on 1 September that there has to be a 'collective answer' by the UN to the problem of Assad.[52] On 11 September, a significant date, Obama postpones any congressional vote on the military operation. Russian Foreign Minister Sergei Lavrov suggests that Russia meets with Kerry to try and resolve the crisis bilaterally. After two days of talks at Lake Geneva, both sides agree on 14 September to a 'Framework for Elimination of Syrian Chemical Weapons'.[53] Syria sucks all energy out of the Russian G20, held in St Petersburg. Cameron's team scramble for a positive story to come out of it, to distract attention from Britain's diminished role, and alight on British humanitarian aid to Syrian refugees. 'We're flying by the seat of our pants, frankly,' says one of the team.

Syria highlights the difficulty in achieving strategic clarity in Cameron's foreign policy, a difficulty that will only mount. After the Syrian defeat, his stature on the world stage diminishes. 'He hates defeat and acutely felt that his authority as prime minister was damaged,' reflects one who worked closely with Cameron. 'I was very struck on subsequent occasions how vociferous he was on foreign policy: "I'm never going to take that risk again."' The humanitarian idealism that motivated Cameron to want to confront Assad and protect his suffering people remains, but his ability to sway events has been fatally undermined. Within the NSC and Whitehall nexus, MI5, MI6 and the Home Office argue with increasing fervour that the real concern for Britain is counter-terrorism (CT). The release by Edward Snowden in June 2013 of the National Security Agency's secret files is another factor focusing minds in the NSC on tackling the risks of CT. Cameron knows how to read the runes. 'OK, our Syria policy is about CT. How does that affect what we do?' says Cameron openly at a meeting of the NSC in early 2014.

The defeat accentuates Cameron's vulnerability in the House of Commons. From now on, he will work hard to avoid bringing any vote to it, above all on Europe because he knows it will be an excuse for his diehard opponents to vote him down. The defeat works deeply into his sense of what he can and can't do. In future, where he believes British action is necessary, as in participation in air strikes against ISIS in Syria, seeking parliamentary approval will be very difficult (although he does win the support of MPs for strikes in Iraq in September 2014). Equally, he continues to support the US in its efforts to bolster the Syrian opposition with training, equipment and covert intelligence. But his ability to offer overt support is much weakened.

Syria marks the ending of the activist phase of Cameron's premiership which, when the Libya intervention appeared to have been successful, was riding high. From now on, he will be much more of a cautious prime minister when it comes to foreign intervention. He is blooded but unbowed. His aides point to the continued slaughter in Syria, which continues unabated. However, whereas his foreign trajectory is downwards, his domestic authority, against all the odds, is on the up.

TWENTY-EIGHT

Essay Crisis Autumn

September 2013–February 2014

The jibe that Cameron is an 'essay crisis' prime minister, who always leaves things too late to do a proper job, is given fresh impetus by the Syria debacle and on into the autumn, at the very moment that Lynton Crosby is attempting to impose consistency and rigour on the whole Cameron operation. First used within government reportedly by Nick Boles, a loyal minister and friend, the expression is picked up by the press in the summer of 2011 and remains a pointed criticism of Cameron's style.[1] Syria disturbs the tectonic plates, and it will take several months for public confidence in Cameron's leadership to return.

His party conference speech in early October is the next big item on the domestic horizon. Speechwriter Clare Foges has the draft ready unusually early. Her brief from everyone is to 'repeat the 2012 speech' but with less focus on the 'global race'. She had come up with the phrase 'the land of opportunity' over the summer, and is pleased to hand over the first draft the week after the Syria vote. All that is lacking, she thinks, is a 'something' to grab the headlines. Cameron gathers his team at Chequers to talk his speech through on the day of Ed Miliband's address at the Labour conference in Brighton. Kate Fall, Ameet Gill, Michael Gove and Steve Hilton, back from California to help craft the words, are all there overnight.[2] Miliband announces a plan to freeze energy prices, which opens up a new front by putting the cost of living at the centre of the debate. None of them expected this, and twenty-four hours of redrafting are required.

They see Miliband's speech as a deliberate tack to the left. Crosby is not present round the dining table, but his influence is heavily felt.

They resist the temptation to give the speech a new focus, but passages are added, full of passion, sometimes anger, arguing that Miliband's repositioning of Labour will endanger the British economy.[3] 'So when Ed Miliband talks about the face of big business, I think about the faces of these hard-working people,' they write. 'Labour is saying to their employees, "We want to put up your taxes, don't come here – stick your jobs and take them elsewhere." I know that bashing business might play to a Labour audience. But it's crazy for our country.' Of Labour's conference proposal to put up corporation tax, he says, 'that is about the most damaging, nonsensical, twisted economic policy you could possibly come up with'. Labour, he says, want to return Britain to '1970s-style socialism'.[4] More than in his 2012 speech, Cameron is thinking ahead to the general election. His message is, 'give us the time, and we will finish the job'. The Foges phrase, 'land of opportunity', makes several appearances, including in the peroration. The text allows him scope to display his compassionate credentials: stressing educational opportunity for all, regardless of background, the desire for everyone under twenty-five either to have a job or be in education, and praising social workers including those who had helped with his own son, Ivan.

The speech in Manchester is more significant than judged at the time. When he comes backstage for his customary glass of beer with his team, he is in a good but not euphoric mood. He feels he has done well enough, but nothing special. He has covered the bases: paying homage to Thatcher, demonstrating strength on foreign policy to help banish memories of the Syria vote, stressing that the NHS is safe in their hands, and providing evidence that Plan A is at last beginning to work. But the real importance of the speech is the ubiquitous influence of Crosby. 'The 2013 speech was indeed a repeat of 2012: it was all about ramming home the message,' as the Australian master himself later says.[5]

Crosby's voice, not Hilton's, is dominant. Hilton added some nice flourishes to the speech, but his brief presence highlights the fact that the thrust of his agenda, for better or for worse, has passed. The influence of Jo Johnson, the new Policy Unit head, is instead pervasive at the conference: some sixty policies are announced in Manchester to give the Conservatives momentum in the final eighteen months of the parliament.

Cameron almost literally has an 'essay crisis' when delivering his words. He likes to take a hard copy to the podium for his big set-piece speeches. The paper copy acts only as a 'security blanket', because he reads from the words in front of him on the autocue. But two hours before he is to deliver the speech, the autocue malfunctions. The text is repeatedly moving all over the screen and no technician can understand why. Cameron several times pops over and asks 'Are you ready yet?' Each time he is told 'Give us a minute', but is not alerted to the reason for the delay for fear that it will cause panic. The malfunction appears to be a glitch with the memory stick, and the whole speech has to be uploaded again. The text has undergone several last-minute additions, so in the final minutes before he delivers it, his team have to check all 6,500 words of the hard copy with what is on the autocue. Cameron sails forth with the speech blissfully unaware that his team are worrying all the time that the same defect will return. For the speech team, it is the most anxious hour of their lives until the final words are safely delivered.

One initiative that Crosby allows in the speech is the trumpeting of High Speed Two (HS2), the planned high-speed railway line between London, the Midlands, the north-west and Yorkshire and ultimately to Scotland. 'Here in Manchester, let me say this: when I say a land of opportunity for all, I mean everyone – north and south. The country has been too London-centric for far too long. That's why we need a new north–south railway line … Just imagine if someone had said, no, we can't build the M1, or the Severn Bridge, imagine how that would be hobbling our economy today. HS2 is about bringing north and south together in our national endeavour,' he says.[6] Osborne had initially championed the idea for a high-speed rail link in 2008 before Labour adopted it, when the details of HS2 were worked out by the then Transport Secretary, Andrew Adonis, in 2009–10. In January 2012, with the hybrid bill still before committee, the government decided to greenlight Phase One, linking London and Birmingham, with construction set to begin in 2017 and a planned opening date of 2026. In January 2013, the primary Phase Two route continuing the track up to Manchester, Leeds and Sheffield is announced, with a planned completion date of 2032.

Cameron and Osborne share an enthusiasm, which grows during the parliament, for what Julian Glover, now a special adviser at the

Department for Transport, describes as 'big, nation-changing projects that could match what they both saw being built on visits abroad, especially in Asia'.[7] The success of the London 2012 Olympics gives them the impetus and confidence that major projects could be achieved on their watch: the financial, engineering and project-management skills are all there. Recent premierships had been cautious on infrastructure, with some rare exceptions: Thatcher authorising the Channel Tunnel, John Major the Jubilee Line extension, and Tony Blair High Speed One, linking St Pancras to the Channel Tunnel line and Europe. The Transport Secretary post had, despite these iniatives, not been one of the front-rank positions in Cabinet, and turnover of incumbents was notoriously high.[8]

The Coalition Agreement in May 2010 signalled positive intentions, backing Crossrail across London, High Speed Two and rail electrification, as well as calling for investment in a national superfast broadband network. However, it came out clearly against a third runway at Heathrow, or expansion of Gatwick or Stansted.[9] Money will be the key to see any of these aims realised. The Treasury are not keen on rail investment, unlike in roads, which brings revenue via fuel duty. Some officials assumed Crossrail would be cancelled or postponed, as it had not been formally funded by the Labour government. 'Don't forget, the Treasury opposed the M25,' Osborne reportedly says.[10] Philip Hammond, the new Transport Secretary, confirms after the coalition's first Cabinet meeting that Crossrail will be constructed, albeit with economies. After the Comprehensive Spending Review in October 2010 is complete, £14.8 billion of funding is agreed for it.[11] Alongside the construction of the London Olympics site, Crossrail will be the major showpiece for Britain's growing ambitions in infrastructure, and indeed becomes one of the biggest construction projects in Europe. The new dynamism is heralded in a little-noticed speech that Cameron gives in March 2012, describing infrastructure as 'the magic ingredient in so much of modern life'.[12]

Whereas Crossrail is secure, HS2 has a big question mark hanging over its future. Cameron comes under considerable pressure in 2011 and 2012 to drop it. The concern is that the debate over it is squandering too much political capital as the proposed route takes it through several safe Conservative seats. He is told it will soak up the government's infrastructure budget for years into the future. The Policy Unit tells him that the economic case doesn't stand up – the Institute of Economic Affairs produces a report suggesting the total cost would be £80 billion, as opposed to the Transport Department's estimate of £43 billion.[13] But Cameron, readily supported by Osborne, never wavers. 'I feel so much of my time is being expended on short-term matters: I want to leave a legacy for Britain,' he would say. The fight appeals to his combative side: as over gay marriage, he relishes a battle, particularly against certain kinds of Tories, who he doesn't worry unduly about upsetting. He thus brushes aside the placards protesting against HS2 that line the road when he goes to Chequers. He would later retort that it is 'a national joke how long it takes to get around the country'.

When appointing Patrick McLoughlin as Transport Secretary in the September 2012 reshuffle, Cameron tells him that 'I'm very keen that HS2 will go ahead.'[14] The appointment is an astute one. As Conservative chief whip for seven years, McLoughlin is well used to working with truculent MPs. He will show understanding to those MPs whose constituencies will be affected, but will constantly urge them to look to the long-term benefits. McLoughlin is a huge fan of the HS1 terminal at St Pancras: 'When I used to go there twenty years ago, you wouldn't want to hang around for five minutes. Now, if I'm half an hour early for a train, I'll go to a bookshop, or have a coffee. It's fantastic; it's a destination in its own right!'[15] He had been told that he would face the wrath of sixty Conservative MPs rebelling against HS2: but when voting takes place at the second reading in April 2014, only twenty-six rebel on the motion.

Overall, how has the 'essay crisis' PM fared on infrastructure? Cameron may not have found a way forward on London's airport problems, handing the judgement over to the Davies Commission after giving a 'no ifs, no buts' promise in 2009 that there would be no third runway at Heathrow;[16] but building Crossrail, investing more in the rail system than at any previous time under British Rail, and promoting the largest road programme for two decades, as well as forging ahead with HS2 – if completed – is not a bad record.

The newfound optimism makes its way into Osborne's Autumn Statement on 5 December, in which the chancellor talks positively about infrastructure projects. 'Britain's economic plan is working, but the job is not done,' he says. 'The biggest risk to that comes from those who would abandon the plan.' Months of frustration and humiliation since the omnishambles Budget are vented in Osborne's speech. Labour and other critics have been 'comprehensively wrong' in their economic prescriptions, he tells the House.[17] 'This was the occasion when I felt that the plan was working, and my numbers were all heading in the right direction,' he later says.[18] However, as one Number 10 official recalls, although 'things might have been coming back under control, the money wasn't coming through in tax receipts'. The growth forecast for 2013 is upgraded in his figures from 0.6% to 1.4%, with the prediction of growth in 2014 upgraded to 2.4%.[19] 'This was the first big revision and the first forecast that started to reflect the improvement,' says Rupert Harrison.[20] Like Cameron's speech at the party conference, the Autumn Statement has one eye on the general election in 2015 and therefore includes politically significant measures such as the introduction of a cap on total government welfare expenditure. For Osborne, and Cameron, it appears that there is real light at the end of the tunnel. Those around Cameron notice the change in the prime minister. For much of 2012, he had not been himself, absorbing the delayed impact of the loss of Ivan (in 2009) and his father (in 2010), notably over the Olympic summer which he wishes they could have seen. But by December 2013, many notice an altogether new confidence in his stride.

A sense of relief may explain his gaffe in allowing himself to take part in what is deemed to be an insensitive 'selfie' with Obama and Danish prime minister Helle Thorning-Schmidt at Nelson Mandela's memorial service in Johannesburg on 10 December. Mandela's long-expected death comes on 6 December, wiping out much of the reporting on the Autumn Statement the day before. That evening, Cameron stands outside Number 10 and delivers a statement, in words written by Foges: 'A great light has gone out in the world. Nelson Mandela was not just a hero of our time but of all time.'[21] He is adamant he will attend the memorial service four days later, which is where the 'selfie' takes place in one of the longueurs of the ceremonies. When the media storm breaks with accusations of poor taste at a sombre occasion, the Danish PM says she will happily have the image erased.

Cameron advises her not to do so, but instead to auction it off for charity.[22]

Cameron returns from a warm Johannesburg to a Britain disappearing under heavy rain clouds. For four weeks, the country has been battered by strong winds and storms that have barrelled across the Atlantic. The St Jude's storm at the end of October had left four people dead and over a half a million homes without power. December is the wettest and windiest month since 1969, with a wind gust of 142 mph being recorded in the Scottish Highlands. Worse comes in January with the wettest month in the south of England since records began more than a hundred years before. Another storm in early February leads to a section of the seawall collapsing at Dawlish in Devon, leaving the railway tracks from London to Cornwall suspended in mid-air.

Owen Paterson, Environment Secretary since the September 2012 reshuffle, returns before the New Year to take personal control of Whitehall's response. He chairs some twenty-five meetings of COBRA in January and February.[23] Cameron has been increasingly anxious; he has history with floods. When Leader of the Opposition, there had been floods in his Witney constituency in July 2007. Despite making a quick visit before flying off to Africa to look at the Project Umubano initiative, a social action project in Rwanda, in which Andrew Mitchell was a leading light, he received a severe lashing from the media for travelling abroad while his constituents were under water. He and his team vow that they must never make the same mistake again. During severe floods in 2012, a woman had barracked him as he was leaving the town hall in Todmorden complaining about government inaction in West Yorkshire.[24] He knows it is a dangerous situation and wants to get the government response right.

On 27 December, he is at Chequers after Christmas with the family watching breakfast television. He's alarmed at the images of rising floodwaters in Kent. He immediately calls the senior private secretary on duty and says, 'I'm leaving at 10.30 for Kent. I've told the cops. Make sure you fix me up a good visit.' This attitude is typical of what even Downing Street insiders describe as his 'essay crisis' behaviour. Some think the significance of the floods is being heavily exaggerated by the media and that 'the scale and magnitude are not nearly as big as how it's being presented'. They worry that sending him on a personal visit too early, while the emergency services are working flat out, runs the risk of distracting them and exacerbating the problem. Others say 'leave it too late and Sky has already called, and it's second-hand news'. But Cameron is insistent that he will go, so the Private Office scrabble around to produce a meaningful visit for him. They manage to find a press officer and a visits officer who live in south London and dispatch them immediately to Kent to find somewhere for him to visit. They alight on Yalding, where the River Medway has burst its banks. The visit is not a success: he's confronted by another angry resident, making for uncomfortable television and news headlines.[25]

Cameron decides to take personal control of the government's response. He chairs his first COBRA meeting on the crisis on 5 February, announcing a further £100 million for flood maintenance and repair.[26] On 10 February, he begins a two-day visit to Dorset, Devon and Cornwall, including Chesil Beach in Dorset.[27] One of his aides describes him as being 'absolutely spooked' by the visit. He returns to Downing Street all fired up and tells his staff that 'this is the most important issue – nothing else that you are doing matters as much as these floods'. He puts Number 10 on a war footing. When Cameron hears that dredging has not occurred in a number of rivers, he explodes. 'Well, why is it not happening?!' The Private Office have to present him with daily reports, the civil-contingencies team start working flat out on it, the Policy Unit is tasked to look at new measures on insurance, while the press office is under no illusion that the PM believes they are dealing with a major national event. Several in Number 10 wonder at his loss of perspective: '"Oh shit, we've got to get Number 10 mobilised. This is a national crisis." But it isn't,' says one. Cameron believes that action on such occasions is better than the alternative: this is one of those moments when Number 10 needs to take a grip. A farcical aspect of his sensitivity to the media comes on a visit to the Somerset Levels where he worries that his Hunter boots make him look too posh. One of the staff is dispatched to Asda to buy cheap black wellingtons, to give him the common touch. That spring, Crosby learns that one of the reasons voters give for saying Cameron is too posh is seeing him on television during the floods wearing a shiny new pair of black wellingtons.

When the Environment Secretary's retina becomes detached in four places, Paterson is immediately booked in for eye surgery and cannot deliver his statement in the House.[28] While Paterson is having his eye operated on, the Communities Secretary Eric Pickles is placed in charge; he promptly launches into an attack on the Environment Agency (EA) for its handling of the crisis. Paterson, convalescing at home, is outraged not only at the public humiliation of the former Labour minister Chris Smith, who had been reappointed the EA's chair by the coalition, but also at the attack on the 'troops'. Paterson texts Smith to say that he personally would like to praise the thousands of EA staff for all the work they have done over Christmas and the New Year. Paterson suspects that Number 10 lay behind Pickles' continuing attacks on DEFRA. On 28 January, Smith is on Radio 4's *Today* programme to defend the EA and mentions receiving a supportive text from Paterson. This statement does not go down well in Downing Street, and Paterson's eventual dismissal edges a notch closer. Pickles refuses to back down and appears on *The Andrew Marr Show* on 9 February, once again criticising the EA, saying, 'I am really sorry that we took the advice ... we thought we were dealing with experts.'[29] Number 10 faces the prospect of the Environment Department and Communities Department being at loggerheads with each other. One crisis is begetting another.

Problems continue for several weeks, with severe flood warnings remaining in parts of Cornwall, Gloucestershire, Somerset, Surrey and Berkshire. Flooding along the Thames continues to affect homes as the river reaches its highest level in sixty years. Cameron, like many of his predecessors as prime minister, believes that the PM alone can deal with such an emergency: he gives the aftermath of the floods forensic attention over the next few weeks, securing the money and overseeing the strategy until, by the end of March, the problems ease. By gripping the government's response from the centre, Cameron has managed a difficult situation the best he can. A symbolic moment comes on 4 April when the railway line at Dawlish reopens. The worst of the floods are over, and communication routes and power lines are repaired after months of disruption. Farther to the east, diplomatic lines are also being restored.

TWENTY-NINE

China Warms, Russia Cools

October 2013–March 2014

'We must reopen our trade links with China,' says an irritated George Osborne in late 2012. For months he has been pressing for a restoration of normal relations with the country. He is looking for all and any possible stimuli that he can find for the sluggish British economy. 'Calm down. Let's hold our nerves and stand by our principles,' is William Hague's response from the Foreign Office. The Foreign Secretary is resistant to any 'kowtowing' to the Chinese, insisting that the economic relationship between both countries remains solid and that the government shouldn't be panicking about the political relationship. 'You get no favours from China by showing you can be pushed around,' one Number 10 aide insists. But Cameron's instinct is to say, 'This is ridiculous. I have made overseas trade to boost the economy a cornerstone of my premiership and I'm not being allowed to go to China. I've got to go to China!'

The problem with China dates back to May 2012, when Cameron and Nick Clegg meet the Dalai Lama in London, causing real anger in Beijing. At the start of Cameron's premiership, it had been all sweetness and light between London and Beijing. On his second day in power Cameron takes Premier Wen Jiabao's call to congratulate him ahead of most other world leaders.[1] He announces he wants to visit China, and six months later, on 9 November, he is on a plane to meet Wen Jiabao and President Hu Jintao before going on to Seoul on a trade trip. Relations are good, if not warm: 'Both sides were trying to work each other out,' says one in the PM's party. Cameron has his first direct experience of Chinese ambivalence towards Britain: there is huge interest and respect for the country's educational institutions, culture and history, and a desire to trade, but also a lingering resentment of Britain's exploitative role during the nineteenth century. This long historical memory strikes with a vengeance when Cameron and his party are asked to remove their British Legion red poppies, because they are associated in Chinese memory with the Opium Wars of 1839–42 and 1856–60. As they enter the Great Hall of the People they are told in no uncertain terms that the poppy is an offensive symbol in Chinese culture. This is distinctly awkward. Should Cameron do as his hosts ask? He refuses. British ambassador Sebastian Wood draws on every tool in his diplomatic bag to smooth over the British refusal to remove their poppies. The discussions themselves prove more perfunctory than substantive. There is some meeting of minds on rebalancing the economy and on climate change, and insubstantial talks on human rights. Cameron sticks by the traditional Foreign Office stance that the British take the last seriously, but won't let the issue overwhelm the importance of good relations between both countries.

Relationships warm considerably when Vice Premier Li Keqiang comes to Number 10 two months later on 10 January 2011. He is viewed correctly as the likely next premier of China. Cameron wants to do everything possible to cement a personal relationship. This means a trip up to the family flat above Number 10, an invitation chosen in part deliberately to contrast with the impersonal vastness of the Great Hall. Li Keqiang is introduced to Samantha as well as to Florence, and given a personal copy of a book by the distinguished English lawyer Lord Denning, *The Due Process of Law*, which Li had translated from English into Chinese when a student at Beijing University.

On 14 May 2012 the event occurs which reverses this newfound bonhomie. It is almost mandatory for each new British prime minister to meet the Dalai Lama at some point. Cameron is less dewy-eyed about him than some of his predecessors like Brown and Blair, but goes along with what he is told will be a deft way of meeting Tibet's great religious leader without overly upsetting the Chinese. The forum selected is the Templeton Prize award ceremony in St Paul's Cathedral, where the two men exchange a few words together. The religious setting is judged appropriate as it softens any political overtones.

Cameron is warned by the Foreign Office that China will make angry comments but 'it will all blow over in three to six months'. As expected, Sebastian Wood is summoned to the Foreign Ministry in Beijing to receive a rebuke from China's vice foreign minister.[2] Shortly after, a visit to Britain by China's chief legislator Wu Bangguo is cancelled by the Chinese government.[3] All as expected: but after six months, Beijing is still fuming and, a year later, on 7 May 2013, a report is made public that the Chinese government are still demanding an apology for Cameron's meeting.[4] Number 10 and the Foreign Office have miscalculated. They have failed to take into account the nature of China's change of leadership that occurs once a decade or so. The struggle for power encourages senior Chinese politicians to position themselves within the regime. Beijing intends to send the British government, and the international community, a strong message about the consequences of interfering in what they see as China's internal affairs. Moreover, the Chinese government is less than thrilled by London's enthusiastic support for the Arab Spring, as it considers the protests a threat to regional order in the Middle East, North Africa and its own backyard.

Pressure from Osborne for a rapprochement is mounting, while Cameron is asking 'Why am I having to pay this heavy price for doing what I was told would not become a major incident?' Angry words flow between Number 10 and the Foreign Office. In Beijing, Wood feels trapped between both, and anxiously seeks a way of unblocking the diplomatic impasse.

The thaw arrives in the summer of 2013. Beijing begins to feel that the punishment has gone on long enough. After all, one senior British official says, 'it all came out as a major victory for the Chinese over Cameron. No leader in the world will now see the Dalai Lama with the exception of Obama.' Having demonstrated their point, the Chinese are eager to enhance their access to currency markets in Europe, seeing Britain as a way of playing Germany off against France. They use several intermediaries to pass messages back and forth to Number 10, including British businessmen. Senior figures in Number 10 are chiefly responsible for brokering the relationship, working closely with the Chinese ambassador in London, Liu Xiaoming. As part of the new accord, the British signal that they have no plans for a repeat meeting with the Dalai Lama, though they fall short of refusing to rule out ever seeing him again. Cameron restates in the House of Commons that Britain accepts Chinese sovereignty over Tibet.[5] Soon afterwards, China's new foreign minister Wang Yi is on the phone to William Hague, and Liu Xiaoming pens an article in the *Telegraph* on 28 June saying that he hopes 'a new chapter in our relations' is beginning.[6] Osborne's trip to China in October 2013 is an early fruit of the new amity. Osborne is deeply interested in China and remains enthused by the possibility of highly profitable links with Britain. Needs must. His focus on building foreign investment between the UK and other countries finds a receptive audience in Beijing. In an effort to help the Chinese government gain greater international recognition for their currency, Osborne starts issuing British government debt bonds in the Chinese currency renminbi the following year, the first Western power to do so.[7] Another thaw is in the air: London mayor Boris Johnson is in the tour party to promote the capital, and much is made of his inclusion by Number 10. In Beijing, Osborne comes under heavy lobbying to support China ahead of the Japanese for the G20 presidency in 2016. Discussions flow back and forwards between Osborne and Hague. The Foreign Office is reluctant, but they eventually concede that the British will back China hosting the G20 very soon, and will say in public that China will make a very good chair for the summit.

The Foreign Office is not enthusiastic about Cameron having a quick follow-up visit to Osborne's. But Cameron insists, and it is arranged for him to visit Beijing with a large trade delegation from 2–4 December. The ambassador Liu Xiaoming, who has accompanied the party, continues to urge the British to at least offer to help on the G20 presidency, and presses his case while Cameron is waiting to see the premier. Cameron debates it with his aides,. They decide against making the offer, but worry that the Chinese might create difficulties at the press conference. But all is well, and it is implicit that, as a quid pro quo, Cameron is not allowed to announce a new Airbus contract. Both sides negotiate a face-saver – an open offer of a state visit for the premier to the UK, which satisfies everyone's dignity. Li Keqiang, who had become premier in March 2013, hosts the Beijing visit, which is judged by both sides to be a success. Messages reach the British

Embassy in Beijing after Cameron's return to the UK that he is regarded as 'a sensible man in the world, a statesman aware of the issues and prepared to debate them'. Cameron and his Chinese hosts agreed to dub their new relationship an 'indispensable partnership'.[8]

Cameron has long believed that one of the foreign policy roles of the prime minister should be to promote British business abroad. In 2010, Hilton and others galvanised Cameron in his belief and the PM would sometimes even describe himself as 'Britain's most enthusiastic salesman'. Cameron had been on an early trip to Turkey and India with a plane full of businessmen. Throughout his premiership, Cameron would take this role to heart and promote British products abroad whenever possible. The *Financial Times* approvingly labelled Cameron's approach as 'mercantilist'.[9] The 'GREAT' Britain campaign is a further manifestation of Cameron's desire to promote Britain for trade and investment. The partnership with China can be seen as a continuation of these aims.

The new bond is cemented when in June 2014 Li Keqiang visits Britain and £14 billion of UK/China deals are announced.[10] A highlight for the visitors is a meeting at Number 10 in the Cabinet Room. Another is Li's meeting with the Queen at Windsor Castle, a rare gesture that illustrates the importance attached to the relationship with China. The pro-democracy demonstrations that erupt in Hong Kong in the latter half of 2014 threaten for a while to unsettle the new friendship and, on 30 November, China bans a visit there by Parliament's Foreign Affairs Committee. Tenacious work within diplomatic channels averts another stand-off. On 13 January 2015, it is announced that Xi Jinping, the General Secretary of the Communist Party and president of China, will make a state visit later in the year: the last time a Chinese president visited was Hu Jintao ten years before, when Tony Blair was PM.[11]

By 2015 diplomatic relations have been restored to where they were in 2010. The rift over the Dalai Lama meeting has been resolved. Some senior figures within the Foreign Office and the armed forces are nevertheless scathing about the government's approach: 'They've had no strategy on China – it's just all compromise, appeasement and reaction, in a knee-jerk way.' But this view does not account for the economic relationship being transformed. The UK became the third biggest destination for Chinese investment during the course of the parliament.[12]

As relations improve with China, they start to go very wrong with Russia. On 28–29 November 2013, European leaders meet at Vilnius in Lithuania to sign an agreement for Ukraine to move closer to the EU. The host nation and the Baltic states are pushing hard to bring Ukraine into the EU camp as another bulwark against Russia. But this pushes Putin too far. To general surprise, because European capitals had not been focusing on relations between Moscow and Kiev, the Ukrainian government announces that it is halting discussions with the EU, opting instead to pursue discussions with Russia.[13] Putin has brought irresistible pressure to bear on Kiev. With rare exceptions, including William Hague and Swedish foreign minister Carl Bildt, who cautions 'be careful how hard you push the Russian bear', few voices anticipate how the Kremlin might react to the West's courting of Ukraine. The focus of most EU countries is on the technicalities of whether Ukraine meets criteria for membership. For some weeks, Cameron has been reluctant to go to Vilnius, complaining that it will be just another big, boring European summit. Sensing that interesting change is in the air, he becomes suddenly engaged and decides he will attend. At the lunch at Vilnius, he sits near Ukraine's President Yanukovych. Cameron had pronounced him a 'crook' after first meeting him at Davos in January 2011, and refuses to have anything to do with him. When aides try to get Cameron to call him to keep him on track with talks about Ukraine and the EU, he sends a stingingly blunt email reply from his BlackBerry: 'No', in brief. After the lunch, Cameron describes him as a 'deeply unimpressive villain'. Things are indeed about to get very interesting in Eastern Europe.

In May 2010, Cameron had come to Number 10 determined to cast a fresh eye over Putin. Over the previous few years, the relationship between Russia and the UK had been very poor. In November 2006, former Russian spy Alexander Litvinenko had been murdered in London with radioactive polonium-210. In July 2007, both countries expelled each other's diplomats. Putin kept the tension high with his demands that Britain hand over billionaire Boris Berezovsky, accused in Moscow of fraud and embezzlement. Russia's invasion of Georgia in 2008 further angered the West and heightened tension.

Cameron is keen to move on from the post-Cold War uncertainties. What matters to him in this new era is promoting the British economy, and globalisation: hence his enthusiasm to establish a different relationship with Putin, and bring down barriers to Russian investment in the UK. So that he is not under any misapprehensions about the kind of man he is up against, Foreign Office officials brief him about high-octane conversations between Putin and Cameron's predecessors as PM. He realises that he will have to be hard-headed and transactional if he is to make any headway, because Putin will pounce on any weakness. Various avenues for closer relations are explored: the British intelligence agencies are willing to share information to help the Russians in preparation for the Winter Olympics at Sochi in February 2014. The Kremlin see this as a great breakthrough, evidence indeed of a British backdown. As early as his visit to Rome in August 2010, Cameron's team are talking to Silvio Berlusconi's staff about helping open corridors to Moscow. Hague visits Moscow in autumn 2010, which goes well. Cameron hopes to have his first meeting with Putin when he is in Zurich for the decision over the 2018 World Cup on 2 December, but that falls through when Putin refuses to attend, claiming FIFA has been subject to a smear campaign.[14] It is not a good omen. Cameron has to wait another nine months before seeing him, in Moscow on 11–12 September 2011, the first time that any British minister or official has spoken to Putin in more than four years.[15] Cameron begins the visit at the Kremlin by seeing President Medvedev, who had been elected in 2008, but Putin is the power behind the throne as prime minister, and indeed is re-elected to the presidency when Medvedev steps down in 2012.

Cameron has a more intensive briefing about this meeting with Putin than for almost any other of his premiership. He is warned that the Russian PM may well begin by attacking him and try to throw him off balance. But he is pleasantly surprised by Putin, who he sees in the much less grand PM's office. Putin begins going through a stack of note cards reciting statistics about how disappointing the balance of trade still is between Russia and Britain. This is not promising: but he is told Putin regularly starts meetings in this way. Then he switches and becomes more positive and personable, recognising that Cameron is sincere in wanting to forge a personal relationship. Putin waxes lyrical about closer co-operation through gas pipelines, and in particular advocates an extension of Nord Stream, which goes through the Baltic Sea to north-east Germany, to allow Russian gas to be delivered to the UK. As a show of good faith, and to get a dialogue moving, Cameron says he will create a premium visa service for Russian business people in return for Russia lifting the ban on British beef, a common policy linkage in British negotiations with Russia that bemused the Russians. In response, the Russians would allow certain British people who had been banned from Russia back into the country.

The visit unlocks a flood of ideas built up over the four years: almost all possibilities for Anglo-Russian co-operation are now on the table, including science, space and energy. The NSC agree to future energy co-operation – despite qualms about getting into bed with the Russians. 'If you are interested in civil nuclear co-operation with Rolls-Royce, or working with us in other countries to secure a design approval for nuclear power stations, we are up for it', is typical of the messages from London. Much of the thinking is from Number 10 or the Cabinet Office rather than generated by the Foreign Office. Periodic phone calls between Cameron and Putin begin, though Putin is apt to be volatile, and typically starts with long silences before launching into a long list of complaints. One of his grittier complaints is over Libya, where he feels Cameron has double-crossed him, and that the British and French intended regime change all along. Syria is another, and growing, source of difference. The trend line, though, is definitely upwards.

The next big event in the relationship between Cameron and Putin is the London Olympics. Putin wants to come over to watch the judo. Yuri Ushakov, Putin's foreign-policy adviser, calls Downing Street and asks 'Will the prime minister see Putin?'

'Of course he will,' the reply comes back.

'Will the prime minister go to the judo with Putin?' he asks.

'Yes, he will.' 'Are you sure?' Even for the Russians, this line of questioning is unusually persistent.

'Yes, certainly. He will not pull out at the last minute,' adds the official, to reassure him.

'Right,' Ushakov says, 'Putin will come.' It is agreed that the leaders will first meet up at Number 10. They have forty minutes in a conversation described as 'fairly consequential', before leaving by car together for the Olympics. Russian judo star Tagir Khaybulaev wins the gold medal. Putin is extraordinarily excited, though the result is expected. 'Shake his hand at the medal ceremony,' Cameron whispers to him.

'Oh no, no, I can't,' says Putin, bashfully.

'Yes you can and you must,' urges Cameron.

So Putin goes down to the podium and he is rewarded when the victorious gold medallist later praises him on Russian prime-time TV.[16] A bigger PR coup for Putin could not be imagined. He is so pleased that he rings Number 10 from his plane (British officials comment wryly that their own phones never seem to work from British planes). 'Can I talk to the prime minister?' he asks. Cameron comes on the line to hear Putin overflowing with enthusiasm: 'Thank you David! That was an astonishing day. So kind of you to do this. I really appreciate it.' It is definitely one of Cameron's diplomatic highlights in his diplomatic-heavy Olympic Games. Cameron is touched and rather taken aback by Putin's response.

Their next significant encounter takes place at the Black Sea resort of Sochi, where Putin has invited Cameron to talk about Syria. Cameron is accompanied by Ed Llewellyn, Hugh Powell, John Casson and Kim Darroch. The meeting has been brokered by Darroch and his opposite number, Ushakov, to explore a middle way on Syria. Cameron's party are hosted at an ornate if somewhat faded villa overlooking the Black Sea. The leaders talk for three hours and by the end are finding some common ground. Cameron reprises his customary toughness about Islamic extremism and the global threat from terror. This chimes with Putin, who has had his own problems with terrorism. Agreements have yet to be reached, but Putin still shepherds the party off to a gargantuan lunch consisting of ten courses, some of which are modelled on British architecture. The pudding is a series of models of iconic buildings in burnt caramel, including Big Ben. Putin wants to push the boat out as far as he can, and has brought in a British chef who has worked at the Savoy. After lunch, he shows Cameron the preparation for the Winter Olympics, which he is overseeing personally. By the time Cameron's helicopter returns, they are, in the words of one aide, 'great, backslapping mates'. The PM's party are in high spirits on the return to London, believing a corner has been truly turned in Anglo-Russian relations and that Cameron will have leverage as the European leader with whom Putin can do business.

But no amount of bonhomie can disguise the fact that Syria is proving a big problem, despite the harmony in Sochi. Differences with Putin come to a head at Cameron's G8 summit at Lough Erne in June 2013. Putin arrives in Number 10 for discussions the evening before, and progress seems to be made. But everything falls apart the next day at the summit itself, when the body language between Obama and Putin is described as 'very bad'. Cameron is trying desperately to achieve a common G8 policy on the way ahead, but the likelihood of securing any meaningful unanimity is disappearing.

The next Cameron/Putin meeting, the last cordial one they will have, comes at the G20 summit at St Petersburg on 5–6 September. Despite continuing differences over Syria, both leaders feel they have a sufficiently close relationship to talk at the end of the day, following a dazzling light show at St Petersburg's Peterhof Palace. The schedule overruns, and consequently the light show doesn't begin until 1 a.m., with Cameron and Putin eventually sitting down to talk at about 2.30. They cover the usual ground: energy, trade and Syria. Both abide by their agreed formula that, where they disagree, they are grown-ups and can transcend differences for the sake of the wider relationship. But it is late, they are prickly, and neither likes being lectured by the other. The conversation takes a bizarre twist and they end up having a 'bickerfest' about gay rights, both wanting to have the last word. Cameron is riding a high horse using arguments fresh from his jousting on gay marriage back home, while Putin argues that Russia's future demography will have problems if gay people are allowed to marry each other, and that the country will not have enough children to secure its future. At times they seem to be enjoying it, at times they seem angry. They are acting like executives at a sales conference who have stayed up too late at the bar. Aides on both sides just wish they'd shut up so they can all go to bed, amazed that they are still talking so late into the night in the midst of such an important international event.

It is Ukraine, however, not Syria, that undoes all Cameron's careful bridge-building. Putin is clear that he will not allow Ukraine to fall into the Western camp. The West collectively fails to recognise that Ukraine is a failing state, divided into an eastern part that looks to Russia, and a western side that looks to Europe. Had it pumped money into Ukraine in the autumn of 2013, and reassured the Ukrainian elite that they had Western support, then Putin might not have had the window to become involved himself. But it is now too late for that, and all too predictably, Yanukovych looks straight towards Moscow.

Angered by Yanukovych turning Ukraine towards Russia, and reneging on an understanding he gave them, protestors demonstrate in Kiev. By late January 2014, thousands begin to join the 'Euromaidan' unrest demanding new elections. Number 10 is in daily conversation with the British ambassador in Kiev, Simon Smith, as the tension rises. On 18 February, violent clashes break out between police and protestors. Security forces start firing on protestors in and around Independence Square, killing at least fifty.[17] Yanukovych's heavy-handed measures achieve little. Four days later, he flees to Russia. The world takes a deep breath and awaits the Kremlin's response. On 27 February, Obama has an inconclusive telephone conversation with Putin. Two hours later, Putin, who is in Sochi, orders thinly disguised Russian soldiers into Crimea. The Crimean Peninsula is a part of Ukraine, but has a large Russian population, and is also the location of the strategically important port of Sevastopol, the home of Russia's Black Sea fleet. Within days the region is annexed to Russia. The response in the West, according to *Time* magazine, is 'disbelief bordering on disorientation'.[18] Within weeks, Russian-backed rebels declare independence in the east of Ukraine. London is stunned: an official from the Foreign Office records: 'Even those of us who were used to dealing with Russia were deeply shocked. Putin was tearing up the rulebook of international diplomacy in such a brazen way.'

Cameron still has sufficient relationship left with Putin to have three telephone conversations with him in February and March. Cameron is blunt: 'Your relationship with us will face increasing difficulties unless you stop the aggression.' Putin replies, 'This is my backyard. The West has repeatedly humiliated me, over Libya, over Syria, etc., for the last ten years.' It is clear Putin feels the US are behind a plan to bring Ukraine into NATO and to push his Black Sea Fleet out of Sevastopol. He believes that Russian interests were under grave peril. Long discussions take place in the NSC over the limited options on offer to them. It is evident that Putin's reading of recent history is very different from theirs. It is equally clear that having an enemy suits his domestic political interests very well. Ministers divide between the ideologues, like Michael Gove and Oliver Letwin, who believe that strong action is necessary, and realists who recognise that British options are few.

Cameron is wide awake to the risk that Ukraine is under, but equally aware that there can be no conceivable military involvement, which might provoke an unstoppable and unpredictably severe military response from the Kremlin. 'From day one, Cameron is clear that we should not make the mistake of encouraging Kiev to fight based on [the assumption] they will have Western military support,' says a Cameron aide. Obama is increasingly stymied too, caught between indignation at Russian intentions and practical realism.

Cameron opts for a twin-track approach: keep talking to Putin bilaterally, while being in the vanguard with the EU pushing for sanctions, which strike him as the most viable weapon available to the West. Ahead of an EU Council on 6 March, he begins lobbying fellow EU leaders to introduce sanctions against Russia, alongside generous financial support to Ukraine. Herman Van Rompuy, who is the chair, is not in favour of a robust response, so before the Council Cameron convenes a meeting in the British delegation office with Angela Merkel, François Hollande, Matteo Renzi and Donald Tusk to try to gird them into resolute action. He hands them a paper, drafted by the NSC. 'We were far from confident that it would be accepted,' recalls Llewellyn.[19] However, events in Ukraine that day, where separatist agitation was accelerating in the east, are a catalyst to action. Merkel is strongly supportive, as is Tusk. The British are gratified at Hollande getting behind it. Renzi does also, but he is too new in office to have much impact. Sanctions are agreed, with travel bans and asset freezes against Russian individuals and organisations, though the British are disappointed that their own role in galvanising the EU does not receive more coverage. At a second EU Council on 20–21 March, Cameron invites himself to the pre-meeting held by the Nordic states, where he encourages them to speak up at the imminent meeting: 'We needed to hear their voice on sanctions,' says an official, 'and they don't always contribute forcefully.' If Cameron hadn't taken the strong line he did at the EU, the British believe it is likely that sanctions would not have been as tough, or lasted so long. After this flurry of activity, Cameron's influence over Ukraine, and more generally on the international stage, begins to fade.

He comes under increasing pressure as the year draws on to focus on domestic and political matters, with the election less than a year away. In 2008, Sarkozy had played a key diplomatic role during the war between Russia and Georgia, but Cameron does not believe he can be a similar broker over Ukraine. 'You are not suggesting that I do this, are you?' Cameron asks when the option is discussed at a meeting of the NSC. An official who was present believes Cameron did not rate his prospects, especially without the backing of Washington. Ultimately, he takes a back seat, saying he is happy for Merkel to lead on Ukraine. She speaks Russian, unlike him, and has a deep understanding of the region: as she tells Cameron, she backpacked around the Ukrainian Donbass as a teenager. Cameron trusts her judgement, that the West must be robust as the best way of de-escalating fighting and danger. She and Putin have over forty conversations about Ukraine. 'She has an empathy for the place and an understanding of the issues that we would have been foolish not to utilise,' says a senior aide.[20] The British are even content to go along with the perception that France is a pivotal ally working with Germany trying to resolve Ukraine, even if France's involvement is largely tokenistic. But jibes that Britain is absent from the top table hurt.

The shooting down over Ukraine of the Malaysian airliner MH17 on 17 July, with Russian-backed forces the likely culprits, strengthens the resolve of the Europeans to stand up to Putin. Cameron himself seems to be an increasingly isolated and mistrusted figure in the EU. His foreign policy, which promised so much in 2010–11, is becoming roundly criticised. The Economist describes coalition foreign policy as 'feeble', while the Spectator dismisses it as 'dismal'.[21] Internally too, voices in the Foreign Office and beyond are critical that Cameron isn't willing to invest the time in foreign policy or to pick up the phone more to European leaders, above all Merkel. To David Richards, the reasons are clear: 'In Ukraine, as in Syria and Libya, there is a lack of strategy and statesmanship. The problem is the inability to think things through. Too often it seems to be more about the Notting Hill liberal agenda rather than statecraft.'[22]

Miliband seizes on this critique to attack Cameron for retreating from the world. Practically, as well as personally, the Syrian defeat at the end of August has diminished Britain's standing in the world, as well as Cameron's self-confidence and willingness to be an activist prime minister abroad. He is deeply frustrated by being unable to shape a more convincing narrative for all the effort that he has put into foreign policy during his premiership. But he's still prime minister and is far from giving up on making an impact on the world stage. He continues with his twin-track policy towards Russia. He is prominent among those at the G7 (Russia having been suspended) in Brussels on 4 and 5 June 2014, who argue that Russia cannot break all the rules of international behaviour and remain in the club. But equally, he keeps his personal line open to Putin, talking at the airport in Paris at the time of the D-Day seventieth commemoration, and at Brisbane on 15 and 16 November at the G20. Cameron felt it offered a 'glimmer of light'. Messages come back to London from the British Embassy in Moscow that Putin 'still respects' Cameron, while finding him at the tough end of EU leaders. Throughout the autumn of 2014 and the spring of 2015, Cameron continues to watch Ukraine nervously, uncertain whether Putin's next move will be to attack eastern Ukraine openly with a full-scale military invasion. All the while, he has to ward off increasingly vocal internal pressures – from the Foreign Office, which is concerned that he is not involved in the discussions alongside Merkel, and the senior military, who want him to sound more threatening in the name of deterrence.

Had Cameron missed a trick in not seeing that Putin was being boxed into a corner with the EU's overtures to Ukraine in 2013? Could he not have used his close understanding of Putin's mindset and insecurities to have counselled that the EU back off for fear of provoking the very response that occurred in 2014? The answers are unknowable. Of course Cameron could do little to solve Ukraine's deep-rooted internal animosities, or counter Russia's resurgent ambitions. But if there was a failure of Western imagination, Cameron must share the blame with his fellow leaders.

THIRTY

2014 Budget: Powering the North

March 2014–February 2015

'From as early as 2010, I'd focused on the 2014 Budget as being a Budget for savers,' says George Osborne.[1] He knew it would be his penultimate Budget before the general election. 'We had in mind that the centrepiece of the Budget would be abolishing the 10p tax rate for savings.'[2] The proposal is well received in the Treasury, in part because of the 10p rate's complexity, especially with some of those least adept at claiming the benefit.

Officials spend several months in late 2013 and early 2014 with Osborne's team coming up with a variety of savings ideas, several of which make it into the Budget. Osborne is attracted by one idea in particular: a turbo-boost for savers, the idea that pensioners will no longer have to buy an annuity, and will be able to draw down as little or as much of their savings as they would like, with restrictions on access to pension pots removed. 'Why don't we just abolish this?' he says when discussing the issue of compulsory annuities with Treasury officials. He has already been bold on pensions, when in the 2010 spending review he raised the state pension age to sixty-six from 2020, a significant but inevitable austerity measure, which will save billions of pounds; this decision is one that many Western governments are realising they must take.

The annuities proposal is different: it is a genuine choice on Osborne's part, and is altogether more bold and innovative. He is petrified it will leak, so is determined to keep it to a tight circle. In the autumn he raises it with the prime minister – 'the first person I always have to square' – who gives it the green light.[3] When he has risky ideas, he likes to consult one of a closed number of wise voices, in this case former chancellor Nigel Lawson. 'The Treasury will be completely against you, as they were against much of what I tried to do,' Lawson tells his young protégé, 'but you should do it nevertheless. It's a great idea.' Osborne takes the permanent secretary Macpherson into his confidence, who tells him, 'I think you should go for it,' adding: 'the Treasury civil servants will tell you not to do it, but that's what they're paid to do'. Then, still more to Osborne's surprise, Macpherson admits that 'we should have done this years ago'. The idea has been around for some time, but low interest rates since the financial crisis have reduced the value of annuities and made the proposal seem even more attractive. Additionally, the plan will raise money.

The Treasury's biggest concern is an increase in means testing, but the plan's reduction in the amount of guaranteed income needed in retirement to access flexible drawdown makes it attractive. Legitimate worries remain about mis-selling abuses, and whether people would go out and blow all their savings on a Lamborghini. Further worries are voiced about the impact on the financial services industry. The move will be highly commercially sensitive, and affect the share price of big insurance companies. Osborne runs it past the minister for universities and science, David Willetts, whom he regards as an authority on pensions (Willetts had been shadow Work and Pensions Secretary from 1999–2005), and also Liberal Democrat pensions minister Steve Webb, both of whom guide him on handling consumer groups.[4] Because it is politic to do so, he also runs it past Iain Duncan Smith, without great personal hopes of learning much.

Debate continues for a long time about whether he should announce the measure in the Budget, or whether he should say he is holding consultations with a view to introducing it. The 'consultation' option is known as Plan B, and Osborne decides to abort it only a week in: 'Come on: you've got to do things,' he says decisively. A key concern in his mind is that if the pensions industry is given notice, it will run a campaign arguing it is a bad idea, and change will never happen. Discreet conversations take place with those who can be trusted in and around the pensions industry. A pivotal figure is Ros Altmann, a leading independent pensions expert and campaigner. She helps orchestrate a campaign of letters to garner industry support for the move, which despite politicising it, helps tip the balance, and makes it difficult for the industry to come across as negative about the proposal without opening itself to the charge of special pleading.

Osborne, ever the showman, is never happier than when he's pulling his rabbits out of his Budget hat. Another rabbit is that from 1 July, stocks and share allowances are to be merged into one new, much bigger £15,000 tax-free limit for individual savings accounts (ISAs), to be called the NISA. It is designed to appeal to savers who are suffering because of the dire interest rates, and at little real cost for the Exchequer.[5] Other measures include support for business, with investment allowances doubling to £500,000, support for exports, innovation and science, and an announcement that an Alan Turing Institute for data sciences is planned.

The detail behind the welfare cap is the other big measure in the Budget. The Treasury has been looking at finding ways to rein in departmental spending over which they have no control; especially now departmental spending is shrinking and they cannot afford any wastage. Its particular concern is where departments have little incentive to control their spending and where the Treasury foots the bill when things go wrong. The 2013 Budget had therefore announced a cap on annually managed departmental expenditure (AME). The spending review that year provided more detail, which was further filled out in the 2013 Autumn Statement which included more details of the 'welfare cap'.[6] As the DWP is a major spending department, the Treasury focuses particularly closely on it. There is also a desire to keep IDS on the 'straight and narrow' with non-Universal Credit projects. 'The PM's priorities, like migrant access to welfare and the household benefit cap, quite often took a back seat compared to Universal Credit,' complained one Treasury official. Osborne thus announces in the 2014 Budget that he will be capping the total amount government is going to allow itself to spend on welfare – excluding pensioner benefits and jobseekers' allowance – to £119.5 billion. This self-denying ordinance means that if government ever wants to spend more than the inflation-indexed figure it will need to seek parliamentary approval.[7] 'Never again should we allow [welfare] costs to spiral out of control and its incentives to become so distorted that it pays not to work,' Osborne says in his speech.[8] The 2014 Autumn Statement and the 2015 Budget figures confirm to the Treasury that the DWP is managing its expenditure better.

Overall, 2014 is a momentous Budget, the set-piece occasion where Osborne proclaims that the government has at last got the economy back under control. 'We set out our plan. And together with the British people, we held our nerve. We're putting Britain right.' But the trumpeting of the return to financial health does not upstage his core theme. 'This is a Budget for the makers, the doers, and the savers,' he says in his closing remarks.[9]

Osborne and Rupert Harrison devise further elephant traps to try to divide Miliband and Balls, who do not totally agree over the future of the British economy. Miliband's initial response is confident: 'The chancellor ... did not mention one central fact,' he says. 'The working people of Britain are worse off under the Tories. Living standards are down, month after month, year after year.' He highlights the 2010 Conservative manifesto, which had promised a rise in living standards, 'but they have delivered exactly the opposite'.[10] Below the surface, idealist Miliband and more pragmatic and business-friendly Balls work to conceal their disagreements. Close colleagues in the court of Gordon Brown since the 1990s, now they are neither ideological soulmates nor even friends, and Osborne and Harrison are determined to squeeze every drop of political capital from their increasingly awkward relationship.

On 31 March, Osborne is in Tilbury Port in Essex to deliver what the *Daily Telegraph* describes as 'his most upbeat assessment of the economy since taking office four years ago'.[11] He lists the government's achievements on the economy: Britain is, he says, 'starting to walk tall in the world again'.[12] The core problem for Cameron and Osborne is that the long-awaited good economic news does not seem to be translating into enhanced popularity. A YouGov poll for the *Sunday Times* before the Budget, on 28 February, has the Conservatives on 34% and Labour on 38%.[13] A YouGov poll in the *Sun* on 31 March, the day of Osborne's Tilbury speech, has the Conservatives remaining on 34%, with Labour down one point on 37%.[14] The worry is UKIP, on 12% at the beginning of March but rising to 13% by its end. The Cameron team has yet to find a successful formula for dealing with this new enemy at their gates.

The 'Northern Powerhouse' idea is one strategy for taking the fight to the Labour heartlands. Ironically it owes its origin to Osborne's failure to win the nomination for the Herefordshire seat of Leominster in 1999.[15] Had he been successful, he would not have become Conservative MP for Tatton in Cheshire in 2001.[16] From his constituency comes his passion for nearby Manchester, which bears fruit in his drive to see it have a single elected mayor (to enhance budgetary control, and to maximise the chances for a Conservative being elected), as well as the merging of its health and social care services. The whole Northern Powerhouse strategy – designed to link Manchester to other leading cities in the north of the country, including Liverpool, Leeds, Sheffield and Newcastle, and give greater power to Manchester City Council – would almost certainly never have happened had he been the MP for Leominster on the Welsh borders.

The idea came from Osborne, but Neil O'Brien – an Osborne special adviser since 2012, and hitherto director of the Cameron-friendly think-tank Policy Exchange – is crucial, as are the Policy Unit's Jo Johnson, Chris Lockwood and Tom Nixon. Second permanent secretary to the Treasury John Kingman and cities minister Greg Clark are both instrumental in driving forward the initiative. The term 'Northern Powerhouse' is coined in the spring of 2014 by Thea Rogers, the uncompromising former BBC producer who joined Osborne's team in 2012. She famously smartened up his image and appearance (including his new Caesar-style haircut), and also got him making regular visits around the country to see business in action. Howard Bernstein, Manchester City Council's chief executive since 1998, is another influence, along with Richard Leese, the leader of Manchester City Council. Bernstein is a key player behind the city's renaissance since the IRA bombing in 1996. He is a particular fan of enhancing transport links across the north.

By the end of 2013, an appetite is growing in the Treasury to take a northern strategy more seriously. There have been many failed initiatives over the previous decades, which had generated cynicism in Whitehall and the regions. There is an impetus to find ideas for long-term improvements to the British economy. England has cities in the Midlands and north which are too small to compete globally, but which could become a real force internationally if only they could be linked with high-speed transport. Initial plans are on a much smaller scale than the Northern Powerhouse, but still include familiar elements such as greater transport links and further devolution of funds. The plans are gestating from the autumn of 2013 through to the summer of 2014, and further influences on their development include the Centre for Cities think-tank and Lord Heseltine's report of October 2013, which advises further development of Local Enterprise Partnerships (LEPs). In March 2014, BBC economist Evan Davis presents a television programme, *Mind the Gap: London vs the Rest*, which captures the zeitgeist.

On Monday 23 June 2014, Osborne gives his first big Northern Powerhouse speech at the Museum of Science and Industry in Manchester. 'There is a hard truth we need to address,' he says. 'The cities of the north are individually strong, but collectively not strong enough. The whole is less than the sum of its parts. So the powerhouse of London dominates more and more. And that's not healthy for our economy. It's not good for our country. We need a Northern Powerhouse too. Not one city, but a collection of northern cities – sufficiently close to each other that combined they can take on the world.' In the run-up to the 2014 conference speech, Osborne becomes particularly excited about the possibilities of a High Speed Three rail link, connecting Liverpool to Hull via Manchester and Leeds.

The plan addresses the problem, growing since before Thatcher's premiership, of the dominance of London and the south-east. Cameron is particularly attracted to the scheme because by May 2014 the gap in unemployment between the north and the south has become at its worst – 5%.[17] The press response to the initiative is positive. Tory moderniser David Skelton writes in the *Spectator* that the north 'needs to think globally'.[18] Cameron sells the idea to the Lib Dems; Clegg is profoundly unhappy. He sees the policy as a threat to Liberal Democrat strength in northern councils and later launches a rival initiative called Northern Futures Plan. He also feels the policy gives greater power to Manchester without a similar initiative for Sheffield, which includes his own constituency. Despite later negotiating a separate deal for Sheffield, Clegg is 'furious' with Osborne at the time and feels it is an attempt to do him political damage, a claim denied by Osborne: 'I had a massive clash with Nick Clegg, which caused a lot of bad blood which was unfortunate, as I never set out to do that.'[19] Upon hearing further details of the Northern Powerhouse in the Autumn Statement, Clegg calls Cameron from a windy Bristol airport telling him it is 'just ridiculous'. 'Why don't you sort it out?' the PM replies. But Osborne is unrepentant. Upsetting Clegg no longer concerns him. Further resistance comes from Ed Balls, who is persistently negative and attempts to sabotage the agenda.

In January 2015, Cameron and Osborne make a rare joint appearance on a platform, at the Old Granada Studios in Manchester, where they lay out the six-point strategy for the Northern Powerhouse, which they follow with a two-day tour of the north-west.[20] They speak at length about the aims of the scheme: increasing long-term growth in the north-west, delivering the largest and most sustained investment in long-term transport, and making the region a global centre of scientific innovation, with a particular focus on material science, biomedicine, super-computing and energy. This is one of a series of regional speeches given in the first quarter of the year; the prime minister and chancellor also travel to north Lincolnshire and Yorkshire together in February, visiting the set of the television soap *Emmerdale*.[21]

Osborne has several claims to being considered a significant and innovative chancellor beyond the evolution and adoption of the narrative of Plan A and austerity. His measures were constantly criticised by opponents for being too harsh, while some on the right believe he should have gone further down the austerity path. As he contemplates his chancellorship, which is likely to end the following May, he knows he neither simplified nor overhauled an overly complex taxation system. The creation of the Office for Budget Responsibility is an achievement, as is his reform to pension age and to annuities, and further regulation of the banking industry. But his Northern Powerhouse initiative, which was not even a twinkle in his eye in 2010, might well be considered his most enduring legacy.

THIRTY-ONE

The UKIP Challenge

2013–2014

'Fruitcakes, loonies, and closet racists': Cameron's description of UKIP to Nick Ferrari of radio station LBC in 2006 is words he regrets as much as any other he has uttered as party leader.[1] No other Conservative leader in modern times has had to contend with such a powerful new party of the right. One reason his party blame him for UKIP's rise is the stellar boost that his 'fruitcakes' comment, oft joyously repeated in UKIP circles, gives the fledgling party. It carries potency because it clearly encapsulates a truth that Cameron feels about UKIP, or at least about some of its supporters – the racist and aggressively intolerant faction, who he despises and who make up some of its most vocal followers. Equally, as Cameron comes to realise, the party is also made up of reasonable people who have become totally disillusioned with the Conservatives and other mainstream parties; people who see their economic security and way of life being threatened by immigration; who see power leeching away to Europe; and who feel the opportunities open to their children for a better life than they enjoyed are under threat.

The perception that Cameron, an Old Etonian and privileged Tory, is dismissing and patronising a large element of the right-inclined electorate who have become unhappy with the direction that the country is taking never entirely goes away. It reinforces the impression that he is aloof, posh, and out of touch with ordinary people. This view receives a turbo-charge in May 2013 when an unnamed insider with 'strong social connections to the prime minister' is reported in the *Daily Telegraph* as speaking about 'swivel-eyed loons', even though they are describing a certain kind of Tory activist, rather than UKIP.[2]

Andrew Feldman strongly denies that he made the remark, following speculation on Twitter and elsewhere on the internet. However, the report is manna from heaven for UKIP supporters, and the best possible recruiting slogan because it seems graphically to epitomise what Tory high command think of ordinary voters.

Cameron's response to the UKIP challenge goes through a number of stages, but he never finds an effective response to it. 'UKIP has certainly been an unwelcome and unexpected factor, with much higher support than we expected,' he says in early 2014.[3] To Graham Brady, chairman of the 1922 Committee, Number 10's response is 'always behind the curve and never established consistency on how to deal with UKIP'.[4] For Liam Fox, great harm is done by the public believing that 'they were being given a cast-iron guarantee on a referendum on the Lisbon Treaty, and it did not transpire'.[5] To Owen Paterson, 'Number 10 massively underestimated UKIP, and abusing them was absolutely crass. My constituency association said: "So this is what Number 10 really think?"'[6] To Matthew d'Ancona, the damage is done by the inconsistency of approach: 'He hasn't handled UKIP well and should have gone in with all guns blazing.'[7]

When Cameron became party leader in December 2005, UKIP was only beginning to be a significant force. Founded in 1993, as a 'non-sectarian, non-racist party [which] does not recognise the legitimacy of the European Parliament',[8] it won twelve seats in the European elections in May 2004. The party trod water for the next six years, and was led into the 2010 general election by Lord Pearson. The party contested 90% of the parliamentary seats with 560 candidates, aiming to win 5% of the popular vote, but ended up with only 3% and without a single MP.

Nigel Farage's election as party leader in November 2010 is, according to the academic Matthew Goodwin, one of the leading authorities on UKIP, the key turning point in its rise. Farage, who previously led the party between 2006 and 2009, immediately starts overhauling the strategy, putting a focus on electoral politics and making gains in Labour as well as Conservative areas.[9] Number 10's first response, which lasts from autumn 2010 until late 2012, is to ignore UKIP. It fails at first to understand that Farage, an adept and popular communicator, is giving voice to a significant slice of the electorate. Now that the Lib Dems are in government, Number 10 believes that the protest vote, which always made up a large portion of Lib Dem support, has needed another outlet: in the shape of UKIP. This fails to explain fully the increase in the party's support, which draws on discontent with the political establishment as a whole and genuine concerns about the level of immigration, especially in areas of the country still depressed after the recession. The Lib Dems also deluded themselves into thinking UKIP's rise would aid their fortunes. 'We've just sat back and watched the Tories chase their tail on UKIP in ways which have been quite helpful for us,' says a senior Lib Dem. It was misplaced optimism.

The Tories' hope that the UKIP vote will gradually subside is proven otherwise by events in 2012. The omnishambles Budget is seen at Conservative Campaign Headquarters (CCHQ) as a significant factor in UKIP's inexorable rise. 'It made us look like a bunch of people who didn't know what we were doing: those who were disillusioned with us went to UKIP instead of Labour and haven't come back.' Gay marriage is the other big recruiter at the time, leading to a second spike, CCHQ believes. Inside Number 10, UKIP is a regular item of discussion at the 8.30 a.m. and 4 p.m. meetings in Cameron's office. The thinking remains that 'there is very little we can do about this. Trying to chase it down the alleyway isn't going to work because of their "we hate the establishment" appeal.'

The events of 2012 force Number 10 into a rethink. The results of this are first seen at the Eastleigh by-election in February 2013, triggered by the resignation of sitting Lib Dem MP Chris Huhne following his guilty plea for hiding a speeding offence a decade before. CCHQ throws everything it has into the campaign to win the seat and stop UKIP, even running a candidate that one top Conservative would describe as 'very UKIPy'. Yet the Lib Dems retain the seat, their first by-election victory under Clegg since the formation of the coalition. It is the closest by-election amongst the top three candidates in over ninety years with UKIP beating the Conservatives into third place, polling 27.8% (only 4% behind the Lib Dems). Conservative woes are magnified two months later at the South Shields by-election, triggered by the resignation of David Miliband, who is departing for a new life in the US. As expected, Labour retain the seat with 50.4% of the vote, but UKIP come second with 24.2%, and the Conservatives drop to third with a miserable 11.5%. This is traumatic for the party, because it shows that UKIP can poll highly even where they had no candidate in 2010, and in the north-east of England, not thought to be a traditionally strong area for them.

Number 10 and CCHQ change tack again and devise a new strategy, 'to neutralise the negatives'. This involves not saying anything that is patronising or dismissive about UKIP members: 'Cameron is internalising this: he knows that he shouldn't call them "fruitcakes" and is shifting off all that rhetorically,' says an aide. Cameron now understands that if UKIP voters are insulted, they may never come back. Policies that are causing UKIP's surge in popularity are to be shelved. Gay marriage has gone too far down the line, so is rushed onto the statute book: 'There is a realisation that it is a divisive issue, and that we have now to mend things,' says an insider. Another says: 'We've got it, we're stopping doing the stuff that's aggravating our supporters and making them go to UKIP. We're taking trouble not to rub people's faces in it ever again like on gay marriage.'

UKIP's popularity, however, still shows no signs of declining. Farage is handed a golden calf: the imminent ending of transitional controls on migrants from Romania and Bulgaria, imposed when they joined the EU in 2007. By 2011/12 with the prospect of the restrictions being lifted, UKIP predict that large numbers of Romanians and Bulgarians will take advantage of work and opportunities not offered in their own countries. Suspicion is fanned elsewhere that an influx of immigration from across the EU is not fired purely by economic reasons: the number of non-UK EU benefit claimants has risen to over 300,000.[10] The government look at ways to see if it can limit the free movement of people, which is a core article of the EU, but are disappointed when their lawyers say there is no possibility. UKIP is thus able to roll together three toxic concepts – the EU, immigration, and benefit cheats – into a single argument. It is a potent mix for Farage.

Pressure mounts on Cameron to take action. Conservative MPs are demanding that he announce that there will be a referendum on Britain remaining within the EU. Fearing he will be bounced into offering a referendum after the May 2014 European elections, which CCHQ is estimating will be a very bad result for the party, he decides to get on the front foot. Hence the Bloomberg speech, delivered in January 2013 (see Chapter 21). Cameron is clear that it will not be a UKIP speech, and that the party will never 'out-UKIP UKIP', and he opens with a 'paean of praise' for European unity, as one of his team put it. The decision to announce an in/out referendum in the next parliament is not without internal critics. To Europhile Ken Clarke, 'the decision to announce the referendum is a reaction to UKIP, the *Mail*, *Telegraph* and Murdoch press. It was also rather foolish of David Cameron and Theresa May to take worries about hordes of Bulgarians and Romanians hitting our shores so seriously, which allowed Farage to conflate immigration and the EU.'[11] Cameron's critics are not only on the right of the party.

The Bloomberg speech does absolutely nothing to win back voters from UKIP. In April 2013, UKIP is polling at 13%.[12] Matthew Goodwin thinks the reason the offer of a referendum – a major concession to Conservative Eurosceptics – does not dent UKIP support is threefold: Cameron himself is not believed because of his 'betrayal' in not having a referendum on the Lisbon Treaty; he is loathed personally; and he is not regarded as a true Conservative by many UKIP voters. They do not thus wish to be led into a referendum by the Conservatives under Cameron, especially as he says he will campaign to remain within a reformed EU. UKIP support is based primarily on instinct and values, and its supporters do not believe Cameron shares them. Lord Ashcroft's research report, '"Are You Serious?" Boris, the Tories and the Voters', suggests that 57% of UKIP voters believe the Conservatives would have a better chance of winning the next general election with Boris Johnson as leader, with 35% saying that this would make them more likely to vote Conservative.[13] It is a disconcerting poll for Cameron's team.

Although the 2013 local elections see the Tories retain control of most of their councils, they lose control of ten and win only 25% of the vote, their lowest figure since 1995. UKIP is close behind on 22%, with a total of 147 seats, an increase of 139. It is the first time that UKIP can legitimately claim to be a party of nationwide support. Jamie Huntman, a newly elected councillor for UKIP in Essex, captures the mood of UKIP defiance when he says 'We are hardly clowns and fruitcakes any longer.'[14] Number 10 consoles itself that the results are better than expected, but they come under relentless pressure from MPs who express concern that they might not be able to win back UKIP defectors in time for the general election.

Number 10 and CCHQ approach the European elections in May 2014 with real trepidation. They cling to the argument that the Conservatives alone are offering a referendum on remaining in the EU, so voting UKIP makes no logical sense. Some members of the 1922 Committee are seriously considering a vote on ending the coalition, fearing that their supporters are losing patience. They decide to wait until after the European elections before initiating such a vote, which is followed by the Newark by-election on 5 June.

In the run-up to the elections, Clegg seizes the opportunity to hold two televised debates against Farage on Europe to highlight the Lib Dems' credentials as the party of the EU. Number 10 discusses how to respond. It understands why Clegg wants to take the risk against Farage as his party is only averaging 9% in the opinion polls, so he needs something to give him a lift. They rate Clegg as a debater and hope he might expose holes in UKIP. The debates prove a mixed blessing to the Conservatives. Clegg comes a poor second to Farage, failing to reproduce the magic which had won him so much credit in the first televised election debate in 2010. He fails to land significant punches, either on Farage personally or on UKIP. The debate may even serve to highlight the Conservatives offering a middle way between the EU rejectionism of UKIP and the enthusiastic support of the Lib Dems. In the European elections on 22 May, UKIP emerge as the overall victors, achieving 27.5% of the vote and twenty-four seats. 'A stunning victory', says the *Independent*.[15] The Conservatives drop to third place, the first time the party has ever not been in the top two in a national election. But the real losers are the Lib Dems, who retain just one of their twelve MEPs, resulting in fresh calls for Clegg to resign.

No tactic has worked against UKIP. The final tack before the general election is to rely on Lynton Crosby, seen by Conservative MPs and many in the party in the country as much more 'sound' on Europe than Cameron himself. Crosby oversees the setting up of professional structures and messaging to allow a more effective response to UKIP. He redoubles the effort to ensure that provocative policies and statements are hidden deep underground. He ensures the

rhetoric is warm towards UKIP voters, while at the same time pointing a relentless searchlight on Farage's personal vulnerabilities and
history. At the heart of Crosby's strategy is placing the Conservatives'
focus squarely upon the long-term economic policy, while insisting
that immigration and Europe, which he believes only feed UKIP, are
never mentioned. Andrew Cooper receives part of the blame for the
article of faith that the UKIP vote would dissipate as a general election
approaches, though, as a senior Number 10 aide admits, 'Frankly we
all thought that. It was Lynton who then crystallised our thinking that
UKIP support wasn't going to go away and that we have to remove the
negatives that are feeding them.' Cameron's long-awaited immigration
speech on 28 November 2014 can be seen as part of this strategy of
taking the concerns of UKIP supporters seriously, by suggesting that
the referendum will be used to extract maximum leverage in the
control of immigration.

The Newark by-election of 5 June 2014, occasioned by the resignation of Conservative MP Patrick Mercer after investigations by the
Commons Committee on Standards, comes two weeks after the
European elections. The party throws the kitchen sink at it: Cameron
himself pays four visits to the Nottinghamshire constituency and the
party amasses a huge army of volunteers from across the country. The
Conservatives retain the seat comfortably with 45% of the vote,
although their majority is halved. The reason that UKIP does not do
even better than its 25.9% is because it still has not fully recovered
from the massive effort it put into the European elections. It lacks the
activists or the money to throw at the by-election. CCHQ believes
that UKIP will return to single digits in the polls by the end of the
summer. But within a few months, a sinister development, apparently
out of nowhere, changes everything.

On 28 August, Cameron is enjoying himself with his team at
Chequers. They are there for a 'start of the new-term meeting', having
a long deep think about how to play the nine months leading up to
the general election. They are sitting in the upstairs dining room. It
has been a decent summer and they are in good heart. Neck and neck
at last with Labour, they have a real sense that they at last have
momentum, and the stubborn polls are beginning to shift in their
favour. One of them picks up a message: 'I don't know if this is a spoof,

but there's a story that Douglas Carswell has resigned.' Cameron immediately senses what this means. Suddenly, all their mobiles start pinging the same message: 'Carswell's going to defect to UKIP.' Cameron breaks up the meeting and they go to watch the television news.

There is a great sense of shock and a deep anger. There had been murmurs that there might be trouble in the autumn, but they have had no intelligence about what Carswell, a known maverick, might be planning. 'Ten of us ploughed into a small room by the front entrance, fixated by what we are seeing on the television,' Craig Oliver recalls: 'it's almost unnerving how the PM takes good and bad news equally.'[16] They begin to debate how they might fight the by-election and what type of candidate they might need. Not putting anyone up against him is an option. The conversation flows back and forth as they examine the options. Feldman is drawn into the debate, as is Crosby. Cameron insists they have to put up a candidate and fight hard to show other would-be defectors the Conservatives will not take it lying down. Crosby texts Boris Johnson to ask if he is interested in standing against Carswell, but the reply comes back at once: 'Thank you, no.' Carswell, they quickly learn, has taken with him files about his Clacton constituency, containing micro-detail about how individuals will vote, almost house by house. It will be a hell of a fight, they all realise.

Carswell is regarded as a serious thinker and person. There is a respect for him among Cameron's team, albeit fairly grudging, as someone who has been consistent in his anti-Europeanism for many years. It is decided that Cameron should release a dignified statement expressing his disappointment – 'it is obviously deeply regrettable' – but they also decide he should highlight the crux of what they see as the paradox at the heart of Carswell's defection: 'it is also, in my view, counter-productive. If you want a referendum on Britain's future in the EU – whether we should stay or go – the only way to get that is to have a Conservative government after the next election and that is what until very recently Douglas Carswell himself was saying'.[17]

Cameron disappears from the discussions to take a call from Theresa May on counter-terrorism, while Crosby returns to London from Chequers by car with Kate Fall and Oliver Dowden. 'The impact of Carswell was very bad,' a Number 10 aide recalls. 'It really affected

MPs, who were worrying about the impact of UKIP on their own re-election.' Farage milks Carswell's defection and is clearly thrilled by the coup. He then creates genuine concern in the Conservative camp by claiming that more defectors might be revealed in due course.[18] Number 10 and CCHQ gear up a couple of notches as they try and work out who he is thinking of, and when the news might come. They assume that Farage is delaying any defections until the party conference, where it will exact maximum damage.

They are not wrong in their guess. On Saturday 27 September, as Cameron's team are travelling up to the conference in Birmingham, they receive news that Conservative MP Mark Reckless is another defector. 'I promised to cut immigration while treating people fairly and humanely. I cannot keep that promise as a Conservative. I can keep it as UKIP,' Reckless announces to loud cheers at UKIP's conference in Doncaster.[19] Craig Oliver is on the train when he hears the news. As he tries to speak to the team from the carriage, his phone keeps cutting out. They all worry that the second defection will knock the entire conference off course and encourage further defections. Cameron is much more affected personally by Reckless's resignation than that of Carswell: he thinks Reckless is not only illogical but purely self-interested, and is both destructive and malevolent. 'He despises people who behave like that,' says an aide. Anger mounts when they learn that a week before he knew he would be defecting, Reckless had allegedly sanctioned the printing of leaflets by his Conservative constituency association, at high cost for the local party.

As soon as Cameron's team arrive in Birmingham on Saturday evening, they meet in the PM's hotel suite: 'I'd always regarded it up till now as the lucky room as it was the place we gathered for the third TV debate in 2010, which he won,' says Kate Fall.[20] Luck is conspicuously absent from the room that night. 'We'd had a big debate the previous week about whether the PM's speech should announce lots of good news then or spread it out over the autumn.' The Reckless story inclines him to want to seek maximum impact from his own speech – 'to put the explosives on the door', as he himself says. They spend a lot of time that evening planning what Cameron will say to Andrew Marr in his interview the next morning. They simply do not know whether more resignations will follow on Sunday, Monday, or on Wednesday, the day the PM speaks. Adam Holloway, Peter Bone and Chris Kelly are all names that are mentioned as possible defectors by the team. 'Both Carswell and Reckless lied to our faces that they weren't going to defect,' says one. They decide that Cameron will downplay it as far as he can, so on Sunday morning he tells Marr that 'these things are frustrating and frankly are counterproductive and rather senseless.'[21] Heavy-duty rubbishing is left to party chairman Grant Shapps, who in his opening speech tells delegates at Birmingham: 'we have been betrayed ... We have been let down by somebody who has repeatedly lied to his constituents and to you – who said one thing and did another ... He lied and lied and lied again.'[22]

Cameron's team are far more contemptuous of Reckless than Carswell, regarding him as 'a little shit'. Just days before, he had had lunch with Michael Gove, now chief whip, and had sworn he was not going to defect.[23] They think he had been swayed by former Conservative financier turned UKIP donor, Stuart Wheeler, who they suspect also influenced Carswell, by leading him to believe that he will lose the constituency to UKIP if he remains a Conservative, and telling him he will have more of a voice for his ideas and enthusiasms if he speaks up from the smaller pond of UKIP. Gove reckons that it is Carswell who persuaded Reckless to follow suit and that the two were a duo.[24] Farage's 2015 book *The Purple Revolution* later reveals that Reckless's defection was always part of his master plan.

Carswell's by-election in Clacton takes place first, on 9 October. Despite a considerable investment of Conservative effort in the constituency, he achieves 59.7% of the vote with a majority of over 12,000. Election specialist John Curtice describes it as the biggest increase in the share of the vote for any party for any by-election in British history (there had been no UKIP candidate standing at the 2010 general election).[25] UKIP's campaign makes much of Cameron's statement in his party conference speech about UKIP being closed down. An article by Matthew Parris in *The Times* on 6 September, in which he allegedly insulted Clacton saying it lacked both 'ambition and drive', is widely circulated by UKIP as further evidence of the patronising attitude of the Conservative establishment towards the party.

The Reckless by-election in Rochester and Strood is held on 20 November. When he defected on the eve of the Conservative conference, there was a hope within the party that they could hold the seat. CCHQ again direct massive resources into the contest. 'We threw everything at it to try to win and this made for a very intense and hard-fought campaign,' says Feldman.[26] Cameron himself goes to the Kentish constituency five times, with the final visit taking place on 18 November, two days before polling.[27] UKIP recruit many new activists over the summer and they too put everything into the contest, which they end up winning with 42.1% of the vote and a majority of just under 3,000. It is a damaging blow for the Conservatives, although there is relief that the UKIP majority is not higher.

The Carswell and Reckless defections change everything. In November 2014, just six months out from the general election, a YouGov poll puts UKIP on 17%.[28] 'I don't think we have ever found a very clear policy on how to deal with UKIP,' confirms one of Cameron's close team that month. Even as late as December, Cameron is still toying with the idea of launching a withering attack on UKIP, saying that only the Conservatives can guarantee the referendum on the EU, and that UKIP will cut the country off from the rest of the world, with a disastrous effect on economic prosperity.

But by early 2015, Crosby's diagnosis is still the only show in town. He helps yank the Conservative case back in a more populist direction. 'Lynton never subscribed to the view the Conservative Party was the "nasty party",' an insider recalls, 'but he thought it was a party full of out-of-touch wankers, frankly, who were privileged and divorced from the lives of ordinary people.' Crosby's polling after the European elections reveals a despair amongst much of the electorate: 'there is a sense of disillusion and frustration that none of the current parties properly are understanding'. But even before the short campaign begins in April 2015, it is Crosby's own prognosis that is coming under attack. UKIP foxed the Conservatives when Farage became their leader just after the 2010 general election, they continued to fox them midterm, and they foxed them all the way through to the general election. Cameron's Conservative critics remained full of anger to the end that he did not handle UKIP better; but did a magic bullet exist that would have shot the UKIP fox?

THIRTY-TWO

The Gove Reshuffle

July 2014

'I'd like you to become chief whip, Michael,' Cameron says to Gove on Tuesday 8 July, six days before the second of his major reshuffles. The prime minister has invited the Education Secretary, one of his closest friends in politics, for their least comfortable drink ever. 'Of course you can stay at Education if you want, but I'd really like you to take on this new job.' Gove admits he is taken aback and doesn't know what to say. Cameron distinctly remembers Gove himself offering mid-parliament to become chief whip to help sort out the ramshackle and rebellious parliamentary party. Along with George Osborne, Gove is one of the very few ministers that Cameron trusts totally and admires. Cameron has not found it easy to find his ideal chief whip in government: Patrick McLoughlin was good but almost too gentlemanly, Mitchell was only briefly in post and much the other way, while George Young, available to fill Mitchell's place quickly, is seen as again too nice to fully grip the very tricky parliamentary party.

Cameron explains his thinking to Gove. A point of critical mass has been reached, education policy is one of the great achievements of the government and he now needs Gove by his side as they put the team in place for the general election and, they hope, beyond. 'You can safely move now because the legislative agenda for this parliament has been completed,' Cameron tells him. As Gove is preparing to leave the study, Cameron adds, 'I would like to have your answer, if possible, by tomorrow morning.' The reshuffle is imminent, and he needs to have the new chief whip in place and part of the debate over several still-undecided changes. Gove goes home deep in thought. He's enjoyed being Education Secretary, and needs more time to complete his disputed agenda. He doesn't want to leave. But he decides never-theless to call Cameron that evening: 'I won't be an unwilling contin-uer in an office in the knowledge you'd rather I move on. So, yes,' he tells the PM. He knows there is more to the move than said.

Cameron hates giving bad news, particularly to friends and loyal political allies, and has listened to powerful voices for and against. He sees the attraction of a Eurosceptic chief whip, unlike both McLoughlin and Young, in preparing for an EU referendum. Against this, Gove and his education reforms are particularly popular in the party and with Conservative commentators, a point made by Osborne. He knows, however he dresses it up, that his remarks are not what Gove wants to hear. He's particularly pained because of the very close personal and family relationship that exists between the Goves and Camerons, including between Samantha and Gove's journalist wife Sarah Vine, a friendship that has protected Gove for several difficult months when the knives were out for him. Sarah had looked after Cameron's children on election night in 2010, and had even been tipped to join the Number 10 team.[1] Close foursomes are rare at the top of politics and rarely last: the Blairs with Alastair Campbell and his partner Fiona Millar was one such, till breaking apart spectacu-larly. 'People accused Cameron of being ruthless towards Gove,' says a close observer, 'but actually, he grappled for months with options other than moving Gove from the education brief, against the advice of his own advisers, until it got to the point that inaction was poten-tially weakening his authority.'

In the few days remaining to the reshuffle, Gove's initial doubts increase. Despite vociferous criticism from parts of the educational establishment, he believes his mission to narrow the attainment gap between rich and poor children, and raise educational standards overall, has begun to bear fruit. 'Everyone here is united in their desire to give the next generation the best possible start in life,' he tells a two-day summit in July 2014. He is joined in addressing the event by education ministers from Poland, Spain and the Netherlands, as well as by Labour's shadow education spokesman Tristram Hunt, and a range of international experts. Surrounded by fellow reformers and educationalists at Lancaster House, Gove's pleasure at the apparent success of his crusade is bittersweet. Amongst those at the summit, he alone knows that this is his last speech as Secretary of State for Education.

Osborne sees more clearly than anyone that Gove's departure from Education will slow hard-fought momentum and cause problems on the right. Only late in the day does he give his consent to it, swayed by the case that in the run-up to the general election, they will both need someone as chief whip they can trust 100%. Cameron and his chancellor hope that Gove will be an authoritative chief whip, akin to John Wakeham for Thatcher and Alastair Goodlad for Major. As late as October 2013 at the party conference, Cameron had been praising Gove to the skies: 'Three and a half years ago, one man came into the Department of Education ... Michael Gove. There he is, with a belief in excellence and massive energy, like a cross between Mr Chips and the Duracell bunny.'[2] 'In October 2013, education was our biggest positive for the government,' says one Cameron aide. By July 2014 the Number 10 team were telling the PM that Gove had become a media and voter liability. What had happened so quickly that was so worrying that Cameron himself reluctantly had to agree? Gove's move was only one in a complex set of ministerial changes in the July 2014 reshuffle. But, given the toxicity and rancour surrounding it, this single move came to overshadow the entire reshuffle.

Where Lansley had stumbled and fallen at Health, and IDS encountered constant woes at the DWP, all had seemed plain sailing for the Education Secretary. The reasons for his success are not hard to divine. Crucially, Gove had the total support of not only the prime minister, but also the chancellor. He had a solid policy platform, inherited from Labour with Andrew Adonis the principal architect, which Brown's Education Secretary, Ed Balls, had not killed off. At the heart of this agenda lay a drive to improve academic standards for all, to attract the best graduates into teaching, halt rampant grade inflation and award financial and managerial autonomy to head teachers. Unlike Lansley, Gove had not tried to reinvent the wheel, but built on existing success, citing Tony Blair as well as Adonis as the true architects of reform.

It helped explain why he had a relatively easy ride from Labour, who left the broad thrust of his policy largely unchallenged and did not posit a distinctive vision of its own, preferring instead to highlight particular issues, such as the need for greater scrutiny over free schools (independent state schools set up by parents, teachers and charities) and for all teachers to have qualified teacher status.[3] Indeed, as the schools minister David Laws says, it was the Lib Dems who saw themselves as the real check on what Gove was doing.[4] He was fortunate too to receive little criticism or challenge from the media. As a former journalist himself, and married to another, he knows many of the key commentators and editors personally: he is assiduous at cultivating journalists, always returns their calls, understands a good story, and feeds the outlets well. While Gove's ultimate goals are simple, the volume and detail of the policies are complex. Few of those writing on education mastered the minutiae of the reforms, such as changes to the English baccalaureate performance measure, clamping down on unauthorised absence and truancy, and making vocational qualifications more rigorous and relevant. These reforms are structural – the transfer of power from local authorities – and far-reaching, as well as beefing up tests, exams and the curriculum which will often take many years to complete.

In Number 10, many of Cameron's team do not fully understand the detail of what Gove is doing. 'He outsources education to Michael completely,' insists David Laws, 'he is one of the few people in Cabinet who the PM rarely challenges and almost never overrules. The Treasury has such a tight grip on other departments. But it's obvious the chancellor totally trusts Michael.'[5] 'David Cameron gave me very clear riding instructions when he appointed me. He was very supportive of the policies I advocated and simply trusted me to get on with it,' says Gove.[6] Cameron himself was, of course, shadow Education Secretary – 'I worked on many of the ideas myself,' he says.[7] He supports the broad principles, the 'standards' and the autonomy agenda, even if the details of what Gove is doing escape him. 'I don't think he or his immediate team appreciated the coherence of the whole education policy reform agenda, or had even heard of E. D. Hirsch,' says one official. (E. D. Hirsch is a Gove guru, an American academic best known for writing *The Schools We Need: And Why We Don't Have Them* and *Cultural Literacy: What Every American Needs to Know*, and for being founder of the Core Knowledge Foundation.)

After becoming shadow Schools Secretary in 2007, Gove drew around him a group of true believers, including special adviser Dominic Cummings, Policy Exchange's Dean Godson, free-school enthusiast Rachel Wolf, and fellow Conservative MP Nick Gibb. In some ways they resembled the group of highly ideological soulmates whom Thatcher gathered around her in the 1970s; where she and her fellow travellers looked to Austrian classical economist and philosopher F. A. Hayek, many in Gove's team looked for inspiration to E. D. Hirsch. Gibb in particular seized on Hirsch's idea that the aspirations of the poor have been limited because they lack the cultural signposts that allow them to access the canon of the Western intellectual tradition, which will allow them to appreciate the higher levels of the curriculum and to move on to a top university. Progressive teaching methods were another bête noire of this group: Gibb was withering in his attacks on progressive teaching, 'child-centred' learning and time being spent at school on pursuits which lack intellectual rigour. Gibb also believed that academic teaching was the key to social mobility: he was full of zeal about research which purported to show that class sizes matter less in improving results than the aspirations of the school and quality of the teaching. All of Gove's team wanted objective data and empirical evaluation to replace subjective and fuzzy judgements, where 'happy and healthy' was an equivalent measure to academic achievement. They believed all schools can and must achieve measurable targets, and that more focus should be given to international comparisons. Where Gibb was particularly interested in the writings of Hirsch, Cummings and Wolf were much more libertarian and focused on school autonomy. The differences within Gove's ideas-rich team over standards and structures, different agendas that were sometimes in conflict, were held together by Gove himself, interested as he was in both.

Becoming Education Secretary in May 2010 is Gove's dream. Adopted by a Labour-supporting family in Aberdeen, educated initially at a state school, he won a scholarship to the independent Robert Gordon's College. He worked hard and gained a place at Oxford. He thinks everyone can succeed, even those from disadvantaged circumstances, if only they have the right education. He used his three years in Opposition from 2007 to develop a coherent reform plan, to visit countries like Finland and the US, and consult experts, rare for an incoming Secretary of State, particularly in recent times. Gove and his team arrive at the DfE all guns blazing but their experience and knowledge of education are not matched by the experience of working in the machinery of state. The shift from Ed Balls's broadly focused Department for Children, Schools and Families to a renamed Department for Education focused on teaching and standards is significant. Gove's team are frustrated by the time it takes for the department to respond to their agenda, and are dismayed by some early departmental errors, exemplified by the bungled announcement to end the Building Schools for the Future (BSF) funding programme. He presses ahead with reform, passing the Academies Act before the summer recess, which allows all state schools to become academies, with greater freedom from local education authority control. In November 2010, he publishes a White Paper encouraging the teaching of modern languages in schools, a tightening of league tables, and a greater emphasis to be placed on each child securing passes in five GCSEs including English and maths.[8] The first signs of a backlash to a perceived restricted curriculum and traditional approach are evident. Steve Hilton from Number 10 shares Gove's mounting impatience with the DfE's weakness in communicating the 'why' and not just the 'what' and 'how'.

From early 2011, Gove becomes more confident in navigating the Whitehall machine, and therefore more assertive. With Coulson's departure, there is no longer anyone preventing Dominic Cummings officially joining Gove's team of special advisers, and, less controversially, he 'opens up' the Civil Service's closed shop of advice, appointing outside advisers to help him develop and deliver innovative policy changes, including Paul Bew on the primary-school assessment, Alison Wolf on vocational education and Charlie Taylor on truancy and behaviour. With the declining influence of Hilton, Gove is also left more alone by Number 10, with the exception of child protection and social work, adoption and fostering reform. At the same time, he continues with the expansion of academies, forges ahead with free schools and drives forward his plans on the curriculum and examinations. Gove is at the peak of his effectiveness and authority from the passage of the Education Act 2011, which receives Royal Assent that

November, through to the summer and autumn of 2013. He advances on many fronts at once, and appears unstoppable, until the tide starts to turn at the end of the year.

Differences with the Lib Dems have been apparent from the outset. In mid-2012 there is a huge battle, when the *Daily Mail* publishes Cumming's thoughts about scrapping GCSEs and the national curriculum, and having a single exam board.[9] A furore breaks out. Such proposals would return Britain to the polarised society of the 1950s, Lib Dems allege.[10] Gove is furious at their reaction. 'I got the PM to agree to replace GCSEs: but when the Lib Dems cut up rough, we had to negotiate a compromise. It was a great shame.'[11] After the September 2012 reshuffle and David Laws' appointment as schools minister, political differences become a serious problem. Gove finds it hard that, whereas the PM will almost invariably give him the green light to whatever he proposes, the default response from Nick Clegg is amber, if not red. He believes Clegg has reached the conclusion that middle-class professionals – particularly those who work in the public sector, who were upset by tuition fee increases and the NHS reforms – are now focusing their attention on Gove's school reforms. Clegg tells Gove outright that his attacks are necessary to placate his own core supporters by emphasising points of difference with the Conservatives. Their personal relationship deteriorates. Cummings allegedly leaks to the *Mail on Sunday* the false allegation that money from DfE has gone to the charity Book Trust because of the charity's relationship with Miriam González Durántez, Clegg's wife. Clegg is furious and believes that Gove and Cummings 'stoop low' to damage him. 'I don't want anything more to do with Gove,' he tells Laws. He says to Cameron: 'I can't work with a Cabinet minister who says one thing to my face and another behind my back.'

Disagreements over local government are a key reason for the acrimony: Lib Dems are aggrieved that the push for free schools and academies is at the loss of local authority oversight and control. Cameron shares Gove's frustration on this: 'We could be doing much more on academies and free schools, but we can't go any further because of the Lib Dems,' he says in January 2014.

The irony is that Gove personally rates Laws, briefly Chief Secretary to the Treasury in May 2010, who had helped protect the education budget from cuts and secured the money for the pupil premium, which gave additional funding to help pupils from disadvantaged backgrounds, in the very first days of the government. He fights for him to become minister of state. But as Gove soon finds, 'I would get David to agree to various policies, but then people would get to Nick, and we lost that support.'[12] To try to improve their frayed relationship, Clegg's staff suggest that Clegg and Gove have a weekly meeting to help keep in step. Gove's office declines: 'It would have been a disaster and only made things worse,' says an insider.

Gove may have survived the Lib Dem roadblocks were it not for an even more fundamental problem. Embedded in his very character are the seeds of his own difficulties. This is epitomised by his reliance on the mercurial if brilliant figure of Cummings, who had worked in Opposition as a special adviser for IDS, but had fallen foul of Coulson, which explains Coulson's antipathy to him. Gove continues to draw on the advice of Cummings despite Coulson blackballing his appointment, and relies on him in the same way that Cameron relied on Hilton's advice. Cummings is a purist with very clear ideas about education and the world. One of these is that Gove must prevail against 'the blob', the education establishment made up of Whitehall, local authorities, university departments and unions, which will try every trick in the book to defeat his crusade. A problem with this binary depiction of the world is that it gives such conservative forces cohesion and a venom that they might never have possessed, emboldening the very enemy which they most wanted to see pacified.

The problems have been simmering, and extending beyond volatile advisers. Suddenly, Gove seems to be fighting on all fronts at once. In early February 2013, he has to abandon his plans for an English baccalaureate, calling it 'just one reform too many at this time'.[13] Ten days later, senior historians write to the *Observer* registering significant concerns about Gove's proposals for the new history curriculum.[14] In March, a hundred academics write 'to warn of the dangers posed by Michael Gove's new national curriculum'.[15] Gove's retort is to call his critics 'Marxists'.[16] That month, the Association of Teachers and Lecturers pass a motion of 'no confidence' against him. In April, the National Union of Teachers do the same unanimously, the first time in its 143-year history that it has performed such an action, and calls for his resignation.[17] A low point for Gove personally is when he is booed at the National Association of Head Teachers Conference in Birmingham in May, in stark contrast to earlier appearances when he had been well received.[18] In October, Poet Laureate Carol Ann Duffy is among nearly 200 academics and authors who write a letter to *The Times*, saying that they are 'gravely concerned' by his policies, and calling for reforms to the national curriculum and exams to be halted.[19]

Number 10 is becoming alarmed at the growing noise. Gove is gently reminded about the fate of Lansley at Health who antagonised the professionals with whom he dealt. Some at such a point would have taken a pause, reflected and rethought their strategy. But Gove's response is to be even more fired up, returning after his Christmas holidays feistier than ever. Pressure from Number 10 is a contributing factor in the departure of Cummings, who claims he left on his own timetable though Downing Street believe that they provided the decisive push. He remains, however, a close confidant of Gove. 'He clearly has some sort of psychic hold over Gove and the Education department. He's a street fighter: but when he talks to us, he's utterly sycophantic,' says one in Number 10, who adds, 'it's nauseating when you know he's being so disloyal behind your back.' Cummings turns his fire on Clegg, who he thinks is partly responsible for Number 10's attempts to rein in Gove. He mounts a full-frontal assault, describing him as 'dishonest' and 'a revolting character' who Cameron 'props up' at the expense of Gove merely in case he might need him in a new coalition after the general election.[20]

Rather than keep his head down, as Number 10 wants, Gove continues to make the front pages, questioning the left's '*Blackadder*' depiction of the First World War, and appearing to fall out with Michael Wilshaw, his chief inspector of schools. Gove and Wilshaw have been a powerful combination working together throughout the first two or three years of government, and public disagreement strikes many as unedifying and puzzling. Wilshaw, a successful state-school head before moving to Ofsted, has been talked up regularly by Gove as sharing the same determination to improve the quality of teaching and standards for all young people. Wilshaw is furious when a DfE memo about Ofsted, written by Cummings, is leaked indicating that senior department figures are 'increasingly alarmed', and that it is 'worth thinking about the whole Ofsted approach with a blank sheet of paper'.[21] Wilshaw lets it be known that he is 'spitting blood' that the department might be briefing against him. Gove continues to respect Wilshaw, though is increasingly concerned about the competence and capacity of Ofsted. Specifically, Gove recognises that the 'Trojan Horse' plot by Islamic extremists to take control of schools in Birmingham was missed and then mishandled. Number 10 is unhappy with Gove continuing to make headlines while Gove is equally unhappy with Wilshaw doing the same, and believes he insufficiently appreciates the impact of some of his media pronouncements on confidence in the school and inspection system.

Differences of emphasis between them, hidden over the preceding years, now come to the surface. Gove wants 'earned autonomy' for free schools and academies, while Wilshaw wants to retain closer scrutiny. Wilshaw is more inclined to keep the status quo, and insufficiently in tune with aspects of the Gove philosophy. Deep inside the DfE, conversations take place about how to address the Ofsted problem. Attention turns to a new chair to work with Wilshaw. Sally Morgan, a senior figure in Blair's Number 10 team, had been appointed chair of Ofsted by Gove in March 2011 at the high noon of bipartisanship, and is concluding her first three-year term. In January 2014, it is announced that she will not be reappointed for a second term. She is a popular and respected figure, and there is predictable outcry and claims she has been 'sacked'. Her response is that Number 10 is now determined to appoint only Conservative supporters to public bodies.[22] The DfE is not unhappy to let that interpretation spread, and there is some truth in it: Number 10 has come under pressure from the media, including the *Mail*, to appoint more right-inclined figures to public bodies. Bar William Shawcross at the Charity Commission, they are mostly still led by New Labour appointees.

The decision not to reappoint Morgan lies far more in fact with the DfE team than with Cameron. Gove thinks a change in chair will help Wilshaw and Ofsted, but admires Morgan and does not like delivering bad news. He leaves others to explain and prepare the ground, which adds fuel to the fire of why he is removing a respected and effective chair. Wilshaw is furious at the intrusion and confused by the decision, and the episode adds further tensions between Gove and the Lib Dems, who think that 'falling out with the chief inspector of schools is not necessary to the work an Education Secretary has to do'.

Gove's wife Sarah Vine is not as popular in all elements of Number 10 as she is with the prime minister. Some regard her as an unguided missile, especially when she enters the fray deploying her raised profile as a weekly columnist in the *Daily Mail*. In early March, she writes about their decision to send their daughter Beatrice to a state comprehensive, Grey Coat Hospital, a very popular girls' school in Westminster. She praises state education as 'a miracle', while dismissing private schools as polarising and built on principles of snobbery.[23] Her article is very badly received in Downing Street, which is hypersensitive to adverse comments about private schooling. With unfortunate timing, Gove appears to exacerbate the problem, rather than to heed the advice to cool it. A week later, quotes from an interview he had given the previous month appear in the *Financial Times* saying that the number of Old Etonians in Number 10 is 'preposterous' and the dominance in public life of just this one school is 'ridiculous'.[24] Cameron's inner circle contains four Old Etonians: Ed Llewellyn, Oliver Letwin, Jo Johnson and Rupert Harrison. They debate whether he has done it to protect Sarah and conclude that whatever his motivation, the impact of the 'noises off' is damaging the old Etonian PM.

By May, Cameron is concluding that his old friend must leave Education. For months he has heard his team complaining that Gove is no longer listening to them, that his advisers are out of control, and that he is failing to communicate his core vision: 'He has singularly failed to get into the mindset of the British people who have no idea what a free school or an academy actually is,' says one. Ameet Gill and Lynton Crosby try to stop him making speeches and to stick to the grid of government announcements, but to no avail. 'We had come to the view that what we needed was someone who would continue the schools policy, but communicate it much better,' says another. Crosby is left to take the public rap for the decision to move Gove. The press laps up this narrative: Tim Montgomerie writes in *The Times* that 'when Crosby told the prime minister that Gove had become a politically toxic figure, he had all the polling data at his fingertips'.[25]

But the decision to move Gove had been taken long before Crosby produced his polling, the conclusions of which are by this time arguably widely known: teachers have lost faith in Gove. The decision had certainly been made well before Cummings' diatribe against Number 10 in mid-June. In the words of the *FT*'s Janan Ganesh, this was when Cummings – albeit no longer a special adviser – 'turned his Gatling gun' from Clegg in May to 'the only man in the country with an even grander office: the prime minister'.[26] In comments to *The Times*, Cummings dismisses Cameron as a 'sphinx without a riddle' whose admiration for his Old Etonian predecessor as prime minister, Harold Macmillan, is 'all you need to know' about him. The comments are less damaging to a Number 10 operation which has been regularly under fire in the media and from Conservative backbenchers than to Gove himself.

In his final few months in post, frequent reports appear in the media about Gove's 'spats' with other ministers. There is resentment in Cabinet and on its committees for his intervening in others' areas with his hawkish support for action in Syria and strongly pro-Israel line. But it is a flare-up in June of his long-running spat with Theresa May that is the final straw. He blames the 'Trojan Horse' episode on a Home Office and security services mindset, influenced by the Prevent strategy, which he believes is intent on 'catching crocodiles' rather than 'draining the swamp' of extremists. For many years, Gove has felt passionate about taking counter-terrorism and radicalisation seriously and dealing strongly with Islamic extremism: his 2006 book *Celsius 7/7*, published in the wake of the bomb attacks in London in July 2005 which killed fifty-two people, likened fighting Islamists to fighting the Nazis.

In an article in *The Times* in June, an 'anonymous source' close to Gove criticises Charles Farr, a senior government counter-terrorism official, who they say typifies the Home Office's reactive approach to terrorism.[27] Farr is the partner of Fiona Cunningham, one of May's special advisers. May and her team are incandescent, and leak a letter from her to Gove asking, 'why did nobody act' from his department over the Trojan Horse affair.[28] The whole spat is getting out of control. Number 10 are furious at the distraction that this argument is causing, and the perception of a Cabinet with two senior ministers squabbling with each other. 'Michael has done this over and over again – had a row internally and then leaked it – and people are frankly fed up with it,' says an insider.[29] According to another aide, 'he had become a liability. He was *too* Michael.' The wonder is that the media are so surprised at Gove's departure from Education.

The right-wing commentariat as expected criticise the PM's move. So do many educationalists and respected figures on the centre left, like former Blair speechwriter Philip Collins. They question Cameron's judgement: of his three welfare ministers, he failed to exercise oversight of one (Lansley), put a second under regular threat (IDS), and dismissed the third (Gove). The *Mail* runs a five-page story attacking what it sees as Cameron's folly on Gove, calling it 'worse than a crime'.[30] When the article is tweeted, conciliatory messages emanate from Number 10 towards the Goves. Cameron's team know they are suffering from the move and do not want to add to their discomfort.

Gove is not the only figure causing difficulties in the reshuffle. Cameron's team need to find space for promotions. They ponder moving the Communities Secretary Eric Pickles, but recognise that he has done a sound job in a difficult department; moreover, his northern, 'authentic' accent is useful to an administration thought to be posh. Their eyes move on to Owen Paterson, Environment Secretary since the September 2012 reshuffle, and Northern Ireland Secretary before. They think that he has done well enough, but that four years as a Secretary of State has been a good innings. They have also been troubled by his gaffes and infelicities, epitomised by a row over the badger cull in parts of the West Country in October 2013 when he said 'the badgers have moved the goalposts', which became a national joke.[31]

Paterson is deeply angry. Nobody had expressed concern to him about his performance, and he resented references in the Sunday papers to his position as being 'vulnerable', which he assumes comes from leaks in Downing Street.[32] 'Owen, you've had a jolly good run in Cabinet, but I've got a party to run and I've got to move you on,' is how Paterson recalls his conversation with Cameron in July.

'If you get rid of me, you are smashing 12 million people in the teeth, because I'm genuinely popular in the countryside,' he responds. 'You will never find anyone who has my rural background. I have not just done what you asked me: I have the confidence of rural people.' He is becoming more and more angry. 'Only I can go to Somerset and stand in a cowshed with a Liberal at five o'clock in the morning and win them over, and then confront hardcore Eurosceptic businessmen in the evening and out-UKIP UKIP. You can't do that.'

'I know, but I can handle UKIP,' Cameron replies.

Paterson gets up to leave Cameron's room in the Commons. As he reaches the door he turns: 'I think you're making a terrible mistake.'

The reshuffle is largely about promoting women and younger talent. Liz Truss, an education minister, is promoted to Environment Secretary. At thirty-eight, she is the youngest member of the Cabinet, and has the additional benefit of having attended a state school (more than half of Cameron's first Cabinet were privately educated). She has been hoping for a move to Education. Paterson is beside himself when he hears the news: 'I think it's bloody disgraceful what the prime minister has done to you. You've been in Parliament for three nano-seconds. You know about education, you wanted to go to education. But here you find yourself dummied into DEFRA, where you have no background at all. This is my phone number. Ring me anytime if you want any help.'

Nicky Morgan replaces Gove at Education. Cameron rates her highly. She is thought to be the most reliable and senior of the available women at minister-of-state level. Other women to receive promotions include Baroness Stowell as Leader of the House of Lords, and Esther McVey who becomes minister of employment. Conservatives and right-wing commentators who approved of Gove's reforms, who are sympathetic to the rural interest, and who are not always the first in line to applaud the advancement of women, are responsible for the generally hostile reception to the reshuffle in Parliament and the media. The reshuffle is, however, well received by women, as a poll in the *Daily Telegraph* suggests.[33]

Relatively overlooked in the reshuffle is the most senior change of all. After four years in the role, William Hague feels he has been Foreign Secretary for long enough. He had originally agreed with Cameron that he would serve in that position until the general election. In early August 2013, only a few weeks before he considered resigning from the government over the Syria vote, he told Cameron that he would stand down from Parliament at the next election. He has had differences on foreign policy, but above all wanted to have his own life back with his wife Ffion and revive his career as a successful author. Hague suggests to Cameron that he would be happy to serve as Leader of the House until the election, which would free him up to have a prominent campaigning role, and allow his successor time to settle in before the election, particularly on the sensitive subject of Europe. Jeremy Hunt is briefly considered as a replacement, but it would be too much of a risk to move him from Health, where he had impressed Cameron, in the run-up to the election. Cameron eventually decides on Philip Hammond, the Eurosceptic Defence Secretary, who had been a prominent figure as shadow Chief Secretary before the 2010 election. Also departing are the veterans Ken Clarke and George Young, both in their seventies.

Cameron has always said that he doesn't like reshuffles and thinks they create more problems than they solve, at least in the short term. If he needs vindication for this belief, the July 2014 reshuffle provides it in spades.

THIRTY-THREE

Scotland Decides

September 2014

'Two days before the vote, David Cameron became the most subdued I've ever seen him,' says an aide. 'He realised that his political fate hung in the balance.' 'It really would have broken his heart if the referendum had been lost,' recalls another. It was his decision alone to call the referendum which could precipitate the end of the 307-year-old union. He knows about British history. He also knows that this would not be like losing a general election. It means he would be forever remembered for just one thing: the PM who broke up the UK. Comparisons are being made with Lord North, prime minister when Britain lost the North American colonies in 1776.[1] 'The only other occasion he was as worried was during the height of the Coulson saga.'

Even among his staff, some think that he was overly hasty in calling for a referendum which even Alex Salmond wasn't demanding, and which dominates his time in the six months leading up to the vote, to the detriment of pressing issues including the economy, UKIP and immigration. The 'essay crisis' jibe is back as Cameron tries desperately to avert disaster, with accusations flying around that he is doing too much, too late. Yes, he feels strongly that the SNP victory in the 2011 Scottish elections pointed towards a need to resolve the issue, but does he really need to force a referendum, and in this, the busiest of parliaments? Has he, in fact – as many in his party believe – conceded too much to Salmond, above all on the timing of polling day, and in the framing of the referendum question? How on earth has he allowed himself to get into this position? Rarely has the job of prime minister appeared lonelier.

Much criticism focuses unfairly on the timing, which results in a drawn-out campaign. Cameron's response is that he doesn't want to impose any set date on Scotland, which in any case he considers subordinate to his main priority in the negotiations: achieving a single in/out question. A more spun-out process will, he argues back, allow more time for the Scottish case to be scrutinised, and for the economic recovery to feed through north of the border.

Back in October 2012, when he and Salmond had signed the Edinburgh Agreement for the referendum to take place in September 2014, the result looked secure, a chance to lance an undoubted boil which might only have become more angry. This was his opportunity to show decisive leadership and to be the prime minister who resolved the Scottish Question for at least a generation. He is happy to give the Better Together campaign a wide measure of autonomy, thinking Alistair Darling will be the reassuring leader who will best serve the cause. Day-to-day dealings are delegated to Osborne. Darling and Osborne respect each other, and talk regularly. Cameron understands totally that he is seen in Scotland as an Englishman and a Conservative, and knows that the campaign has to be led by Scots in Scotland. He sees his role as rising above party politics and using the authority of the PM's office to make the case across the whole of the United Kingdom. Danny Alexander and the Scotland Secretary Alistair Carmichael, who succeeded Michael Moore in October 2013, are now the principal personalities for the government running the campaign north of the border. Increasingly, figures including Lord Strathclyde, Leader of the House of Lords until January 2013, believe that Cameron is allowing himself to be edged out of the debate in Scotland by Labour and the Lib Dems, with their own agendas. Indeed the Labour and Lib Dem powers in Better Together are so convinced of the toxicity of the Tory brand that they block IDS coming to Scotland in April 2014 to launch a paper on welfare and pensions.[2] 'We handed too much over to the Labour Party,' Strathclyde says, 'we paid for the campaign and they ran it – in an uninspiring way.'[3]

From January to September 2014, Cameron visits Scotland on twelve occasions, and delivers six major speeches. From Easter, Scotland becomes a standing item at the 8.30 a.m. meeting in the PM's room. Andrew Dunlop, the Scotland specialist from the Policy Unit, gives a daily update, including the latest polls. Cameron meets Darling regularly and is often on the phone to Scotland. In the latter stages, a daily meeting is convened in Ed Llewellyn's office with all the key staff. The atmosphere becomes palpably tenser by the week.

The Olympic Park in London is the venue for Cameron's first major speech of the year, on 7 February 2014. He wants it to be known that he is taking the lead and deliberately chooses a non-Scottish venue to deliver the speech, which is directed to the whole country and only indirectly to those just in Scotland. His theme is that the rest of the country wants Scotland to remain in the union. The vote may only be exercised by the Scots, but it matters greatly to the rest of the UK. 'Centuries of history hang in the balance,' he says, and if Scotland becomes independent 'there will be no going back ... seven months to save the most extraordinary country in history ... over three centuries we have lived together, worked together, and frankly, we've got together: getting married, having children, moving back and forth across our borders.'[4] He finds the speech liberating, happy he has found his own voice: 'I am as proud of my Scottish heritage as I am of my English or Welsh heritage,' he says. Number 10 are delighted later that month when the speech may have spurred David Bowie to become involved: his acceptance speech at the Brit Awards, read by Kate Moss, ends with the impassioned plea 'Scotland, stay with us.'[5] 'Cameron was the only Conservative who got the tone right,' says Clegg. 'Unlike the Conservative Party which had a complete tin ear, he spoke with a civilised and respectful tone.'[6] Cameron keeps a regular eye on the polls throughout the spring and early summer, which give little cause for concern. Andrew Cooper's regular bulletins suggest all continues to be well: 40% of Scotland's 4 million voters are, he says, still committed to rejecting independence, 30% are committed to 'Yes', while the remaining 30% are undecided.

Ever since the Edinburgh Agreement, Salmond has been goading Cameron to come to Scotland and become directly involved. 'He makes every effort to drag DC into every debate. He wants to personalise the referendum into him vs Cameron, to make it Scotland vs England. But we won't let that happen,' says an aide. Salmond steps up the pressure on Cameron in the autumn of 2013, dubbing him 'feart' for refusing to engage with him in a television debate. 'I seem to have got a new pen pal ... almost on a daily basis,' Cameron tells a fringe meeting at the Tory Party conference that September, referring to the very regular communications he is receiving from Salmond about the debate.[7]

On 26 November 2013, Salmond launches the Scottish government's White Paper on its vision for an independent nation, which Number 10 think is effectively demolished the following day by Darling. While Cameron remains aloof from the street fight, Osborne gets his hands dirtier, mindful that without his pressing, Cameron might never have decided to have the referendum. In Glasgow, in April 2013, Osborne had delivered a hard-hitting speech saying that if Scotland becomes independent, there is no guarantee that currency union will continue. In a speech in Edinburgh on 13 February 2014, he now goes further: 'If Scotland walks away from the UK, it walks away from the UK pound ... there's no legal reason why the rest of the UK would need to share its currency with Scotland.'[8] The evening before delivering it, Osborne phones Ed Balls to ensure that he is in full agreement. Treasury head Nicholas Macpherson provides further endorsement in a letter which concludes that a currency union will be out of the question, a move subsequently criticised for breaching Civil Service neutrality.[9] Number 10 knows that Osborne's strong line will provoke visceral reaction and is therefore a risk, but believe that the Scottish electorate has the time to get over their anger and absorb the underlying message. Salmond dismisses Osborne's intervention as 'bluff, bluster and bullying'. The polls suggest that the speech has indeed created a negative reaction, bolstering those who say they will vote for independence. Within Downing Street, voices are critical of 'George's megaphone message from London', telling the Scots 'they will lose the pound, and that every military base will be relocated to England. But it's not a brilliant way of doing things,' says one. Clegg is also worried about Osborne's strident tone: 'His approach was "Let's go in aggressively, let's hammer Salmond."'[10]

Support for the Better Together campaign is not growing. Fresh impetus is needed. It comes on 2 June with the Strathclyde Commission, unveiled by Lord Strathclyde and Ruth Davidson, leader of the Scottish Conservatives. This recommends giving Scotland further devolution and attracts widespread praise. Strathclyde and Davidson 'may together save the union ... For the first time in decades a Tory idea has been greeted with approval north of the border, being called "revolutionary", "game-changing" and "thoughtful" rather than the usual "pompous" and "arrogant", writes Alice Thomson in *The Times*.[11] President Obama offers another intervention. Number 10 have long been debating who they might encourage to speak up in favour of the United Kingdom. The first missile emanates from the White House, who are very concerned by the prospect of Scottish independence, not least for defence and security reasons. The White House 'tell us privately that they desperately hope Scotland will not become independent', says one diplomat at the British Embassy. Obama knows he is bound to be asked for his view: equally, he is alive to the risk of any intervention being seen as counterproductive. So he runs what he wants to say past Number 10, before announcing on 5 June that he hopes the United Kingdom will stay 'strong, robust and united'.[12]

A few days later on 11 June, the author J. K. Rowling donates £1 million to the 'No' cause, describing independence as 'a historically bad mistake'.[13] It enables Better Together to offer a more vigorous campaign over the final hundred days. On 5 August, Darling and Salmond go head-to-head for the first televised debate. Salmond appears tired and nervous, Darling far more confident: 'Any eight-year-old can tell you the flag of a country, the capital of a country and its currency ... you can't tell us what currency we will have. What is an eight-year-old going to make of that?' Before the second debate on 25 August, this time a victory for Salmond, comes a furore over the NHS. Yes Scotland begin to argue that the NHS will not be safe if Scotland remains within the union: Tory privatisation and spending cuts will harm the quality of provision. It is an effective ploy and Better Together estimate that it cost them over 100,000 votes, amounting to some three percentage points.[14]

Momentum is now firmly with Yes Scotland. On 2 September, a YouGov poll in *The Times* reports that over August, the Better Together lead has shrunk from 14 to 6 percentage points. It is a desperate blow. Carmichael tells Cabinet hours later that 'this is a time to hold your nerve and take the prospect seriously, but we have to stick to the strategy'.[15] Whitehall goes into rapid action, examining how London might extend Scotland's powers, while at the same time looking at what further can be done to warn Scotland of the dangers of independence. Within Downing Street, Cameron's team decide to mobilise more business voices speaking out against independence. At the most secret and confidential levels, discussions are taking place between Number 10 and the Palace about whether the Queen might be willing to express her views before it is too late.[16]

The need for urgency is underlined on 7 September when a YouGov poll in the *Sunday Times* shows that the 'Yes' campaign is now in the lead, with 51% to 49%. Cameron is on his annual visit to Balmoral when the poll is published. Neither head of state nor head of government is remotely amused. Back in London, Jeremy Heywood has been talking to Sir Christopher Geidt, the Queen's private secretary, who is in Balmoral with the PM and his highly respected principal private secretary, Chris Martin, about the constitutional implications for the Queen of a 'Yes' vote. They are mindful of the furore when, during the Silver Jubilee in 1977, she spoke to the nation about 'the benefits which union has conferred, at home and in our international dealings, on the inhabitants of all parts of this United Kingdom'.[17]

Cameron and his team have always been scrupulous about not revealing any conversations which take place with the Queen. No one will know for many years what exactly was said between the monarch and her prime minister. But the conversation over breakfast that morning, when the *Sunday Times* headline reads 'Yes vote leads Scots poll', must have been filled with tension.[18] The Queen keeps her counsel. One week later, after church on Sunday 14 September, she delivers carefully nuanced words to a well-wisher: 'Well, I hope people will think very carefully about the future.'[19] The next day, an ICM poll in the *Telegraph* shows the 'Yes' campaign ahead of Better Together. Many wonder if the panic is overdone; some twenty opinion polls are conducted between 1–17 September by a variety of organisations: the vast majority show 'No' ahead, albeit by a narrowing margin.

The polls galvanise Number 10. The response is: 'What can we throw at this?' 'We are looking for everything we can humanly do to get to the right result. The PM is petrified. It weighs very heavily on his mind. It is a really big deal for him. You can tell when he is really tense because he is tetchy.' Cameron has been deeply shaken. 'Shit, we might lose this', is his reaction. Collectively, Cameron's team feel that

Better Together lacks dynamism, and they have to take more control themselves.

Their cause is helped by the market reaction to the apparent rise in support for independence. On 8 September £2.6 billion is wiped off the value of leading companies with Scottish links on the FTSE 100, and the pound weakens against both the dollar and the euro. The FTSE 100 falls by over twenty points after the polls.[20] On 10 September, Standard Life say they will move parts of their business to England in the event of a 'Yes' vote. On 11 September, Lloyds, which owns the Bank of Scotland and the Royal Bank of Scotland, say they might also consider relocating. These are not random announcements. 'The biggest contribution the prime minister made to the whole campaign, frankly, was getting the banks and pension firms to speak out. It was all orchestrated from London with the PM making calls to business leaders,' says one insider. A core aim of Cameron's team is to shake up the middle classes in Scotland and convince them how bad independence would be for them, in their view. Andrew Feldman is deputed to raise more money and do his bit to galvanise the business community. A rally in support of the union takes place on Monday 15 September in Trafalgar Square, with Sir Bob Geldof, Eddie Izzard and Dan Snow speaking.[21]

Slowly, the 'No' camp begins to regain the initiative in a frenetic final ten days and outstrips the 'Yes' campaign, which is beginning to lose momentum. A major effort is made to sway the press: Cameron, Osborne and Craig Oliver lobby where they can, and Michael Gove writes an article in the *Daily Mail*.[22] Rupert Murdoch, who had flown independently to Aberdeen to test opinion on the ground, is coming off the fence. He reads Gove's piece and wants the same line repeated in the *Sun in Scotland*. The argument convinces him that the union should be maintained and the stance of one of Scotland's best-selling newspapers changes from pro-independence to neutrality.

On 10 September, PMQs are abandoned as Cameron, Clegg and Miliband all fly north to make the case for the union. Craig Oliver is with Cameron in the car on the way from Edinburgh airport to address an audience in the headquarters of Scottish Widows. 'I'm thinking of saying, "You shouldn't vote yes just to give the Tories a kick,"' Cameron tells his communications director. 'Good,' Oliver replies. He thinks it might be an effective way for the PM to show the depth of his feeling. But some in government would rather he doesn't speak at all. 'Can you hide the PM?' Danny Alexander writes in a text to Oliver. The Chief Secretary has been talking to Miliband about the damage the PM might do to the 'No' campaign by adopting a high profile, having been a subdued presence for so long. 'Remember, he is the prime minister. You can't hide him away,' Oliver texts back. They end up having 'quite a robust exchange'. The spat prompts Cameron's team again to wonder whether the Lib Dems and Labour might be putting their own party interests above the overall message.[23] At Scottish Widows, Cameron is in raw and passionate mode as he delivers some of his most powerful words as PM:

> I care far more about my country than I do about my party. I care hugely about this extraordinary country, this United Kingdom that we have built together. I would be heartbroken if this family of nations we have put together – and we have done such amazing things – was torn apart … You make a decision and five years later you can make another decision – if you are fed up with the effing Tories give them a kick and then maybe we will think again. This is a totally different decision to a general election. This is not a decision about the next five years. It is a decision about the next century.[24]

On Monday 15 September, three days before polling, Cameron makes his final visit of the campaign to deliver a speech at the Exhibition and Conference Centre in Aberdeen. His message emphasises what he regards as the risks of a 'Yes' vote:

> We meet in a week that could change the United Kingdom forever … On Friday, people could be living in a different country, with a different place in the world and a different future ahead of it. This is a decision that could break up our family of nations, and rip Scotland from the rest of the UK. And we must be very clear. There's no going back from this. No re-run. This is a once-and-for-all decision.[25]

The speech is written by Clare Foges at her very best. In an unusual move, the text is sent to Gordon Brown to ask for his comments. This is more than a trust-building exercise: they are genuinely interested in his views. Cameron's team have been trying to engage his predecessor in the 'No' campaign since early 2013. They see him as 'an Old Testament preacher', as opposed to Darling, the 'reassuring bank manager'. They certainly don't want Brown to run the campaign, because he is so incorrigibly tribal, but they see his value as an ally. He possesses a unique ability to get out the Scottish Labour vote, helped by his impeccably Scottish background and his left-wing politics. But their early attempts to build bridges are rebuffed. 'If I can't be captain, I'm going to go off and do my own thing', is the sense they have of him. Yet they keep trying. With his track record for twice keeping Britain out of the euro, in 1997 and 2003, they suggest he pen an article on the implications of the referendum for the pound. He agrees but they find him prickly. They are disappointed when a rather dry article appears in the Scottish tabloid the *Daily Record* in November 2013, which Brown refuses to publicise through appearances in the media.[26]

At Easter 2014, Brown has a change of heart, and he signals that he is willing to work with Better Together. They agree he should deliver a speech on pensions, which is helped by material from inside Whitehall. Number 10 even alter their plans to accommodate the speech, which Brown then gives on 21 April.[27] Number 10 are not pleased to hear his suggestion that Cameron and Salmond should debate face-to-face, which Brown knows runs directly counter to the PM's preference not to take part in broadcast debates. In May, Andrew Dunlop sees Brown in his office in the House of Commons. Brown is back to being prickly again, claiming that the campaign is too negative, and plays up the differences between his own views and those of Better Together. But in the final few days, galvanised by the narrowing polls, he springs back into action. He has several phone calls with Cameron, described as 'quite cordial', and accepts that the PM is sincere. Number 10 are pleased that he doesn't brief journalists about the phone calls.

Cameron has been thinking ahead about a new settlement for Scotland in the event of a 'No' victory. After the 2014 Commonwealth

Games from 23 July to 3 August, he signs a joint declaration with Miliband and Clegg, as part of the Better Together campaign. The worrying opinion polls suggest the need, endorsed and egged on by Brown, to come forward with their proposals, which are leaked by Danny Alexander to the *Observer* on 14 September.

On 16 September 'The Vow' is published in Scotland's *Daily Record*. It is conceived by Brown as a way of counteracting the SNP attack on NHS policy, by showing Scotland enjoys a beneficial financial settlement and that the nationalist onslaught is scaremongering. The text of 'The Vow', drafted by Labour's Douglas Alexander, has been the subject of fevered debate with the Conservatives. The eventual wording is firmly anodyne. To the chagrin of Cameron and Osborne, as well as Labour and Lib Dems, the Labour-supporting *Daily Record* refuses to come out for the 'No' campaign. Published with great fanfare on the paper's front page, and addressed to 'The People of Scotland', it promises that the Scottish Parliament is permanent, that it will receive more powers, and that the current system of funding for Scotland, the Barnett formula, will continue.[28] Cameron communicates closely with Brown, who keeps pushing the prime minister to be generous to the Scottish people. Brown takes credit for both the idea and the wording of 'The Vow', if not for the way that it is presented, as if on parchment paper resplendent with burnt edges.[29]

Wednesday 17 September is the final day of campaigning. Glasgow, Scotland's most populous city, as well as the most pro-independence after Dundee, is chosen as the site for mass rallies. The 'Yes' campaigners gather in George Square in the centre of the city. A short distance away, in Maryhill, Better Together meet at the Community Central Hall. Brown gives a speech that is described by *The Economist* as 'the speech of his life'.[30] 'The silent majority will be silent no more,' he says, 'our patriotic identity, proud of our Scottish identity, proud of our distinctive Scottish institutions, proud of the Scottish Parliament that we, not the nationalist party, created.'[31] Brown's speech is so powerful because he finds a passion which Cameron rarely feels able, or comfortable, articulating. Brown is able to find 'the authentic reason for why the United Kingdom might be Better Together', as one insider puts it. Brown's impassioned intervention turned wavering voters back to the 'No' camp. Some even believe he saved the union.

The polls open at 7 a.m. on Thursday 18 September. The turnout, at 84.59%, is the highest for any British election since the introduction of universal suffrage in 1918.[32] Cameron is much more anxious than he had been on the night of the 2010 general election. As the polls close, his close team meet in Number 11 for a takeaway curry. Oliver Dowden has a camp bed set up in his office, the only occasion that he does so over the five years of the parliament. They consume what are described as 'mountains of curry', almost as a distraction to talking about the imminent results, before decamping to Craig Oliver's office on the ground floor of Number 12. In front of them are two television screens. Cameron can't bear to watch. He paces in and out of the room. Lynton Crosby is the most confident, but there is a genuine sense among them all that it could still go either way, even though the most recent indicators have been positive.

At 10.30 p.m. a YouGov poll is released: 54% 'No', 46% 'Yes'. The mood lightens. At about midnight, Cameron says, 'I've had enough. I can't stand it. I'm off to bed.' He says he'll keep his phone on silent so people can text him. The first result is announced at 1.32 a.m. with Clackmannanshire at 54% 'No' and 46% 'Yes'. Orkney follows at 2.03 with 67% 'No', then Shetland at 2.43 with 64% 'No'. Craig Oliver now texts Cameron, saying 'looking good'. Cameron, who has been sleeping fitfully, replies: 'Good. I'll get a couple more hours' sleep.' The PM's party continue to watch the screens in Oliver's office, though they have now moved out into the adjoining open-plan press office in Number 12. Cameron has had speeches prepared in the event of a 'Yes' and a 'No' vote. Meetings have taken place with Heywood and Brown in the days before, confirming what both men might say if Scotland remains in the union. Cameron's team have decided in the event of a 'No' that he will have to come out immediately and talk about 'English votes for English laws' (EVEL), so great is the pressure that they will come under given the concessions made in the last few days, and the hovering presence of UKIP. EVEL, it is hoped, will address the so-called West Lothian Question, whereby Scottish MPs can vote on English-only matters, but not vice-versa under devolution.

'It's no good. I can't sleep,' says Cameron who appears at the door shortly after his text exchanges with Craig Oliver. Dowden comes back at 3 a.m. having had a rest. Cameron is straight down to work making changes to the 'No' speech, which now looks increasingly likely to be the one he will deliver later that morning. At 3.58 Dundee comes out with 57.35% 'Yes', a larger figure than Glasgow which declares at 4.53 at 53% 'Yes'. Shortly afterwards, the BBC's Nick Robinson announces, 'I think we know it now. The United Kingdom is surviving. There will not be an independent Scotland.' The victory in Glasgow, he says, is 'simply not big enough'.[33] Indeed only four out of thirty-two local authority areas across the country vote 'Yes'.

At 5 a.m., Darling is called by Number 10. Cameron congratulates him on the result. Darling reportedly says that the heady post-referendum atmosphere is not the moment to sort out EVEL. To do so, he says, will inflame the SNP by restricting the voting rights of Scottish MPs. Cameron responds that the issue of English votes is one that needs to be addressed at the first opportunity.[34] The wooing and promises to Scotland have created some dismay in England, including among Tory backbenchers. He senses great political danger if he doesn't nip it in the bud emphatically, falling back on the claim that EVEL had been official Conservative policy since 2001, was endorsed by the McKay Commission in March 2013 but had then been blocked by Lib Dem opposition from the then Scotland Secretary, Michael Moore. Cameron also meets stiff resistance from Clegg, having spoken on the phone the day before. 'I'm going to have to lean into the English issue,' he tells Clegg. 'I've got a problem with my English flank and I have to deal with it now.' 'You can say whatever you like, but we don't agree on this – you're not speaking on behalf of the coalition,' replies Clegg. Although Cameron nuances his speech to avoid reference to the coalition, his determination to raise the issue on a cross-party consensus is undimmed.

Just after the Darling call, Cameron's children come downstairs and rush to their father. They sit on his knee. It is the first time that they seem to understand fully the significance of the work their father does: 'Everyone could see how much it mattered to him, and they obviously picked up what was at stake for their father.' At about 5.30 a.m., the close team gather in his study to work on the 'No' text at his desk. At 6 a.m., Edinburgh's vote is declared: 61% 'No'. At 6.18, Salmond concedes: 'Scotland has by a majority decided, *not at this stage*, to become an independent country.'

At 7 a.m., Cameron goes out onto Downing Street to deliver his text, declaring that there will be English votes for English laws: 'The question of English votes for English laws – the so-called West Lothian Question – requires a decisive answer. Just as Scotland will vote separately in the Scottish Parliament on their issues of tax, spending and welfare, so too England, as well as Wales and Northern Ireland, should be able to vote on these issues … We will set up a Cabinet Committee right away.'[35] He says that he has asked William Hague to draw up plans for the new settlement. As expected, the media interpret it as an attempt to outflank his right wing and UKIP, as well as exposing Labour's ambiguity over the policy. Farage is quickly on the airwaves to demand English votes for English laws. Brown promptly telephones Heywood to express his anger at Cameron. Neither is Danny Alexander impressed: 'What it did was just give the nationalists a whole grievance agenda from a minute after the result was declared. It was just dreadful.'[36] Gove stokes fires when he seems to imply in an interview in *The Times* on 20 September that further devolution to Scotland is conditional on progress on EVEL, a claim quickly countered by Number 10.[37] He subsequently explained: 'As chief whip, I was very conscious that the rights of MPs from England and Wales also had to be reasserted. Immediately after the vote, therefore, the PM acknowledged their rights.'[38]

The swiftness and tone of Cameron's statement angers the centre left. 'Any prime minister is a party politician. But a prime minister must also be a national leader,' says an editorial that Sunday in the *Observer*. 'Cameron's handling of the aftermath of the Scotland vote has fallen far short on this count … The clumsy partisanship of Mr Cameron's response has made it look as if he is reneging on a promise.'[39] Brown, and the SNP, are swift to jump on Gove's interview as evidence of betrayal, which despite Number 10's prompt response, they can do little to assuage. Neither are Cameron critics on the right reassured: 'The English will not tolerate another lopsided settlement designed to appease nationalist sentiment paid for by English taxpayers,' says Owen Paterson.[40] The referendum has poked a hornet's nest. The prime minister receives little praise or credit for his months of work and anxiety. Yet he has failed to anticipate the resentment that addressing the 'English Question' in such a precipitous manner just hours after the referendum result would stir – especially among the 45% of Scots who voted to leave the United Kingdom – and the damage it would wreak on the Unionist cause. The SNP may well have gone on to enjoy a surge in support irrespective of Cameron's remarks that morning, but a more statesmanlike and magnanimous approach would have cooled the political temperature north of the border.

A measure of Cameron's extreme tension during the whole devolution denouement is discernible when he makes a rare slip the following Tuesday. To Michael Bloomberg, former mayor of New York, he confides: 'The definition of relief is being the prime minister of the United Kingdom and ringing the Queen and saying, "It's all right, it's OK."' He then tells Bloomberg that 'she purred down the line'.[41] This is a significant breach of protocol and etiquette for a prime minister, and he knows it: he is deeply embarrassed. Compatriots in the White House, however, are only too happy to purr at the result. 'You don't want to do that again,' Obama says to him, only half-joking. EU leaders, notably Spain's Mariano Rajoy, are delighted to see the forces of separatism thwarted, but are also cross with Cameron for raising the separatist spectre so prominently by calling the referendum: 'Please don't open this Pandora's box again,' he is told by Rajoy and others facing separatist agitators.

Earlier that week, a private meeting had taken place in Cameron's room in Downing Street. Only Osborne, Llewellyn, Fall, Oliver and Gove are present. They are considering what will happen in the event of a 'Yes' vote, a very real possibility. Certainly, a defeated Cameron would face calls to resign from the press and the back benches. 'I thought it fanciful he'd be allowed to stay – our feet wouldn't have touched the floor,' recalls one at the meeting. In addition to the loss of a third of Britain's landmass, it would call into question Britain's continued position in international organisations like the G7 and the UN Security Council. There are those who are adamant Cameron should remain: 'Britain would be in a state of crisis and we shouldn't exacerbate a very volatile division by having a prime minister resigning.' His team try to convince him of the need to stay on. None of those present are really sure what is in his mind. The public outcry and anger would be so great, and his personal judgement would come under so much attack, that remaining in power would almost certainly have been untenable. 'The truth is that if the vote had gone against us, he would have been out. He knew that, whatever he might have said to us,' says one. He would almost certainly have jumped before he was pushed. With the prospect of going down in history as the man who broke up the United Kingdom, followed by a dishonourable dismissal, it is unsurprising that in those final few days his mood is so sombre. Even winning the referendum brings little closure or respite, for all the joy so palpably visible on his face at 5 a.m. that Friday morning.

THIRTY-FOUR

EU Tribulations

January–June 2014

It is midday on Friday 27 June 2014. Cameron is at lunch with the EU leaders on the eighth floor of the Council of Ministers office in Brussels. He is insisting on a vote on whether Jean-Claude Juncker should succeed José Manuel Barroso as president of the European Commission, the most powerful post in the EU. Cameron knows that he will lose, but seems not to mind. His fellow leaders, some defiant, some embarrassed with eyes cast down, make their views known via a show of hands. Only Viktor Orbán, prime minister of Hungary, joins Cameron in refusing to support Juncker: they lose by a resounding twenty-six votes to two. Yet Cameron is typically phlegmatic in his response. He returns to the delegation office after lunch, telling his staff how Orbán and he had been heard respectfully in silence. He then compares it to an iconic scene from the film *Spartacus*: after he and Orbán made their stand, most of the other leaders felt compelled to say: 'I am for Juncker', 'I am for Juncker', 'I too am for Juncker'.

'Rarely, if ever, has Britain suffered such a rout on so many fronts in Europe,' writes Andrew Rawnsley in the *Observer* that weekend. Cameron's strategy of pinning all his hopes on Merkel has proved a 'spectacular flop'.[1] In *The Times*, Philip Collins writes that Cameron's EU squabbles all have the same narrative arc: a loud demand, a failure to meet it, and then 'he pretends that his recalcitrance is a virtue that he meant all along'.[2] Nigel Farage milks the result for all it is worth, saying that with his defeat over Juncker, any hopes of Cameron being able to renegotiate Britain's position in Europe ahead of a referendum are gone. Cameron is 'looking like a loser who has learnt nothing, still insisting, though it is rather more difficult, that he can renegotiate our position. He can't,' is the UKIP leader's conclusion.[3] How has Cameron allowed himself to be cornered in this position, with bad headlines on the EU dominating over the following few weeks, when his Bloomberg speech of January 2013 was designed to take the steam out of the whole EU issue before the general election? To understand what happened, the complexities of the EU's changing power balance need first to be unravelled.

The president of the European Commission runs the executive branch of the EU, and can be very roughly compared to its prime minister, as opposed to the president of the European Council, who chairs the regular meetings of the heads of government. The president of the Council, chosen by the heads of state, serves a term of two and a half years. The Commission president is elected on a five-year term by the European Parliament after a candidate is put forward by the European Council. This process is further enshrined in the Lisbon Treaty of 2009. But for several years, the European Parliament has been seeking to enhance its power against the Council, which sets the political direction and priorities of the EU. A directly elected Commisssion president has been a federalist objective for a long time. As an official explains, 'It creates a European politics in which people campaign on a party, and a platform, and a person. It's about the political integration of Europe.' This is a move that the political class in Britain has been slow to detect – despite Britain's permanent representatives to the EU in Brussels, both indicatively ex-Treasury (Jon Cunliffe until November 2013, and then Ivan Rogers), warning about moves afoot by activist MEPs to adopt a process called *Spitzenkandidaten*. This entails the main political groups in the European Parliament – above all the two principal 'families', the centre-right European People's Party (EPP) and the centre-left Progressive Alliance of Socialists and Democrats (S&D) – proposing lead candidates, and then getting behind the one from the group that wins the most seats in the European elections.

Cameron gradually wakes up to the risk that the *Spitzenkandidaten* process poses by enhancing the power of the European Parliament to the detriment of the European Council. 'This concept was never agreed by the European Council. It was not negotiated between the European institutions. And it was never ratified by national parliaments,' he says in June 2014.[4] But Cameron's ability to mould the process is affected by his decision in Opposition to take the Conservatives out of the EPP. 'He didn't realise how important the EPP would become. He did not realise that the European Parliament is all about multilateral relations, and he did not realise how the EPP would grow in importance after Lisbon,' says a despairing diplomat. Cameron's response is robust: 'It would have made no difference if we had been in the EPP. Merkel, Reinfeldt [Sweden] and Kenny [Republic of Ireland] are all in the EPP, and they all disagreed with the *Spitzenkandidaten* process, yet it happened.' Officials have been warning Number 10 since at least 2012 that the appointment of a new Commission president in June 2014 is 'a slow-motion car crash coming towards us'. One senior diplomat thinks that firm action by leaders in the European Council as early as 2012 might just have stopped the car altogether. Had they 'stood up strongly against it, there would have been a fight and the European Parliament would have complained bitterly. But the Council would have had its way. The Council could rightly have said that it had more democratic representation than the Parliament, and could have pulled it off.'

Earnest conversations about a new Commission president begin in the EU Council meetings in October and December 2013. Leaders observe with some dismay that the process is being driven by the S&D and its leader Martin Schulz. At the time it is an open question whether the EPP will mimic the S&D and support the *Spitzenkandidaten* process. Advice flows back to London that, if they do, its two likely candidates will be Juncker or Michel Barnier, France's EU commissioner for internal markets and services. Juncker quickly emerges as the more likely. Reports also flow back to London that 'EU leaders are still in denial about the extent of the momentum within the European Parliament, and cling to the notion that the choice of Commission president is still their prerogative, rather than having it predetermined by the Parliament.'

In November 2013, the pace accelerates dramatically when the S&D group name their *Spitzenkandidat*, Martin Schulz himself. The EPP holds its congress in Dublin on 6–7 March 2014. The British Conservative Party are not represented at it, and Juncker emerges as its favoured candidate.[5] Cameron's own grouping, the European

Conservatives and Reformists (ECR), very much the third power block with representatives from fifteen countries, is unable to assert a strong voice in the debate. The Conservatives are not the only UK party alarmed by the power grab by the European Parliament, and by the activism of its main political families. Labour are panicked at the prospect of Schulz as a candidate. Its relations with the S&D are not strong and its own efforts to block the *Spitzenkandidaten* process fail. The Conservatives continue to maintain that their position is not weakened by not being a member of the EPP, while the Liberal Democrats are the only major party to enjoy close relations with European parties. But even they oppose the *Spitzenkandidaten* and yet are unable to stop the Alliance of Liberals and Democrats for Europe (ALDE) putting one forward. Conservatives eye Juncker with particular alarm as he is no lover of the UK. He favours a social model of Europe, entirely out of tune with the direction that Cameron wants to see the EU take. He is described as 'an old-school dealmaker and schmoozer' who is felt to be past his best: born in 1954, and PM of Luxembourg since 1995, he is one of the world's longest-serving democratic leaders.

Cameron knows he has very few cards left that he can play. He believes Juncker will take Europe in a direction that will create even more hostility amongst the mainstream in Britain, and will not be open to looking sympathetically at Britain's case for a renegotiation. He knows he must block him. The strongest card in his hand is whipping up other European leaders to see that Juncker will not set a good precedent for the modern era, and that ceding so much to the European Parliament will both create an irreversible momentum, and run counter to the EU treaties; indeed this is the prime minister's principal reason for opposing Juncker. In his back pocket he hides his trump card, albeit a weak one, which is that if Juncker is elected, it will make it less likely that Britain will remain within the EU. Several EU leaders are worried by this prospect, including Mark Rutte of the Netherlands, Fredrik Reinfeldt of Sweden, and above all his old friend Angela Merkel. On her broad shoulders he pins his principal hopes. He is later to be blamed for being essentially a one-trick pony by relying too much on her, but it is doubtful if he has other options: and it is hard to know what else he can do but dig in hard against Juncker's appointment. Standing by passively and witnessing Juncker take the presidency without a fight would be an even weaker strategy. Moreover, other European leaders silently hope that Merkel will stop the appointment.

Happily Merkel is in London on Thursday 27 February for her grandest visit of the five years. It boasts the 'top three' ingredients that the capital can offer: a personal audience with the Queen, an address to Parliament, and a private meeting in Downing Street. Merkel is much impressed with Her Majesty, and her entourage are cock-a-hoop that the meeting, at forty-five minutes, lasts longer than scheduled. They are transfixed by the idea that not a word of what is spoken will ever be divulged, envying the discretion around the British head of state. Discussion at Number 10 begins with a bilateral meeting upstairs in Cameron's private flat. Very rarely for Merkel, no aides are present. They talk about Juncker and she strongly advises Cameron not to go in too hard or too quickly against him: get the European elections out of the way first, and then make the case, she says. He comes downstairs with the distinct impression that she 'gets it', that she accepts Juncker is not the right man for Commission president, and that they will find a way of killing off his candidacy. Her message, as he reports it, is 'Don't worry, David. I'm not a fool. I know Juncker isn't the right answer. I will find a way of dealing with that after the elections.' She is equally adamant that the Commission president cannot be Schulz. The pre-meeting over, they have lunch in Number 10's state rooms, joined by their aides. Cameron is in a visibly good mood and the conversation moves to the areas that he feels will need to change for Britain in any EU renegotiation. He is most definitely not in favour, he says, of 'ever closer union' and wants to see reform to the eurozone and the single market, more subsidiarity and constraints on European institutions, and a greater role for national Parliaments. She listens attentively and appears sympathetic to his concerns.

So far, so good. But Number 10 then brief out that Merkel has given qualified support to Cameron's renegotiation stance on the EU. This irritates her and her staff brief that this is not the case. More pointedly, her remarks in the Royal Gallery of the House of Commons contain a blunt message. The great and good of the UK throng to hear her speak, only the second time a German chancellor has addressed

Parliament, the first being Willy Brandt of West Germany at the request of Harold Wilson in 1970. She talks about her respect and admiration for Britain, and its sense of history as proof of its European identity. But she also gives a brief passage in English:

> Supposedly, or so I have heard, some expect my speech to pave the way for a fundamental reform of the European architecture which will satisfy all kinds of alleged or actual British wishes. I am afraid they are in for a disappointment. I have also heard that others are expecting the exact opposite and are hoping that I will deliver the clear and simple message here in London that the rest of Europe is not prepared to pay almost any price to keep Britain in the European Union. I am afraid these hopes will be dashed, too.[6]

She wants to manage the expectations of those investing powers in her, which she is either unwilling or unable to exercise on behalf of Britain. Advice has been coming into Number 10 for a year or more from both Brussels and Whitehall that 'whatever she may say, she may not be able to deliver'. Nevertheless, to Cameron himself, well grounded or not, she remains the one person who can help Britain, both on negotiations, and in ridding him of his Juncker problem. Two weeks after her London visit, they meet in Hanover for a trade fair, and have dinner together in the Guest House of Lower Saxony. Again, she conveys the clear impression to him that she will be able to handle Juncker, if not immediately.

Cameron feels the need to make the case for renegotiation again in an article in mid-March. Deploying almost exactly the same arguments he used to Merkel in Number 10 over lunch two weeks before, he writes 'No to ever closer union. No to a constant flow of power to Brussels. No to unnecessary interference. And no, it goes without saying, to the euro, to participation in eurozone bailouts or notions such as a European Army.' He argues for powers to flow back from Brussels to national Parliaments, for businesses to be liberated from red tape, and for the criminal justice system to protect British citizens unencumbered by the European Convention on Human Rights. He writes that he is happy with EU enlargement, but wants 'new mechanisms in place' to prevent vast migrations. His primary passion is that the EU should be an economic powerhouse: 'So, yes to the single market. Yes to turbo-charging free trade. Yes to working together where we are stronger together than alone.'[7]

He heeds Merkel's advice to cool it on Juncker until after the European elections in May; but behind the scenes, he is working the telephones hard, speaking in particular to both Rutte and Reinfeldt: 'If we let this happen, the European Council will never get another top job: they will be decided by the European Parliament,' he tells them. On 22 April, he has Herman Van Rompuy, president of the Council, to Chequers for an overnight stay. Over dinner, Cameron is pleased to hear his guest criticising the *Spitzenkandidaten* process, and still more to hear him say that he thinks that neither Juncker nor Schulz are right as Commission president. They agree there is a need to place other candidates on the table.

The European elections are held on Thursday 22 May. Like many across the EU, Cameron assumes that the EPP and the S&D will achieve roughly the same number of seats. Merkel tells Cameron not to worry: that if it's a dead heat between the two main parties, it won't be a problem, because neither Schulz nor Juncker will be the answer.' But when the results are declared on 25 May, the EPP emerges as the largest single party, winning 24.2% of the vote and 221 out of the 751 MEPs. The S&D are second with 191 seats while the ECR, to which the British Conservatives are affiliated, come third with seventy seats. In the UK, UKIP emerges as the largest single party, with twenty-four seats and 27.5% of the vote: the Conservatives are third with nineteen seats behind Labour with twenty. The victory for the EPP is a major blow to Cameron, bigger even than the predicted UKIP victory. The EPP's unexpected victory is thought to be because voters in Central and Eastern Europe swung to the right after the Russian intervention in Ukraine.

Overnight, Juncker's claim appears to have become far stronger. Nevertheless Cameron clings onto the hope he will carry the day. Van Rompuy scraps the European Council in May because of the elections, but convenes a dinner at the Justus Lipsius building in Brussels on 27 May to discuss the top jobs. Cameron is on the phone intensively in the preceding days, and believes he has secured general agreement at the dinner that the leaders will reject the *Spitzenkandidaten* process.

Merkel talks about addressing the gender imbalance when choosing their recommendation for the next Commission president: she advocates 'a broad tableau' of contenders.[8] Female candidates being courted at the time include Christine Lagarde from France, Helle Thorning-Schmidt from Denmark, and Dalia Grybauskaite from Lithuania.[9] Van Rompuy sums up by saying: 'Clearly there is a strong feeling that the process shouldn't be concluded quickly and that we should look at other names.' Merkel is transparent in her post-dinner press conference that this is her view, as carried in the *Financial Times* and other papers across Europe.[10] However, Cameron's use of his trump card at the meeting is leaked, and German magazine *Der Spiegel* says that 'Cameron declared to fellow leaders that "If Juncker, a federalist, is appointed Commission president, the chances would increase that the British people would vote to leave in a planned 2017 referendum on EU membership."'[11] A reaction against Cameron is sparked, with some European leaders claiming to have felt 'blackmailed' by him.[12]

Merkel returns home to a hail of protest. 'For days now,' says *Der Spiegel*, 'furious politicians on the editorial pages of newspapers have called on Merkel not to put up with this "blackmail".'[13] Her own party, the Christian Democratic Union (CDU), and its allies, the Christian Social Union in Bavaria (CSU), are angry with her for reneging on previous understandings she had given about supporting Juncker. The CDU/CSU bloc themselves had endorsed Juncker as a candidate on 24 February, and have no sympathy for her volte-face.[14] The *Spitzenkandidaten* had played a major part in the German European election campaign, and therefore the German public have a very different view of their validity. Merkel had agreed with Cameron before the dinner how they would handle the discussion and that she would say at a press conference that there is not just one candidate. Her team cannot blame the British this time for briefing the press, as they themselves briefed the German press just after the dinner. The force of the pro-Juncker reaction against Merkel takes Number 10, and Merkel herself, by surprise: the tabloid *Bild*, owned by Axel Springer, the largest German newspaper group, is unrestrained in its enthusiasm for his candidacy, publishing an article entitled 'Juncker must be president'.[15] She changes her mind very quickly. Her main objective had been to block Schulz: tribalism returns with a vengeance. It is clear that Merkel is going to cave in: 'It is a rare occasion that Merkel loses a domestic political fight,' says a figure in Number 10. 'Merkel had to choose between domestic politics and European statesmanship: in those kinds of situations, she would always choose German domestic politics,' says another. On 30 May, she goes public with the announcement that she wants Juncker to be the new European Commission president.[16]

Cameron is left high and dry, along with Rutte and Reinfeldt. The advice from British officials in Brussels is emphatic: barring a fluke, he will not win. 'You will end up in a position where you will be outnumbered.' Despite this, Cameron insists on standing his ground, 'intent on going down in flames', according to one official. Number 10 provide a number of reasons why he does not want to back down: with the renegotiation in mind, he wants to show the EU he will stick to what he says; taking a resolute position will not jeopardise (and might even help achieve) British success in obtaining a good portfolio in the other top jobs at the Commission; he hopes it will strengthen Britain's voice in the nomination of the other president post, for the Council; finally, he believes that the Commission can do better for its president than Juncker. He knows full well the disparaging remarks made by fellow leaders about the Luxembourger's lack of drive and vision. 'He regards it an example of the egregious way that the EU can operate, where the leaders say one thing in private and another in public.'

Cameron knows his lonely stance will call forth scorn in the UK. Ken Clarke is one of many voices dismissive of his Merkel-or-bust strategy: 'She is the best European leader by a street, but she doesn't walk on water. What she can deliver in European and German politics has constraints … She wants to keep us in the EU, but they misjudged it.'[17] 'Mr Cameron's team has sometimes shown a tin ear for German domestic politics', reflects the *Telegraph* a few months later.[18] On 8 June, in an article in the *Sunday Telegraph*, Boris Johnson causes predictable anger in Number 10 when he dismisses the attempt to block Juncker as the 'quintessence of turd-polishing pointlessness.'[19]

Cameron remains determined to fight to the end. He sees Merkel in Brussels on 4 June at the G7 summit, and invites her for a late-night drink at Rue Ducale, the elegant residence of the British permanent representative. She tells him that she had to look to her own position at home, but now the game is up. 'Look, David, I've got to be blunt,' she tells him. She thought she could stop it but admits she was wrong and it's almost certain now that Juncker will get the Commission job. 'I don't accept that,' Cameron replies, pushing back very hard, 'we shouldn't give in.' Their tone is calm and friendly but underneath it, Cameron is very aggravated, feeling that he has been given undertakings in good faith that she has not delivered upon. Shortly before she leaves at 1.30 a.m. she concedes there is an outside possibility it will be somebody else. 'But I have to say there is no realistic alternative to Juncker,' he recalls her saying, before she sweeps off in her waiting convoy.

They meet again on 9 and 10 June at Reinfeldt's official summer residence in Harpsund, 90 km west of Stockholm.[20] The meeting is Reinfeldt's idea, emerging out of discussions with Cameron. He argues that if only they can get several countries to oppose Juncker, and if their fellow leaders then fear a public spat, they will back off.[21] The discussion on the presidency is deliberately postponed until after dinner on the first day. Cameron's team hope that it will just be the four leaders together 'without hangers-on'. But Merkel 'won't have any of it: typically, she will almost never meet without a trio of her advisers'. Merkel keeps trying to focus the discussion on the programme for the new Commission once it takes up post, as well as on the identity of the new Council president. They sit up talking until two in the morning over several bottles of wine. Cameron keeps bringing their conversation back to first principles and the question of the legitimacy of the European Parliament's action, but Merkel will not have any of this either. She is clearer than ever that it has to be Juncker.

The next morning, Cameron goes for a swim in the lake: 'he likes wild swimming', says an insider. He sets off enthusiastically, joined by some of his aides, while ubiquitous bodyguards look on nervously. Quarrels over Juncker aside, Cameron rates it as one of his most enjoyable short trips of the year. But discussions that morning confirm that the game is up, and Rutte and Reinfeldt know it. They will no longer be fighting Juncker, and in the press conference, Merkel gives no grounds for hoping that the *Spitzenkandidaten* process can be stopped.[22] Cameron leaves Harpsund on 10 June, vowing to stop Juncker, but knowing he will lose.

Whether egged on or not, the British press now weigh into Juncker. He is attacked for over-drinking ('Junck the drunk'), as well as for having a father who fought for Hitler (an unjust accusation, given that his father had been conscripted during Germany's occupation of Luxembourg).[23] The personal onslaughts are read with anger and bemusement in Europe's capitals.

Cameron knows that the hysteria of the domestic press will win him no favours in Brussels, and realises that he needs to turn it into a debate about principle and to focus on the powers that the Commission is giving away. Three days after the meeting in Harpsund, he publishes an article in several European papers outlining his thinking, deploying arguments honed over the previous weeks and months with his fellow European leaders. He dismisses Junker and the entire *Spitzenkandidaten* process:

> We must focus on finding the best candidate for Commission president. Someone who can deliver reform; driving growth and creating jobs; and accepting that Europe's needs may best be served by action at the national level. An honest and trusted broker able to re-engage Europe's voters.[24]

He is immensely frustrated that European leaders have capitulated to the demands of the European Parliament, and is determined that they should vote on the Juncker appointment in order to face up to their actions, even though he knows that Juncker will win. With less than a week to go before the fateful European Council, Van Rompuy visits Cameron in Number 10 on Monday 23 June, towards the end of a long tour of European capitals. Cameron is at his most uncompromising: 'I want to ensure we have a vote in the Council on the Commission presidency,' he tells him. Somewhat taken aback at his directness, Van Rompuy replies as diplomatically as he can that this will not be possible: 'Can you give me a proper vote?' Cameron asks him three times. Three times Van Rompuy replies 'No I can't.' 'If you can't guarantee me a vote I have nothing more to discuss,' Cameron says, almost throwing Van Rompuy out of the room. His brusque treatment of the Council president is the talk of Brussels within the hour, and greatly heightens anxiety in the build-up to the Council.

Cameron leaves for Belgium with low expectations. On Wednesday, both Reinfeldt and Rutte confirm that if there is to be a vote, they will support Juncker.[25] On the afternoon of Thursday 26 June, Cameron and all of his EU counterparts attend a ceremony at the Menin Gate Memorial to the Missing of the Ypres Salient, before dedicating a memorial bench inscribed with the word 'peace' in each of the EU's twenty-four official languages.[26] The venue has been deliberately chosen because of the approaching centenary of the outbreak of the First World War that August. Ypres was the site of incessant fighting on the Western Front throughout the war, and the scene of the greatest concentration of German and British loss of life. After the poignant ceremony, the leaders repair to the medieval Cloth Hall, rebuilt with money from German reparations in the 1920s and 1930s. During the dinner, much of the conversation between EU leaders is about reconciliation in Europe and avoids discussion of the EU's current problems. Cameron's remarks about Britain's role in reshaping modern Europe after the horrors of two world wars are well received. Merkel is distracted by Germany playing the US in the World Cup, and is thrilled by her country's 1–0 victory. The conversation after dinner moves back to the present. Only Cameron and Orbán want to speak about the *Spitzenkandidaten*; to all the others it is a done deal, which will only cause aggravation by bringing it up again now. They don't want to hear Cameron talking about Juncker's nomination being 'an irreversible step which would hand power from the European Council to the European Parliament'.[27] They have had enough of it all.

The next morning, the leaders travel to Brussels for the formal part of the Council. The morning is largely spent on Ukraine and Russia. At lunchtime, the vote that the PM forces takes place. It is a total humiliation for Cameron. Some fellow feeling for his position amongst leaders comes out in the communiqué, which is generous to him, and observes that Merkel will want to consider the British position carefully when looking at the other top jobs shortly to be decided.[28] The next day, Barroso welcomes Juncker to the Commission. Ken Clarke, who knows Juncker, is asked to phone him to help smooth things over. On 30 June, Cameron calls Juncker himself to congratulate him on his new post. They meet on 17 July, which includes an embarrassing 'high five' accompanied by a cringeworthy press statement saying that 'this is how Juncker greets quite a lot of people'.[29]

Two EU issues remain prominent in Cameron's mind: the renegotiation, on which he has decided he must keep quiet until after the general election; and acquiring a top economic job for the UK in the new Commission. On 17 July, Cameron presses Juncker hard: 'I don't rule out giving you an economic post,' Juncker tells him; equally, 'I don't say that I definitely will.' Amongst the several economic jobs up for grabs, commissioner for financial stability and financial services is the favoured one. The British keep up the pressure on Brussels, thinking they may well end up with a lesser economic portfolio such as internal markets, or energy. Juncker's backing is all-important, but it will not be easy given Cameron's relentless efforts to block him. His relations with Cameron's predecessors have not been good either. They were poisonous with Blair, notably after Britain took over the European presidency in 2005, and were arguably worse with Brown, who fell out with him over tax and the position of the City of London.

Cameron immediately starts the search for an ideal candidate. The first thought is an MP, but Cameron reacts strongly against this because it would trigger a by-election. Their search moves to the House of Lords, and they alight on Jonathan Hill, who succeeded Lord Strathclyde as Leader of the Lords in January 2013. Hill had worked for Major as Political Secretary in Number 10, and Cameron thinks that he has the intellect, charm and persuasive skills to succeed in the post.

At a meeting in Brussels several weeks later, Juncker accedes to British wishes and offers Hill the financial services portfolio. This is seen by Number 10 as a good result, because Juncker has yet to allocate the other portfolios and is clearly favouring Britain. Polish prime minister Donald Tusk is nominated for the presidency of the Council, again showing Cameron's influence. Tusk will be useful. Cameron has worked closely with him over Ukraine, and he will be an ally in the event of a renegotiation. On 10 September, Hill is formally nominated as commissioner for financial stability and financial services. Some anti-British feeling is thought in Number 10 to be responsible for hostile questioning of him in front of MEPs, which means that he has to be recalled before being confirmed on 8 October.[30]

With Hill's appointment out of the way, Cameron's engagement with Europe steadily recedes. He at last achieves his initial stated aim of not allowing the EU to distract him unduly. The prize of a renegotiation with the EU on terms that achieve greater legitimacy among the British public lies in the future. If he can enable a rededication of the country to the EU for another forty years, he will be very happy. In the meantime, he knows that his record on Europe has been at best uneven. Though he always claimed that his detachment from the EPP was the right decision, it was taken for narrow tactical reasons to outflank his two Eurosceptic rivals, Liam Fox and David Davis, during the 2005 leadership election. It hampered his ability to make progress in the European Parliament. 'Had anyone thought about the longer-term consequences of where that would land them?' asks one senior diplomat. 'No. Had they taken any palliative action to rebuild relations with centre-right parties on a systematic basis? No. There was no strategy.'

Cameron came to power without a strong vision for Europe, and by 2015 it was political events at home that led him to the grand strategy of the renegotiation and referendum. He and Osborne quickly realised that further treaty change would be needed after 2010, and that Europe was changing far more than they had anticipated in the wake of the eurozone crisis. Cameron became PM not knowing Merkel, though she became the most important and powerful political ally he had in Europe over the five years. When they were in step, such as on the issue of the European budget, his life was much easier. But without her support, he remained very isolated, as the Juncker saga showed all too clearly. As Cameron's first term drew to a close, the question was whether her support would be solid enough to help him achieve the prize of a meaningful renegotiation.

THIRTY-FIVE

Final Autumn

September–December 2014

It is 6 p.m. on Sunday 21 September at Chequers. Cameron is relaxing over a pre-dinner drink with George Osborne and Craig Oliver, discussing the party conference a week away. He is in good spirits, still relieved about the Scottish referendum result two days before. He spent the Friday and Saturday at Dean with Steve Hilton and his wife Rachel Whetstone, who found him in notably 'good spirits'. But as he ponders the future with his two trusted colleagues, he is alive to the challenges ahead and focusing hard on how to meet them. His position in the party is still far from secure. Word has come to Number 10 that, had the Scottish referendum been lost, senior Tories would have started a bandwagon to unseat him.[1] 'There were people who were very much solid, traditional Tory loyalists for whom that was an unthinkable event,' recalls one senior party figure. 'The PM might have found that the Nicholas Soames's of this world, who have been among his greatest cheerleaders, could suddenly become the greatest critics.' The polls remain static and worrying: the Conservatives are averaging 32% against Labour's 35%. Following Douglas Carswell's defection to UKIP three weeks before, chatter is incessant about another imminent defection. Miliband gave two strong conference speeches in 2012 and 2013, and Cameron's team assume he will do so again. The right of the party and the commentariat are still growling about the ousting of Michael Gove and Owen Paterson: they are asking, 'Where's the beef? Does this prime minister have any policies of his own?'

Cameron's challenge is to come up with a message that will excite voters in the fast-approaching 2015 general election. How exactly do they move the rhetoric away from cuts? Lynton Crosby's mantra about the long-term economic plan is forever in their ears, but they feel they need to offer more. Cameron's speech the following week will be his last great opportunity to lay out his stall ahead of the election campaign. 'We need to score, and score demonstrably,' says Craig Oliver. A repetition of the PM's performance in 2011 and 2013, which failed to ignite his audience, must be avoided. Miliband's successful 2013 conference speech, where his announcement of an energy-price freeze set the agenda for several months, provides the catalyst for a policy-rich speech. 'My sense was that Ed Miliband would make another big announcement and what we needed to do was effectively launch the campaign,' recalls one person working on the speech. Since June or July, a small group of five, including Osborne and Rupert Harrison, have been working up a cunning tax plan for Cameron to announce at the conference. If proof is needed about the continuation of the unparalleled bond between prime minister and chancellor, which lasts to the end of the parliament, it can be found in Osborne's generosity in allowing Cameron to make the tax announcement, rather than bagging it for his own speech.

At 7.30 p.m., speechwriter Clare Foges arrives for dinner, and the following morning, Gove, Crosby and Ameet Gill join them to thrash out a final script. Cameron has had a particularly busy September: aside from the referendum, he has been at the UN for the General Assembly and chaired the NATO summit at Newport in South Wales. As a result, 'the speech didn't crystallise until shortly before' the conference, with only six or seven days to go. Foges has been advocating the idea of 'a new British era' to capitalise on the referendum result. 'I am so proud to stand here as prime minister of four nations in one United Kingdom' is her idea for the opening, projecting Cameron as a 'steward of the nation' with a ream of policies he wants to achieve in the next five years. Gove agrees that the text has to be elevated 'above mere transactional details'. But Crosby's emphasis on security, tax announcements and the long-term economic plan prevails. 'Conferring security at every stage of your life' becomes the working theme of the speech.

Cameron, unlike Thatcher, doesn't want to be up half the night before the speech finishing it off. He wants it locked down long

beforehand. The session that morning is therefore crucial. By lunchtime, the main elements are all in place. On tax, he will steal the thun-
der from the Lib Dems, whose conference begins in twelve days, by
announcing that the personal allowance for income tax will rise to
£12,500. More popular still, he will say the threshold on the 40p tax
band will rise from £41,900 to £50,000 by the end of the next parliament. A series of further statements are agreed, to convince voters
that 'there is something in it for them'. For young house buyers, he will
say that 'we will help you get a place of your own' with 'Help to Buy'
and a plan to build 100,000 affordable homes, available only to first-
time buyers. For parents, he will promise a good school for all, and
will chastise shadow Education Secretary Tristram Hunt for his opposition to free schools. For the elderly, there is the promise of future
pension reform. For England, he will 'deliver' on his promise of
'English votes for English laws'. For those tempted by UKIP, immigration will be at the heart of his EU renegotiation strategy, and the
Human Rights Act will be scrapped. For the young, there will be a
place on the National Citizen Service. His strongest anger and passion
will be reserved for Labour's policy on the NHS, which he thinks is
'scaremongering'. He will thus pledge to protect the NHS budget for
England. Cameron's team plot how they will throw the press off the
scent by briefing ahead of the conference that his NHS budget promise will be at the heart of the speech, to give the tax announcements
maximum surprise value.

Miliband knows his own conference speech in Manchester is one of
the challenges of his political career. Once again he decides to deliver
it without notes, as Cameron had done in 2007. Miliband's personal
ratings lag a long way behind Cameron's, at minus 55% to minus 14%,[2]
and he hopes the speech will show he is prime ministerial, a natural
leader. But his hopes are dashed as he delivers a lacklustre performance
and omits mention of the deficit, which becomes the dominant narrative about not only his speech but also the entire party conference,
handing perfect ammunition to critics inside and outside the Labour
Party. Cameron's team are thus in unusually buoyant mood as the week
draws to an end and they prepare to travel to Birmingham.

But on Saturday comes the deliberately timed defection of Mark
Reckless to UKIP. Cameron is mortified and incandescent. Late that

night, when Andrew Feldman has a drink with him in his room, he is still fuming. His old university friend keeps trying to bolster his spirits, telling him how they have more members at conference than anyone can remember and that everyone is in remarkably good spirits. He has only limited success.[3] Cameron's anger mirrors that of his team: 'the fucker has come along and blown everything' is their collective thought that Saturday. But Feldman's optimism proves well placed. By Monday, the team begin reporting that that 'the journos seem pissed off that Reckless hasn't put us on our knees. They keep asking why we are not all depressed by it. They assume we have something up our sleeve.'

Osborne's speech on Monday announces that a future Conservative government will freeze benefits below inflation for a further two years. Its aim is to throw down the gauntlet, saying to Labour, 'This is how we would cut £3 billion from the deficit: what will you do?'[4] Cameron's speech on Wednesday 1 October is his most combative to date:

> A few weeks ago, Ed Balls said that in thirteen years of government, Labour had made 'some mistakes'. Some mistakes? Excuse me? You were the people who left Britain with the biggest peacetime deficit in history ... who gave us the deepest recession since the war ... who destroyed our pensions system, bust our banking system ... who left a million young people out of work, 5 million on out-of-work benefits – and hundreds of billions of debt. Some mistakes? Labour were just one big mistake.[5]

The emotion in Cameron's voice is clear when he delivers the most heartfelt part of his speech, on the NHS:

> From Labour last week, we heard the same old rubbish about the Conservatives and the NHS. Spreading complete and utter lies ... I am someone who has relied on the NHS – whose family knows more than most how important it is ... who knows what it's like to go to hospital night after night with a child in your arms ... knowing that when you get there, you have people who will care for that child and love that child like their own. How dare they suggest I

would ever put that at risk for other people's children? How dare they frighten those who are relying on the NHS right now![6]

For all the bluntness of Cameron's onslaught, Miliband will return to this NHS attack even more forcefully in the election campaign.

To assert his credentials, not only in the forthcoming election but also against any would-be contenders in the Conservative Party, Cameron highlights his qualities as leader. Looking directly at the camera, he says 'you cannot be prime minister of this country, and forget the most important issue that we face', a jibe at Miliband omitting to mention the deficit. To counter the accusations of complacency and the charge that he feels an entitlement to be prime minister, one of the most repetitive criticisms of him, he responds: 'I don't claim to be a perfect leader, but I am your public servant, standing here, wanting to make the country so much better.' To counter the accusations that the Conservatives are heartless, and Labour have a monopoly on care, he claims that the Tories are 'the real party of compassion and social justice'.[7]

After the speech, Rupert Harrison plants himself by Craig Oliver's side for the post-conference briefing. 'I deliberately brought Rupert with me to ensure we had all the answers to the detailed questions we'd undoubtedly be asked. The previous week Labour had got themselves into a tangle – unable to answer key points on a policy, eventually having to gather the lobby round a speakerphone so they could talk to an expert in London,' Oliver says.[8] The press are upbeat. The speech has had an electrifying effect on the audience. 'Gone were the warnings of more pain, more spending cuts, more austerity to come,' reports the BBC's Nick Robinson. 'David Cameron and his party came to Birmingham fearing the worst – more defections and more divisions. They leave here believing they might just still be in with a chance.'[9] The *Mail* titles have not been notably friendly to Cameron over the previous four and a half years, and concerted efforts have been made of late to bring them onside. The speech helps win them back: 'at last he gets it' is their line.[10] To the *Spectator*'s Isabel Hardman, it is 'one of the best speeches he has given since entering government'.[11] Further support comes from *Spectator* editor Fraser Nelson: 'his performance is a reminder of why, even now, he remains the Tory party's single greatest asset ... his speech was a powerful invocation of the strengths of Conservatism ... it was passionate, eloquent, and overall, a speech of a prime minister'.[12] Murdoch has never become a bosom buddy of Cameron's, but *The Times* has warmed. More important than any commentary is the galvanising effect the speech has on the party faithful. The mood of the conference has gone from foreboding at the start, to a Dunkirk defiance, before ending on a high.

The success of the conference does nothing, however, to shift opinion polls. All eyes now turn to Osborne to pull something out of the bag in his Autumn Statement. Throughout October and November, boosted by falling oil prices, the outlook for the economy looks increasingly optimistic. Cameron and Osborne take every chance to travel the country in search of photo opportunities in factories, construction sites and businesses, to highlight the positive employment statistics. The luminous high-visibility vests and hard hats become constant props. Osborne hopes the statement will repeat the acclaim of his March Budget, though the opportunities for reprising the trick are few and narrowing. It may well be the last fiscal event of the coalition: the Lib Dems are saying they will not allow a Budget in the spring of 2015.

Osborne's plans are outlined to Cabinet on Tuesday 2 December. The centrepiece is his reform to stamp duty, a measure the Treasury has favoured for a long time, but has been judged too expensive. No money will be due for the first £125,000 of a property purchase and then 2% will be levied on the portion up to £250,000, which will reduce the burden for first-time buyers in particular. An attraction for Osborne is that the move counters Labour's mansion tax attack, which the Lib Dems don't at first grasp. It is a mark, nevertheless, of the continuing effectiveness of the coalition that no leaking occurs about a sensitive change that would have affected market transactions had it come out. It is to be paid for in two main ways: cutting down on tax avoidance by banks, and by the so-called 'Google tax', which is designed to discourage large companies diverting profits outside the UK to avoid tax.

The Autumn Statement sets out the long-term investment intentions, to allocate money through to the end of the next parliament, so they could announce some goodies 'ahead of the general election'.

Osborne goes over the other measures in the Statement, including increasing the 2014 growth forecast to 3%, up from the 2.7% predicted in March. He announces 500,000 new jobs will have been created in 2014, and that the UK is now the fastest-growing economy in the G7. The deficit, he says, has been 'cut in half' since 2010, and he promises to generate a surplus by 2018–19. Conservatives (if not Lib Dems) around the Cabinet table bang their fists in approval when he finishes the preview. 'We may not have won the election, but it has given us a chance,' says one euphoric Tory present.[13] Vince Cable, a constant thorn over the past four and a half years, introduces a discordant tone, asking how both parties have signed up to such draconian cuts, warning against the setting of unrealistic targets, and the risk they court of broken promises. One person present describes it a 'jaw-dropping moment', seeing it less as an attack on Osborne than a full-frontal assault on his own party leader, Clegg. Cameron gives Clegg a look as if to say 'He's off again', to which Clegg responds with a knowing roll of his eyes – 'See what I have to put up with?'[14]

The Autumn Statement is delivered to Parliament on Wednesday 3 December. Osborne's propensity to showmanship now gets the better of him. 'Our policy of continuing the spending cuts in the first *two* full years of the next parliament, at the same pace as we achieved in this parliament, now produces £4 billion less spending,' he tells the Commons.[15] His aim is to lock shadow chancellor Ed Balls into a vote on signing Labour up to the government's plan on deficit reduction. But the Office for Budget Responsibility, presided over by an exasperated Robert Chote, is sceptical of the figures. He has grown uncomfortable with the government's spending projections, and debates whether they are realistic. He chooses to draw similarities between public spending now and the 1930s. Osborne and Harrison have not anticipated this toxic historical comparison. Suddenly, the headlines are all about the Conservatives' spending intentions entailing a 'return to the 1930s' and 'The Road to Wigan Pier', a reference to George Orwell's bleak account of poverty in the north of England. Osborne protests at the 'hyperbolic coverage', particularly on the BBC.[16] But the damage is done. The frustration is now directed at the chancellor: 'Labour's arguments about the deficit were failing because the economy was beginning to work, and their cost-of-living argument was failing because of the oil-price fall. Suddenly George has handed them an opening,' says an insider. 'The Autumn Statement probably went less well than we had hoped because of the 1930s stuff,' admits one of Cameron's team. It is no understatement. No unforced cock-ups is an article of faith in Lynton-land. Even the issue of immigration – as seen in the next chapter – at last looked as if it had been addressed. Unlike in the autumns of 2012 and 2013 when the skates were under the government, the Conservatives have been the dominant force this autumn. But as the parties leave Westminster for their final Christmas of the parliament, Osborne's error of judgement hands the initiative back to Miliband.

THIRTY-SIX

Controlling Immigration

November 2014

'Enough! I am giving the speech this Friday,' says an irritable Cameron to his team on Monday 24 November. 'We cannot keep talking about it. We have done nothing else for six weeks: I am fed up with the delay. We need to get back to talking about the economy.' The prime minister is rarely this agitated. 'It was a very difficult time in the building,' one insider acknowledges. Others describe it as the most uncomfortable period in Number 10 of the parliament. A crazy cocktail of toxic issues are raising the temperature to boiling point.

On 9 October, Tory defector Douglas Carswell wins the Clacton by-election with 59.7% of the vote, becoming UKIP's first elected MP. The result sees the biggest increase in share of vote for any party in the history of by-elections.[1] The by-election in Rochester and Strood caused by the defection to UKIP of Mark Reckless will be held on 20 November, placing even greater pressure on Number 10. They order a massive effort by CCHQ. Number 10 is under constant fire from Conservative backbenchers and from the press, who are pushing for a definitive statement on immigration and a declaration of the re-negotiation strategy ahead of an EU referendum. The general election is less than six months away. The polls are hardly improving: in mid-November, Labour and the Conservatives are almost neck and neck, with Labour on 33%, and the Conservatives on 32%.[2]

Before the summer recess, Cameron's team debated whether he should make a speech on immigration and the line he might take. The original plan was for a speech in July, which would help to develop a policy on free movement. Farage has managed to shift UKIP's focus from the EU to immigration. Number 10 came up with the idea of restricting benefits to bona fide migrant workers, but a two-week rethink allows the policy to leak to both the Lib Dems and Labour. It results in a speech by Clegg on 5 August calling for tighter controls on migrants from new EU countries, saying that the electorate has 'lost faith' in the government's ability to manage immigration, and that 'everyone who wants to settle in Britain should speak English'.[3] It is strong stuff from the party that has consistently dogged Cameron's attempts to tighten immigration.

As soon as Cameron's team return from the Birmingham party conference in early October, they reopen the subject. What might Cameron say to neutralise this toxic issue? The fault line which emerges is the one that has so often divided the Conservative leadership throughout history: free trade versus protectionism. The supporters of the latter want to 'shoot the UKIP fox' with a very strong pronouncement on immigration. Key amongst them are Craig Oliver, fired up by the red tops, Lynton Crosby, Oliver Dowden and newcomer Max Chambers, who joined the Policy Unit in spring 2014. Among ministers, Oliver Letwin and Michael Gove are strongly in this camp. Gove has yet to adjust to his new role as chief whip, and the polemicist in him gets the better of his judgement as he briefs the press that a cap on EU immigration is possible. It further ratchets up expectations of what Cameron can achieve in future EU negotiations, and adds to the tense atmosphere inside Downing Street.

On the free-trade side stand Osborne and Rupert Harrison, as well as Jo Johnson, head of the Policy Unit from April 2013. The Treasury traditionally favour free trade, seeing immigration as a net gain for the economy, far more so than a source of social or political anxiety. On their side too are the officials in Number 10, who the hardliners think are being obstructive. Llewellyn is strongly on the side of officials, although steered by the pragmatic realisation that Cameron's scope for manoeuvre on restricting EU immigration is very limited. Llewellyn is the supreme Euro realist in Number 10, holding the line against the hardliners: he is also the bridge between both polarised groups. One pragmatist puts it bluntly: 'A cap is not legal. The Europeans will never agree to it, and there is no point in even talking about it.' 'It was one of the very rare occasions where there was serious tension between the civil servants and the political staff,' says another insider. It is the only major occasion when Cameron's briefing-lite personal aides brief against each other. As always, Kate Fall tries to find a middle ground and discover what the prime minister really wants to do and how it can be delivered. Officials warn with increasing force that if Britain pushes the EU too hard it will never achieve its objectives. How did Number 10 manage to get into this invidious position? Is a cap feasible? Is a middle ground even possible?

To understand these questions, we need to go back to before the 2010 general election. In the 2005 election, immigration had featured prominently in the Conservative campaign. 'Every piece of polling told us that it was incredibly important,' Crosby recalls.[4] But once Cameron became leader later that year, immigration was downgraded. He was determined to move the party away from the emphasis that Michael Howard had given the issue. But it still ranked highly with sections of the electorate. In January 2010, with the general election approaching, Cameron told Andrew Marr 'we would like to see net immigration in the tens of thousands rather than hundreds of thousands'. Immigration should return to the levels in the 1990s: 'I don't think that is unrealistic.'[5] Net immigration in 2009 was 196,000: reducing it to tens of thousands will be a tall order. The Conservative election manifesto promised an annual limit on non-EU economic migrants to the UK, prioritising those deemed of most value to the economy, who are to pay a bond on entering the country, which will be repaid on leaving. Hilton was anxious that immigration should not become a focus in the 2010 election campaign. 'There was a view that we had to avoid doing anything which could be construed as "nasty". So we played down the issue,' recalls a senior figure in the campaign. In the Coalition Agreement, the Lib Dems reluctantly accept the Tory ambition to cut immigration, by demanding the end of child detention at immigration removal facilities in return.[6]

The annual net immigration figure for 2010 marks a steep increase to 252,000, a record. Cameron immediately comes under pressure to make a speech on immigration reduction, his first on this issue as prime minister, which he does in the run-up to the May 2011 local elections. Labour's record on immigration he says had been a 'complete mess'.[7] He has learnt that 2.2 million more people came to live in Britain under Blair and Brown than left to live abroad. 'That is the largest influx of people Britain has ever had,' he says, 'and it has placed real pressures on communities. Not just pressures on schools, housing and health care … but social pressures too.'[8] The Lib Dems, who are ideologically opposed to controls on immigration, are not happy with his new macho line. Business Secretary Vince Cable fights hard to ensure firms are not hampered by caps placed on migrant workers, and to prevent a tightening of student visa applications: but Cameron's attitude is hardening. He has come to believe immigration is out of control, and is far more attuned to concerns about the preservation of a traditional British way of life than Conservatives like Osborne. He finds a soulmate in Theresa May: no one else in Cabinet feels as strongly as they do about controlling immigration. 'I am the only person in this government who supports the Home Secretary on immigration,' he is apt to say.

In 2011, the influx of EU nationals is not a major concern, with European and British net migration roughly in balance. Cameron thus focuses on reducing non-EU migration. He turns his fire on stamping out 'shammed, forced marriages', tightening the rules on student visa applications, and scrutinising carefully the welfare system which he says 'for years has paid British people not to work'.

Still the numbers continue to rise. So further tightening follows in 2012. Employer-sponsored visas are introduced to help limit the inflow of skilled workers. British nationals wanting to bring in non-EU spouses are required to have an annual income of over £18,600, which affects more than 30,000 people.[9] More stringent checks are placed on foreign student visa applications, and bogus colleges are closed. These measures combine to make a significant impact from the middle of the parliament, with net migration from non-EU countries beginning to fall.

But at almost the exact moment non-EU immigration comes under control, the problem shifts to EU migration, which from 2013 begins to creep up again. Within Whitehall, two explanations are given. The Treasury attributes it to the continuing eurozone crisis, which makes Britain, with its improving economy, a much more attractive destination for jobs. The protectionists, including many around the prime minister, instead blame Britain's generous and non-contributory benefits system. The Home Office criticises 'less legitimate organisations' for finding ways of bending or breaking the rules, as well as businesses and universities for finding ways around existing procedures and controls.

On 25 March 2013, Cameron delivers a speech on immigration in Ipswich. His aim is to cast a further spotlight on the link between welfare benefits and immigration, and to propose changes to existing benefits law. It is ill-prepared and poorly received. Shadow Home Secretary Yvette Cooper attacks the negative image of migrants he gives, saying that 'most people who come to this country work and contribute' and that his proposals lack any credible plans to tackle illegal immigration or indeed labour market exploitation.[10]

Much of the EU immigration is from southern Europe, but it is immigration from the new accession countries that captures the headlines. Bulgaria and Romania entered the European Union in 2007. Transitional controls on immigration from both countries introduced in 2007 are due to expire on 31 December 2013. With UKIP and the right-wing press stoking up fears of hordes of migrants arriving, Cameron feels he must take further steps. Pressure from the hardliners within Number 10 results in the PM writing an article in the *Financial Times* in November 2013 attacking immigration from the EU.[11] Jon Cunliffe, the British permanent representative to the EU, is delegated to talk to Council president Herman Van Rompuy to explore the scope for limiting 'benefit tourism'. 'Even if the EU doesn't believe that benefit tourism matters, it stills matters in the UK, because every time the right-wing press talks about it, it becomes a huge problem for the government,' Cunliffe tells him. 'I can't touch it. It won't get through the European Court of Justice,' says Van Rompuy. To add insult to injury, he adds, 'Anyway, there is no such thing as benefit tourism.'

An immigration bill is introduced by the Home Secretary in October 2013, aimed at deterring health tourism by requiring temporary migrants to contribute to the NHS, and restricting access to bank accounts for those who live in the country illegally. But it runs into a morass of challenge from all sides – Labour, Lib Dems and backbench Conservatives. The bill, described by Matthew d'Ancona as a 'shambles', receives Royal Assent in May 2014, which has the effect of boosting support for UKIP, rather than detracting from it.[12] After 2013, the focus shifts to border controls, and Britain's decision whether to opt out of police and criminal justice measures adopted by the EU Council of Ministers. Britain would have to opt out of all 130 measures, which would have excluded it from being part of European security co-operation, and then decide which ones to opt back into. Michael Gove is at the forefront of those arguing Britain should opt out all together, but the police and security services are concerned that this will carry significant risks. Theresa May feels strongly that it is not in the national interest to opt out of all them, and they decide to opt out of most of the measures. Labour cleverly exacerbates Conservative divisions by forcing a vote on the concurrent and controversial European Arrest Warrant. Cameron has to make an undignified early return from the Lord Mayor's Banquet to take part in the vote, which the government ultimately wins. It all creates an impression of confusion, especially as it comes on 10 November, a mere ten days before the Rochester and Strood by-election.[13]

These multiple pressures provide the background for Cameron's long-heralded immigration speech in November 2014. After saying in his conference speech that Britain will 'get what [it] needs' on free movement of people within the EU, Cameron further builds up expectations when he reveals his immigration speech will unveil 'the toughest system on welfare for EU migrants anywhere in Europe'.[14] Leaks from Cameron's team suggest he might say that Britain will secede from the EU if it does not change the rules on free movement of people. The *Daily Telegraph* reports that at least six Cabinet ministers will vote to leave the EU if the current regime is maintained.[15] Gerald Howarth, the former defence minister, describes immigration as 'the number one issue in the country ... Our view is that we need to restore to the UK Parliament immediately control over our borders ... We believe that it is not acceptable for our European partners to tell us how to control our borders.'[16] Some senior party advisers argue strongly that they are out of touch with the country on immigration. 'It used to be the case in Britain that if you worked hard, got a good education, got a job, found a husband or wife you can get on in life,' says one of them. 'But immigration means there are now kids with fifteen different languages in one class and the teacher can't educate them. There is a disillusion and frustration, and a sense that none of the current politicians understand it.'

Further disarray occurs when Cameron goes to talk to the right-wing No Turning Back group on 15 October 2014, who are demanding an uncompromising line on EU migration. Cameron intends the meeting to be a way of building trust and confidence, but the group is full of irreconcilables, and damaging leaks later appear of what he said.[17] Number 10 suspect the hand of the right-wing former minister John Redwood. In mid-November, on his way back from the G20 summit in Brisbane, Cameron talks to Tom Scholar, his most senior adviser on the EU in Whitehall. Scholar's advice is bleak: word back from the staff of other European leaders suggests they will say 'we won't back you' if Britain pushes for a cap on EU immigration. Most worryingly, Scholar advises that Angela Merkel will not support a cap. Cameron's team debate whether this is the final decision of EU leaders or mere positioning. 'It is a fine judgement,' says one. But the legal advice to Number 10 is clear: any attempt to impose a cap will be 'shot to pieces', because it would be very likely to require EU treaty change. An influential briefing by the Open Europe think-tank, 'What are David Cameron's options for limited EU migration?', is published in November. It further boxes him in, by saying that achieving unanimity on any EU treaty change required to limit migration would be next to impossible.

Cameron summons senior Cabinet ministers to his office in Number 10 late in the afternoon on 25 November. He is appalled that so many of them have been briefing the press. Former Cabinet ministers, who were not at the meeting, join in the fray. Ken Clarke, who left the government in July, blames Cameron directly: 'By laying so much stress on immigration, he is giving in to the silliest of his critics.'[18] Cameron is exasperated and tells assembled ministers, 'let's not pretend that this is not a serious issue and that we won't face a massive backlash if we don't deal with it. It's about far more than the EU'. Osborne speaks up forcefully: 'we are the pro-business party and we believe in jobs and we need jobs for growth. We will be in trouble if we go into the general election and people are saying we are screwing it up'. Philip Hammond, the new Foreign Secretary, takes a noticeably more Eurosceptic tone. One senior Number 10 aide has had enough: 'what we all need to do is shut the fuck up talking about it'. Another of Cameron's team reflects 'how lonely it is to be prime minister. Your two most senior Cabinet ministers are in two very difficult, different positions. You are utterly alone.'

Years of barely concealed impatience break out into the open. Osborne and Harrison have been sceptical of May's line for a long time. They do not think the Home Office should be erecting barriers to good students coming to the UK, nor indeed to those wanting to come to the UK from China and developing countries. They think that Cameron should have done much more to rein in May, and react strongly against what they see as her increasing leadership pretensions, whipped up by friends in the press, which they regard as 'ludicrous'. For months their anger has been focused on May's two feisty special advisers at the Home Office, Nick Timothy and Fiona Cunningham. Now their hostility is directed on her. With the usual channels breaking down between the Treasury and the Home Office, relations have become very fragile indeed. Briefing and counter-briefing between the Treasury and the Home Office rise to unedifying levels in the latter part of 2014.

John Major is often the figure who Number 10 turn to when boxed into a corner. A senior aide speaks to Arabella Warburton, Major's right-hand figure since his days in Number 10, and they agree that Major should give a speech in Berlin in mid-November. The aim is to make the EU Commission, and specifically Germany, know how much is at stake. Major rises to his theme: 'What we must all realise is that a divorce may be final. Absolute. A reconciliation would be unlikely,' he says, echoing the words that he had used during the Scottish referendum. Whereas the populations of some European countries were falling, Major observes that Britain's population has risen by 7% in the last decade putting 'strains on our health, welfare, housing and education services that we struggle to meet'. He predicts there is a 50% chance that Britain may end up leaving the EU. The speech is a plea to the EU to wake up to the British problem and reach out and help it reach a resolution.[19] It is seen as an indicator of where Cameron's and Number 10's thinking now stands.

The timing of Cameron's own speech is pushed back several times in November. 'Three times Ameet Gill scheduled it in the grid: three times it was uprooted,' says one insider. A resolution comes only in the last few days before the speech is delivered. Craig Oliver produces a formulation of words which says, 'if I can't get what I want, I don't rule anything out'. It throws a bone to the PM's critics on the right wing by indicating that he wouldn't vote to remain in the EU regardless of the renegotiated terms. Ed Llewellyn is now tasked by Cameron to cobble the ideas together into a coherent speech. He has been arguing strongly to delay it for a further two weeks to ensure 'every single operative sentence in the speech could be stress-tested'. He knows, though, that he lacks the luxury of time. The speech has to be well received by four separate and highly divergent audiences: the British public, the Conservative Party, the media and the EU, principally the Commission in Brussels and the Chancellery in Berlin. Llewellyn has just one chance to get it right. He locks himself away in an attic near the Policy Unit at the front of Number 10 and spends several hours drafting it. He speaks to Cameron who is on his way back from Australia to tune the message, as it is clear it is still not right. Llewellyn has been in constant contact with Berlin and Brussels, as he had been when drafting the Bloomberg speech. 'If the speech gets a complete raspberry from Berlin and Brussels, it will go nowhere,' a senior aide admits. Llewellyn worries that a wrongly calibrated speech will affect the British government's reputation for competence in Europe. But Cameron has had enough. He is fed up with the whole topic, and wants it buried before Osborne's Autumn Statement on 3 December, which he hopes will act as a firewall on discussion about it.

On 28 November, Cameron delivers the second most anticipated speech of his premiership (to Bloomberg in January 2013), at a JCB factory in Staffordshire. It opens with praise for how immigration has benefited Britain: 'It clearly couldn't be a UKIP speech, hence the paean of praise for immigration,' says one aide. His determination to curb immigration through more stringent controls is made clear. Specifically he proposes prohibiting claiming of in-work benefits for the first four years of residence in the UK and removal from the country if employment has not been found after six months.[20] But there are no ultimatums. No threats. To the right, it is tame stuff.

Number 10 is more than usually apprehensive about the reception of the speech. The immediate reaction is predictable. Farage quickly criticises Cameron for failing to apologise for his lax immigration policy over the previous four and a half years, castigating him for taking ten years to realise the extent of the problem: 'It's a cynical attempt to kick the issue into the long grass until after the election,' the UKIP leader says.[21] Miliband homes in on Cameron's failure to reduce immigration to the 'tens of thousands', highlighting Cameron's ill-fated statement in 2010: 'kick us out in five years if we don't deliver on immigration'.[22] Green Party leader Natalie Bennett argues that benefit and health tourism are 'non-existent problems' for which Cameron has been unable to produce evidence.[23] When they review the speech forty-eight hours later, however, Cameron's team are pleased. Reports come in that it has been greeted relatively well in capitals across the EU, above all in Germany.[24] The *Daily Mail* regard it as generally sensible, realistic and 'full of common sense'.[25] The right wing in the Conservative Party is not happy, but they were never going to be. They put down a marker that, if the general election is lost, the speech will be seen as a key missed opportunity when Cameron failed to exercise leadership in the national interest. But for the time being, the boil does indeed appear to have been lanced. When interviewed by Marr on 30 November, Osborne doesn't face a single question on immigration: the economy dominates. Even those in Number 10 who had questioned Cameron's judgement on the timing and content of the speech can see that he was right.

Lynton Crosby's directive that, the speech over, the leadership should avoid speaking about immigration is thwarted when, on Monday 13 April 2015, a boat carrying 550 migrants capsizes in the Mediterranean killing some 400, and the following week an estimated 800 are killed in another capsizing. As the destination for boats departing from Libya, Italy is the country most directly affected. Italian prime minister Matteo Renzi is on the telephone whipping up support among European leaders to deal with the crisis. Both he and Donald Tusk, who has now succeeded Herman Van Rompuy as president of the EU Council, seek solidarity from the EU in response. An emergency summit is called in Brussels on 23 April. Cameron, mid-election campaign, is clear that Britain has to make a contribution but is equally adamant, given the toxicity of the debate in Britain, that it will not be able to offer large numbers of places to asylum seekers. Instead, he offers military assets, including HMS *Bulwark*, to help with search-and-rescue missions, and pushes for further action against the networks of human traffickers in North Africa.

No issue so skewered Cameron over his five years in government as immigration. He felt strongly that something had to be done. He found it hard to find an effective response, aware perhaps of the paradox that the economic recovery was largely responsible for the rise in immigration from EU countries still caught in the doldrums. He refused to resort to the jingoism or gung-ho rhetoric that parts of the press – and indeed some in his own team – wished to use. Strongly though he felt about the need to address concerns over immigration, he blankly refused the nuclear options the right wanted.

THIRTY-SEVEN

Farewell Washington

January 2015

The debacle of the Syria vote in August 2013 caused the relationship between the White House and Number 10, apparently impregnable, to fracture. Mistakes had been made by both sides. Number 10 had overstated their capacity to win a majority for action, and hadn't communicated their concern early enough to Washington. The White House had its parallel problem with Congress, and was overly engrossed in the rapidly unfolding situation to communicate fully with London. Both leaders were damaged by the way events played out: they had talked tough, only to pull back from the brink. Strong feelings against the other administration were held in some quarters of each leader's teams, but they passed amid a general acceptance that neither had handled it well. Meanwhile, for a critical ten-month period from September 2013–July 2014, Putin is causing mayhem in Ukraine, and ISIS are advancing in Syria and Iraq.

The White House primarily blames Ed Miliband and Labour for the Syria vote fiasco. Obama's team lobbied Miliband hard to support the government, assuming he and his party would be behind the action, but he refused to do so. 'We just couldn't see how the Labour Party could oppose military action against such a regime for using chemical weapons,' was their response. They suspect Miliband of prioritising political advantage over national security. Obama's team respond to 'personalities and stature': they don't regard Miliband as impressive on either. By the summer of 2014, they conclude they would sooner see Cameron win the general election, even if it means a referendum on British membership of the EU, than have Miliband in Downing Street.

Miliband has a far from successful meeting with Obama in Washington on 21 July, described as 'awkward' by many, which further underlines the Labour leader's lack of gravitas.[1] A starker contrast with Blair's pre-election visit to see President Clinton in 1996 could hardly be made. In April 1996, John Kerr, the British ambassador, said: 'There is no doubt that Blair had the scent of victory about him, and he was already the big draw in Washington.'[2] Miliband's trip, however, is a paltry affair, involving little more than a 'brush-by', as Americans describe it, with Obama.[3] Miliband has already hired as his senior election aide David Axelrod, Obama's influential adviser for the 2008 election, though it does little to warm up relations with Washington. Miliband's team expect much more help and under-standing, believing there to be a special bond between the Labour Party and the Democrats. The White House is not impressed either by Labour's subsequent reaction to the visit. For Miliband, it is a signal failure for a man desperate to acquire the credibility of a prime minis-ter in waiting.

Cameron's team seize on the idea of their own pre-election visit, to publicise their man's credentials and stature ahead of the campaign. One of his senior aides is deputed to open up discussions, mentioning it first to Obama's team during the NATO summit in Wales in early September, which he follows up at the G20 in Australia in mid-November. Cameron's National Security Adviser Kim Darroch flies out to Washington to finalise the plan with Peter Westmacott, the British ambassador. The White House are wary of leaving it as late as February, as 'it will look too nakedly like a pre-election boost'. True, Cameron had gone to Washington in March 2012 and given Obama his whole-hearted support, which 'verged on endorsing him for a second term'. The White House sees the need for reciprocity: 'It is right for us to be doing our bit for him.'

A plan for Cameron to address a joint session of Congress during the visit, which will provide strong images on television news, is dropped because Congress is not in session on the favoured date in mid-January: the Republicans are having a retreat in Hershey, Pennsylvania. The White House nevertheless are happy to offer two slots to Cameron rather than the usual one: a full-length bilateral meeting with the president, and a working dinner. When Miliband's team hear about it, they are incandescent, but powerless. They complain to the media, which is exactly what Cameron's team had hoped for, as they know it will backfire. Cameron's aides are cock-a-hoop at the messages flowing in from a particularly effusive White House, who bill the trip as an 'official visit', and invite Cameron to stay overnight in Blair House, which carries more prestige than staying at the British Embassy. On 15 January 2015, the day that they fly over, a joint article by both leaders appears in *The Times*, committing them to work together to spur growth against a future economic downturn, against terrorist organisations, including al-Qaeda, ISIS and Boko Haram, and to stand up to Russia in Ukraine.[4]

Cameron's party visit the FBI and the National Cyber Investigative facility in Virginia. Cyber terrorism and cyber security are a focus of discussion, especially in the face of increasing domestic concerns about the intrusiveness of proposed new measures. The White House issues a statement saying that 'every day foreign governments, criminals and hackers are attempting to probe, intrude into, and attack government and private sector systems in both of our countries'.[5]

The White House certainly are laying out the red carpet. Photographers capture the leaders walking amiably from the residence to the West Wing. After drinks, Obama leads both teams into the Blue Room for lunch, where he suggests removing jackets, before making remarks about how much he has enjoyed working with Cameron and his team over the last four and a half years. 'We have done a lot of work together' and built good relationships he says, and 'he wants to place that appreciation on the record'. Cameron's team glow at the warmth of the mood music. Then they get down to business. The conversation revolves around US–UK trade, Greece, climate change and Ebola. 'We got the impression from the president's team that they hoped for a much stronger international presence from the UK after the general election,' recalls one official.

The president picks this up again at the two-hour meeting in the Oval Office the following day. Obama describes the UK as a 'remarkable partner'. He is sympathetic that Britain has not felt able to do more in Iraq, though he acknowledges British support for the Kurds, and the RAF flying more sorties to Iraq than any country bar the US. 'I totally understand your position, but I'd really value more action from you if you win the election,' he says. He is most concerned about Britain maintaining the NATO commitment to spending 2% of GDP on defence, and raises it again that morning. If Britain fails to do so, what hope is there for other NATO countries, he wonders. Cameron replies: 'We are looking at it, but I cannot commit to it until after the election.' Discussion then ranges over Syria, internet security and encryption, Russia and Ukraine. The president's team also hopes in the future Britain will commit to air strikes in Syria, do more to fight Boko Haram in Nigeria, and stop Libya falling into the hands of Islamic extremists. Cameron's team anticipate Obama will raise his concern about the EU referendum: they know he is worried at the prospect of Britain leaving. But he remains silent on this. It is a long list. Cameron can, however, help the president on Iran, where Obama is experiencing difficulties. Congress has invited Israeli prime minister Benjamin Netanyahu to address them on 3 March, and have no faith in his policy. Cameron selects a handful of key senators to lobby. The British voice, as a joint negotiator in the talks with Iran, carries some weight on Capitol Hill. Obama appreciates Cameron's intervention. It is evident to them he would prefer a Cameron victory in four months' time. As the party are leaving to return to the UK, one of Obama's senior team says, 'We are rooting for you guys.' Even those apt to find the president aloof are pleasantly surprised by how personable he is on the trip.

Obama's relationship with Cameron is as close as he gets to overseas leaders, which the White House takes pains to highlight. No other relationship, and no other single country, ranks as highly in the White House's priorities as Cameron and Britain. But that is more revealing about Obama's priority and style with fellow leaders. Blair would talk weekly or more to Clinton and George W. Bush. 'I was surprised at how thin the relationship is,' commented a senior British diplomat responsible for relations between both countries under Cameron.

Below the prime ministerial and presidential level, William Hague enjoys a very close relationship with Hillary Clinton, Secretary of State until February 2013, both on a political level – they instinctively feel the same way on many global issues – and on a personal level (he hosts a dinner for her at the British Embassy to mark her retirement from the post in early 2013). Hague rapidly forges a good relationship with her successor, John Kerry, but Philip Hammond, who becomes Foreign Secretary in July 2014, for all his proficiency, lacks the benefit of Hague's experience and gravitas as a former Conservative leader and long-serving Foreign Secretary. The Pentagon become frustrated for a while by what it sees as Britain's lack of activism and willingness to commit more assets to fighting ISIS in Iraq. From early 2014, disenchantment with Britain is being heard from some of the think-tanks that are so influential in Washington. Fundamental questions are asked about the UK's future: will there be another Scottish referendum, and will independence follow? Will Britain break away from the EU, and where will that leave the UK/US relationship if Britain no longer plays the traditional role as the bridge between Washington and Europe? If Britain has lost the appetite for it, does the US now need a special relationship with another country? Such questions do the rounds every few years: they were heard for a time when John Major's government overlapped with Clinton's first administration. France is anxious to fill the slot, but there is no vacancy: the White House knows that no other country has the historical or cultural links that exist between the US and Britain.

Why has Britain not gone further to support the Americans in fighting ISIS in Iraq and Syria? Cameron personally would like to do more, but feels his hands are tied. Like most Western intelligence and security agencies, Britain's National Security Council is wrong-footed when Mosul, not far from the Syrian border in Northern Iraq, falls to ISIS on 10 June 2014. Some 500,000 flee the city to escape the militants. On 18 June, ISIS celebrate their victory by bulldozing part of the desert frontier between Iraq and Syria, symbolically negating the validity of the Western-imposed border that dates back to 1916. The same day, the Iraqi government officially asks the US and UK for military assistance. The Obama administration responds quickly to the call, fearful that the ISIS advance will be swift without it. Cameron's response, however, is that the most he can offer, given the stance of Labour and the Lib Dems, is to help the Kurdish Peshmerga, with whom Britain has had a close relationship over the previous twenty years. British efforts have hitherto concentrated on al-Nusra in Syria, which it regarded as the most dangerous Islamic faction operating in the country. Cameron constantly maintained that the key to stopping the export of terrorism from Syria was the departure of Assad, which he recognised as a step too far at least in the short term. Instead, efforts focused heavily on jihadists returning to Britain, and Iraq was initially regarded as 'an American problem'. But now in mid-2014, ISIS is replacing al-Nusra as the dominant opposition force in Syria, and is quickly crossing over the border into Iraq and towards Baghdad.[6]

By August, alarm is growing about the danger posed by returning jihadists, and at the end of the month, the UK's terror threat level is raised to 'severe'. Cameron publicly commits to fighting radical Islam 'at home and abroad'. In the run-up to the NATO summit in Cardiff on 4–5 September, pressure builds from the White House for Cameron to make a military commitment to combat ISIS in Iraq. Number 10 knows that after the August 2013 Syria defeat it is inconceivable not to seek the support of Parliament, so they ask the White House to bide their time until the Scottish referendum is over. After the earlier Syria defeat, this vote has to be won, so the Lib Dems and Labour have to be on board. Number 10 grows intensely frustrated that 'despite the awfulness of ISIS', the Lib Dems are constantly worrying about the use of force, while Labour are 'unreliable', so support cannot be a 'slam dunk'. Obama tells Cameron he understands, and is content to bide his time. But lower down the food chain in Washington, the grumbling is intense about 'the Brits dragging their feet again'.

As soon as the Scottish referendum has taken place, the pace builds for a vote in Parliament. On 24 September, Cameron asks the Speaker, John Bercow, to recall the Commons on Friday 26. On the 25th, Cameron flies to the UN for the General Assembly, where he devotes much of his speech to 'the mortal threat that we all face from the rise of ISIS', and how the world should unite to 'defeat the ideology of extremism'.[7] Public opinion is moving decisively in favour of air strikes against ISIS, in response to their gruesome atrocities in Syria and Iraq. In early August, 37% of those asked by YouGov approved air strikes and 36% disapproved. By the time he arrives in New York, 57% are responding in favour with only 24% against.[8] A repetition of the disastrous Syria vote thirteen months before is becoming less likely all the time. For Cameron, a second rebuff would be fatal.

While in the US, Cameron has a long phone call with Miliband from his Plaza Hotel suite. Cameron outlines the legal case for British intervention, and runs over the arguments for British strikes in Syria as well as in Iraq. Miliband is adamant: there will be no Labour support for strikes in Syria, a viewpoint echoed by the Lib Dems. This kills any hope of using force in Syria, so Cameron concludes with Miliband that they should restrict any attacks from the air purely to Iraq. Despite Miliband's words, Cameron is still nervous, and tasks Michael Gove with ensuring that the Conservative support will be there, given that the opponents of action against Syria in 2013 are becoming more vocal again. Cameron also remains anxious about the Lib Dems, and whether Labour MPs might split off from the leadership. He accepts that he needs more time for the public to accept any action in Syria. His case this time is strengthened by Haider al-Abadi, the Iraqi prime minister, writing to him asking for support, and the UN Security Council making it clear it also supports the action. On 25 September, the government publishes a summary of its legal advice arguing that international law does not prohibit the use of force if a territorial state requests such support in its defence.

Cameron is thus confident of success when the House of Commons meets on Friday 26 September. He opens the debate by arguing that while there might be 'a strong case' for Britain launching air strikes in Iraq, he does not wish to do so without consensus. He wants British support to be conditional on Iraq 'defending and protecting all [its] people' including its Sunni population. 'Even after ISIS has been dealt with, we should be in no doubt that future British prime ministers ... will be standing at this despatch box, dealing with this issue of Islamist extremism in different forms and in different parts of the world for many years to come.'[9] Miliband then speaks in support of the motion.[10] Broad support is clear for action. The vote is carried easily by 524 votes to forty-three, including six Conservative rebels, twenty-three Labour MPs and one Lib Dem. Three days later, RAF Tornados fly their first armed reconnaissance missions over Iraq. The following day, they carry out their first actual strikes over Iraq.[11]

But the British military contribution in Iraq, while greater than that of any nation other than the US, is still strictly limited. At the White House in January 2015, Cameron confirms that there can be no British escalation until after the general election. In February, Obama asks Congress for approval for military engagement to continue for a further three years. Progress is slow and the Iraqi army struggles against ISIS, though on 17 April, after a bloody two-month battle, Iraqi and coalition forces retake the strategically important city of Tikrit.

Cameron's focus on the dangers of Islamic extremism is one of the leitmotifs of his first five years in government. The security of British nationals is a constant concern, and on those rare occasions when they are taken hostage, he becomes personally involved and will not waver from the policy of refusing to negotiate with terrorists or pay a ransom. Paying ransom money, the British and Americans believe, only increases the numbers of hostages being taken. (He tried, in particular at the Lough Erne G8 in June 2013, to achieve an international agreement to end the paying of ransoms, but other nations were unwilling to follow suit.) During hostage crises, he convenes meetings either in COBRA or his study, attended by the Chief of the Defence Staff, National Security Adviser and head of special operations: 'but it is always his decision alone whether to order British forces into action'.

He does so on three occasions over the parliament. In October 2010, he approves an unsuccessful American military operation to rescue British aid worker Linda Norgrove, held in Afghanistan. A subsequent US/UK investigation concludes that she had been killed by a hand grenade thrown by one of the US soldiers involved in the rescue.[12] In March 2012, the Special Boat Service (SBS) co-operates with the Nigerian army in an unsuccessful attempt to rescue British hostage Chris McManus, who had been taken by Islamic terrorists. Both McManus and Italian hostage Franco Lamolinara are killed by the kidnappers before the special forces can save them.[13] The final attempt, in June 2012, again in Afghanistan, is when the SAS conducts an operation alongside US Navy Seals, which results in the successful rescue of British national Helen Johnson, with seven Taliban being killed in the process.[14] Downing Street is informed at 2 a.m. that the operation has been a success. Cameron is only woken at night on rare occasions. This is one of them, and he stays up until every member of the SAS is safely back in Kabul, and thanks several of the soldiers personally by phone.[15] Another of the rare occasions when he is woken in the middle of the night is when he learns about the killing of Osama Bin Laden in May 2011. The White House has given no forewarning to Downing Street, and wait until the military operation is over before speaking to their British counterparts. When they call at 3 a.m., the duty clerk phones a senior official and asks 'Should we wake the boss?' 'Yes, we should, he will want to know,' is the reply. Cameron is woken and, shortly after, Obama speaks to him, coming across, Cameron notes, as very collected.

ISIS takes some twenty Western hostages in 2014–15, most of whom are released after a ransom. The beheading of two American journalists, James Foley and Steven Sotloff, followed days later by the beheading of a British aid worker, David Haines, by a man with a British accent known as 'Jihadi John' (subsequently revealed to be Mohammed Emwazi), creates a national furore. ISIS release a sickening video of Haines's beheading on 13 September. Emwazi's words at the end of the video are: 'This British man has to pay the price, for your promise Cameron to arm the Peshmerga against the Islamic State ... playing the role of the obedient lapdog Cameron will only drag you and your people into another bloody and unwinnable war.'[16] On 3 October, another video is released by ISIS showing Emwazi beheading British aid worker Alan Henning, a taxi driver from Salford who had volunteered to deliver aid to Syria when he was kidnapped the previous December.

Cameron's fears about young British Muslims returning to the UK from Syria or Iraq determined to commit terrorist offences grow steadily over the parliament. An estimated 600–700 British Muslims have gone out to fight by early 2015, some 20% to al-Nusra and the remainder to ISIS.[17] He clings to his belief that a replacement to Assad in Damascus with more legitimacy is the only enduring answer. The Home Office wants to throw all available resources into monitoring terrorist suspects who return, to deter them from planning terrorist acts which they think will be almost inevitable before long. After the security threat level is raised in August 2014, Cameron asks even more regularly 'How can we get a grip on this?' He constantly presses the intelligence agencies for details of the latest plot and whether there are gaps in their capacity to detect them.

A widespread media fear is an attack on British soil akin to the marauding strike by Islamic extremists in Mumbai in November

2008, which killed 164 people and wounded hundreds more. He constantly drives the Foreign Secretary and the Home Secretary to keep on top of the government's preparedness. 'He takes an obsessive interest in intelligence,' says one member of that community, 'his role as defender of the nation is one he takes very seriously'. Officials comment that few items in the prime minister's box command his attention as much as the classified intelligence reports.

Cameron has made his interest in security matters known from the very outset. He surprises officials in the autumn of 2010 by his close scrutiny of discussions of threats to Britain, ranging from nuclear attack to cyber warfare, terrorism, and natural disasters. His first major opportunity to outline his thoughts on terrorism comes at the Munich Security Conference on 5 February 2011. In Opposition, he had been critical of Labour for not doing more to challenge violent extremism out of concern about alienating the Muslim population. He is in tune with the arguments in Gove's book *Celsius 7/7*, which is critical of those willing to accommodate unacceptable Muslim viewpoints. To help prepare him, he invites a number of thinkers into Number 10, including members of the Quilliam Foundation, an anti-extremism think-tank, such as Maajid Nawaz, a counter-extremism activist who wrote *Radical: My Journey From Islamist Extremism to Democratic Awakening*. Cameron is already clear in his mind that he wants to challenge what he sees as the orthodoxy of not just the previous Labour government, but also Whitehall. When an official asks him to tone down a passage in the draft for fear it might be seen as an anti-Muslim speech, he adds the line: 'Would you advocate inaction if Christian fundamentalists, who believed that Muslims are the enemy, were leading prayer groups in our prisons?'[18]

The speech is to be delivered to an audience of transatlantic security experts, so he is persuaded to build in some standard foreign policy material. But Cameron is clear: while this may be a speech for an international audience in Germany, it is also strongly targeted at his domestic audience. Heavy briefing to the media precedes and follows it. 'The biggest threat we face comes from terrorist attacks,' he tells his audience. 'We will not defeat terrorism simply by the action we take outside our borders. Europe needs to wake up to what is happening in our own countries ... we have to get to the root of the problem ... the origins of where these terrorist attacks lie. That is the existence of an ideology, Islamic extremism.'[19]

Cameron is disappointed that the speech doesn't have more resonance and that he continues to meet complacency about Islamic terrorism, both in Britain and amongst European partners. Laudatory though he is of Theresa May's tenacity over the cases of the radical clerics Abu Hamza and Abu Qatada, he becomes highly frustrated at the slow progress of extradition, which eventually takes place on 5 October 2012 and 7 July 2013 respectively. Lib Dem sensitivities about trampling on civil liberties, regularly articulated by Clegg, are another irritating thorn for Cameron. An early battle comes in 2011 for a replacement to control orders to monitor suspected terrorists, but agreement is eventually reached over new measures, articulated in the Terrorist Prevention and Investigative Measures Act in December 2011.

A number of terrorist attacks on British soil are foiled between 2010 and 2015. On 29 October 2010, for instance, security officials intercept a bomb hidden in a computer printer on a cargo plane at East Midlands Airport that was en route from Yemen to Chicago. The bomb was timed to destroy the aircraft over the eastern seaboard of the US, and had been co-ordinated with another device found in Dubai. However, on 22 May 2013, out of a clear blue sky, comes the most serious terrorist attack of the five years on mainland Britain. While walking near the Royal Artillery Barracks in Woolwich in south-east London, Fusilier Lee Rigby is brutally murdered in front of passers-by in broad daylight by two Islamic fundamentalists, originally of Nigerian descent who had recently converted to Islam. It is what Cameron has always feared: while alertness of the security services and police has thwarted a number of plots, this low-tech attack – involving nothing more than a car and a set of knives bought the day before (though they also possessed an aged unloaded revolver) – has evaded scrutiny. Andrew Parker, who succeeded Jonathan Evans as head of MI5 the previous month, immediately calls the MoD to express his condolences. David Richards phones to reassure him that the armed forces are not blaming the security services for negligence. 'We all know what MI5, MI6, GCHQ and the police do to protect us, so don't worry about that and thanks for everything you have done.'[20]

Cameron is in Paris when he hears of the attack. In his absence, a meeting is immediately convened in COBRA, chaired by Theresa May. Those present are concerned because the BBC has already started to report that the perpetrators are of 'Muslim appearance'. Sensitivities about further attacks are running very high. The security services and police do not know if it is a lone attack or one of a series. Defence Secretary Philip Hammond orders off-duty military personnel not to wear uniform, but Cameron rescinds the instruction the next day. The atmosphere is very jumpy. It is agreed that no one should say anything beyond a bald holding line, as the situation is still regarded as live and dangerous. Boris Johnson says that as mayor of London he has got to say something himself. One of the security staff intervenes to say, 'Well, Mr Mayor, we don't know the full facts yet and it's quite dangerous and potentially lives are at risk if we start saying the wrong things.'

'This is the first terrorist attack since 7/7, and I've got to go out there and say something,' Johnson replies; he takes his own responsibility for keeping London safe immensely seriously too. Boris turns to one of the Number 10 aides and is heard to say: 'Who the fuck is that guy? He needs to get elected before he tells me what to do!' He then goes outside and makes a statement in which he says, 'The fault lies wholly and exclusively in the warped and deluded mindset of the people who did it. What we need now, for the sake of the victim and for the sake of his family, is for these killers to be brought to justice.' Cameron returns promptly from Paris and chairs a COBRA meeting the following day. He is told that there are some 5,000 people living in Britain believed to have terrorist tendencies. He launches an extremism task force, and subsequently the Muslim Brotherhood review.

Islamic fundamentalism is not the only terrorist threat. A few weeks before, on 29 April 2013, Mohammed Saleem is murdered in Birmingham, which the West Midlands police do not at first realise is a terrorist murder. It was committed by Pavlo Lapshyn, a white supremacist who had also attempted to carry out a string of bomb attacks. Cameron's concerns are borne out in two late items of legislation: the Data Retention and Investigatory Powers Act of July 2014, and the Counter-Terrorism and Security Act of February 2015. The former in particular is subject to some last-minute haggling, with May and Clegg working late in Cameron's office, sorting through papers, scrabbling to make final amendments before the bill is signed off.

On 7 January 2015, Cameron is in the prime minister's office in the House of Commons preparing for PMQs, as reports start coming through of a terrorist attack in Paris at the offices of the French satirical magazine *Charlie Hebdo*. With events moving at rapid pace and uncertainty over the numbers involved, it is difficult to know the extent of the attack. One of his staff emails him: 'It looks bad.' Visibly perturbed, he opens PMQs at midday by condemning the 'barbaric attacks'.[21] Reports are still coming in as he travels at 3 p.m. to the British Museum with Angela Merkel to visit 'Memories of a Nation', a special exhibition about German history. The two leaders make a joint statement at the museum about the attacks: 'All of us that live in Europe strongly condemn these attacks and our thoughts go out to the French people,' says Merkel, while Cameron speaks of the 'huge sympathy' he has for the families of those killed: 'We must never allow the values we hold dear, of democracy, of freedom of speech, to be damaged by these terrorists.'[22] It is already getting dark as they arrive back at Downing Street at 4.30 p.m. It is decided to create two precedents that afternoon: first, to have the German chancellor briefed directly by the heads of MI5 and MI6, Andrew Parker and Alex Younger, who has succeeded John Sawers; second, to make a joint call to the French president from the conference telephone in Cameron's office. They are steely if emotional during the phone call, and offer Hollande all the help that they can. By now it is clear that ten employees of the magazine have been killed, along with two policemen. The following day, the 8th, a policewoman is shot dead in Paris by another terrorist, who goes on to murder four people at a Kosher supermarket the next day, before being killed himself.

Hollande decides to make a public display of international solidarity and invites world leaders to Paris on Sunday 11 January. Cameron is initially unsure whether he will be able to attend, but as the momentum from other leaders becomes clear, he changes his plans and decides to go. He flies out that morning with Ed Llewellyn from Northolt to Vélizy-Villacoublay air base, from where he is driven straight to the British residence on the Rue du Faubourg Saint-Honoré. From there, they walk the short distance to the Elysée Palace before buses take them to the Place de la République. Cameron is deeply moved by the public expressions of support for the murdered *Charlie Hebdo* employees. He notes wryly how on most occasions when world leaders travel in coaches, to and from G20s and other summits, the crowd is booing, but here they are applauding wildly, displaying their banners – '*Je Suis Charlie*' and '*Nous Sommes Charlie*'. After the demonstrations, Cameron gives interviews at the British Embassy. He is shocked by the whole episode, struck by how close to home it is and how easily it could happen in Britain. He knows that the quality of British security and police work, and strict legal controls on firearms, have been partly responsible for preventing such vile attacks on British soil; he also knows that luck inevitably has played a significant role.

THIRTY-EIGHT

A Diminished Britain?

September 2014–March 2015

'One of the rare issues on which Cameron will lose his temper is if they try challenging him over development spending,' says an aide. At a time of austerity, Cameron comes under regular pressure about this issue. His dogged commitment to it, while refusing in the final months to commit to a similar pledge on defence, is seen in some quarters as perverse. Criticism reaches a climax on both sides of the Atlantic in late 2014 and early 2015 with even Obama expressing concern at his meeting with Cameron in the White House in January 2015, about Britain's plans for defence spending. Why does Cameron's lead on the world stage, so forthright in his first three and a half years, appear to have gone into reverse?

At the Gleneagles G8 summit in July 2005, chaired by Tony Blair, the G8 committed itself to spend 0.7% of gross national income on overseas development. When Cameron became Conservative Party leader in December 2005, he retained Andrew Mitchell, who was committed to the target, as shadow International Development Secretary. For five years in Opposition, he and Mitchell worked very closely to make development a priority area for the Conservatives.[1] Why did Cameron give it such high standing? Christianity is not an overt force in Cameron's life, as it is for some who are strong support-ers of development. Political factors certainly played a part: the party needed to reposition itself and shed its 'nasty' and reactionary image, and development was an ideal symbol. But the crusade is about much more than that. He understands the benefits for Britain of the diplo-matic clout and authority that an emphasis on 'soft power' can provide. In July 2007, he visited Rwanda when his own Witney constituency was suffering from floods, which brought him his first serious taste of adverse publicity on his development priority. Aides speak of the 'special place that Rwanda has in his heart', dating in part back to his sense that the party had not done enough in response to the genocide in 1994. On his 2007 visit he committed the Conservatives to achieving the Gleneagles target within six years, and spoke powerfully about his personal commitment to the cause of development. The 0.7% figure in the 2010 Conservative manifesto, a commitment eagerly supported by the Lib Dems, readily finds its way into the Coalition Agreement. Danny Alexander, in charge of the 2010 Spending Review, oversees a debate about whether the figure should apply immediately or be delayed until 2015: 'In the end we decided that it should be met by 2013, which secured broad agreement,' he says.[2] Cameron and Mitchell, now Secretary of State, reserve a third of this budget for conflict prevention, and helping to support fragile states.

Cameron continues to invest time and political capital in this area, going far beyond support for the 0.7% figure. In 2011, he delivers a major speech in Lagos, arguing that Africa should be seen as a place of opportunity, and that democratic capitalism is superior to authoritarian capitalism (the little dig at the Chinese does not go unnoticed).[3] He believes economic and political freedom, rather than aid, best lift people out of poverty, and he wants spending to focus on measurable objectives such as immunisation. Right-wing critics of development policy constantly irritate him, and shortly before his Lagos speech, he deliberately takes a question from a *Daily Mail* journalist at the end of the Deauville summit in May 2011, using it as a chance to attack all the reasons critics give for opposing the 0.7% figure.

The critical point on the 0.7% commitment comes in early 2012, with the economy still not responding, and further cuts to be found. Mitchell, aware of the threat, approaches Osborne to persuade the Treasury to stick to the 0.7% commitment, recognising that 2013 is the year in which the government had agreed to reach it. Throughout 2012 into 2013, the prime minister is still one of the very few to actively support 0.7%. In 2013, Justine Greening, who replaced Mitchell at International Development in September 2012, comes under intense pressure from the MoD who are quick to make their case in public. She outmanoeuvres the MoD.[4] Within the Quad, even

Clegg begins to say, 'You know, it would make our lives much easier if we push back the 0.7%.' Cameron considers this and speaks to Osborne about it, but in the end, they come out against change. Why, especially at a time of such intense pressure? The reasons include: Cameron's personal commitment; a desire to avoid war with charities and non-governmental organisations, including with popular figures like Bob Geldof; and critically a desire not to break promises. Cameron and Osborne look to Australia, where the prime minister Kevin Rudd had received widespread opprobrium in 2010 after deferring his carbon cap-and-trade commitment. Both PM and chancellor have also absorbed the lessons of Clegg reneging on his tuition-fees pledge. 'We won't make any new friends by dropping it, we'll still have the *Daily Mail* on our back, and we'll look like people who have no principles' is their view. The 0.7% target is reached in 2013, and Britain is the only G8 country to do so (the US spends less than 0.2% – although its GDP is six times greater than that of the UK), while Sweden, Norway, Denmark, Luxembourg and the UAE are the only other nations to reach it. Despite consistently meeting the target for three decades, the Netherlands falls short in 2013.[5]

In the summer of that year, Cameron reads *Why Nations Fail: The Origins of Power, Prosperity and Poverty* by Daron Acemoglu and James A. Robinson, a book which further underpins his belief that open political and economic institutions, rather than autocracies, are the most likely to create sustainable success and prosperity. He is also persuaded by Mitchell to accept Ban Ki-moon's invitation to co-chair the UN high-level panel on development to explore future targets after the Millennium Development Goals. While in New York in the summer of 2014 he writes an article for the *Wall Street Journal*, in which he argues against corruption and for greater transparency in the developing world.[6] He texts Mitchell to thank him for persuading him to accept the position. Somalia is a country in which the prime minister invests a great deal of personal effort, trying against the odds to bring more stability. A conference in May, organised by Mitchell before his departure, successfully galvanises international support. Cameron takes a strong lead in July 2014 at the Girl Summit, which Justine Greening asks him to co-host, and he speaks movingly about female genital mutilation.

A difficulty had arisen at the end of June, immediately prior to this summit, when, with the support of Mitchell, the Lib Dem former Scotland Secretary Michael Moore tabled a private member's bill to enshrine the 0.7% target into law.[7] This is a moment of peril for Cameron, as it would lock the government into spending more than £12 billion annually on development. A handful of Conservatives make it noisily clear that this is a step too far. Cameron and Osborne are in a corner and know they have no way out except to support the measure, or see the Lib Dems take the credit and have opprobrium rain down on them. Instead, Parliament faces down fire from some on the right wing of the Conservative Party, notably Philip Davies and Jacob Rees-Mogg. Deft work from Greening and Conservative whips sees the bill pass the Commons by a majority of 146 to six, but passage through the House of Lords is trickier with some opposition, including from heavyweight establishment figures like former chancellor Nigel Lawson and former Cabinet Secretary, Robin Butler.

When Ebola erupts in Africa in September 2014, he again takes a lead. That month, Obama says to him: 'Look, this really is urgent, I need you to take care of Sierra Leone, François Hollande to take care of Guinea, while we do Liberia.' The joint effort is significant in arresting the spread of the disease. Along with his support for gay marriage, Cameron's commitment to international development is his principal stand for liberal and humanitarian values. It wins him few friends in his party, and brings particular turbulence in the months leading up to the general election with many, not just on the right, wanting more money on defence; but his commitment is striking.

The development/defence trade-off sticks in the craw of Cameron's right wing and the military. When the question had been raised in 2013 as to which country would host the biannual NATO summit in September 2014, Cameron willingly put up his hand: it would coincide with the end of Britain's thirteen-year war in Afghanistan, and he is eager to show the world that Britain takes its commitments to NATO and international security very seriously. Number 10 is conscious that the country has not held a NATO summit since the last summer of the Thatcher era in July 1990, marking the end of the Cold War. With Putin on the warpath, the spectre of an aggressive leader in the Kremlin becomes a real concern. The dominant issue of the summit will inevitably now be how to deal with Russian aggression in Ukraine.

To help gain fresh perspective, Cameron convenes a meeting in late July 2014 in the large dining room at Number 10. A range of political and military figures are invited, including former Labour Defence Secretary and NATO Secretary General George Robertson, former Chief of the General Staff Mike Jackson, and former Labour Foreign Secretary Margaret Beckett. Michael Fallon, who has just taken over from Philip Hammond as Defence Secretary, starts out chairing the meeting until Cameron takes over. The PM gives an overview for twenty minutes, and then listens to the range of views. One person present describes it as 'a bit of a charm offensive to seek our views as to what might come out of the NATO summit'. Cameron is conscious of the force of history bearing down on him from the east. He wants the summit to make an impact.

Number 10, though, has become disillusioned with the official Whitehall machine's attempts at producing the distinctive agenda Cameron wants, so Downing Street special adviser Daniel Korski and colleagues in the Policy Unit seize the initiative, collating a number of ideas. These include a joint expeditionary force for NATO, and an Armed Forces Declaration, a tribute to the sixty-fifth anniversary of NATO's formation. Crucially, the agenda includes a fresh commitment to meet the target, first formulated in 2006, of spending a minimum of 2% of GDP on defence. The Treasury and officials in Number 10 counsel against mentioning 2%, arguing that it is unaffordable. The Whitehall machine is so sceptical about whether agreement could indeed be reached on such a broad agenda that an aide has to go round foreign leaders before the official photo, pen in hand, to get them to sign up to a presentational version of the Armed Forces Declaration.

Newport and Cardiff in South Wales provide the venue for the summit, with roads closed for weeks as part of a massive security operation, including twelve miles of security fencing acting as a 'ring of steel'. The summit is indeed hyped as 'the most important since [the] fall of the Berlin Wall in 1989', which is not without foundation.[8] For Number 10, a core subtext is using the summit to push the EU towards sanctions on Russia in response to its aggression in Ukraine, which again receives less media notice than they would have liked.

Cameron is pleased that the summit does indeed reinvigorate a sense of collective security among member states after several years of the alliance's focus not being on threats to Europe itself. But while many of the debates and serious-sounding resolutions quickly fade from international memory, the commitment to the 2% for defence spending does not. The 2% figure, about which Cameron feels strongly, is barely discussed in the National Security Council before the summit. As one senior British officer wondered at the time, 'I think the PM may be painting himself into a corner on this.' Sure enough, the commitment, hastily conceived, comes back to haunt him. The military are not going to let him forget it.

Many still have lingering resentments dating back to the 2010 Spending Review and the Strategic Defence and Security Review (SDSR), believing that defence has been overly clobbered in the austerity cuts. A particular cause of concern is the decision to scrap Harrier jets and decommission the *Ark Royal* (the Royal Navy's sole aircraft carrier) earlier than planned, and without replacements for the best part of a decade. The military dismiss the SDSR as a mere cost-cutting exercise, and pin their hopes on a new strategic review in late 2015 properly identifying the priorities for Britain's role in the world.[9] Retired generals, admirals and air chiefs are rising out of their armchairs and finding common voice with serving officers – a dangerous alliance, especially when conjoined with right-wing Conservative backbenchers. Information starts to be dripped into the media, which is regularly reminded that in October 2010 Cameron had announced that Britain 'will require year-on-year, in real terms, growth in the defence budget in the years beyond 2015'.[10] Despite this weight of criticism, Number 10 continue to believe that it called the 2010 SDSR right: 'We didn't need tanks and heavy equipment as the generals wanted. We need flexible forces and linked battlefield functions such as ISTAR [information, surveillance, target acquisition and reconnaissance systems] for today's battles against ISIS,' says one aide.

Are Cameron and Osborne now on different sides of the argument? They were certainly at one in the early years in power, believing that Labour had wasted billions of pounds on defence, and had run the MoD poorly. They protect the equipment programme in 2010, and appoint Hammond as Fox's successor in October 2011, hoping his sharp financial brain will help ensure value for money. But where Cameron sees the romance of the British armed forces, and revels in being a staunch defender of his country, Osborne focuses more on the pounds and pence. He is adamant that if the government is going to make savings and complete the job of deficit reduction, cuts will have to be made in defence spending, 'or we have no hope of balancing the budget by 2020'. Treasury officials are fiercely behind him in their belief that there is still huge wastage in defence: 'There are too many admirals, too many generals, too many chauffeurs,' one says. They argue forcefully in late 2014 and early 2015 that the procurement budget is excessive, and that the quality of Britain's defence and foreign policy will not be jeopardised by planned cuts. 'Defence is good for a billion' is how the service chiefs characterise the Treasury's attitude to their spending. They have read the Treasury's steely-eyed world view perfectly. With the economy set to expand, the Treasury believe that committing to a fixed target of 2% will pin down far too much money on defence, create an awkward precedent for other departments (Education might demand protection too), and prevent the completion of deficit reduction. Osborne blankly refuses to let the 2% commitment be included in the Conservative manifesto for the 2015 election. Elections, as Crosby would agree, are not won on defence.

Month after month, the pressure mounts on Cameron. Senior backbenchers including Bernard Jenkin and Rory Stewart, chairman of the Defence Select Committee, are leading the sceptics. In February 2015, the committee criticises the 'strikingly modest' role that British forces are playing in fighting the ISIS.[11] The military's close connections with backbench Conservatives are now seriously fuelling the criticisms within both camps. Cameron is becoming so irritated by the barrage of criticism that it further emboldens him to resist making a definite pledge for Britain to maintain the 2% figure. He retorts that he has made a ten-year commitment to increase equipment, and to maintain the ground forces at their current level, and to stick by Trident. 'You've got Putin buggering around, you've got ISIS, you've got Obama doing crazy things with Iran and we are not backing our own defence,' retorts one former Cabinet minister, throwing up his arms in horror. Cameron succeeds in neutralising defence as an issue during the election campaign, when only UKIP and the Democratic Unionist Party commit to the 2% target. Beneath the surface, are the questions being asked about Britain's place in the world damaging to Cameron's leadership? Why is the media-savvy PM not responding more to what the right-wing press want him to do?

The last nine months of the parliament witness the most critical questioning of Britain's standing on the world stage since the 1970s. The speculation can be traced in part to a cool wind blowing across the Atlantic from Washington. The criticism finds expression, albeit in private, during Cameron's White House visit in January 2015. On the flight home, Cameron refers to American concerns about Britain and how, unusually, the president had come back to this several times. Something of the White House's questioning seeps into Washington's political bloodstream. Number 10 doesn't believe that the president is orchestrating it, though some more junior White House aides might be. In March, head of the US army General Raymond Odierno launches a public salvo. Because of cutbacks, he says, Britain will no longer be able to commit division-sized forces to future combat operations, adding that he is 'very concerned' about the falling proportion of defence spending in the UK.[12] Throughout the spring, British ambassador Peter Westmacott reports back to Number 10 about Washington's concerns regarding Britain's 'strategic drift'. There are still more damaging broadsides from nearer to home: the International Institute for Strategic Studies reports in February that the cuts have resulted in a 20–30% reduction in Britain's defence capability.[13] Then a report in March from the respected Royal United Services Institute claims that the British army could now be reduced to its smallest size since 1770, with just 50,000 troops.[14] It receives widespread publicity on both sides of the Atlantic. Number 10 think the claims alarmist and absurd. But the criticism keeps rolling in.

On 5 May, just two days before the general election, Vice President Joe Biden spends an hour with the British chiefs of staff, who are making a call to their opposite numbers in Washington. He tells them: 'We Americans have a higher bar for you Brits than for the rest. You are a pillar of NATO and we expect you to show the way. We have elections coming up next year, and middle-class America is fed up with having to cough up the money to sort out security in Europe.'

The concern is this: the US accounts for more than 70% of NATO's military spending. Britain might have the fifth largest defence budget in the world, but Washington worries that if Britain isn't prepared to commit to the 2% in the future, there is little hope that other nations will follow suit.[15] Disillusion in Washington finds its sharpest expression in an article in the *Washington Post* in May which makes a powerful claim: 'after an extraordinary 300-year run, Britain has essentially resigned as a global power'.[16] The piece that most gets under the skin of Cameron, though, appears in the *Financial Times* in the same month arguing that 'Britain [has] decided it's going to turn in its deputy sheriff's badge and let the US play the role of world policeman alone'.[17] He is visibly upset and irritated, telling his team that the piece is grossly unfair.

Disillusion with the British government from within the American military, defence and security community is actively fed by their counterparts, many retired, within the United Kingdom. Richard Dannatt – former Chief of the General Staff, briefly official adviser on defence to Cameron in Opposition, and a constant critic of both Blair and Brown – is the most vocal. Dannatt constantly jabs away at Number 10. Almost equal an irritant is Richard Shirreff, the British general who served as Deputy Supreme Allied Commander in Europe until 2014. In February 2015, he says that Britain has become a mere 'bit player' on the world stage and in the midst of the most serious international crisis for fifty years Cameron has gone AWOL.[18] One aide dismisses him as 'totally off the wall'. Shortly after, the former Chief of the Air Staff Michael Graydon attacks the British government's policy as 'disappointing and, indeed, frankly shameful'.[19]

Criticism of Cameron for lacking a clear strategic sense of foreign policy, widely aired in David Richards' 2014 memoir *Taking Command*, is becoming a common perception. Relations in Cameron's final months before the election become strained and ragged within the Whitehall national security community. Suddenly, he is in everyone's sights. Service chiefs and officials turn on him for preventing the National Security Council (NSC) co-ordinating foreign, defence and security policy as they would like. Some say he lacks the strategic grasp of Clegg or Osborne, and lacks a vision of Britain's place in the world of a Thatcher or Blair. He is criticised for making hasty rather than considered judgements. He is accused of not trusting his advisers and officials at large beyond his close circle and his Number 10 team. He is said to begin NSC meetings by asserting 'this is an important issue and you know what I think, but nevertheless let's go through the arguments', thereby discouraging others from speaking up. His team are nonplussed by the accusations: 'Yes he has strong views, but if he didn't, he would be criticised for being indecisive.' The Foreign Office is no longer as assertive as it was in the early years of the coalition. Whereas initially Cameron's appointment of Hague, and the latitude he gave him, restored some pride and authority to the Foreign Office lost in previous years, there is a widespread view that its influence diminishes towards the end of the Hague era. By late 2014, almost every aspect of Cameron's effort on foreign affairs is under attack. How much justice is there in the criticisms?

His lead on Libya in 2011, lauded at the time in many quarters, is accused of failing to anticipate the destabilisation of the country by Islamic extremists. 'We had no security presence on the ground, a huge failure, and no coherent drive from the centre to stabilise the country', says one retired official. Ed Miliband joins in the criticism during the election campaign, alleging that Cameron's failures in Libya after 2011 have contributed to the refugee crisis in the Mediterranean.[20] Though Miliband's attack is criticised for its opportunistic timing, his argument strikes a chord. Cameron is accused of naivety and romanticism in his response to the Arab Spring in general, and failing to recognise fully the unsavoury elements amongst those protesting against the status quo. Libya certainly became a failed state after 2011, and it remains an open question whether his intervention in 2011 made matters worse. Would staying out, as in Syria where Assad remained, have been better? Certainly, no lasting peace has been established, but he may have prevented mass bloodshed on the streets of Benghazi in 2011. After the trauma of Iraq, however, no voice on the NSC was recommending putting British boots on the ground. Equally, any attempt to bring in UN peacekeepers would have been vetoed by Russia, given Putin's strong antipathy to Anglo-French action in Libya. Effort was expended to try to help a transitional government take root, to no avail. If post-2011 Libya is chalked up as a failure for Cameron, it is not for want of his trying to find a humane way forward.

On Russia, Cameron is criticised for not gaining more leverage from the relationship he built up with Putin from 2011 to 2013, which might have deterred the Russian leader's aggression in Ukraine. He is criticised for snubbing Putin at the Sochi games in February 2014, and for not being a direct part of the German-led talks on Ukraine. 'We should be in there,' say diplomats: 'he took his eye off the ball.' During the D-Day seventieth-anniversary celebrations in Normandy in June 2014, Merkel invited Hollande to join her for conversations with Ukraine's president, Petro Poroshenko. Obama tells Cameron: 'I don't think I want to be part of this,' and Cameron agrees to stay out too. Cameron's advisers believe they do not need to be directly involved, and have great faith in Merkel to lead the discussions and to keep them regularly informed. Criticism of torpor over Ukraine discards the strong stance that Cameron made at EU Council meetings and the NATO summit on sanctions against Russia. Cameron describes Britain's role as being 'the strongest pole in the tent', pressing for sanctions in the first place, keeping the US and EU aligned over them, and ensuring they remain in place when others waver.

On China, Cameron is attacked for needlessly provoking the country at a time of leadership transition when, with hindsight, it is said that Clegg could have met the Dalai Lama. As a consequence, he ran a serious risk of damaging Britain's relations with China, before eventually handing the Chinese a major moral victory, as incoming world leaders are now much more reticent to meet the Dalai Lama. This criticism has substance, if underplaying the importance Cameron and Osborne gave to repairing the economic relationship.

On his relationship with the US, Cameron's desire to avoid the overfamiliarity of Blair, and the perceived neediness of Brown, produces a relationship arguably too detached, with insufficient work put in to build up links between the teams below the leaders themselves, such as those between the Defence and Foreign Secretaries and their American counterparts (with the exception of Hague's close relationship with Hillary Clinton). But Obama nevertheless thinks Cameron his closest overseas ally during 2010–15; the relationship may not be as close as Thatcher–Reagan or Blair–Clinton/George W. Bush, but it establishes equilibrium and serves British interests well. Cameron deserves credit for establishing this bond with the president, even if Whitehall could have been more adept at building close relations with Obama's team, for all their very different outlooks and views of Britain from their opposite numbers under Clinton and George W. Bush, particularly after the departure of the sympathetic Thomas Donilon, Obama's National Security Advisor, in June 2013. The US certainly wanted Britain to do more in Iraq, but the two pillars on which its own policy was based proved misjudged: faith in the Baghdad government, whose leadership under prime minister Nouri al-Maliki proved unsatisfactory, and faith in the Iraqi army.

On the EU, he is criticised for being overly concerned by his own right wing, which led him in Opposition to pull out of the centre-right EPP grouping in the European Parliament, creating difficulties with Merkel. Merkel liked Cameron personally, and they reached a mutual understanding of their different approaches to the EU. But it took time after 2010 for her to see him as a serious political player. It is hard to discern a clear strategy or forethought on Europe, or to see more than a series of tactical withdrawals and pyrrhic victories, until 2013, with the EU budget cut and the announcement of the referendum. He is criticised too for not doing more to build coalitions of support, which are vital in the EU. Cameron's freedom of manoeuvre over Europe nevertheless is severely limited by his uncompromising Eurosceptic backbenchers, who have inflicted considerable damage on the four previous Conservative leaders, and who harbour a deep hatred towards him personally. Equally, he can when the occasion demands build support in Europe, or over Libya in 2011, the European budget in 2013 and Ukraine in 2014–15. But his record on the EU at best is mixed.

While there is some justice in these criticisms, cumulatively they take little account of the difficulty that any leader would face in trying to find consistency in the anarchic world of these five years, with the rise of Islamic extremism, a prolonged economic crisis in Europe, and a reticent US president. Cameron is vulnerable to attack on his foreign and defence policy mostly from the autumn of 2014 onwards when he allows himself to be overly focused on the general election. 'There are no votes in defence or foreign policy' may have been an article of faith with him and his team. But he allowed himself to be too swayed by Osborne who will not commit to 2% on defence before the election, and Crosby who will not relax his tub-thumping insistence on the long-term economic plan. Game, set and match to the long-term economic plan, but it comes at a price.

Cameron's foreign and defence policy achievements are not empty. He has partial success in achieving his three objectives in foreign policy: to safeguard the British nation; exploit opportunities for selling British products abroad; and to provide a moral lead and practical help on the world stage. He shows judgement and resolve in getting Britain out of Afghanistan in 2014, stoking up anger among elements of the military for doing so. His decision to stick by the development pledge helps save lives and gives Britain moral authority at the UN. His standing up to what he sees as the bloated defence community may, if the 2015 SDSR is well conceived, prove politically to be on a par with Thatcher confronting her antagonists who had vested interests in maintaining the status quo – the professions and trade unions. Aside from questions over Libya in 2011, and his lack of groundwork before the Syria vote, he avoids major blunders in foreign policy, keeps the country safe, and harbours hopes that his non-doctrinaire approach to the EU, coupled with his strong relationship with Merkel, might yet achieve a new settlement between Britain and Europe – something that eluded all his predecessors since the 1970s.

THIRTY-NINE

The Coalition Endures

November 2014–March 2015

'Why do we need to have a Budget at all? Why would I give that to you?' says Clegg angrily to his Conservative colleagues. He is adamant in the weeks before Christmas that Osborne will not have his final showcase. The Lib Dems are thoroughly disillusioned with the big fiscal events of Autumn Statements and Budgets, sick of seeing the Conservatives take the credit when they go well while the Lib Dems are marginalised. 'They should have come to the realisation about Budgets earlier, frankly,' says Rupert Harrison. 'But they've finally realised they'd never got anything good out of them. It's George standing in front of Number 11, and it's basically seen as George's event.'[1] Privately, Osborne thinks it is very stupid of them to let him have this Budget. David Laws, an increasingly strident figure for the Lib Dems, says that if there is to be a fiscal statement, it must be on a 'care and maintenance' basis only (i.e. addressing matters that need annual attention), with no crowd-pleasing political content. Clegg is refusing to budge.

But Osborne needs his spring Budget – for the Conservative Party, with the election coming up; for himself; and, so he says, for the country. His acrimonious dispute with Clegg over Northern Powerhouse has badly soured their personal relationship since the summer. Osborne has always seen Clegg as naive but is now beginning to see him as a loser. Osborne, more than anyone in the government, calls such shots in these final months before the election.

The Budget is the most difficult of the three major arguments between the coalition partners in the final nine months, the other two being the Data Retention and Investigatory Powers Act of July 2014 and the Counter-Terrorism and Security Act of February 2015. Some differences had come over the Autumn Statement in December and the NHS winter crisis: but a way through these had been negotiated relatively easily. To officials trying to hold the government together, the greatest worries come from increasing differentiation, with the Lib Dems needing to be seen to offer alternative policies as the election approaches; squabbles over who would claim credit for initiatives; and leaking, which first manifested itself after the boundary changes dispute, and which becomes considerably worse in the final months. Up to that point, the government has been less prone to leaking than many of its single-party predecessors. By the autumn of 2014, Lib Dems are sick of being pushed around and used as fodder for Conservative policies, and demand more say; the Conservatives are equally angry at the Lib Dems portraying themselves in the media as humanising the mean-spirited, nasty Tories.

Yet despite all this, Osborne gets his spring Budget, and a full-on one too. How has he managed to convince the Lib Dems to let him go ahead? Deception plays a part. He convinces the Lib Dems that an annual spring Budget is a necessity for reasons of income and corporation tax, and other necessary financial provisions. Osborne's team meticulously assemble the technical and legal arguments, such as the Office for Budget Responsibility's obligation to produce reports, which point to the Budget being inescapable. 'Surely it can be delayed?' the Lib Dems pertinently ask. 'No, it can't,' they are told blankly. In fact, as Osborne knows all along, the Budget could very well have been postponed until after the general election.

Over a series of Quads in the early weeks of 2015 Osborne sets to work battering away at remaining Lib Dem reservations, offering them what one Number 10 insider describes as 'a succession of goodies that he had for months squirrelled away under the table'. 'Let's start on the things we can agree on,' he says to Clegg and Danny Alexander, 'and let's see what comes out of these discussions and whether we can find things for you.' Further increases in the personal allowance (this time from £10,600 to £11,000 by 2017/18) are indispensable parts of coalition Budgets, with both parties, as ever, claiming the credit. To soothe Danny Alexander's and Scottish Lib Dems' concerns over North Sea oil taking a battering from reduced oil prices, Osborne agrees to a cut in petroleum revenue tax from 50% to 35%, and a range of further measures to support the struggling industry. He then agrees to the idea of Steve Webb, the Lib Dem pensions minister, to allow people to sell their annuities. To placate Lib Dem worries about banks and multinationals moving profits offshore, Osborne assents to further restructure measures, and agrees to raise the bank levy. Finally, to meet the concerns of Clegg over mental health provision, he agrees that mental health services in England will receive £1.25 billion in extra funding during the next parliament. 'If you want me to do all this, fine, but we will have to have a Budget,' he tells them, like a clever schoolboy who knows he has just pulled off a cunning wheeze.

Thus Osborne scales the first of his challenges over his final Budget: securing Lib Dem agreement for it to go ahead. He then meets Cameron and Lynton Crosby to ask whether they feel an attention-grabbing policy is needed, but they agree that any such rabbit might distract the party from Crosby's relentless themes of the long-term economic plan and Ed Miliband's weaknesses as party leader. 'All very fascinating,' says Crosby drolly at a meeting of Cameron's team, listening to a succession of economic ideas to scintillate the public, 'but voters only need to know two things about the economy: one, it was broken five years ago by the other lot; second, it's OK now under us.'[2] Osborne's wish to make a splash on savings and pensions reform is thus roundly vetoed.

Osborne is left with an economic and political challenge: to produce a Budget to persuade the electorate to vote Conservative while ensuring that the numbers still add up respectably. In February, his team focus heavily on the Office for Budget Responsibility (OBR). The Office for National Statistics' economic revisions in the summer of 2013 showed that Britain hadn't suffered a double dip, but only a single one.[3] Information from the OBR filters into Osborne's office suggesting that, with tax receipts at last picking up, debt as a percentage of GDP will fall. 'The fact that the debt target might be in sight gave Osborne's team great heart,' says an official, 'coming after all the lows and highs of the previous years since 2010.' For Osborne, getting national debt falling as a share of GDP is 'a vindication of our approach over the years since 2010. Everyone thinks I promised to eliminate the budget deficit; what I actually promised to do was to get debt falling as a share of national income by the end of the parliament. So that was very important for me, even though it didn't make headlines in the press,' he says.[4] The better economic news plays its own part in bringing Lib Dems onside.

Osborne delivers one of his most political of all Budgets. The bank levy, and abolishing the 55% tax charge on pension pots, help to disarm Labour. So too does a reduction in the amount of budget surplus he wants by the end of the next parliament, thus neutralising Labour's attack after the Autumn Statement about public spending reaching its lowest levels since the 1930s. The standard devices of taxing banks more, along with some well-drafted anti-tax-avoidance measures, provide the cash for some Osborne goodies, including a fully flexible ISA designed for older voters, and a new Help to Buy ISA aimed at first-time buyers, described nakedly by one of Osborne's team as 'big, classy, election campaign policies'.

Osborne is in defiant form when standing up to deliver his Budget shortly after 12.30 p.m. on 18 March. He might have been denied his wish for pyrotechnics in terms of fresh announcements, but no one can stop him exercising his flamboyance in language. 'Today, I report on a Britain that is growing, creating jobs and paying its way ... we'll have paid off the debts incurred in the South Sea Bubble, the First World War, the debt issue by Henry Pelham, George Goschen and William Gladstone ... Growth is up; unemployment is down; borrowing is down in every year of the forecast; we reach a surplus – all contributing to a national debt now falling as a share of national income. Out of the red and into the black – Britain is back paying its way in the world today.'[5] He concludes, 'Today I present the Budget of an economy that is stronger in every way than the one we inherited ... Living standards: on the rise. Britain: on the rise. This is the Budget for Britain, the come-back country.'[6]

Osborne's final Budget denies Miliband some killer lines of attack he would have had if it had come some months earlier, but he presses his case hard in response. His principal theme is that the Budget is from a government 'who are not on [the people's] side ... the chancellor ... made no mention of investment in our National Health Service and our vital public services'. He attacks the 'colossal cuts' in policing, local government and defence, and, in anticipation of a core Labour refrain in the imminent election campaign, warns that 'they will end up cutting the National Health Service. That is the secret plan that dare not speak its name today'.[7] The Budget is, however, generally well received, and not just in quarters that one would expect in a feverish pre-election climate. The *Sunday Telegraph* salutes Osborne as 'Prince George', carrying a picture of him resembling Machiavelli.[8] The *Observer* the same day carries a poll finding that 43% of voters think he is 'a good chancellor' against 24% who believe the opposite.[9] His caution is also praised: whether or not at Crosby's insistence, he has resisted the temptation for gimmicks and has substantially kept his promise that it would not be a pre-election Budget with giveaways. 'Considering the electoral temptation to give something to everyone … he gambled that voters would thank him for his fiscal discipline and back him,' says *The Times*.[10] Applause is not universal, however, and writing in the same paper the following day, the astute Philip Collins is far less impressed: 'Mr Osborne did not chant, as he incited his pantomime audience to sing along, two important facts about the meagre recovery: "Productivity Down! Immigration Up!" It must have slipped his mind that the deficit in the balance of payments is the worst in peacetime since 1830 … we got a recovery based on household debt, consumer spending and government schemes to stimulate the housing market, a glass menagerie of a recovery, both precious and fragile at the same time'.[11]

The Budget overall is a hugely cathartic experience for Osborne. The months of strain and self-doubt that followed the 2012 Budget have all evaporated. He feels vindicated in his often bitterly contested judgements on the economy. His mind is switching to securing similar vindication for his wider political judgements. He feels that he could play a central role in devising the government's day-to-day strategy alongside being chancellor, countering those who had argued from the outset, especially after the omnishambles Budget, that he should concentrate on being chancellor alone. Many of the core political judgements of the past five years have been influenced heavily by his forceful advice, including pulling out of Afghanistan, calling the Scottish referendum, heating up the rhetoric during the AV referendum, sacking Andrew Lansley, bringing in Mark Carney at the Bank of England and Lynton Crosby at CCHQ, emboldening Number 10 to bounce back assertively after the Syria vote defeat, and facing up to the military on defence spending. It is clear from the very beginning that Osborne, not Clegg, is the real deputy prime minister.

Treasury officials are struck from the outset by Osborne, who is a very different kind of chancellor from his predecessors. 'I'm not prepared to countenance any anti-Number 10 gossip or thinking in the Treasury,' he tells them in May 2010. This is not what Treasury mandarins are used to hearing. Even when PM/chancellor relations are good – as often between Major and Clarke (1993–7), and in the early days of Brown and Darling in 2007–8 – there has always been a certain wariness and worldly cynicism amongst Treasury officials about what Number 10 might be cooking up. This is an altogether different world. 'Dave and George are not going to waste time or emotional energy fighting each other,' said Hilton in early 2010, with a John-the-Baptist-style enthusiasm. 'Oh yeah,' many thought, 'you just wait. How naive.' But his prediction proved correct.

Osborne signals the change in style by the way he organises his day, which barely changes over the next five years. 'He would start the morning working from his office in Number 11 before going to the 8.30 a.m. meeting in the prime minister's room in Number 10. He would arrive at the Treasury just after 9 a.m., then spend the middle part of the day either there or in Parliament, before returning to Number 10 for the daily meeting at 4 p.m., spending the rest of his day at Number 11. His day, physically and politically, is bookended, starting and finishing in Downing Street.' Officials whose careers span thirty or more years have never known a relationship between prime minister and chancellor anything like as enduringly close. There are no personnel or doctrinal issues, no need for Cameron to draw on figures in Number 10 to offer countervailing economic advice, as Thatcher did with Alan Walters, or Blair with Derek Scott. Cameron instead works closely with Jeremy Heywood and then Chris Martin, his two most senior former Treasury advisers in Number 10, who work to eliminate the customary mistrust between both offices. Cameron indeed favours Treasury advice over that of the Foreign Office, seen in the appointment of Ivan Rogers and Tom Scholar as his two key advisers on the EU, both of whom are ex-Treasury, rather than Foreign Office as is usual. As well as studying economics as part of his degree, Cameron worked in the Treasury in the 1990s, which further helped his instincts chime naturally with its officials.

Osborne might often be the better tactician, but Cameron's is always the more dominant voice. Osborne always defers to him, and not just out of respect for his seniority in rank and age. Shorn of Cameron's reassurance and support, Osborne would not be able to perform as he does. Indeed were it not for Cameron and his team sticking by him at key moments, principally the aftermath of the omnishambles Budget, he would not have salvaged his reputation. During Osborne's dark months, and they were very dark, it is Cameron who sustains him. Osborne always knows that. Deferring to and respecting Cameron is an article of faith, which he never doubts or lets anyone challenge in front of him. The success of the government, such as it is, is due above all to the relationship between these two men, with Osborne's daring and showmanship balanced by Cameron's innate caution.

But how good is Osborne as chancellor from 2010–15? Many charges are levelled against his stewardship of the economy over the five years. The central one is that the core programme of austerity, of questionable economic substance, may well have delayed economic recovery. Then comes the shift towards a mild Keynesian stimulus in 2012, with softening fiscal targets and 'Funding for Lending', whilst at the same time denying there was any Plan B and that Plan A was all that mattered. There are a host of other concerns: a worrying and potentially dangerous legacy of poor productivity improvement, a serious deficit in the balance of payments, and insufficient help for the worst-off in Britain, who in many cases saw their lives become even less secure. Others point to a failure to eliminate the deficit, with debt remaining at 80% of GDP, and a recovery significantly based on a fall in oil prices, as well as on household debt and consumer spending. The criticisms roll on and on. Janan Ganesh, Osborne's biographer, is indeed right to say, 'we should reserve judgement on Mr Osborne'.[12] This is ever the case with chancellors. Even after ten or twenty-five years' perspective, judgements are tentative, and even then will be substantially value-driven. By 2015, the British economy is judged to be the strongest in the West, alongside the United States: at least some of that success must be due to Osborne's judgements, especially considering the economy's starting point in 2010.

We are on surer ground when describing Osborne's footprints than assessing their impact. Devising Plan A, and the immediate decision to announce in-year spending cuts in May 2010, the Emergency Budget and the Spending Review, define Osborne's whole chancellorship from the outset. He goes on to invest considerable political capital in maintaining a consensus behind this strategy, domestically and internationally. The creation of the OBR in 2010 is a significant innovation, which brings order and clarity to both Budgets and Autumn Statements and, though it buffets him at times, it means he is able to live less hand-to-mouth than Darling or Brown had done before him. He will be remembered as a pension reformer: although the increase in state pension age would have happened anyway, his change to annuities is a genuine choice rather than a fiscal necessity. His overhaul of the banking regulatory system is another significant innovation, including the Financial Policy Committee, the Prudential Regulatory Authority and the Vickers Report's recommendations, albeit changes which fade in public perception as concerns over the behaviour of banks move down the public agenda. He pushes big infrastructure projects, including HS2, Crossrail and the Northern Powerhouse: the last, changing the relationship between the Treasury and the regions, may be seen as one of his most enduring legacies. He has a major impact on welfare reforms, but little on schools, beyond support for Gove who he trusts implicitly. Universities attract much more of his attention, where he lifts the cap on university places. He protects the science budget and pushes universities and British companies to be less insular, not least in relations with China. Finally, cutting the 50p tax rate is very much his own decision, taken because he thinks it is the right thing to do economically and philosophically. It is of a piece with his competitiveness agenda and changes to corporation tax. Overall, he is proud to be the most pro-capitalist Conservative chancellor since Nigel Lawson in the 1980s.

Osborne shares credit too for the survival of the coalition. His fall-out with Clegg contrasts with the loyalty and respect he shows to Danny Alexander, which is mutual. Their relationship is periodically stressed, particularly towards the end when Alexander chooses to present the Lib Dem 'Alternative Budget' on 19 March, the day after Osborne's own. The case for presenting their own spending figures is reasonable, but the theatrical form that Alexander chooses, together with a yellow Budget case, is thought to be risible, not only by Osborne and Cameron but also the House at large, which is almost universally hostile. The worst moment in the Osborne/Alexander relationship comes during the election campaign when Alexander, troubled by Lib Dem ratings, leaks Treasury advice revealing that IDS has sent the Quad a proposal for nearly £8 billion of cuts in welfare.[13] Osborne responds quickly by text: 'Come on, I thought we'd agreed not to do this! Hope all is going well for you in Inverness.'

Cameron remains close to Clegg till the very end, although the relationship is severely tested when the Lib Dems realise that the Conservatives are making a full onslaught on their marginal seats. On election night, Cameron sends him a text wishing him luck: 'This democracy lark is a nerve-jangling thing,' it reads. They both believe that there is a strong likelihood that they will be in government together after the election. At the end of one of their final bilateral meetings, they ask officials and aides to leave the room. 'We talked in a relatively perfunctory way about what might follow. It was all rather British,' says Clegg.[14] 'We're going to have to leave that until our next coalition,' they joked, discussing unresolved issues. Cameron is far more positive than any of his Cabinet about the prospect of a future coalition government. He thinks Clegg is a bit naïve and can be self-indulgent, but he also has a genuine affection and respect for him. Clegg has defied the sceptics in his party who said that the coalition would not endure, or who argue that they should come out of it in the final months and fight alone. To do so, he says, would hand even more of the kudos for the government's successes to the Conservatives, and call into question all the sacrifices that have been made. And yet he had seriously considered resigning a year earlier after the devastating results the Liberal Democrats suffered at the European elections. 'We saw a catastrophic loss of support,' Clegg recalls. 'For a few days after the results, I considered going, but I didn't talk to the PM; just my wife Miriam and Paddy [Ashdown].'[15] Had he resigned in May 2014, the remaining months of Cameron's premiership would have been very different.

According to William Hague, for Cameron 'there was never any doubt in his mind or mine that the coalition would continue right up till the general election'.[16] Any threat to the coalition's survival comes in fact much more from the Conservative Party than the Lib Dems. Backbenchers who have always resented the coalition, and feel they were bounced into it, are prominent in pressing Graham Brady and the 1922 Committee to hold a vote on whether the party should come out of it. 'The matter was discussed,' says Brady. 'There were certainly some members who wanted this to happen in the spring of 2014, but never sufficient.' After the local elections that May and the Newark by-election in June, the unrest dies away.[17] Number 10 argues very strongly to the 1922 Committee leadership that pulling out of the coalition would bring disaster: minority government with defeats every few days on the floor of the House, an inability to pass Budgets and financial measures, and the electorate presented with the impression of a shambolic government. (Although as Brady and Number 10 know, some backbenchers so hated Cameron that such a dystopian prospect would have been an incentive, not a deterrent.)

Clegg flexes his muscles in the final few months, in particular on foreign policy, wanting a tougher position on exports to Israel and a more assertive policy in the Middle East. Officials think 'that kind of activism could have led to problems on foreign policy had it carried over into a second term'. The final Quad is held on 9 March, just before the Budget. The final Cabinet meeting comes two weeks later on 24 March. There is a full agenda, beginning with mental health, introduced by Clegg and Jeremy Hunt. Then Oliver Letwin, the company secretary of the coalition, gives a Panglossian survey of the coalition government's achievements. Then follows a discussion on ISIS, Syria and Iraq. All know his seminal role in the coalition.

Cameron has been giving some thought to the final Cabinet. While out on a run, he comes up with the idea of concluding it with a small celebratory drinks party. When he is sent the proposed Cabinet agenda to peruse in his red box a few days before, he writes in the margins, 'I've got quite a nice idea: let's get everyone a beer from the constituency brewery.' His idea is to have the meeting in the afternoon or evening so that everyone could relax together. Clegg is enthusiastic about the idea and says: 'I'd like to get some crisps from my constituency too.' Crowded diaries do not permit any deviation from the normal meeting time, however, so all attendees are presented at the usual morning meeting with the beers with a label saying, 'Co-ale-ition. An unconventional pairing ... that lasts the distance'. The beer is produced by Wychwood Brewery in Cameron's constituency and is accompanied by a pot from Clegg of crisps made by Henderson's of Sheffield. It falls some way short of the bronze medal that Churchill gave all members of the coalition government in 1945, but the gesture is still appreciated. Emotions run high around the Cabinet table. They are all conscious, at least a little, of the historic significance of their surviving five years of coalition government together: 'We've come so far, and we should be proud of what we've done together,' Cameron says to them. He and Clegg are not the only ones around the table expecting to be back together in six weeks. Both parties have had teams working informally on a new coalition agreement, the secrecy dictated mostly by the knowledge that such plans are abhorrent to the wings of both parties.[18]

Within days, though, the gloves are off. Clegg vents months of frustration at Osborne when, on 5 April, he describes him as 'a very dangerous man with a very dangerous plan and I'll do everything in my power to stop it.'[19] After months of phoney war, the real fight at last has begun.

FORTY

'If we lose'

March–May 2015

'I don't get it. This is one of the best campaigns I've ever seen. All our candidates are saying: "We are getting such a good sense on the ground." Yet it's not making any impression on the polls or in the way the media is reporting the campaign,' says an exasperated Cameron. It is Saturday 25 April, and he is holed up in Chequers, taking stock in the Hawtrey room of a disappointing first four weeks of the election campaign. With him are Craig Oliver, Liz Sugg, Lynton Crosby and Crosby's business partner Mark Textor, who is running the party's polling. The meeting has been called because of the chorus from the media, which is damaging to the party, saying that the Conservative campaign is failing because the polls aren't shifting. While Ed Miliband and Labour are performing ahead of expectations, the Conservative campaign, and Cameron in particular, are under attack for being listless and overly regimented. They need to regroup and discuss adjustments that might be required. Cameron is aware of the personal criticism. He has heard it all before: back in the 2010 campaign, he was accused of lacking passion and coming over as detached, as if he didn't truly want to be prime minister, or feeling that he had a God-given right to the job.

The day before, Friday 24 April, sees Cameron campaigning in Clacton, Essex. It is a long day and his performance is flat until his final question, when he suddenly sparks into life, saying 'I will tell you what I am fighting for: I am fighting for families, for all that really matters.' His team suddenly jump to their feet, and one says 'Wow, where did that come from?' Cameron is still revved up when he speeds back to London in his car: 'I've had enough of being told I'm not fighting for this, or not fighting that, or not fighting UKIP. I am going to give it straight.'[1] But his mood collapses on Saturday. The day begins badly, with an article in *The Times* saying that 'five years of Number 10 seem to have killed the Tory leader's appetite for winning voters … Cameron is the skulking warrior who'd rather be in his tent. He does not need the electorate and, as Tory high-ups fear, he is not even desperate to win.'[2] This view is echoed elsewhere: 'Privately, Cabinet ministers [are] dismayed at Cameron's performance and his lack of obvious desire and passion to win,' says the *Daily Telegraph*.[3]

That morning, in Croydon, he muddles up which football team he supports, saying 'I would rather you support West Ham' when he meant Aston Villa: aides say he is feeling exhausted, had earlier driven past West Ham, and is not thinking straight. Such slips trouble him. He realises it will be widely reported, and he is angry with himself. A meeting has been called at Chequers to address these destabilising concerns. Cameron knows he needs to come across with more passion and intensity if he is to convince wavering voters, and an email from Andrew Feldman telling him this reinforces the message. Cameron is naturally reticent, feeling he shouldn't act the showman, but Feldman tells him that he agrees with those saying he needs to show more aggression to impress upon voters what is at stake and how much this election matters. Cameron's mind is clearing by the time he joins the core campaign team for the meeting at Chequers.

Do they need to tear things up and start again? Craig Oliver reminds him of one of his favourite expressions about panic: 'There's no need to set your hair on fire and run around screaming,' he tells the PM. 'The fundamentals are right. The media is bored of writing that our campaign is boring. Let's give them the excuse they need to write something else.' Crosby adds forcefully to Oliver's argument. 'Let's use this criticism and turn the negativity to our advantage,' he says. Sugg tells Cameron, 'You are the best person to be prime minister. Go and show them why. Go out and fight. What will it be like to wake up on 8 May and feel like you haven't given it every drop of effort?'[4] Sugg had bumped into Oliver that morning in the hallway of 11 Downing Street and they compared notes: Oliver is one of those who believe the polls are wrong, but still thinks it is essential at this point in the campaign for Cameron to go up a gear. The team are unanimous that he needs to energise himself more, and agrees a statement to put out, that he will become more passionate as they enter a new stage in the campaign.

The next morning, Sunday 26 April, aides notice a difference. The PM is tangibly more animated and has resolved in his own mind to let things rip. On the helicopter on the flight west to Yeovil in Somerset, he frantically writes down what he might say. An aide urges him on: 'This is a turning point. Go for it.' Cameron is almost too distracted to notice, absorbed in his usual routine of writing five pages of notes, then boiling them down to three, then one, then bullet points. His nose is still in his text as he is whisked away from the helicopter by car, driving past Paddy Ashdown's house with posters for David Laws, the local MP, prominently on display. They arrive at a village in the constituency and are shown to the room at the back of the hall. 'He was very fired up and ready to go. He bounded out of the room and jumped up on stage.' His aides and protection team immediately notice a different prime minister. He has a new quality about him.

Cameron carries the energy forward to the launch of the small-business manifesto on the Monday. Again, he springs up onto the stage at the Institute of Chartered Accountants in London, praising those starting small businesses for 'taking a risk, having a punt, having a go, that pumps me up'. There is no stopping him: 'If I am getting lively about it, it is because I feel bloody lively about it.'[5] For the next few days, 'It was a change of style, sleeves rolled up, no suit or tie – in the round, it felt different,' says Osborne.[6] Cameron has the kick-start he has needed. He starts feeling much better about himself: the lows are behind him and he begins enjoying the campaign again.

The strategy of the campaign – the focus on economic competence and Miliband's leadership – remains exactly as before, as does the emphasis on the SNP and on vital Lib Dem marginals. But a new self-belief is apparent in the team for much of the last ten days. They feel they have managed to change gear mid-campaign, in contrast to Labour 'which has Miliband stuck in his suits, speaking from a lectern', says one. 'It worked in the first weeks of the campaign to present him as prime ministerial. But over a long campaign, it became monotonous.' 'They haven't managed to reach inside themselves and find the thing to change: we have,' says another. While they see Miliband's campaign falter, and succumb to gimmicks, they maintain their focus.

The Conservative campaign is the most strategic and scientific in the party's history. Crosby runs it with military efficiency from CCHQ in the open-plan office in Matthew Parker Street near to Parliament. At the centre of the office is 'the pod' with Crosby sat in the middle. To his right sits Stephen Gilbert, who runs the 'ground war', the battle for marginal seats, and to his left sits Craig Oliver, running the 'air war', dealing with the media. Oliver has been working out of both Number 10 and CCHQ but bases himself permanently in CCHQ for the last few weeks of the campaign. Also at the desk is Mark Textor, whose speciality is the latest micro-targeting techniques. Textor crunches the overnight polls. Party chairman Andrew Feldman is important too, especially with his personal relationship with the PM. Party co-chairman Grant Shapps is effectively sidelined after a number of skirmishes with the media, including a controversy over his former business dealings. Jim Messina, campaign manager on Obama's 2012 re-election campaign, gives advice principally on social media and online messaging in the latter stages. No other figures come close in importance to this group during the entire campaign.

Crosby stresses the need to be proactive. They cannot let themselves be distracted by the media into making reactive statements that threaten the overall clarity of the campaign. Key to this vision is the economy: 'The notion of our five-point economic plan is that we are working for something better for people in the long-term, and are not just a bunch of opportunist politicians making short-term interventions,' he says.[7] Parties lose elections, he believes, when the voters aren't sure what the core message is. Hence the imperative need for a plan for the future, underpinned by iron discipline. 'On the whole, the campaign was very disciplined. One or two people needed some counselling, as always happens, but on the whole, it was pretty straightforward,' he says.[8] A series of Sunday evening meetings with Cameron's inner circle had started before Christmas, where Crosby argues that the route to success is via the Lib Dem marginals, as Gilbert and his team had already identified. If all these seats can be taken, and Labour is held at bay in the marginal seats won in 2010, an outright majority is possible. Given Crosby's force of character and understanding of voters in the marginals, even Cameron's team are reticent to challenge his expertise. But they still push him back: 'Can we really take all the seats off the Lib Dems?'

To Oliver, the genius of Crosby lies in his ability not only to spot that the route to victory is ruthlessly targeting Lib Dem seats, but his ability to deliver it too.[9] Cameron and Osborne flirted with the idea of an advertising blitz at the start of the year, with a series of billboards across the country, as in 2010, but Crosby is sceptical about the value of mass advertising campaigns, which play to the egos of politicians rather than targeting specific voters. In January they are presented with one of a number of poster ideas from Saatchi: 'WELL DONE YOU' it states simply, in black type on a white background. There is silence in the room for about a minute. Everyone looks at each other before Cameron says: 'Maybe I'm not getting this, but isn't that rather patronising?' The Saatchi representative retorts: 'That's the point – it's supposed to be controversial and prompt a debate.' Osborne, initially attracted to the idea of a big poster campaign, now worries that the idea risks presenting a complacent view of the economic recovery. The proposed poster is shelved.

Even before Cameron calls the general election on 30 March, a regular rhythm is established at CCHQ. At 5 a.m., Gilbert chairs the first meeting of the day, where the field team collate information from the previous day to assess what needs to be done. At 5.45, Crosby then chairs a meeting of Gilbert, Oliver and Textor, drawing on Gilbert's information, Textor's overnight polling and a report from CCHQ on the morning bulletins and newspapers. At 6.30, the third meeting of the day sees Llewellyn and Fall come from Number 10, and at 7.30, Cameron and Osborne join them, often face-to-face, but sometimes by conference call, where they discuss the key media appearances and interviews for the day. The final morning phone conference follows at 8.15 with the Cabinet, during which they are briefed by Crosby and Oliver. The day is bookended with a final meeting in the evening, again either face-to-face or by conference call. Cameron and Osborne always participate, and it is often the most decisive exchange of the day.

Visits by Osborne and Cameron across the country are co-ordinated to complement each other. The public face of the 2015

Conservative campaign is essentially a double act between the two men, while other actors have only walk-on parts. Osborne had jointly run the campaign in 2010. He takes great pride in his skills as a campaign manager. But he doesn't cavil now at ceding control to Crosby – partly because Crosby is meticulous in securing his and Cameron's agreement for every single decision of importance. Whenever morale amongst the inner group dips with the refusal of the polls to move, or due to the constant media criticism, Crosby raises their spirits. He repeatedly focuses the team on his research, showing where the campaign needs to focus and which voters need to be targeted, especially in the critical Lib Dem marginals. Textor time and again underlines Crosby's view that the election is winnable and that Cameron and the team should not start doubting themselves.

Crosby's iron discipline trumps even the manifesto, launched at Swindon University Technical College on 14 April, the day after Labour's manifesto launch. Entitled *Strong Leadership. A Clear Economic Plan. A Brighter, More Secure Future*, the manifesto is the fruit of fifteen months of work overseen by Jo Johnson. Despite this, Cameron had ordered it to be rewritten in February around the theme of 'security'. The policies did not change, but the structure did, with a new emphasis placed on security at every stage of life. It includes the doubling of free childcare for three- and four-year-olds to thirty hours a week, an extension of the right to buy, and a guarantee that those on minimum wage will pay no income tax by the end of the next parliament. But the emphasis on the campaign remains a focus on leadership and economic competence, rather than policy prescription. Party research shows that the public are sceptical about the details of policies, and the decision is therefore taken to keep the campaign focused rigidly on the key issues.

Cameron's biggest regret of the 2010 general election is that he agreed to the three televised debates during the 'short' campaign, which he feels sucked the oxygen out of it, absorbed far too much of his own time, and left him just a few days at the end to put his case to the country personally. Cooper, Feldman, and, above all, Crosby are clear that the same format must not be repeated in 2015. Oliver and Llewellyn are in the middle, concerned about the potential damage if Cameron is blamed for refusing to participate and none take place. It becomes apparent that they cannot avoid them altogether. Cameron personally believes that because a fixed-term parliament means that broadcasters know when the election will be, debates can be planned for February or early March, well before the campaign begins.

The team have two overriding concerns. They have been saying for months that Miliband is a weak leader; so if he takes part in a head-to-head with Cameron, 'anything better than Miliband defecating on the stage will be a plus for Labour'. Farage, they believe, is a fading star; so any extra television exposure for him will only add to his credit. There are months of negotiations. Cameron's team become locked into a major fight with the broadcasters, who they say are ignoring their requests for an early spring debate and are then trying to bully them into participating. The broadcasters, they believe, then add insult to injury by wanting UKIP to be represented. The negotiations produce 'a lot of drama', according to one senior aide. They have a fine judgement call: balancing the certainty of the accusation that Cameron is scared of participating against the high risk that Miliband and Farage will receive a boost, as Clegg did in 2010. They decide to hold their line. Oliver has to face down broadcasters threatening to 'empty chair' the PM. Oliver's discussions with the BBC's director of news and former editor of *The Times*, James Harding, produce the idea of a single, seven-way leader debate to include the leaders of the SNP, Plaid Cymru, UKIP and the Greens, as well as the three established parties. By giving Nicola Sturgeon, whose popularity in Scotland is on the rise, such a high profile, Cameron's team believe the potential damage to Miliband and Labour could more than outweigh any damage Farage might do the Conservatives. Agreement is reached eventually on the seven-way debate, as well as back-to-back interviews with Cameron and Miliband in front of a live studio audience, and a 'challengers' debate', omitting Cameron and Clegg, to be held on 16 April. They further agree that Cameron will appear alongside Miliband and Clegg at a special BBC *Question Time* on 30 April, as happened in the 2005 campaign.

On 5 March, Downing Street announces formally that Cameron will take part in only one televised debate, with the seven party leaders. Jim Messina's counsel has been important in helping them reach this decision, arguing from his experience in the US that a seven-way debate would be substantially less risky to the Conservative cause than a two- or three-hander. A backlash does indeed come, articulated strongly in *The Times*: 'Number 10's arrogant "final offer" to participate in just one seven-person debate before the campaign officially starts risks reinforcing the worst stereotype of the Tories as high-handed "born to rule" grandees.'[10]

The first television contest that Cameron faces is Jeremy Paxman on Channel 4 and Sky News on 26 March, alongside Miliband. Cameron has not trusted the former *Newsnight* presenter since he was interviewed as a leadership candidate in November 2005. After being asked if he knew what a 'pink pussy' was, the two fell out badly, and Cameron has tried to avoid Paxman ever since. He is unusually nervous before the programme, knowing that Paxman has nothing to lose, and as the incumbent he will be given the harder ride of the two interviewees. When the interview begins, his anxiety is palpable. Cameron's team are not surprised by Paxman's aggressive questioning, particularly over 'zero hours' contracts. Cameron is unsettled by the encounter, but when he talks it over afterwards with the team, his spirits rise, and he thinks he did better when interacting with the studio audience.

A week later on 2 April comes the seven-way debate on ITV, moderated by Julie Etchingham. Cameron is selected to speak last. He spends ten to fifteen hours preparing for it, a significant chunk of his time, though far less than he spent in 2010. Bill Knapp, who had worked on Obama's 2008 election campaign and who had helped Cameron with the debates in 2010, is brought back from the US to offer advice. His core strategy is not to get dragged into the argument, but to let the other speakers slug it out. Llewellyn and Fall think Cameron makes a strong start with his initial speech, then fades a bit, but overall they are happy, principally because neither Miliband nor Farage shine. 'Do no harm' is the advice Cameron has taken to heart, an approach that his team feel is vindicated by the public reaction to his performance. Sturgeon is widely perceived to have 'won' the debate, and as soon as it is over, Crosby pushes out the line that Sturgeon is therefore a disaster for Miliband.[11]

By the time of the fourth and final television event, the *Question Time* debate on 30 April, Cameron has had his pump-up experience, and goes into it feeling much more confident than for the Paxman interview. The first two questions are tricky, but on the whole he manages to put across all his core lines. By this stage in the campaign, his team are thoroughly disenchanted with the BBC and are pleased that the public, rather than journalists, will be asking the questions. In a theatrical masterstroke, Cameron brings out the Liam Byrne note from 2010 ('I'm afraid there is no money'), once again reminding voters of the perceived economic irresponsibility of Labour. 'That is the situation I inherited,' Cameron says. In contrast, Miliband has a poorer night, stumbling over the questions on spending, before literally stumbling as he leaves the stage. Labour's modest improvement in the polls during the early stages of the campaign has halted.

To Crosby, *Question Time* is one of the pivotal moments in the campaign, because it brings Cameron and Miliband slap up against voters. Focus groups have consistently been showing the Conservative leadership that, when presented with a forced choice between a Miliband-led coalition with the SNP, and a Conservative majority government, they prefer the latter. Combined with other factors – including Miliband's interview with comedian and self-proclaimed revolutionary Russell Brand, and the controversial 'Ed stone', the large stone tablet carved with Labour pledges – Miliband's waning credibility is damaged further. The inner circle at CCHQ has not been greatly troubled by the Labour leader. 'Whenever we reviewed the picture in our marginal seats,' says Stephen Gilbert, 'we could see that Miliband remained a big problem for Labour. His ratings marginally improved for a time, and then went back down again, but on the critical measure of who was the preferred PM, it was Cameron all the way.'[12] Overall, even if Cameron's television appearances do not have an unequivocally positive impact on voters, they certainly do not have the negative impact which they had in 2010. 'We felt vindicated,' says one of his team. 'The television set pieces didn't get in the way of the campaign. Even though it was a hard fight to get the outcome we did, we felt that we had called it right.'

If the television debates didn't swing votes to the Conservatives, what did? Fears over Labour's economic credibility and about a Labour government propped up by SNP support are key. A month after the Scottish referendum in September, an Ipsos MORI poll put

Labour 29% behind the SNP in Scotland.[13] As early as November 2014, Conservative focus groups are picking up concerns about a rampant SNP, and they are brought to the attention of the leadership at CCHQ. In January, however, the Conservative Party in Scotland reports that the SNP are not as strong as is being made out and might win only twelve to fifteen seats. But then the polls strengthen again for the SNP, and a wipeout for Labour in Scotland becomes increasingly likely. This is welcome news for the Conservatives: with Labour going into the election with 258 seats, they will now need to gain some one hundred seats to offset the Scottish losses if they are to gain a majority – an almost impossibly steep hill to climb.

In January, CCHQ devises a campaign to target Conservative–Labour waverers, and those considering voting UKIP, urging them to vote Conservative or risk ending up with the SNP holding the balance of power. The idea is mooted of flipping the public perception that Clegg is dancing to Cameron's tune. Thus is spawned the poster campaign depicting Alex Salmond with a miniature Miliband sticking out of his top pocket. Digital images are created of Miliband in front of Number 10, arm in arm with Salmond. The media pounce on this negative campaigning, especially when allied to the lack of priority given to fresh policy initiatives, but high command decide this line of attack is a risk well worth taking. It meshes cleverly the Conservatives' two core themes: Miliband's weakness as a leader, and the damage that could be done to economic stability if a Labour/SNP coalition government were to be formed. All the economic progress made since 2010 will be put at risk, they argue. The team at CCHQ report throughout April that 'every night on the doorsteps we are finding that the line is working in every type of target seat: the voters are very anxious about the economy, and about Ed Miliband, propped up by the SNP, putting the country back to where it was,' says Stephen Gilbert.[14]

Buoyed by the success of the strategy, Crosby and Gilbert propose to Cameron that the party puts up posters of Salmond in the West Midlands and Sturgeon in West Yorkshire. They talk about it to Osborne, who thinks 'this could be the game changer, because nothing so far seems to have made a big difference in the polls and this could shift things'.[15] It forces Miliband again and again to rule out

Labour forming a coalition with the SNP. To Clegg, the shift in focus to fear of a Labour/SNP coalition makes all the difference to the outcome. 'Ten days before the election, the exam question given to the electorate changed. It was no longer "Do you favour left or right on the economy?" It was "How can we stop Salmond and Miliband?" On the doorstep it was unbelievable. Again and again and again, we saw the evidence of that plan working.'[16]

The other key to the Conservative victory was locked into place months before the campaign started: to hold all marginal seats vulnerable to Labour (and perhaps take a few off them), while making the principal battleground winning as many of the Lib Dem-facing seats as possible, especially in the south-west. CCHQ feed the line to the media that the party needs only twenty-three seats to win an outright majority. While technically correct, this disguises a far more sophisticated targeting strategy. The initial focus on just fifteen Lib Dem seats (where their majorities were most at risk) increases to twenty-eight in the final ten days of the campaign. Lib Dem incumbency, with strong relationships built up with constituents often over many years, is the obstacle. The tactic deployed is to target and then put the squeeze on a small number of different types of voters identified by the party's private polling. CCHQ ensure the Conservative candidates in these seats work hard to prove their credibility with constituents and then convince them that if they don't vote Conservative, they would end up with Miliband backed up by Salmond and the SNP. A relationship is built with those who are receptive through personalised letters and visits. Specific messages are tailored to a number of voter types in each constituency: several thousand versions of a standard letter are used to communicate with them. Labour, in contrast, invest their money into sending out vast volumes of literature to all groups without the same segmentation, and amassing an army of volunteers across the country rather than targeting particular seats.

Ten days before polling day, Crosby and Gilbert tell Osborne and Cameron that they should redouble their targeting of Lib Dem seats and should aim for the lot. 'It was another key moment,' says Osborne, 'we'd always expected to pull back a bit and not go for the safe Lib Dem seats like Yeovil, Twickenham and Thornbury, and Yate. But we changed tack and started to aggressively target the Lib Dem seats across the field.'[17] Old hands at CCHQ said that they had never seen such an energetic Conservative campaign on the ground: 'You always get the candidates telling us "It's better on the doorstep than the polls are showing." But this was different. We knew we were doing well in the seats we needed to be winning, and all the Lib Dem seats were very much in play,' says Gilbert.[18] Cameron's team are frustrated by reports in the media about Labour's more energetic campaign, while giving little credit to the Tory operation.

Yet, despite the focus on the Labour/SNP coalition fear, despite the full-frontal attack on Lib Dem seats, despite even Cameron being pumped up, the headline polls on voting intention refuse to budge. The lack of reward for all the effort begins to seep into every pore in the Conservative Party, right the way up to the prime minister. 'Every day, we looked, and it was 32 to 33, 34 to 35, 35 to 35. The polls refused to budge. I can't claim we weren't affected by the polls and we didn't begin to ask "Surely, they can't *all* be wrong all the time?"' says one of the team. Sugg, who travelled every day with Cameron, admitted 'the constant refusal of the polls to shift was demoralising. It bore down on us. We constantly asked ourselves, "What more can we do?"'[19]

Criticism of the Conservative campaign is ubiquitous. Column inches are dedicated to how the focus on the economy hasn't worked, that Miliband hasn't imploded and that the campaign is boring and lacks flair. Osborne's pledge on 11 April to spend an extra £8 billion on the NHS is seen as a panic measure which damages Tory credibility on the economy. But Cameron and Osborne refuse to believe Labour scaremongering on the health service. Andrew Cooper records at the end of April that Cameron is remaining 'amazingly calm, positive, steady, not panicking, refusing to be dragged off the grid, he's worn-out but determined'.[20] But the strain *is* taking a toll. Craig Oliver talks about how 'the constant mantra that the Conservative campaign isn't working because the polls aren't moving, was an echo chamber of self-reinforcement'.[21] Some of their ire focuses on Lord Ashcroft's detailed constituency polling: 'His bloody polls wind everybody up. The national polls refuse to reflect our internal polls. It makes us all very nervous,' says another in the high command. The BBC is another target of their anger. Osborne is one of those seething at the relentless BBC narrative that the Tory campaign is boring, which contrasts with everything he hears out on the stump. Constant pressure is put by CCHQ on the BBC to probe Miliband's pledge that Labour will not form a coalition or do any deal with the SNP. 'You are not asking him the right questions,' CCHQ keep telling the BBC. 'Sturgeon is clear that she will want to talk to Labour. The idea that Labour can sustain a government without a relationship with the SNP is absurd.' The BBC are irritated by this continual barrage, but nevertheless put pressure on Labour about their intentions, who in turn keep denying they will get into bed with the SNP. Salmond and Sturgeon make Labour squirm, saying that they would put backbone into a Miliband government. Cameron's team sense that they have Miliband on the run.

Osborne remains optimistic about the final result: 'If you have a big lead on the economy, which increased as the election approached, and a big lead on leadership, I thought that in the end it would turn to us,' he says.[22] He and Cameron refuse to believe in the sincerity of Labour's core argument that the Tories are out to privatise or damage the NHS. They genuinely believe that their own arguments on the economy are right and in the interests of the country. They feel that they have the better of the argument, and that Miliband failed to take on his own party in 2010 on the economy. In Carlisle, at the conclusion of his thirty-six-hour tour of Britain in the run-up to polling day, Cameron says: 'We are not trying to cut the deficit because we are sort of demented accountants obsessed by numbers. We are doing it because we want to go home at night, look our children in the eye and say this generation did the right thing and did not leave an unsustainable debt for you to pay off because that is not the sort of people we are in this party and this country.'[23]

Fighting Labour is one anxiety on the final day of the campaign. Fighting the Conservative Party is another. On the evening of Wednesday 6 May, Cameron returns to his home at Dean from his final tour planning to have a long rest in anticipation of a sleepless thirty-six hours ahead. Every night during the campaign, Cameron has been receiving red boxes from Downing Street, though the paperwork inside is considerably thinner than usual, consisting of little more than intelligence reports, diplomatic telegrams and a small number of government decisions that require his consideration. But this night is different: his Private Office has put in a huge pack of papers on the EU negotiation so that he can think this stance through with colleagues on Thursday in the event of questions on Friday morning before the expected coalition talks begin. He flicks through his papers before falling into a deep sleep.

On the morning of polling day, 7 May, he goes to vote in the nearby village of Spelsbury. At 10 a.m., the praetorian guard converge on a 'neutral house' in Oxfordshire, undetected by the media, to plan all conceivable electoral scenarios. The PM himself has summoned the secret meeting, which includes Osborne, Hague, Letwin, Llewellyn, Oliver, Fall and Crosby. They spend the most time thinking through the scenario that they might have the most seats but fewer than Labour and the SNP combined.

The discussion flows back and forth over the different scenarios. What kind of coalition will they be able to form, the best outcome in the minds of most of them? 'I can't construct a scenario in which we receive over 300 seats,' says one of his team. 'It's just not going to happen.' 'Our working assumption was that, if we manage to get back into Number 10, it would be a coalition government,' says another. But they will need to achieve support for it from the 1922 Committee. The 1922 Executive know they have a truculent parliamentary party, whose hardliners feel they were bounced into a coalition precipitously in 2010 without due consultation, and they are simmering. The 1922 Committee, and especially chairman Graham Brady and the Executive, are very clear that they will not allow themselves to be bounced into another coalition; to be railroaded twice is more than their jobs are worth.

The SNP will not consider any deal, which leaves the Lib Dems and the Democratic Unionists from Northern Ireland. It is equally likely that they would have more seats than Labour but that Labour and SNP together would hold a working majority in the Commons. They discuss claiming that such an arrangement would lack legitimacy, given Miliband's repeated denials of a partnership with the SNP during the campaign. Conservative fears that Labour will be forced into a deal with the SNP are underlined when, in the hour before the final opinion polls are announced, Miliband's team begins a heavy briefing operation based on the Whitehall bible, the *Cabinet Office*

Manual (paragraph 2.12), which they use to argue that, if the polls are correct, a Conservative government will be illegitimate because it couldn't pass a Queen's Speech, whereas they could, even though they will have fewer seats.[24] This is seen as a tacit acceptance of Labour having to work in partnership with the SNP. Final party polling suggests the Conservatives are looking quite good against the Lib Dems, but may struggle in the seats that they are defending against Labour.

Just before lunch, they are joined by Michael Gove and Cameron's parliamentary private secretary, Gavin Williamson, so that they can change the focus of the discussion towards party management. They agree that a leadership election will be called for, if the Conservatives do badly. There is little they can do to fend it off. The apprehension is that if the Conservative vote is low, below 32–33%, and Miliband is able to form a government, disaffected Conservative backbenchers will go on the *Today* programme and call for an immediate leadership election. 'The 1922 Executive were aware of plenty of colleagues who were open in their view that if we lost the election, Cameron would obviously have to go,' says an insider. A senior BBC figure two weeks before had said that 'already people are lined up to go on the media on Friday morning to say he has to stand down'.

The core question on the table is how they are to respond in the event of the expected failure to win a majority. They all believed, or hoped, that the polls would improve as the crucial day approached. They have not. Over lunch, the team must now discuss delicate matters they have not wanted to touch until now, but can avoid no longer. If Cameron has to stand down, how can they head off rivals? Cameron himself has inadvertently raised the stakes on his own future in an interview six weeks before, on 24 March. James Landale, a fellow Old Etonian and the BBC deputy political editor standing in for the sick Nick Robinson, had put an awkward question to Cameron, and he had answered it. As an aide says, 'James had been very charming and beguiling all day, and had asked him earlier by a sports pitch what his personal intentions for the future were. Cameron parried it, but when he came back to the house, Sam was there and he finds it harder not to conceal the full truth with her present.' Cameron blurted out that 'Terms are like Shredded Wheat – two are wonderful but three might just be too many.'[25] The admission that if he wins the general election he will not stand again, even if widely known in the Westminster village, sends shock waves through the whole political system, and as a disclosure coming on the eve of the campaign it is inept, if not worse. He is only being honest in admitting that he will not stand again, and feels it is the right thing to say, but it raises the question: when will he go? In 2019? 2018? 2017? He hopes his admission of the elephant in the room might reduce pressure on him to go. This is naive. It has intensified it.

Cameron has been Conservative leader for a full ten years, which is a feat in itself: only four other leaders in the twentieth century survived as long (Bonar Law, Baldwin, Churchill and Thatcher). The Conservative Party is notoriously brutal to its leaders: within the previous decade, it had effectively dismissed his four predecessors. Challenges to a Conservative leader are the norm, not the exception. His survival for so long has had as much to do with the absence of a viable successor as it has his own skills and qualities. Who might try to unseat him? David Davis, after two unsuccessful bids, is ruled out. So too is Liam Fox: the Adam Werritty episode in 2011 raised the question of confidence in his judgement and damaged his reputation. No other serious candidate on the right is evident. In the centre, the most obviously popular candidate is Boris Johnson. He could have struck in 2012–13 when Cameron and Osborne were at their most vulnerable, but his position as London mayor and the fact he isn't an MP ruled out a challenge. Boris is quiescent from 2013 onwards, partly through the mediation of Crosby, but also because Osborne subtly lets it be known to Boris that if he wants Treasury support for his legacy as mayor, he must play by the rules. Clegg is one of those surprised at the way that when Boris asks for money for London, he is treated with kid gloves by Osborne and Cameron.[26]

Theresa May is the other contender from the centre. Like Boris, she is not notably popular with the parliamentary party, although she has more support now than when she had considered running for the leadership in 2005. She is believed to be raising her leadership flag over the Home Office with a speech to a ConservativeHome conference in March 2013 on her 'three pillars of conservatism', which provokes a vitriolic response from Osborne as well as Gove, and damages her relationship with Number 10 from that point on. This is odd, when so many of her policies and instincts, not least on immigration, chime with Cameron's own.[27] Aside from a Eurosceptic challenge from the right, which is never going to materialise, there is no clear philosophical alternative to Cameron being offered by any potential candidate. The electoral logic of the coalition would remain unaltered for the rival candidates too, and they would almost certainly have to adhere to Plan A, the central plank of the government's policies. May's speech arouses such indignation precisely because it appears to offer an alternative outlook for the leadership. As the parliament grinds on, the 1922 Executive becomes aware of talk of a possible challenge from the 2010 intake, though they can never assess reliably whether the support for the Adam Afriyie challenge is genuine enthusiasm for the candidate, or designed merely to prise open a serious contest.

The risk of a leadership challenge to Cameron had been reduced by the introduction by William Hague when party leader of new rules requiring 15% of MPs to write letters to the chairman of the 1922 Committee to trigger a vote of confidence. The change deliberately discourages a challenge because, assuming the chair is acting with integrity, no MP knows if their letter is the first or the last needed. Had a confidence vote in Cameron been triggered he would have won it comfortably, but with a very significant minority voting against, 1922 insiders say. Such a vote would have been damaging for him, and could have precipitated a chain of events leading to his departure. (Although from the first time Cameron came into danger in 2007, Hague himself has made it known that if the leader goes, he would go too.[28])

The 1922 Committee executive say that they will have a conference call on the Friday after the election to take stock of the position, before convening a full meeting of the parliamentary party on the Monday morning. Cameron's team that polling-day lunchtime sense that there are a worrying number of backbenchers who would relish a fight, and would prefer to go into Opposition than be part of another coalition with the Lib Dems, so they aim to corral a group of supporters made up of ministers, traditional loyalists and those who hope for promotion in the following five years, to vote down the refuseniks. For several weeks, Gove and Gavin Williamson have been working to identify possible candidates. Their task is made much harder because several heavyweight loyalists, such as former ministers Tony Baldry and Stephen Dorrell, who could have happily told the 1922 Committee to 'stop panicking', are standing down as MPs at the election. Having figures known to be Number 10 stooges would be pointless. They worry that they might not be able to find sufficient supporters to champion their cause. Equally they are unsure of the precise numbers of those willing to speak out against them.

After lunch, at about 2 p.m., Cameron leaves for Dean. An hour later, speechwriter Clare Foges arrives to work directly with the PM. She finds an apparently empty house, sits down and waits. After a short while, Cameron comes downstairs and says, 'Right, shall we begin the speeches?' He wants three separate speeches drafted. Best-case scenario is they have enough seats to form a coalition with the Lib Dems or the DUP: he dictates a few thoughts to her which she works up into a speech, completed later by him and Osborne. The second speech anticipates Labour being behind but trying to form a majority with the SNP. Llewellyn has distilled the thoughts from the midday meeting and emailed them to Foges, arguing that Labour has no democratic case for forming a coalition as the electorate voted on the basis that Miliband had expressly ruled out such an arrangement.

The third speech is the bleakest. With the house still quiet, Cameron airs various thoughts which Foges takes down, before working them up into a speech on her laptop. Later that afternoon, a very small group of Cameron, Samantha, Osborne, Llewellyn and Fall go for a walk through the woods near Cameron's house. They continue to discuss post-election outcomes. All the while, they are receiving mixed messages; some reports are optimistic, others pessimistic talking of high Labour turnout. At one point, Cameron asks, 'Are you sure we don't need to have "speech zero"?' This is in the event of the Conservatives winning an overall majority. The collective feeling is that, in the very unlikely event of that happening, it will be easy enough for him to construct what he needs to say. As one member of the group says, it would be a 'nice problem to have'.

Afterwards they settle down on garden chairs for drinks on the patio. 'I'm going to read you the speech,' Cameron tells them. They go very quiet. They all know that this is effectively the 'if we lose' speech. It opens, 'It is clear that we have not won and that I will have to go. I will be seeing the Queen later this morning.' He goes on to say poignantly, 'I hope they will say I did my duty. Being the prime minister of this country is the best job that one can possibly have. I wish Ed and Justine every success in doing it. Thank you for giving me the opportunity to serve.' The state of the country when he walked through the front door of Number 10 five years ago comes next, and he lists some of the achievements, including creating 2 million jobs. 'I will stay on as party leader until July but will not be making any comments or sharing any thoughts on my successor,' he concludes. The mood that evening amongst them all is 'very bleak'. As he talks, Fall, Sugg and Foges have tears in their eyes. Everyone is hugely emotional. Cameron has convinced himself that he will not be prime minister in twenty-four hours. They talk about plans for him and Samantha leaving Downing Street. They are annoyed by news, as it happens incorrect, that the Milibands are demanding they are out by Saturday morning, which they feel contrasts with the courtesy they extended to Gordon Brown in May 2010. Cameron is extremely down that evening: 'The mood had turned very dark,' recalls one present.

At 7.30 p.m. they have a supper of steak pie which Cameron had brought down from Scotland the previous day. Apprehension mounts as the evening wears on. The final polls have not made for good reading. YouGov has Labour and Conservative tied on 34%.[29] ICM, which they, along with many, read as the gold standard, comes out at 35% each.[30] Populus says it is going to be extraordinarily tight: 'The reality is that, when we were confronted by this, our confidence ebbed away,' says one. At 9 p.m. two conference calls take place by prior arrangement. The first is with the media spokespeople at CCHQ, the second with Cabinet ministers. Cameron thanks them for all they have done during the campaign and they briefly discuss how to respond to the various scenarios. Ever conscious of the way that remarks said early on can shape the environment, Cameron urges his ministers to remain calm and disciplined until they know the whole picture. At 9.20 p.m. they go through from the dining room to the living room and put on the television. His phone rings: 'We're going to be fine. We're going to get 300,' Feldman tells him.

'I don't know,' Cameron replies despondently. 'I'm just not sure it's possible.'

'We're really confident that our voters have come out in numbers. Internal tracking says we're going to be 300,' his old friend says before signing off. Those still in the team from 2010 – Llewellyn, Fall and Sugg – sit in the same seats to watch television as they did five years before. A car arrives to take Osborne off for a helicopter flight up to his constituency of Tatton in Cheshire. Like millions of others in the country, Cameron and his team huddle round the television waiting anxiously for the clock to strike ten o'clock.

'The sweetest victory'

7–8 May 2015

To Cameron's team gathered round the television at his home in Dean in Oxfordshire, the seconds tick agonisingly slowly until, as Big Ben strikes 10 p.m., David Dimbleby announces: 'We are saying the Conservatives are the largest party. Here are the figures which we have. Quite remarkable this exit poll. The Conservatives on 316, that's up nine since the last election in 2010. Ed Miliband for Labour, seventy-seven behind him at 239, down 19. If that is the story, it is a quite sensational story.'[1] Cameron's team cannot believe what they are hearing. There is a long pause before they cry out in joy and start hugging each other wildly. 'Sensational David, an extraordinary night if, *if*, that exit poll is right,' says Nick Robinson shortly after. His words inject a note of caution. 'Hold on, it's only an exit poll,' say Cameron's team. 'Why might it be any more right than all the other polls which have us level pegging?' The final prediction from CCHQ had the Conservatives up to 315; so maybe the exit poll is right, they wonder.

Cautious optimism gradually replaces the depression of earlier in the evening. Cameron, Ed Llewellyn and Kate Fall hold conference calls with Lynton Crosby in London and George Osborne in Tatton. Crosby impresses on them the need to remain cautious and they agree that Cabinet ministers should not stray from this line. An email is immediately circulated to them before they take to the airwaves. Crosby believes that they will finish in the 315/316 area, but says it all depends on a very small number of voters in the seats they are defending against Labour. Can they hold these? 'We know we've killed the Lib Dems, but what happens if we can't hang on to our trickier seats?' Cameron starts to worry about who they will partner in a government if the Lib Dems are wiped out: 'Look, if we get 316 we'll be fine, we needn't worry about the Lib Dems,' he is told. 'Oh my God, yes. I don't care – we can go it alone,' he exclaims. He is finding it difficult to take it all in, and is in a state of shock: 'He is very emotional, genuinely stunned,' says one.

The mood quickly falls when the BBC report a YouGov poll which puts the Conservatives on 284, completely in line with the opinion polls, and which is based on a big sample on polling day. 'It was an emotional rollercoaster,' says one. Glued to the television, they debate which is right: the near unanimity on the opinion polls, or the exit poll, which was accurate in both the 2010 and 2005 elections. The guru here is Craig Oliver, who had been the editor of the BBC's general election results programme in 2010. They all turn to him as he confirms that the exit poll in 2010 was indeed 100% accurate, and he explains why he has so much faith in John Curtice, the renowned psephologist behind the exit poll. While waiting for the first results, a party watching television at the home of the president of Cameron's constituency association, PR adviser Peter Gummer, rush down the street to congratulate Cameron's team. There is general excitement, but also agonising uncertainty. The plan was for Cameron to have gone upstairs for a couple of hours' sleep after the exit poll was declared, but he is far too much on edge.

The first result to be declared, the safe Labour seat of Houghton and Sunderland South at 10.55 p.m., tells them little except for the total collapse of the Liberal Democrat vote from 13.9% and 5,292 in 2010 to just 2.1% and 791. Cameron's team remain on a knife-edge until other results come in. It takes an unusually long time for the first results to be declared in the Conservative/Labour marginal seats. There is palpable relief as the early results confirm the prediction of the exit poll rather than the YouGov poll. At 1.48 a.m., Nuneaton declares. This is one of those marginal Conservative seats in the Midlands vulnerable to Labour, which Labour needs to win. Huge effort has been poured into the constituency in support of the candidate Marcus Jones, with Cameron paying a personal visit. They all know how much the result matters. Labour needs a 2.3% swing to win it; but the swing is in the other direction, 4% towards the Conservatives whose vote increases by 2,000 votes. 'That was the big confirmation,' records Llewellyn. To Osborne, the other key vote that night is one not even highlighted by the BBC, North Warwickshire, where the Conservative majority increases from fifty-four to 2,973, while Labour suffers a 4% fall in the vote. 'Those two results were hugely significant. It told us that we might be on track for an overall majority,' recalls Osborne.[2] Shortly after 2 a.m., Cameron's party leave Dean for the count in Witney's Windrush Leisure Centre. The sound of the Sky helicopter tracking the convoy brings out the crowds from the villages who wave as they shoot past. At 2.44 a.m. Cameron walks into the leisure centre, facing a wall of photographers, cameramen, reporters and supporters. He is shown to a small upstairs gym full of equipment smelling of sweaty socks. Llewellyn peels off to go to CCHQ. The remaining party set up temporary camp before becoming glued to the television.

At 3.29 a.m., the Lib Dem Ed Davey's result in Kingston and Surbiton is declared, revealing a Conservative gain for James Berry with a majority of nearly 3,000. 'Hang on, we might just have the numbers we need,' says Liz Sugg.[3] At 4.32 a.m., they hear Boris Johnson speaking after his success in Uxbridge: 'The people of Britain after a long and exhausting campaign have finally spoken.' Fall says it is at about this time that they start to realise they will win a majority.[4] Cameron asks for some paper and one of his favoured blue Sharpie pens. He turns to Craig Oliver and says, 'I suppose we'd better write a speech soon – what shall we say?'

'You should reclaim "One Nation" – it's what you think and who you are. We want people to know that even if they didn't vote for you, you have something to say to them. You want to be their prime minister too,' Oliver replies.

It chimes immediately with what Cameron had been thinking. 'I think you're right – we should never have let Miliband try to take that away from us. We *should* reclaim it.' He also believes that it would contain an implicit reference to the sensational result in Scotland, where the SNP are on course to win all but three seats. A few minutes later, Osborne calls from Tatton and Cameron runs the idea by him. He likes it.[5] 'Yes, that is the right thing for you to say now,' the chancellor says. Cameron then sits at a chair and writes out his script. The Telford declaration at 4.45 a.m. and Gower at 5.11 a.m., both

Conservative gains from Labour, tell them not only that they have fought off the Labour attack, but that they are making inroads into long-held Labour territory. At 5.23 a.m., Miliband speaks after his Doncaster result: it is 'a very disappointing and difficult night for the Labour Party'.

At 5.43 a.m., after successfully holding his own seat, Cameron delivers his first public utterance of the night. 'If you want a home that you can own of your own, if you want security and dignity in retirement, we are on your side … I want my party, and, I hope, a government I would like to lead, to reclaim a mantle that we should never have lost, the mantle of one nation, one United Kingdom.'[6] His core idea is that he doesn't want there to be an adversarial relationship between government and the people; he wants to reach out to the whole country. At 5.52 a.m. he gets in his car, sitting beside Samantha, with his team in other vehicles. As they drive east towards the rising sun, he is on the phone talking and sending messages. It is now daylight. 'Cornwall North, my God!' texts one aide to him from the car behind after the result is declared, another Conservative gain from the Lib Dems – a seat they had held for twenty-three years.

Cameron speaks to Llewellyn about the plans. It is now clear that an overall majority of indeterminate size will be achieved; Cameron is still finding it hard to believe. Then he calls Crosby: 'I'm going to give you a massive hug, Lynton,' he tells him. He is in regular touch with Osborne whose result in Tatton is declared just as Cameron's car pulls up to CCHQ in Westminster at 7.15 a.m. He is in a state of some euphoria. Crosby, Feldman, Gilbert and Textor are there to greet him in the lobby. They take him into the large open-plan office: 'Thank you. You are an amazing team,' he tells them while standing on a filing cabinet placed on its side. 'Five more years! Five more years!' chant his rapturous audience in return. Somebody present films his speech and puts it on YouTube. Cameron compares the victory to elections that he has known, 1987, 1992 and 2010, and tells them that 'this is the sweetest victory of them all … The pundits got it wrong. The pollsters got it wrong. The commentators got it wrong.'[7] After much hugging and cheering, he is swept back down to the car.

At 7.30 a.m. he arrives back at Number 10. When he sees his staff waiting for him, headed by his principal private secretary Chris

Martin, he gives them all hugs – 'unusual, because although he's a very nice man, he's not usually tactile', says one of his team – before going upstairs to the flat to see the children off to school. At 8 a.m. he comes back downstairs. Christopher Geidt, the Queen's private secretary, is in the main corridor, finalising arrangements for the day. The plan had been for the Queen to stay at Windsor in the expectation that coalition talks would last some days, but she was to return to London if necessary, so the prime minister could have an audience with her. However, by 6 a.m., when it looks like Cameron would be back, and it would be like a 'normal' election, Downing Street and Palace officials discuss how to respond. Keen to avoid speculation that the Queen had been working on the assumption of coalition talks, arrangements are made for her to return to Buckingham Palace. Difficulties arise over the precise form of words to be released about her meeting with Cameron: officials suggest the press be told that the Queen will see the prime minister 'at the conclusion of the coalition government' and that the prime minister 'now has the intention of forming a Conservative government'.

At 8.05 a.m., the BBC predicts that Cameron will receive 329 seats, with a majority in single figures. The news is brought to Cameron while he is talking in his study to Jeremy Heywood and Chris Martin about immediate plans for the day. At 8.16 they learn that Ed Balls has lost his Morley and Outwood seat to the Conservatives, a massive defeat for the Labour cause. Not since Michael Portillo lost his seat in Labour's landslide in 1997 has such a heavyweight figure been so brutally ejected. Before going up to the flat for a couple of hours' sleep, Cameron shares his thoughts with aides about what he might say in the keynote address he will shortly have to deliver, reiterating that 'I want to make a speech with One Nation sentiments in it.'

At 10.30, he is back down in his office. 'I can't sleep, I'm too excited,' he tells his staff. He is exercised about the statement he will shortly deliver, one that will further define his second term, and contextualise his first. Drafts are handed to him, one of which contains the phrase 'closing the gap between rich and poor'. He doesn't like this. 'Too Milibandy,' he says. He wants something more in tune with what he said in the manifesto and during the campaign. Officials are buzzing around outside his office. They are as surprised as anyone to find him back in the room that morning: 'In their wildest dreams, the team might have been hoping for a coalition but defeat was the most likely scenario the day before, and here they are back in power,' says an aide. At 10.55 a.m., Cameron's train of thought is interrupted by an aide saying that Miliband is on the line: 'I was just calling to offer my congratulations. You won a famous victory. Most of the pollsters said it wasn't going to happen,' says Labour's leader, who has led his party to one of its worst defeats.

'That is very kind of you,' Cameron replies. 'You are right about the pollsters. I had no idea what the outcome was going to be. You spoke with real credit, good arguments, some points I know I need to address. What you said this morning about bringing the UK together and treating governments of the UK with real respect was right. We've all got to rebuild Scotland. Ed, I wish you the best of luck. We've not always agreed with each other, but worked effectively where we needed to and maintained cordial relations outside the Chamber. Thank you for the call.'

'Give my best to Sam and the kids,' Miliband says.

'Same to yours. Gruelling for both families,' Cameron replies.

'Take care,' says Miliband, signing off. It is a brief call. Miliband is about to offer his resignation as party leader. Both men are utterly drained and exhausted, but the tone is conspicuously gracious. Immediately after it, Cameron turns to his team: 'We should say something about Ed in my remarks,' and the words are then inserted. 'We should say something nice about Nick too,' he adds. That is also done.

At 11.10 a.m., Oliver Letwin arrives at his office. Cameron wants him to remain at his right hand, responsible for the Cabinet Office. Rumours abound that Clegg is going to resign. It had been a disastrous night for the Lib Dems. The polls had suggested they might retain twenty-five to thirty seats. Ultimately, they keep just eight, losing every single seat in their traditional heartland of the southwest. The Queen is still not settled back at Buckingham Palace: there is no hurry for Cameron to see her. So at 11.20, he spends twenty minutes in his office pondering his new Cabinet. Little preparation has taken place, as they had not expected to be back. Officials normally start planning for reshuffles well in advance, and have all the moves neatly mapped out. Now they have barely anything in place. Additionally, Cameron will have twenty-five more jobs to appoint to Conservatives than he did five years before. The big offices of state have already been decided: Osborne will remain at the Treasury, May at the Home Office, Hammond at the Foreign Office and Fallon at Defence. Uncertainty hangs over the future of Gove, who has proved to be a rebarbative chief whip. In the run-up to the EU referendum, a more emollient character will be needed. Also with 331 seats, the final Conservative majority is just twelve, and a lot of massaging of the party will be required. Mark Harper, widely liked across the party, is chosen. But what job to give Gove? Will he take Justice Secretary? He will, with all the status of the Lord Chancellor's job wrapped up in it.

At 11.24 a.m., Cameron learns that Farage has resigned as leader of UKIP, having failed to win Thanet South, the seat on the Kent coast which he made such a personal mission. 'There was this extraordinary feeling that all our political opponents had been put to the sword. Ed Miliband forced to resign, Ed Balls losing his seat, the Lib Dems decimated, Nick Clegg resigning, Farage not even getting a seat. All our critics over the previous five years had been completely confounded,' says Osborne.[8]

While Cameron is preparing to leave for the Palace, his team watch the chairman of the 1922 Committee, Graham Brady, being interviewed on television. The last five years have seen a constant battle against backbenchers, with many of them arguing Cameron could not win an outright majority. For a moment, they feel the pleasure of vindication.

At 12.24 p.m., Cameron is driven through the front gates with Samantha to see the Queen. After twenty minutes, he leaves the Palace and returns to Downing Street. On the way, he consults with his team about his speech, and they say, 'Take your time. Get ready for it, don't be hurried.' He decides that he is not quite ready, so he comes back into Number 10. Twelve minutes later, he emerges in front of the cameras: 'I've been proud to lead the first coalition government in seventy years, and I want to thank all those who worked so hard to make it a success; and in particular, on this day, Nick Clegg. Elections can be bruising clashes of ideas and arguments, and a lot of people who believe profoundly in public service have seen that service cut short. Ed Miliband rang me this morning to wish me luck with the new government; it was a typically generous gesture from someone who is clearly in public service for all the right reasons.'

He concludes: 'This is a country with unrivalled skills and creativeness; a country with such good humour, and such great compassion, and I'm convinced that if we draw on all of this, then we can take these islands, with our proud history, and build an even prouder future. Together we can make Great Britain greater still. Thank you.'[9] He finishes speaking at 1.16 p.m., and reaches for Samantha, who is watching with the team from the steps outside Number 11, the same place they had stood five years earlier. Elated, he clasps her hand and walks back towards Number 10, before turning for the cameras. At 1.17 p.m., the front door closes behind them.

Cameron 2010–2015

The Verdict

What then are we to make of 'Cameron at Number 10' during 2010–15? We should not judge prime ministers as if they all served on a level playing field. Some come to power blessed with advantages, none more so in recent years than Tony Blair who in 1997 inherited a strong economy, enjoyed a large majority and led a unified Labour Party. Cameron's inheritance in May 2010 was one of the most challenging for fifty years, worse than the situation Wilson faced in 1974 or arguably even Thatcher in 1979. Yes, he had the good fortune to face Ed Miliband as Labour leader – Miliband's brother and leadership contender in 2010, David, would have posed a greater challenge – and to have no serious rivals around the Cabinet table to spark a leadership election. Boris Johnson, the one figure with more popular appeal to Tory voters than him, was ruled out by not being in Parliament. Where Blair had, in Gordon Brown, a chancellor who undermined him, significantly damaging his effectiveness as premier, Cameron had a chancellor who enhanced his own authority and effectiveness. Cameron was fortunate too to have William Hague affirming his leadership, especially earlier in his premiership, with all the authority and experience a former party leader carries. His decision to form a coalition with the Liberal Democrats usefully shielded him from unpopular decisions, particularly over public spending cuts. By entering the coalition, the Liberal Democrats believed they were taking a brave decision – albeit one that would cost them dear at the polls.

But there the blessings end. Cameron's difficulty in managing his party was exacerbated by his failure to win an overall majority in May

2010. He came to power at a time of the worst economic crisis since the 1930s. His response was to say that the coalition was 'governing in the national interest' – a phrase which imbued his speeches and statements for most of his first twelve months in power. The constraints of the economy and coalition politics were never far from the surface. Like Konrad Adenauer, chancellor of West Germany (1949–63), Cameron displayed uncanny instincts for holding his party and coalition together, but did not win over hearts and minds.

Cameron came to power at a time of widespread anti-establishment feeling and disillusion across the nation. It contributed to British politics being in an unusually febrile and volatile state after 2010. The stellar rise of UKIP in 2013–14 threatened the most dangerous split on the right for generations. Cameron had the Conservative press on his back from 2011–13 partly in anger at his setting up the Leveson Inquiry. As with John Major, but unlike with Margaret Thatcher, he had few cheerleaders among the right-wing commentariat or Tory grandees. Most were unwilling or unable to give him credit for his strengths and achievements, or to credit his difficulties. The Fixed-Term Parliaments Act 2011, designed to bind the coalition together, denied him the opportunity to call an election at a moment of his own choosing, depriving him of a critical tool in disciplining his party. He faced a turbulent House of Lords, an assertive judiciary, rampant Scottish nationalism, and EU laws that constrained his ability to limit immigration from the EU.

Such difficulties explain some if not all of Cameron's problems. His unforced error in presiding over a confused message in the 2010 general election proved to be crucial. Direction of the Conservative campaign was split, and the prospectus divided between the optimistic if inchoate 'Big Society' and the overdone pessimism of austerity on the economy. The election could have been won outright against a discredited prime minister and Labour Party, and a country disillusioned with thirteen years of Labour rule. Cameron was thus to a significant extent the author of some of his own problems during these five years. He was determined not to preside over the same divided campaign in the 2015 election. Vindication followed with the party achieving an overall majority, its first in twenty-three years. Cameron's outright victory confounded the predictions of opinion pollsters and many commentators from both sides of the political spectrum. Critics said he only won because of last-minute fears of an SNP–Labour alliance, but research suggests economic arguments and Cameron's qualities over Miliband were decisive. Victory shattered Miliband's Labour Party as well as Clegg's Liberal Democrats. Both parties lost their leaders after the general election and immediately descended into disarray. The Conservatives, despite their slender majority, gained a political hegemony and confidence in the months that followed which they have not known since before Black Wednesday in 1992.

On perhaps the greatest political issue of his day, the European Union, which had torn his party apart for fifty years since Macmillan first tried to gain British entry in 1961, Cameron should be criticised for arriving in office with little coherent plan beyond a naive aspiration that it must not overshadow his premiership. When he produced a strategy in January 2013 with the referendum pledge, he too often gave the impression that he was reacting to events rather than mastering them. That said, no Conservative leader since Britain joined the European Community in 1973, Thatcher included, had held the party together on Europe. His grasping the referendum might yet bring the party a degree of unity on the EU, or at least acceptance, that it has lacked for forty years.

Cameron's deficiencies as a long-term, strategic thinker are another criticism, notably in foreign policy. Again and again in these pages, we see a short-term, reactive premier, the Cameron often portrayed in the press. But the attack should not be overplayed or judged devoid of context. If Cameron lacked principles, how do we explain his standing by Plan A on the economy, gay marriage and the decision to spend 0.7% of GNP on international development? He expended considerable political capital in remaining fixed on each of these policies. The five years were characterised by an uneasy mix of dogged adherence to such policies while displaying marked flexibility on others. He stuck by what he deemed the most important factors: coalition survival and economic recovery. Circumstances openly militated against long-termism, and flexibility is a virtue as well as a vice; often for Cameron it was additionally a necessity.

The economic recovery of 2010–15 defined the character of the coalition and Cameron's premiership. Economists will argue whether the deficit should have been cut more quickly, or slowly, and whether it was the global economy rather than government policy which was more responsible for the restoration of economic fortunes. Osborne's failure to eliminate the structural deficit during the life of the parliament, a commitment abandoned after only two years, brought much criticism at the time, though government spending as a proportion of GDP fell from some 45% to 40%, which is a significant reduction in such a short period. In only five years in power, Cameron and Osborne achieved a reduction in public spending as a proportion of GDP approximately equal to the reduction achieved by Thatcher during the whole of her eleven years in power. By 2014 Britain had the fastest growth rate in the G7, with a strong record on job creation, and falling unemployment (2.2 million more were in work than in 2010), helped by low inflation and low interest rates.

Cameron and Osborne stuck by Plan A, albeit with modification, in the face of severe pressure, particularly during 2011–13. Public spending cuts were painfully felt, particularly by the young, who saw their benefits decline while pensioners were protected. Recovery was hampered by the continuing eurozone crisis and slowdown in global economic growth, but was helped by the fall in oil prices. Productivity remained sluggish by international standards, and real wages struggled to recover to pre-recession levels. The rise in living standards was skewed towards the south-east, which only began to be addressed by Osborne in his Northern Powerhouse strategy from mid-2014. Cameron invested great energy for a prime minister in his role as 'chief salesman' for the UK abroad, galvanising British companies to export, though export growth remained disappointing. He and Osborne worked hard to inject a more entrepreneurial spirit into British industry, symbolised by Tech-City in East London.

Osborne's contribution to this government and Cameron's premiership was seminal. Like Cameron, he grew in stature over the five years, recovering strongly from his personal errors of judgement early on, notably the failure to win the 2010 general election and the omnishambles Budget of 2012. He was responsible for much of the tactical thinking of the government, though Cameron would overrule if Osborne was being too tactical or he considered his judgement was wrong. The most instinctive political operator in Cameron's team,

Osborne also possessed the quickest and subtlest mind. He was the most media-savvy and calculating of Cameron's team: the others, including Cameron, could be almost guileless by comparison. Cameron delegated Budgets and fiscal events to Osborne, but he was always the more dominant, as when he prevented Osborne from reducing income tax to 40% in the 2012 budget, deterring him from laying into the Lib Dems and gaining tactical advantage at the expense of long-term strategy. He gave him cover and succour when deeply wounded for much of 2012. They spoke to each other almost every morning and every evening over the five years, enjoying the most successful and harmonious political relationship at the top of the last hundred years. The secret of the success was the way they complemented each other: to an uncanny degree they thought as one.

Osborne always knew when to bite his lip, defer to Cameron's seniority, and, uniquely in modern British politics, neither the PM's nor the chancellor's teams ever briefed against the other. There were differences of emphasis, certainly, and in these, Cameron's view prevailed. Osborne would have preferred to have been more aggressively liberal on social issues, more of a neocon on foreign policy, tougher on colleagues and backbenchers, and more of a tax and economic reformer, though it was the economic situation rather than Cameron that was the principal restraint. Cameron, the older figure by five years, was always more of a shire Tory, while Osborne was more of an urban liberal.

School reform took prominence among domestic achievements, the work of one minister above all: Michael Gove. He ferociously drove through a series of controversial reforms to make exams more rigorous, to improve the quality of teaching and to give schools more autonomy, establishing an altogether new breed of 'free schools', while greatly accelerating Labour's programme of academies. When Gove was moved in July 2014, his successor Nicky Morgan was given clear instructions to continue his crusade, albeit with a more conciliatory approach. The success of the education reform agenda is far from established, however, with many academies struggling to meet expectations set for them, while the mark on social mobility will not be seen for many years.

Welfare was the second major domestic achievement, with Iain Duncan Smith introducing significant if contentious reforms to the benefits system to ensure that welfare was targeted at the most deserving, and those out of work were encouraged back into employment. He stuck doggedly to his flagship policy, Universal Credit, and against the odds, remained in office throughout the parliament and into the next. Many of his welfare reforms have already contributed towards fiscal consolidation and shifting the terms of the public debate on welfare. Health policy was more uneven still, with two very different phases: a difficult two years when Andrew Lansley tried to introduce some important if flawed reforms to the NHS, and a second when Jeremy Hunt drove through amended reforms and pacified the NHS so that it was not the predominant issue at the 2015 election. The reforms remain highly controversial, the subject of avid continuing debate, while fundamental issues of affordability are left unresolved. At the Home Office, often the most difficult department of state, Theresa May ran a tighter ship than many of her predecessors, battled to control non-EU immigration, and oversaw a reduction in crime despite severe cuts in the Home Office budget. Domestic successes came in several other areas, including public sector reform, but not in others, with plans for elected mayors in major British cities being largely rejected in local referenda. The record on new housing, the environment and reducing poverty, even with Lib Dem interventions, remained weak. With much of the domestic policy agenda still awaiting validation and in want of overall coherence, Cameron has further to go before he can be seen as a great social reforming prime minister.

Northern Ireland enjoyed its most peaceful five-year period since the 1960s, due in part to Cameron's June 2010 acknowledgement of the culpability of the British army on Bloody Sunday in 1972. In mainland Britain, despite cuts, austerity and high unemployment, civil unrest and trade union disruption were largely avoided, with the notable exceptions of the protests over student tuition fees in November and December 2010, and the riots in London and other cities in the summer of 2011. Fusilier Lee Rigby in May 2013 was the only British citizen to be murdered due to Islamist terrorism on British soil during the five years, despite a considerable rise in threat levels. Many plots, including some of 7/7 proportions, were foiled, through the skill, resourcing and legal powers of the intelligence services and police, together with a degree of good fortune. The

London Olympics proceeded without incident in the summer of 2012. Cameron spoke forcefully about combating terrorism in February 2011, and would have wanted to go further in these five years to combat the threat both in the UK and abroad. He determined to do more if he secured a second term, perhaps recognising that not enough had been done to engage with leaders in the Muslim community. But throughout 2010–15, his close personal alertness to the threat of terrorism on the streets of Britain, and his wish to reduce the risk, was forensic.

Cameron's record as a leader abroad, however, is much more mixed. He seized the initiative over British troop withdrawal from Afghanistan in 2014, and worked hard to try to ensure that the hand-over to the Afghans was smooth. Credit is due for the timely and orderly way he brought Britain's involvement in this long-running war to an end. Another lesson he learnt from Blair's government was to avoid any hint of 'sofa government' as seen during the Iraq War in 2003. He thus set up the National Security Council soon after the general election in 2010, which met weekly and which he himself chaired. The organisation's first great test came over British intervention in Libya. This was driven by Cameron personally, backed by all members of the NSC and in Cabinet, and additionally supported by a United Nations resolution. The conclusion of the war and the downfall of Gaddafi in the autumn of 2011 brought Cameron short-term acclaim. He hoped, along with many others in the heady initial days of the Arab Spring, for a new dawn of democracy sweeping across the Arab world. This optimism faltered during the following years as it became clear that Libya had descended into violence and tribal infighting, and with Syria falling into civil war. His attempt to involve Britain militarily against Assad in August 2013 after he used chemical weapons against his own people produced his biggest foreign policy reversal of these years. The Commons defeat, and the deteriorating position in Libya, the two big question marks of his premiership, contributed to a loss of assertiveness by him in the final year and a half leading up to the general election in 2015. Humanitarian instincts drove him to intervene in Libya in 2011, and to try to intervene in Syria in 2013. He was not the first British leader whose aspirations in the region were to be thwarted by forces far more powerful than anything they could control. He can be criticised certainly for acting; equally, inaction would have resulted in opprobrium, and possible risk.

The recovery of the British economy and Cameron's relationship with President Obama, trumpeted again in a late visit to Washington in January 2015, were significant in countering the widespread narrative about a loss of British influence on the world stage. Britain's standing in the world in 2015 was certainly no higher than it had been in 2010, with many arguing it had diminished. It is thus hard to discern a consistent shape and intent of Cameron's foreign policy during these five years, though he succeeded in keeping Britain safe, improving the relationship with the US after the Brown years and in promoting the British brand abroad. But it was not a time of heroes. Other national leaders in the West struggled to assert themselves on the world stage. Obama, Hollande, and leaders across the EU all experienced difficulties given the economic climate, the rise of China and India, Putin's aggression in Ukraine, and militant Islam's success in Syria and Iraq. Only Merkel in Germany emerged with credit from these difficult five years, though continuing difficulties facing the eurozone dented her authority.

If Cameron is seen to have succeeded on his big challenges during 2010–15, and to have introduced some important reforms along the way, then it follows that his team in Number 10 is unlikely to have been poor, as commentators frequently alleged over the five years. Number 10 went through a steep learning curve after May 2010, at times anarchic and ill-disciplined with Hilton there, but operating with increasing efficiency and effectiveness from 2012–13, for which Cameron's three principal lieutenants – Ed Llewellyn, Kate Fall, and Craig Oliver – must take credit. All three eschewed becoming figures in their own right, unlike many in the courts of Thatcher and Blair. If this was in part a dual premiership with Osborne, it was also equally to some extent a collective premiership.

Cameron will leave office before 2020, and the ultimate verdict of history on him will depend on three principal questions: how he resolves Britain's place in Europe, the continuing success of the economy, and resolving the Scottish (and English) questions. Reforming public services, and keeping Britain secure from the threat of terrorism, are other areas. But much can be said now about his achievement during 2010–15. He won two referenda, the first on AV and the second on Scotland, if not by a decisive margin on the latter, and with many questions left open. The startling resurgence of the Scottish National Party and its transformation of electoral politics north of the border sent shock waves through the British body politic, which he has yet to pacify and resolve.

He has led the Conservative Party for a turbulent nine and a half years; his three predecessors survived just eight years between them. The party is stronger and more unified after the 2015 election than it has been since Thatcher fell twenty-five years before, though it is questionable whether he has redefined modern conservatism in his image and whether the early journey to 'detoxify' the Tory brand will ever be completed. More pressingly, it remains to be seen how Cameron will manage the internal fallout from the EU referendum, whatever the result, and whether deep-seated divisions will return as damagingly as ever. If he can lead his party and the country into a new and settled accommodation with Europe, it will rank as the greatest of all his achievements.

Cameron's mark on the nation is still taking shape, though the contours of his premiership between 2010 and 2015 are clear. At the outset of the book, we pondered whether Cameron had claim to be considered as the twenty-first-century Stanley Baldwin. While Baldwin's place in history has been damaged by his failure to prepare the country sufficiently for war, he nevertheless bestrode the politics of the early twentieth century. He provided reassurance domestically during one of the most volatile and uncertain periods in British history. Though the circumstances of 2010–15 are markedly different, Cameron's achievements in governing a country emerging from a major financial crisis, charting a course through a divided Europe and amid an international order rocked by terrorism and fundamentalism, rank alongside Baldwin's. It will be a measure of the success of Cameron's second term if he can provide the leadership for Britain on the *world stage* which Baldwin so spectacularly failed to do in the 1930s.

The government of 2010–15 compares favourably with Thatcher's first term 1979–83, and comfortably outshines Blair's from 1997–

2001. While the achievements of the government of 2010–15 were uneven, by holding the coalition together, and providing stability at a time of economic renewal, he will be considered – whatever else may happen in the remainder of his premiership – as a figure of real historical interest and substance.

Acknowledgements

We would like to thank above all the team of researchers who worked with us on the book. We were fortunate to have had our principal researchers Jonathan Meakin and Illias Thoms from start to finish. Illias concentrated primarily on domestic politics and policy including the economy, welfare and health reforms, while Jonathan handled US relations and foreign policy more generally, including Afghanistan, Libya, Syria, Russia and China. Both conducted some interviews, oversaw the production of briefs and incorporated feedback from readers, as well as contributing to the writing of the chapters themselves, both intellectually and factually. Hayley Carr, who worked with us for much of the writing phase, was critical in organising the office, facilitating the interviews and the throughput of work, and ensuring the successful completion of the book.

The team worked as a small and close-knit group putting in quite exceptionally long hours, seven days a week. We would also like to express our deep gratitude to, in order of length attached to the project, Jennie Doyle and Khurram Jowiya, Beth Oppenheim, Mark Davies, Ruari Hutchinson and Alison Warrick. We have always said to research teams we have worked with in the past that, in order to be successful, we must work at least as hard as Number 10. Each individual rose to this challenge and more. We are sure they will all go on to remarkable careers and we wish them every success.

We would also like to thank those (necessarily anonymous) ministers, aides and officials, Conservative and Liberal Democrat politicians, staff members and activists for interviews and for reading either the whole book or specific sections and providing comments to ensure the accuracy of the story.

We would like to thank professors Vernon Bogdanor, George Jones and Dennis Kavanagh for reading an early stage of the full book, and Christopher Everett, Mike Finn and Anthony Goodenough for reading the proofs. Philip Collins and James Naughtie provided useful insights towards the end of the project. A final thanks to Professor Stuart Ball, as ever, for advice on Conservative history.

We were very fortunate to have *Cameron at 10* published by William Collins. In particular we would like to thank our editor, Martin Redfern, for guiding us through the project with such professionalism, skill and attention to detail. We are hugely grateful for the sterling work by our copy-editor David Milner, and to the indexer, David Atkinson. Also at William Collins we would like to thank the stellar Kate Tolley, Katherine Patrick, Caroline Crofts and Minna Fry for their expertise. From the outset, we had a very clear image of what we wanted *Cameron at 10* to offer, and we would like to thank Andrew Parsons and Saddika Ozkan at I-Images for providing some of the superb photographs that illuminate the story. Andrew Enston also deserves credit for assisting with photographic selection.

Our final thanks go to Susan Thomas for co-ordinating the safe storage of all the research material at the Bodleian Library, and the British Academy/Leverhulme small-grants team, including Dr Ken Emond, Claire McDonagh and Ratha Saravanakumar, for supporting our primary research to further the field of humanities and social sciences.

Peter Snowdon in particular would like to thank Anthony Seldon. From mentor to collaborator, Anthony has been a great source of wisdom and encouragement for nearly twenty years. Andrew Gordon, at David Higham Associates, has been exemplary, offering sound advice from the outset. I am grateful to all my colleagues at the BBC for their support, in particular Jamie Angus, Victoria Wakely and Ollie Stone Lee at the *Today* programme, as well as Nick Robinson, Norman Smith and other colleagues in Westminster. Malcolm Balen provided valuable and insightful comments from start to finish. As on many other projects, Daniel Collings has been a constant source of wisdom and encouragement. Finally, I would like to thank my family and especially my wife Julia, for her love, heroic patience and support. My son, William (nearly two years old at the time of writing), will be relieved that *Cameron at 10* will not feature in his selection of bedtime stories – at least for a while!

Anthony Seldon in particular would like to thank the following: first and foremost Peter Snowdon, whom I have known since he was an A level student. I have watched his career progress with pride as he has developed into a fine writer and shrewd political judge. At Wellington College I would like to thank my outstanding PAs Angela Reed and Hani Edwards, and all my colleagues, governors and students. I would like to thank the vast numbers of contacts in and outside Whitehall and academic life with whom I have worked for thirty years on these inside books. Finally, I would like to thank my wife, Joanna, and my three children, Jessica, Susannah and Adam. Without them, the writing of this book would have been impossible.

Bibliography

Acemoglu, Daron, and James A. Robinson, *Why Nations Fail: The Origins of Power, Prosperity, and Poverty* (Crown Business: 2012)

Adonis, Andrew, *5 Days in May: The Coalition and Beyond* (Biteback: 2013)

Allen, Graham, and Iain Duncan Smith, *Early Intervention: Good Parents. Great Kids. Better Citizens* (Centre for Social Justice: 2008)

Bell, Anthony, and David Witter, *The Libyan Revolution, Part 1: Roots of Rebellion* (Institute for the Study of War: September 2011)

Bell, Anthony, and David Witter, *The Libyan Revolution, Part 2: Escalation and Intervention* (Institute for the Study of War: September 2011)

Bell, Anthony, and David Witter, *The Libyan Revolution, Part 3: Stalemate and Siege* (Institute for the Study of War: October 2011)

Bell, Anthony, Spencer Butts, and David Witter, *The Libyan Revolution, Part 4: The Tide Turns* (Institute for the Study of War: November 2011)

Brien, Stephen, *Dynamic Benefits: Towards Welfare that Works* (Centre for Social Justice: 2009)

Chalmers, Malcolm, *Mind the Gap: The MoD's Emerging Budgetary Challenge* (Royal United Services Institute: 9 March 2015)

Cockburn, Patrick, *The Rise of Islamic State: ISIS and the New Sunni Revolution* (Verso Books, reprint: 2015)

d'Ancona, Matthew, *In It Together: The Inside Story of the Coalition Government* (Penguin, second edition: 2014)

Department for Education, *The Importance of Teaching: The Schools White Paper 2010* (2010)

Elliott, Francis, and James Hanning, *Cameron: Practically a Conservative* (Fourth Estate, third edition: 2012)

Fairweather, James, *The Good War: Why We Couldn't Win the War or the Peace in Afghanistan* (Jonathan Cape: 2014)

Farage, Nigel, *The Purple Revolution: The Year That Changed Everything* (Biteback, second edition: 2015)

Ford, Robert, and Matthew Goodwin, *Revolt on the Right: Explaining Support for the Radical Right in Britain* (Routledge: 2014)

Ganesh, Janan, *George Osborne: The Austerity Chancellor* (Biteback, second edition: 2014)

Gove, Michael, *Celsius 7/7* (Weidenfeld & Nicolson: 2006)

Hazell, Robert, and Ben Yong, *The Politics of Coalition: How the Conservative–Liberal Democrat Government Works* (Hart Publishing: 2012)

Hirsch Jr., E. D., *Cultural Literacy: What Every American Needs to Know* (Houghton Mifflin: 1987)

Hirsch Jr., E. D., *The Schools We Need: And Why We Don't Have Them* (Random House: 1996)

International Institute for Strategic Studies, *The Military Balance 2015* (11 February 2015)

Journal of Public Heath, 'A Qualitative Study of the "Bedroom Tax"' (15 March 2015)

Kornelius, Stefan, *Angela Merkel: The Authorized Biography* (English translation, Alma Books: 2013)

Laws, David, *22 Days in May: The Birth of the Lib Dem–Conservative Coalition* (Biteback: 2010)

Macwhirter, Iain, *Disunited Kingdom: How Westminster Won a Referendum But Lost Scotland* (Cargo Publishing: 2014)

Norman, Jesse, *Edmund Burke: The Visionary who Invented Modern Politics* (William Collins, second edition: 2014)

Oliver, Neil, *A History of Scotland* (Weidenfeld & Nicolson: 2009)

Purnell, Sonia, *Boris: A Tale of Blond Ambition* (Aurum Press, second edition: 2012)

Reconstruction: Plan for a Strong Economy (Conservative Party: 11 September 2008)

Richards, David, *Taking Command* (Headline: 2014)

Salmond, Alex, *The Dream Shall Never Die: 100 Days that Changed Scotland Forever* (William Collins: 2015)

Seldon, Anthony, and Mike Finn (eds), *The Coalition Effect, 2010–2015* (Cambridge University Press: 2015)

Seldon, Anthony, and Guy Lodge, *Brown at 10* (Biteback, reprint edition: 2011)

Seldon, Anthony, *Blair* (Free Press, second edition: 2005)

Seldon, Anthony, *Major: A Political Life* (Weidenfeld & Nicolson: 1997)

Snowdon, Peter, *Back from the Brink: The Extraordinary Fall and Rise of the Conservative Party* (HarperPress, second edition: 2010)

The Coalition: Our Programme for Government (Cabinet Office: 2010)

Timmins, Nicholas, *Never Again* (Institute for Government/King's Fund: 2012)

Wellings, Richard, *Failure to Transform: High-speed Rail and the Regeneration Myth*, IEA Current Controversies Paper No. 48 (April 2014)

Wilson, Rob, *5 Days to Power* (Biteback: 2010)

Documentaries

Boris Johnson: The Irresistible Rise, BBC film, Michael Cockerell, 25 March 2013

The Liberal Who Came to Power, BBC Radio 4, 17 February 2014

Under Attack: The Threat from Cyberspace, BBC Radio 4, 8 July 2013

The Syria Vote: One Day in August, BBC Radio 4, 10 November 2014

Five Days that Changed Britain, BBC Parliament, Nick Robinson, 10 January 2011

Notes

Interviewees who agreed to be quoted by name are referred to below, in addition to other published sources. To avoid endlessly repeating the words 'Private interview' and 'Private information', off-the-record references are not cited individually.

Introduction

1. For an analysis of the policy record of the coalition government, see Anthony Seldon and Mike Finn (eds), *The Coalition Effect, 2010–2015* (2015)
2. Benedict Brogan, *Daily Telegraph*, 5 October 2011
3. Stuart Ball, *Portrait of a Party: The Conservative Party in Britain* (2013), p. 468
4. Interview, Stuart Ball
5. Interview, Vernon Bogdanor
6. Anthony Seldon, 'Chumocracy', *Sunday Times*, 5 May 2013

Chapter 1

1. Interview, Tom Fletcher
2. Interview, Sir Simon McDonald
3. Interview, Tom Fletcher
4. Interview, Ed Llewellyn
5. Interview, Liz Sugg
6. Interview, Laurence Mann
7. Interview, Tom Fletcher
8. Interview, Laurence Mann
9. Interview, Tom Fletcher
10. Ibid.
11. Ibid.
12. Ibid.

13. Interview, Patrick McLoughlin
14. Interview, Laurence Mann
15. Ibid.
16. Interview, Ed Llewellyn

Chapter 2

1. Anthony Seldon and Guy Lodge, *Brown at 10* (2010), p. 144
2. Ibid., p. 151
3. Francis Elliott and James Hanning, *Cameron: Practically a Conservative* (third edition, 2012), pp. 53–72, 109–30
4. Interview, George Osborne
5. Ibid.
6. Interview, Ed Llewellyn
7. Interview, Oliver Letwin
8. Peter Snowdon, *Back from the Brink: The Extraordinary Rise and Fall of the Conservative Party* (2010), p. 314
9. *Reconstruction: Plan for a Strong Economy*, Conservative Party conference, 11 September 2008
10. Interview, Rupert Harrison
11. *Guardian* website, 9 October 2008
12. Seldon and Lodge, *Brown at 10*, pp. 282–3; *The Times*, 27 December 2014

13. Interview, Matthew Hancock
14. Interview, Oliver Letwin
15. Interview, George Osborne
16. Hansard, 22 April 2009, column 243
17. Seldon and Lodge, *Brown at 10*, p. 258
18. Ibid., pp. 258–9
19. Interview, Rupert Harrison
20. Interview, Matthew Hancock
21. George Osborne, 'It's ridiculous to pretend that there won't be cuts', *The Times*, 15 June 2009
22. George Osborne, Conservative Party conference speech, 2009; Snowdon, *Back from the Brink*, pp. 372–4
23. Snowdon, *Back from the Brink*, p. 372
24. Interview, George Osborne
25. Janan Ganesh, *George Osborne: The Austerity Chancellor* (2012), p. 221
26. Martin Kettle, 'George Osborne's speech did the business', *Guardian* website, 6 October 2009
27. *Telegraph* website, 6 October 2009
28. *Guardian*, 7 January 2010
29. Snowdon, *Back from the Brink*, p. 389
30. Ibid., p. 390
31. Ibid., p. 389
32. George Osborne, Mais Lecture, 'A New Economic Model', February 2010
33. Conservative election poster, 'We can't go on like this. I'll cut the deficit, not the NHS', January 2010

Chapter 3

1. Interview, David Cameron
2. Interview, Liz Sugg
3. Interview, Nick Clegg
4. Interview, Oliver Letwin
5. Ibid.
6. Interview, Kate Fall
7. See Anthony Seldon and Guy Lodge, *Brown at 10* (2010), pp. 454–68
8. Interview, Lord O'Donnell
9. See David Laws, *22 Days in May: The Birth of the Lib Dem–*

Conservative Coalition (2010); Rob Wilson, *5 Days to Power* (2010); Andrew Adonis, *5 Days in May: The Coalition and Beyond* (2013)
10. Interview, William Hague
11. Interview, David Laws
12. Interview, William Hague
13. Interview, Lord O'Donnell
14. Interview, Kenneth Clarke
15. Interview, Oliver Letwin
16. Interview, George Osborne
17. Ibid.
18. Interview, William Hague
19. Interview, Nick Clegg
20. Interview, Lord O'Donnell
21. Ibid.
22. Ibid.
23. Interview, Graham Brady
24. Interview, Laurence Mann
25. Interview, Lena Pietsch
26. Interview, Jonny Oates
27. Interview, Laurence Mann
28. Interview, Andrew Cooper
29. Interview, Lord O'Donnell
30. Interview, Oliver Letwin

Chapter 4

1. Interview, Paul Kirby
2. Interview, David Laws
3. Ibid.
4. Interview, Steve Hilton
5. *Reconstruction: Plan for a Strong Economy*, Conservative Party conference, 11 September 2008
6. BBC News, 24 May 2010
7. David Laws, *22 Days in May: The Birth of the Lib Dem–Conservative Coalition* (2010), p. 232
8. *Observer*, 30 May 2010
9. Interview, Paul Tucker
10. Interview, Danny Alexander
11. Matthew d'Ancona, *In it Together: The Inside Story of the Coalition Government* (2013), p. 47
12. *Guardian* website, 22 June 2010
13. See Chapter 24 for a full account of the battles between the Treasury and DWP
14. Interview, Sir David Richards
15. Hansard, 19 October 2010, Column 798

16. *Securing Britain in an Age of Uncertainty: The Strategic Defence and Security Review*, p. 32
17. BBC News, 20 October 2010
18. Hansard, 20 October 2010, column 949
19. BBC News, 21 October 2010
20. Hansard, 20 October 2010, column 965
21. Interview, Lena Pietsch
22. Ibid.

Chapter 5
1. Interview, Jonathan Caine
2. Interview, Owen Paterson
3. Interview, Tom Fletcher
4. Interview, Jonathan Caine
5. David Cameron speech to the Commons, *Guardian*, 15 June 2010
6. Interview, Tom Fletcher
7. Interview, Jonathan Caine
8. Ibid.
9. Hansard, 15 June 2010, columns 739–42
10. *Guardian*, 18 June 2010
11. Interview, Julian King
12. BBC News, 11 October 2011

Chapter 6
1. Interview, Sir Sherard Cowper-Coles
2. Interview, James Fergusson
3. Ibid.
4. Ibid.
5. Interview, Sir Nigel Sheinwald
6. Interview, Liam Fox
7. Interview, Sir Simon McDonald
8. Interview, Oliver Letwin
9. Interview, Sir Peter Ricketts
10. Ibid.
11. Ibid.
12. Interview, Tom Fletcher
13. Diary, Sir Nick Parker, 11 June 2010
14. Interview, Liz Sugg
15. *New Statesman*, 4 December 2008
16. *Rolling Stone*, 22 June 2010

Chapter 7
1. Interview, Tom Fletcher
2. *Guardian*, 8 September 2010

3. Ben Brogan interview with David Cameron, *Daily Telegraph*, 25 September 2010
4. Interview, Tom Fletcher
5. *Guardian* website, 18 April 2010
6. Interview with ITV before 2010 election, quoted in the *Guardian*, 8 September 2010
7. Interview, Lord Feldman
8. *Guardian* website, 27 July 2010; ibid., 28 July 2010
9. Interview, Tom Fletcher
10. *Guardian*, 25 August 2010
11. *Daily Mail*, 24 August 2010
12. *Guardian*, 25 August 2010
13. Gordon Brown, House of Commons, 25 February 2009
14. Interview, Lord Feldman
15. Interview, David Cameron
16. Ibid.

Chapter 8
1. *Telegraph* website, 4 October 2010
2. *Guardian*, 27 January 2007
3. Matthew d'Ancona, *In It Together: The Inside Story of the Coalition Government* (2013), p. 74.
4. Francis Elliott and James Hanning, *Cameron: Practically a Conservative* (third edition, 2012), p. 451
5. *Guardian* website, 9 July 2009
6. *Guardian*, 25 February 2010
7. Elliott and Hanning, *Cameron: Practically a Conservative*, pp. 452–3
8. *Observer*, 10 July 2011
9. *New York Times*, 5 September 2010
10. *Daily Telegraph*, 21 December 2010
11. *Guardian* website, 5 January 2011
12. Ibid., 21 January 2011
13. David Cameron, Andy Coulson Resignation Statement, 21 January 2011
14. Interview, Lord Feldman
15. *Independent*, 22 January 2011
16. David Cameron, Twitter, 6 October 2012
17. *New Statesman*, 'Cameron's Ten Biggest U-turns', 17 February 2011
18. BBC *Panorama*, 25 April 2012

19. Hansard, 30 June 2011, column 55WS
20. BBC News, 13 July 2011
21. Hansard, 20 July 2011, column 921
22. BBC News, 20 July 2011
23. Hansard, 13 July 2011, column 314
24. *Guardian* website, 25 April 2013
25. BBC News, 4 July 2014
26. Ibid., 24 July 2014
27. *Daily Telegraph*, 25 June 2012
28. *Guardian* website, 21 November 2014

Chapter 9
1. Interview, Liam Fox
2. BBC News, 21 February 2011
3. *Guardian*, 20 February 2011
4. Cabinet Secretary's Review of papers relating to the release of Abdelbaset al-Megrahi, Cabinet Office, 7 February 2011
5. Anthony Bell and David Witter, *The Libyan Revolution, Part 2: Escalation and Intervention* (Institute for the Study of War, September 2011), p. 14
6. *Guardian* website, 22 February 2011
7. *Guardian*, 6 March 2011
8. Dell and Witter, p. 18
9. Interview, Sir David Richards
10. David Gardner, *Last Chance*, quoted in James Buchan, 'On a Knife edge', *Guardian*, 3 May 2009
11. Interview, Liam Fox
12. Patrick Wintour and Nicholas Watt, *Guardian*, 2 October 2011
13. Interview, Sir Simon McDonald
14. Matthew d'Ancona, *Sunday Telegraph*, 20 March 2011
15. Wintour and Watt, *Guardian*, 2 October 2011
16. d'Ancona, *Sunday Telegraph*, 20 March 2011
17. Interview, Sir Peter Ricketts
18. Interview, Sir Peter Westmacott
19. Bell and Witter, *The Libyan Revolution, Part 2*, pp. 24–5
20. *Sunday Telegraph*, 26 March 2011
21. *Guardian*, 25 March 2011
22. Interview, Sir David Richards

23. Wintour and Watt, *Guardian*, 2 October 2011
24. Ibid.
25. Ibid.
26. Ibid.
27. Anthony Bell, Spencer Butts and David Witter, *The Libyan Revolution, Part 4: The Tide Turns* (Institute for the Study of War, November 2011), p. 17
28. Ibid., p. 21
29. Interview, Gabby Bertin
30. James Forsyth, *Spectator* blog, 20 September 2011

Chapter 10
1. Interview, Lord O'Donnell
2. Interview, Patrick McLoughlin
3. Interview, William Hague
4. Interview, Julian Astle
5. Interview, Nick Clegg
6. Matthew d'Ancona, *In It Together: The Inside Story of the Coalition Government* (2013), p. 79
7. Interview, Matthew Elliott
8. *Guardian*/ICM poll, 3 December 2010
9. *New Statesman*, 11 May 2011
10. Reuters/Ipsos MORI Political Monitor – AV Questions, 25 February 2011
11. Janan Ganesh, *George Osborne: The Austerity Chancellor* (2012), p. 273
12. ConservativeHome, 16 February 2011
13. Interview, Lord Feldman
14. Tim Montgomerie, 'The Story of the AV Campaign', http://conservativehomeblogs.com/avstory/, 5 July 2011
15. http://www.bbc.co.uk/news/uk-politics-12504935
16. Interview, Matthew Elliott
17. *Guardian*/ICM poll, 18 April 2011
18. Interview, Stephen Gilbert
19. Interview, Nick Clegg
20. BBC Radio 4, *The Liberal Who Came to Power*, 17 February 2014
21. Ibid.
22. Interview, David Willetts
23. *Guardian*, 3 March 2011

24. BBC Radio 4, *Today*, 3 May 2011
25. Interview, Nick Clegg
26. Interview, Oliver Letwin
27. BBC Radio 4, *The Liberal Who Came to Power*, 17 February 2014
28. Interview, Danny Alexander
29. Interview, Julian Astle
30. Interview, Oliver Letwin
31. Interview, Nick Clegg

Chapter 11

1. Neil Oliver, *A History of Scotland* (2009), p. 294
2. Interview, Ed Llewellyn
3. Severin Carrell, Nicholas Watt and Patrick Wintour, 'The Real Story of the Scottish Referendum: Britain on the brink', *Guardian*, 15 December 2014
4. *Daily Mail*, 19 August 2013; Ed Lowther, 'How Scottish is David Cameron?', BBC News website, 7 February 2014
5. BBC News, 14 May 2010
6. Ibid.
7. Interview, Danny Alexander
8. Ibid.
9. Interview, Andrew Dunlop
10. Carrell, Watt and Wintour, *Guardian*, 15 December 2014
11. Hansard, 10 January 2012, column 51
12. Carrell, Watt and Wintour, *Guardian*, 15 December 2014
13. Ibid.
14. Interview, Andrew Cooper
15. http://www.gettyimages.co.uk/detail/news-photo/prime-minister-david-cameron-gives-a-speech-at-the-apex-news-photo/139060650
16. ConservativeHome, 7 October 2011; interview, Julian Glover
17. Transcript of David Cameron's Scotland speech, 16 February 2012
18. Ibid.
19. *Sunday Times*, 14 October 2012
20. Interview, Ed Llewellyn

Chapter 12

1. Matthew d'Ancona, *In It Together: The Inside Story of the Coalition Government* (2013), p. 140
2. Interview, Liz Sugg
3. BBC Radio 4, *Today*, 9 August 2011
4. BBC News, 9 August 2011
5. *Guardian* website, 9 August 2011
6. Ibid.
7. Ibid.
8. Ibid.
9. Ibid.
10. Boris Johnson, interviewed in *Boris Johnson: The Irresistible Rise*, BBC film, Michael Cockerell, 25 March 2013
11. d'Ancona, *In It Together*, p. 145
12. *Guardian* website, 10 August 2011
13. Ibid.
14. BBC Radio 4, *The World at One*, 10 August 2011
15. BBC News, 10 August 2011
16. Interview, Craig Oliver
17. Hansard, 11 August 2011, column 1,053
18. Ibid., column 1,131
19. Ibid., column 1,057
20. Interview, Steve Hilton

Chapter 13

1. Interview, Lord Feldman
2. Matthew d'Ancona, *In it Together: The Inside Story of the Coalition Government* (2013), p. 188
3. Interview, David Cameron
4. Peter Snowdon, *Back from the Brink: The Extraordinary Rise and Fall of the Conservative Party* (2010), pp. 224–42
5. Steve Hilton to Tim Chatwin, email, 21 December 2009
6. Interview, David Cameron
7. Interview, Steve Hilton
8. Ibid.
9. Interview, Tim Chatwin
10. Interview, Oliver Letwin
11. Interview, Francis Maude
12. Interview, Michael Lynas
13. Interview, Lord O'Donnell
14. Interview, Steve Hilton

15. David Cameron, Big Society Speech, 19 July 2010
16. *Financial Times*, 23 July 2010
17. Interview, Tim Colbourne
18. *Guardian*, 14 February 2011
19. *Independent*, 15 February 2011
20. Interview, Steve Hilton
21. BBC News online, 23 May 2011
22. *Spectator*, 25 May 2011
23. *Daily Telegraph*, 6 July 2011
24. Interview, Lord Kerslake
25. *The Times*, 20 January 2015

Chapter 14
1. Interview, David Cameron
2. *Sun*, 26 September 2007
3. David Laws, *22 Days in May: The Birth of the Lib Dem–Conservative Coalition* (2010), p. 185
4. *Liberal Democrat Manifesto* (2010), p. 67
5. Interview, Nick Clegg
6. BBC News, 8 September 2011
7. *Guardian* website, 24 October 2011
8. Interview, David Cameron
9. *Guardian*, 5 December 2011
10. *EurActiv.com*, 5 December 2011
11. Interview, Tim Colbourne
12. Nick Clegg, *The Andrew Marr Show*, 11 December 2011
13. Interview, Lena Pietsch
14. Hansard, 12 December 2011, column 519
15. Interview, Andrew Cooper
16. *Spectator* website, 14 December 2011
17. BBC News, 13 December 2011
18. http://www.boston.com/news/world/europe/articles/2011/12/15/uk_insists_it_will_help_europes_new_fiscal_pact/
19. *Daily Mail*, 'Day PM Put Britain First: Defiant Cameron Stands Up To Euro Bullies', 10 December 2011
20. Interview, Tim Colbourne

Chapter 15
1. David Cameron, Conservative Party conference speech, 4 October 2006

2. Andrew Lansley, Conservative Party press release, 11 July 2007
3. David Cameron, speech to the Royal College of Nursing, 11 May 2009
4. David Cameron, speech to the Royal College of Pathologists, 2 November 2009
5. *The Coalition: Our Programme for Government* (2010), p. 24
6. Sir David Nicholson, NHS Alliance conference, 18 November 2010
7. David Cameron, Foreword to the Spring 2008 Conference Paper
8. Nicholas Timmins, *Never Again*, Institute for Government/King's Fund (2012); *Independent*, 10 July 2012
9. Matthew d'Ancona, *In It Together: The Inside Story of the Coalition Government* (2013), p. 99
10. Simon Stevens, *Financial Times*, 15 July 2010
11. d'Ancona, *In It Together*, p. 106
12. Timmins, *Never Again*, p. 96
13. Ibid.
14. *Guardian* website, 6 April 2011
15. Robert Hazell and Ben Yong, *The Politics of Coalition: How the Conservative–Liberal Democrat Government Works* (2012), p. 182
16. *Observer*, 10 March 2012
17. Interview, Lord Feldman
18. Interview, David Cameron
19. 'NHS Five Year Forward View', 23 October 2014

Chapter 16
1. 'Statement by the President on the Passing of Leonard Nimoy', the White House, 27 February 2015; Anthony Seldon and Guy Lodge, *Brown at 10* (2010), p. 229
2. Barack Obama, Westminster Hall, 25 May 2011
3. *Guardian*, 14 March 2012
4. *Time* website, 14 March 2012
5. BBC News, 13 March 2012
6. Matthew d'Ancona, *In It Together: The Inside Story of the Coalition Government* (2013), p. 232

7. Interview, Sir Peter Westmacott
8. d'Ancona, *In It Together*, p. 232
9. Interview, Jonny Oates.

Chapter 17
1. Matthew d'Ancona, *In It Together: The Inside Story of the Coalition Government* (2013), p. 232
2. Interview, Rupert Harrison
3. Janan Ganesh, *George Osborne: The Austerity Chancellor* (2012), p. 281
4. BBC News, 1 February 2012
5. James Browne, 'The 50p income tax rate', Institute for Fiscal Studies (2012); Ganesh, *George Osborne*, p. 283
6. Interview, Julian Astle
7. Interview, Nick Clegg
8. Tim Montgomerie, 'Tories should support more property taxes if proceeds are used to cut other, more harmful taxes', http://conservativehomeblogs.com, 29 August 2012
9. Interview, Nick Clegg
10. Interview, Julian Astle
11. Interview, Danny Alexander
12. Hansard, 21 March 2012, column 810
13. Interview, George Osborne
14. *Guardian*, 28 August 2012
15. Interview, George Osborne
16. *Daily Telegraph*, 28 March 2012
17. *Financial Times*, 6 March 2012
18. BBC News, 23 April 2012
19. Interview, George Osborne
20. BBC News, 29 May 2012
21. *Guardian*, 7 June 2012
22. Interview, Andrew Cooper
23. Interview, Danny Alexander

Chapter 18
1. Interview, Lord Feldman
2. *Guardian*, 4 September 2011
3. David Cameron, Twitter, 6 July 2014
4. *The Times*, 25 February 2015
5. Interview, Ed Llewellyn
6. *Daily Telegraph*, 26 July 2012
7. BBC Radio 4, *Under Attack: The Threat from Cyberspace*, 8 July 2013

8. BBC News, 31 December 1999
9. *Daily Telegraph*, 30 July 2012
10. *Guardian*, 3 September 2012
11. Ibid.
12. Interview, George Osborne
13. Interview, Lord Feldman
14. Interview, Iain Duncan Smith
15. Ibid.

Chapter 19
1. YouGov, 27 June 2012
2. Politico, 27 October 2011
3. *Conservative Manifesto* (2010), p. 67
4. *Liberal Democrat Manifesto* (2010), p. 88
5. BBC Radio 4, *The Liberal Who Came to Power*, 17 February 2014
6. *The Coalition: Our Programme for Government* (2010), p. 27
7. Interview, Oliver Letwin
8. *The Times*, 27 June 2012
9. *Guardian* website, 27 June 2012
10. Jesse Norman, *Observer*, 1 July 2012
11. Ibid.
12. Interview, Lord Strathclyde
13. Interview, Julian Astle
14. *Guardian* website, 6 July 2012
15. Ibid.
16. Ibid.
17. Ibid.
18. ITV Meridian News, 9 July 2012
19. Interview, Jonny Oates
20. *The Times* website, 9 July 2012
21. Hansard, 10 July 2012, column 188
22. BBC News, 11 July 2012
23. Matthew d'Ancona, *In It Together: The Inside Story of the Coalition Government* (2013), p. 288
24. Nick Clegg statement, BBC News, 6 August 2012
25. Interview, Liam Fox
26. *The Coalition: Our Programme for Government*, p. 27
27. Interview, Nick Clegg
28. Interview, Julian Astle
29. Interview, Jonny Oates
30. Interview, Lena Pietsch
31. Interview, Lord Feldman
32. Interview, William Hague

33. Interview, Nick Clegg
34. Interview, Oliver Letwin
35. *The Coalition: Together in the National Interest* (2013), p. 6

Chapter 20
1. *Sunday Times*, 23 December 2012
2. *Guardian*, 28 November 2014
3. *The Times*, 26 September 2012
4. *Guardian*, 26 September 2012
5. MailOnline, 30 September 2012
6. Interview, Andrew Cooper
7. Matthew d'Ancona, *In It Together: The Inside Story of the Coalition Government* (2013), p. 299
8. Ibid.
9. Interview, Matthew Hancock
10. Interview, Andrew Cooper
11. Interview, David Cameron
12. Interview, Kate Fall
13. Interview, Lord Feldman
14. *Daily Mail*, 11 October 2012
15. *Independent on Sunday*, 21 October 2012
16. ComRes, ibid.
17. *Sunday Times*, 21 October 2012
18. *Daily Telegraph*, 27 July 2012
19. Interview, Oliver Letwin
20. *Forecast Evaluation Report*, OBR, 16 October 2012, p. 8
21. Interview, Danny Alexander
22. *Guardian* website, 5 December 2012

Chapter 21
1. *Financial Times*, 13 January 2014
2. *Evening Standard*, 16 January 2013
3. Coalition Agreement, p. 19
4. *Guardian* website, 29 June 2012
5. Ibid.
6. *Sunday Telegraph*, 1 July 2012
7. *Guido Fawkes* website, 28 June 2012
8. Letter from David Cameron to John Baron, 18 September 2012, https://html1-f.scribdassets.com/f6wos38sg1uedld/images/1-0529bb1be2.jpg
9. BBC News, 31 October 2012
10. Ibid.
11. Stefan Kornelius, *Angela Merkel: The Authorized Biography* (translated 2013), Kindle edition 3284
12. Ibid.
13. Interview, Ken Clarke
14. Interview, Graham Brady
15. Private information
16. Interview, David Cameron
17. Hansard, 23 January 2013, columns 304–5
18. Ibid., column 306
19. See Anthony Seldon, *Major: A Political Life*, 1997
20. *Guardian* website, 14 February 2013
21. *Daily Telegraph*, 9 February 2013; *Guardian*, 9 February 2013
22. *Daily Telegraph*, 13 May 2013
23. Interview, Owen Paterson
24. Interview, Ken Clarke
25. *The Times*, 7 May 2013
26. BBC News, 15 May 2013
27. Ibid., 29 October 2014
28. *Guardian*, 7 November 2013

Chapter 22
1. *Guardian*, 4 October 2005
2. Interview, Steve Hilton
3. *Guardian*, 4 October 2006
4. David Cameron, Downing Street reception, 9 April 2014
5. YouGov, 13 June 2012
6. BBC Radio 4, *Today*, 2 September 2011
7. *Pink News*, 28 November 2013
8. *Guardian*, 5 October 2011
9. Interview, Andrew Cooper
10. Channel 4 News, 15 March 2012
11. www.c4m.org.uk, 15 March 2012
12. Matthew d'Ancona, *Evening Standard*, 30 May 2012
13. *Daily Telegraph*, 28 May 2012
14. Ibid., 6 October 2012
15. Interview, Alan Duncan
16. Interview, Laurence Mann
17. George Osborne, 'Obama proves you can win in tough times', *The Times*, 13 November 2012
18. *Daily Telegraph*, 10 December 2012
19. Matthew d'Ancona, *In It Together: The Inside Story of the Coalition Government* (2013), p. 310

20. Ibid., p. 311
21. Ibid., p. 313
22. Gary Gibbon, Channel 4 politics blog, 6 February 2013
23. *Daily Telegraph*, 5 February 2013
24. *New York Times*, 6 February 2013
25. Interview, Graham Brady
26. Interview, Phillip Blond
27. *New York Times*, 6 February 2013
28. BBC News, 5 March 2013
29. Interview, Liam Fox
30. *Daily Telegraph*, 20 May 2013
31. Ibid., 25 May 2013
32. *Daily Mail*, 4 June 2013
33. Gibbon, Channel 4 politics blog, 4 June 2013
34. *Guardian*, 16 July 2013
35. David Cameron, 2013 Party Conference Speech, 2 October 2013
36. *Pink News*, 28 March 2014
37. Ibid.
38. Ibid., 15 July 2013
39. Interview, David Cameron

Chapter 23
1. Paul Goodman, *Daily Telegraph*, 29 December 2012
2. BBC Poll Tracker, 20 January 2015
3. Martin Ivens, *Sunday Times*, 9 September 2012
4. *Spectator*, 6 October 2012
5. *Guardian*, 7 October 2012
6. Ibid.
7. BBC News, 27 November 2012
8. Interview, Lord Feldman
9. *Guardian*, 18 November 2012
10. *Observer*, 21 July 2013; Sonia Purnell, *Just Boris* (2012)
11. Interview, Lynton Crosby
12. Ibid.
13. Ibid.
14. Matthew d'Ancona, *In It Together: The Inside Story of the Coalition Government* (2013), p. 231
15. *The Times* website, 12 June 2013
16. *Mail on Sunday*, 14 April 2013
17. BBC News, 12 July 2013
18. Sky, 12 July 2013
19. *Guardian* website, 12 July 2013
20. *Sunday Times*, 3 November 2013

21. Interview, Lynton Crosby
22. David Cameron, CBI Speech 2013, 4 November 2013
23. Interview, Lynton Crosby
24. ComRes, *Guardian*, 12 December 2014

Chapter 24
1. Interview, Iain Duncan Smith
2. Ipsos MORI poll, 12 July 2013
3. Philip Collins, *The Times*, 28 November 2014
4. Peter Oborne, *Daily Telegraph*, 16 February 2015
5. Iain Duncan Smith and Graham Allen, *Early Intervention: Good Parents. Great Kids. Better Citizens*, Centre for Social Justice (2008)
6. Stephen Brien, *Dynamic Benefits: Towards welfare that works*, Centre for Social Justice (2009)
7. Interview, Iain Duncan Smith
8. *Daily Mail*, 11 January 2015
9. 2010 Spending Review, p. 68
10. BBC News, 11 January 2015
11. David Cameron, *Sun*, 1 February 2012
12. See Chapter 18
13. *Daily Mail*, 13 November 2011
14. Press release, the Trussell Trust, 16 October 2013, http://www.trusselltrust.org/foodbank-numbers-triple
15. BBC News, 20 February 2014
16. Ruby Stockham, Left Foot Forward, 4 July 2015
17. *Journal of Public Heath*, 'A Qualitative Study of the "Bedroom Tax"', 15 March 2015
18. National Housing Federation, 27 May 2014
19. Interview, Philippa Stroud
20. Interview, Iain Duncan Smith
21. Interview, Lord Kerslake
22. Interview, Philippa Stroud
23. Peter Oborne, 'With Universal Credit, Work Might Finally Pay', *Daily Telegraph*, 15 February 2014
24. Matthew d'Ancona, *In It Together: The Inside Story of the Coalition Government* (2013), pp. 86–98;

Matthew d'Ancona, 'The reinvention of Iain Duncan Smith: is he the man to save the Tories?', *Guardian*, 15 February 2015

25. Gov.uk, 'Plans Advanced for Accelerated Roll-out of Universal Credit After Success in North-West', 29 September 2014

26. National Audit Office, 'Departmental Overview: The Performance of the Department for Work and Pensions 2013–14', 28 October 2014

27. Interview, Oliver Letwin

Chapter 25

1. Interview, George Osborne
2. Interview, Rupert Harrison
3. *Channel 4 News*, 25 January 2013
4. *The Economist*, 23 February 2013
5. Vince Cable, *New Statesman*, 6 March 2013
6. Matthew d'Ancona, *In It Together: The Inside Story of the Coalition Government* (2013), p. 336
7. Interview, George Osborne
8. Interview, Oliver Letwin
9. d'Ancona, *In It Together*, p. 336
10. Hansard, 20 March 2013, columns 947–9
11. *Daily Mail*, 21 March 2013; *The Times*, 21 March 2013; *Daily Telegraph*, 21 March 2013
12. Sky News, 16 April 2013
13. *Guardian*, 19 April 2013
14. *Guardian*, 20 March 2013
15. BBC HARDtalk, 9 August 2012
16. Bank of England, Forward Guidance press release, 7 August 2013
17. ONS, Gross Domestic Product Preliminary Estimate, Q1 2013, 25 April 2013
18. BBC News, 27 June 2013
19. George Osborne, Mansion House Speech 2013, 19 June 2013
20. ONS, Gross Domestic Product Preliminary Estimate, Q2 2013, 25 July 2013
21. *The Times*, 23 August 2013
22. *Independent*, 20 August 2013
23. *Financial Times*, 8 October 2013
24. ONS, Gross Domestic Product Second Estimate, Q4 2013, 26 February 2014; *Financial Times*, 6 June 2014

Chapter 26

1. Bloomberg, 8 April 2013
2. Gov.uk press release, 'Death of Lady Thatcher', 8 April 2014
3. Francis Elliott and James Hanning, *Cameron: Practically a Conservative* (2012), p. 68
4. Ibid., pp. 91–2
5. BBC News, 13 September 2007
6. Anthony Seldon, *Major* (1997), pp. 252–5, 325–8
7. Simon Heffer, lecture, Wellington College, 9 March 2015
8. Interview, Vernon Bogdanor
9. Interview, William Hague
10. Peter Snowdon, *Back from the Brink: The Extraordinary Rise and Fall of the Conservative Party* (2010), p. 214
11. Interview, David Cameron
12. BBC News, 17 April 2013
13. *Sunday Times*, 28 April 2013
14. Hansard, 10 April 2013, columns 1,613–16
15. Ibid., columns 1,616–17
16. *Guardian* website, 13 April 2013
17. *Guardian*, 17 April 2013

Chapter 27

1. Médecins San Frontières, press release, 24 August 2013; Al Arabiya News, 21 August 2013
2. BBC News, 24 September 2013
3. 'The Opposition Advances in Damascus', Institute for the Study of War, 9 August 2013
4. *Daily Telegraph*, 15 September 2013
5. *Foreign Policy*, 6 December 2012; *Time*, 18 September 2012
6. *Daily Telegraph*, 10 August 2012
7. BBC News, 20 November 2012
8. *Daily Telegraph*, 10 November 2012
9. *Guardian*, 12 November 2012

10. David Richards, *Taking Command* (2014), Kindle version 76%
11. Interview, Sir David Richards
12. Richards, *Taking Command*, Kindle version 77%
13. CNN, 23 January 2013
14. BBC News, 15 March 2013
15. Early Day Motion 189, 5 June 2013
16. *The Week*, 17 June 2013
17. *Sunday Times*, 16 June 2013
18. Gov.uk, 'The 2013 UK G8 Presidency'
19. *Daily Telegraph*, 20 August 2012
20. Interview, Nick Clegg
21. 'Chemical Weapon Use by Syrian Regime: UK Government Legal Position', 29 August 2013
22. Interview, Ken Clarke
23. Ibid.
24. https://twitter.com/david_cameron/status/372321743064793088
25. BBC Radio 4, *The Syria Vote: One Day in August*, 10 November 2014
26. *Sun*, 28 August 2013
27. BBC Radio 4, *The Syria Vote: One Day in August*, 10 November 2014
28. Interview, Nick Clegg
29. *LA Times* website, 28 August 2013
30. *The Times*, 29 August 2013
31. *Daily Telegraph*, 28 August 2013
32. *The Times*, 29 August 2013
33. Interview, Nick Boles
34. Interview, Nick Clegg
35. Interview, Michael Gove
36. Hansard, 29 August 2013, columns 1,425–39
37. Ibid., column 1,555
38. *Guardian*, 30 August 2013
39. BBC News, 4 September 2013
40. Ibid.
41. BBC Radio 4, *The Syria Vote: One Day in August*, 10 November 2014
42. Interview, Laurence Mann
43. CNN News, 31 August 2013
44. *Spectator*, 29 August 2013
45. *The Times*, 30 August 2013
46. *Time* magazine website, 30 August 2013
47. *The Economist*, 30 August 2013
48. Interview, William Hague
49. Interview, Julian Astle
50. Anthony Seldon, Diary, 1 September 2013
51. *Washington Times*, 30 August 2013
52. Associated Press, 1 September 2013
53. *LA Times*, 14 September 2013

Chapter 28

1. Patrick O'Flynn, *Daily Express*, 20 August 2011
2. *Mail on Sunday*, 29 September 2013
3. *Spectator*, 2 October 2013
4. David Cameron, Conservative Party conference speech, 2 October 2013
5. Interview, Lynton Crosby
6. David Cameron, Conservative Party conference speech, 2 October 2013
7. Julian Glover, 'The Coalition and Infrastructure', in Anthony Seldon and Mike Finn (eds), *The Coalition Effect, 2010–2015* (2015), p. 214
8. Ibid., pp. 210–11
9. *The Coalition: Our Programme for Government* (Cabinet Office, 2010), pp. 14, 16, 31
10. *Financial Times*, 20 August 2013, cited in Glover, 'The Coalition and Infrastructure', op. cit., p. 219
11. www.crossrail.co.uk/about-us/funding (accessed 29.05.2015)
12. *The Times*, 19 March 2012
13. Richard Wellings, *Failure to Transform: High-speed Rail and the Regeneration Myth*, IEA Current Controversies Paper No. 48, April 2014
14. Interview, Patrick McLoughlin
15. Ibid.
16. *Richmond and Twickenham Times*, 21 October 2009
17. Hansard, 5 December 2013, column 1,101
18. Interview, George Osborne
19. Hansard, 5 December 2013, column 1,102
20. Interview, Rupert Harrison
21. David Cameron, 6 December 2013

22. *Daily Telegraph*, 15 December 2013
23. Interview, Owen Paterson
24. BBC News, 28 June 2012
25. *Guardian* website, 27 December 2013
26. Ibid., 5 February 2014
27. *Daily Telegraph*, 10 February 2014
28. Interview, Owen Paterson
29. BBC, *The Andrew Marr Show*, 9 February 2014

Chapter 29

1. *Daily Telegraph*, 12 May 2010
2. *Daily Mail*, 15 May 2012
3. *Guardian*, 25 May 2012
4. *Independent*, 7 May 2013
5. Hansard, 8 May 2013, column 22
6. *Daily Telegraph*, 28 June 2013
7. *Financial Times*, 14 October 2014
8. BBC News, 3 December 2013
9. Janan Ganesh, *Financial Times*, 23 March 2015
10. Gov.uk, 'UK and China agree £14 billion of trade and investment deals', 17 June 2014
11. *Daily Telegraph*, 14 January 2015
12. *Financial Times*, 27 October 2014
13. *Irish Times*, 29 November 2013
14. BBC News, 1 December 2010
15. Ibid., 12 September 2011
16. Reuters, 2 August 2012
17. BBC News, 12 February 2015
18. *Time*, 20 March 2014
19. Interview, Ed Llewellyn
20. Private information
21. Michael Clarke, 'The Coalition and Foreign Policy', in Anthony Seldon and Mike Finn (eds), *The Coalition Effect, 2010–2015* (2015), p. 360
22. Interview, Sir David Richards

Chapter 30

1. Interview, George Osborne
2. Ibid.
3. Ibid.
4. Matthew d'Ancona, *In It Together: The Inside Story of the Coalition Government* (2013), p. 374
5. Martin Lewis, www.moneysavingexpert.com, 19 March 2014

6. *Spending Round 2013* (HMT, 2013), p. 26; *Autumn Statement 2013* (HMT, 2013), p. 7
7. *Budget 2014* (HMT, 2014), p. 26
8. Hansard, 19 March 2014, column 785
9. Ibid., columns 781–94
10. Ibid., column 795
11. *Telegraph* website, 31 March 2014
12. George Osborne, 'Chancellor speaks on tax and benefits' speech, 31 March 2014
13. *Sunday Times*, 28 February 2014
14. *Sun*, 31 March 2014
15. Janan Ganesh, *George Osborne: The Austerity Chancellor* (second edition, 2014), p. 89
16. Paul Goodman, http://conservativehome.blogs.com, 3 March 2015
17. ONS, Regional Labour Market Statistic, 14 May 2014
18. *Spectator*, 24 June 2014
19. Interview, George Osborne
20. Gov.uk, 'Long term economic plan for the north-west set out by Prime Minister and Chancellor', 8 January 2015
21. Gov.uk, 'Prime Minister and Chancellor visit the set of *Emmerdale*', 5 February 2015

Chapter 31

1. LBC, 26 November 2012
2. *Daily Telegraph*, 18 May 2013
3. Interview, David Cameron
4. Interview, Graham Brady
5. Interview, Liam Fox
6. Interview, Owen Paterson
7. Interview, Matthew d'Ancona
8. *Guardian*, 26 May 2014
9. Interview, Matthew Goodwin
10. *Daily Telegraph* website, 28 November 2014
11. Interview, Ken Clarke
12. BBC Poll of Polls, April 2013
13. '"Are you serious?" Boris, the Tories and the Voters', Lord Ashcroft polls, p. 9
14. Jamie Huntman, *Guardian*, 3 May 2013

15. *Independent*, 26 May 2014
16. Interview, Craig Oliver
17. BBC News, 28 August 2014
18. *The Times*, 29 August 2014
19. BBC News, 27 September 2014
20. Interview, Kate Fall
21. BBC, *The Andrew Marr Show*, 28 September 2014
22. *Daily Telegraph*, 29 September 2014
23. BBC News, 1 October 2014
24. Interview, Michael Gove
25. *Financial Times*, 10 October 2014
26. Interview, Lord Feldman
27. BBC News, 18 November 2014
28. YouGov/*Sun*, 10 November 2014

Chapter 32
1. Matthew d'Ancona, *Sunday Telegraph*, 20 July 2014
2. *The Times*, 2 October 2013
3. Alan Smithers, 'The coalition and society (II): Education', in Anthony Seldon and Mike Finn (eds), *The Coalition Effect, 2010–2015* (2015), p. 289
4. Interview, David Laws
5. Ibid.
6. Interview, Michael Gove
7. Interview, David Cameron
8. DfE, *The Importance of Teaching* (2010)
9. *Daily Mail*, 20 June 2012
10. *Daily Telegraph*, 21 June 2012
11. Interview, Michael Gove
12. Ibid.
13. BBC News, 7 February 2013
14. *Observer*, 17 February 2013
15. *Independent*, 19 March 2013
16. *Daily Mail*, 23 March 2013
17. *Independent*, 2 April 2013
18. BBC News, 18 May 2013
19. *The Times*, 1 October 2013
20. Andrew Gimson, ConservativeHome, 15 May 2014
21. *TES*, 24 April 2015
22. BBC News, 1 February 2014
23. *Daily Mail*, 5 March 2014
24. *Financial Times*, 14 March 2014
25. *The Times*, 17 July 2014
26. *Financial Times*, 16 June 2014

27. *The Times*, 4 June 2014; BBC News, 8 June 2014
28. *Independent*, 4 June 2014
29. *Daily Mail*, 10 June 2014
30. Ibid., 16 July 2014
31. BBC News, 9 October 2013
32. *Independent*, 8 June 2014
33. *Daily Telegraph*, 20 July 2014

Chapter 33
1. CNN News, 8 September 2014; *Herald Scotland*, 6 September 2014; *Daily Mail*, 4 September 2014
2. *Guardian*, 16 December 2014
3. Interview, Lord Strathclyde
4. *Guardian* website, 7 February 2014
5. *Daily Telegraph*, 20 February 2014
6. Interview, Nick Clegg
7. *Daily Telegraph*, 30 September 2013
8. http://www.bbc.co.uk/news/uk-scotland-scotland-politics-26166794
9. *Guardian*, 15 December 2014
10. Interview, Nick Clegg
11. *The Times*, 4 June 2014
12. BBC News, 5 June 2014
13. *Guardian*, 11 June 2014
14. Ibid., 16 December 2014
15. Ibid.
16. Ibid.
17. Silver Jubilee Address to Parliament, 4 May 1977, http://www.royal.gov.uk/Imagesand Broadcasts/Historic%20speeches%20and%20broadcasts/Silver JubileeaddresstoParliament 4May1977.aspx
18. *Sunday Times*, 7 September 2014
19. *Telegraph* website, 14 September 2014
20. *Guardian* website, 8 September 2014
21. Bloomberg, 15 September 2014
22. *Daily Mail*, 13 September 2014
23. Interview, Craig Oliver
24. BBC News, 10 September 2014
25. Scottish Conservatives website, 15 September 2014
26. *Daily Record*, 23 November 2013
27. *Guardian*, 21 April 2014

28. *Daily Record*, 16 September 2014
29. *Guardian*, 16 December 2014
30. *The Economist*, 19 September 2014
31. City AM transcript, 17 September 2014
32. Sky News, 19 September 2014
33. BBC News, 19 September 2014
34. *Guardian*, 15 December 2014
35. Gov.uk, 19 September 2014
36. *Guardian*, 15 December 2014
37. *The Times*, 20 September 2014
38. Interview, Michael Gove
39. *Observer*, 21 September 2014
40. *Sunday Times*, 21 September 2014
41. Sky News, 23 September 2014

Chapter 34

1. *Observer*, 29 June 2014
2. *The Times*, 27 June 2014
3. *Sunday Telegraph*, 29 June 2014
4. *Guardian*, 13 June 2014
5. *Observer*, 7 March 2014
6. *Guardian* website, 27 February 2014
7. *Sunday Telegraph*, 15 March 2014
8. *Financial Times*, 27 May 2014
9. *Sunday Times*, 1 June 2014
10. *Financial Times*, 27 May 2014
11. *Der Spiegel*, 4 June 2014
12. Ibid.
13. Ibid.
14. *Wall Street Journal*, 24 February 2014
15. Mathias Döpfner, 'Juncker muss Präsident werden', *Bild*, 30 May 2014
16. BBC News, 30 May 2014
17. Interview, Ken Clarke
18. *Daily Telegraph*, 4 November 2014
19. *Sunday Telegraph*, 8 June 2014
20. *Guardian*, 11 June 2014
21. *Daily Telegraph*, 29 June 2014
22. Deutsche Welle, 10 June 2014
23. *Sunday Times*, 8 June 2014; *Sun*, 8 June 2014; *Channel 4 News*, 27 June 2014
24. *Guardian*, 13 June 2014
25. *Wall Street Journal*, 25 June 2014
26. BBC News, 26 June 2014
27. Ibid.

28. *Independent on Sunday*, 29 June 2014
29. MailOnline, 17 July 2014
30. BBC News, 8 October 2014

Chapter 35

1. *Guardian*, 18 September 2014
2. Reuters, 2 November 2014
3. Interview, Lord Feldman
4. Nick Robinson, BBC, 29 September 2014
5. *Spectator* website, 1 October 2014
6. Ibid.
7. Ibid.
8. Interview, Craig Oliver
9. Nick Robinson, BBC, 1 October 2014
10. *Daily Mail*, 1 October 2014
11. *Spectator* website, 1 October 2014
12. Ibid.
13. *Sunday Times*, 7 December 2014
14. Ibid.
15. Hansard, 3 December 2014, column 308
16. BBC Radio 4, *Today*, 4 December 2014

Chapter 36

1. John Curtice, *Financial Times*, 10 October 2014
2. BBC News, 16 November 2014
3. Ibid., 8 August 2014
4. Interview, Lynton Crosby
5. *Daily Telegraph*, 10 January 2010
6. *Guardian*, 24 April 2015
7. Interview, David Cameron
8. *Daily Telegraph*, 14 April 2011
9. *Guardian*, 24 April 2015
10. *Guardian* website, 25 March 2013
11. *Financial Times*, 26 November 2013
12. Matthew d'Ancona, *In It Together: The Inside Story of the Coalition Government* (second edition, 2014), pp. 393–4
13. BBC News, 19 November 2014
14. David Cameron, Conservative Party conference speech, 1 October 2014; *Daily Telegraph*, 27 November 2014
15. *Daily Telegraph*, 27 November 2014

16. *Huffington Post*, 28 November 2014
17. *Spectator* website, 15 October 2014
18. Interview, Ken Clarke
19. *Daily Telegraph*, 13 November 2014
20. BBC News, 28 November 2014
21. UKIP website, 28 November 2014
22. *Guardian*, 29 November 2014
23. BBC News, 28 November 2014
24. Ibid.
25. MailOnline, 28 November 2014

Chapter 37
1. Guy Lodge and Illias Thoms, 'The coalition and the Labour party', in Anthony Seldon and Mike Finn (eds), *The Coalition Effect 2010–2015* (2015), p. 541
2. Anthony Seldon, *Blair* (2004), p. 367
3. *The Times*, 22 July 2014
4. *The Times*, 15 January 2015
5. White House Fact Sheet, US–United Kingdom Cybersecurity Cooperation, 16 January 2015
6. Patrick Cockburn, *The Rise of Islamic State: ISIS and the New Sunni Revolution* (2015), p. 27
7. David Cameron, speech at the UN General Assembly, 25 September 2014, https://www.gov.uk/government/speeches/pm-speech-at-the-un-general-assembly-2014
8. YouGov, 26 September 2014, https://yougov.co.uk/news/2014/09/26/isis-how-majority-came-favour-air-strikes/
9. Hansard, 26 September 2014, columns 1,255–68
10. Ibid., columns 1,268–72
11. BBC News, 30 September 2014
12. *Sunday Telegraph*, 17 October 2010
13. *Daily Telegraph*, 8 March 2012
14. Ibid., 3 June 2012
15. Ibid.
16. *Guardian*, 14 September 2014
17. *New York Times*, 18 February 2015
18. David Cameron, speech on radicalism and Islamic extremism, Munich Security Conference, 5 February 2011

19. Ibid.
20. Interview, Sir David Richards
21. *Guardian* website, 7 January 2015
22. Ibid.

Chapter 38
1. Interview, Andrew Mitchell
2. Interview, Danny Alexander
3. *Telegraph* blog, 28 January 2011
4. Interview, Justine Greening
5. *Guardian* website, 9 March 2015; OECD website, DAC member profile: the Netherlands (accessed 8 July 2015)
6. *Wall Street Journal*, 5 June 2014
7. *The Times*, 1 July 2014
8. *USA Today*, 31 August 2014
9. *Daily Telegraph*, 4 June 2015
10. Hansard, 19 October 2010, column 799
11. 'UK should do more in Iraq, says Committee', Parliament website, 5 February 2015 (accessed 13 July 2015)
12. Ibid., 2 March 2015
13. International Institute for Strategic Studies, *The Military Balance 2015*, 11 February 2015
14. Malcolm Chalmers, *Mind the Gap: The MoD's Emerging Budgetary Challenge*, Royal United Services Institute, 9 March 2015
15. *Washington Post*, 21 May 2015
16. Ibid.
17. *Financial Times*, 11 May 2015
18. BBC News, 6 February 2015
19. *The Times*, 23 April 2015
20. Ibid., 27 April 2015

Chapter 39
1. Interview, Rupert Harrison
2. *The Times*, 19 March 2015
3. BBC News, 27 June 2013
4. Interview, George Osborne
5. Hansard, 18 March 2015, column 770
6. Ibid., column 779
7. Ibid., column 780
8. *Sunday Telegraph*, 22 March 2015
9. *Observer*, 22 March 2015
10. *The Times*, 19 March 2015

11. Ibid., 20 March 2015
12. *Financial Times*, 16 March 2015
13. *Guardian*, 30 April 2015
14. Interview, Nick Clegg
15. Ibid.
16. Interview, William Hague
17. Interview, Graham Brady
18. *Sunday Times*, 10 May 2015
19. *Guardian*, 6 April 2015

Chapter 40
1. Interview, Liz Sugg
2. *The Times*, 25 April 2015
3. *Daily Telegraph*, 16 May 2015
4. Interview, Liz Sugg
5. *Guardian* website, 27 April 2015
6. Interview, George Osborne
7. Interview, Lynton Crosby
8. Ibid.
9. Interview, Craig Oliver
10. *The Times*, 10 March 2015
11. *Daily Telegraph*, 4 May 2015
12. Interview, Stephen Gilbert
13. Ipsos MORI, 30 October 2014
14. Interview, Stephen Gilbert
15. Interview, George Osborne
16. Interview, Nick Clegg
17. Interview, George Osborne
18. Interview, Stephen Gilbert

19. Interview, Liz Sugg
20. Interview, Andrew Cooper
21. Interview, Craig Oliver
22. Interview, George Osborne
23. *Guardian* website, 6 May 2015
24. *Cabinet Office Manual* (2011), paragraph 2.12, pp. 14–15
25. BBC News, 24 March 2015
26. Interview, Nick Clegg
27. Theresa May, 'We will win by being the party for all', ConservativeHome Victory 2015 conference, 9 March 2013
28. Interview, William Hague
29. YouGov, 6 May 2015
30. ICM/*Guardian*, 6 May 2015

Epilogue
1. BBC, 7 May 2015
2. Interview, George Osborne
3. Interview, Liz Sugg
4. Interview, Kate Fall
5. Interview, Craig Oliver
6. David Cameron, victory speech in Witney, 8 May 2015
7. YouTube, 8 May 2015
8. Interview, George Osborne
9. David Cameron, victory speech in Downing Street, 8 May 2015

Index